M3/S

£180

3 Volume set

£80

Alfred and Mary Paley Marsall in the late 1870s.

The Correspondence of
Alfred Marshall, Economist

THE CORRESPONDENCE OF
ALFRED MARSHALL, ECONOMIST

Volume 1. Climbing, 1868–1890

A Royal Economic Society Publication

Edited by

JOHN K. WHITAKER
University of Virginia

CAMBRIDGE
UNIVERSITY PRESS

Published by the Press Syndicate of the University of Cambridge
The Pitt Building, Trumpington Street, Cambridge CB2 1RP
40 West 20th Street, New York, NY 10011-4211, USA
10 Stamford Road, Oakleigh, Melbourne 3166, Australia

First published 1996

Printed in the United States of America

Library of Congress Cataloging-in-Publication Data
(Revised for v. 2- v. 3)

Marshall, Alfred, 1842–1924.
  The correspondence of Alfred Marshall, economist.

  Includes bibliographical references.
  Contents: vol. 1. Climbing, 1868–1890—vol. 2. At
the summit, 1891–1902—vol. 3. Towards the close,
1903–1924.
  1. Marshall, Alfred, 1842–1924—Correspondence.
2. Economists—Great Britain—Correspondence. 3. Neo-
classical school of economics. I. Whitaker, John K.
(John King). II. Title.
HB103.M3A4 1996   330.15′7   95-8022
ISBN 0-521-55888-3 (v. 1)
ISBN 0-521-55887-5 (v. 2)
ISBN 0-521-55886-7 (v. 3)

A catalog record for this book is available from the British Library

ISBN   0-521-55888-3 Hardback

CONTENTS

ACKNOWLEDGEMENTS

Over the long decade during which this work has been in preparation, I have incurred substantial debts for information, advice, and assistance. Major contributions from the following are gratefully acknowledged: R. D. C. Black, A. W. Coats, P. D. Groenewegen, G. C. Harcourt, D. E. Moggridge, the late Sir Austin Robinson, and Rita McWilliams Tullberg; while Donald Winch, acting on behalf of the Royal Economic Society, has been invariably supportive and patient of delay. I also wish to acknowledge valuable assistance on particular matters from: G. Beccatini, G. Busino, R. H. Coase, I. M. Drummond, M. Gallegati, W. B. Gaynor Jr., Philomena Guillebaud, S. Hashimoto, J. P. Henderson, the late K. H. Hennings, A. Kadish, A. L. Levine, J. Löwe, T. Raffaelli, R. P. Sturges, Z. A. Silberston, J. G. S. G. van Maarseveen, and D. A. Walker. A series of able graduate-student research assistants eased what has been essentially a one-man task: J. von der Borch, whose aid with letters in German was invaluable, K. Choi, J. Lutzker, D. Mullin, M. Szechowicz, and, last but not least, C. Steen. Generous research leaves from the University of Virginia also aided the task considerably.

I am particularly grateful to the Faculty of Economics and Politics of the University of Cambridge, the copyright holder, for permission to reproduce Marshall materials, especially from the substantial collections held in the Marshall Library, Cambridge. For access to privately held manuscript material, and for permission to reproduce it, my overwhelming debt is to Richard D. Freeman for his great generosity with regard to the extensive and important Foxwell Papers in his possession. Thanks with respect to particular items are also due to the late S. R. Dennison (Robertson Papers), P. D. Groenewegen (G. Darwin letter), A. Heertje (Levasseur Papers), and the late Rosamond Könekamp (Jevons Family Papers).

Permission from the following persons or bodies to reproduce materials from the collections held by the indicated institutions is gratefully acknowledged. For details of the specific collections and items involved see the comprehensive listing of archival material by source that is appended to Volume 3.

In Cambridge: The Syndics of Cambridge University Library; The Mistress and Fellows of Girton College; The Librarian, King's College; The Principal and Fellows of Newnham College; The Master, Fellows and Scholars of St John's College; The Master and Fellows of Trinity College.

In Oxford: The Master and Fellows of Balliol College; The Librarian Bodleian Library (also J. R. Wynter Bee on behalf of the Hon. Mrs Crispin Gascoigne for the Harcourt Papers); The Librarian, Nuffield College; The Librarian, Oriel College.

In London: The Librarian, Bishopsgate Foundation; The British Library Board (also T. Farmiloe for the Macmillan Archive); The Librarian, British Library of Political and Economic Science; The Archivist, King's College; The Librarian, University College Library; The Librarian, University of London Library (also Mrs B. Norman-Butler for the Booth Papers).

Elsewhere in the UK: The City of Manchester Leisure Services Committee, with regard to The Manchester Central Library; The Director and University Librarian, John Rylands University Library of Manchester; The Librarian, University of Newcastle-upon-Tyne Library (also C. J. Bosanquet for the Bosanquet Papers); The Deputy Keeper of Records, Public Record Office of Northern Ireland, Belfast (also Mrs M. T. Scott for the Scott Papers, and Martin, King, French, Ingram, Solicitors, Limavady, for the Ingram Papers); The Librarian and Archivist, Sheffield University Library.

Elsewhere in Europe: The Curator of Manuscripts, Amsterdam University Library; The Archivist, Bundesarchiv, Koblenz; The Librarian, Bibliothèque Cantonale et Universitaire, Lausanne; The Librarian, Lund University Library; The Librarian, Royal Library, Stockholm; The Archivist, Staatsbibliothek zu Berlin; The Board of Trinity College, Dublin.

In North America: The Librarian, Rare Books and Manuscripts Library, Columbia University; The Curator, Harvard University Archives; The Librarian, Baker Library, Harvard University; The Librarian, Houghton Library, Harvard University; The Librarian, University of Illinois Library, Urbana-Champaign; The Manuscripts Division, Library of Congress; The Librarian, Thomas Fisher Rare Book Library, University of Toronto; The Archivist, State Historical Society of Wisconsin; The Librarian, Yale University Library.

Permission to reproduce various previously published materials was generously granted by the following: The Royal Netherlands Academy of Sciences and Letters; the Econometric Society; the Royal Economic Society; Macmillan and Co.

Librarians and archivists around the world, too many to mention by name, have been uniformly helpful, but special thanks must be recorded to the late A. H. Finkell and D. Ross, successive Marshall Librarians; to Frances Willmoth, Marshall Library Archivist; to M. Underwood, Archivist of St John's College, Cambridge; to Angela Raspin, Archivist of the British Library of Political and Economic Science; and to B. E. Clevenger Jr., of the Reference Department, Alderman Library, University of Virginia, whose guidance to unfamiliar sources proved invaluable.

The portraits included in Volumes 1 and 2 are reproduced by permission of the Librarian, University of Bristol, those in Volume 1 having been retouched from the faded originals. The portrait included in Volume 3 is reproduced by permission of the Librarian, Marshall Library, Cambridge.

Publication subsidies from the Royal Economic Society and from St John's College, Cambridge (Marshall's old college), have made publication possible. Scholars everywhere should benefit from this generous support, which is gratefully acknowledged.

GENERAL INTRODUCTION

Alfred Marshall, eminent English economist and founder of the 'Cambridge School of Economics', was born in 1842 and died in 1924. His heyday proved to be the decisive period in the establishment of economics as science, as profession, and as academic subject. His own contribution to each of these developments was major.

The familiar selection from Marshall's correspondence included in *Memorials of Alfred Marshall* in 1925 has proved an invaluable and frequently invoked source of insight. Less laboured, less painfully qualified, and certainly less inhibited, than his carefully wrought publications, these letters have long added new dimensions to the understanding of his life, thought, aims, and character. Since 1925, further items from Marshall's correspondence have been published, and even more have been quoted and offered as telling evidence. A comprehensive edition of the extant correspondence seems, in the words of the late Lord Robbins, an 'essential desideratum' for Marshall scholarship.[1] Precedent for such an enterprise exists in the similar editions already published for major economists of Marshall's era, such as William Stanley Jevons, Léon Walras, or Vilfredo Pareto. More general justification might be found in the peculiar ability of informal correspondence to reawaken dead voices, to illumine character, mindset, and personal relationships, and to provide valuable insights to biographer, exegete, and intellectual historian.

The preparation of a comprehensive edition of correspondence requires, in the first instance, that the pertinent documentary raw material be assembled. This assemblage proved no mean task in Marshall's case. He appears to have made no systematic effort to preserve letters received or retain copies of letters sent. The Marshall Papers, held in the Marshall Library, Cambridge, include some items in each category, and there is also a miscellaneous holding of letters from Marshall preserved by their recipients and eventually donated to the Library, most significantly numerous letters to his long-time colleagues Herbert Somerton Foxwell and John Neville Keynes. But much of the traceable correspondence is widely dispersed, consisting of letters preserved in the papers of a correspondent.

The scattered and haphazard nature of this raw material means that there are gaps, some apparent, others only surmisable. In particular, very few family letters have been preserved, so that the extant correspondence is primarily professional. There is clearly a risk that further letters will come to light eventually, truly exhaustive search being impracticable. Yet the available material seems sufficiently complete, rich, and interesting, that such a vague hazard ought not to inhibit going ahead with what is to hand.

The term 'correspondence' is somewhat elastic. Here, as is standard practice, letters published in newspapers and magazines are included, as are the open letters or 'flysheets' that Marshall circulated to the Cambridge University Senate when controversy pended. More idiosyncratic is the inclusion of Mary Paley's correspondence, subsequent to her marriage to Marshall in 1877, if letters appear to be written to, or on behalf of, the couple. In addition to 'correspondence', thus extended, various pertinent and otherwise inaccessible documents, hardly construable as letters, are reproduced in footnotes and appendices, or in the guise of 'enclosures'. The edition is, therefore, best viewed as one of 'correspondence and related documents'.

A comprehensive edition of correspondence aims to reproduce all *significant* letters, suitably edited and documented, so that the user has access to the full body of available material and not merely a selection of highlights. Some letters are patently too trivial or impenetrable to merit inclusion, so that a modicum of selectivity can enhance an edition's readability and usefulness. Editorial judgements about exclusion do raise awkward questions of principle, however. Can the needs and interests of the potential future audience be seen at all clearly? In the face of such doubts it has seemed best in the present work to resolve disputable cases in favour of inclusion.

Documents chosen for reproduction must be transcribed and then incorporated into a text where they are supported by explanatory footnotes and by a system of cross-referencing and indexing. The general approach to these tasks that has been adopted here may be explained briefly as follows. A more detailed account is provided in the ensuing section on 'Editorial Practices'.[2]

Transcription has aimed to reproduce the original as closely as is consistent with readability. The objective has been to preserve the general character of the original, especially any indications of haste and spontaneity, rather than to capture each stroke of the writer's pen with pedantic fidelity. Readers need to be reminded that hasty scribblings—although often revealing—are less accurate than carefully honed publications in representing a writer's *conscious* position. Too often, casual phrases from a letter are made to bear too heavy an evidential weight, a risk enhanced by over-polished editorial transcription.

Explaining the origins of documents, and elucidating the obscure allusions they contain, are the most daunting editorial tasks. Ironically, points of little potential interest to users frequently pose the greatest difficulties, requiring exploration of alien areas of scholarship and unfamiliar information sources. Given the inefficiency and unreliability of such explorations, it has frequently seemed better to admit ignorance than falsely pretend to knowledge. The alternative of eliding awkward incidental passages from the documents reproduced has been resisted, however (except in footnote quotation). Such elisions tax the reader's confidence and make it more difficult for scholars to assess interpretations that others have placed upon partial quotations.

Everything cannot be explained: a modicum of prior knowledge must be assumed of users. The primary audience for the present work is conceived as historians of economics, together with scholars interested in the intellectual and institutional history of the social sciences. The explanatory material is geared to such an audience, but, given the vagueness with which the audience can be envisaged, an erring on the side of explaining the obvious has seemed best.

Settling on an editorial apparatus is to some extent a matter of trial and error, influenced by the character of the material being edited. The needs of two quite different types of user must necessarily be compromised. The first seeks a graphic narrative of the subject's activities and concerns. The second wants information on a specific point, and approaches the work as a reference tool. The elaborate and reiterated cross-referencing and indexing required by the second type of user, if all salient passages are to be retrieved from any starting-point, may seem unnecessarily obtrusive to the first type of user, proceeding chronologically. The aim in the present work has been to develop an apparatus that is comprehensive without being unnecessarily obtrusive, although whether this aim has been achieved the reader must judge. Details are provided in the following section.

Marshall's correspondence, presented chronologically, is divided into three volumes. The present one covers the years between 1868 (the date of the first available letter) and 1890. This was the period during which Marshall established himself as a world-renowned economist. It culminated in the 1890 publication of his *magnum opus*, the book entitled *Principles of Economics*. The second volume deals with the years 1891 to 1902, which saw Marshall in the full tide of professional and professorial activity, the acknowledged leader of British economists. The final volume covers the years 1903 to 1924, the year of Marshall's death. It opens with the culmination of his successful campaign to establish a new Tripos in Economics and Politics in Cambridge. But the dominant feature is his long struggle, following retirement in 1908 from his Cambridge chair, to fulfil his frustrated literary ambitions. These were achieved to a degree by the publication of *Industry and Trade* in 1919 and *Money Credit and Commerce* in 1923.

Each of the three volumes is essentially self-contained. However, comprehensive indices covering all the volumes are placed at the end of Volume 3. There also will be found a detailed listing of the archival sources used. This includes a specific archival reference for every item mentioned in the body of the work, where normally nothing more than the collection name is stated.

The description of editorial practices given next is followed by a short biographical sketch of Alfred Marshall. The family background is sketched in

Appendix I of the present volume, completing the material designed to be
introductory to all three volumes.

[1] L. C. Robbins, Review of *Early Economic Writings of Alfred Marshall*, *Economica*, 44 NS (February
1977), pp. 91–2

[2] For a fuller discussion of the general issues involved in editing correspondence see my 'Editing
Alfred Marshall' in Donald H. Moggridge (ed.), *Editing Modern Economists* (AMS Press, New York,
1988), and my 'Quandaries in the Editing of Correspondence: The Case of Alfred Marshall', in
the symposium 'Editing Economists and Economists as Editors', Pascal Bridel (ed.), *Revue
Européenne des Sciences Sociales*, 30 (January 1992), pp. 69–80.

EDITORIAL PRACTICES

Whenever the original could not be traced (for example, letters published in *The Times*) the original printing was taken as the source and reproduced as closely as possible, apart from the standardization of layout and typography. If the original manuscript or typescript of a letter was traced, the transcription follows it as faithfully as is compatible with comprehensibility. The original spelling, capitalization, punctuation, accents, and abbreviations are reproduced, but layout is standardized (for example, postscripts squeezed into the heading of a letter are placed at the end). Missing periods are added at the ends of sentences in a few cases. Editorial insertions into the text are accounted for in footnotes and are normally enclosed in square brackets. Alterations made by the writer during composition are described only when the change seems to be of some interest.

It should be observed that Marshall's own spelling veers between 'labor' and 'labour', 'shew' and 'show', and so on. He rarely uses the apostrophe, letting the context indicate possessive usage, and persistently writes the name of the publisher Macmillan as MacMillan. Marshall's abbreviations are for the most part self-evident, but it might be noted here that the frequently used abbreviation 'Mo Sc' stands for 'Moral Science(s)'. Other abbreviations whose meaning may not be clear are explained in footnotes.

The heading of each letter gives the full name of writer or recipient and the actual or presumed date of writing, uncertain portions of dates being indicated by parentheses and question marks. In most cases the date also appears in the body of the letter, but often in an abbreviated form likely to cause confusion unless clarified. The date of a published letter is that of publication unless there is specific information as to the date of composition or transmission.

The first footnote to each letter gives the source, using abbreviated versions of the names listed at the beginning of each volume in the case of manuscript sources. Unless the contrary is indicated, the original may be assumed to be an autograph signed letter. The first footnote also typically describes the evidence on dating whenever the date is not explicit in the body of the letter. Postmarks and addresses from envelopes and postcards are noted should they seem informative, but since such facts are unavailable in most cases a systematic recording has not been attempted. After building Balliol Croft in 1886, Marshall almost invariably wrote on notepaper with a printed head from that address (the fullest version being Balliol Croft, 6 Madingley Road, Cambridge). Rather than continually reproduce this address in the body of each letter, the fact that a letter came from that address is indicated in the first footnote.

The first footnote includes a précis of any letter not written in English. It also details any previous 'substantial' printing: that is, any reproduction extending beyond partial quotation. There are often deviations between the version given here and such a previous printing, but no attempt has been made to record all such differences.

The 88 letters reproduced in 1925 in *Memorials of Alfred Marshall* call for special mention, since the originals of all but a few can no longer be found. That many of the letters had been pruned for printing is abundantly clear from the printed versions. That some rephrasings and elisions were also undertaken silently is demonstrable from a comparison of the printed version and the original when the latter has survived. Obviously, whenever the original version was available it was taken as the source, but in other cases there was little alternative but to reproduce the *Memorials* version. The alternative of omitting such letters seemed unappealing given their significance and wide currency. In mitigation it should be noted that the editing of the *Memorials* letters by A. C. Pigou, although unacceptably intrusive by modern standards, does not seem to have seriously distorted the substance.

Identifications of persons mentioned in letters or footnotes are handled in three ways. Certain names, for example Plato or Shakespeare, are taken as too well known to require further identification. Other names are briefly identified on first mention in the body of a volume, all subsequent mentions *in the same volume* being explicitly cross-referenced back to this identification. The remaining names mentioned in a volume are listed and briefly identified in the 'Biographical Register' included *in that volume*. Occasionally they are also minimally identified on mention by clarifying the full name, and possibly other salient facts, when this may aid the reader or resolve an ambiguity. Thus, if the mention of any individual is not accompanied by a short biographical note, or an explicit reference to one, then a brief biographical outline should be found in the Biographical Register of the volume being used, the only exception being names assumed too familiar to require further explanation. However, to avoid costly repetition, those individuals listed in the biographical registers of Volumes 2 or 3 who have already been described in the register of an earlier volume will not have the full description repeated, but will be accompanied by a reference to the earlier description with only the briefest of identifications.

The general aim has been to include in the registers names that recur frequently or are likely to be familiar to most, but perhaps not all, users. It should be noted that the biographical register for a volume may not include all writers or recipients of the letters included in that volume and that different volumes may treat the same individual differently.

The biographical sketches provided are inevitably skimpy, frequently little more than dates and a one-phrase characterization. The sketches for individuals included in the biographical registers are somewhat fuller, especially for those most closely associated with Marshall, but even then only the most salient points are noted, without any attempt at biographical comprehensiveness. With very few exceptions, biographical information has been drawn from the following standard sources:

(i) J. Eatwell, M. Milgate and P. Newman (ed.), *The New Palgrave* (Macmillan, London, 1987); (ii) H. Higgs (ed.), *Palgrave's Dictionary of Political Economy* (Macmillan, London, 1925–6); (iii) E. R. A. Seligman and A. Johnson (ed.), *Encyclopedia of the Social Sciences* (Macmillan, New York, 1930–5); (iv) D. Sills (ed.), *International Encyclopedia of the Social Sciences* (Free Press, New York, 1968); (v) Joyce M. Bellamy and J. Saville (eds.) *Dictionary of Labour Biography* (Macmillan, London, 1972–); (vi) J. A. Venn, *Alumni Cantabrigienses, Part II, 1752–1900* (Cambridge University Press, Cambridge, 1940); (vi) *The Balliol College Register, Second Edition 1833–1933* (Oxford, 1934); (vii) *Newnham College Register 1871–1971* (Cambridge, 1979); (viii) L. Stephen and others (eds.) *Dictionary of National Biography* (*with Twentieth Century Supplements*) (Oxford University Press, London, 1917–); (ix) *Who Was Who* (Black, London, 1920–); (x) A. Johnson (ed.) *Dictionary of American Biography* (Scribner, New York, 1927–).

Publications referred to in a letter or footnote are fully identified upon first mention in a volume and this initial identification is cross-referenced on all subsequent mentions of the publication *in the same volume*. But to aid the user, such cross-references are accompanied by an abbreviated title that will often sufficiently identify the publication involved. An exception to the above procedure occurs in the case of a few frequently mentioned works which are identified throughout a volume by the abbreviated title defined in the List of Abbreviations for that volume. References to *The Times* commonly give page and column in the form (16d), for p. 16, col. 4.

Two qualifications to these general procedures for identifying individuals or publications should be pointed out. In cases where mention of an author's name is merely a way of alluding to a publication, the identification of that publication is taken as a sufficient identification of the individual, so that the individual may not appear in the register unless inclusion seems justified on other grounds. Second, when works are mentioned in reading lists, course descriptions, etc., appended as 'enclosures' to letters, or reproduced in footnotes, it has not always seemed necessary or feasible to provide a full bibliographic description of every work mentioned. This manifests a more general policy of not providing explanations of explanations.

Letters are arranged chronologically and numbered sequentially throughout and between all three volumes. Cross-references within a volume are in the form [200], [150.2], [159.3, 4], where [200] denotes letter number 200, [150.2] denotes footnote 2 of letter number 150, and [159.3, 4] denotes footnotes 3 and 4 of letter 159, and so on. Cross-references between volumes are infrequent, being restricted to substantive matters. A reference in Volume 2 to the first volume would take the form 'Volume 1, [203.1]', and so on. Cross-references between adjacent letters, although probably redundant for the reader proceeding sequentially, are included to aid other types of user. References to appendices can be taken to refer to the appendices of the volume being used unless there is a specific indication to the contrary.

Prior to receiving its charter in 1887, the Royal Statistical Society was known simply as the Statistical Society. For pre-1887 references to the organization and its journal, this name is rendered as [London] Statistical Society, except in the biographical registers, where [Royal] Statistical Society is used for simplicity. The Royal Economic Society was known as the British Economic Association before receiving its charter in 1902. The name used in references is the one appropriate to the date involved. The name of the organization's journal, the *Economic Journal*, has been unchanged since its first volume in 1891 so that no distinction by date is required.

ALFRED MARSHALL: A SKETCH

Alfred Marshall was born on 26 July 1842 in the London suburb of Bermondsey into a comfortable lower middle class home, his father, William Marshall, being a clerk (later cashier) at the Bank of England. The family subsequently moved to the suburb of Clapham where most of Alfred's boyhood was spent. His father was a stern taskmaster, but Alfred's youth seems to have been moderately happy. He was educated at the Merchant Taylors' School, a venerable London day school, revealing an acute mind and a particular aptitude for mathematics—a predilection his father discouraged. But with a loan from an Australian uncle and an open exhibition to St John's College, Cambridge, Marshall entered Cambridge University in 1862, preparing for the Mathematical Tripos, the University's most prestigious degree examination. He emerged in 1865 in the distinguished position of Second Wrangler, topped only by the future Lord Rayleigh, a result ensuring Marshall's election to a Fellowship at his College. In 1868 he was also appointed as Lecturer in Moral Sciences at St John's, his interests having meanwhile drifted from mathematics and physics towards a concern for the philosophical and moral foundations of human behaviour and social organization. Henry Sidgwick and William Kingdom Clifford were important influences among his intimates, while a heady if perplexing infusion of German idealism and Darwinian evolutionism, the ideas of Kant, Hegel, and Spencer especially, leavened the pragmatic British utilitarian tradition that he derived through John Stuart Mill and Sidgwick. Marshall was always to be strongly influenced by idealist and evolutionist ideas, although he never quite managed to reconcile them with the dominant British tradition.

Set to lecture, somewhat against his inclination, on political economy, Marshall rapidly became engrossed in this novel subject and by the early 1870s had determined that his life's work would lie in the transformation of the didactic old political economy into a new science of economics, open to the progressive intellectual and social movements of the day. During the next few years he absorbed the literature of his subject, both theoretical and applied, and began to write out his own theoretical ideas. He mastered the classical tradition of Smith, Ricardo, and Mill and was encouraged towards a mathematical approach by early acquaintance with the works of Cournot and Thünen, marching independently some way along the paths blazed in the early 1870s by Jevons and Walras. He became an effective and inspiring teacher. Prominent among his early pupils were Herbert Somerton Foxwell, Henry Cunynghame, John Neville Keynes (father of Maynard), Frederic William Maitland, and Joseph Shield Nicholson. Marshall was also involved in the movement, instigated by

Sidgwick, to provide lectures for women students and admit them informally to university examinations—formal membership in the University being quite out of the question. Among the women students to whom Marshall taught political economy was Mary Paley, one of the first students of the foundation that was to become Newnham College. In 1876 she and Marshall became engaged. They were married in 1877. Marriage required Marshall to resign his Fellowship at St John's, celibacy requirements not being removed at Cambridge until 1882. He found a new livelihood as first Principal of the fledgling University College, Bristol, where he also became Professor of Political Economy, Mrs Marshall assisting with the teaching. The position did not really suit Marshall, who was anxious to get on with his own writing and not temperamentally suited to the tasks of administration. The difficulties of the situation were worsened by the parlous financial position of the College—it was one of the least prosperous of the mushrooming civic foundations of the period—and by a disabling illness (the diagnosis was kidney stones) that restricted his ability to get out and about. In 1881 he resigned his posts to spend a year recuperating on the Continent, and there, in a prolonged sojourn in Palermo, the composition of the *Principles* began in earnest.

In the mid-1870s Marshall had written much of the manuscript of a book on foreign trade and protectionism, visiting North America in the summer of 1875 for the purpose of studying at first hand the benefits and disadvantages of protection in a new country. The manuscript was eventually abandoned, but in 1879 Sidgwick had four of its theoretical chapters printed for private circulation under the titles *The Pure Theory of Foreign Trade: The Pure Theory of Domestic Values.* These brilliant chapters—arguably the high-water mark of Marshall's achievements as a pure theorist—were not widely circulated, but they did begin to establish his reputation among economists at large. More immediately important in this regard was the publication in 1879 of *The Economics of Industry,* coauthored with Mrs Marshall. This had set out as a primer of political economy, but Marshall had taken an increasing hand in it, and although it ostensibly remained an introductory text it was in fact—as discerning critics such as F. Y. Edgeworth noted—a quite sophisticated statement of Marshall's views on his subject, especially on the theory of distribution. In later life he took an unreasonable dislike to this first book but it has distinct merits.

The years as Principal, although apparently unproductive, marked the beginning of Marshall's emergence as a major economist at the national and international levels, the few minor publications he had produced before 1879 scarcely hinting his latent powers to the world outside Cambridge. Elevation to the Principalship had also brought Marshall to public prominence and opened up to him the wider world of affairs, especially through friendship with Benjamin Jowett, the redoubtable Master of Balliol, who moved in the highest circles and was an influential member of the Council of University College, Bristol. He frequently stayed with the Marshalls on his visits to that city.

It was probably through Jowett's generosity that the Marshalls were able to return to Bristol for the academic year 1882–3 during which Marshall served as Professor of Political Economy at the College, giving a notable series of public lectures on issues raised by Henry George. And it was doubtless with Jowett's blessing that Marshall took up in 1883 the Balliol lectureship to candidates for the Indian Civil Service made vacant by the sudden death of Arnold Toynbee. Marshall had a considerable success at Oxford, but the unexpected death of Henry Fawcett, who had been Professor of Political Economy at Cambridge since 1863, opened up the irresistable prospect for Marshall of a return to his own University in the position he most coveted. With the death of Jevons in 1882, Marshall—despite the meagreness of his published output—had become the undisputed leader of the modern scientific school of economics in Britain. His election to the chair was virtually a foregone conclusion. He took up his new duties in January 1885, also being elected to a Professorial Fellowship at his old college, St John's, where he joined forces with Foxwell. Then aged 42, Marshall was to remain in these positions, absorbed in a ceaseless time-consuming round of teaching, organizing, public service, and University affairs, until he retired voluntarily in 1908 at age 66 to free himself for the writing which had hitherto been squeezed into the jealously guarded (and not ungenerous) University vacations. These were predominantly spent away from Cambridge, the Austrian Tyrol and the south coast of England or the Channel Islands being favourite venues.

The administrative and teaching burdens of Marshall's Professorship were to absorb much of his energy, indeed frustratingly so. Cambridge was changing rapidly, and it was no longer possible for the Professor to give his few required lectures to 'Poll men' (ordinary degree students), leaving honours teaching to college tutors and lecturers, as Fawcett had done. But the degree structure had not been correspondingly modified and political economy, holding only a subservient place in the Moral Sciences and Historical Triposes, did not have the freedom necessary in Marshall's eyes to develop advanced work or appeal to the best students. He took every opportunity to enlarge the scope for attracting and training students to the high calling, as he saw it, of an economist, at the cost of antagonizing Sidgwick and other colleagues, and later of considerable friction with Foxwell, culminating in an irreparable breach in 1908.

Marshall was not cut out to be a successful University politician, although he was to take a prominent role in opposing in 1896 the granting of Cambridge degrees to women, taking for once the popular side. The frequent shrillness and exaggeration of his views on University and educational matters alienated more than it persuaded others. But his great strength lay in a dogged perseverance. By persistent if sometimes inept and tactless manœuvring he eventually achieved in 1903 his goal of an independent Tripos in Economics and Politics. But the victory was somewhat pyrrhic—few if any resources were provided, Cambridge as a whole having just failed rather lamentably in an attempt to raise substantial private funding in competition with the thriving civic universities. Nevertheless this success, even if only a qualified one, was vital in paving the way for the full flowering of the Cambridge School of Economics in the inter-war period.

Though the years of his Cambridge Professorship were frustrating in many ways, Marshall did produce significant disciples, the most important being Alfred William Flux, Charles Percy Sanger, Arthur Lyon Bowley, Sydney John Chapman, Arthur Cecil Pigou (who, to Foxwell's chagrin, was to be Marshall's youthful successor in the Cambridge chair), David Hutchison Macgregor, Charles Ryle Fay, Walter Thomas Layton, and John Maynard Keynes, son of John Neville and the most famous of all. Several of these did not take economics as part of a degree, however, being more akin to today's post-graduates.

The signal achievment in the years of Marshall's Professorship was the publication in July 1890 of his *Principles of Economics, Volume I* by Macmillan's. Composition had commenced in 1881–2, but progress had been slowed by several factors. The moves to Oxford and Cambridge were major interruptions, the former requiring an extended course of reading on Indian matters. At Cambridge he was faced with the need to promote his subject. As a leading figure in the growing community of economists he was drawn, rather reluctantly, into professional activities outside Cambridge, while as an increasingly public figure he was faced with invitations to appear before government inquiries, write articles on economic issues for the quarterlies, and so on. The 1880s saw his most copious flow of occasional writings as well as his most important discussions of monetary issues, especially through his extensive evidence to the Gold and Silver Commission, 1887–8. He offered the *Principles* to Macmillan's in 1887 as a two-volume work, projecting completion of the first volume later in the year and the second volume in 1889. This forecast proved hopelessly over-optimistic, and the second volume was never to appear.

When *Principles of Economics, Volume I* finally appeared in July 1890 it attained a small place in British publishing history as the first book to be marketed under the net book agreement, which strove to establish resale price maintenance in a previously anarchic market. The early reception of the work must have been highly gratifying to its author. Seldom can a book on economics have been so widely and respectfully reviewed in the popular press—virtually every newspaper in Britain noticing it favourably. The enlightened and constructive tone of the work, and the putting behind of both sterile doctrinal controversy and the pessimistic pronouncements of the old political economy, all recommended the work to the lay reader. Marshall, always anxious to reach an audience beyond the scholars and students of the academy, must have been delighted by this indication that the wider world was listening. The academic reviewers too, although not wholly uncritical, left no doubt that a major work had appeared upon the scene, one which would have a considerable impact on the subject. Marshall's standing as one of the world's leading economists had been cemented.

The essential theoretical ideas of the *Principles* were not basically different from Marshall's earlier statements. Nevertheless, the *Principles* had a richness and complexity, a breadth and ripeness of wisdom, that went considerably beyond his earlier writings, displaying a subtlety of conception and an awareness of the profound complexity and interrelatedness of economic phenomena.

The success of the first volume of the *Principles* was gratifying, but much remained to be done. Marshall was soon dissatisfied with various aspects of the published work and nettled by various criticisms or misunderstandings of it. Being both sensitive to criticism and extremely reluctant to enter into controversy, or even into serious debate—after 1890 he seems to have taken little interest in the theoretical work of others—his general reaction was to rewrite to enhance the clarity and explicitness of his statements or to incorporate silently the changes needed to meet or accommodate criticisms. Only in a few cases were criticisms addressed explicitly in occasional publications. There thus occurred a long and extensive process of reorganizing and rewriting of the first volume which continued over the entire eight editions appearing during Marshall's lifetime. Despite extensive expositional changes his views do not seem to have changed significantly, nor is it clear that the incessant polishing always improved the work which tended to lose its vitality and focus.

The most pressing task facing Marshall in 1890 was completion of the promised second volume of the *Principles*, intended to deal with various applied areas. There were many distractions, both in the University and outside, in addition to the rewriting of the first volume and the preparation of a condensation of it to replace the early *Economics of Industry*. (The replacement appeared in 1892 as *Elements of the Economics of Industry*, incorporating material on trade unions not drawn from the larger work.) The 1890s saw Marshall engaged in considerable public service, especially his extensive duties as a member of the Royal Commission on Labour, 1891–4. By about 1895, when he vowed to avoid all escapable obligations in an attempt to bring his second volume to completion, labour problems were assuming a more prominent role in his plans for the work and the treatment of foreign trade had ramified into a major historical study. Much material was collected and drafted, but it proved impossible to organize satisfactorily. By about 1900 the impetus had been largely spent, although the plan to write a second volume was not formally abandoned until 1907, and it was 1910 before the title of the first and only volume of the *Principles* was changed to *Principles of Economics: An Introductory Volume*. Looking back in 1907, Marshall confessed that it had gradually become clear to him that four volumes at least would have been needed to achieve his earlier aims. In lieu of his abortive second volume he now proposed to bring out an independent volume entitled *National Industry and Trade*.

Marshall drifted almost accidentally into writing this proposed work. In 1903, with the tariff controversy at its height in Britain, he was asked to provide a private memorandum on foreign trade policy for the then Chancellor of the

Exchequer, and responded with his 'Memorandum on the Fiscal Policy of International Trade'. Basing his plans partly on the thoughts already embodied in this Memorandum, he then proposed to Macmillans that he prepare a short topical treatment of international trade questions to appear probably in 1904. But like all Marshall's books this one grew in his hands. In 1907 portions of it were already in print, but its focus had moved away from topical issues to the more fundamental ones of the evolution of national industrial leadership and the consequences of monopolistic combinations of producers and workers. Progress remained slow even after Marshall retired from his Professorship in 1908. Declining strength and ill health reduced his ability to work, but a greater obstacle lay in the rapid changes transforming the world economy. Continual recasting and rethinking were called for if the book was not to be superseded by events. The outbreak of war exacerbated this difficulty, and all thought of publication had to be set aside until more settled times. By 1916 the title of the book on which Marshall had been working for some twelve years had reached its final form of *Industry and Trade* but the work was now to extend to more than one volume. In August 1919, when Marshall was aged 77, *Industry and Trade* at last appeared. Predominantly historical and descriptive, it covered only the first part of the scheme envisaged in 1907, and it had been with some difficulty that Marshall had been persuaded to drop 'Volume I' from the title. The book was respectfully received, but failed to have the impact on either economic thought or economic policy that it might have had if published twenty years earlier when he was at the height of his powers.

Marshall's ability to work was now ebbing fast, and in the last few years remaining to him he set himself to rescue what he could of the materials he had accumulated over his life. Remarkably, in the light of the long history of recurrent delay and indecision, *Money Credit and Commerce* appeared in 1923. For the most part it is a pastiche of Marshall's earlier writings on international trade and money, most of them dating back to the 1870s and 1880s, and is a disjointed and disappointing work.

After the completion of *Money Credit and Commerce*, Marshall toyed with his earlier occasional writings and his evidence to official inquiries, with the aim of republishing portions, especially those dealing with the role of government and 'aims for the future', the main outstanding items on his past agenda. He made no progress and died on 13 July 1924, aged 81. After his death, two of Marshall's famous pupils went some way towards fulfilling his last intentions. In 1925 Pigou included many of Marshall's occasional writings in his edition of *Memorials of Alfred Marshall*, while in 1926 Maynard Keynes edited Marshall's contributions to government inquiries in *Official Papers of Alfred Marshall*.

The years after the return to Cambridge in 1885 pased in a regular cycle with few highlights. Mrs Marshall taught economics at Newnham for many years and also acted as a kind of editorial assistant to Marshall. But their initial intellectual partnership was not to be revived. Assisted over many years by the faithful servant Sarah Payne, Mrs Marshall devoted herself above all to smoothing Marshall's way, ministering to his needs, and relieving him from life's vexations. Any intellectual ambitions she may have had were sacrificed, but she found solace in painting and an independent social life, as well as in teaching and social service. She survived her husband by almost twenty years, dying on 7 March 1944 at age 93.

Balliol Croft, the house the Marshalls built after returning to Cambridge, became after occupation in late 1886 the centre about which Alfred's life rotated during his remaining years. There, when in Cambridge, was his study and writing done, and to there came for advice, guidance, and exhortation, a stream of students and incipient writers of prize essays or fellowship theses. Until he retired, Marshall gave his lectures regularly in the University's Literary Lecture Rooms on Trinity Street, where Room 5 was his special preserve, but College played little part in his life. He was not a clubbable man, evading many social activities on the plea of feeble health and the need for a strict regimen. As the acknowledged leader of British economists he was prone to lead from the rear. Yet he was not a recluse. Balliol Croft saw a steady stream of visitors, American and German economists as well as British, but also many individuals from other walks of life. Exasperating as he could be to his colleagues, Marshall also had an elusive magnetism. He had a charm for the young, who savoured his eccentricities and were inspired by his high and unselfish enthusiasm for his subject and his hope to make economics serve the common good. The influence he exerted on his students was by no means the least part of his legacy.[1]

---

[1] See Appendix I, below, for a description of family background and a list of publications bearing on Marshall's biography. A full bibliography of Marshall's writings can be constructed from the chronologies prefacing the volumes of the present work, while *Memorials*, pp. 500–8, supplies an annotated one. Many of Marshall's occasional writings are reproduced in *Memorials* and *Guillebaud*. The latter also includes variant passages from the first seven editions of *Principles*. *Early Economic Writings* reproduces the 'Pure Theory' chapters of 1879, together with many early manuscripts, while most of Marshall's contributions to government enquiries are reprinted in *Official Papers*. (For full descriptions of the cited works see the list of abbreviations.)

This sketch is based, in part, upon my 'Alfred Marshall und seine *Principles of Economics*', in H. C. Recktenwald (ed.), *Alfred Marshall's Lebenswerk: Eine kritische Analyse aus moderner Sicht* (Vademecum zu einem Neo-klassiker: Verlag Wirtschaft und Finanzen GmbH, Düsseldorf). The permission of the publisher is gratefully acknowledged.

ABBREVIATIONS

BLPES   British Library of Political and Economic Science

Diaries   Diaries of John Neville Keynes (Cambridge University Library, Additional Manuscripts, 7831–9, covering 1874–1890)

Early Economic Writings   *The Early Economic Writings of Alfred Marshall, 1867–1890*, ed. John K. Whitaker (Macmillan, London, 1975, for the Royal Economic Society: 2 vols.)

Economics of Industry   Alfred and Mary Paley Marshall, *The Economics of Industry* (Macmillan, London, 1879, revised 1881)

Guillebaud   *Alfred Marshall's Principles of Economics: Ninth (Variorum) Edition*, vol. 2, ed. Claude W. Guillebaud (Macmillan, London, 1961, for the Royal Economic Society). (Vol. 1 is simply a reprint of the eighth edition of the *Principles*.)

LW   *Correspondence of Léon Walras and Related Papers*, ed. William Jaffé (North Holland, Amsterdam, 1965: 3 vols.).

Memorials   *Memorials of Alfred Marshall*, ed. Arthur Cecil Pigou (Macmillan, London, 1925, for the Royal Economic Society).

Mill's *Principles*   John Stuart Mill, *Principles of Political Economy with Some of their Applications to Social Philosophy* (Parker, London, 1848: several further editions). The standard edition is that appearing as *Collected Works of John Stuart Mill, Volumes Two and Three* (University of Toronto Press, Toronto, 1965).

Official Papers   *Official Papers of Alfred Marshall*, ed. John Maynard Keynes (Macmillan, London, 1926, for the Royal Economic Society).

Principles (1)   The first edition of the *Principles*: Alfred Marshall, *Principles of Economics: Volume I* (Macmillan, London, 1890).

Principles (2)   The second edition of the *Principles* (Macmillan, London, 1891).

Principles (8)	The eighth and final edition of the *Principles*: Alfred Marshall, *Principles of Economics: An Introductory Volume* (Macmillan, London, 1920).
Reporter	*The Cambridge University Reporter*, the official organ of Cambridge University since 1872. Published weekly in term time.
Ricardo's *Principles*	David Ricardo, *On the Principles of Political Economy and Taxation* (Murray, London, 1817, revised 1819, 1821). The standard edition is that appearing as *The Works and Correspondence of David Ricardo, Volume One*, ed. Piero Sraffa (Cambridge University Press, London, 1951, for the Royal Economic Society).
Scope and Method	John Neville Keynes, *The Scope and Method of Political Economy* (Macmillan, London, 1891).
Wealth of Nations	Adam Smith, *An Inquiry into The Nature and Causes of The Wealth of Nations* (Strahan and Cadell, London, 1776, with three further editions). The standard edition is that appearing as *The Glasgow Edition of the Works and Correspondence of Adam Smith, Volumes One and Two* (Clarendon Press, Oxford, 1976).
What I Remember	Mary Paley Marshall, *What I Remember* (Cambridge University Press, Cambridge, 1947).
WSJ	*Papers and Correspondence of William Stanley Jevons*, ed. R. D. Collison Black and Rosamond Könekamp (Macmillan, London, 1972–81, for the Royal Economic Society: 7 vols.).

LIST OF MANUSCRIPT COLLECTIONS[1]

BLPES, F. Y. Edgeworth Papers.
BLPES, Passfield Papers.
BLPES, H. Solly Papers.
Bristol University Library, Archives.
British Library, Macmillan Archive.
Bundesarchiv, Koblenz, L. J. Brentano Papers.
Cambridge University Library, Diaries of J. N. Keynes.
Cambridge University Library, University Archives.
Columbia University Library, J. B. Clark Papers.
Columbia University Library, E. R. A. Seligman Papers.
Foxwell Papers [privately owned].
Girton College, Cambridge, Archives.
Greater London Record Office, Papers of the Toynbee Memorial Fund.
Harvard University, Baker Library, Foxwell Papers.
Jevons Family Papers [privately owned].
John Rylands University Library, Manchester, W. S. Jevons Papers.
King's College, Cambridge, O. Browning Papers.
King's College, Cambridge, J. M. Keynes Papers.
King's College, London, Archives.
Library of Congress, Washington D. C., D. A. Wells Papers.
Marshall Library, Cambridge, J. N. Keynes Papers.
Marshall Library, Cambridge, Marshall Papers.
Newnham College, Cambridge, Archives.
Nuffield College, Oxford, F. Y. Edgeworth Papers.
Oriel College, Oxford, L. R. Phelps Papers.
Palgrave Family Papers [privately owned].
Public Record Office, Northern Ireland, J. K. Ingram Papers.
Royal Economic Society Archive.
St John's College, Cambridge, Archives.
State Historical Society of Wisconsin, Madison, R. T. Ely Papers.
Trinity College, Cambridge, H. Sidgwick Papers.
Trinity College, Dublin, C.F. Bastable Papers.
University College, London, Archives.
University College, London, K. Pearson Papers.
University of Lausanne, Fonds Walras.
University of London Library, C. Booth Papers.
Yale University Library, W. G. Sumner Papers.

---

[1] See the listing of archival materials by source appended to Vol. 3 for further details of these collections and for precise archival identifications of them.

BIOGRAPHICAL REGISTER

As explained in the description of editorial practices above, this register describes all individuals mentioned but not specifically identified in the body of the present volume with the exception of a small number of names deemed so well known that identification would be otiose. It does not include all correspondents. Unless otherwise indicated, reference is to Cambridge on academic matters and Britain on general matters.

Anderson, James (1739–1808). Scottish writer on economic development and agriculture. Author of *Observations on the Means of Exciting a Spirit of National Industry* (1777) and other works. An early contributor to rent theory.

Ashley, William James (1860–1927). A leading economic historian. A student at Balliol (BA 1881) he remained in Oxford as a teacher of economics and history until 1888. Thereafter Professor at Toronto 1888–92, Harvard 1892–1901, and Birmingham 1901–25. A supporter of Chamberlain's schemes for tariff reform and a critic of deductive economics. Knighted 1917.

Auspitz, Rudolf (1837–1906). Austrian businessman and economic theorist. Co-author with Richard Lieben (1842–1919) of the important *Untersuchungen über die Theorie des Preises* (1887–9).

Bagehot, Walter (1826–77). Journalist, editor of *The Economist*, banker, and writer on economic, political, and literary topics. His main economic works are *Lombard Street* (1873) and *Economic Studies* (1879).

Balfour, Arthur James (1848–1930). Conservative statesman and writer on philosophic and theological subjects. Educated at Trinity, Balfour's inclinations were philosophic and literary, but he played a distinguished part in public life. Entering Parliament in 1874, he served under the premiership of his uncle, the Marquess of Salisbury (1830–1903), as Chief Secretary for Ireland 1887–91, and then as First Lord of the Treasury and Leader of the House, 1891–2 and 1895–1902. Balfour in turn served as Prime Minister 1902–5, but his Cabinet was rent by the tariff-reform question and severely defeated at the polls. He joined the coalition government in 1915 and was created Earl Balfour in 1922. His *Notes on Insular Free Trade* (1903) were a remarkable production for a Prime Minister. Balfour's sister, Eleanor Mildred, married Henry Sidgwick.

Bastable, Charles Francis (1855–1945). Irish economist and legal scholar, professor of political economy at Trinity College, Dublin, 1882–1932, and also Regius Professor of Laws 1908–32. An influential textbook writer, author of *Public Finance* (1892), *The Theory of International Trade* (1893), and other works.

Bastiat, Frédéric (1801–50). French proponent of laisser-faire and brilliant, if shallow, writer on economic topics. Author of *Sophismes Économiques* and *Harmonies Economiques*.

Bateson, William Henry (1812–81). Master of St John's College, Cambridge, 1857–81. Third Wrangler 1836. Vicar of Madingley 1843–7. A prominent actor in University reform and an early supporter of Marshall. More an administrator and organizer than a theological scholar.

Bentham, Jeremy (1748–1832). Eminent social philosopher and propounder of utilitarianism.

Berry, Arthur (1862–1929). Cambridge mathematician and Fellow of King's. Under Marshall's influence, dabbled in economic theory during the late 1880s and early 1890s and taught mathematical economics for the Moral Sciences Tripos from 1891 to 1900. Helped administer Cambridge extension teaching from 1891 to 1895, leading to a breach with Marshall over the role of women.

Blanqui, Jérôme-Adolphe (1798–1854). French writer on economic topics, author of *Histoire de l'Economie Politique en Europe* (1837), a pioneering study of the history of economics.

Böhm-Bawerk, Eugen von (1851–1914). Austrian economist, civil servant, and statesman. A leader of the Austrian School of Economics, best known for his critical and constructive writings on capital theory, especially *A Positive Theory of Capital* (1889).

Bonar, James (1852–1941). Economist and civil servant. Born in Scotland and educated in Glasgow, Oxford, and Germany. A career civil servant, he never held a regular position as a teacher of economics. His interests were primarily in the history of economics and theories of population, especially the work of Malthus. Author of *Philosophy and Political Economy* (1893) and other works.

Booth, Charles (1840–1916). Shipowner and social investigator. Organizer of the surveys described in his monumental *Life and Labour of the People of London* (1891–1903). He became in the 1890s a prominent proponent of old-age pensions, and was to take Joseph Chamberlain's side in the tariff-reform controversy of 1903, becoming a notable member of Chamberlain's Tariff Commission.

Brassey, Thomas (1836–1918). Politician, naval administrator, and expert on naval affairs, with an interest in wages questions. The son of Thomas Brassey (1805–70), engineer and railway contractor. Became first Lord Brassey in 1895 and Earl, 1911.

Brentano, Ludwig Joseph, or 'Lujo' (1844–1931). German economist with a special interest in labour questions. A moderate member of the German Historical School. Professor at Munich from 1891 to 1914.

Browning, Oscar (1837–1923). A famous Cambridge character, active in the teaching of history at Cambridge, and in pressing for an expanded role in the University for the study of politics. Fourth Classic in 1860, he taught at Eton until 1875, leaving under a cloud for King's where he became College Lecturer in History, having held a Fellowship since 1859. He built a considerable reputation for the College's teaching in this field and later became University Lecturer. He was also involved in teacher education. In 1909 he left Cambridge in dudgeon for Bexhill, then Rome. His eccentricities, like his girth, were on the grand scale.

Burt, Thomas (1837–1922). Trade union leader of the moderate 'Old Unionist' stamp and Liberal politician. Starting life as a mineworker, Burt served as general secretary of the Northumberland Miners' Mutual Confidence Association, 1865–1913. He was an esteemed Member of Parliament for Morpeth 1874–1918. He was, with Marshall, a member of the Labour Commission, 1891–4, and served as Secretary to the Board of Trade, 1892–5.

Caird, James (1816–92). Agricultural expert, government adviser, and copious writer on agricultural matters. The advocate of 'high farming'. Knighted 1882.

Cairnes, John Elliot (1824–75). Irish economist, perhaps the most eminent adherent of the later Classical School. A follower, though not uncritically so, of John Stuart Mill. Lived in London from 1865, serving as Professor of Political Economy at University College, London, from 1866 to 1872. Author of *The Character and Logical Method of Political Economy* (1857), *Some Leading Principles of Political Economy* (1874), and many other works.

Cantillon, Richard (1697–1734). Irish born banker, active mainly in France, and author of the posthumously published *Essay on the Nature of Commerce in General* (1755), one of the first systematic works on economics, virtually rediscovered by Jevons in 1881.

Carey, Henry Charles (1793–1879). American economist and social philosopher. Retired from business at age 42 and devoted himself to economic and social topics, on which he was a prolific author. The leader of the Pennsylvania protectionists and a critic of the Ricardian School.

Chevalier, Michael (1806–79). Eminent French liberal economist, immortalized in the Cobden-Chevalier Treaty. His works are now little remembered.

Clark, John Bates (1847–1938). Leading American economist, particularly noted for his work on the marginal-productivity theory of distribution, especially *The Distribution of Wealth* (1899). Professor at Columbia University from 1895 to 1923. Before this he taught primarily at Smith College.

Clifford, William Kingdon (1845–79). Mathematician and philosopher, one of the most brilliant minds of his generation. Second Wrangler in 1867, Clifford became a Fellow of Trinity in 1868 and was Professor of Applied Mathematics at University College, London, 1871–9. His meteoric career was cut short by the collapse of his health. One of Marshall's Cambridge intimates in the late 1860s.

Cohn, Gustav (1840–1919). German economist, a specialist in public finance and transportation. Professor at Göttingen from 1884. Studied railway problems in England in the 1870s.

Cossa, Luigi (1831–96). Italian economist, noted for his wide and cosmopolitan knowledge of the literature of economics. Professor at Pavia from 1858.

Cournot, Antoine Augustine (1801–77). French mathematician, philosopher, and economist. Author of the celebrated *Researches into the Mathematical Principles of the Theory of Wealth* (1837), an epochal work in mathematical economics. Served as a university administrator for most of his career.

Courtney, Leonard Henry (1832–1918). Politician, lawyer, journalist, and economist. Second Wrangler 1855. Fellow of St John's 1856. Called to the Bar 1858. A Member of Parliament from 1876 to 1900 and holder of several minor government offices, including service as Financial Secretary of the Treasury 1882–4. A member, with Marshall, of the Labour Commission, 1891–4. From 1865 to 1881 he wrote leaders for *The Times* and from 1872 to 1875 was professor of political economy at University College, London (thus Cairnes's successor and Jevons's predecessor). Essentially a follower of J. S. Mill, his interest in economics was not deep, but he was an early supporter of the British Economic Association. An enthusiast for proportional representation, a supporter of women's suffrage, and an opponent of imperialism, he became Baron Courtney of Penwith in 1906.

Cunningham, William (1849–1919). Economic historian and churchman. Senior Moralist in 1872. He combined teaching, first in Cambridge extension lecturing and then as a College or University Lecturer in Cambridge, where he was associated with Trinity, with active churchmanship, rising in the latter to the rank of archdeacon. Although an early student of Marshall's, Cunningham soon became something of a thorn in his side. The two differed on methodology, on curricular reform, and on economic policy, Cunningham being a staunch opponent of free trade and anything smacking of laisser-faire, as well as a proponent of empire. He is best known for his influential *The Growth of English Industry and Commerce* (1882). In addition to his other activities, Cunningham served as Tooke Professor at King's College, London, from 1891. He was, over the years after 1885, the most vocal opponent of Marshall's schemes for the reform of economics teaching in Cambridge.

Cunynghame, Henry Hardinge (1848–1935). Civil servant, polymath, and amateur economist. One of Marshall's early students (Second Moralist 1873) Cunynghame developed under Marshall's influence an interest in the topic of his later book *Geometrical Political Economy* (1904). An active career in law and the civil service, together with his wide enthusiasms, prevented his involvement in economics being more than intermittent and kept him from developing further his undoubted talent as an economic theorist.

Darwin, Charles Robert (1809–82). Eminent naturalist, author of *The Origin of Species* (1859).

Darwin, George Howard (1845–1912). Mathematician and astronomer, second son of Charles Darwin, the naturalist. Second Wrangler in 1868 and a Fellow of Trinity 1868–78 and 1884–1912. Plumerian Professor of Astronomy and Experimental Philosophy, 1883–1912. Before settling on a scientific career he had toyed with the law, being called to the Bar in 1872, and had dabbled in various subjects, including economics. An early supporter and defender of Jevons's marginalist theory, this early interest in economics does not seem to have been sustained in later life. Knighted 1905.

Dunbar, Charles Franklin (1830–1900). American economist. After an extensive business career, Dunbar became Professor of Political Economy at Harvard in 1871, thereafter serving his department and institution in various administrative roles in conjunction with his professorial duties. Editor of the new *Quarterly Journal of Economics*, 1886–96, and best known for his *Chapters on the Theory and History of Banking* (1891).

Ede, William Moore (1849–1935). One of Marshall's early students (first class in the Moral Sciences Tripos of 1871), Ede undertook extension lecturing in the 1870s, teaching political economy in the north of England. He also assisted the Marshalls with the proofs of the *Economics of Industry* (1879). Ordained in 1872, his career was devoted primarily to the Church. Rector of Gateshead 1881–1901, Dean of Worcester 1908–38. A close associate of Brooke Foss Westcott (1825–1901) during the latter's years, 1890–1901, as Bishop of Durham.

Eden, Sir Frederick Morton (1766–1809). English businessman and writer on economic topics, remembered especially for the careful factual research embodied in his *The State of the Poor* (1797).

Edgeworth, Francis Ysidro (1845–1926). One of the most eminent economic and statistical theorists of his age, and an admirer and supporter of Marshall. Of Anglo-Irish stock, a nephew of Maria Edgeworth, he studied at Dublin and Oxford, obtaining a first in 'Greats' in 1869. His 1881 publication, *Mathematical Psychics*, is probably his greatest, and certainly his best known economic work. After a slow entry into academic life, he taught for some years at King's College, London, where he became Tooke Professor in 1890. In 1891 he became Drummond Professor at Oxford. First editor of the *Economic Journal* (1890–1911), his writings are notable for their brilliant elusiveness.

Elliott, Thomas Henry (1854–1926). Career civil servant, secretary to the Board of Agriculture and Fisheries 1892–1913. Elliott's civil-service work in various departments led him to take a general interest in economic issues and he was an early supporter of the British Economic Association, serving for some years as its secretary. Knighted 1902.

Ely, Richard Theodore (1854–1943). American economist, educated at Columbia University and in Germany. A founder of the American Economic Association and a seminal influence on the American school of 'Institutional Economics', associated with the University of Wisconsin, where Ely taught from 1892 to 1925. Before this he had taught since 1881 at the Johns Hopkins University.

Farrer, Thomas Henry (1819–99). Civil servant and writer on economics. Educated at Balliol, Farrer was called to the Bar in 1844 but ceased to practise upon entering the civil service in 1850. Serving in the Board of Trade, of which he was Permanent Secretary, 1865–86, he was actively involved in much economic legislation. A fervent free-trader and Cobdenite, he published extensively on economic matters. In retirement he joined the London County Council and sat on various Royal Commissions, including the Gold and Silver Commission of 1887–8. He was created Lord Farrer in 1893, having been knighted in 1883.

Fawcett, Henry (1833–84). Economist and politician. A follower of J. S. Mill, Fawcett's best known work is his *Manual of Political Economy* (1863). A student at Trinity Hall, and Seventh Wrangler in 1856, he was subsequently blinded in a shooting accident. Nevertheless, he was elected to Cambridge's Professorship of Political Economy in 1863, and to Parliament as a Liberal in 1864. He gave regular series of lectures in Cambridge, some later published in monograph form, but otherwise played a limited role in University teaching and affairs. He served as Postmaster General from 1880 until his unexpected death.

Fawcett, Millicent Garrett (1847–1929). Wife and amanuensis of Henry Fawcett and subsequently a leader in the agitation for women's suffrage. Born Millicent Garrett, and married in 1867, she was the author of *Political Economy for Beginners* (1870) and *Tales in Political Economy* (1894). A founder of Newnham College.

Flux, Alfred William (1867–1942). Economist and statistician. Flux came under Marshall's influence after graduating as Senior Wrangler in 1887. A Fellow of St John's from 1889, he left Cambridge in 1893 to teach economics in Manchester and then Montreal. Returning to Britain in 1908 as Statistical Adviser to the Board of Trade, he devoted the remainder of his career to improving official statistics. His writings were predominantly of an applied and statistical character, but he had strong theoretical skills. His *Economic Principles* (1904) was the first Marshallian textbook.

Foxwell, Edward Ernest (1851–1922). The younger brother of Herbert Somerton Foxwell, and like him a member of St John's, Ernest obtained a disappointing second in the Moral Sciences Tripos of 1874. He became a successful Cambridge 'coach' or tutor, and also undertook extension lecturing. He served as Professor of Economics at the Imperial University of Tokyo, 1896–9. An expert on railway matters, the topic of his few publications.

Foxwell, Herbert Somerton (1849–1936). Economist and bibliophile. Born in Shepton Mallet, Somerset, Foxwell studied at University College, London, and then at Cambridge, where, at St John's, he was Senior Moralist in 1870. Under Marshall's influence, Foxwell developed early an interest in economics to which he was eventually to devote his career. A Fellow of St John's from 1874, with an interruption 1898–1905 due to marriage, he was also College Lecturer in Moral Sciences, 1875 to 1905, and subsequently the College's Director of Studies in Economics. From 1876 his Cambridge teaching was combined with regular teaching at University College, London, first as lecturer and from 1881 as professor, in succession to Jevons. Subsequently, this was combined with lecturing at the London School of Economics. Foxwell's main interests in economics lay in monetary and financial matters, and he mixed frequently with men of affairs in London. His publications are scattered and of an applied character. He is best known for his magnificent collections of the early literature of economics. His scepticism about economic theory, his quixotic temperament, his alliance with various causes, especially the bimetallist movement in the 1890s, and conflict over teaching and curricular matters, gradually cooled the warm regard and friendship between Marshall and Foxwell that had existed before 1885. The tariff-reform issue of 1903 proved a further source of difference between the two. There was a final breach in 1908 over Marshall's unwillingness to support Foxwell as his successor to the Cambridge chair.

George, Henry (1839–97). Radical American economist, orator, and politician. Best known for his *Progress and Poverty* (1879) and as progenitor of the single-tax movement. Ricardian rent theory played a prominent role in George's thought.

Giffen, Robert (1837–1910). Economist and statistician. Born and educated in Scotland, Giffen embarked upon a career in journalism. This led to service as assistant editor of *The Economist* under Bagehot, 1868–76. Giffen then entered the civil service, heading the statistical department of the Board of Trade and becoming in 1882 the Board's assistant secretary. He retired in 1897. A prolific writer on applied economics and statistical topics, Giffen was a pioneer in the construction of economic statistics. He edited the *Journal of the [Royal] Statistical Society*, 1876–91, and was a founder of the British Economic Association. Knighted 1895.

Gladstone, William Ewart (1809–98). Liberal statesman and one of the major actors on Britain's political stage in the latter half of the nineteenth century. Initially a Conservative, he became the dominant force among the Liberals from 1859, serving with distinction as Chancellor of the Exchequer and then as Prime Minister on various occasions, 1868–94. His political hopes and his party's unity foundered on the rocks of the Irish question. In the interstices of an arduous political career, he published extensively on theological and literary topics.

Gonner, Edward Carter Kersey (1862–1922). Economist, educated at Oxford. As a young graduate, Gonner came under Marshall's influence during the latter's period in Oxford, 1883–4. From 1888 until his death Gonner taught at University College, Liverpool, subsequently the University of

Liverpool, becoming Brunner Professor of Economic Science in 1891. His interests within economics were mainly historical or practical, and his most important work was his *Common Land and Inclosure* (1912). He is also remembered for his editorial work on Ricardo. Knighted 1921.

Goschen, George Joachim (1831–1907). Statesman and financier of German descent. Educated at Oxford, he became a director of the Bank of England in 1856 and a Member of Parliament in 1863 as a Liberal and subsequently a Liberal-Unionist. He held several government offices, most importantly as Chancellor of the Exchequer under Lord Salisbury, 1887–1892. An occasional writer on economic topics, author of *The Theory of Foreign Exchanges* (1861), and an opponent of tariff reform, Goschen was the first president of the British Economic Association. He was created Viscount Goschen in 1900. His *Essays and Addresses on Economic Questions* (1905) collect his occasional pronouncements.

Gossen, Hermann Heinrich (1810–58). German civil servant and writer on economics. His remarkable development of marginal utility theory in his *Entwickelung* (1854) was unnoticed and practically unknown until brought to light by Jevons in 1879.

Hadley, Arthur Twining (1856–1930). American economist. Hadley spent much of his life in New Haven, the place of his birth, being a student and, after 1891, professor at Yale, and then serving as Yale's President, 1899–1921. He studied under Wagner in Berlin and spent some years as a freelance writer and lecturer on railway issues. The author of *Railway Transportation* (1885).

Howell, George (1833–1910). Labour leader, politician, and author. Rising from humble circumstances, Howell became a prominent figure in the trade-union movement and served as a Liberal Member of Parliament from 1885 to 1895. He wrote ambitious works on labour questions, his *Conflicts of Capital and Labour* (1878) being the best known, and bequeathed his economic library to the Bishopsgate Institute.

Ingram, John Kells (1823–1907). Irish polymath and follower of Comte. Ingram's entire career was associated with Trinity College, Dublin. A critic of deductive political economy and an advocate of a holistic, historical approach. Author of *A History of Political Economy* (1888), among many other works.

Jevons, Harriet Ann (1838–1910). Harriet Ann Taylor, third daughter of John Edward Taylor (1791–1844), founder and proprietor of the *Manchester Guardian*, married William Stanley Jevons in 1867. After his death she played an important part in collecting and publishing or republishing his work.

Jevons, William Stanley (1835–82). Economist, statistician, and logician. Born in Liverpool and educated at University College, London, Jevons spent five years in Australia as a young man. His *Coal Question* (1865) and his seminal *Theory of Political Economy* (1871) paved the way for his emergence in the 1870s as the leading British economist. His important monetary writings were collected in *Investigations in Currency and Finance* (1884). Jevons taught at Owens

College, Manchester, 1863–76, and was professor of political economy at University College, London, 1876–80. He died in a drowning accident.

Jones, Richard (1790–1855). Economist and clergyman. Educated at Cambridge, Jones succeeded Malthus in 1835 as Professor of Political Economy at Haileybury. A critic of the deductive method of Ricardo, and an advocate of a more inductive and comparative approach.

Jowett, Benjamin (1817–93). Greek scholar and educational leader. Jowett became a Fellow of Balliol College, Oxford, in 1838 and was Tutor from 1842 to 1870 and Master from 1870 until his death. He served as Regius Professor of Greek at Oxford from 1855. For some years, especially after his participation in *Essays and Reviews* (1860), he lay under suspicion of heresy. Jowett was a dedicated reformer in University and College matters, and a supporter of university extension, improved secondary education, and better training for the Indian Civil Service. Balliol took the lead under Jowett's influence in encouraging its students to prepare for public service and take on the burden of Empire. Jowett strove to further the careers of his protégés, of whom Marshall was one, by introducing them to the already established. He took an amateurish interest in political economy and occasionally lectured on the subject.

Kautz, Gyula (1829–1909). Hungarian economist and politician, trained mainly in Germany, and a follower of the older German Historical School of Roscher. Kautz is noted for his work in the history of economics.

Keynes, Florence Ada (1861–1958). Florence Ada Brown, a student at Newnham, 1878–80, married John Neville Keynes in 1882. As her children grew she became an active leader in charity organization and local affairs.

Keynes, John Neville (1852–1949). Logician, economist, and educational administrator. Born in Salisbury, Keynes was educated at University College, London, and Cambridge, where he had a long-time association with Pembroke College. Senior Moralist in 1875, Keynes became Marshall's rather reluctant protégé. He taught logic and some economics in Cambridge for many years, serving as University Lecturer in Moral Science, 1884–1911. But his main activities were administrative, first with the University's Local Examinations and Lectures Syndicate, and after 1910 as the Registrary, the University's chief administrative officer. Keynes published *Studies and Exercises in Formal Logic* (1884) and *Scope and Method of Political Economy* (1891), both works of substantial merit. But by 1891 his scholarly ambitions and his interest in economics had waned, together with his patience with Marshall. Thereafter, he devoted himself increasingly to administrative duties in the University and to private and family life, not least to the proudly anxious upbringing of his extraordinary son, the economist John Maynard Keynes (1883–1946).

Laughlin, James Laurence (1850–1933). American economist. Educated at Harvard, Laughlin taught at Harvard and Cornell before moving to the new University of Chicago in 1892 to head its economics department. A hard-money man, Laughlin's largely forgotten publications focus on monetary issues. He edited the *Journal of Political Economy* for many years.

Launhardt, Carl Friedrich Wilhelm (1832–1918). German engineer and economist, a pioneer of mathematical economics. Launhardt spent most of his life in Hanover, his birthplace, where he was associated with the Polytechnic Institute (subsequently University). His most important economic work was his *Mathematische Begründung der Volkswirtschaftslehre* (1885), an application and development of marginalist ideas.

Laveleye, Émile Louis Victor de (1822–92). Belgian economist of wide interests and socialist inclinations. Professor at the University of Liège. His writings are little remembered.

Lavergne, Louis Gabriel Léonce Guillhaud de (1809–80). French agricultural economist and politician, noted for his studies of the rural economy in Britain and France.

Leslie, Thomas Edward Cliffe (1827–82). Irish economist. Leslie was educated at Trinity College, Dublin, and was professor of jurisprudence and political economy at Queen's College, Belfast, from 1853 until his death, residing predominantly in London, however. A critic of the deductive method in political economy, Leslie espoused a more factual and comparative approach in his applied writings. His influential economic essays were collected in his *Essays on Political and Moral Philosophy* (1879).

Levasseur, Pierre Émile (1828–1911). French historian and economist, noted for his studies of the history of the working classes. He also wrote on monetary history.

McCulloch, John Ramsay (1789–1864). Economist. Born and educated in Scotland, McCulloch was a discriminating follower of Ricardo. A voluminous writer on economic and commercial topics, McCulloch lived in London after 1820. His best-known work is his *Principles of Political Economy* (1825). He was the first Professor of Political Economy at University College, London, 1828–37.

Macleod, Henry Dunning (1821–1902). Economist of somewhat idiosyncratic views. Born in Scotland and educated at Cambridge, Macleod became a voluminous and opinionated writer on economic and monetary matters. An inveterate applicant for academic posts, he never obtained one, although he was permitted to lecture in Cambridge for a short time in the late 1870s.

Macmillan, Alexander (1818–96). Publisher. Younger brother of Daniel Macmillan (1813–57), founder of the publishing firm of Macmillan and Company. Initially booksellers in Cambridge, the brothers commenced as publishers in 1844 and moved the main business to London.

Macmillan, Frederick Orridge (1851–1936). Publisher. Elder son of Daniel Macmillan, the founder of Macmillan and Company. Frederick's career was devoted to the family business, in which he rapidly took a prominent and eventually dominant role, helping establish the firm as one of the world's leading publishers. A leader in the publishing industry, he was largely responsible for the Net Book Agreement of 1890, in which Marshall's *Principles* played a significant part. He was knighted in 1909.

McPherson, David (1746–1816). Historian, born and educated in Scotland. Compiler of the *History of Commerce* (1805) and other chronicles pertaining to economic history.

McTaggart, John McTaggart Ellis (1866–1925). Hegelian philosopher. In 1888 McTaggart obtained a First in the Moral Sciences Tripos and also won the Marshall Prize. For some years he assisted Marshall's elementary teaching by vetting the papers of students. A Fellow of Trinity from 1891, McTaggart was lecturer in Moral Sciences from 1897 to 1923. He took little further interest in economics and, perhaps partly because a staunch feminist, soon drifted apart from Marshall, opposing the establishment of the new Economics Tripos in 1902–3.

McVane, Silas Marcus (1842–1914). American economist. Born in Canada and educated at Harvard, he taught political economy and history at Harvard, 1875–1911. As an economist, a conservative Classical die-hard, but of some subtlety.

Malthus, Thomas Robert (1766–1834). Economist and pioneer in the study of population. Educated in Cambridge, Malthus, an ordained clergyman, became in 1805 professor of political economy at the East India College, Haileybury. Immortalized by his *Essay on the Principle of Population* (1798). His subsequent *Principles of Political Economy* (1820) echoed his amicable disagreements with Ricardo.

Mangoldt, Hans Karl Emil von (1824–68). German economist. A teacher at Göttingen and Freiburg, Mangoldt is remembered mainly for his *Grundriss* (1863), a theoretical work anticipating marginalist ideas and Marshallian partial-equilibrium analysis.

Marshall, Agnes (1845–?). Younger sister of Alfred. Died in India. See Appendix I.

Marshall, Charles William (1841–?). Elder brother of Alfred. See Appendix I.

Marshall, Henry (1821–80). Paternal uncle of Alfred. See Appendix I.

Marshall, Louisa Maria (1818–1907). Paternal aunt of Alfred. See Appendix I.

Marshall, Mabel Louise (1850–1912). Youngest sister of Alfred. Married Erneste Delabeare Guillebaud (1856–1907). See Appendix I.

Marshall, Mary Paley (1850–1944). One of the initial group of students attending what was to become Newnham College, Mary Paley attended Marshall's lectures for women and successfully sat the Moral Sciences Tripos papers of 1874. Returning to Newnham in 1875 as a teacher, she and Marshall became engaged in 1876 and married in 1877, with the consequence that Marshall had to resign his Fellowship at St John's. The two moved to Bristol, where Mary soon began to teach political economy to the day students at the

University College, Marshall being the College's Principal. The *Economics of Industry* (1879) appeared under their joint names. It had been commenced by Mary alone, but Marshall had taken an increasing hand after their engagement. Mary published little after this, but she did return to teaching economics at Newnham when the two came back to Cambridge in 1885, continuing to do so until 1908, when she began to serve in an advisory capacity as Director of Economic Studies, withdrawing finally in 1916. Although sacrificing her own interests to a considerable degree in order to smooth Marshall's path, she maintained a sphere of freedom, and a degree of independence, which produced a late blossoming in her last two decades. Her continued engagement in economics permitted her a role in Marshall's writing as critic and editor, as he acknowledged in his prefaces. Mary was an enthusiastic water-colourist, an avocation for which she showed a modest talent. For further details see Appendix I.

Marshall, Rebecca (1817–78). Mother of Alfred, née Oliver. See Appendix I.

Marshall, William (1812–1901). Father of Alfred. See Appendix I.

Martin, John Biddulph (1841–97). Banker and economist. After education at Oxford, Martin entered the family bank. A member, and eventually president, of the [Royal] Statistical Society, he published articles on monetary and banking issues. One of the founders of the British Economic Association.

Marx, Karl Heinrich (1818–83). German philosopher, economist, socialist, agitator, and habitué of the British Museum. Author of *Das Kapital* (1867).

Menger, Carl (1840–1921). Austrian economist, the progenitor of the Austrian School of Economics. Menger's *Principles of Economics* (1871) was one of the founding works of marginalism. Professor of political economy at Vienna from 1879 to 1903, his polemics against Schmoller on methodology gave rise to the infamous 'methodenstreit' of the 1880s.

Mill, John Stuart (1806–73). English philosopher. The leading philosophical and social thinker of his age, educated by his father, James Mill (1773–1836), to carry on the utilitarian cause. Mill's contributions to economics were significant and went well beyond polishing Ricardo. His *Principles of Political Economy* (1848) dominated the Anglo-American scene for the next 30 to 40 years, to be superseded only by Marshall's *Principles*.

Munro, Joseph Edward Crawford (1849–96). Lawyer and economist. Born in Ireland and educated in Belfast and Cambridge, where he obtained a First in the Law Tripos of 1875. Called to the Bar in 1876. He served as professor of political economy and jurisprudence at Owens College, Manchester, 1882–92. This brought him into the ambit of economists and involved him in the study of economic issues, but he was primarily a legal scholar and authority.

Nicholson, Joseph Shield (1850–1927). A member of Trinity, Nicholson obtained a First in the Moral Sciences Tripos of 1877, having previously studied at King's College, London, and in Edinburgh and Heidelberg. He won the Cobden Prize at Cambridge in 1877 for his essay *The Effects of Machinery on Wages* (1879) and remained in Cambridge until 1880 as a private tutor. From 1880 to 1925 he served as professor of political economy at the University of Edinburgh. He wrote mainly on monetary topics. His three-volume *Principles of Economics* (1893–1911) remained in the tradition of Mill and avoided any semblance of discipleship to Marshall, who does not seem to have had a strong influence on Nicholson.

Paley, Mary (1850–1944). See Marshall, Mary Paley.

Palgrave, Robert Harry Inglis (1827–1919). Banker and economist. Palgrave joined at age 16 the banking firm of Gurney and Company in its Great Yarmouth office, eventually becoming a partner. His business concerns and responsibilities did not deter him from undertaking research and writing on economic and statistical matters and he became an authority on the financial sector. He was closely involved in various scholarly organizations, especially the [Royal] Statistical Society, the British Association, the Institute of Bankers, and eventually the British Economic Association. In the 1880s he was an unsuccessful applicant for the chairs in economics at Oxford and Cambridge, and embarked on the organization and editing of the *Dictionary of Political Economy* (1894–9), the work for which he is best remembered. Knighted 1909.

Pantaleoni, Maffeo (1857–1924). Italian economist and occasional politician. One of the leading Italian economists of his era, Pantaleoni taught at Pavia and Rome. His *Pure Economics* (1889) owed much to Marshall's privately printed *Pure Theory* chapters (1879) and was an influential second-round contribution to marginalism. More generally, Pantaleoni looked beyond the marginalist paradigm to a broader and more evolutionary basis for economics.

Pearson, Karl (1857–1936). Mathematician, bio-statistician, eugenicist, and polemicist. Pearson was Third Wrangler in 1879, becoming a Fellow of King's in 1880. From 1884 he was Goldsmid Professor of Applied Mathematics and Mechanism in University College, London, and eventually served as Galton Professor of Eugenics in the University of London, 1911–33. During the 1880s his interests ranged widely over literature, philosophy, and science, but by the 1890s he was concentrating increasingly upon bio-statistics and genetics, becoming a major figure in the development of statistical theory. He founded the journal *Biometrika* in 1901 and edited it for many years. The Eugenics Laboratory at University College, headed by him from 1906, was prominent in the study of social pathologies. An enthusiastic controversialist, Pearson had a running dispute in 1910–11 with Marshall and John Maynard Keynes (1883–1946) over the effects upon children of parents' alcoholism.

Perry, Arthur Latham (1830–1905). American economist. Perry was educated at Williams College and taught there for many years as Professor of History and Political Economy. A follower of Bastiat, and an exponent of free-market free-trade views, Perry is known mainly as a successful but superficial writer of elementary textbooks on economics.

Phelps, Lancelot Ridley (1853–1936). A member of Oriel College Oxford for 64 years, becoming a Fellow in 1877 and serving as Provost, 1914–29. Phelps's teaching was wide in scope, ranging from classics to political economy. In 1885 he succeeded Marshall and J. N. Keynes as lecturer to the Indian Civil Service probationers at Oxford. Heavily involved in Oxford's poor-law administration and local government, he became a recognized authority on poor-law matters and was an influential member of the Royal Commission on the Poor Law, 1905–9. A member of the Oxford group, linked to the Christian Social Union, that launched in 1890 the *Economic Review*, a competitor to the projected *Economic Journal*.

Porter, George Richardson (1792–1852). Statistician. Failing as a sugar broker, Porter devoted himself to economics and statistics, becoming in 1834 head of the statistical department of the Board of Trade, and in 1841 the Board's joint secretary. One of the founders of the [Royal] Statistical Society and author of *The Progress of the Nation* (1836–43).

Potter, Beatrice (1858–1943). See Webb, Beatrice.

Price, Bonamy (1807–88). Economist. Born in Guernsey and educated at Oxford, where he took a double first in mathematics and classics in 1825, Price taught at Rugby School from 1830 to 1850. After some years of involvement in business, he was elected in 1868 to the Drummond Professorship of Political Economy at Oxford, in succession to J. E. Thorold Rogers who had made himself too unpopular to secure re-election. Price held the chair until his death, being re-elected twice. He was diligent in his duties and published several works on economics, but showed little originality.

Price, Langford Lovell Frederick Rice (1862–1950). Economist and economic historian. Price was educated at Oxford ('Greats' 1885) where he came under Marshall's influence. Appointment as lecturer to the Toynbee Trust led to his *Industrial Peace* (1887), for which Marshall wrote a preface. A Fellow of Oriel College, Oxford, from 1888, he remained for the rest of his career as a teacher in Oxford, turning increasingly towards economic history and away from Marshall's style of economics. He assisted with the proofs of Marshall's *Principles* and reviewed the book sympathetically, even fulsomely, in the *Economic Journal* of 1891. An early supporter of the British Economic Association, he eventually drifted into the opposing historicist camp, more in sympathy with Ashley and Cunningham than with Marshall or Edgeworth. The latter's ineffectiveness in promoting economic study at Oxford was a further irritant.

Pryme, George (1781–1863). Lawyer and economist. Sixth Wrangler in the Mathematical Tripos of 1803, Pryme became a Fellow of Trinity in 1805. Called to the Bar in 1806, he practised law for many years, serving also as Member of Parliament for Cambridge from 1832 to 1841. After 1816 he lectured regularly on political economy in the University and was granted the title of Professor of Political Economy in 1828. He bequeathed to the University a collection of economic books and pamphlets. Pryme showed no great originality as an economist and his chief claim to fame is as Cambridge's first professor of political economy, although the chair Marshall was to hold was established only after Pryme's retirement, Henry Fawcett being its first incumbent.

Quesnay, François (1694–1774). French physician and economist, leader of the Physiocrats and inventor of the 'Tableau Économique' which took a prominent role in Physiocratic thought.

Ramsay, William (1852–1916). Chemist. Educated at Glasgow, Ramsay was Professor of Chemistry at University College, Bristol, 1880–7, and subsequently at University College, London, 1887–1912. At Bristol he also served as Principal, 1881–7, succeeding Marshall. Recipient of the Nobel Prize for Chemistry in 1904 for his pioneering work on inert gases, he was one of the leading chemists of his day. Knighted 1902.

Rau, Karl Heinrich (1792–1870). German economist. For many years a professor at Heidelberg. His Smithian *Lehrbuch* (1826–37) was the most successful German text on political economy of its era and went through many editions, some of which introduced a graphical representation of supply and demand.

Ricardo, David (1772–1823). Economist and financier. Ricardo's *Principles of Political Economy and Taxation* (1817) was a seminal work for the British Classical School.

Rogers, James Edwin Thorold (1823–90). Economist and economic historian. Tooke Professor at King's College, London, 1859–90 and Drummond Professor at Oxford 1862–8. His radical views and abrasive style prevented his re-election to the latter chair in 1868, but he was eventually re-elected in 1888 and held the chair until his death. A supporter of laisser-faire policies, but a critic of deductive economics, Rogers is best remembered for his monumental *History of Agriculture and Prices in England* (1886–1902).

Roscher, Wilhelm Georg Friedrich (1817–94). German economist, the leader of the 'older' German Historical School of Economics, emphasizing inductive methods and the study of patterns of economic development, but not bitterly anti-theoretical. Teaching at Leipzig from 1848, his *System der Volkswirtschaft* (1854) was the leading German text of its era. He also produced major studies of the history of economic thought.

Sax, Emil (1845–1927). Austrian economist. Born in Austrian Silesia and educated in Vienna, Sax was a professor at the University of Prague, 1879–93. His work was independent of Menger's, and his writings on general economics, public finance, and transportation, are now little remembered.

Say, Jean-Baptiste (1767–1832). French economist, whose *Traité* (1803) became the dominant exposition of Smithian ideas but went well beyond Smith in its emphasis on utility and its statement of the 'law of markets'.

Schäffle, Albert Eberhard Friedrich (1831–1903). German sociologist and economist. Professor at Tübingen, 1860–8, and Vienna, 1868–71. Active in public life in his earlier years, he devoted himself after 1871 to copious writing on economic and social matters. Best known for his *Quintessence of Socialism* (1874).

Scheel, Hans von (1839–1901). German statistician. An adherent of the German Historical School, and a leading 'socialist of the chair', Scheel taught at Halle and Berne before entering in 1877 the German imperial statistical bureau, becoming its director in 1891.

Schmoller, Gustav von (1838–1917). German economist, leader of the 'younger' and more strident German Historical School of Economics. Schmoller was professor at Berlin, 1882–1913, from which position he dominated German economics. His disputes on methodology with Menger gave rise to the 'methodenstreit'. His publications were predominantly historical.

Schönberg, Gustav Friedrich von (1839–1908). German economist, an adherent of the 'younger' German Historical School led by Schmoller. Schönberg wrote on social issues, including industrial relations, but is remembered mainly for the editorial work on his *Handbuch* (1882), a leading encyclopaedia of economics in its day.

Seligman, Edward Robert Anderson (1861–1939). American economist. Trained at Columbia University and in Europe, Seligman taught at Columbia from 1885 to 1931. An expert in public finance, he rivalled Foxwell as a collector of early economic literature. Extensively involved in public affairs, he was also a founder of the American Economic Association.

Senior, Nassau William (1790–1864). Economist and lawyer. Educated at Oxford, Senior was the first incumbent of its Drummond Professorship of Political Economy, 1825–30, and was re-elected to the chair in 1847, holding it until 1852. He was widely involved in governmental inquiries as adviser, advocate, and Commissioner. Operating within the general Ricardian framework, he nevertheless made significant departures and his ideas on utility, abstinence, and method were particularly noteworthy. His *An Outline of the Science of Political Economy* (1836) is the most systematic of his somewhat fragmentary economic writings.

Sidgwick, Henry (1838–1900). Philosopher and occasional writer on economics. Graduating as Senior Classic, Sidgwick became in 1859 a Fellow of Trinity. Initially teaching classics, his interests moved towards the moral sciences. Resigning his Fellowship in 1869 because of religious scruples, he continued as College Lecturer in moral sciences, taking the leadership among the small group, including Marshall, of those teaching for the Moral Sciences Tripos. He became Knightsbridge Professor of Moral Philosophy in 1883. Following the publication of his *Methods of Ethics* (1874), Sidgwick became increasingly interested in economics, an interest culminating in his *Principles of Political Economy* (1883). Although primarily drawing on Millian ideas, Sidgwick broke new ground in his discussion of the role of government. After Marshall's return to Cambridge in 1885, there was considerable friction with Sidgwick over the administration and reform of the Moral Sciences Tripos. Sidgwick was a promoter and advocate of women's education in Cambridge, taking a leading role in the establishment of Newnham College. Marshall, initially an enthusiastic supporter of this movement, gradually drifted into resolutely opposing further advance, and this further estranged him from Sidgwick.

Smith, Adam (1723–90). Scottish economist and philosopher, author of *Theory of Moral Sentiments* (1759) and *Wealth of Nations* (1776), the latter the fountainhead of the British Classical School of Economics and one of the most celebrated works in the literature of economics.

Sorley, William Ritchie (1855–1935). Philosopher. Born in Scotland, Sorley was educated at Edinburgh and Cambridge, where he gained a first in the Moral Sciences Tripos of 1882. He was Professor of Philosophy at Cardiff, 1888–94, and Aberdeen, 1894–1900, before returning to Cambridge to succeed Sidgwick as Knightsbridge Professor of Moral Philosophy, 1900–33. He became a Fellow of Trinity in 1901. In the later 1880s he was one of the early lecturers for the Toynbee Trust, publishing an essay on *Mining Royalties* (1889).

Stanton, Vincent Henry (1846–1924). Theologian. A student at Trinity, Stanton was Twentieth Wrangler in 1870. He was a Fellow of Trinity 1872–1924, Ely Professor of Divinity 1889–1916, Regius Professor of Divinity 1916–22, and Honorary Canon of Ely 1916–24. In the 1870s he taught political economy to extension classes.

Stephen, Leslie (1832–1904). English man of letters. Educated at King's College, London, and Cambridge, where he was Twelfth Wrangler in 1854, he held a Fellowship at Trinity Hall, 1854–67. His *Sketches from Cambridge by a Don* (1865) and his *Life of Henry Fawcett* (1885) are informative on the Cambridge of his era. Stephen had a continuing interest in political economy, his views on it being essentially classical, and his most notable contribution in this regard was *The English Utilitarians* (1900). His progeny became central members of the Bloomsbury Group.

Stuart, James (1843–1913). Born in Scotland and educated at St Andrew's and Cambridge, where he was Third Wrangler in the Mathematical Tripos of 1866, Stuart became a Fellow of Trinity in 1867. He was Cambridge's Professor of Mechanism and Applied Mechanics, 1875–89, after which he moved into the business world. He was a Member of Parliament, 1884–1900 and 1906–10. Stuart was mainly responsible for the establishment of Cambridge extension lecturing in 1873 and for providing early leadership to it.

Sumner, William Graham (1840–1910). American economist and sociologist. Educated at Yale, and in Europe, he returned to Yale in 1872 as Professor of Political and Social Science. Noted for his staunch belief in laisser-faire and his Social Darwinism, Sumner's interests moved increasingly into sociology.

But his earlier, and primarily economic, writings focused on monetary issues and protectionism.

Thornton, William Thomas (1813–80). Friend and colleague of John Stuart Mill and writer on economic and social issues, sympathetic to cooperation and trade unions. His *On Labour* (1869) was the stimulus for Mill's recantation of the wages-fund doctrine.

Thünen, Johann Heinrich von (1783–1850). German economist, landowner, and agriculturalist. Thünen's remarkable *Der Isolierte Staat* (1826–63) opened up new ground in location and distribution theory, and in the application of mathematics to economics. Drawn from the experience of administering his own estate, Thünen's work appealed strongly to Marshall, who claimed to have been considerably influenced by it.

Tocqueville, Alexis Charles Henri Clérel de (1805–59). French writer and historian, author of *Democracy in America* (1835–40).

Todhunter, Isaac (1820–84). Mathematician and noted Cambridge mathematical coach. Senior Wrangler in the Mathematical Tripos of 1848 and a Fellow of St John's from 1849 until his marriage in 1864. He returned as Honorary Fellow in 1874.

Tooke, Thomas (1774–1858). English merchant and economist, born in Russia and active in the Anglo-Russian trade. Tooke became an expert on monetary matters and was a chief spokesman of the 'Banking School' in the debates surrounding the Bank Charter Act of 1844. His *History of Prices and the State of Circulation* (1838), subsequently extended with the aid of William Newmarch (1820–82), was a remarkable factual inquiry which buttressed Tooke's opposition to the quantity theory of money and its 'Currency School' proponents.

Toynbee, Arnold (1852–83). Economist and economic historian. Educated at Oxford, Toynbee became upon graduation lecturer to the Indian Civil Service probationers at Balliol, despite having taken only a pass degree. An inspiring teacher and a passionate supporter of social causes, Toynbee, along with Thomas Hill Green (1836–82) did much to awaken 'Young Oxford' to the plight of the poor. Toynbee mistrusted the a priori approach of earlier economists, and his posthumously published *Lectures on the Industrial Revolution* (1884) gave impetus to the rise of economic history in Britain. His flame burned too brightly to last, but his example and influence helped turn younger Oxford scholars against the main tradition of British economics continued by Marshall.

Toynbee, Charlotte Maria (c. 1840–?). Charlotte Maria Atwood married Arnold Toynbee in 1879 and outlived him by many years. She was active in promoting the posthumous publication of his essays and lectures.

Turgot, Anne Robert Jacques (1727–81). French philosopher, economist, and administrator, associated with the Physiocrats. His *Reflections on the Formation and Distribution of Wealth* (1770) is a masterpiece of theoretical analysis.

Twiss, Travers (1809–97). Lawyer and economist. Twiss's career was devoted mainly to the law, and he served as Regius Professor of Civil Law at Oxford from 1855 to 1870. He did, however, hold the Drummond Professorship of Political Economy at Oxford for one term, 1842–7, and this gave rise to his *View of the Progress of Political Economy in Europe*, one of the earliest histories of the subject.

Venn, John (1834–1923). Logician and University historian. Sixth Wrangler in the Mathematical Tripos of 1857, Venn was a Fellow of Caius from 1857 to 1923. After holding a couple of curacies, he was College Lecturer in Moral Science from 1862. His interests, immortalized in the Venn diagram, were primarily in logic and probability, and his *The Logic of Chance* (1866) was a significant contribution to probability theory. He devoted much effort to College and University history.

Walker, Francis Amasa (1840–1897). American economist, statistician, and university administrator. Rising to the rank of Brigadier General in the Union forces during the US Civil War, and frequently referred to thereafter as General Walker, he next served the US government in various capacities at the Budget Office, the Bureau of Statistics, and the Indian Bureau, but most importantly by supervising the Censuses of 1870 and 1880. Meanwhile he taught political economy at Yale's Sheffield Scientific School from 1871 to 1880. From 1881 until his death he served as President of the Massachusetts Institute of Technology, also teaching economics there. He published several works on economics, most significantly *The Wages Question* (1876), and in his later years became a prominent exponent of international bimetallism. He was a founder and the first president of the American Economic Association. He and Marshall met on several occasions.

Walras, Léon (1834–1910). French economist, the pioneer of general-equilibrium theory, and a founding father of marginalism. After a chequered early career, Walras taught at the Academy (later University) of Lausanne, 1870–92. There he published his great work *Elements of Pure Economics* (1874–7). An advocate of land nationalization, something of a radical on matters of economic and social policy, and indefatigable in promoting his ideas through correspondence with other economists.

Ward, James (1843–1925). Abandoning a career as a Congregational Minister, Ward entered Cambridge in 1872 and gained a First in the Moral Sciences Tripos of 1874. He was a Fellow of Trinity from 1875 to 1925 and served as Cambridge's Professor of Mental Philosophy and Logic from 1897 to 1925. He was a leader in the introduction of psychological studies in Cambridge. Although once a student of Marshall's, the two came to differ, especially on issues concerning the Moral Sciences Tripos.

Webb, Beatrice (1858–1943). Beatrice Potter, the daughter of Richard Potter, a wealthy industrialist, became involved in social enquiry in the 1880s, assisting Charles Booth, her cousin, in his massive survey of London. She then undertook, against Marshall's advice, a study of cooperation resulting in her *The Cooperative Movement in Great Britain* (1891). Marriage in 1892 to Sidney Webb initiated their famed partnership, with its prodigious production of monumental studies, its Fabian advocacy, its involvement in the affairs of London and the nation, and its crucial role in the foundation of the London School of Economics.

Webb, Sidney James (1859–1947). Born in London in modest circumstances, Webb was employed at age 16 as a clerk. He entered the civil service in 1878, remaining until 1891 when he took a seat on the London County Council. An early member of the Fabian Society, largely through friendship with George Bernard Shaw (1856–1950), he rapidly rose to leadership and by the later 1880s was playing a crucial role in elaborating and advertising the Society's views. At this stage he took some interest in economic theory, being an early contributor to the infant economic journals of the time. His marriage to Beatrice Potter in 1892 launched the famous partnership. After this, his interest in economics proper languished, as the pair turned to studies of administrative history.

Wells, David Ames (1828–98). American economist and administrator. Trained in geology and chemistry, Wells came to economics through journalism, his first book on economic matters being *Our Burden and Our Strength* (1864). Commencing in 1865, he held various governmental positions, mainly concerned with the administration of taxation, and also lectured sporadically at Yale, Harvard, and other institutions. A hard–money man, and a leading advocate of laisser faire policies, he published extensively on economic issues, *Recent Economic Changes* (1889) being his best-known work.

Whewell, William (1799–1866). Philosopher, mathematician, and scientist. A leading figure for many years in Cambridge and British scientific circles, Whewell was Master of Trinity from 1841 until his death. His wide-ranging interests extended to political economy, which he hoped to impel in a more inductive direction. He published four memoirs (1829–50) offering a critique of Ricardian economics and edited Richard Jones's *Literary Remains* (1859). He also published *Six Lectures on Political Economy* (1862).

Wicksteed, Philip Henry (1844–1927). Wicksteed's interests were wide-ranging. A Unitarian minister, 1867–97, he was also heavily involved in university extension lecturing, 1887–1919, lecturing on literature and philosophy as well as economics, and becoming an authority on Dante. In the 1880s, stimulated by the ideas of Henry George, he mastered Jevons's *Theory of Political Economy* and used its approach in criticism of Marx and also in the exposition and elaboration offered in Wicksteed's own *Alphabet of Economic Science* (1888). His most important theoretical contribution to economics was his *Coordination of the Laws of Distribution* (1894). *Commonsense of Political Economy*

(1910), his most wide-ranging work, showed affinities to the ideas of the Austrian School of Economics.

Young, Arthur (1741–1820). Agricultural expert and economist. Young's careful descriptions of agricultural conditions and methods, based on his extensive travels, were influential and remain important source material. He was less successful as a systematizer and economic thinker, his main economic work being *Political Arithmetic* (1774–9).

CHRONOLOGY FOR ALFRED MARSHALL, 1842–1890

1842	Born in Bermondsey (26 July).
1852–61	Attended the Merchant Taylors' School, London.
1861–65	An undergraduate at St John's College, Cambridge.
1865	Second Wrangler in the Mathematical Tripos of 1865.
	Substitute teacher of Mathematics at Clifton College.
	Elected Fellow of St John's College.
1865–68	Mathematical coaching: increasing involvement in philosophy, psychology and political economy.
1868	Appointed as College Lecturer in Moral Sciences at St John's.
1871	Published a review of W. S. Jevons, *Theory of Political Economy* in *Academy* (1 April): see *Memorials*, pp. 93–100.
1871–5	Involved in the teaching of women students at what was to be Newnham College.
1873	Presented his economic theories in a paper to the Cambridge Philosophical Society: see *Early Economic Writings*, vol. 2, pp. 283–5.
1874	Published his essay 'The Future of the Working Classes': see *Memorials*, pp. 101–18.
	Published short articles on 'The Laws of Political Economy' and 'The Province of Political Economy' in the *Beehive*, a radical labour journal (April–May): reprinted in R. Harrison 'Two Early Articles by Alfred Marshall' *Economic Journal*, September 1963.
	Mary Paley sat successfully the papers for the Moral Sciences Tripos.
1875	Visited North America (June–October).
	Mary Paley returned to teach at Newnham (October).
1876	Published his essay 'Mr Mill's Theory of Value' in the *Fortnightly Review* (April): see *Memorials*, pp. 119–43.
1877	Married Mary Paley (17 August).
	Resigned his positions at Cambridge.
	Appointed first Principal of University College, Bristol, founded 1876, and also its Professor of Political Economy.
1878	Mary Marshall began to teach political economy to the day students in Bristol.
1879	The book *Economics of Industry*, jointly authored by Alfred and Mary Paley Marshall, published by Macmillan.

Marshall's unpublished chapters on 'The Pure Theory of Foreign Trade: The Pure Theory of Domestic Values' printed and circulated by Henry Sidgwick: see *Early Economic Writings*, vol. 2, pp. 111–236.

1880   Gave evidence to the official enquiry into 'Intermediate and Higher Education in Wales and Monmouthshire'.

1881   Published a review of F. Y. Edgeworth, *Mathematical Psychics*, in *Academy* (18 June): see *Early Economic Writings*, vol. 2, pp. 265–8.

Revised edition of *Economics of Industry* published.

Resigned positions at Bristol.

1881–2   Extended stay on the Continent (September–August), wintering in Palermo. Composition of *Principles* (*1*) begun.

1882   Returned to Bristol as Professor of Political Economy.

1883   Gave public lectures on 'Progress and Poverty' in Bristol.

Appointed lecturer at Balliol College, Oxford, in succession to Arnold Toynbee, with responsibility for teaching political economy to Indian Civil Service probationers.

1884   Elected to a non-stipendiary Fellowship at Balliol.

Published his essay 'Where to House the London Poor' in *Contemporary Review* (March): see *Memorials*, pp. 142–51.

Appointed Professor of Political Economy in the University of Cambridge in succession to Henry Fawcett (December).

1885   Elected a Professorial Fellow of St John's College, Cambridge.

Delivered and published his Inaugural Lecture, 'The Present Position of Political Economy': see *Memorials*, pp. 152–74.

Presented a paper to the Industrial Remuneration Conference, subsequently published in the Proceedings of the Conference.

Published 'Theories and Facts about Wages' in the *Cooperative Annual:* see *Guillebaud*, pp. 598–614.

Published 'Graphic Methods of Statistics' in the *Jubilee Volume* of the [Royal] Statistical Society: see *Memorials*, pp. 175–87.

Provided a preface for a reprint of W. Bagehot, *Postulates of English Political Economy*.

Mary Marshall resumed teaching at Newnham.

1886   Submitted written evidence to the Royal Commission on the Depression of Trade and Industry: see *Official Papers*, pp. 1–16.

The building of Balliol Croft completed (August).

1887   Published 'Remedies for Fluctuations of General Prices', *Contemporary Review* (March): see *Memorials*, pp. 188–211.

Supplied a preface for L. L. F. R. Price, *Industrial Peace*, a work sponsored by the Toynbee Trust: see *Memorials*, pp. 212– 26.

Published a note 'The Theory of Business Profits', *Quarterly Journal of Economics* (July), responding to criticisms by F. A. Walker: see *Guillebaud*, pp. 670–5.

1887–8   Gave written and oral evidence to the Royal Commission on the Values of Gold and Silver (December-January): see *Official Papers*, pp. 17–195.

1888   Published a note 'Wages and Profits', *Quarterly Journal of Economics* (January) responding to criticisms by S. M. McVane: see *Guillebaud*, pp. 822–7.

1889   Delivered and published his Presidential Address 'Cooperation' to the Cooperative Congress at Ipswich (June): see *Memorials*, pp. 227–55.

1890   *Principles (1)* published (July).

          Delivered and published his Presidential Address 'Some Aspects of Competition' to Section F of the British Association for the Advancement of Science at Leeds (September): see *Memorials*, pp. 256–91.

          Inaugural Meeting of the British Economic Association, London (November).

LIST OF LETTERS REPRODUCED IN VOLUME 1

LETTERS 1–332

1. To the *Cambridge University Gazette*, 2 December 1868[1]

The Previous Examination[2]

A time when the overcrowding of the Senate House by the Candidates for the Previous Examination is attracting attention is singularly appropriate for raising the question whether there is any one type of Examination which can satisfy the various requirements of all classes of men in the middle of their University career. Mr. Sidgwick has suggested (*University Gazette*, No. 3), that to the present Pass Examination there should be added an Examination for Honours in Elementary Mathematics.[3] I want to go a little further.

I should like that beside the 'Previous' Pass Examination there should be a 'Previous' Honour Examination in Latin, and a 'Previous' Honour Examination in the applications of Elementary Mathematics to Physical Science: that for either or both of these, any one who chose might be a candidate: that it should not be required of Candidates for any Tripos, except the Classical, to have gone through the 'Previous' Pass Examination, provided they had taken Honours in the former of these two Examinations: and that the same exemption should be granted to Candidates for any Tripos except the Mathematical, provided they had taken honours in the latter of them. A man, who failed in one of these Honour Examinations, might either receive a 'Certificate of satisfaction' from his Examiners, or be compelled to go through the Pass Examination of the succeeding year.

It seems to me scarcely possible to overestimate the benefit which the adoption of some such scheme as this might confer on men of nascent energy, by saving them from the intense demoralisation of deliberately and elaborately doing things badly for the sake of a rambling Pass Examination.

Mathematical men are, I think, often deeply injured by the systematic superficiality of their Classical studies. If the time which they spend on Latin and Greek were concentrated on Latin alone, it would in most cases enable them to read Virgil and Lucretius with ease and with pleasure, and to obtain much of that culture which arises from a real acquaintance with the great minds of a great nation. With regard to their own subject, they are taught to consider as mere cram a knowledge of the language of any new method of investigation without a thorough grasp of the idea of that method. Yet the University course compels them, their Schoolmasters, and their College Tutors to conspire together in order that they may attain some verbal knowledge of two languages, even where there is no hope that they will ever acquire any grasp of the ideas, to the expression of which the chief value of the languages is owing. Can such a practical lesson be without effect on their Mathematical studies; and on their future life? Let any one look at the present 'Accidence Paper.' Let him reflect that, for many at least of those Mathematical men who do not intend to take Holy Orders, it represents, not the means to, but the absolute end of, their Classical study; and let him say whether its grittiness does not set his teeth on edge. A Mathematical man who devotes much time to his Classical 'Subjects' may be thereby compelled to forego the acquisition of a new scientific method, besides losing places in his Tripos. In exchange he is enabled to 'get up' some extra pages of a Latin or a Greek book and to learn aorists[4] a few more aorists, genders, and genitive cases. He reads his author too slowly and painfully to be able to enter into his spirit: he might have entered into the spirit of the method which he loses. Can his private tutor be blamed for hinting to him that it is only virtue that can be its own reward, and for exhorting him not to allow his Classics to interfere more than is absolutely necessary with his 'work.' But, if he were likely to read Latin in that liberal and appreciative manner which an Honour Examination can foster, different advice would often be given; even if it were only with a view to that freshness which a man would bring back to his Mathematical work after an intelligent contact with a mind like that of Lucretius. Nor would the pupil feel that in following such advice he was sacrificing his material interests.

The effects of an Honour Examination in the applications of Elementary Mathematics to Physical Science would be for the present more limited; but they would be similar in kind. A knowledge of Algebra may be thorough without being extensive. Most Classical men are compelled to attend lectures on Algebra for a whole year. These in general teach them scarcely any new methods, suggest no new ideas, are barren of practical results, and often, by their endless manipulations of unmeaning symbols, weary them into a hatred or a scorn of Mathematics. It would be, I think, much better if those who, on coming up, have a sound, though limited, knowledge of elementary Algebra and Trigonometry were encouraged to go on at once to Mechanics and Hydrostatics. A hope of being speedily initiated into the chief methods by which the world has attained its present knowledge would be to a large class of Classical men an irresistible attraction, even if their labours were not to be directly requited. Nor does it seem to me that so high a training of the reasoning faculties can be so easily obtained in any other way. It is difficult to say what should be the exact limits of the examination. But, I think, some such a book as that of Mr. Balfour Stewart on Heat, which is singularly rich in methods and in results, might well be added to the list of subjects proposed by Mr. Sidgwick.[5] Taking favourable cases, and assuming unnecessary analysis to be rigorously excluded, I am even sanguine enough to hope that a labour no greater than is demanded for the present 'Three Days' course[6] might suffice for attaining (with or without the aid of the Differential Calculus) a thorough grasp of the Principle of the Conservation of Energy, the connecting link between the Physical Sciences.

Setting aside, however, the cases in which there exists an enthusiasm for this kind of knowledge, or even a strong interest in it, much may be expected from the scarcely lower motive of an honest shame. There is a growing tendency to expect from either sex, and from every rank in life, some knowledge of the more prominent physical phenomena. The cook, who insisted on filling the kettle quite full of water 'for fear the steam should have room to get in and burst it,' is considered to be behind her age. There are, perhaps, many graduates of Cambridge who could not explain clearly why her caution was at once unnecessary and futile; but the number of those who are not ashamed of such ignorance is rapidly diminishing. It seems to me to be very important that the University should take advantage of, and guide this tendency. At present some men read painfully a little dry Mathematics, then forget them, and afterwards read casually some popular works on Natural Phenomena works which are often bad, and always hampered by the want of Mathematical Symbols. Instead of this, men might be led, by a course which would not only interest them, but also afford intellectual training of the highest possible type, to a real insight into the main principles of Physics. An intelligent curiosity thus once excited would be continually stimulated by various occurrences in after life. And, so far at least, the direct influence of the University on their habits of thought would not cease when they left its walls. The proposed Examinations might be made subservient to this great object in other ways, particularly through their relations to the smaller Triposes.[7]

Alfred Marshall.

---

[1] *Cambridge University Gazette*, 2 December 1868, p. 67. The *Gazette*, published weekly in term time between October 1868 and December 1869, was established to provide a vehicle for the circulation of University news and the discussion of University issues. A bound set is preserved in the rare-book room of the Cambridge University Library.

[2] The Previous Examination or 'Little Go' had to be passed by all undergraduates. It was normally sat (in the Senate House) in the fourth term of residence (the Michaelmas term of the second year) and covered a Greek Gospel, both a Latin and Greek classic, Paley's *Evidences of Christianity*, the first three books of Euclid, and elementary arithmetic. Those studying for an honours degree in one of the 'Triposes' were also required to pass in 'Additional Subjects' which were mathematical in character—a feature favouring candidates for the Mathematical Tripos. Honours candidates were permitted to take the Previous Examination after two terms of residence providing that all parts were sat at the same time. Reform of the Previous Examination and of the Ordinary BA which was taken by the large lump of undergraduates not attempting honours—the so called 'Poll men'—were perennial Cambridge issues. For details see Denys Arthur Winstanley, *Later Victorian Cambridge* (Cambridge University Press, Cambridge, 1947), pp. 144–84. Also see Christopher Brooke, *A History of the University of Cambridge*, vol. 4, 1870–1990 (Cambridge University Press, Cambridge, 1993).

[3] Henry Sidgwick, 'University Legislation,' a letter published by the *Cambridge University Gazette*, 11 November 1868, p. 22. Sidgwick proposed replacing the 'additional subjects' of the Previous Examination, taken on a pass-fail basis, by a new examination in 'Elementary Mathematics, pure and applied' that intending Tripos candidates could attempt for classified honours as well as for a pass.

[4] The inclusion of this word was probably a printer's error.

[5] Balfour Stewart, *An Elementary Treatise on Heat* (Clarendon Press, Oxford, 1865). Sidgwick's letter had suggested the following topics: 'Euclid, Algebra, Trigonometry, Statics, Hydrostatics, Dynamics (with some Conic Sections), and easy Astronomy.'

[6] The 'Three Days' were the examinations in the Additional Subjects of the Previous Examination.

[7] The smaller Triposes at this time were the Moral Sciences (1848), Natural Sciences (1848), and Law and History (1868). The two long-established large Triposes were the Mathematical and the Classical, the former being the more prestigious and competitive.

2. To the *Cambridge University Gazette*, 9 December 1868[1]

The Previous Examination

Mr. Sidgwick in his letter on University Legislation[2] calls attention to the probable diminution in the number of those who can venture to carry on two separate studies to the end of their University career, and to the general tendency to specialisation which exists here as elsewhere. It is to be expected, and, I think, to be wished, that the smaller Triposes should increase in size and in number at the expense not only of the Poll but of the last class in the Mathematical and in the Classical Tripos.

History does not indeed point out a better preparation for any future study which a man will have leisure and inclination to pursue than a successful course through one of our great Triposes. They afford to Cambridge a singular power of testing and of promoting thoroughness in one pursuit; and hence, by inculcating a hatred of unthoroughness in all pursuits, of doing what art can do to create genius. A man however who has been in the last class of one of these Triposes, if he does not adopt a scholastic life, frequently settles down at once to practical work: having no interest in the knowledge which he has acquired here, he makes it his first business to forget it: and he has not learnt while here to look at his own special pursuit from the point of view of a genuine student. His mental growth in one direction may have been considerable. And there is one direction in which, if his habits of thought had once begun to extend, they would have been likely to have been fostered by the circumstances of his daily life, and to have been serviceable to the world. But these directions are not the same. The increase of competition and the growing allurements of ephemeral literature render it daily less easy for him to make it a part either of his business or of his pleasure to overcome the difficulties which lie at the commencement of a new line of study. The spontaneous development of a new form of intellectual energy is a very hard task. It is probably altogether too hard for him. About the principles and the history of his profession he knows nothing, and he cares nothing. The old channels of his thought are cut off: no new ones are formed: and he stagnates. The number of those, who think that the intrinsic values of Classical or Mathematical studies are sufficient to compensate for such a result as this, is rapidly diminishing. And there is a growing feeling here and elsewhere that Cambridge may safely defy any University in the civilised world to produce a set of men who, without being specially idle or specially stupid, have made less of their advantages than these men. Occasionally one hears similar remarks applied to men who have taken somewhat higher degrees than these.

The four Minor Triposes which we already have, (to say nothing of those in Theology and in Modern Literature and History, which we probably soon shall have), might be wonderfully effective in removing this reproach, if the University encouraged men to read for them.[3] But the University does not.

A man on coming up frequently does not know what his future career will be: he is perhaps unwilling to lose the credit of his school work: if ambitious, he does not like to content himself with the scanty honours of a Small Tripos: and he most probably decides, rightly enough under the circumstances, to read for one of the others. And thus, if after all he is but an ordinary man, and if his life is not a scholastic one, he probably becomes narrow and lethargic in his intellectual habits, in consequence of the difficulties which the University threw in the way of his obtaining some special teaching in addition to his general training.

There seems to be only one way of removing these difficulties without interfering with the interests of any of those men for whom an almost exclusive devotion to Classics or to Mathematics might be ultimately advantageous. And that is by instituting some such Honour Examinations in the middle of the University course as those which I proposed last week. A man would then be able to carry out during the first half of his time here one or both of the chief branches of his school work. Meanwhile his social habits would be formed without danger of his being brought under the influence of a professional clique. At the end of it he would receive from the University a certificate of his preliminary training, which would be of use to him in after life, and fully satisfy his just ambition. He would then know tolerably well his wishes, his prospects, and his powers: and he could then choose the Tripos for which he should read. If he elected to continue his Classical or his Mathematical studies, he would certainly be in no worse a position than he would have been under the present arrangement. But if not, he might, under the guidance of a Minor Tripos, devote his whole energies to obtaining a sound knowledge of the principles of the subject in which he was most interested. Under this new *régime* indeed there would be such an improvement in the number and in the calibre of the candidates for the Minor Triposes, that the name itself would almost cease to be appropriate.

I must not stray into a discussion of the position which the proposed examinations would take as preparatory for these Triposes. But Mr. Sidgwick, while urging the importance of preliminary training in Elementary Mathematics, makes special reference to one of them—the Moral Sciences Tripos. In relation to it, he insists on the direct benefit of some acquaintance with the subject matter of Mathematics.[4] I should also lay special stress on the indirect benefit of a training in scientific method, in spite of the authorities 'which can be quoted against me.' Doubtless, scientific methods may be misapplied. But it is a coincidence which cannot be altogether devoid of significance that, on the one hand, most of those who have created epochs in the study of mind have had some acquaintance with mathematics, and many of them have been great mathematicians; and, on the other hand, the authorities referred to have been in general better qualified to exemplify than to detect that one-sidedness which arises from the inability to apply a scientific method to those cases in which it is wanted.

There remains a point of some practical importance. I would suggest that, in order to induce classical men to take an interest in the 'Previous' Examination in Latin, it should be joined to an Examination in Greek; and that two lists should be published—one representing the marks for Latin alone—the other, those for Latin and Greek together. Either list might be divided into three classes, each containing three or more divisions. A similar arrangement might, if necessary, be applied to the Previous Examination in Mathematics. These two examinations would then absorb a very large number of University and College examinations, and save examiners and examinees much unwholesome work.

In conclusion I cannot do more than hint at the use which they might subserve, in case it should ever be judged desirable to include in either of the main branches of our University studies a greater variety of subject matter than could be conveniently represented in one Tripos.

Alfred Marshall.

---

[1] *Cambridge University Gazette,* 9 December 1868, p. 55.

[2] See [1.3].

[3] There appear to have been only three minor Triposes at this time: see [1.7]. Perhaps Marshall was counting the medical degree. A Theology Tripos was established in 1871, Triposes in Semitic Languages and Indian Languages in 1872, and the Law and History Tripos was divided into two separate Triposes in 1873. For details see Winstanley, *Later Victorian Cambridge* [1.2], pp. 185–209.

[4] Sidgwick had stated in his letter [1.3] that 'the importance of this preliminary training in Elementary Mathematics can hardly be exaggerated; and any development of new triposes will only make it more felt. As a teacher of Moral Sciences I feel it most strongly. One of the most important branches of Moral Sciences is the enquiry into the nature and conditions of knowledge; which, without such preliminary training, runs great risk of degenerating into shallow dialectics.'

3. To the *Cambridge University Gazette*, 14 April 1869[1]

The Previous Examination

While some modifications in the rules for the Previous Examination are under discussion, I wish to suggest, as a step in the right direction, a small change with regard to it. I propose that there be added to it a Latin paper of a somewhat higher type than those which it now contains: that this be a voluntary paper; but that no knowledge of Greek be required from a man who passes in it. If this be done, mathematical men will be enabled to spend on English and Latin literature that portion of their time and energy which they now devote to Greek accidence and Greek vocabularies. But further, University men have not been less severe than others in their criticisms of those parents who are more anxious about the number than the thoroughness of their daughters' accomplishments. Yet, since the compulsory examinations at Oxford and Cambridge[2] necessarily direct the teaching in the best schools, or at all events in the best parts of them, a parent is forced, often against his will, to make his son 'accomplished,' after some fashion or other, in each of two dead languages, or to forego the advantages of a really good school education for him. By taking the step which I have suggested Cambridge would abdicate her share in this tyranny.

I cannot however abstain from again expressing the opinion that nothing short of University Honour Examinations in the middle of our course can encourage a man while here to devote himself mainly to that pursuit which directly, or indirectly, will have the most influence on his thought in after life; while he yet gives to some second study enough time and energy to obtain a thorough grasp of it. Nor does it seem that the growing evils of College Examinations can be checked in any other way.

Alfred Marshall.

---

[1] *Cambridge University Gazette*, 14 April 1869, pp. 125–6.
[2] These compulsory examinations were the Previous Examination in Cambridge and Responsions in Oxford. Each required both Latin and Greek.

4. To the *Cambridge University Gazette*, 10 November 1869[1]

The Previous Examination

To the scheme for putting the Previous Examination for Honor men in their second term, the objection is much urged that all the advantages which would be thus gained would be increased by putting it at the end of their first term. It is assumed that it could not be put at the beginning of their first term, because their Tutors would be unable to guarantee that the candidates they sent in for it were *bonâ fide* Honor men. Means however are required of enabling Tutors to form a rough estimate of their pupils' abilities before lectures begin. The *special* College Examinations for this purpose would be superseded if the Previous Examination took place very early in October and all Freshmen were re-commended to go in for it. It would only be necessary to publish a list of those who passed in all the subjects, 'additional' as well as 'ordinary;' but an account of the letters which their pupils had obtained in the various subjects would be sent privately to the several Tutors. A trifling redistribution of funds would be required; but labour would be saved to the University educational body as a whole. The already heavy clerk's work of the Senior Examiner would be increased; but this would be taken off his shoulders by the Vice-Chancellor's clerk, whose appointment is, we hope, to follow on, if it does not precede the abolition of Vice-Chancellor's dinners. The education of the schoolboy and the employment of the Poll-man would not be interfered with; but the University would no longer declare that a diffused mediocrity of attainments was a worthy object to which to direct the energies of the Honor man even for one term. At the same time any change that placed the Pass Examination earlier in the course would render it more easy and more necessary to have in the middle of the course Honor Examinations, which would stamp with public recognition any *thorough* mathematical or classical work which a man had done up to that time.

Alfred Marshall.

---

[1] Printed with other letters on the topic, *Cambridge University Gazette*, 10 November 1869, p. 226.

5. To the *Cambridge University Reporter*, 22 February 1871[1]

Celibacy in the University

Mr Morgan has done good service by pointing out some of the effects of the rules which enjoin celibacy on Fellows.[2] I wish to approach the subject from a point of view somewhat different from his.

The working of our University institutions seems to be as follows. We elect to Fellowships each year a number of students selected by a method which is, or by slight modifications may be made, at least as good as any other. A very large portion of the very ablest of these, if estimated by a Tripos standard, and probably a still larger portion if estimated by a broader standard, go out of residence almost immediately. One of the chief motives in most such cases, and in many almost the sole motive, is the hope of winning a position in which they will be able to marry. Of those who remain probably not one fourth devote themselves deliberately to a celibate life, or look forward with confidence to being able to marry without abandoning their studies for some practical work, in most cases that of a parish priest. Their position is similar to that of a farmer who has a short lease and who expects no compensation for improvements. A man wearied with teaching, fascinated by the excitements of term time and the allurements of vacation, must have a strong interest in his study, if, with small prospects of developing its results, he lays the laborious basis of that thorough knowledge which can be fully acquired only in a lifetime. In what proportion of cases is this done? How far is it true that but few mathematical teachers have read much beyond the text-books which they teach; and that it is difficult to find men competent to lecture on the subjects recently introduced into the Tripos? How far is it true that the reason why original questions are not more often set in the higher subjects at present in the Tripos, is that but few examiners have obtained the grasp of these subjects which would be derived from an extensive mathematical reading? How far is it true that, putting aside mere compilations, the contributions to classical and mathematical literature which issue from Cambridge are but few in number, while the brilliancy of those few serves but to show how much may be effected in a life deliberately devoted to study? How far all this is true I do not know; but I have heard it often asserted; and it cannot be wholly false. In so far as it is true, how far is it due to our system? and how far would the evil be removed by that remedy which Mr Morgan proposes, namely the simple abrogation of the rules relating to celibacy?

Let us look at the effects of such a change. The privilege would enable many very able men to continue very important work. On the other hand it would in many cases fall to those who would never have obtained their present posts had the abler men who have made way for them known that this privilege would be granted: posts which it might be possible to fill, after the concession of the privilege, with men of firstrate ability. Moreover, if this change were made, vacancies would be diminished in number, while the value of the Fellowships would be increased. The pursuit of Tripos success would be even more intoxicating than now; the tendency to reaction after it even greater than at present: and there would be no possibility of removing those who fell into comparative lethargy.

If we are to have many married lecturers we must, I think, follow to some extent that portion of the German system which has reference to the appointment of teachers; and which, whatever the other portions of the system may be, appears to be much more successful than our own. The rough test which an examination at the age of twenty-one or twenty-two can afford, should be used to confer the means and privilege of studying and teaching here only for a limited number of years. A second and later selection must decide who are to have the privilege of adopting for life the profession of a Cambridge student and teacher. The first election is guided by definite examination results: and is thoroughly well conducted by the comparatively unprofessional bodies who now elect. But the second election could be based on no such test; and it would be a great advantage if it were conducted by a body who had some special knowledge of the branch of learning which it was supposed the candidate had advanced or was likely to advance. Such a board would be a University board: and thus the Fellows of

Colleges would be saved the experience, painful in a large College and very painful in a small one, of having to decide in doubtful cases whether to pass a sort of vote of want of confidence on a very intimate friend. What title this second election should confer is a matter of indifference. But the person so elected would be required besides performing College duties to deliver lectures on that particular branch to which he had devoted himself, lectures which would form part of an organised system for the whole University.[3] Besides retaining his Fellowship independently of marriage he would receive a fixed annual sum from College or University funds: while yet, as in Germany, part of his income would depend upon the number of his hearers; and he would be kept to his work by the competition of younger lecturers. At the age of, say, fifty-five he would be compelled to retire unless he received special permission to hold his post for some years longer. A liberal retiring pension would be provided for him. The funds for this and other purposes would be obtained from the diminution in the number of Fellowships which would be rendered feasible by the rule by which the tenure of all Fellowships, as far as granted by the first election, would be limited to, say, ten years from the B.A. degree.

If this plan were adopted, the ablest men would in general feel that their best chance of obtaining early a position in which they could marry would be by staying in Cambridge and devoting themselves to some special study. In their first stage they would have every motive that hope and fear can give to be vigorous in their work. And in their second when lecturing on that particular branch of their subject which they had by this time mastered and were now engaged in extending, they would be likely to feel an interest, an enthusiasm in their lectures which cannot be attained in any other way whatever.

Alfred Marshall.

[1] Printed on pp. 205–6 of the *Reporter*, 22 February 1871. The *Reporter* commenced publication in 1870 independently of the University, following the pattern established by the *Gazette*. After its first two years it became the official organ of the University and ceased to publish letters apart from those included in the authorized record.

[2] Henry Arthur Morgan, *The Tenure of Fellowships Considered Especially with Reference to College Tutors and Lecturers* (Privately printed, Cambridge, 1871). This pamphlet by a Fellow of Jesus College was summarized on p. 207 of the *Reporter*, 22 February 1871. It emphasized that the bar to marriage of Fellows meant that experienced College Tutors or Lecturers could rarely be retained, and that an occupation viewed as merely temporary gave little incentive to improve performance.

[3] At this time the system of University Lectureships and Readerships had hardly begun. Only the Professors held University, as opposed to College, appointments.

6. To the *Cambridge University Reporter*, 1 March 1871[1]

The Previous Examination

Much has been written recently upon the details of the Previous Examination. Perhaps many plans in the legislation of recent years would have been avoided if there had existed an opportunity for discussing the convenience of students, of lecturers, and of examiners in as full a manner as has been done in this case. But such discussions proceed on the assumption that the general form of the Examination is to be retained. It may therefore be worth while, before they proceed further, to enquire whether it can remain much longer a mere Pass Examination.

There are three classes of students for whose wants the present Examinations provide tolerably well, viz. those who cannot or will not learn anything thoroughly: those who intend to adopt as their profession the study or teaching of Classics or Mathematics: and, lastly, those who intend to pursue some other profession, but have a liking for Classical or Mathematical studies, and will probably have leisure after their degree sufficient to enable them to lay the foundation of a thorough knowledge of the principles on which the practice of the rest of their lives will be founded. But there is a large and increasing number of men in a position similar to that of those last mentioned, except that they are not likely to have this leisure. And for these there is no adequate provision.

A man, who after ending his Classical or Mathematical studies plunges at once into active work on which they have no direct bearing, finds himself at first especially weak on the practical side. He dreads the consequences of his blunders to himself and to others. He feels, perhaps rightly under the circumstances, that the most urgent and pressing necessity for him is to acquire the rules of thumb of his profession and the habit of applying them readily. It should be the special privilege of a highly educated man to be master of his rules. Instead thereof the rules obtain mastery over the man. He struggles perhaps at first, and makes some bitter remarks on his College education: but he succumbs under the pressure of work; and after a time is no longer conscious of his yoke. Had he overcome the preliminary difficulty at College, and obtained even a slight knowledge of the principles on which these rules are based, each new rule that he came across in practice would find its proper place in his system: his rules would increase his grasp of principles, his principles would enable him to understand his rules. Soon he would feel strong enough to modify old rules and to make new ones; to promote practice by applying to it science, and to promote science by supplying it with inductions. It is a common remark that, while we have in England able practical men and able scientific men, we are lamentably deficient in practical men who understand science. What a boon it would be to England if men more often supplied at the University the missing link between their school work and the business of their lives: if the lawyer more often learnt something here about the history and principles of Law; if the medical man had more often obtained some thorough knowledge of Chemistry and Physiology; if the statesman and the clergyman had more often studied something of ethical and political Philosophy! And yet under our present system a man can very often hardly be blamed for not supplying this missing link. At the commencement of his course there is frequently as to his future profession some uncertainty which cannot be quite cleared up until he has ascertained what his real powers are. The easiest and surest roads to University distinctions and rewards are through Classical and Mathematical studies. It is not unnatural that he should be unwilling to lose all credit for the work he has done at school; and that, in his uncertainty, that which might ultimately be his real interest falls into the background; particularly if the first question which he is likely to be asked at home relates to the market value of his expectation of future emoluments. These difficulties would be all at once removed by the simple plan of allowing him to have the results of his Mathematical and Classical work registered by a University Honor Examination in the middle of his course.

I think then that the Previous Examination should be made a thorough Examination in Classics and Mathematics. Three lists should be published, one corresponding to the marks for Mathematics, one to the marks for Latin alone, and one to the marks for Latin and Greek added together. A man who got honors in Latin should be excused from passing in Greek. But with this exception each man should have to pass in Classics and Mathematics as at present; and besides the honor lists for the several subjects, a list of those who had passed in all should be published as at present. For a third class in the Latin list some attempt at Latin Prose and an 'unseen' translation paper should be required, but none at Latin verse.

This scheme would possess the following advantages besides those already pointed out. Every person who preferred the old mode of examination would be able to avail himself of it unchanged. But freedom would be given to those who preferred, or whose parents and schoolmasters preferred for them, that they should learn to write Latin prose and to read freely Latin authors, instead of getting up small portions of a few Latin and Greek books in such a manner as to have no chance of imbibing from them any literary culture. Again these Examinations would afford a good substitute for, nay an improvement on, those double degrees which are becoming more rare under the influence of increasing competition in either Tripos. It would not seldom happen that a man, who distinguished himself in after life for scientific or literary attainments, would be able to look back with pleasure and just pride to having obtained for Classics or Mathematics respectively a high place, perhaps one of the very highest, in an University Examination in the middle of his course. I hope even that it would be the rule, and not the exception, that Mathematical men who come from good schools would try for a first class in the Latin Examination. Many men again, who now never read for any but pass Examinations, would be induced to read for one at least in preparing for which they would be energised by striving to acquire knowledge instead of being demoralised by struggling to conceal ignorance.

Lastly they would supply a means of awarding University and College

Scholarships; and for various reasons a large number of Examinations would be rendered superfluous.

Alfred Marshall.

[1] Printed on pp. 222–3 of the *Reporter*, 1 March 1871. See [1.2].

7. From Henry Sidgwick, July or August 1871[1]

Trin. Coll.

My dear Marshall

We have just settled the women, after some delay. Miss Larner gets the scholarship: but it is doubtful whether she will come till X^mas—her father is ill.[2]

I was somewhat disappointed in her work: it was precise and clear but certainly jejune—bookwork always written out well, once or twice admirably: but difficult points shirked.

I should have said (if I had not heard anything of her before) that she was well prepared but scarcely promising. She was clearly head in P.E (60 out of 100, next 54) second by 2 marks in Log. We only gave two firsts in Group D, both distinguished in Logic.[3] After some hesitation I did not give any distinction. (60 was supposed to be just on the line). The average was decidedly high in P.E. I only plucked two out of 13. I got Venn to fix the standard for passing level (as nearly as he could) with that of Poll men in June. The second class standard was considerably above this again: this included Miss. M. Kennedy, whose work agreeably surprised me: it was decidedly intelligent, no absurdities, and no bad blunders: everything apprehended to a certain point.

She got with me 49 marks to Miss Larner 60: about the same in Logic.

My plans for lecturing next term are still rather vague, on account of Miss L's uncertainty.

As for Evolution, I quite understood the view you expressed last term, but I do not think I agree with you, and I am quite sure I do not with Karl Marx. This Spiessbürger is after all only our old friend the 'Bourgeois' for whose wicked selfishness Political Economy is supposed to have been invented: when I first read socialistic tracts I was much impressed with the breadth of view implied in this contemptuous term: but on reflection the Bourgeois after all appeared to me the heir of the ages, as far as he went: and so of Bentham's Normal man. I say I do not quite know whether I agree with you: for I do not know whether you mean more than to insist on the *limitations* of Benthamism and the need of supplementing it with some historical sociology. But I certainly do not think it the *special* function of the Philosophy of Jurisprudence to develop dynamical conceptions. On the contrary I feel as if a grasp of the Utilitarian method of determining rules had been of the greatest value to myself, and how few M.P's have really got it any critical debate will indicate. It seems to me that the tendency just now, owing to the positivists, is rather over-historical than otherwise.

However I do not really know if we should disagree: I think I told you that I had worked out principles of *constitutional* jus[4] for B's normal-mensch in two or three lectures; so much t[o][5] my own satisfaction that I am perhaps biassed in favour of the method.

Here it is too hot to work: I am reading novels.

Yours ever | H. Sidgwick

[1] Trinity College, Sidgwick Papers. Marshall noted on it 'July or August 1871 written to me in Switzerland.'

[2] Felicia Larner (1851–1932) and Mary Kennedy (1845–1939), together with Mary Paley (who was to marry Alfred Marshall in 1877), were three of the group of five students which, arriving in October 1871, formed the nucleus for what was to become Newnham College. Sidgwick was a prime mover in this scheme and Marshall an active supporter. See *What I Remember*, pp. 10–21; Rita McWilliams-Tullberg, *Women at Cambridge* (Gollancz, London, 1975), pp. 50–69.

[3] This refers to the Cambridge Higher Local Examination which was open to women. Group D covered the 'moral sciences.' P.E. is Political Economy and Log. is Logic.

[4] Law?

[5] Letter apparently omitted.

8. To Members of the Cambridge University Senate, 22 May 1872[1]

[*The Previous Examination*]

Doubt has been expressed as to whether a member of the Examinations Syndicate could have been in earnest when he 'found running through the various portions of its Scheme a wonderful harmony and unity.'[2] This may be a reason for regretting that a vote is to be taken on the Report at so short a notice; but it is not surprising.[3] A little search, however, will discover a common basis supporting all its chief proposals. Through all of them the old principle is rigidly maintained that a man's study must be not only thorough but broad; while each of them sweeps away a host of vexatious interferences with the liberty of each individual student to choose for himself his own course of study. It does not appear that a man is injured by having his reading tested in an examination, but only by allowing his reading to be warped for the sake of an examination. The scheme proposes, as far as is possible without being unduly cumbrous, to diminish the evils of examinations by increasing the number of ways in which a course of reading may be tested by them.

I will confine my attention to one of its purposes—that of providing increased facilities for the study of the principles of sciences other than mathematics and scholarship. It has been maintained that the existing University arrangements suffice for this purpose. I wish to answer this argument.

We live amid a steadily growing 'ardor of industrialism.' The temptations are daily increasing which urge a man engaged in practical life to devote every action to the direct attainment of some immediate end. However great his intellectual vigor, the bustle of his practice renders it difficult for him unaided to commence the study of the principles of the sciences which bear upon it. If the first painful steps in the study could be taken here, his later progress in it need not be full of toil; his routine work would be a series of opportunities of scientific observation, experiment and reasoning: he would develope science and be developed by it. There are some men who can take these steps here without difficulty. Pollmen can; Fellows of Colleges in their luxuriously busy leisure can; but other men in general cannot do it without foregoing all public recognition of the work that has mainly occupied the previous ten years of their lives. If the school-work of such a man has been thorough, he puts himself at a manifest disadvantage if he obtains Honors only in a small Tripos in which he competes on equal terms with men of a narrower education. In most cases he decides to obtain credit for his school work at whatever cost. He may not be conscious that in so deciding he to some extent sacrifices the advancement of himself to that of his worldly interests: nor even if he be, will the University have exhaustively discharged its entire duty by blaming him for his decision. In a conflict between the improvement of a man's worldly interests and that of himself the weight of his parents' influence will generally be thrown into the balance in favor of the former: and on this ground, if on no other, the conflict ought to be removed. Honor Examinations (let them be called by what name they may) in the middle of the course would do this almost completely. Thorough work in Classics and Mathematics done by those who did not enter for the Classical or Mathematical Tripos respectively would be stimulated and rewarded; and students would not be asked to commit themselves definitely to any one pursuit while they were yet scarcely more than schoolboys.

It is however urged that a man may now devote nine or seven months, if he has them to spare, after taking a place in one of the larger Triposes, to reading for one of the smaller. He may; if he is himself inclined, or if he can be induced by others to cut and dry for an examination the thoughts that have had so short a life. The Regulation that opens this course to him may do more good than harm;[4] but it cannot be said that it much diminishes the number of those men who, though possessing the ability necessary for applying science to practice, have no familiarity with those particular sciences, the rules of which they practise—or do not practise.[5]

Alfred Marshall.

---

[1] An untitled printed flysheet or 'fly' sent to the voting members of the University Senate. Such flys were a characteristic feature of Cambridge academic politics, being circulated energetically when controversial issues were due for a vote in the Senate. From a bound volume of miscellaneous pamphlets preserved in the Library of St John's College, Cambridge. The date is pencilled at the foot in an unknown hand.

[2] This probably alludes to another fly, not identified. Marshall was a member of the Syndicate, appointed on 30 March 1871 to consider the Regulations for the Previous Examination and the General Examination. (The latter was the second examination taken by the ordinary-degree candidates. These candidates also had to attend, and be examined upon, the lectures offered by a Professor as well as taking a 'special' examination in one of a list of subjects that included political economy.)

[3] The Syndicate reported on 27 April 1872 and its Report was discussed by Senate on 17 May and voted upon on 30 May. The Report was quite radical, permitting French and German to be substituted for Latin or Greek and providing for an Initial Previous Examination to be taken by selected students immediately upon entering the University. After considerable manœuvring it was substantially rejected. Greek was to remain compulsory until well after Marshall's death. See *Reporter*, 15 May 1872, pp. 280–95; 22 May 1872, pp. 315–19; 5 June 1872, pp. 344–53; 4 February 1873, pp. 62–9; 11 February 1873, pp. 76–82. Also see Winstanley, *Later Victorian Cambridge* [1.2], pp. 163–71.

[4] After passing Part I of the Classical or Mathematical Triposes, either of which was sufficient to earn an honours degree, students were free to take another Tripos rather than proceeding to Part II.

[5] The account of the discussion on 17 May 1872 of the Syndicate's Report records the following remarks by Marshall (*Reporter*, 22 May 1872, p. 318):

> Mr Marshall thought that although Classics and Mathematics were perhaps the very best training for many, there was an important class to whom it was otherwise. It would be an advantage to a Mathematical man to finish his Classical gymnastics with Latin, and then to read French and German enough to read and understand books, instead of Greek only just enough to make it difficult wholly to forget it. It was an additional advantage of the scheme, that it enabled Mathematical men to compete in Latin with Classical men, without spending labour to acquire a knowledge of Greek accents and genitive cases. He called attention to the increasing hurry and scramble of after-life, leaving little leisure for study: to the great size of each science, requiring a larger portion of life to be given to its study than formerly. Hence, therefore, it was necessary that gymnastic education should end earlier: not however much earlier than it did some time ago. He spoke of the ill reputation of English lawyers on the continent, saying that foreigners were accustomed to describe them as men of good native ability, but knowing nothing of principles. He thought it would have been a boon to them to have studied the history and principles of law before they left Cambridge. There was a greater and more varied opportunity afforded now for the application of ability and thought to many subjects. Gymnastic training was most useful when it taught a man to regard thoughtfully the things that came before him in after life. So Chemistry was better than Differential Equations for a medical man; his faculties would be better exercised in after life if he read the former instead of the latter. He advocated a wider choice of study in opposition to tying men down to a course adapted to a past time. It was of little use to open one set of men's intellectual faculties by a higher education, when they were to have another set of intellectual faculties exercised in the world.

9. From Edwin Abbott Abbott, 25 May 1872[1]

City of London School | E.C

25/5/72

My dear Marshall,

I have looked through the Report of the Syndicate, more particularly Parts II, III & IV, and I very much wish I could come up to vote for it.[2] Without committing myself to every detail in these parts, I quite go with the principle of them. I sincerely trust the Report, as a whole, will be adopted.

As for Part II, I believe it will have the effect of raising the standard both of dead & of modern languages. Teachers will no longer have to inflict both Greek & Latin upon pupils that will never get a single literary idea from either: and French & German will gain more respect & attention.

The peculiar training (for I quite admit there is a peculiar training) given by the dead & not by the modern languages, will be supplied by Latin alone, or by Greek alone, to a degree quite sufficient for such pupils as we are now considering. If Greek and Latin, both, were to be insisted on much longer, I fear an increasing number of able scientific & mathematical students might find Cambridge inacceptable to them.

I wish Part IV had been in force when I was an undergraduate. I can never look back without regret at $3\frac{1}{2}$ years spent in the study of little else but the mere words, apart from the subject matter, of classical authors. I take it for granted that, when the Honour Previous Examina[n] is started, the Classical Tripos will become even less of an examination in mere composition-work than it is now.

I believe the great bulk of Head Masters will welcome these changes. Of course each of us will have idiosyncracies. I should have preferred as the alternative for one dead language, English and French, or English and German, instead of French and German.

With best wishes for the success of the Report.

I am, Dear Marshall | Yours very truly | Edwin A Abbott

[1] Trinity College, Sidgwick Papers. Edwin Abbott Abbott (1838–1926) had been Senior Classic in 1861 and had been elected a Fellow of St John's in 1862. He was headmaster of the City of London School from 1865 to 1889.

[2] This refers to the report of the Syndicate on the Regulations for the Previous Examination and the General Examination: see [8.2, 8.3]. Part I added algebra to the required mathematics. Part II proposed the substitution of French and German for Greek; Part III an Initial Previous Examination to be taken on entry: Part IV additional Previous examinations for honours in mathematics and classics. All these proposals were eventually rejected.

10. From Henry Whitehead Moss, 28 May 1872[1]

The Schools, | Shrewsbury.
May 28. 1872.

My dear Marshall

I am afraid that I cannot help you. If I came up at all, I should vote against parts I and IV, against the former as I would against any scheme which proposed to add a feather's weight to the excessive burdens now laid upon candidates for classical honours, against the latter partly for the same reason but principally because I think that it would be in effect nothing more than a superfluous anticipation of the mathematical and classical triposes, and would attract none or next to none of the 'poll' men. I like Part III, and sympathise with the principle of Part II, but I could wish that in the latter some security had been provided for the thoroughness of the examination by a definition of the subjects and that no advantage had been given to 'Students who offer themselves for examination in Latin only' over those who wish to be examined in Greek only.

Yours very truly | H. W. Moss

---

[1] Trinity College, Sidgwick Papers. See [9.2] for the background. Henry Whitehead Moss (1841–1917), Senior Classic 1864 and Fellow of St John's 1864–7, was the headmaster of Shrewsbury School from 1866 to 1908. The following note was added by Marshall on the reverse:

Dear Sidgwick | I had misunderstood Moss about Part IV. Abbot says that the Head Masters Meeting was put off | Yrs | AM.

Sidgwick and Marshall were both members of the Syndicate whose report was at issue (see [8.2]). For Abbott see [9.1].

11. From William Henry Bateson, 10 June 1872[1]

St. John's Lodge,
10 June, 1872.

Dear Sir,

The Master and Seniors are desirous of obtaining full information in regard to the instruction given in the College by the College Lecturers, and would be obliged to you if you would aid them in their inquiry by furnishing replies to the annexed questions as soon as you conveniently can.

I am, | Dear Sir, | Yours very truly, | W. H. Bateson.

[Enclosure]

1. How many distinct courses of Lectures, including papers set in the course of Lectures, each Lecturer gave in each Term of the year ending at Michaelmas 1872?

2. What was the subject of the Lectures in each course?

3. What number of Lectures was given in each course?

4. How many names were there in the List of those who ought to attend each course?

5. What was the actual attendance?

6. What course was adopted by the Lecturer with regard to defaulters?

7. Are any additional courses of Lectures required, in the opinion of the Lecturers in that particular department (Classical, Mathematical, &c.) with which the Lecturer is himself connected, either

(a) for Candidates for Honours,

or (b) for Candidates for the Ordinary Degree?

8. Might any of the present courses of Lectures be dispensed with?

9. What new courses of Lectures will be required in consequence of the establishment of new Triposes as avenues to degrees?

10. Has the Lecturer any suggestions to make

(a) as to how the system of College Lectures may be rendered more efficient;

(b) how regularity of attendance may be best secured;

or (c) how, generally, the whole question of College Lectures and attendance at them should be dealt with?

---

[1] Printed letter and enclosure sent to College Lecturers at St John's College, Cambridge. W. H. Bateson (1812–81) was Master of the College from 1857 to 1881. A copy of the enquiry is in the College Archives. For general background on the College's history see Edward Miller, *Portrait of a College: A History of the College of Saint John the Evangelist Cambridge* (Cambridge University Press, Cambridge, 1961).

12. To William Henry Bateson, 16 October 1872[1]

St John's College,
October 16, 1872.

My dear Master,

It is probable that, owing to a variety of causes, the Master and Seniors have but an imperfect acquaintance with the details of the arrangements for teaching Moral Sciences in the College. I have for some time felt that I ought to communicate with them on the subject: but have scarcely known how to do so.

I therefore answer your printed letter of enquiries with much fulness and minuteness.

QUESTIONS I. II. III.

I enclose a printed notice in which are detailed the courses of lectures delivered by me in the past year.[2] It was circulated in June 1871.

The terms on which Students were admitted to the lectures were the same as for the present year. I enclose a copy of a printed list which was circulated in October, 1872.[3]

I charge no fees to Johnians for looking over their answers to my sets of papers.

That portion of Question I., which refers to papers, cannot be answered briefly. Three lectures a week were delivered in each course. A paper of questions was given out in each week with the exception, in some cases, of the first week of the course. Students were encouraged to write their answers in my rooms. Their answers were returned to them at the commencement of the next lecture, with corrections and sometimes lengthy notes in red ink. This lecture was in every case entirely devoted to giving, with full explanations, my own answers to the questions. I made special reference to the answers sent up by the students only in those cases in which a point had been made or an error committed which might be suggestive to the rest of the class. Each student was encouraged to ask for further explanation after lecture, if the answer given in lecture, together with the written comments on his own answer, did not suffice to make the matter clear to him. By this means unnecessary repetitions were avoided; while the written comments obviated those misinterpretations and misrecollections to which verbal corrections are liable in all subjects, but particularly in the Moral Sciences.

Besides the five courses of papers given, as above described, in connexion with my five courses of lectures, it will be seen that I gave four papers specially for Questionists. These were corrected and answered in the same way as the others. From six to eight hours were occupied in writing red-ink corrections to the answers to each of these papers. During much of this time I was occupied with the work of out-college men. For this I received no fee, but in return for it Johnians received gratis an even greater amount, as it happened, of private attention from Mr Sidgwick, Mr Levin, and Mr Jackson.[4]

My lectures in general began at the same time as the Mathematical lectures; and in some cases, not being interrupted by College examinations, continued a week longer.

The examination in Moral Sciences, and the examination for College Essay Prizes, involved considerable additional work. (They are both necessary: the latter has made me acquainted with some men who promise to be successful students of Moral Sciences.)

Much time—on the average probably more than three hours a week during Term—was occupied in private, but official, conversation with students on the general course of their studies, and on special difficulties. The corresponding work for a student of Mathematics or Classics is performed in general by his College Tutor or his private tutor.

Excluding the work referred to in the last two paragraphs, I spent on my direct public work as a lecturer on the average at least seventy hours a Term.

(Of course I do not include time spent directly or indirectly in preparing lectures, or in making papers of questions: or again in correcting the answers of members of other colleges for which I was remunerated by separate fees. These fees amounted in the year to somewhat less than £20.)

I wish the above elaborate statement with regard to the amount of work I perform to be considered as not implying any complaint. But in my answer to Question VII. I shall argue that more lectures are required. I have desired to shew that, independently of my inability to lecture satisfactorily on a greater number of subjects than I do at present, I cannot fairly be expected to increase the amount of my official work.

QUESTION IV.

I receive no 'list of Students who ought to attend my lectures,' nor is it possible that I should. Students do not always even acquaint their College Tutors with their intention of reading Moral Sciences before coming to me the first time for advice. In general, after a lengthy conversation I give them definite advice as to the courses which they should attend in their first Term of reading. As their acquaintance with the nature of the subjects lectured on, and with the style of the various lecturers increases, I encourage them to take upon themselves an increasing share of the responsibility of directing the course of their studies.

QUESTION V.

In the October Term 20 students entered themselves for my lectures, of whom 14 were Johnians. This large number was due to there being only one set of lectures on the subject, and to the attendance of some Questionists at two out of the three lectures in each week. (The papers were devoted to the wants of the Junior Students.) On these two days the average attendance was about 12 Johnians and 4 others: on the third day in the week it was about 9 Johnians and 3 others.

In the Lent Term and in the Easter Term I had two classes in Political Economy. Some men attended in both classes: some changed from one to the other. I have preserved no register; but I am pretty sure that the average attendance during the Lent Term and the earlier part of the May Term was in the Senior Class not less than seven and in the Junior not less than nine. During the latter part of the May Term the attendance was irregular. Several Bachelors reading for Fellowships at Trinity attended my lectures.

The number of Johnian Students of Moral Sciences has been, is, and (as I shall presently argue) is likely to be large as compared with those of Students from other Colleges.

Thus Johnian students have together received more assistance from the Lecturers of other Colleges than the Students of other Colleges have together received from me.

QUESTION VI.

I have not employed, and do not wish to employ, any other mode of inducing the regular attendance of Johnians at my Lectures than that of conversing privately with them on the advantages and disadvantages of it in each particular case. Putting out of consideration part of the May Term, I have found in my whole experience only two Johnians who without reasonable cause have been persistently irregular in attendance at my lectures.

But the attendance at my Lectures of members of other Colleges, and the attendance of Johnians at Lectures other than mine, has often been bad. I regard this evil as requiring serious attention: I shall consider it at length further on (Question X.). I may state here that, as an experiment, Mr Sidgwick and I propose to send to each other at the end of each week lists of the attendance of Johnians and Trinity men respectively at our lectures.

QUESTION VIIa.

More Lectures are required.

Neglecting the wants of the Questionists, there ought to be available for our Students an advanced and an elementary course of Lectures in each Term on each of the four subjects of the Tripos, or nearly so.[5] The work would be fairly though not thoroughly done if in the year twenty courses of Lectures were delivered in St John's.

This is impossible. We are then compelled to avail ourselves of the aid of the Lecturers of other Colleges. But, since we must do this, it can no longer be assumed either that the Lecture arrangements can frequently be modified to suit the wants of individual Johnians, or that every course of Lectures delivered will succeed in obtaining the full confidence of Johnians. Thus with the system of intercollegiate Lectures from thirty to forty courses, independently of Professors' Lectures, are required in the University.

The study of Moral Sciences has suffered severely during the past year from a lack of elementary Lectures. In each Term several men have complained to me that much of the time they have spent in the lecture-room has been wasted in consequence of their not having been able to understand what was said by the lecturer. The reason for this is that the Study of Moral Sciences is progressing, and there are few classes in which there are not present some men of decided ability and considerable knowledge. In Moral Sciences particularly it is difficult for a Lecturer to avoid addressing himself mainly to his more advanced pupils.

It is, as far as can be ascertained, mainly in consequence of the absence of elementary lectures that several Johnians have in the course of the year abandoned the study.

Nor is there the least doubt but that others have been deterred from beginning the study through hearing of the difficulties with which beginners had to contend.

(Other reasons for wishing that the number of lecturers on Moral Sciences may be increased are, (i) that in consequence of greater specialisation on the part of the lecturers, their lectures might gradually obtain a higher value: and (ii) there would be less danger that if one or two lecturers happened to leave Cambridge the whole system of teaching might be deranged. This danger is at present not small.)

It is clear then that more lectures are wanted. But it is not so clear that St John's College is specially called on to supply more lectures. I wish to say a few words on this point.

I have already called attention to the fact that St John's has almost always had a disproportionately large number of Moral Sciences' Students. There is a reason for this over and above the fact that there has for a long period been one lecturer, at least, on the subject here.[6] This reason is that, in general, there come to St John's College a disproportionately large number of Students, who, having had no special advantages at school, are yet qualified by their energy and intellect to make good use of such advantages as may be offered to them. It has been the peculiar glory of our College to bring special advantages within the reach of such men.

Such men are frequently attracted towards Moral Sciences; for these Sciences above all others are adapted for being thought over by men rather than for being learnt by boys. Such men at first require somewhat elementary lectures; and the absence of suitable lectures presses heavily on them, if, as is likely to be the case, they are unable to afford the expense of reading with a private tutor.

It may I think be concluded that, if there were two lecturers on Moral Sciences in the College, the number of Students would in the course of time increase considerably.

(It is due to the Seniors that I should here give the reasons which caused me to ask Mr Foxwell to deliver a course of Lectures on Logic as deputy for me during this Term. I have of course already obtained the Master's approval of my so doing. The reasons were three: (i) there was an urgent need for a set of Lectures on Logic (this is evidenced by the size of Mr Foxwell's class, about 14). (ii) In order to do myself the full Johnian share of the work, I should have been compelled to lecture on some subject besides Political Philosophy and Political Economy; and as a consequence I must have interrupted the course of reading by which I am endeavouring to enable myself to lecture on these subjects less inefficiently. (iii) I wished to provide gratis a set of papers for those Johnians who had attended my lectures on Bentham in the October Term of last year. Moreover, I felt confident that Mr Foxwell was one of those members of the College (for there are others) who would be able to deliver such a course of lectures efficiently and to command the attention of Students. The event has so far amply justified my expectation.

In the Lent and Easter Terms I shall give, as before, an elementary and advanced set of papers myself.)

VIIb.

There is scarcely any provision for the Special Examination for the Ordinary Degree in Moral Philosophy and Political Economy. But these Examinations are likely to be modified so that Students for them can make use of the elementary lectures for students for the Tripos. The need for such lectures will be hereby increased.

I suppose it is hardly within my province to make any remarks on the College Lectures on Whately's Logic.

QUESTION VIII.

No.

QUESTION IX.

Should a History Tripos be founded, it is probable that the number of Students who desire to obtain some knowledge of Political Economy will be increased. Their wants may perhaps be somewhat similar to those of Students in the Indian Civil Service, for the instruction of whom there is at present no suitable provision.[7]

QUESTION X.

My answer to Question VI. points to a change as desirable ultimately. But there is no urgent need for its being adopted immediately. I think that some person should be formally entrusted with the duty of giving officially counsel to the Johnian students of Moral Sciences. He should pay special attention to the regularity of their attendance at lectures delivered by other than Johnian lecturers. With such lecturers he should be brought officially into communication. (Post cards do the work well enough for the present.) It should be his duty to become acquainted with the private circumstances of each Johnian Student of Moral Sciences, with the details of the history of his study, with the reasons of his success or failure in each portion of his study, with the nature of the difficulties which most hamper him, with his tastes, his hopes, and his aims. He should thus be able to mark out for each student a plan of reading adapted to his individual wants. He should prevent him from going too fast or too slowly, and above all from reading desultorily or unsystematically.

I have dwelt somewhat at length on this point, partly because I think that in this direction the experience of Moral Sciences' Studies is likely to be useful to other studies in which the intercollegiate system is beginning to be made use of.

The account above given of the difficulties to be overcome with regard to the teaching of Moral Sciences may throw light also on the course to be pursued with reference to the growing need for specialisation on the part of our lecturers on other subjects. It brings out into strong relief the importance of having a large number of young men engaged in lecture work. I think that the vigorous life of the college would be promoted if a considerable number of Junior Fellows were told off to lecture each on some special department of knowledge, with the stimulus of delivering a small number of lectures in that department. If the number of courses, at all events of courses for Honour men, which each younger lecturer delivered were small, and those few courses were on a subject in lecturing well on which he might fairly be expected to take a pride, the care devoted to the preparation of lectures would, I think, attain quickly a very high standard. I venture to suggest therefore that no new appointments be made, for some time at least, to the posts now held by our classical and mathematical lecturers; but that as vacancies occur the work performed now by one such lecturer be distributed between two or more new lecturers.

This system tends to cause students to be instructed by teachers who have no personal acquaintance with them. It is thus becoming continually more important that we should efficiently discharge our duty of supplementing public teaching by official but private and detailed guidance for each several case. For this end I think we require a much more careful organisation than at present exists. Without it we shall not succeed in putting a student who does not read with a private tutor in a position even approximately as good as one who does: we shall not avoid the shortcomings of continental Universities.

In conclusion, I am doubtful whether I ought to apologize more for the length of this letter, or for not having written one of similar scope a long time ago.

I am, | My dear Master, | Yours very truly, | A. Marshall.

The Rev. the Master of St John's College.

Postscript.

November 23, 1872.

The average attendance at Mr Foxwell's lectures from the commencement of the Term to the present time has been a little over ten, of whom barely seven have been Johnians. In my class the total number has averaged twelve, of whom about five are Johnians. There have been thirteen students of Moral Sciences during the Term, of whom two have been Questionists.

[Enclosure 1][8]

Lectures on Moral Sciences.

October Term, 1871.

Professor Maurice on Moral Philosophy (subject to be announced at the beginning of the October Term).

Professor Fawcett on Political Economy (for those who require the Certificate).

Mr Venn on Logic.

Mr Sidgwick on Mental Philosophy (Descartes, Bain, and parts of Hamilton).

Mr. Sidgwick and Mr Jackson on Moral Philosophy (Aristotle's Ethics).

Mr Marshall on Moral Philosophy (Bentham).

Lent Term, 1872.

Professor Fawcett on Political Economy (on Socialism).

Mr Venn on Logic, continuation.

Mr Sidgwick on Mental Philosophy (Locke, Cousin on Locke, and the Historical Parts of Hamilton).

On Moral Philosophy (The English Moralists). Tu.Th., Sat., at 9.

Mr Levin on Mental Philosophy (Descartes, Hamilton, Bain).

Mr Marshall on Political Economy, Elementary (Mill). On Political Economy, Advanced.

It is probable that Mr Levin will also give a set of Lectures for the 'Special' Examination in Moral Philosophy.

Easter Term, 1872.

Professor Maurice on the History of Moral Philosophy.

Dr Campion on Political Economy.

Mr Venn on Logic, continuation.

Mr Sidgwick on Moral Philosophy (Kant).

Mr Levin on Mental Philosophy (Ferrier, Cousin on Kant). Mr Marshall on Political Economy, Elementary (Mill), continuation. On Political Economy, Advanced, continuation.

[Enclosure 2]

Lectures on Moral Sciences.

October Term, 1872.

Mr Sidgwick. On Ancient Ethics—Plato and Aristotle. (M., W., F., at 12, beginning 16 October.) On Psychology—Bain and Stewart, Book I. (Tu., Th., Sat., at 12, beginning 15 October.)

Mr Levin. On Mental Philosophy. (M., Th., at 12, beginning 17 October.) On Logic. (Tu., Fr., at 12, beginning 15 October.) On Moral Philosophy. (W., Sat., at 12, beginning 16 October.)

Mr Marshall. On Bentham's Moral and Political Philosophy. (M., W., F., at 10.45, beginning 16 October.)

Mr Foxwell. On Logic. (In Mr Marshall's rooms, Tu., Th., Sat., at 10.45, beginning 15 October.)

Lent Term, 1873.

Mr Venn. On Logic. (In continuation of Mr Foxwell's Lectures.)

Mr Sidgwick. On Ethics, especially Stewart, Book II., Butler, and Whewell. On Mental Philosophy—Locke, Cousin on Locke, and Hamilton.

Mr Levin. Continuation of Lectures in preceding Term.

Mr Marshall. On Political Economy—Mill. On Political Economy for advanced Students.

Easter Term, 1873.

Mr Sidgwick. On History of English Ethics and Kant's Ethics. On Mental Philosophy—Kant and Ferrier.

Dr Campion. On Political Economy.

Mr Venn, Mr Levin, and Mr Marshall: continuation of Lectures in preceding Term.

These lectures will be open without charge to Members of St Peter's, Clare, Pembroke, Gonville and Caius, Corpus Christi, Queens', St Catharine's, St John's, Trinity, and Downing Colleges, and of Trinity Hall: and they will be open on payment of a fee of £1 for each set to all other Members of the University. A series of papers will be given, generally speaking, in connection with each set. The fee for each series of papers will be £2.

Questionists belonging to any of the above-mentioned Colleges will be at liberty to attend any of the lectures in the October Term; and a series of papers, for which no fee will be charged, will be given specially for them by Mr Venn and Mr Marshall, at 12 o'clock, as follows:—

Mr Venn. On Moral Philosophy, 9 and 16 Nov. On Mental Philosophy—Psychology, 16 Oct., Metaphysics, 26. Oct., History of Philosophy, 2 Nov. Logic, 23 Oct., 6 and 20 Nov.

Mr Marshall. On Political Philosophy, 23 Nov. On Political Economy—Theory, 19 and 28 Oct.; History, 13 Nov.

The lectures of Prof. Birks and Prof. Fawcett are advertised separately.

---

[1] Printed in the pamphlet *Replies of College Lecturers to the Inquiries of the Master and Seniors of St John's College Cambridge* (Privately printed, Cambridge, 1872). The printed version has marginal summary notes omitted here. Copies of this rare pamphlet are in the St John's College Library and the Cambridge University Library. 'Questionists,' mentioned at various points, were degree candidates. For the origins of the term see Alfred I. Tillyard, *A History of University Reform from 1800 A.D. to the Present Time, with Suggestions Towards a Complete Scheme for the University of Cambridge* (Heffer, Cambridge, 1913), pp. 34–5.

[2] Reproduced as Enclosure 1.

[3] Reproduced as Enclosure 2.

[4] Thomas Woodhouse Levin (?–1904), BA 1861, St Catherine's College, author of *The Logic of Money* (Bell, London, 1887) and also of philosophical works, appears to have been a recognized teacher but not to have held any College or University appointment. Henry Jackson (1839–1921) of Trinity became Regius Professor of Greek in 1906. The intercollegiate lecture system was rapidly developing around this time, with Moral Sciences teaching in the van (see Enclosure 2 for details).

[5] The four subjects of the Moral Sciences Tripos were (i) Moral and political philosophy, (ii) Mental philosophy, (iii) Logic, (iv) Political economy. Political economy was also one of the 'special' subjects for the ordinary BA, and when the Historical Tripos was established in 1873 it included a required paper on 'Political economy and economic history' (*Reporter*, 18 December 1872, p. 134).

[6] Joseph Bickersteth Mayor (1828–1916), Fellow of St John's 1852–64, and Josiah Brown Pearson (1841–95), Fellow 1865–80, appear to have both taught Moral Sciences in St John's College during the 1860s.

[7] Both Cambridge and Oxford Universities had an arrangement whereby candidates for the Indian Civil Service were in residence for two years before taking up their duties. Normally these probationers did not take degrees. (See for example *Reporter*, 30 November 1875, pp. 127–9.)

[8] The notices reproduced as Enclosures 1 and 2 are similar to those regularly published in the *Reporter*. Professor Maurice is John Frederick Denison Maurice (1805–72), the famous Christian Socialist, who was Knightsbridge Professor of Moral Philosophy from 1866 to 1872. Dr. Campion is William Magan Campion DD (1820–96) of Queens'. Professor Birks is Thomas Rawson Birks (1810–83), who succeeded Maurice as Knightsbridge Professor in 1872.

13. To Herbert Somerton Foxwell, 10 August 1874[1]

Friog, N. Wales
10 Aug 1874

My dear Foxwell,

Your class will not be a 'Continuation': many of your hearers will be beginners: but some of them will have been to Miss Marshall.[2] Really I do not see much use in any adaptation of one set of lectures to the other: but I think Miss M. was quite right in wanting to know your opinion. I have sent her most of what you say, leaving out your pretty humilities. Of course perplexities & difficulties would be out of place. Firmness of grasp and practical acquaintance with the social relations of industry seem to be the main requirements from the lecturer.[3]

I too have been struck by the stodginess of the Swiss character: but I have regarded it rather as the cause than as the effect of their social equality: though in some directions doubtless social-equality does foster stodginess. But I had sought to explain away facts that were inconvenient. Democrats always do, you know. So I found the explanation of their character mainly in the dormouse life they live[4] in winter & the bad air they then breathe, but above all in the difficulties of communication. Till recently many valleys were as shut off from the world as a solitary island in the Pacific, or nearly so, I fancy. Then too when the nation first awakened to life, war was its one capability: consequently the boldest, most enterprising spirits went out to be shot down as mercenary soldiers leaving no children—at all events at home. Again just those parts which have been least depressed by bad means of communication have been battlefields for endless wars. And is not it true that every country in which generations have grown up amidst the brutalities & terrors due to the violence of murdering banditti have had their senses dulled to the finer influences of life?

I know very little of France, but I am surprised at your speaking of it as a country without any wealthy middle class.

I do not know Geneva; I wish I did: I will some time, I hope. I have a deep curiosity to see the mother of the two strongest enthusiasms the world has seen since Catholicism degenerated from a faith into a creed.

Yours ever | A. Marshall

---

[1] Foxwell Papers. Envelope postmarked 'Dolgeli Au 10 74' addressed to Hotel de Cygne, Luzern, Switzerland.

[2] This refers to extension lecturing that Foxwell proposed to undertake in the North of England. The implied further correspondence on the matter is untraced. Miss Theodosia Marshall (no relative) was a member of the Leeds Ladies' Educational Association and must have given some preliminary lectures on political economy. See John Fletcher Clews Harrison, *Learning and Living, 1790–1960* (Routledge and Kegan Paul, London, 1961), especially p. 230. For general background see Edwin Welch, *The Peripatetic University: Cambridge Local Lectures 1873–1973* (Cambridge University Press, Cambridge, 1973).

[3] Marshall subsequently reported to William Stanley Jevons that 'He [Foxwell] has given elementary lectures in Political Economy at Leeds with great success, and great benefit to himself. He has a clear and easy style, and is remarkably successful in interesting beginners in their work.' (Quoted in a letter from Jevons to John Robson, 2 November 1875, *WSJ*, vol. 4, pp. 144–5. Marshall's letter to Jevons has not survived.)

Marshall had served in the spring of 1874 as an examiner for extension courses in political economy given by William Cunningham and William Moore Ede in the North of England. He reported to the organizing Syndicate:

> The short courses of Lectures, which have during the last three months been delivered in these towns, appear to have completely succeeded in the aim to which they were directed, of introducing the classes to the subject, of giving them a general acquaintance with the nature of the problems with which Political Economy deals, and of the method by which they must be treated. Ninety-one out of ninety-four papers which were sent up deserve certificates to the effect that the writers have attended the lectures with profit and have clear notions on some of the elementary principles of the subject; while forty Candidates (of whom 10 are from Bradford, 7 from Halifax, 7 from Keighley, and 16 from Leeds) deserve a higher certificate to the effect that they have, with the aid of the lectures, mastered the leading outlines of the subject, and laid a foundation for a thorough study of its more difficult problems. A few papers shew that considerable power of dealing with questions of some complexity has been already obtained.
>
> I am of opinion that the success of this introductory course of lectures has been such as fully to justify the attempt to proceed to more advanced courses, in each of which one or two of the more difficult portions of the science might be treated exhaustively. (*Reporter*, 2 June 1874, p. 426.)

Marshall's articles in the *Beehive* 18 April, 2 May 1874 seem to have sprung from his visit to Halifax. See Royden Harrison, 'Two Early Articles by Alfred Marshall,' *Economic Journal*, 73 (September 1963), pp. 422–30.

[4] In the original 'live' is written 'life'.

14. From William Stanley Jevons, 7 January 1875[1]

Parsonage Road, | Withington, | Manchester.
7 Jany. 75.

Dear Mr. Marshall,

Ever since our most agreeable visit to Cambridge I have been intending to write to you & say how much I was interested in the answers in political economy. While at Cambridge indeed, I called at your rooms in hope of seeing you but found you had gone down, or rather to be strictly accurate I was on the way to do so when informed that you had gone down.

I thought that nearly half the candidates gave very intelligent answers, showing that they had not merely crammed up a little of Mill but had been induced to enter more into the subject as a study of their own. What interested me most of all however was the way in which some of them applied the graphical method no doubt according to your views. I did not understand the particulars of all the figures as some of the men in the hurry of writing seemed to think the examiners must know all about the figure if they merely sketched it out. I understood enough however to think that the way in which you had applied curves to questions of taxation & the like was very successful. I have no doubt that there is a great field open for the investigation of economy in this way and I wish that you could be induced to print what you have already worked out on the subject. I do not know whether your proposed articles or books were to touch on this subject.

I am reading Sidgwick's book[2] with much interest. It is exceedingly acute & full of novelties, but cannot be said to be easy reading. It cannot have very many readers, but no one who pretends to be well read in moral philosophy can pass it over without careful study.

Believe me, | Yours faithfully, | W.S. Jevons.

[1] Marshall Papers. Reproduced in *WSJ*, vol. 4, pp. 95–6. Jevons, then a Professor at Owens College, Manchester, had been visiting Cambridge as one of the examiners for the Moral Sciences Tripos, which had commenced as usual on the last Monday in November. This was the occasion on which Mary Paley sat the papers.
[2] Henry Sidgwick, *The Methods of Ethics* (Macmillan, London, 1874).

15. To Herbert Somerton Foxwell, 27 January 1875[1]

12 Victoria Road | Clapham Common

My dear Foxwell

I am very sorry indeed that you are unwell. It is a great pity: but I trust to your natural 'go' to keep you up.

I have no good book on Cooperation. The best account of it on the whole is I think that in Thornton on Labor (last edition of course).[2] There was an article on it by Brassey a few months back in the 'Contemporary' which was very suggestive, & presented the difficulties clearly. It was spoken of as an inaugural address at the Cooperative meeting at Halifax last year: & impressed the Cooperators much.[3]

I wish one could get a translation of 'Ce qu'on voit'[4] separately. I should rather like a circular to be sent from large town lecturers to the publishers to tell them that if they liked to print off an edition of it separately, it would be sure of a sale; but that, if they would not, a rival translation would be made & published elsewhere: the threat perhaps being left in the background.

I have heard nothing of the Tripos beyond the list. I had no notion Turner would be where he is. I never thought he was solid, but I expected that he would in Exam: get the credit of solidity.[5] On the whole I think the list good. It is one of several instances that I have noticed in which men get into their right places in the Tripos after having been in wrong places in earlier Exams. I don't mean that I prefer our plan on the whole to the new Nat: Sc: Tripos Plan.[6] I have not written to your brother to congratulate him.[7] In fact I have been occupied in my mothers sickness. After hovering at the gate of death for five weeks, she has taken a sudden start & is now out of immediate danger.

Yours ever | A Marshall

---

[1] Foxwell Papers. On mourning paper, probably commemorating Marshall's younger brother Walter (see Appendix I). Sent to 28 Westbourne Terrace, Mount Preston, Leeds, where Foxwell was giving extension lectures: see [13.2, 3]. Addressed from the Marshall family home. Envelope postmarked 'JA 27 75'.

[2] William T. Thornton, *On Labour; Its Wrongful Claims and Rightful Dues* (Macmillan, London, 1869; second edition 1870). See *Early Economic Writings*, vol. 2, pp. 262–3, for Marshall's evaluation of this work.

[3] Thomas Brassey, 'Co-operative Production', *Contemporary Review*, 24 (July 1874), pp. 212–33. The occasion giving rise to this article is not mentioned.

[4] Frédéric Bastiat, *Ce qu'on voit et ce qu'on ne voit pas* (Guillaumin, Paris, 1850). Bastiat's last pamphlet is included in the later editions of his *Sophismes Économiques*. Marshall probably had in mind the recent translation by Patrick James Stirling of the fifth edition of the latter: *Economic Sophisms* (Oliver and Boyd, Edinburgh; Simpkin and Marshall, London; 1873). A translation of Bastiat's pamphlet by W. B. Hodgson had actually been published independently but was doubtless out of print by 1875: *What is Seen and What is not Seen: or Political Economy in One Lesson* (Smith, London; Ireland, Manchester; 1859).

[5] Foxwell had been one of the examiners for the Moral Sciences Tripos of 1874 [14.1]. Hawes Harison Turner (1851–1939) of Trinity had obtained a second class. He served from 1875 to 1898 as secretary to A. J. Balfour.

[6] The Natural Sciences Tripos had been amended in November 1874 to encourage specialization. For details see D. A. Winstanley, *Later Victorian Cambridge* [1.2], pp. 198–203.

[7] Foxwell's younger brother, Ernest, had obtained a Second Class in the Moral Sciences Tripos of 1874. His candidacy does not seem to have interfered with Foxwell's acting as examiner.

---

16. To Herbert Somerton Foxwell, 31 January 1875[1]

My dear Foxwell,

I have just done a cool thing. I have ordered two books to be sent to you from Tomlins.[2] It is clear that you ought to have them: & by ordering them I have saved time. They are i Kauffmans adaptation of Schäffle:[3] this though not well 'adapted' is the best book in English on Communism & Socialism generally. But Owen is rather snubbed: & up in the North Owen's name is great: so I have told Tomlin to get for you Booth's life of Owen.[4]

I am awfully glad you are getting together.

I left my Mother progressing with rapid strides. But I hardly know when I have felt more washed out than I do today. I daresay this will pass off: but as I could offer you in exchange for your lively letter nothing better than glump, I will subside at once.

Yours ever | A Marshall

[1] Foxwell Papers. On mourning paper to the same address as [15]. Envelope postmarked 'Cambridge JA 31 75'.

[2] A bookseller.

[3] Moritz Kaufmann, *Socialism: Its Nature, its Dangers, and its Remedies Considered. Founded on the German Work 'Kapitalismus und Socialismus'* [*1870*], *by Dr. A. E. F. Schäffle* (King, London, 1874).

[4] Arthur J. Booth, *Robert Owen, the Founder of Socialism in England* (Trübner, London, 1869).

17. To William Stanley Jevons, 4 February 1875[1]

S.J.C
4 Feb 1875

Dear Professor Jevons,

I thank you for your paper on the Mathematical Theory of Political Economy which I have just received. I read it with interest some time ago in a newspaper.[2]

I incline to think that the substantive difference between us is less than I once supposed.[3]

We appear to be held apart more by the divergence of our views with regard to Mill than by any other cause. As a result of many courses of lectures on Mill I have been convinced that his work, instead of being full of plausible sophistries, appears at first sight & perhaps even more at second sight to contain fallacies where really there are only incomplete truths.

I admit however that the theory of Political Economy is in its infancy; that Mill was not a constructive genius of the first order, & that, generally the most important benefits he has conferred on the science are due rather to his character than to his intellect.

Believe me | Yours faithfully | A. Marshall

I am glad Mr George Darwin has attacked the first chapter of Mr Cairnes 'Leading Principles'.[4]

[1] Reproduced in *WSJ*, vol. 4, p. 100. The original manuscript is in the John Rylands University Library, Manchester, Jevons Papers. S.J.C. is St John's College.

[2] 'The Progress of the Mathematical Theory of Political Economy, with an Explanation of the Principles of the Theory', a paper given to the Manchester Statistical Society on 11 November 1874. This paper was published in the Society's *Transactions*, Session 1874–5, pp. 1–19, and in shortened form in the *Journal of the* [*London*] *Statistical Society*, 37 (December 1874), pp. 478–88. The text of the latter version is reproduced in *WSJ*, vol. 7, pp. 75–85. Newspapers of the day often gave full, if not verbatim, reports of scientific papers and addresses, so that Marshall may well have stumbled upon one. However, he was being disingenuous, having actually published an anonymous review of Jevons's paper: see [18.2].

[3] Marshall had reviewed Jevons's *Theory of Political Economy* (Macmillan, London, 1871) less than favourably: *Academy*, 3 (1 April 1872), pp. 130–2, reprinted in *Memorials*, pp. 93–9.

[4] George H. Darwin, 'The Theory of Exchange Value' *Fortnightly Review*, 17 (February 1875), pp. 243–53; John Elliot Cairnes, *Some Leading Principles of Political Economy Newly Expounded* (Macmillan, London, 1874). Darwin was at this time a young Fellow of Trinity.

18. To Herbert Somerton Foxwell, 4 February 1875[1]

My dear Foxwell,

I thank you much for your letter. I am going to utilize you. You have already seen the inclosed: but you have only just read the paper of which it speaks.[2] I am now writing something about Cairnes:[3] it is more subdued than this about Jevons: but as I am to sign my name I am in some fear lest people should think it pert. Would you mind telling me if you think that, had I signed my name to the inclosed, it would have been thought atrociously pert.[4]

I am glad you know Miss Marshall.[5] I know her only by correspondence: but I believe she is a great power for good.

I am delighted too that you are going on well generally. I wish you would tell me some Tripos gossip: at least I would like to hear a little about the marks.[6] I know nothing at present. Why should not your brother read P. Ec. for the next 9 months & lecture at some big town in October.[7] My mother is, I am thankful to say, very much better.

I am writing to Jevons to thank him for his pamphlet & repeat in a very subdued tone what I said in the Academy.[8]

I have no jokes of my own to send you. So I send some from 'Englands greatest humourist.'[9] Hoping to receive the kernels by return of post I am sincerely
    Yours ever | A. Marshall

[1] Foxwell Papers. On mourning paper to the same address as [15]. Envelope postmarked 'Cambridge FE 4 75'.

[2] Marshall enclosed a printed proof copy of a note he had written on Jevons's paper of 11 November 1874 to the Manchester Statistical Society [17.2]. Marshall's note, essentially a short review, had been published anonymously in *Academy*, 6 (21 November 1874), p. 558. The note must have been written very shortly after November 11 as the editor of Academy had requested return of proof on 17 November. Since Marshall had reviewed Jevons's *Theory of Political Economy* for *Academy* in 1872 [17.3], it seems likely that the initiative was the editor's, and that he had sent Marshall a newspaper report of Jevons's lecture, most probably the one appearing in the *Manchester Examiner and Times*, 12 November 1878. Jevons noted that reports had appeared in three Manchester newspapers which circulated widely and sent a copy of the *Examiner* report to Walras. (*WSJ*, vol. 4, p. 102.)

[3] This probably refers to Marshall's signed essay 'On Mr. Mill's Theory of Value', *Fortnightly Review*, 19 *NS* (1 April 1876), pp. 591–602: reprinted in *Memorials*, pp. 119–33. However, the considerable delay in publishing this criticism of Cairnes may indicate that Marshall had in mind some other paper which failed to be published.

[4] Marshall's superior tone and patronizing attitude did indeed make his note on Jevons 'pert'. This hitherto unknown publication of Marshall's will be reprinted elsewhere, it is hoped.

[5] See [13.2].

[6] See [15.5].

[7] See [15.7]. Ernest Foxwell did in fact eventually devote himself to 'coaching' and extension lecturing, but details have not been ascertained.

[8] See [17].

[9] This item was not sent as [19] makes clear.

19. To Herbert Somerton Foxwell, 7 February 1875[1]

S J C

7 Feb

Dear Foxwell,

Thanks for your letter. I suppose I forgot to inclose a paper of 'nuts to crack' written by the Arch-humourist—C. Spurgeon. I cannot find the paper now.[2]

I did not answer about 'Supernatural Religion'. It seems to me that Lightfoot gains many victories on small points: but is beaten on large ones.[3] But the matter does not excite me. A little while ago, shortly before S.R. was published I got excited about it: but I became so *absolutely* convinced that Christ neither believed nor taught any of the leading dogmas of Christianity that I now look upon the fray with the languid interest of a mere spectator.

I know very little about bill-brokers except what I have learnt from 'Lombard Street'.[4] As I understand the matter bill brokers make their living by discounting bills at a rate a trifle higher than they have to pay themselves.

A banker fights shy of a bill which requires technical or personal knowledge to enable him to see into its merits. Such a bill goes to a specialist broker who has made it his business to become acquainted with the circumstances of the individual & his trade.

But perhaps you mean how is it that Bankers themselves will discount bills at one per cent *per annum* when they can get more than three on the absolute security of Consols?[5] This puzzled me for a long time: but I believe I have found the solution. No broker would dream of discounting a bill for a long period say a year at this rate or any like it. But a banker—or any other capitalist—may have some cash on hand—say £10,000—which he is pretty certain not to want for some time. If a sudden stringency of the market came he might want it: but *ex hypothesi* there are no signs of stringency on the horizon. Of course if one of the Sultan's wives were to put him out of temper by parting his hair crooked & he were without warning to tweak the Russian Ambassador by the nose the market might get tight in a week: but nothing much short of this would cause a man to suffer much loss from having discounted a bill for a short period.

But why does he not buy Consols & sell them at the end of one, two, or three months as the case may be? Because *ex hypothesi* Consols are tremendously high: if he wanted money a short time hence, it would probably be because there were some slight incipient signs of stringency, & these might easily cause a fall in Consols which would bear a great ratio to the interest to be got from them in the period in question. Of course a *very* low rate of interest is almost always due to a reaction from over-speculation.

Yours ever | A. M.

---

[1] Foxwell Papers. On mourning paper to the same address as [15]. SJC is Saint John's College.

[2] See [18]. The paper mentioned has not been identified. Charles Haddon Spurgeon (1834–92) was a popular preacher, noted for his employment of humour, who published a spate of sermons and homilies.

[3] Joseph Barber Lightfoot (1828–89) published a sequence of seven articles in the *Contemporary Review*, 25–27 (December 1874–February 1876), republished as *Essays on the Work Entitled Supernatural Religion* (Macmillan, London, 1880). The articles were a reaction to the appearance of the anonymous *Supernatural Religion: An Inquiry into the Reality of Divine Revelation* (Longmans, London, 1874–7: three vols.). The author was Walter Richard Cassels. Lightfoot of Trinity was Hulsean Professor of Divinity 1861–75, Lady Margaret Professor of Divinity 1875–9, and Bishop of Durham 1879–89. The controversy over Supernatural Religion was only in its early stages at the time of the present letter.

[4] Walter Bagehot, *Lombard Street: A Description of the Money Market* (King, London, 1873), especially ch. 11.

[5] Consols are irredeemable government bonds.

20. To Herbert Somerton Foxwell, 9 April 1875[1]

My dear Foxwell,

I wish I could come to Leeds: I should like to much: but I can't. I thank you very much for the kind invitation.

The nearest approach to what you want, that I know of, is 'Joint Stock Companies—a practical treatise on their promotion, management & winding up' by R.S.E. Farries Published by Rich^d [?] & Co London 3rd Ed 1874.[2] It is not exclusively legal: & it is of moderate size, smaller than Thomson's 'Laws of thought.'[3] It does not discuss the P.E. of Joint Stock Companies: I do not quite see how that can be treated till we get the long promised treatise on 'Things in general'.[4]

But in one of the best monographs[5] ever written—'the Principles & Practice of banking', by Gilbart—there is an instructive chapter on 'The administration of Joint Stock Banks, with an inquiry into the cause of their failures'.[6] Very much of what is said here is of general application to Joint Stock Companies. Gilbart, you know, had a great deal to do with the making of the London & Westminster Bank. His book is likely to be in a public library. It is expensive (16s, I think).

I am sorry your brother was ill at the Mo: Ph: exam:[7] we have not been able to award a prize.

The list is astonishing[8]

Class I	Class II	Class III
Anderton	——	Warren
Ryland		Horny
Hurndall		Parker

Jacobs was second bracketed with Nicholson: but, as perhaps you know, he was examined at Trinity & [therefore] does not appear on our list.[9]

Hurndall did not tell me he was unwell, nor did he appear so : but his papers were those of a jaded man.[10]

I very much want your photo.

Would you care to coach a very promising beginner for half a term, say the month of May. If so I would recommend one to go to you, & he probably would. Or you might begin on May 7th.. that would work very well.

Yours most sincerely | A. Marshall

[1] Foxwell Papers. On mourning paper to the same address as [15]. Envelope postmarked 'Cambridge AP 9 75'.

[2] Richard Spearman E. Farries, *Joint Stock Companies: Being a Practical Treatise on Their Formation, Management and Winding Up Under ' The Companies Act of 1862'* etc. (Farries Brothers, London, 1865: third edition 1874). The publisher of the third edition of this very rare book is not given in standard bibliographic sources and Marshall's writing of the name is indecipherable.

[3] William Thomson, *Outlines of the Laws of Thought* (Pickering, London, 1842) revised as *An Outline of the Necessary Laws of Thought: A Treatise on Pure and Applied Logic* (Pickering, London, 1849) with many subsequent editions and reissues. Presumably Thomson's work is mentioned only with reference to its size, not its contents.

[4] This allusion remains obscure.

[5] Marshall wrote this word as 'monograms'.

[6] James William Gilbart, *The Principles and Practice of Banking* (Bell and Daldy, London, 1871). This combined posthumously two works on banking by Gilbart (1794–1863), who became manager of the London and Westminster Bank in 1834 and was a prominent figure in banking circles of his day.

[7] This probably refers to Foxwell's youngest brother William Arthur (1853–1909), admitted to St John's in 1874 with a London BA, who eventually became a physician.

[8] The list apparently refers to the results of the Intercollegiate Examination in Moral Science. The students listed were all from St John's. William Edward Anderton (1853–1937) obtained a first class in the Moral Sciences Tripos of 1875; Frederick Ryland (1854–1902) was bracketed as second moralist in the Tripos of 1876; William Evans Hurndall (1845–1895) got a second in the Tripos of 1875; William Warren (1853–1923) got a first in the Tripos of 1877: the son of a bricklayer he was a Fellow of St John's 1880–7; Frederick William Horny (1856–?), born in Vienna, got a second in the Tripos of 1876, as did George Parker (1853–1937).

[9] Joseph Jacobs (1854–1916) of St John's was first moralist in the Tripos of 1876, when Joseph Shield Nicholson of Trinity, subsequently a prominent economist, was bracketed second with Ryland.

[10] Hurndall eventually became a congregational minister, as did Anderton.

21. To Rebecca Marshall, 5 June 1875[1]

Steam Ship 'Spain'
Saturday 5 June 1875

My darling Mother

We expect to be in New York at some time tomorrow. So I will get a letter ready to be posted as soon as we arrive. We have had a prosperous voyage, though there were two days of weather considerably rougher than is generally experienced at this time of year. I was however never thrown completely off my food, & as soon as the weather got moderate I began to enjoy the voyage again.

On the whole it has been very enjoyable. I have heard it said that a busy man never gets leisure completely; unless he takes a long voyage. And there is some truth in this saying. The weak point of the passage has been the utter absence of ladies worth talking to; at least there is no one with a strong character as far as I can find. Most of them are agreeable, many of them refined: but they have no 'go'. Partly because I have been rather spoilt; partly because, according to the general confession the ladies are slow, or as one man put it, when the Ship Surgeon was abusing the 'Smoking room' for neglecting the ladies—'You can't get a pack of hounds to hunt when there is nothing to hunt'—partly for the one reason, partly for the other, I have hardly spoken to the ladies. Of the men I have seen a good deal. And some of them have plenty of character. Thus the first notes that I have made, have been of 'character'.

After some consideration I have decided on the following plan of operations. I shall as usual make my business notes on Cambridge paper of the same size as all my other lecture-notes. But I shall not attempt to draw a hard & fast line between business-notes, & what may be called travellers notes. Indeed as my main object is to form notions about men & manners, it would be very hard to draw such a line. But I will from time to time select such of my notes as appear to contain matters that would be interesting to you, & send them home.[2] I will ask you to be so good as to send them on to Aunt Louisa, who is likely, I think, to be interested in some of them. I will however ask both you & her to do me one favor; that is, not to make any folds in the paper in addition to those which I make. For my lecture notes stand up on end in wooden cases; & as some of these will take their stand there, I do not wish to have their standing strength diminished by unnecessary creases.

The notes will be put together primarily with the purpose of refreshing my own memory. But as I should have to make such notes anyhow, I am enabled by this plan to let you know much more about what is interesting me than I could if I had to write additional & separate accounts for home. If there should be anything that I do not wish to be shewn to others I will mark it as 'private'.[3] Thus e.g. you can send on this letter to Aunt Louisa without hesitation. Of course I do not want the letters to be preserved; only the 'Notes'.

You may be amused at our meal hours. They seem to me to be absurd.

      a heavy meat Breakfast at 8
      a meat lunch at 12
          dinner—   4
      a light tea   7

These are the four meals that most of the passengers eat. But [it][4] is possible to get a sandwich between nine & ten in the evening. I do this; & by eating no meat at lunch & nothing at tea, find I get on very well.

We saw a splendid Iceberg the other day: about 120 f[t].. high on a base of about 200 feet each way. The form was pyramidal & the workings of the weather on its surface had made fine bold forms: it was about a mile off, & could only be seen properly by a telescope: thus we lost most of its brilliancy. The Captain said that it was an extremely rare occurrence to find an iceberg in a latitude so low. But I forget now what the latitude was; I think about 43.

The 'emigrants' are 500 in number more than half German & Swedes. There are many children among them.

I will stop now: but very likely will add a postscript tomorrow morning when we are in sight of New York.

Give my kindest love to my Father & the Girls

Your very loving | Alfred Marshall

Arrived at last.

The entrance to N. York is grander in every way than that to London: only I was surprised at not seeing nearly so much shipping as on the Thames.

Partly because of my not being accustomed to colour during the voyage the banks of the Hudson struck me as being gloriously green. Moreover, it was well set off by the colour of the houses. I shall, I see already, have a great deal to say about the Americans taste for strong colours.

What I have seen of the city, I like much more than I had expected.

I will write again soon. You will I think be safe in writing to Niagara Falls any time before the 22nd.

I have some doubts whether Aunt Louisa will care for the long papers inclosed: only I recollect, that she liked reading our journals from the Lakes.[5] Of course I should have no objections to my letters being sent on to Uncle Harry but he would have the most decided objection to reading them.[6]

[Enclosures]

June 2. 1875   *Sketches of Character*

On board S.S. Spain bound to N. York.

A-*Boardman*.[7] 6f^t.. 2. Age 24 perhaps, was a middy, tells following tale with great pride. A Spanish man of war had laid herself across a spanish harbour to compel the payment of certain harbour dues alleged to be due by some American & English ships lying in the harbour. They telegraphed to Gibraltar: & the ship in which Boardman was was sent to clear the passage. Shortly after they were started the signal was put up for their recall. The Captain told Boardman who was in charge of the signals that he must not see it. He shut his eye put up the telescope & reported that he could see nothing. The[y] steamed up: cleared for action, loaded guns &c. To their horror they found the Spanish ship putting up steam: the spanish Captain came on board their ship & gave way. 'In all his life he had never known so much cursing' as took place on board his ship when they found they were to have no fight: ie for the sake of a bit of amusement in the way of fighting, they were willing to engage two countries in war.

He is a handsome, dashing, rakish, sort of fellow: a dare-devil: but with splendid stuff in him. He was invalided out of the navy. He would not be dependent, but went out to the neighbourhood of Chicago, entered an engineer's shop: & is now working with his own hands: but will probably become wealthy.

He with a friend was going out of a saloon & found a man standing with his revolver to the teeth of another. He & his friend let fly at the same instant with their fists. The man fell: & then fired his revolver but did no harm. Boardman wrenched it away, breaking one of his fingers. Nothing came of the matter.

In one saloon he remarked on the large number of bullet holes in the walls & ceilings 'Oh yes' said the waiter quietly 'we often have warm work here'. He saw one row that evening. Only one man was hit & he only in the shoulder. He was carried home in a cab; 'nothing came of it'.[8]

He heard a story of some miners in, I think, the Oregon district. A commercial traveller was staying in one of the houses: three miners were playing cards: A man passed by, & wanted to rest; of course he was invited in: he soon joined in the game. Presently another man came by, with a gun slung over his shoulder. He took a seat. The commercial traveller noticed that the stranger began to win steadily (they were playing for heaps of gold-dust) & presently saw the second stranger, who could see the cards of the three miners signalling to the first stranger. He waited for some time so as to be certain. He then without uttering a word shot the first stranger dead. The second bolted, the three miners started in chase. They soon returned bringing his corpse. 'That is the way rough justice is done out there' said Boardman. Nothing came of it.

Boardman told me some of his private adventures whence I concluded that a revolver was a requisite for a traveller in the West. Ultimately Boardman found I had no taste for 'Saloon' life. He pitied me evidently: but, when he became quite convinced of it, assured me with good-natured but repeated emphasis 'You won't want a revolver'.

S.S. Spain Liv:-N.Y   *Sketches of Character*

3 June 1875

A little, travelled Swiss—age probably 45, with gentle pretty wife age perhaps 18: gentle, simple mild, but apparently honest & true, he had obviously done his best in the world, but the world had played with him & though still gentle he had become, as he himself said embittered against it; but it was a soft plaintive anger that he shewed.

Once in New York a man was shot down by his side in the streets. He was arrested by the police & imprisoned. 2000 dollars bail was demanded, he repeated with earnestness 'if I had not been able to give bail I should have been kept in prison for months. Is that just.' He wanted the world to be so pure that unlimited discretion could be given judges to deal with each case entirely on its own merits: then the judge might (perhaps) have let him free. He gave the bail the next day, but was detained in N.Y for months, waiting for the trial to come off, & neglecting his business: at last he sacrificed his bail & returned to Europe, but his prospects in life were already blighted; & he never recovered his position.

He is most comically jealous about his wife. He keeps her to his side all day long, whatever is going on. She is gentle, open, apparently willing to talk to others: & a favorite on board: but if any man whatever makes any remark whatever to her, his little face becomes like a pocket thunderstorm: whence much amusement.

One form of his embitterment against the world in general is his attitude towards religions, which is one of steady negation. His wife was asked to take part in singing hymns &c in the Service last Sunday. He caused some merriment by saying 'Well dear! You have done worse things than that before now.'

He has been a great deal in Peru: & made some sweeping statement about old Peruvian civilisation having been greater than any modern civilisation. But when pressed for his reasons he could only say that they had built some great fortifications that shewed great genius for the masonry work; & that Peru had been governed for a long while by one race. No doubt he had had originally more materials for forming a judgement on. But all that he said was a caution against trusting the conclusions of unscientific observers without an opportunity of cross-examining them.

S.S. Spain. Liv:-N.Y.   *Sketches of Character*

3 June 1875

An Irish Priest: amiable, erudite, with considerable dialectical power, but not otherwise powerful. Had many discussions with him about philosophy. Many of his remarks seemed original & forcible: but there is no evidence that they were his own. He was at one time fascinated by metaphysical speculations; but though more successful in this branch than in others (he then was I think at a Belgian University) he revolted from them & was impelled to the 'common-sense' of the 'English' school: This turned out to mean Reid, Stewart, & Hamilton.[9] This struck me as eminently characteristic. It was characteristic that he should like Reid & co (though probably there are many Roman Catholics who base their systems on German abstractions). But it was eminently characteristic that he should subsume the English school under the Scotch, or rather that he should be unconscious not only of the purport of English inductive work, but even of its prominence. Yet he fought well about Bishop Berkeley. There was indirect evidence that his reading had been under some control at all events; e.g. he had not read Hume.

We discussed monasteries & nunneries. I wanted to know whether he had any notions as to means whereby the pettiness that is supposed to be rampant there might be got rid off. Though his mode of carrying on a discussion is in general complaisant & subdued, he here at once adopted a confident, almost aggressive, but yet studiously inoffensive & even captivating tone. Pettiness is a natural element in all institutions founded on the experience of the moment: it is not to be found in Catholic institutions. Their rules have come down from distant times, the wisdom of many successive generations has been built into them: in them self-sacrifice is accepted as a means & also as an end, implicit obedience to the authority of centuries is demanded & is conceded. He had seen much of them: he knew no life happier than theirs: every one who knew them could testify to the marvellous cheerfulness which reigned in them.

I felt that this one-sided statement was audacious; & replied that I had seen the faces of an enormous number of nuns at various times, that they did not bear out what he said. He seemed to be conscious that he had been injudicious in overstating his case but he was very firm in maintaining that the remedy which I proposed, viz an increase of the independence of the individual was the worst possible change. Absolute, implicit obedience, & offering up of self was the vital condition for success. It did not seem to occur to him that it is wrong to maim the spirit as it is to maim the body.

I found that he had very strong 'national' opinions: I spent many hours in discussing Irelands relations to England. As are most such people, he is a curious compound of sagacity & openness with bigotry & narrowness. He would confess or rather insist that it was foolish to dilate on Englands wrongs to Ireland in the past, but he was morbidly sensitive about Englands antipathy to the Irish; & his proofs of this antipathy seemed to depend mainly on the history of the distant past.

I avowed myself as an advocate of 'federalization' or at least of some such plan as that of Earl Russell's for local parliaments,[10] provided a scheme for working it could be found. He had complete faith that ere long some able man would be found to solve the problem: but volunteered a suggestion of a difficulty. If the Irish Parliament had to be consulted on matters of taxation, their consent would hardly be obtained for taxes in support of a war against America or France. They were bound to France he said not only by religion, but by sympathies & by gratitude for the friendly interest that France had taken in them in the past: they were more closely bound to France than to any other nation.

It was an error to suppose that any Irish except an insignificant tail of the 'residuum' of the Fenians, would wish, if they had the power, to disturb those holders of property whose ancestors had acquired it by Saxon 'confiscations.'

Of the services which an Irish parliament could do for his country, he discussed at length only one: It would protect Irish industries. Here again he brought forward some arguments inconsistent with the first principles of Political Economy: but when pushed he gave way. Taking his case as a whole, & discounting some statements as to matters of fact which he made, but which were probably one-sided, I came to the conclusion that it was not strong.

In particular he failed to give any good answer to the question. 'If the Irish are, as you say, naturally industrious, & not devoid of a genius for manufactures,

why have the Irish not developed their manufactures as easily as those towns
e.g. in the Eastern Counties of England, which have no special natural
advantages. He could only say that (i) *some* Irishmen succeed as manufacturers
in the United States, & that some at least of these are of *purely* Irish blood, &
(ii) Irish manufactures used to flourish before they were destroyed by English
tyranny. But with regard to this last point he was inattentive to the facts that
since that time (i) the character of the English people has changed (ii) the change
that has come over the mode of conducting manufacture is such as to give a
higher premium than before to the specially Anglo–Saxon qualities of enterprise,
daring without recklessness, the power to organize & the power to command &
to obey.

    Still there were, scattered among his arguments many instructive bits. His
strongest point was this; if manufactures were forcibly started, though the
country as a whole would perhaps suffer in consequence some immediate loss,
this loss would be soon recovered, because men who now refuse to work, would
then be induced to work. In support of this he urged the repugnance of Irish
men for working as hired laborers on the land; & the old insecurity of capital
invested by a farmer in his land. 'Gladstones Act,[11] though I am perfectly
convinced it was made with the best possible intentions, has in one respect had
a result the opposite of what was proposed. The compensation which a tenant
can claim for improvements is forfeited if he have sublet (without leave) his
farm. Suppose the sons of a farmer to be growing up: he does not care to pay
them a daily wage: he is likely rather to take them into partnership, this
partnership is extremely likely to be capable of being presented as a subletting
and the farmer makes his sons emigrate. Ireland is starved for want of hands'.
It is possible that there may be some slight difficulty here; that the definition of
'subletting' in the act requires alteration: but on the whole the conversation
made me think more highly of the act than I had done before.

S.S. Spain Liverpool. N.York   *Sketches of Character*

June 3 1875

Rev^d.. W^m.. Nullen. Missionary of the B.C.F.M.[12] An American who had been
20 years in Natal & is now returning. Had long discussions about Langibalele
& Colenso.[13] Though in most respects apparently fair & open, he appeared to
me to have a twist[14] in his mind on this matter. As regards Colenso he accused
him of being a special pleader but when pressed for the facts was compelled to
admit that the interpretation he put on Colenso's acts was not the only one
possible. Though apparently mild in character generally, he spoke in uncompromising terms about the necessity of enforcing from the natives instant
obedience at the expense of any amount of severity: but he had no tangible
arguments to give in favor of this position. His defence of the Natal Government
amounted to this: we undertook to govern the Zulus by Kaffir law & not by

English. Our treatment of Langibalele, though harsher than would have been possible under English law, was not as severe, as a Kaffir chief in the same position as the Governor would have been legally *justified* in sending a messenger to take Langibalele's life: & we only expelled the tribe. But he could not shew that the severity of the government was needed save by reference to the general principle that Kaffirs must be ruled with an iron hand. On the whole a 'Positivist', who holds that modern Christianity leads men to adopt a high moral code of behaviour with regard to those only who are strong enough to make men feel the evil results of retaliation, would have triumphed in listening to him.

He let out that the orthodox people in Natal generally had made tremendous capital out of a forced journey that Colenso made, without resting on the 'Sabbath'. He confessed that laziness was the dominant feature of Kaffir character: & obviously chuckled over the diplomatic blunder that Colenso had made in the matter.

He let out also that the Kaffirs are so ignorant & thoughtless that they just believe whatever the missionaries tell them. (He would probably have been more cautious in his admissions on this subject if he had heard the conversation shortly before to the effect that the united efforts of all the missionaries who have ever been to India have not succeeded in converting one single member of the Brahmin or thinking class, & scarcely anybody at all except the most ignorant & depraved, even these being generally entirely unaffected as regards morality. This testimony from Evans a member of the Indian Civil Service[15] is worth recording in confirmation of similar testimony. It would not be worth very much when taken alone.)

[1] Marshall Papers. Addressed to the family home, 12 Victoria Road, Clapham, S.W. Marshall visited North America in the summer of 1875 to explore its socio-economic conditions and to examine the effects of protectionism, spade work for a book on foreign-trade problems he was then writing. (See *Early Economic Writings*, vol. 1, pp. 52–66; vol. 2 pp. 3–236, for details.) He sailed from Liverpool on the SS Spain, landing in New York City on Sunday 6 June, and sailed from New York on the SS Erin on Saturday 2 October. The following rough itinerary is implied by the letters and enclosures [21,–32] written while abroad. 6–8 June New York City; 9–11 June Albany and vicinity; 12–13 June Springfield; 14–27 June Boston and vicinity; 28–30 June Providence and Norwich; 1–6 July New Haven and Hartford; 7–9 July New Lebanon, Oneida, and Rochester; 10–12 July Niagara; 13–16 July Toronto, Guelph, Hamilton, and Buffalo; 17–18 July Cleveland; 19 July Oberlin. After this the available detail is much reduced. Chicago was probably reached on 22 July and the next month was spent in travelling to the West Coast, San Francisco and Virginia City being among the places visited. St Louis had been reached on the return journey by Sunday 22 August and was probably left on 26 August. Travelling via Indianapolis (26 August), Cincinnati, Columbus, and Canton, Pittsburgh had been reached by Sunday 5 September. After several days in Philadelphia (he was there on 18 September), New York City had been reached by 23 September. Whether an intention to visit Washington DC was implemented remains unclear.

[2] These notes will be appended as 'enclosures' to this and the further letters [22–32] that Marshall wrote from North America. This device seems justifiable given the close relationship between the notes and letters, even though it is not always clear whether or when each particular note was sent. In a few cases it is clear that the notes were not sent.

[3] Recourse to this procedure is not apparent.

[4] Word apparently omitted.

[5] Untraced.

[6] The grounds of his likely objection are unsurmisable.

[7] Subsequently Boardman—not further identified—was overwritten as Portman.

[8] Opening quotation mark omitted in the original.

[9] Thomas Reid (1710–96), Dugald Stewart (1753–1828), and Sir William Hamilton (1788–1856) were all Scottish philosophers. For general philosophical background see William Ritchie Sorley, *A History of British Philosophy to 1900* (Cambridge University Press, Cambridge, 1920).

[10] Lord John Russell (1792–1878), first Earl Russell, British statesman and Prime Minister, took some interest in Ireland, but it is not apparent to which of his proposals Marshall is alluding here. See Spencer Walpole, *The Life of Lord John Russell* (Longmans Green, London, 1891: 2 vols.).

[11] The Landlord and Tenant (Ireland) Act, 1870 (33 & 34 Vict., c. 46). Gladstone was Prime Minister when the Act, which sought to improve tenants' rights, was passed.

[12] Probably the Board of Commissioners for Foreign Missions, founded in America in 1810. No further details about Nullen have been discovered.

[13] John William Colenso (1814–1883) was the famous Bishop of Natal, deposed for heresy in 1863. Langalibalele (1818–89)—note the correct spelling—a Zulu chief, was banished in 1874 by a special court invoking native law, a result protested by Colenso.

[14] The word 'twist' could possibly be 'taint'.

[15] The most likely person is Henry Farrington Evans, educated at Corpus Christi College, Oxford, who had been in India since 1867. See the first edition of the *India Office List* (Harrison, London, 1886).

22. To Rebecca Marshall, 12 June 1875[1]

Massascit House | Springfield Mass
12 June 1875

My dear Mother,

I wrote last just after arriving at New York. I did not stay there long: partly because I intend to stay there a few days on my way back: partly because the population of New York is chiefly of foreign birth.

I came up the Hudson, by steamer, on Wednesday, stopped at Albany till yesterday & arrived here today.

I was reminded in New York of the towns of Holland at almost every step: I found this partly explained when I read that in the early days of New York bricks used to be imported from Holland. The bright red wash that the Dutch use has a marvellous effect in lighting up the streets. I found the same to some extent in Albany again: & it turns out that the Dutch element was exceptionally strong in the early times of Albany.

A hostile critic of American architecture would accuse it of striving too much for effect. De Tocqueville says that he was impressed by the sight of many pleasure villas built in Greek style of marble, shining from the banks of the Hudson as he sailed into New York. He went next day to examine the best of them & found it was made of wood. He was disgusted and savage. That was in /35.[2] Things may have altered since then. Anyhow I did not find anything like as much sham as I expected. I found in the larger buildings uniformly thoroughness & solidity, as far as the eye could judge: though I am told the building is not so strong as it appears to be. I do not deny that some of their architects seem to me to have been audacious & to have failed. But there is originality daring & strength about their work: more than there is, so far as I know, about the work of any other nation. I believe that they will ere long give the world the first genuine architecture it has had since genuine Gothic was broken up by the erudite servility of the Renaissance.

The Americans have a habit of inserting huge letters into a vast sheet of light, & open wire netting,[3] & hanging the advertisement across the street. It is incomparably the most effective mode of advertising that I have seen. But, to say nothing of more sentimental objections, it prevents one from seeing the street. I think it should be put down by law: or at least curbed.

I stayed at the Fifth Avenue Hotel. It is the first Hotel of New York: probably the most important Hotel in the World. For Hotels are important in America. As I cannot ever see a better specimen of an American Hotel, I will give you an account of this. It is built of white marble: outside nothing else, inside white marble except where it is necessary to have something else. It is not particularly large: at least there are many hotels in America which are larger. It has beds for 1100 people. On the ground floor there is a large Hall with seats, where people chat. In this Hall there is a huge marble bar behind which stand the manager or submanager & his two assistants. They are all cultivated gentlemen in appearance: probably drawing immense salaries. They award rooms, answer inquiries & receive payment of accounts. The leading notion here, as throughout America as far as I can tell, about accounts is that life is not long enough for accurate accounts. The plan therefore is this. You are charged for the meal that happens to be going on when you enter the house whether you eat it or not: & thereafter you are charged a certain number of dollars a day: in first class Hotels $5, in others $4 or $3. So that, excepting when carriages, washing or such things have to be paid for, the accounts are short. For, I should have said, on the same floor with the 'Office' there is what is called a 'Bar';—where spirituous liquors & all kinds of concoctions—the American drink mixer is as professional an artist as the French Cook—are sold & payment made over the counter. On the ground floor also is a large smoking & newspaper room: below, are the basement smoking & billiard rooms. On the ground floor also is a little telegraphic apparatus. This is worked by one man in 'Wall Street' (the New York 'Lombard Street') currents are sent from there by one & the same movement to every place at which they wish to have the latest news. At each of these places a wheel with letters on it is made by the shocks to turn round till the right letter is opposite to a band of paper when it is jerked against the paper & the letter in question is printed off. No one is wanted to look after the machine. Many yards of paper are printed off without being looked at by anyone. But if any two people in the 'Fifth Avenue Hotel' want to make a bargain about stocks, they go to this machine take up the strip of paper between their fingers & read it backwards till they come to a quotation of the stock in question. Thus they are as well posted as if they were on the Exchange itself.

Above are dining rooms, breakfast rooms, bordering[4] endless bedrooms; & the first necessary of existence in a large hotel in hot weather viz a steam lift which *without ever stopping* from 7 am till midnight goes up & down. The meal hours are breakfast 6.30 to 11, lunch 1 to 2, dinner 2 to 7, tea 6 to 9, supper 7 to 11.30 For each meal there is a printed card giving the fare; (or rather for each of the chief meals Breakfast, Dinner, Supper (Tea & Lunch are not given at most hotels)).[5] You go in as often as you like; you eat as much as you can of as many dishes as you like, & you pay for everything bed, meals, service $5 a day.

If you reflect that for dinner you have a choice of sixty or seventy dishes, many of them very recherché you cannot call this dear. It would cost more[6] to live as well at Clarence's Hotel.

The Hotel at Albany at which I was was second class, not perfectly clean. I paid $3 a day. I thought it much dearer than the superb luxury of the 'Fifth Avenue Hotel' for $5.

There is not much tide at New York. The largest steamers come straight to land, by a clever arrangement. The shore is scooped into a number of long recesses; & in each is found room for one steamer. So that each steamer discharges its cargo from its entire broadside straight into its own shed. The river steamers here are quite different from those in Europe. The best of them have paddle wheels

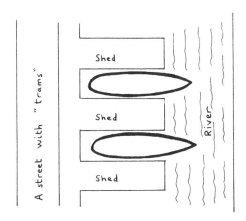

of about 40 feet diameter, with three decks & room for about 1000 passengers. Of course they go much faster than screw steamers of the same size & horse power would; but they would not work in a storm at sea.

The Hudson is rather like 'The Rhine', ie the Rhine between Bingen & Bonn. On the whole I liked it better than the Rhine: there were fewer rocky details, but more mountainous grandeur, very much more variety, & of course a greater breadth of water. I believe that with the exception of the upper part of the Mississippi & perhaps the Saguenay of Canada, it has the finest river scenery in North America. I spent two days & a half in going over Manufactories at Albany & in the neighbourhood thereof. I have written many notes about them: but I shall not send them home because they would be hardly intelligible without some explanation & because I want to correct such observations as are open to error by questions asked in other places.[7] I shall, I think, go on to Boston tomorrow (I am writing on Sunday now) & stay there some time. As at present advised I propose to travel thence as follows: (but shall not take tickets that will commit me definitely to any route) Boston-Providence-Norwich-Hartford-Montreal-Ottawa across to the St Lawrence-down the rapids to Montreal-Albany-Niagara Chicago (possibly S^t.. Paul & down the Mississippi till I meet the Pacific railroad again, if not) straight to San Francisco-the Yosemite Valley,-Denver-Kansas City,-S^t.. Louis-Louisville-Cincinnati (arriving there late in August) spend the first half of September in the iron, coal, & oil region of Ohio, & the latter half in the Manufacturing districts of which Philadelphia & New York are centres, leaving for England on October 2nd. I think I am safe in giving Chicago as an address for letters posted on or before the 28th.. I had intended to tell you of my washing bill. They charge in New York $1.$\frac{1}{2}$ for every dozen items. After my voyage I had a good deal to be washed, e.g. I sent 11 collars. My bill was nearly $4. Generally speaking people here will not be bothered to charge small prices for anything: they go in for averaging prices; & they will not do anything however small save for high pay.

I went into a church this morning at random (every place of worship is a church here). It turned out to be a Congregational church. The singing & the responses shewed marvellously good drill. The preacher was lively but of no great ability. He talked a good deal about communism, & made the ordinary mistake of mixing up its history with that of Communalism. His theology was decided, but he did not obtrude it. I intend to go to a great many services, to see what goes. He was of course dressed in ordinary costume, & free & easy in manner. There was no tinge of sacerdotalism in him. But the end of the church where he was was crowded with superb flowers all natural ie in pots—I like the notion.

Give my kindest love to every one | Your very loving Alfred

[Enclosures]

New York   *The Drama*
7 June 1875

'Big Bonanza' at 5th.. Avenue Theatre. Written by an American for Americans about Americans. Had run over 100 days. Theatre small: actors few, but in the main good. Chief persons a thriving & genial 'Wall-Street' man, & his cousin a 'Scientist'. Business man, kind & generous to every one, particularly the

Scientist: on one point alone is he impatient. The Scientist talks of students as men of brains in contrast to Business Men: & vows that if he would deign to do such a thing he could make his fortune in a trice. Business man dares him to try: he does; he behaves like a silly child, trusts a casual acquaintance to put him up to 'tips': has the good luck to be put up to a genuine tip which is to 'sell Bonanza'. But he is ignorant enough to think that in order to sell a thing on the Exchange he must have the thing: & sets to work to buy. Bonanza comes down, & he would have been nearly ruined if the Business man had not on his own responsibility prevented his orders from being executed. Meanwhile the business man had pushed a patent which the scientist had taken out for a new dye, & sold it for him for $20,000. The play was the most characteristic thing I have seen here in that (i) it represented the business man as a sort of deity; & the 'scientist' as a mere nincompoop. (ii) it patronised the scientist; he was good for something: he could help to dye carpets. (iii) The main joke of the play assumed the audience to understand that you need not have 'Big Bonanza' shares in order to sell them: which few of a London audience would know.

8 June. At Union S^t.. Theatre: reputed one of the best. Adaptation of French Drama called the Orphans.[8] Everything was told in direct unmistakeable language: nothing was left to be inferred. Thereby the vulgar were forced to understand the whole movement: & as the vulgar are the most important people in a theatre, French 'breadth' of treatment is I suppose commercially correct. But there was no high art in the play & most of the actors spoke like school children repeating a lesson. This of course French comedians do not.

American Shopmen   *Sketches of Character*

June 7 1875. Went into a largish shop in New York to buy a hat. A civil, intelligent, gentlemannered, businesslike, elderly man waited on me. 'What size is yours', & without waiting for an answer or saying more he took my hat off my head looked at it; tried it on his own head, moved it up & down to see how it felt, took it off, looked at it again, tried it on again, hunted over a large box, selected a hat, walked up to me, said with quiet unassuming but complete confidence, 'that will fit you'. It fitted me exactly. Whereas in general I have to try on many hats before I get the right one. Some Englishmen would not have liked his trying on their hats: but they would have tried on any number of his hats with the greatest composure; not insolently, but as a matter of course. My friend was such a perfect democrat that it did not occur to him that there was any reason why he should not wear my hat: his manner was absolutely free from insolence. May the habit become general! If it does some go-ahead Yankee will find space in his advertisements for a line:—

'Our shopmens heads warranted perfectly clean'.

American Shopmen   *Sketches of Character*

10 June 1875

Went into a leather shop to buy a box.[9] The shopman patronised me & gave me an introduction to the Superintendent of the penitentiary there (New York State) 'the best in the world'. Had been in England with Barnum: had had charge of the saddles. Repeated that he liked it immensely. You are so free: there is the same law for rich & poor. Here there is not—money will do anything, anything.

June 10, 1875. Albany N.Y   *Invention*—American

Large Stove works. 'Are many inventions made by the men?' Answer from youth who shewed me over & was obviously in authority 'No: at least as a rule: they are almost entirely made in the shop. One & only one invention of importance has been made here by a working man. He got $100 for it; He might have sold it, if he had waited & managed properly, for $20,000. If inventions are made by a working man at all, it is in general not by those brought up in the trade who have stuck to it, but by men who have had a good education to start with; & who have knocked about in the world & shifted from one occupation to another.' 'How do you account for the superiority of the American inventive faculty over the English.' 'Chiefly by the difference in the habits of the consumers: English people are contented with the things to which they are accustomed. Americans are always on the lookout to see if they cannot find something better suited to their purposes than they have already. The demand for ingenuity calls forth the supply.'

June 10, 1875. Albany N.Y   *Invention*—American

Large reaping & mowing machine works. Conversation with one of the men in the carpenters shop. Had been working for the firm in various parts of America for 20 years.

'Why do American mowing & reaping machines cut out the English'. 'We are quicker in making changes: we make lighter machines: the advantage our wood gives us is not important: we do not (here) use hickory except for the teeth. We have just brought out a patent which will enable us to throw up (so as not to let it sweep off the corn) any one or more of the arms of the reaping machine. We have only just succeeded in making reaping machines which will work on rough land: now we can send reaping machines anywhere where mowing machines will go.' 'The American machines are lighter than the English. Does this have any effect on the length of time they will wear?' 'Not much, if they are handled properly. It is the fashion now to have iron frames: these are light, though not so light as they look: but they are liable to be broken.'

June 10, 1875. At Albany N.Y.   *Irish*—In America

In large stove works very many Irish & Germans. The former not so good as the latter—reasons (i) more given to drink (ii) 'not so apt to ask reason why'.

In adjoining agricultural implement works less hard work, more intelligence wanted, & the men were chiefly Americans. Their faces were a brilliant contrast to those in the former works. I am told that moulding &c is mainly done by Irish.

June 11. Going over three iron works intermediate between Albany & Troy made enquiries about the Irish: in all three many Irish were employed; the same character, as far as I could judge, throughout. One man, a German told me that the Irish seldom got into posts of command in private firms: but their party organization enabled them to get into many of the best posts under government. One man told me that Americans, or at least some of them, went in for making tools of the Irish, taking the best posts themselves & letting the Irish have the second level.

June 11, 1875   *Inventions*—American

Went over large Bessemer works between Albany & Troy. The book keeper (English), & the chemist (German) who (the latter) shewed me over, told me that they turned out nearly twice the amount of steel that was done in England with the same plant. America will soon, not only hold her own against England, but even export. Their excellence consists possibly to some extent in the superior energy of their men (he was not sure about this) but chiefly in their mechanical improvements. I rather suspect him of comparing America now with England of some time back. I could not understand all the improvements of which he spoke: one was very simple, the steel ingot when got into the form of a rectangular parallelopipedon was brought into the rollers that were to roll it out, by a number of rollers constituting the platform on which it rested: a motion backwards or forwards was given to these by a series of cogwheels, the power being hydraulic & applied by a man who sat at his ease looking on at the operation.

This was pretty, but not of much importance. The German complained much of the conservatism of the English manufacturers. Twenty years ago they were unquestionably ahead in all lines: they rest on their laurels: they are proud: if an Englishman makes a move, the Americans will have the new plan or rather some one or more trifling improvements upon it in work at once: *they* are not too proud or lazy to go over the water & hunt for new notions. The English are.

There is a decided growth of an aristocratic set in America: this will be important: at present it is small; & men outside it go up & down with enormous rapidity. 'My grandfather may have been worth a million dollars, & I now working as a day-laborer:—as likely as not'. In the continual shifting a man with a turn for invention has a great chance of getting to the top. I said 'Then the large number of your working classes who have the habit of thinking for themselves, does indirectly promote inventions, to a greater extent than it appears. If many inventions are not made by those who work with their hands, many are made by those who have worked with their hands'. I understood him to assent to this.

Another thing of importance, he could not judge of how much importance, was the American law of patents. In England any one can patent anything (or nearly so A.M.). So that when his patent is infringed, he has to prove in a court of law that his patent was for a substantive invention: unless he is a rich man this breaks him. In America no patent is allowed except for a substantive invention; the courts of law recognise the granting of the patent as a proof of the reality of the invention: thus the poor man is secured. An American patent only costs $100. Everything is patented.

He recommended me to examine a brilliant piece of Yankee invention at the neighbouring[10] [horse shoe works].

Horse shoe works (near Troy). An elaborate notice was painted up 'No admittance, no passes given'. I went boldly into the office. The subordinates did not think of giving me leave: my card was sent in to one of the firm: he cross examined me with some care & then said, 'As you are a stranger I have great pleasure in sending you over.' I was chaperoned by a policeman. The central operation was this: a bar, of which the adjoined [see Figs.] represents approx:

the transverse section, was put red hot into a machine. A sort of hook caught it & pulled it back, thus giving it the general outline of the shoe. Then came two moulds down on it which gave it the rims & holes for the nails, &c. They could make 60 a minute running extra high speed: but the average amount per minute from one machine was 40 or 45. It seemed to me to be a brilliant adaptation of an old idea rather than original invention of a high order.

The works were run by a water wheel, fed from a large pond on the neighbouring high lands: the water was brought in a large iron tube & shot out forwards over the wheel. It ran all the winter in spite of the ice; but got a little slack in the dry season. Scarcely a drop of water fell over: the water rushed in with great force: this finally convinced me that for large wheels the water should be shot forwards. The diameter of this wheel was I should guess about 36 feet, width 8 feet.

The bellows were worked by a steam engine: this steam being provided gratis thus:—the flames from each puddling furnace being forced to make the detour of a boiler (a boiler for each furnace) before escaping up the chimney [see Fig.].

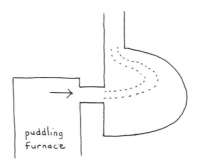

At the Bessemer works I watched some preparations for moulding. I thought the sand was not cut so clean as I had seen it done in England: but [weskits?][11] were put on which I had not seen before. The great improvement of modern times seems to be the pouring the moulten steel into a reservoir in the centre of many moulds & letting it flow in at the bottom of these so as to rise up: thus uniformity is attained, & the mould is not injured. I do not know whether this is done in England.[12]

In a large shop for repairing the cars of the N.Y.C. & H.R.R.[13] at Albany I found what appeared to me an undue preponderance of hand labor: such as I should have expected in Central Europe rather than in America: but in such a point as this a repairing shop does not give trustworthy evidence.

12 June 1875   *American Manufactures*

Went over a huge cotton mill (Harmony) at Cohoes, three miles north of Troy. Unlimited supply of water power. One turbine drives a gigantic factory. It was better built, with more ambition than most English factories: but not superior to Saltaire or Listers.[14] Had long talk with a young overlooker, who could not guess how many hands were employed but thought monthly wages amounted to about \$36,000. Monthly wages seemed to be in his room \$5–20, in others \$15 to 30. Much more than half of the workers were Irish & French; the latter the more numerous. Then of course overseers &c had higher pay. But I did not gather that wages were much higher than in England. He assented & asserted that prices were higher here; he had married an Englishwoman whose parents had kept a shop: & she told him that American flour was sold in England at a lower price than in America. (Of course she would not know what allowance to make for the variations of harvests, but the remark is worth something.) The machinery was almost entirely imported from England. In no case was it, as far as I could gather, new in principle.

¹ Marshall Papers.
² Alexis de Tocqueville, *Democracy in America* (Longman, Green, Longman, and Roberts; London, 1862; first French edition 1835), vol. 2, book 1, ch. 11, 'Of the spirit in which the Americans cultivate the arts'.
³ That is, the netting is both light and open.
⁴ Possibly 'bordering' should be 'boudoirs'.
⁵ The closing parenthesis and full stop are not in the original.
⁶ The word 'more' was substituted for the phrase 'two or three times as much'.
⁷ Despite this disclaimer the relevant surviving notes are appended here as an 'enclosure'. See [21.2] for explanation.
⁸ The advertised title of this play was 'The Two Orphans'. See for example *New York Times*, Sunday 14 February 1875, where a detailed synopsis of 'The Big Bonanza' is also printed.
⁹ Presumably this transaction took place in Albany.
¹⁰ This is the end of a page and an omitted page might be suspected if the pagination were not continuous.
¹¹ Illegible word.
¹² The following note appears to have been inserted subsequently: 'I believe this method is open to grave objection'.
¹³ The New York Central and Hudson Rail Road.
¹⁴ Sir Titus Salt (1803–76), a leading worsted manufacter and philanthropist, founded Saltaire in Yorkshire as a model company town. The engineering firm of R. A. Lister and Co. was located in Dursley, Gloucestershire.

23. To Rebecca Marshall, 20 June 1875[1]

Boston 20 June 1875

My very dear Mother

I am delighted to hear of Fanny's engagement.[2] I am writing to her. Thankyou & the girls for your letter. Tell May I read Charles' letters & liked them extremely.[3] Since I last wrote I have seen a immense number of things & of important persons. I have been staying with Mr. Eliot, President of Harvard College, the great University of America.[4] While there I had no time to write anything more than pencil jottings in my pocket book. Thus I am behind hand this week.

I arrived in Boston on Monday last. Went on Tuesday to Mr. Eliot: saw with him the great festivity in the 17ᵗʰ.. 'the centennial celebration of Bunker Hill', & came here again on Saturday. I suppose you know that Boston is the intellectual capital of America as Edinburgh is of Scotland. It is the Capital of the New England States: for all purposes: & it has collected around it almost all the great literary Men of the Country. There is more polish in it, & probably less misgovernment than in any other great town.

It is proud of being more like European towns, & especially like English towns than any other great town. Still the American 'go', though controlled, & absolutely free from swagger here, is to be seen here.

Thus on the whole it is I think one of the most delightful spots on earth.

It is of course hot in summer, & cold in winter: but the suburbs, such as Cambridge, in which Harvard University is, & where many of the leading literary men live, has shade & easy access to splendid wilderness.

Probably you knew that many of the leading men here are Unitarians, I was astonished to find how many. Almost all the leading churches in Boston are Unitarian: & in the leading literary society there is scarcely anyone who is not Unitarian. Of course there is a great variety of belief included under this common name. Though the churches which are now Unitarian were originally Congregational, they use, or at least some of them use, the English liturgy with a very few alterations. Putting on one side all those which are necessitated by their rejection of the doctrine of the Trinity, I think that the rest are so far as I have observed improvements, startling improvements. I had no notion there were so many small flaws in the English liturgy till they were pointed out to me, when I heard the minister shunt off for a while onto a new path, here & there. Seeing that they had used their discretion I turned to the marriage service to see if they had altered that; & to my intense delight found that their woman does not promise to *obey* the man.

Tuesday Morning.

I must send off this letter: short as it is. You will have seen an account of the Centennial Procession in the Newspapers. I met many interesting people at Mr Eliots & the houses he took me to. The most celebrated of these people was General Sherman: strong, lively, rather rough, but withal a man whom one could not help liking.[5] Yesterday I dined at Mr Norton's.[6] The Editors of the 'Atlantic Monthly' (Mr Howells) & the 'Nation' (Mr Pigott, I think) (far the ablest paper of America) & one or two other men—Professors—were there.[7] Conversation was good & lively. During the first part of the evening the lead was taken by Mr Howells who belongs to the lighter order able men. He was full of stories of Mark Twain, & Bret Harte. When Bret Harte came to stay with him he said 'Why it must be quite dangerous to let off a pistol here; in whatever direction you fired you would bring down a two-volumer' (literary man). Of humour such as this presented under the mask of buffoonery, the Americans seem to have almost a monopoly. A good instance of this is the story of the fishing boy in the extract I send you.[8] Almost every Newspaper (the Nation is the only exception of which I know, & I have seen a score of papers) has a humourous Column: & so far as I know every 'Railway-time-tables' has some pages devoted to it. Of course some of the fun is rough & some of it is no fun at all.

In ordinary conversation too there is a great deal of humour.

Mr Norton is artistic: Professor in Art; & a severe school; defining Art as command over form. In spite of this artistic severity, he has scientific & philosophical interests of the old English (Baconian) type. I do not know of anyone else like him.

He is instructive; because his talk is constructive. Mr Eliot, great as is his practical power, is not much more than a useful factor in conversation he does not originate much. I am just going to run over to Lowell a manufacturing town, then I go to Norwich, to see at leisure Mr Wells:[9] He is said to have no practical power, & to be unfit for political life. But he is said, even by those who judge his tactics most severely, to possess more of just that kind of information which I am striving to obtain than any other man in America. I propose to go up the Connecticut River Railway to Montreal: then to Ottawa, down the St Lawrence Rapids to Montreal, to Albany, Niagara, Chicago. It is almost certain that if you write to me at Post Office Chicago within three or four days after getting this, your letter will reach me there. I will leave at Chicago instructions about having letters forwarded.

your loving Alfred

[1] Marshall Papers. See Appendix I for details on Marshall's family.
[2] Peter Groenewegen conjectures that 'Fanny' is Marshall's cousin Susan Francis (1852–?), daughter of Thornton Marshall. The promised letter to her has not been traced.
[3] 'May' is presumably Mabel Louise, Alfred's younger sister: 'Charles' was his older brother, probably writing from India. No family letters to Alfred have been preserved.
[4] Charles William Eliot, 1834–1926. President of Harvard 1869–1909.
[5] Presumably William Tecumseh Sherman (1820–91) of Civil-War fame, then Commander of the US Army.
[6] Charles Eliot Norton (1827–1908), Professor of the History of Art at Harvard.
[7] Presumably William Dean Howells (1837–1920). The editor of the Nation at this time was Edwin Lawrence Godkin and 'Mr Pigott' remains a mystery. The names were interlined and the parentheses are not in the original.
[8] Not preserved.
[9] David Ames Wells: see [24].

24. To David Ames Wells, 23 June 1875[1]

Boston, Parker House N° 100
23 June 1875

Dear Sir

As you were so good as to say that you would consult with M^r.. Baker about my staying in Norwich,[2] & to request me to let you know what would be the most convenient time to me to come there, I write now to say what my plans are. I propose to leave Boston for Providence on Saturday, & shall be ready to come on to Norwich on Tuesday. But if there should be any reason whatever for my doing so, I could go to Norwich by a somewhat longer route, so as to arrive there a few days later. Apologizing for thus trespassing on your kindness,

I have the honor to be, | Dear Sir, | Yours truly | A. Marshall

The Hon: | David R. Wells[3]

[1] Library of Congress, D. A. Wells Papers. 23 June was a Wednesday.
[2] See [26] below.
[3] Marshall's error.

25. To Rebecca Marshall, 26 June 1875.[1]

Saturday | 25 June 1875

My very dear Mother

I write you a line now because it is uncertain whether I will have time to write again for a few days. My time has not ceased to be fully occupied. I have seen since last Tuesday the largest watch Factory (at Waltham) & the largest organ Factory (Mason & Hamblins[2]) in the World, & six other factories. The Work has been heavy as the weather has been hot. It has involved a good deal of railway travelling—Oh! I must not forget the State Prison, where men are taught many kinds of Manufactures, their work being let out to Contractors at almost 75 cents (2/6) a day.[3] Such leisure time as I have had has been mainly given up to writing notes of my experiences. Some of these were written at odds & ends of times in my pocket book;[4] & are 'fixtures': the rest even I do not like to send you.[5] They would not be very interesting to you without explanation, & I can scarely spare them. Oh! I think I have said this before.

I go to Providence on Monday. On Tuesday to Norwich: where I shall be busy: then Northwards.

Tomorrow I want to go to some chapels & to make some calls. I wonder how you are getting on. I shall not get to Niagara for a long time any how; though I have some thoughts of cutting off the Montreal part of my trip. I shall not decide about this until I leave Norwich. Meanwhile I am not able to give you any address beyond Chicago. I have decided not to bind myself to go to California till it is absolutely necessary to do so. There are very strong reasons for going there. Still as I should save £50 by cutting off this part of the trip, I do not intend to bind myself to go there until I know for certain that I will have time to see what I want to see there.

I have just bought an illustrated paper for you.[6] On the whole it has disappointed me. I learn that though dated June 26 it was really published before the 17th..

Still you may care to look at it. You should read Holmes' poem. It had great popularity, not of course on its literary merits, for it is but a rough imitation of Tennyson; but because it hit off the sentiment of the hour. It is characteristic. Also some of the advertisements, though not really the best I have seen, are amusing.

Sunday evening. It has been hotter than ever today. I went to a Unitarian church in the morning & a Baptist church in the afternoon. Rufus Ellis,[7] the Unitarian was one of the two ministers called upon by the state to offer up prayer during the Centennial Celebration: a fact worth noting since in England public feeling is rather opposed to the Unitarians.

Rufus Ellis is however not very far removed from the English church in his opinions: & his Sermon was awfully slow; as slow as an English Sermon.

If we beat the Americans in the higher walks of literature they are out of sight ahead of us in popular preaching. Of course Rufus Ellis' audience was an aristocratic one: perhaps that had something to do with his being slow. There was a wonderful amount of 'go' about the Baptist Services: unfortunately the preacher was an Englishman—good of his kind. I send you the paper that was given to every one.[8] You will from that see the connection in which the 'afternoon preaching' stands to the other work.

The Hall was a very large one, with a magnificent organ. The Audience mainly composed of Boston shopkeepers & their families: people under 25 being in a marked majority.

i   Hymn 3 was sung by the whole congregation.

ii An extempore prayer lasting two minutes was said.

iii A short Anthem was sung by four voices two male, two female, all singers of a very high order.

iv Twenty verses of an epistle were read, so selected as [to][9] supply the congregation with the content of the text on which the sermon was preached.

v   A collection was made, by about twelve men, each moving quietly indeed, but rapidly.

vi Hymn 4 was sung by the whole congregation.

vii The Minister in charge gave a clear statement in free & easy colloquial language of the arrangements for the week; & apologized for having put on the Englishman to preach after having advertised himself.

All this occupied about 12 minutes. Yet everything was in perfect order. The latter part of the Afternoon & the evening I spent in two long Conversations i with Prof Everett, a young man 34, say, son of the famous Everett, educated at Cambridge England, blatant but acute: & ii with Mr Norton.[10]

I got them both to talk about Unitarianism. They spoke from widely different points of view. The only things that it is worth while to say here are that (i) The growth of Unitarianism was gradual & imperceptible for a long time, until an accident caused men to have to take a definite standpoint, when they concluded that they were Unitarians. In general, but not always, the pastor & congregation went together. (ii) Unitarianism is at all events not gaining ground on the whole. The rest of the conversation was mainly on literary topics.

I am sleepy, & have two or three very heavy days before me.

Good bye | Kindest love to All | Your very loving | Alfred Marshall

I fear that Some of the discussions with Emerson about philosophy will bore you. Still, I think, You will on the whole like to see the papers I send.[11]

They say the weather never is much hotter than it has been today. If so, the heat will not be so hard to be borne as I had expected. Still it is bad enough to make exercise a bore.

[Enclosures]

Mason & Hamblins[12]   *American Manufacture*
Organ Factory, Cambridge, Mass
22 June 1875

Was shown over by intelligent man apparently sub-manager who understood the whole work. The characteristic of the firm is the way in which every operation is broken up into a great number of portions, the work of each individual being confined to a very small portion of the whole operation. 'Does this prevent the growth of intelligence?' 'I think not: whatever a man has in him, that comes out of him. We don't take men even for common work who have not their wits about them. The pay here is very low for men who do not use their wits: a man who does use his wits gets to save time in small ways, & so ultimately obtains a very high wage. If a man has no brains we get rid of him: There is plenty of opportunity for this in consequence of the fluctuations of the market. If a man has some brains, he stays on at his work; but if he has any ambition, he must get to know all that goes on in the shop in which he is working: otherwise he has no chance of becoming foreman of that shop. Men do sometimes make inventions in lines not their own: but, in fact, most improvements in detail are made by the foremen of the several shops; & improvements on a very large scale are made by a man who does nothing else. He is an Englishman.' 'How are your workers arranged according to nations.' 'They are chiefly Americans. Our package case makers are chiefly English; the designer of our carving is a Frenchman (Frenchmen have almost a monopoly of this kind of work: they have a natural talent for form, or at least for "trumperiness"). The tuners are chiefly American, the only exception being an Englishman. Germans would be too slow to make their money. Several Englishmen are foremen.' 'You pay by the piece?' 'Yes: but in many cases we let out the whole work done in a shop to one or two foremen. The men who work in that shop say they work for "Mason & Hamblin", but really they are in no way responsible to us; but only to the "Boss".' 'Do you take apprentices?' 'No: the only thing at all like this that we do is to bind some of them by a legal document to serve us three years: e.g. the tuners who are not good for much until they have become accustomed to the special tone of our organs. It is not true here that the tuners or other skilled & highly paid laborers get at first lower wages than the lads who are in the unskilled shops. We pay e.g. the tuners at starting a fair wage & simply select the best: the high wages they ultimately obtain are the equivalent of their special faculties.' 'The wages of the tuners are very high: but they cannot work more than eight hours a day: at least we do not like them to. There is an immense amount of undeveloped musical talent in the American nation.'

He shewed me many of the little inventions by which they aimed for perfection. There seemed to be nothing specially original in the shop. I had seen before everything in the way of machinery they had to shew except a marvellous lathe: but that was not their own. Their improvements were in small details as regards manufacture, e.g. numerous contrivances for securing that certain parts should be air-tight, that certain others should work easily. The Englishman had invented the harp-stop.

June 24, 1875   *American Manufactures*
Pacific Cotton Mills.
Lawrence *&c*. Comp printed papers about them.[13]

They started with cotton as it is imported & finished off print dresses ready for market. I have no reason to think there was anything original in the works: but one or two things I saw there for the first time. The patterns of the prints were bought by the treasurer in Boston: wh has a staff of designers there: when made a water color sketch was sent down: this was enlarged & engraved onto a piece of copper. A woman then traced over the pattern: & as she took each stroke a multiplier caused an exactly similar stroke to be taken by each of ten diamond points [see Fig.] on the shellack enveloping a roller. This was submitted to acid:

pattern

& the men then engraved properly the outlines thus indicated: afterwards the roller served to print one color. 'But the work done by the women is skilled work'. 'Yes: only it requires no judgement: mere attention'. Which was characteristic. In the printing shops, Englishmen chiefly were engaged. Steadiness & patient industry are not in fashion among Americans Mr Rollis said (I think in this connection). They will not work through a long apprenticeship (see Apprenticeship).[14] They had a chemist with a large laboratory, who tested everything. He was a German. In the repairing shop the workers were chiefly Americans. (This & what follows applies to all the textile works I have been over here including the Lowell Manufacturing works (carpets) & both cotton mills, Lowell.) Generally promotion takes place according to merit not dependent in the main on technical preparation. The firm selects overseer of a room & the second hand (or vice-overseer). The third hand is selected by the overseer, who also choses all the women in the room. Anyone can weave ordinary cloth: but comparatively few can weave carpets. When a vacancy occurs the overseer puts on any woman he likes: he soon sees whether she can do the work. The carpet weavers obtain high wages. 'Do the carpet finishers obtain high wages'. No; anyone almost can do that: & the work is clean; no oil: many women who will not go into any other work in the mills go there.

Lowell & Lawrence   *Apprenticeship*
24 June 1875

Mr Rollis paymaster at Pacific works said that Americans would not stand the tedium of a long apprenticeship. If set down to work for a period of seven years, they would throw up their place after doing a few years of the work, start off West probably, in the hope sometimes fallacious of bettering themselves: & throwing away all their shop training. Thus e.g. good carpenters are scarce to be found: a man buys a box of tools & is at once a carpenter. *I* 'In that direction then trades unions might do some good'. He shied at the mention of Trades Unions; but when pressed admitted this point.

In the 'Lowell Manufacturing Company's' carpet works an English overseer when asked to compare the advantages of the workman in England & America gave the following among others. 'In America people take so much more pain about teaching you than in England. Here every one really does have a chance. They don't have it in England. In England men are very negligent about teaching: the long apprenticeships there cause men often to spend twice or three times as long in learning to do a thing as they need; & meanwhile people do not teach them carefully: they had rather not.' Pressed for reasons he gave one which is worth noting, though apparently wild. 'Many English overseers have shares in the Mill in which they work: so they look out for good hands ready made: they do not want to be bothered with new hands who might spoil the work. In America an overseer would not be allowed to hold such shares; even if they were in open market, he might get the sack if he bought any; so he has no interest in excluding learners'. Every statement here requires to be confirmed.

Chickering Piano Works[15]   *American Manufactures*
June 25 1875

Went over with a small but intelligent youth. 500 men employed, almost exclusively American. All frames overstrung ie the long strings strung over, in a different plan from the small strings [see Fig.]. A very large portion of the work was being done in duplicate, triplicate, or even twenty fold: mechanical appliances did not obtrude themselves, care & judgement were required from

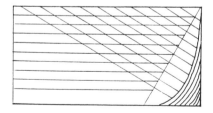

many of the workers in a very high degree. Many of them had able, almost powerful & artistic faces. The boy spoke of their earning 50$.[16] He shewed me a piano which was to cost more than $1000. Also one horizontal semi-grande, apparently very well made, but with single strings which their firm had sent out in the year 1823.

Ralph Waldo Emerson[17]   *Sketches of Character*
25 June 1875.

Like his portraits: but his eyes light up his countenance. I had been invited to dinner, but through error arrived in afternoon. The party was breaking up as I came. But he was kind: no touch of hauteur about him.

He knew more Oxford than Cambridge men: thought Oxford led in Classics: e.g. 'the great work' Liddell & Scott:[18] *I* 'But Scott is, I believe, a Cambridge man, & is said to have done almost all the work'. Change of subject. He knew Tom Taylor, a Cambridge man: also one 'Owen'; *I* 'I do not know him'.[19] He went on however for ten minutes telling me how he met this Owen, & what character he had, though there was nothing of special interest about him. This was one of several instances of the dreamy old-man-garrulity which rambled on speaking more for himself than for his hearer. They were the only symptoms of age I noticed in his talk, unless I should add his determination to interest himself in what had interested [him?][20] (of this more hereafter). He was immensely anxious to hear Ruskin lecture at Oxford. The lecture was sweet & gentle in tone, & exquisite in style: but Emerson was aghast at the tone of deep, settled, despairing melancholy with which Ruskin in a private conversation afterwards spoke of the future of the world. Emerson protested. Ruskin said 'I cannot help it' & went on as before. Emerson could not endure it & hurried away. *I*: 'I was not prepared for this account of him'. *E*: 'But it is so: all his friends spoke to me hopelessly about him, Carlyle & others' (I forget what others). Here his son broke in, (he is established as a doctor in Concord, which is but a country village) 'But Mr Carlyle told me that Ruskin was the one man in England who looked at things from the right point of view'. *E* 'Yes: but just after saying that he told me that he had learnt more from Froude[21] than from any other man. Whence I gathered that he used praise somewhat recklessly'.

I asked him whether he thought that Carlyle's complaints about the deterioration of work, as regards honesty & thoroughness, had any support from the circumstances of America. *E* 'There is hardly anyone who is less able to give an opinion on this matter than I: but I imagine that American goods must on the whole be tolerably good, because the American consumer knows, on the average, so much more about the quality of the goods he buys than the English consumer does.' The latter part of the answer, even more than the former, convinced me that he was more of a recluse than I had imagined. *E*. 'Tell me what young men there are in England rising to carry on Carlyle's work'. *I*. 'I know of none. Literary work proper of the highest order has not been done by our younger

men. During the last few years Science has been so prolific of new notions, that our more enterprising minds have thrown themselves upon these: they have not that complete mastery of the new notions they handle, & that leisure which are necessary for high literary work'. 'Yes, I know Science has been very active with you lately, but surely with all your intellectual wealth, you must have some literary men.' 'Well, we have some young men of great literary power; but their development has been one-sided.' I took as instances Swinburne & Clifford.²²
E 'What that horrid, corporeal, loathsome Swinburne! I read his 'Songs',²³ & have heard some stories about him. Surely he has nothing great in him.' *I*, 'If you have only read his Songs, you know only his worst side. His sensuous vileness does not obtrude itself in all his works. Some of his prose writings, though perhaps not great, are more full of good things than the writings of perhaps any English literateur'. *E* 'But surely in your Country Tennyson is the commanding figure. Where there is a commanding figure in the field anyone who diverges wholly from his manner should be put aside at once.' I am sure that this is the substance of what he said: I thought it monstrous, but was quiet; saying only that I had spoken of Swinburne as onesided, & half-developed; & that I thought that history shewed that mere literary power was often accompanied by sensuality. He went on to speak in terms of extravagant eulogy of Tennyson & Wordsworth. 'I read many articles from your reviews: an American Magazine is devoted to reprinting selected articles chiefly English:²⁴ I read this: You seem to have abundant power (he was obviously thinking of literary criticisms) only I do not like what your writers say about poetry. I have decided views about that: & your critics do not know properly what that is (he here spoke as one having authority). There has been a rage in England for crying up Shelley as a poet: that is a mistake: Shelley was a great genius, but he was not a poet. Two or three of his small poems are good, but he is not a great poet.' I did not draw him on about this, I wish I had.

He returned to Clifford, & wanted to hear about him. I explained why Cliffords views about immortality &c, might be put aside; & went on to describe him as a representative of the work of the present generation about Continuity. E did not even know what this meant, in its modern use. Another indication that he is a recluse. Then we talked about Cliffords interest in the problem whether two straight lines can inclose a space. This also was new to E. He was amused, but a trifle scornful. This piqued me. So I fired off Helmholz's case of beings living on the surface of a sphere.²⁵ He listened hard & with effort. I waited for a reply. 'Well', he said at last 'it is a very ingenious argument: but it has no practical bearing.' I should have dropped the matter; but I had just seen him described in an American guidebook as 'the greatest living trans-cendentalist'; so I seized the opportunity to get on the subject of Kant: & said 'Directly, no doubt: but indirectly it seems to me to bear on fundamental questions of theology & morality. e.g. Kant says the mind may know certain moral & theological propositions certainly & a priori; for it does so know certain physical propositions. I searched his book to find what instances he gave of this: when I found that all these were deprived of value, I changed my attitude to some extent with regard to the other propositions.' *E.* 'Well it seems to me that Kants argument was a trumpery one, & it is fairly matched by a trumpery answer.' This remark one would accept as a matter of course from 9999 men out of 10,000. But from 'the greatest living transcendentalist' I had expected at least some sympathy with Kant's difficulties. He was obviously not at ease when speaking of mathematical notions; & was glad to shift his ground. 'But are no men working at subjects of more practical interest: take Shakspeare for example, how did he come to exist? how was it that a man so incomparably greater than any one who has ever existed, or than anyone who seems likely to exist, should have been so neglected by his contemporaries. Herrick a contemporary, & a real poet never mentions his name; Ben Jonson awards him praise, but the sort of praise a man bestows on one whom he regards as inferior to himself: he had no notion whatever that Shakspeare was, so to speak, the whole world, & he himself nobody'. I said that it was more wonderful that Shakspeares sonnets had been underrated, than that his dramas had. E. assented. E. said 'There is scarcely any psychological problem more interesting, than the question how a man so far ahead of others came into existence.' The suggestion contained in this remark appeared to me to be the most important thing he offered to me. He was going on to speak of the thoroughness of German work about Shakspeare, when I had to leave to catch the train.

He seemed to me to be a gentle but keen spirit, to whom Nature has not granted to an exceptional extent the power of working through her problems; but to whom she has given the rare & choice faculty of asking questions of her; of asking them with exquisite grace & with fervent, but somewhat subdued emotion. I do not wonder that many women find in him their high priest.

His house was comfortable, but not large, or luxurious. Plain in style, probably old: inside few pictures: these good.

Dinner at the Saturday Club   *Sketches of Character*
26 June 1875

Present Mr Emerson, whose guest I was, D^r.. Holmes Judge Gray (chief justice of Massachusetts: probable Chief Justice of the U.S.), another lawyer who had declined chief justice of Mass: (an older man), Mr Norton, Dr Howe, & two or three others, every one eminent, whose names I forget.[26] The conversation did not come to a head where I was: it was chiefly personal, & travellers conversation: very good dinner conversation but nothing more. D^r.. Holmes was holding forth about sonnets at the other end of the table: but I could scarcely catch a word of what he said. He was maintaining at one time that Shakspeares sonnets were a series of pairs of verses: each sonnet was not a completely & elaborately built up whole: He was a compact little man: with every indication of ability but none of genius: Judge Gray has a magnificent head, enormously high; & he is a young man. A characteristic bit of sparring may be quoted: the lawyer (not Judge Gray) had been talking about some one who was made Professor at Harvard while he the lawyer was a student. 'He was made professor because he had taught mathematics to the Class in which I was with such brilliant results', & his eyes twinkled. 'Ah! yes' said quietly the man next to me 'if he succeeded in teaching mathematics to that class, he was equal to anything, he earned his promotion.' I forgot[27] that Emerson talked a good deal about Kant in terms of the highest adulation. He had heard Sir W. Hamilton[28] lecture but thought him lifeless; he delighted me by saying that Hamilton had never had vogue in America. But he surprised me by limiting his admiration for Locke almost exclusively to his character. He thought Hume a much abler man: subtler, though his flashes were rare.

[1] Marshall Papers. Probably written from Boston. The letter was evidently written on Saturday 26 June and dated as 25 June in error.

[2] The correct spelling is Hamlins.

[3] In the original 2/6 (two shillings and sixpence) is interlined without parentheses.

[4] Not traced.

[5] Despite this disclaimer, the relevant surviving notes are appended here as an 'enclosure'. See [21.2] for explanation.

[6] Not identified.

[7] Rufus Ellis (1819–85), then pastor of the First Unitarian Church in Boston.

[8] Not traced.

[9] Word omitted.

[10] William Everett (1839–1910), Cambridge BA 1863, author of *On the Cam* (Sever and Francis, Cambridge, Mass., 1865), classical lecturer at Harvard 1870–7. Son of Edward Everett (1794–1865), scholar, statesman, and orator. On Norton see [23.6].

[11] See enclosures that follow.

[12] See n. 2 above.

[13] These printed papers have not been traced.

[14] See the next enclosure. Mr Rollis is identified there as the works' paymaster.

[15] In Boston.

[16] Presumably weekly.

[17] Ralph Waldo Emerson (1803–82) of Concord near Boston, the famous essayist, poet, and lecturer, leader of the New England transcendentalists. A friend of Thomas Carlyle (1795–1881), British historian and man of letters.

[18] H. G. Liddell and R. Scott, *A Greek-English Lexicon Based on the German Work of Francis Passow* (Oxford University Press, Oxford, 1843).

[19] Presumably Tom Taylor (1817–80), critic and playwright: editor of *Punch* 1874–80. Owen cannot be identified.

[20] Word unclear.

[21] James Anthony Froude (1818–94) the British historian, also a friend of Carlyle. Ruskin is, of course, John Ruskin (1819–1900), British author, artist, and critic. Emerson's fourth and youngest child, Edward Waldo Emerson (1844–1930), graduated from Harvard Medical School in 1874 and was a lifelong resident of Concord.

[22] The poet Algernon Charles Swinburne (1837–1909); William Kingdon Clifford.

[23] Presumably A. C. Swinburne, *Songs Before Sunrise* (Ellis, London, 1871).

[24] Probably the *Eclectic Magazine of Foreign Literature Science and Art*, published 1844–1907, mainly in New York.

[25] Hermann Ludwig Ferdinand Helmholtz (1821–94), German scientist. See his 1870 lecture 'On the origin and significance of geometrical axioms', reprinted in his *Popular Lectures on Scientific Subjects: Second Series* (Appleton, New York, 1881).

[26] 'Emerson' appears to have been the father, not the son. Holmes was probaby Oliver Wendell Holmes (1809–94), doctor and essayist. Horace Gray (1828–1902) had been Chief Justice of Massachusetts since 1873 and was appointed to the US Supreme Court in 1881, although never becoming Chief Justice of the US. Dr Howe is probably Samuel Grindley Howe (1801–76), physician and philanthropist, husband of Julia Ward Howe who wrote the Battle Hymn of the Republic. On Norton see [23.6]. The unnamed lawyer has not been identified.

[27] What follows appears to be an addendum to the preceding account of the interview with Emerson.

[28] See [21.9].

26. To Rebecca Marshall, 5 July 1875[1]

Hartford | Connecticut
5 July 1875

My very dear Mother,

I have had a busy, laborious, but most instructive week. On Monday I went from Boston to Providence. I stayed there one day, & went over with the manager a firearms factory which is exporting its rifles. The manager is one of the most enterprising & powerful men of business I have seen. He explained his success by reference to the immense freedom he gave to his men to do the work in their own way subject to his approval.

On Tuesday I went to Dr Bakers at Norwich. Norwich situated among cliffs & rocks on the banks of a broad river is one of the most charming towns I have seen. The Bakers were very kind, old fashioned people; Their niece Miss Nunn sister of the Miss Nunn at Cambridge who had sent me there, was an active minded able person, with very agreeable manners age 26–32.[2] They have, as is the fashion here, a carriage on four spider-leg wheels to hold two. The old couple proposed that Miss Nunn should take me out for a drive: She would have driven had I been incapable; as it was, she only steered. I enjoyed it immensely: at a tête-à-tête she was first rate; so I manouvred, with success, to get a similar drive at the only other time when I had an hour to spare, the next evening. Her views were just those which an enterprising, earnest-minded woman brought up in the Country might be expected to have. I find a great charm in such people. I do not care for naivety alone: any more than I like sugar alone: but when mingled with enterprise it is very delicious; of course it would not take the place of strong diet: for steady support I would have the strength that has been formed by daring & success: but such evening drives are among the luxuries of life.

The day time was occupied in close talk with Mr.. Wells of whom I have spoken before.[3] He told me an immense amount: but his time was valuable & he was not very well: so for a good part of the time he handed me over to 'Judge' Bowles: a man aged about 35, a student of Political Economy, with his eyes open.[4] He took me to see several factories. On Thursday I went to Newhaven.

On Friday I called on two Professors of Political Economy Sumner & Walker at Yale College.[5] Yale College is the second University in importance in America. The orthodox people support it more than Harvard, as it is free from the Unitarian 'taint' of Harvard. It claims to have the same position relatively to Harvard that Cambridge claims to have relatively to Oxford: ie to turn out men, less showy indeed but more thorough than its rival. The teaching seemed to me to be on a severer & more cautious plan than that at Harvard. But I fancy they do not get as good material among the students as at Harvard. Certainly the average social position of the students there is lower.

In the evening Prof Sumner took me to a sort of grande levee somewhere in the town, where a lot of big-guns were assembled—e.g. the Governor of Connecticut, a genial, intelligent 'English gentleman' in appearance, & a far more important man the Governor of North Carolina who has probably a very high future in store.[6] I was not exactly one of the lions but I was 'a strange animal.' So the host introduced me to almost every one in the room: which was a bore. There was scarcely any one there with whom I should not have liked to talk for an hour: but to talk for two minutes, to go through the labor of the preliminary small-talk & then giving the conversation a wrench, so as [to][7] turn it upon something important, & then to be at once interrupted and have to do the same with someone else—this is poor fare.

I spent from Saturday afternoon to Monday morning at Prof Sumners. He had been educated in America & Göttingen, & had stayed a long while at Oxford.[8] He says he is too hard worked to do much[9] constructive work: I am not sure that he has the nature fitted for discovering epoch-making truths: but in every other respect he is a man of enormous ability. His varied learning & training, & great natural acuteness, judgement, & critical power, combined with a passion for thoroughness, make him on the whole the most instructive companion I have had. He has not the cool classic, finish of style that Mr Norton[10] has; he has not the enormous knowledge of America that Mr Wells has: but his training enabled him always to see what was the information I wanted, & to give it in clear orderly form; he had mastery at once over principle & fact.

He had no turn for physical science: but believes that the higher portions of philology afford a complete scientific training: for 'Science requires you to define & analyse, so as to know what you mean, & then to prove: nothing more'. This seems to me characteristic of a powerful mind which has been nurtured chiefly on literary & philosophical work. I think a man who has only these powers has every element necessary for a scientific genius except a scientific genius: that this genius does its work by constructing; & that for this work each several science requires its own peculiar cast of genius: so that in general a genius in chemistry could not have been a genius in botany or geology.

My discussions with him were almost entirely on economical & political questions: & I will say no more of them.[11]

I told his wife & sister in law that I was glad to have come to America: if only for this to discover that American girls are not entirely given up to the task of preserving their complexion: I thought this was the main business of the American girls who loaf about Europe.

They were abundantly gracious; but after some hours began to talk about the English girls whom they had met on their travels. 'The English girls are very lively,[12] but they are sadly unable to take care of themselves. Once on the Continent of Europe I got to know very intimately two English girls. We Americans used to make up excursion parties: large parties: but we never had any one to look after us: we were able to do that for ourselves. But all my entreaties could not induce the mother of these English girls to let them come with us when she could not go herself to watch them. American girls are much more trustworthy than English: they do not require to be watched at every turn.' This nettled me: so I said—'English mothers do not follow their daughters about when in the presence of men in order to watch them: but in order to provide them in emergency with that protection & defense which the more self-possessed American girl has learnt to be able on all occassions to provide for herself.' They were polite & seemed to assent to this: but on thinking the matter over I could not help feeling that it is probably true that the average American girl is more trustworthy than the average English girl. Not only is she more acute & more ready, but she has herself, I think, more under control. The fourth of July is being celebrated today.[13] Crackers & fireworks in the street are awfully annoying. People hasten their departure from the big cities in order to avoid the fourth of July. It is a Pandemonium of boys. It must be stopped soon.

Kindest love to all | Your very loving | Alfred

I can not give any further address

---

[1] Marshall Papers.

[2] Emily A. Nunn was an American student who was resident at Newnham Hall in the Lent Term of 1874–5. She later married Charles Otis Whitman (1842–1910) the biologist. No further information about the Baker family has been ascertained.

[3] See [23], [24].

[4] Not identified. Perhaps a member of the Bowles dynasty, owners and editors of the *Springfield Republican* with whom Wells was closely associated.

[5] William Graham Sumner and Francis Amasa Walker. A letter of introduction to Sumner from Wells is preserved in the Sumner Papers, Yale University Library. It reads:

Norwich. July 1. 75 | Dear Sumner | I want to introduce to you Mr. Alfred Marshall who is associate professor with Fawcett at Cambridge, England. He visits New Haven to see you & Walker & learn what he can about economic matters in this country. Please give him the right hand of fellowship. | Yours ever | Wells

[6] Charles Robert Ingersoll (1821–1903) was Governor of Connecticut, 1873–7. As [27] makes clear, it was the Governor of *South* Carolina—Daniel Henry Chamberlain (1835–1907: Governor 1874–6)—who was also present. He was to withdraw from political life after losing power in South Carolina and became in 1883 Professor of Constitutional Law at Cornell University.

[7] Word apparently omitted.

[8] See Harris Elwood Starr, *William Graham Sumner* (Holt, New York, 1925), the standard biography.
[9] The word 'much' was inserted as an afterthought.
[10] See [23.6].
[11] See Vol. 3 [1128] for Marshall's recollection, in a (1922 ?) letter to James Phinney Munroe, of his discussion with F. A. Walker on this visit.
[12] The word 'lively' might possibly be 'lovely'.
[13] July 4th was a Sunday, hence the delay of celebrations until the 5th.

27. To Rebecca Marshall, 11 July 1875[1]

Niagara Falls
10 July 1875

My very dear Mother

I have just got your two letters & the newspapers.[2] I have read the letters, both yours & the girls' with great interest & hope to derive much benefit from the newspapers; I was anxious to know more than the American papers tell me about the Master & Servants Act.[3]

I am very sorry to hear so poor an account of my Father's feet. I trust he may soon be set up again. It is a very good thing that you sent for Dr.. Cronin.[4]

I am extremely sorry that my notes were illegible: I took more pains about writing them than I am wont to do about notes intended to be read only by myself. Probably the rolling of the ship had a greater effect on me than I thought. I hope the notes, that I have sent, written on firm land have been a little better. If not, I shall have to [be][5] ingenious & invent some other excuse. I think I shall say I was in general tired when I wrote them; which won't be much of a fib after all.

My last letter at all events was written under difficulties. I had a bad toothache, & earache. At last I got some chloroform & held it in my mouth over the gum. From comparing this with other experiences, I am inclined to believe the measure to be on the whole profitable. The next day Tuesday was intensely hot. I went over a large factory in the morning, & then called by appointment on Governor Ingersoll[6] who took me over the State House, & shewed me the two legislative chambers. (Rep: Assembly & Senate) of Connecticut in Session. The former consisted mainly of 'farmers': (the word farmer here means independent cultivator of land, whether he owns it or not: it is almost impossible to let land for agricultural purposes here). The Senate was much smaller, quieter; very business like, & with apparently no taste for 'spouting'. Governor Ingersoll was very kind & attentive; too much so: he gave up two hours to me, took me to a club gave me a lunch of ham & a luxurious American drink called 'mint-julep': made me talk all the time to a hard headed & powerful, but painfully taciturn lawyer—Such men require an enormous amount of talking too: it is a heavy labor to purvey for an elephant—& sent me home with such an awful headache & face-ache that I did nothing but lie on my bed & read guide-books for the rest of the day.

I have been knocked up on each of the two hottest days we have had. It happens that I have exposed myself & fatigued myself a good deal on each of them. In general I have been very well: I have no great fear about the future provided I do not do too much. I think I had been doing too much in the week before last.

I have now decided somewhat to curtail my plans. I have already cut out the Montreal branch of the tour. I intend to penetrate someway inland from Toronto. The class of people that I want to see are, I am assured on all hands to be found in the district around Toronto, & are not in large numbers in lower Canada. I am to start for Toronto on Tuesday (12th), I think.[7] (While I think of it, it was Governor Chamberlain Governor of South Carolina; not of North Carolina, from whom so much is expected, as I told you in my last letter.[8]) On Wednesday I travelled to New Lebanon the chief settlement of the Shakers. I slept at the Settlement & came on the next day to Oneida, near which is the most important communistic settlement outside of the body of the shakers.[9] I spent five or six hours at the Community & came on to Rochester on Friday: Saw Rochester & came on here yesterday. The weeks work has not been an especially heavy one: but I feel as though I had passed through a great deal in it. Although I had read largely about them before, the contact with Communists, having thoughtout theories of life so widely different from those in common vogue was highly instructive. I send you a paper of the Shakers. I have many of their publications.[10] They go in against the Art of 'the World'. The spiritual kingdom is gradually evolving music for itself; the supply of shaker tunes is very large, a new one in almost every number of their journals, & many others besides: & gradually doubtless they will evolve a Spiritual Architecture. This was said in answer to my question why they did not spend some of the energies on adorning their buildings: these approach nearly to cubes. Yet I must confess there is a sort of picturesqueness about them when taken together with the scenery.

The brother who was told off to wait upon me, & with whom I spoke more than with anyone except Elder Evans[11] (the leader of the whole movement), was a young Swede: an angelic character. A student at a Swedish University, he had been dissatisfied with the customary views of life, & becoming interested in some accounts of the Shakers, he visited America in order to see them, & became convinced that here alone in the world was the spirit of early Christianity worked out in life. He was the son of a Swedish judge, well off in the world but he brought what money he had with him into the common stock: Now his father has died & left him a fortune: but he does not dream of departing.[12] His face is sweet & strong: features massive, at least somewhat massive, upper lip thin & often pulled firmly by the muscles, as though he were in the habit of attaining victory over self not without struggle, mouth straight (this is the weakest line in his face) he is cheerful though always quiet, utterly devoid of self assertion, which is more than I can say for Elder Evans. Agriculture & horticulture are the occupations that the Shakers most affect; & if you saw only the cotton frock which he wears, the brown cotton trousers clay-stained towards the feet & the rough uncouth shoes below you would think he was an ordinary agricultural laborer. But in his face you would perceive the refinement of the true gentleman. There are few men with whom I would so readily change lots as with him: but I would rathest stay where I am.

Niagara. Niagara is a great humbug: worse than the Alps. It takes longer for a man to discover how much greater Niagara is than it seems than it does to discover that an Alpine valley which appears to be only a mile broad is really six miles broad. It grows on one gradually that a river half a mile in breadth & in the center of the fall 15–30 feet deep is falling 160 feet perfectly clean fall (at least in the most important places) {of course a stream several feet deep when flowing at its usual pace becomes only a few inches deep when it falls over a precipice.} Below the Falls the river is only 1000 feet broad & flows quietly on; but it is 180 feet deep. I am bringing home some glass stereoscopic slides of it which, if not broken on the way, will give you a better notion of it than I have time to give now.

I tear out of last months time-table the only information I yet possess about the Chic[ago] & Pac[ific] railway. I will look out for more: but cannot be sure of getting any more.

I trust you are getting on again; I am so sorry you were thrown back by your walk downstairs, Mother dear.

Address for letters posted before August 1st Post Office St Louis Missouri U.S.

Kindest love to all. Hope to get better news of Pater at Chicago

Your loving | Alfred

---

1 Marshall Papers. The original, which must have been written on Sunday 11 July, appears to have been incorrectly dated to the 10th, although the date, being overwritten, is far from clear.

2 Not preserved.

3 A deputation of trade unionists to the Home Secretary on 24 April had protested the laws of conspiracy and requested amendment of the Master and Servants Act 1867 (30 & 31 Vict., c. 141). The Government obliged with the Employers and Workmen Bill which was enacted during the summer (38 & 39 Vict., c. 90). See *The Times*, 28 April (13f), 30 April (6f), 27 June (6c), 13 July (9c), 17 July (18e), 30 July (7a), 3 August (7a), 6 August (7a), 9 August (7c).

4 Presumably the family physician. See [32.3].

5 Word apparently omitted.

6 See [26.6].

7 Presumably Tuesday July 13. See n. 1 above.

8 See [26.6].

9 For information on the Oneida and New Lebanon communities see Charles Nordhoff, *The Communistic Societies of the United States* (Harper, New York, 1875), especially pp. 151–79, 259–301.

10 None of these items has been traced.

11 Frederick William Evans (1808–1903), who presided over Mount Lebanon for 57 years.

12 See Nordhoff, *Communistic Societies*, pp. 152–3 where the same individual is described.

28. To Rebecca Marshall, 18 July 1875[1]

Cleveland, Ohio
18 July 1875

My very dear Mother,

I have just returned from a short run in Canada. I was lucky in being taken up by M^r.. McKellar a member of the ministry of Ontario, who until recently had charge of the emigration department, among others.[2]

From him & from others to whom he introduced me I obtained much useful information about the prospects of emigrants. He took me over the Agricultural College, & Government Model Farm at Guelph. I then went over some factories at Hamilton, the chief manufacturing town of Canada, & at Buffalo & came on here. I am to stop at Oberlin, a mixed college for men & women tomorrow, & expect to get your letters in Chicago on Thursday.

I send you a map of the Union Pacific Railroad, with my route past & proposed marked out by pinholes, which will be easily seen if you hold the map up to the light.

I have not quite decided by which route to go from Chicago to Omaha, & with regard to my route after leaving S^t. Louis, the only things which I have quite settled are that I must pass through Cincinnati, Canton, Pittsburg, Washington Philadelphia & New York. I shall probably at some point get a little more into the region of slavery (defunct) than in the plan jotted out.

You will observe that I have twice gone over one piece of railway—from Albany to Springfield. This I did chiefly in order to visit the Shaker Village, which I had passed through once unawares. I am also to pass over a long strip of the Pacific Railroad twice: for I cannot avoid doing so except by taking ship at S^t.. Francisco.

The map is worth study as a specimen of American Advertising. In almost every general ticket agents office, & their name is legion, are exhibited time tables with maps by each of the large railways: of which anyone who will may take a copy. The one I send is indeed the finest of all but there are several nearly as elaborate. I have another copy; & could have obtained any number I wanted.

I like very much what I have seen of the Canadians; the elder generation resembles the more intelligent & active of our farmers; the younger is in some points like the youth of the United States; but has more English frankness, generosity, & ingenuousness as it appears to me. They have most of the virtues of their 'republican' neighbours, in my eyes. The lads are independent, without being unmannerly, perfectly masters of themselves: & the girls are mistresses of themselves. There is a complete absence of aristocratic exclusiveness in social matters: &, as far as I can gather—I have to speak at second hand, but on good authority—thorough freedom in the management of their own concerns for young women—freedom I call it, because it appears to me individually to be right, & wholesome, but it would be regarded as dangerous license by the average

Englishman; I do not mean only the Englishman of the severer type, but the average Englishman with ordinary, easy-going notions.

Still the Canadians have some dull faces amongst them; on the average they have not so much 'go' as their neighbours; & they seem willing to confess that much of what 'go' they have has been obtained by conduction & convection from the United States. Of course I am not in a position to compare the two nations as a whole. But I think that nine Englishmen out of ten would find themselves more happy & contented in Canada than in the U.S; though I myself if I had to emigrate, should go to the U.S.

The most important conclusion to which I have come is that though Canada's slow progress is in the main attributable to her physical conditions, she is now delayed not nearly so much by her severe winter, as by her want of Coal.

I shall be very glad to get the letters at Chicago which will tell me how you & my Father have been getting on since you wrote to Boston.[3] I will give P.O. Pittsburgh Pennsylvania as address for letters posted before August 8. I shall not leave there before August 23: but I may not get there before September 10th..

Kindest love to Pater & the girls, | Your very loving Alfred Marshall

The weather has on the whole been mild; I have not suffered from the heat in the least. I am very well. I have just heard a Sermon (Presbyterian) on total abstinence declaring in the most uncompromising way that moderation is utterly inefficient.

[1] Marshall Papers.

[2] Archibald McKellar (1816–94) was commissioner of public works, minister of agriculture, and provincial secretary of Ontario from 1871–5.

[3] See [23, 27]. Possibly the latter letter had been forwarded from Boston.

29. To Rebecca Marshall, 22 August 1875[1]

                                                      St. Louis 22 Aug: 1875

My very dear Mother,

If your last letter had been contained in a white envelope, I should have been wrapped in anxiety as to what could be going on at home. As I had given no address intermediate between Chicago & S[t]. Louis I made up my mind in expectation of one here. But the man at the Post office told me there was nothing for me. I had noticed a violet envelope, & asked him to shew it to me. He did so, & it was yours. The address was well & elegantly written. But in a letter addressed to Poste Restante elegance is the last virtue of importance: a bold, round clear hand should be aimed at. Please to tell Agnes of this.

I am very delighted that you & my Father are getting on so well. I feel quite envious of my Father's musical successes. If I had time I should feel sorely tempted to endeavour to follow his example. I am extremely glad that he is going in for this form of recreation: it is probably the best he could have, & good every way.

I am much distressed about Charles' accident: but I trust it may not be so bad as you fear. I am glad Agnes & May are to sing at the workhouse: I hope they will not sing exclusively hymns. It is as bad for the mind to feed exclusively on hymns & such-like as it is for the body to feed exclusively on meat.

I send you a 'Harper'. I bought it because the picture about the riflemen seemed to me to be clever: but the rest of the paper is only up to Summer level.[2]

I saw a good deal of the wild population of Virginia City[3] before I left. The stronger virtues of men are present in the men to a very high, an exceptionally high degree: but they have no other virtues. The next generation might be a splendid race if the gentler virtues were present among the women. But there is scarcely a virtuous woman in the state of Nevada. The women have all the faults of the men; many more besides; & none of their virtues. They say San Francisco used to be in the same condition. Outwardly all is changed there: but inwardly things remain much as they were. The weak point of the Far West lies in their women.

Characteristically enough men are more 'down on', more intolerant of the 'woman's rights' movement there than any where else as far as I have observed. Indeed the movement seems never to have had any considerable vogue there.

Fortunes have been made there in a most marvellous way. A man of the name of Mackay[4] carried a pick 5 or 6 years ago & is now worth from 75 to 80 million dollars. Almost 8 or nine other men, chiefly of similar origin combine more or less with Mackay & rule California. Most of them are Irish. The mass of Irishmen are the lowest class here in every way: but there are an immense number of hugely rich Irishmen.

My journey from Virginia City here was devoid of any special features of interest. The Missouri valley is full of swamps, negroes, Irishmen, agues, wildly luxuriant flowers & massive crops of corn: ie Indian Corn.

The gentleman to whom I had a note of introduction here is out of town. Which is a great bore. He is one of those whom I was specially anxious to meet.[5] The town is unhealthy, worse than Chicago, & I should have hurried away had not a Mr Woodifield, an English Engineer whom I met on the train fallen ill. A good deal of my time has been spent in his room. (I am now writing on Tuesday[6] but I think I can safely go away tomorrow.) I am very careful: I have to be: I shall be glad to get away. St Louis is the least interesting town I have been in. The inhabitants have neither the 'go' of the Yankee nor the polish of the Englishman. Still there is a good deal of solidity about the place. There are 120,000 Germans here. I think I gave Pittsburg & Washington as addresses. The only other address I can give is Hoffmann House New York. I am to leave on October 2nd..: So there is no use in writing later than the 19th..

Kindest love to my Father & the Girls | Your very loving Son | Alfred
I am very well.

[Enclosure]⁷

*Virginia City*⁸

Miners wages were up to $10 a day. Now are $4 a day for everyone who works
in the mines bar foremen. Much quieter than it was a few years ago, gambling
on smaller scale: less shooting. Still anyone who worked for $3.95 underground
would infallibly be hung or shot. If it were not for the union wages would be
down to $2, or 2 1/2 as they are with the miners of California: but the union
4000 or 5000 strong with plenty of six shooters for tyrannical masters is strong
enough to prevent them from going lower. So say several men with whom I
spoke. The superintendent of, I think, the Savage Mines⁹ said that the masters
had willingly consented to the $4 a day: because¹⁰ things are so dear here they
know men could not live for much less. They work in shifts of 8 hours viz 11.
a.m–7 p.m.; 7 pm to 3. a.m; 3–11 a.m. There are in general in the hot places
3 or 4 men at each job: they relieve one another, those off work going into a
cool place: so that few work more than 3 hours a day. The heat is bad to men
new to the work: but on the whole the work is about 'the lightest in the world.'
Those at work underground are chiefly Irish & Cornish men, some American.
The Irish here shew no antipathy (as at Merthyr Tydvil¹¹) to underground
work. The (Savage) Superintendent had never known pay independent of work
before: but the plan answers here marvellously: the work done is more than
elsewhere under similar difficulties. The foreman in each place should know how
much work each man does, & when slack times come discharges the worst. A
good workman will often be kept on above ground if work below is slack. They
make a rule to discharge a man who cuts his work 2 times running: at the
Virginia Consolidated they do it if a man cuts his work once: thus they weed
out drunken fellows.

The four men who control the Virginia Consolidated & many of the other
mines here; as well as the water supply from Lake Washoe¹² (in the regulation
of the price of which however the town has something to say: moreover the
mines could pump up water for themselves without very great difficulty) are all
Irish. Mackay & Fair who live in Virginia City: Flood & O'Brien who live at
San Francisco.¹³ Mackay was a laborer at $4 a day. By speculating he had made
a little: once when rather 'tight' he threw his pick away & vowed he would
work no more. Now he is the richest man on the coast. Fair is said to be a
splendid manager; apparently the ablest of them. Fl & O'B were seven years ago
small w[h]isky shop (a low den) keepers in San Francisco. The four have worked
together.

A typical dodge for increasing wealth is as follows. A Bonanza is discovered.
It is kept quiet, covered up: old hands who know the difference between good
ore & bad kept out of the way: the works pursued in other directions, great
expenses incurred, call after call made on the shareholders. This lowers price of
shares (i) because it makes people think lightly of the mine (ii) because those

who have shares have to sell some of them in order to pay the calls on the others. Then they buy largely: then they open out the best deposits: & give every facility to people who want to inspect the mine. They see a solid almost limitless mass of ore, they are encouraged to pick specimens to take them home & get them analysed: then the furor sets in: when it has got to its maximum the chief people begin to unload. Thus the Virginia Consolidated leaped up to 800 in February & are now at 320.

Several of the Gold Hill mines[14] were set on fire some time ago. Shares fell from 300 to $2.50. (Money happened to be scarce.) The Manager of Crown Point[15] was then worth perhaps $10,000. Now he is one of the richest of millionaires. He knew the mine was as good as ever & bought in. It is characteristic that people concluded (without any evidence as far as I know) that they were set on fire on purpose.[16]

The Sutro Tunnel is being driven in to tap the mines from Carson river: it is more than 2000 feet below Virginia City: it is to be 4 miles long: A charge of $2 is to be made for hauling the ore out per ton: now the cost is about $13 per ton. $8,000,000 dollars were raised for it, chiefly in England. The money used here generally has not been obtained from abroad, at least directly: but from San Francisco. Of course the San Francisco people have borrowed abroad.[17]

Virginia City[18]

Grand men with huge limbs & bright eyes, a strong will & a ready hand—full of daring & enterprise, impatient of restraint; but with a vast depth of true & tender feeling down at the bottom of their hearts, that welled up ever & anon: indeed men with all the stronger elements of greatness: men who might be the fathers of a noble generation.

But few have wives: & those in general the lowest of the low, the last women on earth to be fit to supplement by womanly virtues, the rough virtue of the men: but the Irish will not marry such but fetch out wives to them.

---

[1] Marshall Papers: it seems probable that additional letters were written home on the four weekends intervening between Sunday 18 July and Sunday 22 August, but none has been preserved, as is also the case for all letters from home. See Appendix I for identification of the family members mentioned. The family affairs alluded to remain obscure.

[2] See *Harper's Weekly*, 19/974; Saturday 28 August 1875 (actually published some days previously). The cartoon, entitled 'A Challenge to All Nations', shows the US inviting all the Rifle Teams of the world to a friendly competition during the 1876 centennial of the USA.

[3] The silver-mining town in Nevada—see enclosure.

[4] John William Mackay (1831–1902) had worked for $4 a day when he first came to the Comstock, but was now its most prominent figure.

[5] Possibly William Mason Grosvenor (1835–1900), editor of the *St. Louis Democrat* and author of *Does Protection Protect?* (Appleton, New York, 1871), the answer being 'yes'. Marshall acquired a copy of this work.

[6] Presumably Tuesday 24 August. The closing parenthesis was omitted from the original.

[7] See [21.2] for explanation.

[8] Marshall arrived in this short-lived boom town on the fabulous Comstock Lode at an interesting point in its history. There had recently been a serious fire and the collapse of the Bank of California, engineered by the 'Big Bonanza Firm'—the Virginia Consolidated Mine group led by Mackay—had precipitated a dramatic drop in the prices of shares in the silver mines which were the town's *raison d'être*. For graphic accounts of the personalities and events of this colourful era see: *History of Nevada with Illustrations and Sketches of its Prominent Men and Pioneers* (Thompson and West, Oakland, 1881. Reprinted with an introduction by David F. Myrick; Howell-North, Berkeley, 1958); Wells Drury, *An Editor on the Comstock Lode* (Farrar and Rinehart, New York, 1936. Reprinted, University of Nevada Press, Reno, 1984).

[9] Probably a 'Colonel' Gillette who was superintendent of the Savage mine around this time. See Drury, *Comstock Lode*, p. 34.

[10] Written as `·.·` in the original.

[11] The coal-mining town in South Wales.

[12] The recently engineered water supply in fact came from Lake Marlette in the Sierras, crossing the Washoe Basin.

[13] James Graham Fair (1831–94), James Clair Flood (1825–88), William Shoney O'Brien (1826–78). Marshall's information is broadly correct, although Flood was born in New York, not Ireland.

[14] Gold Hill was a town abutting Virginia City.

[15] John Percival Jones (1829–1912) who had become a US senator for Nevada in 1873.

[16] See *History of Nevada*, [n.8], pp. 592 and 620–1.

[17] The Sutro tunnel, an adit designed to provide ventilation, drainage, and access for the deep mines on the Comstock by approaching from a lower elevation, was completed in 1878 after much opposition from vested interests.

[18] This fragment may have been composed retrospectively.

30. To Rebecca Marshall, 5 September 1875[1]

Pittsburgh Sep 5, 1875

My very dear Mother

There are no letters for me here. I say that not because I am disappointed: for I got a letter recently, & I suppose you have not heard from Charles in the interim: but in order that no letter may drop out without your knowing of it. I send you a newspaper. There is nothing in it that is worth looking at excepting some of the explanations of the prints. Many of the prints are, I think, good.

I inclose a bill of fare that I stole today.[2] I found that my habit of going to second class hotels involved so much inconvenience in towns in which I expected to make acquaintances that I go to first class hotels in these cases. Here I think I should have gone to a first class hotel anyhow. For none but a first class hotel would go to the expense of the perpetual washing & scouring that it is needed in 'the sootiest town on this planet'. At a second class hotel they would have had nearly as many dishes: but they would have been more sloppy. The charge here is $4: at a second class hotel it would be $2.50 to $3.50. The dinner today was rather better than usual: that put it into my head to steal the bill.

I did not quite like Cincinnati quite so much when I left it as when I wrote to you.[3] There are too many Germans of the lower classes there, who have come to America somewhat late in life. They remain boors. But the next generation will be American citizens of a high type. In Columbus I had only time to see the Penitentiary; where, as in most at least of the large American prisons, a large variety of complex manufactures is carried on. Men are let out to a separate Contractor for each branch at 75 Cents a day he teaches them: & they work for him. The system is I think so incomparably superior in all its results to other systems that it must in the course of time become universal.

M[r] Bolton, the steel manufacturer at Canton, Ohio, to whom I had a letter of introduction from M[rs].. Bulley[4] taught me more by his deeds than his words. He is too much absorbed in steel making to give much thought to questions of public policy. His energy & his habits of business were instructive. He is fighting a battle with the Yankees, & confident that he is beating them; as well as the Sheffield people. I am convinced that if all American iron masters understood their trade as well as he does, they would want no 'Protection'. He is an Englishman. He was very kind. He lives with simplicity: nay extreme frugality. He looks forward to coming home & he has only just got over the preliminary difficulties which attend the starting of a business. From letters of introduction which he has given me to Pittsburgh,[5] I shall, I believe obtain the means of having American 'Protectionist' doctrines expounded at me by the ablest expositors of them. Than which at the present moment there are few things which I more desire.

Here is the scene [see Fig.]. There averages half a mile of flat land on each side of each river: this is crowded with iron works & other buildings. Beyond this flat land in every direction there are hills rising very abruptly from two to six hundred feet & sprinkled with houses. (To be continued in the next number.)[6]

Kindest love Alfred.

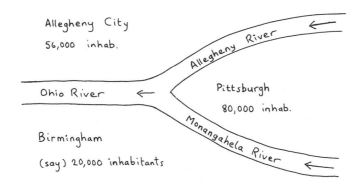

[Enclosure]⁷

26 Aug 1875   *Wages*
Indianapolis.

Machinists averaging about 2 1/4–2 1/2 Carpenters the same: they used to be
$ 1/2 behind machinists.[8]

Puddlers about 4 used to be much higher. Heaters in rail rolling mill about
4 for first heatings: for final re-heatings before the bar is rolled out about 7. They
used some time ago to get 9 & 18 respectively. This told me by one of first
heaters: who said we are paid 'Not for what work we do, but for what we know':
ie the labor is highly skilled.

Hickory-buggy-wheel works: large: work continuous: no rest: somewhat
severe: much of it requiring some nous: highest wages 2 1/2: used to be 3 1/2:
beginners of course less: average now 2.

Cincinatti: on way to spoke to German stonemason. Said wages were 2 1/2—3
1/2: used to be 5 or more. Carpenters about 1/2 a dollar behind. Masons could
expect work during about 8 months in the year: but he had worked the whole
year round working in winter in a beer cellar.

[1] Marshall Papers. See [29.1].
[2] Neither the bill of fare nor the newspaper has been preserved.
[3] This letter, probably written on the preceding Sunday, 29 August, has not been preserved.
[4] Possibly the mother of the three Bulley sisters who had been Mary Paley's fellow students at
   Newnham. However, the reading of the name is subject to doubt. Mr Bolton, a UK emigrant,
   remains unidentified.
[5] It would appear that Philadelphia was intended. That city was the home of the Pennsylvania
   protectionist school led by Henry Carey (see the enclosures to [31]).
[6] Since over two weeks supervened before the composition of the next surviving letter it seems likely
   that an interim letter has not been preserved.
[7] See [21.2] for explanation.
[8] These and the subsequent numbers appear to be daily wage rates in dollars.

31. To Rebecca Marshall, 23 September 1875[1]

Hoffmann House
New York 23 Sep: 1875

My very dear Mother

I did not write from Philadelphia partly because I was pressed for time partly
because I thought I might get a letter on arriving here. But I am not surprised
at not finding one here, for I have come here sooner than I intended.

My chief motive in hurrying on was to have plenty of time to have a bad
tooth doctored. A Philadelphia dentist declined to promise a satisfactory
treatment unless I came twice with a weeks interval. I could not do this, & so
he recommended me to have it done in New York. I am only just in time to
save one of the most important grinders. The dentists here are very able men:

charges to match. The New York Dentist cleaned the tooth out carefully. 'Now, how will you have it stopped: with composition it will cost $3: with platinum $4: with gold $12. Gold is the only thing that is thoroughly secure.' My conclusion is that putting aside the question of losing the tooth, gold is the cheapest merely as saving the time lost on having the tooth stopped again (together with the time lost after it has been stopped in objurgation of things in general). But $12 is big sum.

In Philadelphia I spent many hours in conversation with the leading protectionists.[2] And now I think, as soon as I have read some books they have recommended me to read, I shall really know the whole of their case: & I do not believe there is or ever has been another Englishman who could say the same.

I again missed some interesting people to whom I had brought notes of introduction, but who were not in town: but I could not have been much better off. A Colonel Hawley[3] whom I met took me up, asked me to dinner & brought me into contact with some of the leading politicians of Pennsylvania. Colonel Hawley has charge of the buildings &c for the centennial exhibition at Philadelphia. I suppose you have seen accounts of these buildings: they are immensely larger than any other exhibition buildings have been.

I have some introductions here, I do not know whether they will come to much. If I can get time I shall take a three or four days run up into the anthracite coal region north west of here, leaving my heavy luggage at this Hotel. I have engaged my berth by the 'Erin'; which is to sail on second of October. I shall go straight to Cambridge & arrive there just after lectures have commenced, I hope. I will run down to see you a few days later, probably at some time in the week beginning on October 17th.. But I can make no plans definitely before arriving in Cambridge. For as I shall [be][4] there after work has commenced, I shall have to let the other lecturers arrange the hours of my work so as not to interfere with theirs. It is a long time now since I heard from home: I last heard in St.. Louis: & the time seems longer than it is. It would do me an immense amount of good to get a letter saying that you including Charles are all well.[5]

Please to give my very kind love to my Father & the girls

Your very loving Son | Alfred Marshall

[Enclosures][6]

Sep 5, 8. 1875   *American | Glass Manufacture*
Birmingham Pa.[7]

   i water glasses, funnels, water jugs &c of 'flint glass'. Men rather rough, boys very much so. Work requiring skill but not very high skill.
  ii window glass works consisting of
     i blowing house
    ii flattening house
   iii cutting house.

Work in former two very hot: hotter than in the other & flint glass houses: requiring enormous skill: wages very high: men almost universally intelligent &, though rough, yet refined.

   Operation

i   blow the holder [see Fig.] the end being solid

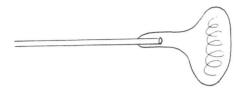

ii   heat the end
iii swing it & blow it till it has this form [see Fig.]

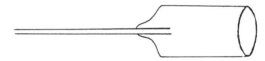

iv   crack it by rubbing red hot iron along one generating turn of cylinder
v   slowly heat it
vi   pass it on revolving disk to hotter oven where it is flattened by pressure of a rod, & a sort of wooden hoe rubbed on it
vii lift it into a crate & leave it a while in a cooling oven.

Nailworks   *American Manufactures*
Pittsburgh 7 Sep 1875

   Two long rooms of machines: all similar in principle but as I understood a trifle more skill required for making large nails than small. Two chisels meet & cut off from a strip of iron a wedge [see Fig.]

It is then turned over & caught in a 'die', which holds it while a horizontal blow is given at the thick end so as to make the head.

   For the small nails the pay is $1.81 a cwt: each man or lad makes nearly 2 cw^t.. in a day. A 'cutter' has four machines in general which he keeps in order: he hires the lads that work them. The general arrangement is for him to get half pay: thus the lad gets say 1\frac{1}{2}$, the cutter $6.[8] The work of the 'cutter' is high class & tolerably continuous: the machines are continually wanting some repair: they seldom run for more than four or five hours without wanting a chisel ground or something of the sort. The work of the lads is very simple.

7 Sep 1875   American Manufactures | *Petroleum*
Alegheny valley. Petrolia. Karns City[9]

A Derrick [see Fig.]. Used to be 40 feet high: now 80 to let in a long pipe
at once

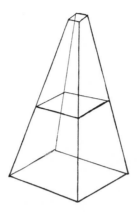

Bore by a steel chisel let up & down by a manilla rope. Chisel not fastened to
rope directly: but by a catch thus:-
a long rod, six feet long, just above the chisel to which the chisel is loosely hooked
[see Figs.]. Thus if the chisel is jammed the rod pulls it with a jerk. The shape

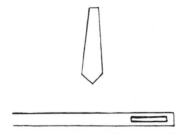

of the edge of the chisel is *always* worn thus [see Fig.]. Bore a nine inch hole till
you get below water level say 600 feet: fill up with iron piping so as to keep

water out & bore a narrower tube till you reach the oil sand: at the bottom of
it put a lifting pump.
    Gas used for furnaces of boilers: in one case used to light a town. Mr Wuth[10]

went to see a hole from which gas emerged in 5 inch column at 200 lb pressure: 'enough to drive 5 or 6 rolling mills'. Each man his own tanks: a company, or an individual pumps from these tanks into tanks of its own: which form a long series going down to a refining town.

18 Sep 1875   *H. C. Carey*[11]

Comfortable House. Large Drawing room. Good pictures. Hale & hearty, age 83. In dressing gown. At previous (short) interview he had burst out[12] with 'England always goes in for whatever suits her own interest'. I said 'I should say at once that I am Englishman & that I find a good motive for Englands conduct when you can see nothing but what is bad,' voice rather derb.[13] He was somewhat staggered: but in the second interview avoided dropping into the original line.

Had been a free-trader when young. Struck by fact people moved west: attributed it to free trade which caused exportation of manure. Struck again by remnants of houses, or orchards, 'a peach tree here, an apple tree there on barren hills.' This set him to criticising Malthus. With great trouble I nailed him to the question 'Do you reject the law of diminishing returns in an old country, the rate of agricultural progress, & the rate of emigration being given'. He could not give a direct yes: but he jumped off—why should people stay where they are born. Cairnes is diffuse & says nothing new except that things had a 'normal' value. McLeod talks nonsense. 'Oh! but English economists do not indorse McLeod'. 'Well but Chevalier does'. 'Chevalier is not trustworthy on such points'. 'Chevalier is a humbug: dishonest: a free trader for gain in opposition to his convictions. McCulloch is even worse'. Jevons too has written a book full of mathematical nonsense.[14] He says value depends on utility. The jackass does not know that the utility is great only when the value is small. When Faraday[15] first discovered how to produce electricity his methods were very expensive. There was very little of it, & therefore it did very little good: but its value was high. 'Oh! but he does not mean total utility: he means utility per unit'. 'I don't know what he means' & he burst away to say something else. I think it was that no one knew anything who could not understand what was meant by value. 'Value depends on cost of *re*production'. I tried to nail him about this but could not succeed. I nailed him on the question why do you urge 'protection' for Ireland, & yet maintain that Alabama has no right to erect custom houses round herself. He winced: but said, 'Oh I do not *say* that Ireland ought to have protection'. He spouted at me his old views at great length. The interview lasted $2\frac{3}{4}$ hours: out of which he was talking $2\frac{2}{3}$ hours.

He said his father had left Ireland because he found he would spend so much time in prison if he did not: I understand him to say that his father was a protectionist but I do not see how that is consistent with the fact that he himself was at first a free trader.[16]

[1] Marshall Papers.

[2] Prominent Philadelphia protectionists besides Henry Charles Carey (see enclosure) were William Elder (1806–85), Joseph Wharton (1826–1901), and Robert Ellis Thompson (1844–1924). Marshall acquired some of their writings and was particularly impressed with Thompson who was Professor of Social Science in the University of Pennsylvania. See *Early Economic Writings*, vol. 2, pp. 89–111; Joseph Dorfman, *The Economic Mind in American Civilization 1606–1865* (Viking, New York, 1946), pp. 789–825.

[3] Possibly Joseph Roswell Hawley (1826–1905) of Connecticut, chairman of the US Centennial Commission and a convinced protectionist, or perhaps a younger relative of his.

[4] Word apparently omitted.

[5] See [29.1].

[6] For explanation see [21.2].

[7] A suburb of Pittsburgh — see the map in [30].

[8] That is, running a machine yields $3.00 a day of which $1.50 goes to the operator and $1.50 to the cutter, who supervises four such operators. One cwt. (hundredweight) equals 112 1bs.

[9] Petrolia and Karns City are small towns north of Pittsburgh reached by the 'Alegheny' (correctly, 'Allegheny') valley.

[10] Not identified.

[11] Henry Charles Carey (1793–1879), prolific and idiosyncratic writer on economic subjects and leader of the Pennsylvania protectionist school. (This account was previously reproduced in *Early Economic Writings*, vol. 2, pp. 92–3.)

[12] In the original 'out' is written as 'ought'.

[13] Defined as a rare usage meaning 'rough, uncrystallised, massive' in the *Oxford English Dictionary*. Perhaps Marshall was falling back on the German usage ('compact, solid, rough').

[14] *The Theory of Political Economy* [17.3]. The preceding allusions are to Thomas Robert Malthus, John Elliot Cairnes, Henry Dunning Macleod, Michael Chevalier, and John Ramsay McCulloch.

[15] Michael Faraday (1791–1867), eminent physicist.

[16] Marshall's doubts were unfounded. See Dorfman, *The Economic Mind*, p. 790. The senior Carey, Mathew Carey (1760–1839), had been well known as a writer on economic and social topics.

32. To Rebecca Marshall, 25 September 1875[1]

Hoffmann House
25 Sep. 1875

My darling Mother

I am delighted indeed to get your letter which has just arrived & to learn that you are all going on well you, Pater, Charles, & all. I will candidly confess that I was beginning to worry a little more than I ought about you.[2]

I have been devoting a good deal of attention to that particular branch of American industrial enterprise which concerns itself with decayed teeth: & I have an extremely high opinion of it. I have just payed my third visit to the dentist, he has worked at me for two hours. He then hoped, I would be tired. 'No: I want to get it over' 'Ah! well: I cannot give you any more time now you must go home & have lunch & come again, in three hours time'.

Meanwhile I scratch a few lines to you to express my admiration of his art. He is indeed a German by birth: but thoroughly americanised.

I hope so soon to be able to tell you orally all that I have to say, that I will now go off to my lunch.

Kind love to all. | Your very loving Son | Alfred

I am very well: neuralgia & toothache have been the only things that have troubled me: my teeth on one side were worse than I expected. The tooth that has given such exceptional trouble was the one which I took to Mr Cronin[3] a year ago & told him I was certain it was going wrong.

Last new American dodge. A set of false teeth, three or four of which exhibit gold stoppings. Of course no one would stop false teeth: teeth with stoppings in them must be 'natural'.

[1] Marshall Papers.

[2] See [29.1].

[3] Presumably the family dentist. Perhaps related to the Dr Cronin consulted about feet? See [27]. Indeed, the *Post Office London Suburban Directory* for 1876 lists Augustus Cronin, dentist, and Edward Cronin, physician, as both practising at 185 Brixton Road S.W., not far from the Marshall family home [21.1].

33. From Thomas Edward Cliffe Leslie, 3 June 1876[1]

21 Delahay Pl | Westminster S.W

June 3

My dear Sir

I take leave to send to you a copy of the essay on the Philosophical Method of Pol. Economy of which I spoke.[2]

The number of Hermathena for which it was written has been delayed, so that my Essay is not exactly published at present, but I got some copies for distribution. One of these was the subject of a favourable article in the Pall Mall Gazette of Tuesday May 30.[3] I sent another to Mr Léonce de Lavergne who has written to say that he is disposed to concur entirely in my views, & that he had always thought the abstract method defective.

In spite of his feeble health M de Lavergne is one of the most influential political men in France, & one of its most highly esteemed economists, & I think I may augur from the expression of his concurrence that when my ideas obtain fuller development in the book which I hope soon to publish,[4] they will meet with a good deal of acceptance in France.

Indeed I am firmly convinced that the life of the old à priori method depends on the lives of a few individuals influential with the Press of this country, & giving it at present an artificial existence.

Pardon me for stating so a conclusion which you may reject & believe me

Dear Sir | Very truly yours | T E C Leslie

[1] Marshall Papers.

[2] T.E. Cliffe Leslie, 'The Philosophical Method of Political Economy' *Hermathena*, 2 (1876), pp. 265–96, reprinted in Leslie's *Essays in Political Economy* (Hodges Figgis, Dublin; Longmans Green, London; 1888), pp. 163–90. There is no record of the apparent prior contact of Leslie and Marshall.
[3] 'Political Economy A Hundred Years Old', *Pall Mall Gazette*, 23 (30 May 1876), p. 10.
[4] No such book was to appear. (Leslie died in 1882.)

34. Fragment of a proposal to Macmillan and Company, (April ?) 1877.[1]

Theory of Foreign Trade etc.

Probably not more than 160,000 words (exclusive of marginal notes): almost certain not to exceed, 200,000 words. Some portions of MSS. (chiefly those pencilled at side) to be in smaller type. Types large and small those of Cambridge Shakespeare. Wish the price to be low rather than high but not extraordinarily low.[2]

Outlines of Political Economy

Part I Economics of Industry
Part II Economics of Commerce and Finance
Each part to consist of 24 chapters.
The chapters of Part I will average probably not more than 3000 words certainly not more than 3300 (i.e. the Part will contain probably not more than 72,000 words or 185 pages, certainly not more than 80,000 words or 205 pages). Type somewhat similar to that of Macmillans' Primers, price not to exceed 1/6. Copyright after ye second edition to revert to Miss Paley.[3]

[1] Marshall Papers: an edited version of Marshall's very rough draft. This fragment outlines the plan for two publishing projects that Marshall must have invited Macmillan and Company to consider at this time. The proposal may have been made in person. In any case, no trace of a covering letter survives. The 'Outlines of Political Economy' was intended to be jointly authored with Mary Paley. Previously published in *Early Economic Writings*, vol. 1, p. 58.
[2] Marshall had already completed large portions of this manuscript, but it was never to be published by him. The surviving portions are reproduced in *Early Economic Writings*, vol. 2, pp. 3–236: for the background see vol. 1, pp. 57–66.
[3] Mary Paley, at the instigation of Professor James Stuart, the leader of the Cambridge extension movement, had embarked upon a political-economy primer for extension audiences. Marshall had taken a hand after their engagement in May 1876 and it was eventually published in 1879 by Macmillan and Company as *The Economics of Industry*. The projected companion volume never appeared.

35. From Alexander Macmillan, 17 April 1877[1]

A. Marshall Esqre   Macmillan & Co.
St Johns College   Publishers to the University
Cambridge   of Oxford, 29 & 30 Bedford
                                            Street, Covent Garden, W.C.
                                               London. April 17, 1877

My dear Mr Marshall,

I am glad to say that Mrs Fawcett does not object to our publishing your & Miss Paley's book.[2] The main point that she dwelt on was that both in title & form it should be made to appear as little as possible a rival to hers. This I assured her you would be anxious to do.

The terms on which we would be willing to publish this book would be of the same kind as we publish the Primers on. That is we pay a certain sum on publication calculated after a certain number of copies were sold to repay our outlay & yield an equivalent profit to us. After that we should pay a royalty for every copy sold. All these amounts could only be definitely settled when the size & cost of the book were ascertained. But we could pretty well fix it when the MS. was in our hands complete. I suppose you would like to have the MS. back for thorough revision & completion.

We had agreed as I understood that we should publish your larger book on the terms that we take all risks of publication & share equally with you any profits that may arise. This we are willing to do & I understand you also agree to these terms.

In looking over your MS.[3] it struck us that considerable improvement might be made in both the literary form & in the actual construction of the book. I have taken the liberty of sending the MS. to a friend who has an adequate knowledge of Political Economy but who is specially a man of fine literary taste.[4] You will not mind I hope our getting his suggestions. I trust both your books may succeed in our hands. With very sincere regards to Miss Paley & yourself believe me

Yours very truly | Alex Macmillan.

---

[1] Marshall Papers. Previously reproduced in *Early Economic Writings*, vol. 1, p. 59.

[2] Millicent Garrett Fawcett, the wife of Henry Fawcett, was the author of *Political Economy for Beginners* (1870), also published by Macmillan, a potential competitor of the projected work.

[3] Of the book on foreign trade.

[4] Not identified.

36. From Alexander Macmillan, 14 May 1877[1]

A. Marshall Esqre   May 14. 1877.
St Johns College
Cambridge

Dear Mr Marshall

We are returning your MS by rail today. Our reader had been busy & only sent it back this morning. He had seen your articles in the Fortnightly,[2] and thought highly of them as to substance & thinks also highly of this. But as regards the style, his judgement is that though fairly clear it rather wants vividness & the reader is not carried along. Perhaps the word that might convey best what he means might be that it is rather too merely meditative, as if you were thinking your own thought without fully bearing in mind the audience. He uses the word *intricacy*. I dont know whether this will help you much. I daresay as you go along you will find out the faults yourself. I would suggest reading bits of it aloud to a friend & seeing where & in what way he found it hard to understand. If once you get one sentence right in that sense it will lead to the rest coming right.

We will be ready to begin printing whenever you like. Perhaps we might as well have the agreements drawn up for both this book and the other smaller book. Have you thought of an exact title for the Educational book? We must avoid its being too like Mrs Fawcetts.[3] Also in drawing up the agreement are we to insert Miss Paleys name & how?

My kind regards to her.

Yours very truly | Alex. Macmillan.

[1] Marshall Papers. Partly reproduced in *Early Economic Writings*, vol. 1, p. 60. The printed letterhead is identical to that of [35].
[2] Marshall had published only one article in the *Fortnightly Review* ('On Mr. Mill's Theory of Value,' [18.3]).
[3] See [35.2].

37. From Thomas Edward Cliffe Leslie, 21 June 1877[1]

21, Delahay Street, Storey's Gate, London, S.W., June 21st, 1877.

My dear Mr. Marshall,

Let me assure you that I should hear with real pleasure of your appointment to the posts of Principal and Professor of Political Economy at University College, Bristol. Political Economy seems to me to stand in urgent need of investigators with attainments such as yours and following your method.

Believe me, very sincerely yours, | T. E. Cliffe Leslie.

[1] From a printed set of testimonials submitted to Marshall as part of his successful application for the post of Principal of University College, Bristol. See Appendix II for further details and for the texts of those testimonials not written in the form of letters to Marshall.

38. From William Stanley Jevons, 23 June 1877[1]

2, The Chestnuts, West Heath,
Hampstead, N.W., June 23, 1877.

Dear Mr. Marshall,

I have just received your letter informing me that you have decided to apply for the posts of Principal of University College Bristol, and Professor of Political Economy. There can be no doubt that the College is to be congratulated on counting you among the candidates, but as you have many intimate friends who will speak of your remarkable fitness for the Principalship I will restrict myself to saying that in appointing you to the Professorship, they will add to their staff of Professors one of the most able and experienced teachers of Political Economy in England.

It is known to many how much attention you have bestowed, and how thorough have been your inquiries in certain branches of the science. Your forthcoming work on the theory of Foreign Trade is looked forward to with much interest by those acquainted with its contents, and will place you among the most original writers on the science.

I consider it superfluous to say more, for I cannot imagine that there is likely to be any other candidate comparable to you in fitness for the joint posts for which you are going to apply.

I am, yours very faithfully, | W. Stanley Jevons.

[1] From a printed set of testimonials: see [37.1]. Reproduced in *WSJ*, vol. 4, pp. 204–5.

39. From Thomas George Bonney, June 1877[1]

My dear Marshall,

Your very high position in the Mathematical Tripos and the reputation which you have since acquired as an authority in Political Economy and other branches of the Moral Sciences are sufficient proof of your great mental power, and your remarkable success as a Lecturer in the former subject shows your ability as a Teacher. But further, no one can be long in your society without perceiving that, in addition to extensive knowledge, you have unusual vigour, boldness and originality of thought. This is manifested by your mode of dealing with subjects of which you have not made a special study. From what I have heard I fully believe you would be successful in addressing large audiences; and you are able to express your own views, so as to conciliate rather than to irritate even those who are strongly opposed to you. You have always taken a decided line in questions of a political nature, yet I think there are not many men in Cambridge who have fewer enemies and more friends than yourself. I am quite sure that no institution of which you were Principal would be allowed to become inert or to languish: for you appear to me to possess not only unusual energy and a high sense of duty, but also to have great fertility in originating plans combined with a very practical idea of how to carry them into effect.

Believe me, very sincerely yours, | T. G. Bonney, B.D., F.S.A. and G.S. Fellow, Lecturer, and late Tutor S.J.C., and Cambridge Preacher at the Chapel Royal Whitehall.

[1] From a printed set of testimonials: see [37.1]. T. G. Bonney (1833–1923), clergyman, scientist and climber, had been 12th Wrangler in 1856 and a Fellow and Tutor of St John's. He was Professor of Geology at University College, London, from 1876 to 1901.

40. From Alexander Macmillan, 16 July 1877[1]

Alfred Marshall Esqre   16 July, 1877
2 South Buildings
Clapham Common

Dear Mr Marshall

The question of raising the price of your book[2] raises two questions, one mainly in your ken, and the other mainly in ours, but both demanding, I think, consultation.

1. Can you fulfil the conditions under which you undertook to write a book for a specific purpose, and as I gathered, for a particular audience at a fixed price—1/6—? If by raising the price you narrow your purchases, say by one half, then you gain nothing if your royalty is *barely* doubled, which the increased price to 2/- would scarcely admit of. This requires careful consideration.

2. If you raise the price at all I think it should be to 2/6. Whoever is willing to give 2/- will hardly notice the extra 6[d].

Can you & Miss Paley come & see us tomorrow or Wednesday? Please drop a post card fixing any hour between 11 & 1, or between 2 & 4.

Yours very sincerely | A. Macmillan.

[1] Marshall Papers. The printed letterhead is identical to that of [35]. *The Post Office London Suburban Directory* for 1876 lists Mrs. Adley as the resident of numbers 2 and 3 South Buildings, Clapham Common. Since William Marshall, Marshall's father, resided at this time at 12 Victoria Road, Clapham, it seems likely that Marshall was staying temporarily in rooms or a private hotel.
[2] *Economics of Industry.*

41. From William Jack, 19 July 1877[1]

July 19. 77

My dear Sir

We have been thinking over the whole matter in the light of your statistics & of your Mss.

We find
   654 students attending Pol. Econ. classes
   120 examined,

during year.[2] Assuming all of the 654 to use the book, & considering that each of the 120 will in course of time become a center of Educational influence, we should think that 2000 might fairly represent the sale in the first years of which alone anyone would like to speak beforehand. Probably too the book requires a good deal of the readers attention, a quality which will make it at once excellent for students—& perhaps a little too high pitched for what one might call an eighteen penny audience. On the whole, feeling pretty confident that a very considerable portion of the sale is equally secure whether the price is 1/6 or 2/6 seeing that the book will not look dear at 2/6, & that the second volume ought probably to sell at the same price and would not probably have so large a sale, we should decidedly advise 2/6 not 1/6 as the proper price.

   The terms we could offer are
1.   £50 to cover the first 4000 copies sold in England
2nd. 5[d]. per copy on every copy beyond the 1st. 4000 sold in England. Half for America.

   We should urge you to make the final form as satisfactory as you can, to stereotype & to be content till a good many thousand have been used, with such corrections as stereotype plates permit. Whenever in your opinion & ours any completer revision is necessary, we bear all the mechanical cost & you undertake the literary work. It is for our mutual interest & for your reputation that the book should be kept fully up to the latest date.[3]

   Faithfully yours | William Jack
Alfred Marshall Esq
We return the Mss to you in M[r] Bowes'[4] care.

---

[1] Marshall Papers. The printed letterhead is identical to that of [35]. Reproduced in *Early Economic Writings*, vol. 1, pp. 60–1 n. The letter concerns the proposed *Economics of Industry*. William Jack (1834–1924), 4th Wrangler in 1860, Professor of Natural Philosophy at Owens College Manchester from 1866–70, and editor of the Glasgow Herald from 1870–6, was at this time an editorial adviser to Macmillan and Company. He became Professor of Mathematics at Glasgow University in 1879.

[2] These figures presumably refer to extension teaching in general, not just the Cambridge-sponsored classes.

[3] This stereotyping procedure was followed and no substantial rewriting was to take place over the book's life.

[4] Robert Bowes of Macmillan and Bowes, the Cambridge branch of the business.

42. From William Jack, 26 July 1877[1]

July 26, 1877

My dear Sir
   I find that a letter was written to M[r] Bowes asking him to send the Mss on to your address.

I am delighted to hear that you have been elected to Bristol and I offer my heartiest congratulations.[2] The future of higher education in the West of England will very much depend on you, and I suppose you have at Bristol pretty much an open field.

Should we proceed to set up another specimen page or so now or will you be so much engaged now that we ought to wait till hearing from you again? Remember only that there are scarcely any 250 pp books nicely printed & on good paper sold for less than half a crown, that more pages are not necessary for the *look* of the book, & that 500 pp for the double book will be quite long enough.

Very truly yours | William Jack

Alfred Marshall Esq
I hope Miss Paley will let me add my congratulations to her.[3]

[1] Marshall Papers. The printed letterhead is identical to that of [35]. See [41.1].
[2] Marshall had been appointed Principal and Professor of Political Economy at University College Bristol on the preceding day, Marshall's thirty-fifth birthday. For an account of the early history of the college see Basil Cottle and James Wilson Sherborne, *The Life of a University* (University of Bristol, Bristol, 1951).
[3] The marriage of Alfred Marshall and Mary Paley was to take place on 17 August 1877.

43. To Herbert Somerton Foxwell with a postscript by Mary Paley Marshall, 11 September 1877[1]

SJC
11 Sep

My dear Foxwell
I send you my rosewood reading desk. I love it too much to sell it & cannot use it at Bristol. You once praised it; so you too may become fond of it.

Yours ever | A. Marshall
read & approved | MPM

[1] Foxwell Papers. Not posted. SJC is St John's College.

44. To Herbert Somerton Foxwell from Mary Paley Marshall, 24 January 1878[1]

1, Glen Oran Villas, | Apsley Road, Clifton
My dear M^r. Foxwell
We are exceedingly obliged to you for all the trouble you have taken about the piano. M^r. Marshall is writing to M^r. Stamford[2] about it at once. The 'pocket' sounds very attractive & I think if it can be got for the price you named, we shant be able to resist the temptation. We are thinking of having an Evening

& inviting all the College staff, & I think now we shall put it off & wait till our musical instrument appears.

I am rather concerned about the lady students & Perry; partly because I fear I may have had something to do with it. I was at Cambridge for a couple of days last term, & took Perry's Introduction to P.E. to read in the train.[3] I was a good deal struck by some passages in his chapter on value, & thought his illustrations forcible & well expressed. I know I showed the book to some of the students at Newnham, & I believe I told them that if the rest of the book were as good as what I had read, it might be worth reading. I have since read the rest, & am quite disappointed. But I ought to have written & told them so at Newnham. It is possible that what I said when there may have lead to this wholesale purchase, & if so I am extremely sorry. I am writing to tell Miss Rowe[4] (who is one of my correspondents) that I consider the book, with the exception of the parts I first read, as harmful rather than otherwise, & will ask her to tell the others so. In this way I hope I may make some reparation for my rather hasty remarks.

I suppose Term is just beginning at Cambridge. We seem to be in the middle of ours here. M^r. Marshall is at College else he w^d. join me in kind regards

Yours very sincerely | Mary Paley Marshall

---

[1] Foxwell Papers. Postmarked 'JA 24 78'. Clifton, although once separate, was by this time a residential suburb of Bristol.

[2] Presumably Stamford was a mistaken rendering of Stanford [45.7]. Marshall's rendering of Stanford in [45] is unambiguous and likely to have been more accurate through greater familiarity.

[3] Arthur Latham Perry, *An Introduction to Political Economy* (Scribner Armstrong, New York, 1877), which seems to have been adopted as a textbook at Newnham.

[4] Annie Emily Rowe (1855–1946), a student at Newnham 1877–8: subsequently a headmistress in South Africa.

45. To Herbert Somerton Foxwell, 28 January 1878[1]

1 Glen Oran Villas | Apsley Road, Clifton

My dear Foxwell,

I am not quite sure that I understand what you mean about Mill.[2] I think he means to classify the agents of production as

i personall (ie labour)

ii material $\begin{cases} a & \text{'land' ie all wealth which is not produced by human} \\ & \text{effort \& is not the result of saving: e.g. rivers} \\ b & \text{capital, machinery, improvements in land, canals} \\ & \text{\&c which are the result of effort \& saving.} \end{cases}$

I do not think it is true that Rent is a result of the Law of D.R.; but that it is the result of a limitation of the sources of supply, taken together with a limitation of the produce which can be got from any one source: this second limitation takes the form of the Law of D.R. with regard to a very large class of things: but it seems to me that this is an accident & not essential to the nature of rent. Nor do I regard inequality of the fertility of the several sources of production as a necessary condition of rent. Only when it happens that (i) the Law of D.R. applies, & (ii) there is inequality of fertility, then the Law of Rent applies in just that form in which Ricardo laid it down.[3] When these conditions are not present, we have I think Rent still: ie the owner of any natural monopoly is[4] able to obtain payment for the use of it & this payment is regulated by economic laws; These Laws may be called Laws of Rent; but they would differ in form from Ricardos Law, because of the difference in kind[5] of the limitation of supply. It seems to me that this is really Mills view, see Bk III of Ch V §3. I don't feel at all sure that I have given you my views on the point on which you wanted them. If not, I will try again.

About Perry.[6] I recommended my wife to read him as a study of style. I think he has wonderful powers of exposition. I believe he has done very good service in his generation; but on account of his proclivities towards MacLeod I should not recommend him to beginners. I got to like his style before I knew of these proclivities; perhaps I should otherwise never have got to like it.

Stanford[7] has written very kindly about the piano: it is really very good of him. I fear I have troubled him rather about the case. We don't care what it is provided it is not a bright coloured wood. A dark rosewood would do as well as anything. I am writing to tell him this.

Many thanks to you too about it from *us*.

Yours ever | A Marshall

---

[1] Foxwell Papers. Envelope postmarked 'Clifton JA 28 78.'

[2] Foxwell must have been commenting on the manuscript of the *Economics of Industry*, but the implied prior communication cannot be documented and may have been verbal. The specific allusion is to book i of J. S. Mill's *Principles*. 'D. R.' stands for 'diminishing returns'.

[3] See Ricardo's *Principles*, ch. 2.

[4] The word 'is' was repeated in the original, occuring at a turn of page.

[5] The word 'kind' replaced the deleted word 'form'.

[6] See [44.3]. MacLeod is Henry Dunning Macleod.

[7] The person advising on the purchase of a piano was probably Charles Villiers Stanford (1852–1924), who was organist of Trinity College and conductor of the Cambridge University Musical Society from 1872 to 1893. He became a renowned conductor, composer, and teacher and served as Professor of Music 1887–1924.

---

46. To Herbert Somerton Foxwell from Mary Paley Marshall with postscript by Alfred Marshall, 19 April 1878[1]

1, Glen Oran Villas, | Apsley Road, Clifton
April 19th.

My dear M[r]. Foxwell

There is some chance of the question being raised on the Council whether I may teach next year at University College. M^r. Marshall & I are very anxious for many reasons that I sh^d. May I ask you to give me a testimonial of my efficiency. What I sh^d. be very glad to have from you as my Examiner, & as the Examiner of some of my pupils, is a statement that I have some Economic knowledge, & that I am able to teach what I know. Also that I did not seem to make myself or my subject odious, or exert a bad influence on the students.

It sh^d. not be addressed to the Council of the College, for indeed the Council have not as yet constituted any post in the College w^h. could be held by a woman. For the same reason it w^d. be better not to have it said in Cambridge that I am applying for the post.

Yours sincerely | Mary Paley Marshall

I am going to write her a testimonial too: but mine must be all facts no sentiment. I can speak of her work on the Correspondence scheme;[2] but I can't say that those who are put on it are the elite of the literary & scientific world with the same force as you could. Yrs. AM

---

[1] Foxwell Papers. Mary Marshall was granted permission to teach the day classes in political economy. For details see John K. Whitaker, 'Alfred Marshall: The Years 1877 to 1885', *History of Political Economy*, 4 (Spring 1972), pp. 1–61.

[2] This probably refers to the scheme for the Education of Rural Young Women by Correspondence, initiated in 1871 by Henry Sidgwick in conjunction with the Cambridge Association for the Higher Education of Women. See McWilliams-Tullberg, *Women at Cambridge* [7.2], pp. 233–4, n. 24; Blanche Athena Clough, *A Memoir of Anne Jemima Clough* (Arnold, London, 1903), pp. 133–4.

47. To Herbert Somerton Foxwell, 26 April 1878[1]

1, Glen Oran Villas, | Apsley Road, Clifton.

Beloved Fox,

I can't honestly say your testimonial is strong enough in its praises. But it is one of the strongest I have ever seen: so I know I ought to be contented. It will certainly help us immensely.

I am thinking of doing my curves before my Theory of Foreign Trade.[2] Every minute till October will be taken up with part I of the Manual,[3] which is an awfully hard thing to do. But we find we are getting to write much faster than we used to, so I hope we will really do it by October. There is no hurry about the matter but I would like to have your views at some time on the question whether to bring out Foreign Trade or Curves next.

Yours ever | AM

---

[1] Foxwell Papers. Envelope postmarked 'AP 26 78'. Foxwell's testimonial has not been traced.

[2] By this time Marshall seems to have decided not to proceed further with his foreign-trade volume, even though it was substantially complete. Instead, he proposed developing two separate monographs from the material. See [50].

[3] *Economics of Industry*.

48. To Herbert Somerton Foxwell, 27 May 1878[1]

University College, Bristol
27 May 1878

My dear Foxwell,

You can read any portion of my letter that you think fit at the Board. But it seems to me that they are both, & particularly no 2, rather longwinded for such a purpose.[2]

Regarded as a working man Howell is certainly not illiterate; but when he tells the early history of English gilds he is obviously speaking of things of which he knows little.[3] Moreover he almost avowedly writes as a special pleader for Trades Unions; & the statements of fact which come from the mouth of a special pleader are less convincing than those which are made by a historian. I should not have believed many of the things he states if I had read them first in his book; & though he has copied hundreds of sentences & paragraphs verbatim from Brentano,[4] he never shews where Brentano's responsibility ceases & his begins. Howell is a book which I think & hope most students will read; but on account both of its matter & manner I think it is not well fitted for the Tripos.

I had wanted to read Walker on Money[5] before writing to you again. What little I have had time to read of him tends to confirm my old impression. I should hardly like to vote against him, but I am not in a position to vote for him.

I have no time for argument; otherwise I would like to discuss the 'Wages-class' question now. But I will put down without argument some propositions which seem to me to be true, & to be inconsistent with Walkers conclusion.[6]

i   The essential problem of the Wages question is, what are the proportions in which the produce of industry (labour + capital) is divided between wages of labour & interest on capital.

ii   The produce of industry includes all the effects of industry for which people are willing to pay a price, not only commodities: thus it includes railway travelling, musical entertainments, medical advice &c.

iii   The produce of industry includes the effects of the work not only of *a* the agricultural labourer but also of *b* the gardener who trains creepers over the house, of *c* the hired waiter (whether hired from a Capitalists office for servants, or hired directly) when he arranges flowers on the dinner table & *d* of the domestic servant who does the same. It includes the effects of the work not only of *a* the professional milliner but *b* the dressmaker who comes to work in the house by the week & *c* the housemaid who mends the stockings. It includes the work not only of *a* the painter who polishes up the house but also of *b* the boy who polishes up the boots & *c* of the ladies maid who polishes up her employers head.

iv If it were true as Walker says that for the purposes of the Wages problem those are not wage receivers who are not employed as a means to profit, it would be true that there would be no wages problem, at all events of its present form in a country in which every household was self sufficing. For then every servant would be a domestic servant. But provided there were freedom of movement for the servants from one master's employ to another (& perhaps squatting on uncultivated land & shifting for themselves may be thrown in) the wages problem would in all its fundamental characteristics remain, I think, unaltered. Of course the problems of value would not exist in their present form in such a country. And therefore it might be difficult for people to borrow Capital without minutely stipulating how the debt was to be paid back with interest. But this being done the Profits—or as I prefer to say the Interest—problem would I think be very nearly the same in fundamental principle as it is now.

I must go on with my work—College work I mean. The day lectures were scarcely a tenth part of my work.[7] Indeed I almost liked them, because no one could say I was neglecting the College when I was in the lecture room, & very often I hardly got 5 minutes in the day outside the lecture room in which to think about Pol. Econ. But partly because I have a private secretary I wont have so much Principals work next year as this I hope.

Yours very sincerely | A Marshall

[1] Foxwell Papers.
[2] The letter referred to here has not survived. The allusion is probably to the deliberations of the Moral Sciences Board in Cambridge in regard to lists of books for the Moral Sciences Tripos.
[3] George Howell, *The Conflicts of Capital and Labour Historically and Economically Considered: Being a History and Review of the Trade Unions of Great Britain, Showing their Origin, Progress, Constitution, and Objects in their Political, Social, Economical and Industrial Aspects* (Chatto and Windus, London, 1878).
[4] Lujo Brentano, *On the History and Development of Gilds and the Origin of Trade Unions* (Trübner, London, 1870).
[5] Francis Amasa Walker, *Money* (Holt, New York, Macmillan, London, 1878).
[6] The following discussion relates to the views put forward in Francis Amasa Walker, *The Wages Question* (Holt, New York, 1876).
[7] These were to be taken over by Mrs Marshall starting with the next session.

49. To Herbert Somerton Foxwell, 29 May 1878[1]

29 May

My dear Foxwell,

Blanqui[2] is in the College Library. I should not like it to be put into the Tripos on my responsibility. But you can read the table of contents in a few minutes & then taking for granted that Blanqui is a good safe man just a trifle above mediocrity, with a humdrum but not slow style, you will be able to vote on him pretty well. My own opinion is that it is a very great evil for students to go through a P.E. Course & to know nothing of the order of evolution of the economic phenomena of modern times. A study of Blanqui will go about as far to remove this ignorance as the study of so small a book can be expected to go.

About Walker[3]—I am awfully sorry I have been attacking a pet doctrine of yours. But I can't help it now. The difference between Walker & myself goes deeper I fear than a disagreement as to doctrines at the bottom of p 215.[4] I think one of the most useful things in his book is the insistence on the importance of the 'entre-preneur'.

But so far from holding, as I *think* he does, that the main wages problem relates to the position which the entrepreneur holds relatively to unskilled labour, I hold that the main problem is that of the division of the produce of industry into interest or the reward of abstinence, & wages, including the wages of the entrepreneur, or the remuneration of labour.[5]

It seems to me that in the country I supposed wages disputes could exist; there could be organised & federated trades unions, trades councils, strikes, lockouts; disputes about piece-work, hours of labour, overtime, number of apprentices, introduction of machinery, as well as of course wages (real-wages, there might happen to be no money). There could be arbitration, courts of conciliation &c &c. There could not be disputes as to whether production should be stinted to avoid glutting the market, because there would be no market to be glutted. But otherwise a trades-union in such a country might borrow the constitution & rules of one of our Unions, I think.

Yours ever | A Marshall

My wife has been reading & comparing Howell & Brentano with great care. She thinks Brentano is incomparably superior to the first chapters of Howell.[6]

---

[1] Foxwell Papers. Envelope postmarked 'Clifton MY 29 78'.

[2] Jerome Adolphe Blanqui, *Histoire de l'Économie Politique en Europe....* (Guillaumin, Paris, 1837: fourth edition 1860).

[3] See [48.6].

[4] Where Walker puts forward the view that domestic servants are not in the 'wages class'.

[5] Such a view was to be forcefully expressed in the Marshalls' 1879 *Economics of Industry*.

[6] See [48.3, 4].

50. Draft for a letter to Macmillan and Company, (June?) 1878[1]

In a letter dated July 26 1877 Mr Jack asked 'Shall we proceed to set up another specimen page or so now, or will you be so much engaged that we ought to wait till hearing from you again.'[2] I answered that for some time to come we should be unable to proceed with the book. {I have delayed writing to you till we[3] could see our way to finishing the book off.} I think I am able to say now confidently that if no unforseen event occurs, we shall be able to get it out by the end of this Vacation.[4] {I have given to the book every minute of time that I could snatch from my College work.}

You may recollect that Mr. Macmillan and yourself urged us to abandon the notion that the book could conveniently be partly rewritten between the first & second edition; & that you advised us to try at once to put it into a form in which we should be content for it to remain.[5] We have followed this advice & have entirely rewritten already {the central and most important half of the book Ch. VI–XVIII} more than half the book.[6] There is still about a quarter of the book which wants to be rewritten, & all of it requires a little finishing. But on the whole we are very much better satisfied with the book than we were at this time last year. We have put into it a good deal more original matter than it had then. But we think that it is not only better arranged, but also much more readable than it was before. And though I can't promise to remain satisfied with it always, I think there is much less chance of our becoming ashamed of it than there would have been if we had driven it through press last year.

I do not think that on the whole we have increased the amount of matter in the book {at all events not considerably}. It will I think still be well contained in the 250 pp. of kind of which you sent us a specimen. But as you know we would very much rather, now that the book is to be sold for 2/6, have 280 or 300 pp. somewhat less crowded; though we admit [it][7] is as good-looking a page as we ever saw with so large an amount of print in so small a space. If then you would kindly send us another specimen page or two now we should be very much obliged to you.

With regard to the book on Foreign Trade, I have come to the conclusion that it will never make a comfortable book in its present shape. My present notion is that I have three books before me all of which I hope to get out tolerably quickly {before the end of 1881} in the following order. They are:

(i)   a book on the method of diagrams {distinct from but allied to the methods of analytical mathematics} applied to economic theory including Foreign trade curves
(ii) a book on Foreign trade for general readers
(iii) the supplementary volume (on Banking Foreign Trade and Taxation) to that which is now nearly ready.

I could get the curves ready for the Press in a very short time. The Foreign Trade would take me a little longer. The supplementary small book would take us a good deal longer still. {I may perhaps ask for some advice on the question of the order of publication of these three books.} I find that Prof. Fawcett's book,[8] interesting as it is, has taken up less than I thought it would of the ground I want to cover.

We may be passing through London in the latter half of July: but otherwise we shall not have an opportunity of calling on you unless we come to London on purpose. We could do this if there were a strong reason for doing so: but we are rather stingy of our little store of time.

A.M.

[1] Marshall Papers. Reproduced in *Early Economic Writings*, vol. 1, pp. 61–3. Portions in curly brackets were struck out. The references to a possible visit to London in July and to completing the book by the end of 'this' vacation suggest a June date.

[2] See [42]. Marshall's quotation is not exact.

[3] 'We' was originally written 'I'. By this time Marshall seems to have taken the work largely into his own hands.

[4] That is, by October.

[5] See [41]. An original intention to address the letter to William Jack rather than the Macmillan Company is still revealed in this sentence. Mr. Macmillan is Alexander Macmillan.

[6] Eventually the volume was divided into three books of respectively 8, 13 and 9 chapters, so that these chapters would appear to have comprised the latter chapters in book i ('Land, Labour and Capital') and the bulk of book ii ('Normal Value').

[7] Word apparently omitted.

[8] Henry Fawcett's *Free Trade and Protection* (based on lectures given in Cambridge in the autumn of 1877) was published by Macmillan in May 1878.

51. To Herbert Somerton Foxwell, 3 July 1878[1]

3 July 1878

My dear Foxwell

I am not in a good temper with you because you did not pitch into my last letter. I spouted some of the book at you about the wages problem in a country in which no goods were bought or sold & ∴ none made for profit. I know you don't agree with what I say, but I should like to hear why, in order that we may see the error of our ways before we go into print on the subject, ie when we are wrong, & when we are right find out what extra explanation is needed.[2] But I will try to smother my ill temper & answer your questions.

I don't much recommend the history of economic science; though I most strongly recommend the history of economic phenomena. I spent a good part of a year on it, made voluminous notes, lectured on them twice, came to the conclusion that anything like an elaborate treatment was not profitable for me & most unprofitable for the class; & have seldom used my notes since.[3]

There are absolutely no English works on the subject except McCulloch, McLeod, & Travers Twiss.[4] This last is of some little use, it is out of print & extremely scarce, but it is in the University Library. French books on Pol: Econ: have as a rule disappointed me. Two brilliant exceptions are Lavergne's 'Les Economistes Francais du XVIII^m Siecle. 1870', (you should anyhow buy this 7f.50.) & Turgot's 'Reflexions sur les Richesses' Univ: Lib. There is a magnificent collection of the writings of the Physiocrats by Daire in the Univ: Lib:—it is out of print: it should be read pari passu with Lavergne.

I have very often tried to read Say as a disagreeable duty: but his dulness has beaten me every time. I have heard several others say the same. I don't believe there is anything to be got out of him.

You should look at McCulloch, 'Treatises on Economic Policy' as well as his life of A. Smith. Also the little article on primitive Political Economy by Jones. If you won't read German I can't recommend much about early mediaeval & ancient Econ Theories. But for various reasons you may be interested in looking at some portions of the last chapter of Lecky's Rationalism & of Hallams Middle Ages (particularly in connection with Italian Economy).

I believe, by the bye, there is some good Pol Econ in Italian. I have thought of learning Italian on purpose.

I forgot to mention Recherches Historiques sur le Système de [John] Law par E Levasseur 1854. I did not get it till I was tired with Law. It is obviously longwinded but probably good. Levasseur is able.

Of course you will look at Blanqui, commonplace as he is; the way in which he recognizes the solidality between economic phenomena & economic history is improving.[5]

You never told me what was done about the Tripos list.[6]

Thankyou for reminding me that I ought to write to Nicholson to thank him for his essay.[7] I was surprised with the result, though less than I should have been if I had not known that Keynes had spent a good deal of his energies in writing an attack on Cliffe Leslie.[8] He cut out the most aggressive portions of it, but I expect his essay was weakened by the loss of blood. Nicholson's was of the kind that I expected from him, but abler than I expected: original in side remarks rather than on any main issue.

We are now getting a little breathing time & are working hard at the book. We expect to get it ie 'The Economics of Industry' out this Vac."

Yours ever | A Marshall

---

[1] Foxwell Papers. On mourning paper (see [52.2]). Envelope postmarked 'Bristol JY 3 78'.

[2] This line of argument seems to have been largely eliminated from the finished version of the *Economics of Industry.*

[3] Many notes answering this description are preserved in the Marshall Papers. A few fragments are reproduced in *Early Economic Writings*, vol. 2, pp. 252–61.

[4] The works alluded to here and in the following paragraphs appear to be: John Ramsay McCulloch *The Literature of Political Economy* (Longman, Brown, Green and Longmans, London, 1845) and *Treatises and Essays on Subjects Connected with Economical Policy; with Biographical Sketches of Quesnay, A. Smith, and Ricardo* (Black, Edinburgh, 1853); Henry Dunning Macleod, *The Principles of Economical Philosophy* (Longmans, Green, Reader and Dyer, London, 1872–5: 2 vols.); Sir Travers Twiss, *View of the Progress of Political Economy in Europe since the Sixteenth Century* (Longman, Brown, Green and Longmans, London, 1847); Léonce de Lavergne, *Les Économistes Français du XVIIᵉ Siècle* (Guillaumin, Paris, 1870); Anne Robert Jacques Turgot, *Réflexions sur la Formation et la Distribution des Richesses* (Paris, 1766); Eugène Daire (ed.), *Physiocrates . . .* (Guillaumin, Paris, 1846); Jean Baptiste Say, *A Treatise on Political Economy; On the Production and Distribution of Wealth* (A translation of the fourth edition of Say's *Traité d'Économie Politique:* first edition Paris, 1803; Longman, Hurst, Orme and Brown, London, 1821); Richard Jones, *Primitive Political Economy of England* (Austin, Hertford, 1852: from the *Edinburgh Review*, April 1847): reprinted in William Whewell (ed.), *Literary*

Remains, Consisting of Lectures and Tracts on Political Economy by the Late Rev. Richard Jones (Murray, London, 1859); William Edward Hartpole Lecky, *History of the Rise and Influence of the Spirit of Rationalism in Europe* (Longman, Green, Longman, Roberts and Green, London, 1865); Henry Hallam, *View of the State of Europe during the Middle Ages* (Murray, London, 1818); Pierre Émile Levasseur, *Recherches Historiques sur le Système de [John] Law* (Guillaumin, Paris, 1854); Jerome Adolphe Blanqui, *Histoire de l'Économie Politique en Europe* (Guillaumin, Paris, 1837: fourth edition 1860).

[5] An alternative reading of 'imposing' might be suspected but does not seem justifiable.

[6] The point at issue remains obscure, but see [48.2].

[7] Joseph Shield Nicholson had been awarded Cambridge University's triennial Cobden Prize for an essay on the set topic of 'The Influence of Machinery on Wages'. Nicholson's essay was published as *The Effects of Machinery on Wages* (Deighton Bell, Cambridge, 1878). See *Reporter*, 30 September 1876, p. 619; 5 March 1878, p. 322.

[8] John Neville Keynes had submitted a 365-page essay for the Cobden Prize. He had commenced in early February 1877, under Marshall's guidance, but had learned in March that Cliffe Leslie would be one of the adjudicators. (The others were Henry Fawcett, *ex officio* and John Budd Phear (1825–1905) nominated by the Cobden Club. Phear, who had been a Fellow of Clare, was at this time Judge of the High Court of Bengal.) On 25 April Keynes confided to his diary 'He [Marshall] advises me strongly not to send in what I have written about Cliffe Leslie in my Cobden Essay. But I am not sure at all that I shall take his advice'. The finished essay was submitted in June. See *Diary*, entries for 8 February, 5 and 9 March, 25 April, 20 and 22 June, 1877.

52. To Herbert Somerton Foxwell, 1 September 1878[1]

My dear Foxwell,

I, having just lost my own mother, can feel with you. She was to me, what yours was to you.[2] And my sisters miss her much as yours do their mother. But they are older than yours & agree with my Father on most religious questions: so that they are on the whole happy.

We have now the proofs of the first nine chapters.[3] The first few must, we think, be sent back to the printer soon. But we will send you duplicates of them to glance through, & the remaining chapters to be read through, so that you will find them at Weston,[4] when you go there. Then you must come & see us & talk over them.

I suppose Weston S.M. is enough address: we don't want to lose them in the post.

Yours very sincerely | A Marshall

Mary sends you her warm sympathy & kindest regards.

[1] Foxwell Papers. On mourning paper. Envelope postmarked 'Clifton SP 1 78'.

[2] Marshall's mother had died on 16 June 1878, aged 61, at Sutherland House, Great Malvern, Worcestershire, the home to which his parents had retired. (Information provided by Peter Groenewegen.) See Appendix I.

[3] For the *Economics of Industry*. In the published version the first nine chapters comprised book i, 'Land, Labour and Capital'.

[4] The Foxwell family home was at Weston-super-Mare in Somerset.

53. To Herbert Somerton Foxwell from Mary Paley Marshall, 22 September 1878[1]

Glen Oran Villas | Apsley Road
Sep 22nd.

My dear Mr. Foxwell

I am sending you Book II Chs I–VI wh. is as much as we have ready for the final reading before sending to the press.[2] You kindly said you wd. look it through & so we are venturing to give you this further trouble.

We took 6 days of real holiday last week at Lynton,[3] as we shd. not have had another opportunity before Term began; but now on our return there is such an accumulation of College work besides the Inaugural address that Alfred says he shan't be able to touch the book again till after Term has begun.[4] But we thought that if you could give us some hints about these chapters they wd. be of immense value when we are able to work at them again. It is a great disappointment to us that the book cant be out as soon as intended.

What a grand place Lynton is. I like it better than any place I know in England. We went there by sea, & we came back by that wonderful road over Porlock Hill. Every day we took a huge walk & did not pay any attention to rain of wh. we had enough & to spare.

We came back to find the house still full of workmen. We have now no sitting room but the Boot room! Alfred has to be at the College all day long however, so it does not much matter.

With our kind regards & with very many thanks for your kind help, yours very sincerely
M P Marshall

Be sure & do not trouble about the chapters if you cannot do it conveniently. We feel that we have already been too merciless in our demands on your time.

---

[1] Foxwell Papers. On mourning paper.
[2] In the published version of the *Economics of Industry*, the first six chapters of book ii dealt with value, rent, and the general problem of distribution, the remainder of the book dealing with the specifics of distribution.
[3] The resort in North Devon.
[4] Marshall delivered his public lecture 'Some Aspects of Modern Industrial Life' on 7 October 1878. See Whitaker, 'Alfred Marshall: The Years 1877 to 1885' [46.1], pp. 53–61, for the detailed summary which appeared in a Bristol newspaper.

54. To Herbert Somerton Foxwell from Mary Paley Marshall, 10 October 1878[1]

University College Bristol

My dear Mr. Foxwell

Let us have chaps I–III back as soon as you have read them, but not sooner. We have a great craving for views on them & anything that you or Mr. Sidgwick can give us will be accounted a great & valuable favour. Alfred w^{d}. scarcely allow me to send you a copy of the Inaugural, he sternly resisted my sending one to M^{r}. Sidgwick for he says he had to do it so rapidly & amid so much other work, that he is not at all proud of it. I do not of course agree with the last remark.[2]

The College is fairly at work now, & looks I think prosperous in all respects except funds. I gave my first lecture yesterday, & I shall have a class of 14 or 15 I think.

With kind regards, | Yours very sincerely | M P Marshall.

[1] Foxwell Papers. Envelope postmarked 'Bristol OC 10 78'.
[2] See [53.4].

55. To Herbert Somerton Foxwell, 27 October 1878[1]

My dear Foxwell,

I agree with almost everything you say in substance: but many of the things which you 'desiderate' seem to us to belong to the Theory of Market Values.[2] This is the case e.g. with monopoly & scarcity values, & with 'non competing groups' except insofar as Mill's (not Cairnes') doctrine of grades belongs to & is quoted in Book II. I think you know I have a great contempt for what Cairnes says on the subject, on mental as well as on moral grounds.

But what you have written has been extremely useful to us. It has made us determine to shew our hands much earlier than we had intended to. We are now writing a new beginning Chap IV in which we endeavour to answer before hand the objection that the theory of Normal Values is not directly applicable to labour-&-capital-politics: we insist that all class & social groupings belong to the Theory of Market Values.

About separating Wages of Management from Interest in the Normal Theory: I hardly feel more certain of anything than that in future generations every one will do it.

I find the work of the book continually increase, & the time I have to give to it continually becoming less than I had expected. The book certainly can't come out before Xmas. I hope it may be ready by the middle of January.

We are writing to the Sidgwicks to say we fear we must postpone our visit to February.

With very hearty thanks for your abundant & most important help we are Yours very sincerely | A Marshall

[1] Foxwell Papers. Envelope postmarked 'Bristol OC 27 78'.

[2] The *Economics of Industry* draws a fundamental distinction between 'normal' (long-run competitive) value, dealt with in book ii, and 'market' (short-run and/or non-competitive) value, dealt with in book iii. For example, the effects of monopoly and collective action, including the actions of trades unions, are relegated to book iii. The references which follow are to the treatments in J. S. Mill's *Principles*, especially book ii, ch. 14, and Cairnes's *Leading Principles* [17.4], especially part i, ch. 3.

56. To Herbert Somerton Foxwell, 4 November 1878[1]

My dear Foxwell,

I could not understand your last letter at all until I got out your syllabuses, which I am ashamed to say I have not looked at for some time.[2] I now think we differ very little.

But I don't like your use of Profits

    you —— our —— Wages of Management

     I think you overrate ⎱ the importance of the 'Market' theory relative to

    you —— we underrate ⎰ the 'Normal' theory of the division of the produce.

And so you are not likely to do more than gently forgive the persistence with which we direct our efforts to arguing that Normal Wages of Management are governed by laws similar to those which govern other wages.

Your criticisms have been of enormous help to us; & in consequence we are rearranging the chapters we sent you so completely that we are almost rewriting them. We have followed your advice in almost all cases except those in which you have obviously misunderstood our meaning. But in these cases we have made violent plunges in the hope of making ourselves more intelligible to our next reader.

Sidgwick has sent me his paper on Mills theory of value in which his distinction between scarcity & 'monopoly' value occurs.[3] Something that you said about my having overlooked this distinction makes me think you don't understand our view. For this reason I send you a part of the proof of that Chapter on Rent which we cut out of Book I on Sidgwicks advice. Part of this chapter we have put into Chap III[4] of Book II. The rest of it we are going to put partly in the last chapter of Book II,[5] partly with a long discussion of monopolies wh. we have already written in Book III.[6] For what Sidgwick & you call Monopoly Values we treat along with Market Values: & what you call Scarcity values we treat along with Rent. Please return the proof: it is the only copy we have. I think Sidgwicks paper is admirably written. Of course I agree with almost every word of it.

Yours ever | A Marshall

[1] Foxwell Papers. On mourning paper. Envelope postmarked 'Bristol NV 4 78'.

[2] This probably refers to syllabi for extension classes taught by Foxwell. It was customary to print such syllabi, often so detailed as to be mini-essays. Those in question here have not been traced or identified.

[3] This unlocated paper on Mill's theory of value must have been one of a series privately printed by Sidgwick for a Cambridge discussion group on political economy that he had organized when his interests turned to this novel subject. (What appear to be two such papers are included in a collection of Sidgwick pamphlets held by the University of Southern California.) Sidgwick published three economic essays in the *Fortnightly Review* for 1879, but none incorporates the material in question, his 'The Wages-Fund Theory', *Fortnightly Review*, 26 NS (1 September 1879), pp. 401–13, being the most pertinent.

[4] This could conceivably be read as 'Ch. IV'. Book ii, ch. 3, of the *Economics of Industry* is entitled 'Rent', while book ii, ch. 4, is entitled 'Rent in Relation to Value'.

[5] See book ii, ch. 13, of the *Economics of Industry*, 'Relation of Normal to Market Value'.

[6] See book iii, ch. 4, of the *Economics of Industry*, 'Monopolies. Combinations'.

57. To Herbert Somerton Foxwell, 10 January 1879[1]

1 Glen Oran Villas, | Apsley Road, Clifton
10 Jan 1879

My dear Foxwell

We are most deeply indebted to you for wading through that mass of bad writing & cross corrections. You have done us an enormous service.

We don't say that we have a theory to explain produce = wages + interest. But we do think we have.

Speaking for myself I can say that I have been working hard at that difficulty which Sidgwick raises[2] at all events since 1869. I know this because I know that when I reviewed Jevons Theory of Pol Econ for the Academy,[3] that difficulty was prominent before me in consequence of my having been already in the habit of thinking of wages as the discounted value of produce; & not being clear in my own mind as to the mutual causal relations of the various elements. There was nothing that I looked at with greater interest than his equation[4]

$$\text{produce} = \text{profit} + \text{wages}.$$

I did not think his solution valid, I knew I had not one myself: & when asked a year or two afterwards to write a primer[5] I declined *simply* because I knew I had not solved the question; & intended to write a big book on wages before writing a primer. I took foreign trade before wages; because I thought I could get that over quickly; & I knew I could not write a theory of wages quickly. But many years have passed since then; & in every year I have given more time to this question than to any other question whatever, except those about which I have been writing.

All this is very egotistical:—but I feel a little drawn at your saying that Sidgwick said no one had seen the difficulty except Jevons.

I have not finally abandoned 'wages = discounted value'. I think something may be made of the phrase yet; but not much. I think it is an impostor because it seems simpler than it is, & to explain more than it does. Still if, as I hope, I ultimately write a big book on wages, I think I shall give the phrase two or three chapters.

Thus your criticisms are of enormous value in showing us that we have not brought out in sufficiently clear outline our main theory. This means another delay for the book: but the matter is vital.

In some respects I think you would see our position much more clearly if the book were in print; & you could see all at once. Most of what you say about the accumulation of capital, & about demand is I think duly considered in its proper place.

In your last criticism you said we had given too little space to the ordinary Adam-Smith-account of differences of wages in diff. employments. Now you say we have given too much. Very likely you have been right in each case. We think you are right in almost everything you say: part of what you say about the use of 'may' is an exception. It is impossible to thank you too much for saying it before we have gone over the book a third time & sent it to the press.

Yours very gratefully | A Marshall

¹ Foxwell Papers. Addressed to 4 Clarement Crescent, Weston super Mare.
² See pp. 411–13 of Sidgwick's 'The Wages-Fund Theory' [56.3] for an elaboration of his views. In a shorter privately printed earlier version (see [56.3]) to which Marshall possibly alludes here, Sidgwick had stated 'when the "Wages-fund Theory" is cleared away, the general problem of distribution is, according to ordinary economic doctrine, left simply indeterminate. I must, however, notice an ingenious, and (I believe) original solution of the problem that has been offered by Professor Jevons . . .'.
³ See [17.3].
⁴ Jevons, *Theory of Political Economy* [17.3], p. 259.
⁵ Nothing is known of the circumstances of this request.

58. To Herbert Somerton Foxwell, 14 February 1879¹

1, Glen Oran Villas, | Apsley Road, Clifton.
14 Feb 1879

My dear Foxwell,
   You are indeed to be pitied in your second great loss.² I know it is one of those losses that cannot be lessened by the sympathy of others; & that time alone will heal it: but time will heal it, time & the outward growth of life.
   I am very glad that Bateson Bonney & Taylor are our three representations.³ The news of the election is the best news I have heard from Cambridge since I left. There are others who as individuals have strong claims. But I don't think any other set of three would be nearly as good as this set.
   Thanks for your interesting account of Blackburn.⁴ We will certainly send

McColl[5] a copy of our book when it is out, as bar accidents it will be early in this summer. But at present it is not progressing. Another attack a little worse than the last has made my doctor turn & rend me. I mean he has shut me up at home & forbidden me to do anything for a week.[6] When he lets me out I must give some Gilchrist lectures that ought to have been going on now, & meanwhile the book must wait.[7]

There is no great news here. Mary is on the Council of the High School for Girls. Our Council has selected an architect & will I trust soon build: but there is some doubt about it.

Remember me to the dear old College.

Yours ever | A Marshall

Thanks too for your account of Sidgwick's club.[8] I am always glad to hear what goes on there.

I think it is a very important truth that there is not much use in having a special theory of foreign trade; but I think it is a good deal more important a truth that there is some use in having one.

[1] Foxwell Papers.

[2] See [52]. Presumably the death of another member of Foxwell's family, but not his father who survived until 1886.

[3] William Henry Bateson, the Master, Thomas George Bonney [39.1] and Charles Taylor (1840–1908), Fellows, had been selected to represent St John's College in negotiations over the reform of the College's Statutes with the Statutory Commission. This had been established by Parliament in July 1877 to institute reforms at Cambridge. Taylor—mathematician turned theologian—was to succeed Bateson as Master in 1881. See Miller, *Portrait of a College* [11.1], p. 95; Winstanley, *Later Victorian Cambridge* [1.2], chs. 7 and 8.

[4] The Lancashire mill town?

[5] Probably Norman McColl (1843–1904), who took a first in the Moral Sciences Tripos of 1866 and became a Fellow of Downing in 1869. He edited the *Athenaeum*, 1871–1900.

[6] It was at this time that Marshall was struck by a disabling illness, diagnosed as kidney stones, which seriously restricted his activities for some years.

[7] A press report of Marshall's lecture (repeated in several locations) on 'Water as an Element of National Wealth', appeared in a Bristol newspaper on 6 March, and is reproduced in *Memorials*, pp. 134–41. The Gilchrist Educational Trust was active in sponsoring popular lectures nationally, not merely in the Bristol region. See Harrison, *Learning and Living* [13.2], p. 242; Whitaker, 'Alfred Marshall: The Years 1877 to 1885' [46.1], p. 24.

[8] See [56.3].

59. From William Stanley Jevons, 12 May 1879[1]

address Hampstead
12 May, 79

Dear Mr. Marshall,

I have for some time back felt very guilty about retaining a book of yours (Rau)[2] which you kindly sent me some years since. I have been always on the point of finishing with it and always delaying. However now my new edition of the 'Theory of Pol. Econ^y' is almost out of the printers hand and I have no further excuse for keeping your book. I have posted it to-day registered & hope you will get it safely. I have to thank you much for your kindness.

I hope you will be interested in my new preface. Mr. Sidgwick having sent me a copy of your printed papers[3] I have been able to refer to them tho not as much as I shd have liked the work having been mostly done before I received the copy. Your problems are rather stiff and I have hardly succeeded in mastering them.

Hoping that Mrs Marshall is pleased with her lecturing work & satisfied with her class, which however is seldom the case with a teacher.

I am, | Yours faithfully, | W.S. Jevons.

[1] Marshall Papers. Reproduced in *WSJ*, vol. 5, p. 63.

[2] Karl Heinrich Rau, *Grundsätze der Volkswirtschaftslehre* (Winter, Heidelberg, 1826: eighth edition Leipzig, 1868–9). This work is included in the 'List of Mathematico-Economic Books, Memoirs [etc.]' appended to the second edition of Jevons's *Theory of Political Economy* (Macmillan, London, 1879). Some editions included a demand–supply diagram—probably the reason for Jevons's interest. Marshall told Seligman in 1894 that he possessed only the eighth edition (Vol. 2, [443]). But at some point he acquired the fifth edition of 1847 (now in the Marshall Library). The diagram appears on p. 580.

[3] Sidgwick had arranged to have four of the chapters from the technical appendix to Marshall's abandoned foreign-trade volume privately printed for the use of his Cambridge discussion group (see [56.3]). A few copies were sent to economists outside Cambridge. A facsimile edition was published in 1931 as Alfred Marshall, *Pure Theory of Foreign Trade: Pure Theory of Domestic Values* (Reprints of Scarce Tracts in Economic and Political Science, 1; London School of Economics and Political Science, London). See *Early Economic Writings*, vol. 2, pp. 111–236 for the fullest available text.

60. To Herbert Somerton Foxwell, 12 May 1879[1]

Glen Oran Villas, | Apsley Road, Clifton

Beloved Foxwell

Add one more to your many good & kind deeds & tell me what you think of Arnold of Trinity who is now a candidate.[2] Has he 'the to know to do'? Is he genial?

Yours eternally | A Marshall

Ive been to London to see a doctor. He encourages me: says I will in all probability be nearly as strong as ever by the end of the summer.[3]

[1] Foxwell Papers. Postmarked 'MY 12 79'.

[2] Edward Vernon Arnold (1857–1926), Senior Classic in 1879, was an applicant for the classical professorship at University College, Bristol. He was not appointed.

[3] An earlier letter to Foxwell (Foxwell Papers, 10 May 1879) seeking advice on other applicants for the classical professorship had added:

> I wish I could come up: but I cant. My doctor's a bully, thats a fact. He wont let me do anything I can help.

61. To Herbert Somerton Foxwell, 18 June 1879[1]

University College, Bristol
18 June

My dear Foxwell

Many thanks for your interesting letter. I like Zincke's article,[2] but there are several things in it I don't quite believe: I am not even quite sure that rents generally will go down: though no doubt some will. I think the important question is that of American competition: & that Zincke has dealt with very slightly: in particular he does not say how much of the present lowness of price of American produce in England he puts down (i) to the Railway wars in America, & (ii) to the purchase of U.S. & other bonds by Americans in the English market.

I am glad about McLeod.[3]

Ede is here examining for the Higher Local

We are all very busy | Yours | A. Marshall

[1] Foxwell Papers. Addressed to the Savile Club, London. A duplicated insert listed student entries at University College, Bristol, in the academic years 1877–8 and 1878–9. The table shows the numbers for political economy.

	Day		Evening	
	Men	Women	Men	Women
1877–8	1	11	30	13
1878–9	1	25	47	7

[2] F. B. Zincke, 'Pauperism and Territorialism', *Fortnightly Review*, 25 NS (June 1879), pp. 807–23. Foster Barham Zincke (1817–93) was an antiquary who wrote several articles on land tenure and the state of the rural population.

[3] This allusion is obscure. Henry Dunning Macleod had been an authorized lecturer for the Moral Sciences Board in Cambridge. A cessation of his lecturing activities was perhaps the cause for gladness.

62. To William Stanley Jevons, 30 June 1879[1]

1, Glen Oran Villas, | Apsley Road, Clifton
30 June 1879

Dear Professor Jevons,

I take up the pen with some shame to acknowledge your letter of May the 12th, and the safe arrival of 'Rau'. When your letter came I was in an unusual press of work which as I was not very well, I could hardly get through; and when the pressure was over I forgot your letter till just now.

I am looking forward with the greatest interest to the new edition of your book. During the last two years I have been too much occupied with practical work to do any considerable amount of study or writing. I hope better days are in store and I think soon I may begin on a book of curves of which the papers sent you by Mr. Sidgwick will form the basis. The pure theory of international values I don't much care about. I don't think it can be made easy without curves, and I think I shall leave it very much as it stands; but in the rest of the book I propose to give only a subsidiary place to curves, and to develop the application of the theory somewhat. In this way I hope to contribute my mite towards that work of 'real'-ising the results of abstract quantitative reasoning in Economics of which I recognize in you the chief author. The *Economics of Industry*, the 2s. 6d. book which my wife and I are writing, is nearly finished. You may be sure that one of the first copies that are bound will find its way to Hampstead.

Yours faithfully, | A. Marshall.

---

[1] *Memorials*, p. 371, reproduced in *WSJ*, vol. 5, p. 66. The original has not been traced.

63. To Herbert Somerton Foxwell from Mary Paley Marshall, (September?) 1879[1]

Dear M[r]. Foxwell,

We think that the time has about come when you said you w[d]. be home & w[d]. like to have some proofs, so we send you a goodly pile. The last chapter—Cooperation—& the end of Book III ch VIII are being printed just now, & we will send you it in a day or two. We have run out of good proofs of the first part, & are obliged to send rather mutilated copies. Isnt it a grand thought that the book will be in the binders hands this week & will probably make its public appearance in about 3 weeks time.

I hope you had good weather & a pleasant time abroad & with our kindest regards

Yours very sincerely | M P Marshall

P.S. Please pardon the half sheet. I forgot your aversion thereto.

M^r. Marshalls health is about the same as when you saw him.[2]

I am sorry to find that we have not a spare copy of the later chaps of Book III. I will send it in a day or two.

[1] Foxwell Papers.
[2] See [58.6].

64. From Benjamin Jowett, (September?) 1879[1]

> Address Professor Campbell's | St Andrews

Dear Mr Marshall

I was very sorry to hear of your intended resignation, which will, I fear, prove a great blow to the College. But I can hardly ask you to reconsider a determination at which you have arrived on grounds of health, after careful thought.[2]

I will ask you, however, to consider one or two alternatives which do not interfere with your decision 1st whether you would remain with us for one year more until the building is carried out and the College is a little more in hand: We shall not get another principal who will do as much for it as you could have done. We could, I am sure, lighten the mechanical work during this year. 2nd whether without continuing to hold the Principalship you could retain the lectureship in Political Economy. This would give M^{rs}. Marshall a field and she would be able to take a part in the ladies' education of Clifton which has been & would be of so great value.

I write in haste (excuse pencil for I scribble this in the waiting room of a railway where there is no ink and the train has just come in). It would be of importance if it can be arranged that your intention should not be known until it is actually carried out. Untrue reasons are likely to be given for it. I shall not mention it to any one.

I am so sorry to hear of your illness independently of the consequences of it to the College. This kind of illness though not dangerous is depressing & one cannot help fancying oneself at times worse than one really is. I hope that you & M^{rs}. Marshall will come & pay me a visit as soon as you can. I am always interested to hear about the books on Political Economy though I do not think that I rightly understand the mathematical formulas. With best regards to M^{rs}. Marshall

Ever yours truly | B Jowett

[1] Marshall Papers. Jowett is known to have been in Scotland in the Autumn of 1879. Lewis Campbell (1830–1908) was Professor of Greek at St Andrew's University from 1863 to 1892. He subsequently served as one of Jowett's editors and biographers.
[2] See [58.6]. Marshall's resignation was delayed to 1881: see [99]. Jowett was a member of the Council of University College, Bristol, and was to become Marshall's mentor.

65. From Benjamin Jowett, 6 October 1879[1]

Oxford
Oct. 6. 1879

My dear Professor Marshall

I think that the Calendar had better be sent to each of the Fellows of Balliol & New College.[2]

I shall be very glad to have the little book[3] and congratulate you on the completion of it.

No one, I believe, except myself & Mr Budd,[4] know of your intended resignation: Do you think it is quite impossible to make some arrangement such as you hint at for the reduction or partition of the work of the Principal? I would like you to give some thought to this & not to be deterred by imaginary difficulties: I feel certain that the course which you are taking is not the best for us, & that unless you are absolutely compelled to it by ill health I doubt whether it is the best for you: 1. Because you cannot devote your whole time to writing: 2. The result of writing is uncertain & it is better to have a resource besides. 3. because the comfort of writing & sometimes the power to write depends a good deal on being in easy circumstances, so as to be able to go any where & see any one: 4 The anxiety of a small income (though I do not know your circumstances) and the monotony which it involves is as trying as a certain amount of mechanical work: 5 I do not anticipate that the work of the College would be as great in the future as in the past. 6. There is no professorship at Cambridge in your subject likely to be vacant.

My idea would be that you should have a V. Principal say at a salary of 300£ a year chosen & paid by yourself (with the approval of the Council). Will you consider all this, before finally deciding.

Ever yours | B Jowett

---

[1] Marshall Papers.

[2] Balliol and New Colleges, Oxford, had taken a prominent part in the foundation of University College, Bristol, and provided financial support. Jowett represented Balliol College on the Council of the new institution.

[3] The *Economics of Industry* which was to be published very shortly.

[4] Francis Nonus Budd (1824–99), a local solicitor, then Chairman of the College Council.

66. From Charles John Clay, 7 October 1879[1]

University Press, Cambridge
Octr 7th 1879

Dear Sir

We expect to have copies of your book completed tomorrow. They will be in the binder's hands by Friday I suppose, and will not long rest there—as I have no doubt that the covers have been prepared before this by Macmillan's orders. We are using every exertion to get the work done quickly.

I am much obliged by your kind appreciation of our workers which is very gratifying.

I am | Dear Sir | Yours very truly | C. J. Clay

P.S. We are in communication with Macmillan about the book—there will be no time lost in London you may be satisfied[2]

---

[1] Foxwell Papers. Sent to Foxwell with [67]. Clay (1827–1905) was the senior partner in Richard Clay and Sons, printers to the University.

[2] The urgency arose through the desire to have the *Economics of Industry* available for the opening of the new academic year.

67. To Herbert Somerton Foxwell from Mary Paley Marshall, 12 October 1879[1]

1, Glen Oran Villas, | Apsley Road, Clifton
Sunday

My dear M[r] Foxwell

It was very good of you to write us word to jog on Mac.[n] & we have just done so. We were in hopes that things were progressing fast, & send you Clays note[2] to show that he is doing his part. We knew there had been very tiresome delays but we thought they were getting past. We are not proud of the 'shopping'[3] of the book. We don't feel that we have solved the great problem of the use of commas & we know we havent been consistent in their use. But as to quotations we think we have a theory, but perhaps it isn't the right one & perhaps we havn't acted up to it if it is.

Yours on behalf of the Firm A.M & MP.M (unlimited) | MPM.

P.S. We hope you are better. Alfred is having better times just now, in fact he seems really stronger than he has been for a long time. But as it is he seems only just able to get through his work. The College is flourishing & the entries are plentiful.

---

[1] Foxwell Papers. Postmarked 'OC 12 79'.

[2] See [66].

[3] Neither the reading nor the sense of this word is clear.

68. From Alexander Macmillan, 13 October 1879[1]

Oct 13 1879

Dear Mr Marshall

We are doing our best to get your book out, and arrangements are going on for the distribution of copies to the Lecturers &c. I am sending you a copy in limp cloth which I hope you & Mrs Marshall will like. I had a good many specimens before me ere I decided. The *boards* would not do *Economically*. I think that even artistically it is not so nice to look at, and to handle surely the limp cloth is most convenient. The book will be out for sale early next week I hope.

Yours very truly | Alex. Macmillan

---

[1] Foxwell Papers. The printed heading is identical to that of [35].

69. To Herbert Somerton Foxwell, 18 October 1879[1]

                                          1, Glen Oran Villas, | Apsley Road, Clifton.

Private

My dear Foxwell,

I have put off writing to the Master,[2] because I do not want to trouble him so long as I do not know my own mind. And a suggestion has been made here that some of my work can be taken off me—that which I think properly belongs to the Secretary—my income being reduced. I could easily give up £100 or £200 a year, & shall stay if anything of this kind can be managed. But I don't think it can: meanwhile time is going on fast. Sidgwick writes that there are practically no Moral Sciences men. So I suppose it would not do for me to think of coming back as a Mo: Sc: lecturer.

But in my last year at Cambridge I had a large class (22) more than half of which consisted of the best Historical men. Do you think S^t.. Johns would have me as a Historical Sciences Lecturer with the understanding that I looked after the men generally & taught economic history, economics, & perhaps political philosophy including Bentham &c.

We got the first copy of our book the day before yesterday. You will get one soon.

About Personal Capital I forgot to say that Capital is a thing—perhaps the only thing in economics—which we can't define to our own satisfaction ([comp ye?][3] square brackets in chap. on distribution in Book II[4]). But what we have said about Personal Capital is consistent. All human strength we regard as personal wealth: we regard it as capital in so far as it is destined to be used, say in running a coal barge on the Thames but as wealth which is not capital in so far as it is used say in the Oxford & Cambridge boat race.[5]

In fact as we are not satisfied what is the right use of capital we have tried in this one instance consciously to be conservative.

Still we wish we had not that quotation from Mill in the chap on Capital.[6]

In haste | Yours ever | A M

---

[1] Foxwell Papers. The envelope is postmarked 'OC 18 79'.
[2] That is to W. H. Bateson, the Master of St John's College. Projected reforms at Cambridge were improving prospects for married fellows and lecturers. See [58.3].
[3] Illegible.

[4] See *Economics of Industry*, book ii, ch. 6, s. 5 (pp. 98–100) which deals with the concepts of income and capital. Square brackets are used in the book to partition off more advanced sections.

[5] These distinctions are not at all explicit in the *Economics of Industry*. See especially book i, ch. 1, ss. 5–7, and ch. 3, s. 8 (pp. 5–7, 20).

[6] See *Economics of Industry*, book i, ch. 3, s. 1 (pp. 13–14) for an extensive quotation from J. S. Mill's *Principles*, book 1, ch. 4, s. 1. (The quotation is of the second paragraph of that section, omitting the last sentence, and deals with the definition of a manufacturer's capital as 'that part of his possessions [including money] . . . which is to constitute his fund for carrying on fresh production'.)

70. To Herbert Somerton Foxwell, 19 October 1879[1]

1, Glen Oran Villas, | Apsley Road, Clifton.
19 Oct

My dear Foxwell,

I have decided, in order to avoid delay, to write the Master by this post. If you think there is any chance that the College would be willing to have me as a lecturer, you might perhaps clear up matters a little by a talk with him.

Yours, as you deserve, | ie unscrupulous about troubling you | A Marshall

[1] Foxwell Papers.

71. To Herbert Somerton Foxwell, 23 October 1879[1]

1, Glen Oran Villas, | Apsley Road, Clifton.
23 Oct 1879

My dear Foxwell,

The Master wrote that the question of lectureships was closed during the uncertainty as to what the commissioners would do.[2] I hope you may have seen him. Until you wrote I had not the smallest notion that a lecturer on history was being talked of.

I don't know what to do. I should be happier at Cambridge & all things considered, my wife says, she would, on a small income than here with my present one even if the Council can take off part of my work. I shall not know what they can do till after the 19th.. of November. And meanwhile I hardly know what to say to those members of the Council whom I talk to about it. I think there is no use in writing anything more till I hear again from you.

What you say about the book is too good: but we are indeed made happy by it.

How is it that you have not had a copy sent you by Macmillans from us. We put you almost at the top of the list, & people here whom we put at the bottom have had it sent to them?

You understand that I have not resigned, & have not even told the Council as a body that I am thinking of doing so. If I had a good retreat at Cambridge I should resign straight off; if not I should only resign in case they found that they could not make any great change in my position. Every body here is very kind: I have nothing to complain of, but that the post is in consequence of unforseen causes, heavier than the Council thought & I thought it would be when I was elected.

I will not come back to Cambridge to play the part of cuckoo, & turn you out of your own nest. I wish we could have a talk.

Yours in haste | & gratitude | A Marshall

A 'good retreat' at Cambridge is a retreat with a moderate income (£150 is enough) but above all it is a place to which people want me to come. E.g. if people said we want a history lecturer who can teach history & not one who can teach what is already taught; so that we only half like having Marshall back, I think I had better not come. This is what I fear.

[1] Foxwell Papers.

[2] The Statutory Commission (see [58.3]) was bringing its work of reform towards a close at this time, but much remained unsettled. The letter from Bateson has not been preserved.

72. To Herbert Somerton Foxwell, 25 October 1879[1]

1, Glen Oran Villas, | Apsley Road, Clifton.
25 Oct 1879

My dear Foxwell,

I thank you for your most kind letter. As to your offer to resign half your salary to me, it is just like you: but there is no consideration whatever that would induce me to accept that offer or anything at all like it. Really we have no claim to pity. It may be that this post can be so modified that I can stay in it. But if not we shall go away & live perhaps for one or two years on our means together with the savings of the last two years: We should indeed lump the five years 1877–81 together, & consider that as we had done more than our share of money making in the first half, we might do less in the second half.[2] After a rest I should look out for some lecturing work, perhaps in Cambridge perhaps in Scotland or anywhere in fact.

During this year or two we may perhaps live in an out of the way farm house, but it is not unlikely that we should live in lodgings in Cambridge during part of the year; so that I might have the use of the University Library & Mary might have access to Newnham. Mary is indeed urging me very strongly to resign unconditionally in order that we may do this. And if [I][3] consulted my own inclination I should do it. But to say nothing of other considerations I should as things are not feel justified in going away from this College in its present state if the Council wanted me to stay & were able to relieve me of the Secretarial part of my work. As to my being made a Fellow, I never thought that possible for a moment. I recollect that everyone condemned Christ's for electing Peile, though his case was a thousand times stronger than mine in every way.[4] I don't think my letters to Cambridge can have done any harm (beyond giving several kind people some trouble that has come to nothing) except in one way; about which I am rather anxious. You tell me that there was some thought of electing [an][5] outsider to an ordinary Fellowship with the purpose of making him lecture on history. I can conceive that some sensitive people may be now not quite so eager to do this as before, on the ground that after what has passed it might seem a little slight to me. If this happened I should be deeply distressed. My hobby for years was that the College should have a real bonâ fide historical lecturer; & nothing would delight me more now than to hear that in default of any bonâ fide historian within the walls, the College had elected [an][6] outside historian to a Fellowship.[7]

What you say about the book's faults in Book I is we think in the main true. We noticed it ourselves when it was too late. We would give a great deal to be able to cut out the quotations from Bastiat & one or two from Mill (that on pp 13, 14 is the only one about which we care very strongly),[8] & to rewrite & amplify chaps I & III.[9] However we adhere to our original notion that a long discussion on scope & method should come either in the preface or at the end of the book: not at the beginning. And we have always had some thought of writing two or three chaps of that kind at the end of Economics of Trade & Finance.[10]

We have however another plan which is to write a third companion volume on the outlines of economic history, in which confusions about terms would be treated in the only way in which they can be satisfactorily dealt with; ie historically. If we live long enough such a book will be written by us or one of us: we did not speak of it in the Preface, because the smallness of this book has given us so much trouble that we don't want to promise to write another *small* book. But about utility & value, I am not sure that I know quite what you want—we are distinctly against putting a *little* of the history of economic theory into a book of this kind. And the kernel of the distinction is in Book II Ch I.[11] Indeed it has always seemed to me that one great use of the doctrine of Final utility, is that it super-annuates the old discussions about value & riches. However I think something should have been said of it somewhere, perhaps one word in Book I Ch I, & two words in Book II Ch II.[12] Would an addition similar in substance, (thought not in form of course) to the first part of the inclosed lecture,[13] satisfy your demands.

The more fully & the more frankly you speak of such things the better a friend you will be—No: you can't be better than you are—the more use will your friendship be to us.

We can't see that we have followed Mill very much in the earlier part except in that unfortunate quotation about capital which we put in too hastily & are much ashamed of. We should like to know what it is that we have done wrong. However I expect we shall be told very soon.

We should of course be most delighted to hear that you were going to review us in the Fortnightly: even if you do chastise us, you will do us an immense service.[14]

Some time tell me whether when next I get time for work again I should go on with the curves or with the Economics of Trade & Finance.

Yours everlastingly (in spirit as well as in length of letter) | A Marshall

We are not surprised that the style of Book I is worse than that of Books II & III. We felt ourselves writing more easily & therefore we supposed better as we went on.

---

[1] Foxwell Papers.

[2] Marshall had been guaranteed a minimum income of £750 per year at Bristol, but insisted on a £50 reduction when Mary Marshall took over the day classes. See Whitaker, 'Alfred Marshall. The Years 1877 to 1885' [46.1], pp. 5–9, for details.

[3] Word apparently omitted.

[4] John Peile (1838–1910), Fellow of Christ's since 1860 and University Teacher in Sanskrit since 1865, married Annette Kitchener in 1866, sacrificing his fellowship. He was, however, re-elected in 1867, an unusual procedure. He was Master of the College from 1887 to 1910.

[5] Apparently written as 'at'.

[6] Apparently written as 'at'.

[7] Such an appointment does not seem to have been made at the time, perhaps because of uncertainties about the futures of University and College Statutes (see [58.3]). In 1884 Joseph Robson Tanner (1860–1931) and James Bass Mullinger (1834–1917) were appointed as College Lecturers in History (Miller, *Portrait of a College* [11.1], p. 103).

[8] The *Economics of Industry* opens (pp. 1–2) with a long, if freely rendered, quotation from Frédéric Bastiat's *Harmonies Économiques* (Guillaumin, Paris, 1850) extolling the remarkable coordination of society implied by exchange and the division of labour. See pp. 48–50 of the 1880 translation, *Harmonies of Political Economy*, by Patrick James Stirling (Oliver and Boyd, Edinburgh; Simkin and Marshall, London). Bastiat's famous story of the candlemakers' petition is retold on p. 18 of the Marshalls' book, but there is no quotation or even reference to the source in Bastiat's *Sophismes Économiques* (Guillaumin, Paris, 1846). John Stuart Mill is quoted on various matters on pp. 5, 8, 13–14, 19, and 107 of the *Economics of Industry*. See [69.6] for details of the pp. 13–14 quotation on capital.

[9] These chapters are entitled 'Introductory' and 'Capital'. The new preface added to the second edition of the *Economics of Industry* (Macmillan, London, 1881) observed that 'The first chapters were printed at a time when it was proposed to give the volume a more elementary character than was ultimately found advisable; and the difficulties which surround the definition of economic terms were ignored as far as possible' (p. vii).

[10] The preface to the *Economics of Industry* had explained that 'An inquiry into the subjects of Banking, Foreign Trade and Taxation is deferred to a companion volume on the "Economics of Trade and Finance"'. Also see [34, 50]. The promised book never appeared and was apparently never commenced.

[11] This chapter is entitled 'Definitions. Law of Demand'. It highlights the distinction between value in use and value in exchange and introduces the idea of marginal or 'final' utility, relating it to the 'law of demand'.

[12] These chapters are entitled 'Introductory' and 'Law of Supply'. It is difficult to see where the proposed discussion could fit into the latter. Perhaps it was ch. 1 of book ii, not ch. 2, that was meant.

[13] Probably a hand-written lecture note, not traceable.

¹⁴ The *Fortnightly Review* did not review the *Economics of Industry*, nor does Foxwell appear to have written a review. For some discussion of the reviews that did appear see *Early Economic Writings*, vol. 1. p. 68.

73. To the Editor, *The Times*, 27 Oct 1879[1]

Sir,—A statement made by you recently, to the effect that University College, Bristol, may be regarded as a 'chapelry served by Balliol preachers,'[2] seems likely to give rise to the impression that this college has as yet no permanent staff. The fact is that travelling University lecturers finished their preparatory work here three years ago, and in 1876 a college was founded which now has 14 resident professors and lecturers. Between them they give 59 separate courses of lectures, besides laboratory instruction, and more careful attention is paid to the work of individual students than travelling lecturers could find time for. The college thus justifies its name by offering instruction of the same character as that given at the Universities, and the fact that it had in last session 576 students, exclusive of medical students, shows that there is a demand for such teaching. Balliol and New Colleges, Oxford, have aided us by contributing liberally to our funds; and their representatives on our council have helped us by their advice in our endeavour to enable the citizens of Bristol to apply science in their business and to obtain culture in their leisure.

I am, Sir, yours faithfully, | A. Marshall, Principal, U.C.B.

University College, Bristol, Oct. 27.

¹ Published in *The Times*, 30 October 1879.
² A leading article in *The Times*, 22 October, on Firth College, Sheffield, had remarked:

> This bodily immigration of Oxford and Cambridge into Bristol and Sheffield and Nottingham is the most interesting educational experiment of the period. Cambridge commenced the movement by its scheme of what is called University Extension. . . . Oxford, or rather a single College in Oxford, carried the undertaking a step further. The intermittent ministrations of itinerant tutors it consolidated and crystallised by establishing a permanent lecturing body at Bristol. The Bristol College is a kind of chapelry served by Balliol preachers.

74. To Herbert Somerton Foxwell, 2 November 1879[1]

2 Nov 1879

My dear Foxwell

I wish you had written your last letter a year & a half ago. Everything you say would have led to some alteration though there are some points on which we don't quite agree with you.

I think no harm & some good would have come from putting our definitions of value in use & value in exchange in Book I Ch I.

I am sorry you spent a whole lecture on p 6: because that shews that you are not coming round, as I almost hoped you were, to the view which I have now held for a great many years about definitions.[2]

For some years I used to begin my elementary course with two quotations one from Mill's Logic & another from Kants Kritik to the effect it is a mistake to spend time at the beginning of a science on inquiries into definitions & method.[3] Then at the beginning of the advanced course when men had gone through Mill once,[4] I used to jaw away for several hours about them.

Of course I have spent a good part of the last ten years in considering the questions raised in Sidgwicks article on method,[5] & have views more or less satisfactory to myself about most of them. (I agree with him more than I do with most writers on the subject: but it does not seem to me that he has gone quite to the bottom of the subject.) But I maintain that there is no part of our little book the proper understanding of which would be to any considerable amount assisted by a preliminary discourse on method & definitions. We have however always known that when we discuss Money in the Economics of Trade we shall be unable to ignore the difficulty about the relation between money & capital, & that about the standard of value.[6]

However we quite admit that since we have admitted so many difficulties into Books II & III, we ought to have pitched the key a little higher in the first chapters of Book I.

We have not expressed ourselves clearly about capital. We wanted not to raise the difficulty about saving in the definition: we have decided that though the arguments on either side are very strong & nearly equal, it is on the whole best not to call natural agents capital except in so far as capital has been invested in them.

About Wealth I cannot understand why you object to the definition of material wealth on p 6.[7] Personal wealth stands on a different footing.

In my lectures the key stone sentence is [that][8] Giffens method of measuring wealth is right for some purposes, not for others.

When you are talking of national wealth, I don't think the condition 'capable of being exchanged' should be insisted on: that is all.

I think it a crime to use a word in two senses only when you don't know what you are doing: the inverse rule to that which divides murder from homicide.

I don't know what is to happen here. I have been on the point of sending in a formal resignation for some days; & shall probably do it soon.[9] But it is just possible that some scheme may be started for taking the heavier & duller part of my work off. Everybody we have spoken to has been very kind about it.

I will let you know more as soon as I know it myself.

Yours ever | A. M.

[Enclosure: Draft for letter to the Council, University College, Bristol.][10]
This is the first draft of my letter. It is of course strictly private: not to be left about.

Gentlemen,

I deeply regret that the state of my health compels me to place in your hands my resignation of the post to which you appointed me. I am already attached to the College by many ties; I believe it has a great future before it; and very strong reasons are required to make me decide that I must leave it at this critical time. But the administrative work which has fallen on me, has been heavier than I expected when I came here; and, though some of it will be less in the future than in the past, yet the reorganization of the College finances will involve so much extra work during the next few years as to put a great strain upon me even if I should lay aside my studies: and this I am not willing to do.

If I could have devised a plan which would have much diminished my share of the College work, I should have asked you to consider whether you could adopt it, and should have wished to defray the expenses of it myself. But I cannot find any such plan that has a sufficiently good prospect of working well to justify me in laying it before you.

I must therefore offer you my very hearty thanks for the most kind and thoughtful consideration which I have always received at your hands, and ask you to relieve me of my duties as soon as it shall be convenient to you to appoint my successor.

I remain, Gentlemen, | Your obliged servant | A M

---

[1] Foxwell Papers. Envelope postmarked 'Bristol NV 3 79'.

[2] *Economics of Industry*, p. 6, deals with the distinction between material and personal wealth and also that between productive and unproductive labour.

[3] John Stuart Mill, *A System of Logic* (Parker, London, 1843); Immanuel Kant, *Critique of Pure Reason* (1781). It would be hazardous to guess just which passages Marshall had in mind.

[4] The allusion here is most probably to J. S. Mill's *Principles*.

[5] Henry Sidgwick, 'Economic Method', *Fortnightly Review*, 25 NS (1 February 1879), pp. 301–18.

[6] See [72.10].

[7] '*Material Wealth* consists of the material sources of enjoyment which are capable of being appropriated and therefore of being exchanged'. *Economics of Industry*, p. 6.

[8] Word inserted for clarity. See Robert Giffen, 'Recent Accumulation of Capital in the United Kingdom', *Journal of the [London] Statistical Society*, 41 (March 1878), pp. 1–31, reprinted in his *Essays in Finance, First Series* (Bell, London, 1880).

[9] See enclosure.

[10] Duplicated with the preliminary note added by hand. Marshall did not in fact resign the Principalship until 1881. See [99].

---

75. To Herbert Somerton Foxwell, 20 November 1879[1]

University College, Bristol
20 Nov 1879

My dear Foxwell,

I have to thank you for your long & useful letter.[2] I won't answer it now, because answers by word of mouth are better than by letter: & you must manage to stay with us for a day or two in the Christmas Vacation, if you possibly can. We should like very much to see you.

The Council met yesterday & passed a resolution asking me to stay & empowering the Chairman[3] (who was known to think that I ought not to have secretarial work to do & that I ought to have time to study) to approve for one year any arrangements I might make for lightening my work. I have known during the last few days that such a resolution was likely to be passed: I mean a resolution somewhat to this effect. Of course I have accepted the offer.

Yours ever | A Marshall

[1] Foxwell Papers.
[2] Not traced.
[3] See [65.4].

76. To William Stanley Jevons, 8 December 1879[1]

1 Glen Oran Villas | Apsley Road, Clifton
8 Dec 1879

My Dear Jevons

My wife and I have often wondered what you would think of our book: we were more anxious for your good opinion of it than for anyone else's. I nearly decided to write to you about it just after the book had gone to the binders, for I then happened to read again your article on 'The advantages of capital to industry'. I met with it in your second edition and thought it must be an addition to your older theory: but I found it in your first edition also: this proved that I had read it carefully once, though I had forgotten all about it.[2] It is quite clear that under the circumstances we ought to have referred to this article when writing §3 of our Book II Ch. X.[3] It is not unlikely that you may have noticed other cases of the same kind; but we have never consciously repeated any doctrine that we could possibly have 'assimilated' from any recent writer without giving a reference to him.

We feel immediately proud of your having adopted our book for the Examination of the Banker's Institute.[4] It is one of the many obligations we owe to you.

Yours very truly | A Marshall

[1] King's College, Cambridge, J. M. Keynes Papers. From a transcript supplied to Keynes by Jevons's son, Herbert Stanley Jevons (1873–1945). The original was attached to Jevons's copy of the *Economics of Industry*, now lost.
[2] See 'The Advantage of Capital to Industry', pp. 242–5 of the first edition and pp. 254–7 of the second edition of W. S. Jevons, *Theory of Political Economy* ([17.3], [59.2]).
[3] Book ii, ch. 10, of the *Economics of Industry* is entitled 'Interest'. Section 3 deals with producers' demand for capital as a function of the rate of interest.
[4] For the (less than flattering) background to this adoption see Jevons's letter to H. S. Foxwell of 14 November 1879 in *WSJ*, vol. 5, pp. 79–81.

77. To Herbert Somerton Foxwell from Mary Paley Marshall, 14 December 1879[1]

1, Glen Oran Villas, | Apsley Road, Clifton.

My dear M[r]. Foxwell

We shall look forward with great pleasure to seeing you on the 29th. We are asking M[r]. Nicholson[2] to come at the same time, but do not yet know whether he can do so. We are gradually coming to the end of our Term & finish by the end of next week. M[r]. Marshall seems really stronger, he has been much better since our plans have become more settled.

You know we are going to have a telephone wire between our house & the College, so that he may administer from afar.

I am hoping for some skating when you come. We are also expecting our minds to be greatly chastened & improved by your hints on the book.

Ever yours sincerely | Mary Paley Marshall

[1] Foxwell Papers. Postmarked 'DE 14 79'.
[2] Presumably Joseph Shield Nicholson.

78. To Herbert Somerton Foxwell, 14 January 1880[1]

1, Glen Oran Villas, | Apsley Road, Clifton.
14 Jan 1880

My dear Foxwell

Beeton was here on Sunday to dinner, with Miss Clough. We were all much charmed & a little amused by his enthusiasm.[2] He told me much that was useful as to the details of procedure on the Stock Exchange.

I have not written out for you the contents of the rival books 'Economics of Trade & Finance' & 'Pure Economic Theory' because I have pretty well decided on the latter: & I shall not have much time to give to either one or the other before I come up to Cambridge at the beginning of the May Term. Ede[3] is strongly in favour of my doing the curves next.

There is no vacancy here in the post of Secretary, nor likely to be. The arrangement with Main[4] is designed to enable the present Secretary to go on.

If you see Webb[5] tell him he has not answered my letter about Donkin's Acoustics.[6]

Best remembrances to all old friends | Yours ever | A Marshall

Thanks for the paper about the Statistical Society. I filled it up & sent it in. I propose to become a life member.[7]

[1] Foxwell Papers.
[2] Henry Ramié Beeton (1851?–1934), stockbroker, businessman, and amateur economist. A friend of Foxwell. Miss Clough is most probably Anne Jemima Clough (1820–92), Principal of Newnham College, Cambridge (on whom see B. A. Clough, *A Memoir* [46.2]).

³ William Moore Ede, who had taken a first in the Moral Sciences Tripos of 1871, is acknowledged in the preface to the *Economics of Industry* as a source of advice and assistance.
⁴ John Frederic Main (1854–92), 10th Wrangler 1876, was Professor of Mathematics, Mechanics and Engineering at the College. The precise nature of the arrangement remains uncertain.
⁵ Robert Rumsey Webb (1850–1936), Senior Wrangler 1872, was a Fellow of St John's from 1872 to 1936. He became a well-known mathematical 'coach'.
⁶ William Fishburn Donkin, *Acoustics, Theoretical, Part I* (Clarendon, Oxford, 1870). The nature of Marshall's query is unknown.
⁷ Presumably a membership application for the [London] Statistical Society. Marshall became a Fellow on 20 January 1880, compounding his subscription for life by payment of twenty guineas. See *Journal of the [London] Statistical Society*, 43 (September 1880), p. 409.

79. To Herbert Somerton Foxwell, 24 January 1880[1]

24 Jan

My dear Foxwell,

Can you let me know the number of the 'Mind' in which the Math^l. paper on Hedonism occurred.[2] I want to get it. Was it by any chance by a man of the name F Y Edgeworth. Jevons had lent him my papers on economic curves, & he has just written a polite letter about them in which he seems to imply that I should know who he is. But I don't: do you?

Yours ever | A Marshall

[1] Foxwell Papers.
[2] Francis Ysidro Edgeworth, 'The Hedonical Calculus', *Mind*, 4 (July 1879), pp. 394–408.

80. To Francis Ysidro Edgeworth, 8 February 1880[1]

31, Apsley Road,[2] | Clifton.
8 Feb 1880

Dear Sir,

I had heard of your paper in Mind[3] & had intended to read it; but I had forgotten your name, & it was not till after I had written to you that it occurred to me you might be the author of that paper. I have now read nearly all the book you sent me;[4] & am extremely delighted by many things in it. There seems to be a very close agreement between us as to the province of Mathematics in the sciences that relate to man's actions.

As to the interpretation of the Utilitarian dogma, I think you have made a great advance: but I have still a hankering after a mode of exposition in which the dynamical character of the problem is made more obvious; which may in fact represent the central notion of happiness as a process rather than a statical condition.

I am sure your work on your present lines has a great future before it.

Yours very truly | A Marshall

F. Y. Edgeworth Esq

[1] BLPES, Edgeworth Papers. Neither Edgeworth's side of the ensuing correspondence nor Marshall's previous letter have been traced.
[2] This replaces the previous postal address of 1 Glen Oran Villas. Both addresses refer to the same house.
[3] See [79.2].
[4] F. Y. Edgeworth, *New and Old Methods of Ethics* (Parker, Oxford and London, 1877).

81. To Francis Ysidro Edgeworth, 28 March 1880[1]

31, Apsley Road, | Clifton
28 March 1880

Dear Sir

A series of other engagements have left me but little time for thinking about the applications of Mathematics to Economics. I am now beginning to have more time at my disposal and have just found your letter among my papers.

I do not quite recollect what called forth your query about the meaning of the word dynamical: indeed my views on the subject are too immature to be formulated briefly: but a hint of my meaning is contained in the fact that I think there is room for question whether the Utilitarians are right in assuming that the end of action is the sum of the happiness of individuals rather than the vigorous life of the whole.

As regards the applications of geometrical rather than analytical reasoning to economics, I have not such decided views as you suppose.

When tackling a new problem, I generally use analysis, because it is handier: And in the book which I am just going to begin to write I shall retain (in footnotes) a little Mathematical analysis for questions which I can't reduce under the grasp of curves. But—partly because curves require no special training, partly because they bear more obviously on the science of Statistics—I intend never to use analysis when I can use geometry.

You say: 'It has doubtless occurred to you that the curves of supply & demand for labour may intersect in several points'. I am not sure that I follow you: do you mean the labour of *one* trade or of all trades? And do you mean the supply at any instant: or do you refer to the laws of growth of population? My experience of the exact treatment of supply & demand in reference has been disappointing. The intricacies of the question are so numerous, the difficulties connected with the time element so great, that I have never got any curves relating to it which have satisfied me for many months after I first drew them.

Hoping that you will not forget your kind promise to send me some detailed criticisms of my papers.[2]

I am yours sincerely | A. Marshall

[1] BLPES, Edgeworth Papers.

[2] That is, the chapters on *The Pure Theory of Foreign Trade: The Pure Theory of Domestic Values* (see [59.3]).

82. To Herbert Somerton Foxwell, 30 April 1880[1]

31, Apsley Road, | Clifton.
30 April 1880

My dear Foxwell

Thanks for your interesting papers.[2] I have read them rapidly being very busy: if I may I will keep them till I can read them more carefully. I can't tell how far we differ about rent. I think not much: of course the value of corn in a country where there are many landowners is governed by altogether different laws from those which apply to the case where all land is owned by one man: in other words rent does not enter into Exp: of Prod^n.., but the 'Monopoly Profit' of say a patentee does.

If you look at the Theory of Domestic Values p 30 you will see a hint of a view of rent which seems to me similar to yours. Only for practical purposes I prefer the view taken in the Economics of Industry.[3] I spent a long time many years ago in debating whether I would throw overboard the latter view for the former for the purposes of *pure* theory. I decided in the negative; & though I have opened the question two or three times since, the conclusion has always been the same. Still the fact that as I understand Cunynghame & you prefer the former even for *applied* theory causes me to doubt as to whether I may not change.[4] But I think you don't in your lectures bring out the difference between that part of the value [of][5] a thing which is due to the temporary limitation of supply of the means of producing it, & that which is due to the permanent limitation, and there are several broad statements in your lecture notes which I should like to narrow & 'condition'; but very likely you did this yourself in delivering the lectures.

You took away with you the lecture notes which you had sent us, when you were last here.

As to being anticipated by others; if I am I shall be unfortunate, but if I were to publish hastily I should I think be wrong. I give every moment I can spare to the work: but with my limited strength, & my College occupations that is but little. I am very much better but I still can't stand physical exertion, & this limits my power of recovery if ever I get over done. But the summer is coming, & I shall soon be able to get my share of fresh air. N.B. if you hear any rumours as to the chance of there being a vacancy for the Professorship of Pol Econ,[6] will you kindly let me know *at once*.

I think Blackley's scheme[7] is most important: & should be discussed with care & energy: but I don't see my way to saying it will i work ii dispense with out-door

relief. I don't think he is very sharp at seeing objections: I shan't quite believe
in him till he writes a big book in which he fairly meets all objections.

Yes: indeed I am glad about the elections.[8]

Everything is going on well here except that we dare not canvass for money,
until the heat of the Tories' anger at their defeat has cooled down.

Yours very sincerely | A Marshall

I am writing to Blackley in answer to a letter of his, at least I shall write as
soon as I can.[9]

[1] Foxwell Papers.

[2] Not traced. Probably handwritten lecture notes.

[3] See the facsimile reprint of Marshall's *The Pure Theory of Foreign Trade: The Pure Theory of Domestic Values* [59.3]. On the cited page he introduces the possibility that rent may be measured by the quasi-triangular area above a supply curve rather than by that under a marginal product curve, the formulation adopted in the *Economics of Industry*.

[4] Marshall appears to have been alluding to Henry Hardinge Cunynghame 'Notes on Exchange Value', a printed lecture syllabus (London, 1880?).

[5] Word apparently omitted.

[6] The reference is presumably to Fawcett's Professorship in Cambridge.

[7] William Lewery Blackley (1830–1902), clergyman and author, had been proposing a national insurance scheme for some years. His articles were collected and republished in his *Collected Essays on the Prevention of Pauperism* (Paul, London, 1880).

[8] The Liberal Party had been returned to power in the very recent general elections, setting the stage for Gladstone's second administration. But the allusion could be to College or University elections.

[9] No such correspondence has been traced.

83. From Alexander Macmillan, 22 June 1880[1]

<table>
<tr><td>Professor Marshall
31 Apsley Road—
Clifton</td><td>Macmillan & Co.
Publishers
29 & 30 Bedford Street, Covent Garden, W.C.
London, June 22. 1880.</td></tr>
</table>

Dear Prof. Marshall

The sales of 'Economics' has been about 1600 of which nearly 1400 were sold during the first six months. The last three have been a little over 200, but these are of course not educational months, and we will not expect to do much till late August & early September & then on through the winter months again.

I would rather not use[2] the invidious comparisons which you justly feel to be doubtful. I dont think they do good & they awake antagonisms of a not very noble nature.

When you have your new book into some shape & can tell us its probable size we shall be very glad to hear from you.

We have been glad to hear that your health has so much improved and it is pleasant to know from yourself of the improvement.

Very sincerely yours | Alex. Macmillan

[1] Marshall Papers. Apparently in response to a letter from Marshall, not preserved.
[2] Presumably in advertising the *Economics of Industry*.

84. To Herbert Somerton Foxwell, 14 July 1880[1]

31 Apsley Rd | Clifton

My dear Foxwell,

We are just starting for North Devon & in packing up have come across these papers of yours which have been very useful to us;[2] but wh we now return with many thanks.

There is a vacancy for a Registrar for the College: but I have not sent your brother[3] a paper: because I think they want a man of business rather than of academic training: & I am not sure that he w^d.. like the work of canvassing for subscriptions, which is the most important thing that the Registrar has to do.

We have just found some reports of lectures of yours, that we think you asked us for some time ago.

We hope you are flourishing | Yours eternally | A Marshall

[1] Foxwell Papers. Postmarked 'JY 14 80'.
[2] Possibly the papers mentioned in [82].
[3] Presumably Ernest Foxwell.

85. To Sarah Emily Davies, 11 November 1880[1]

31, Apsley Road, | Clifton.
11 Nov 1880

Dear Miss Davies,

I am sorry I cannot sign the memorial which you sent me.[2]

I think the right course for the University to follow is to offer to men & women a new degree—not B.A.—for which neither residence in Cambridgeshire, nor passing Previous Examination[3] in its present form is required. I cannot see why women who can be taught well in local colleges should be refused recognition for their work by the older colleges, unless they consent to neglect what may be their urgent duties to their families.

Yours sincerely | A Marshall

[1] Girton College, Cambridge. Sarah Emily Davies (1830–1921) was the founder and first Principal of Girton.

[2] Presumably the Girton Memorial of 16 April 1880, seeking the admission of women to the Cambridge BA degree. See McWilliams-Tullberg, *Women at Cambridge* [7.2], p. 77 (also pp. 70–84 for the general background).
[3] See [1.2].

86. To Herbert Somerton Foxwell, 21 November 1880[1]

31, Apsley Road, | Clifton.
21 Nov 1880

My dear Foxwell,

I am not surprised at your desire for the chair at University College.[2] I have been thinking about it a great deal during the last fortnight: my wife wishes me to stand. But unless some new light should be thrown on the subject, I am not likely to consider myself at liberty to do so. In fact my duty to my wife as well as my duty to this college restrain me. When I was doubting whether to stand for the post at Edinburgh, I had to consider the latter alone; for my wifes position would not have been worsened by our going to Edinburgh.[3] But at that time the College was changing its Secretary, & after consulting several people I convinced myself, I am not sure after all whether rightly or not, that I had no right to stand: though if I had gone to Edinburgh I should have changed a life that is not very happy for one of perfect happiness.

I am not very happy here: not because I dislike my work; but because I do not really like it: & it is a pain to me to see one month after another pass away with practically nothing done that I really care for. I am better in one sense, that is I have scarcely any pain: but this is purchased at the expense of almost complete abstinence from movement & therefore from fresh air. This keeps my vitality low: & I am not able to do as a stronger man might, much effective study in the hours that remain free from my College work. It is however true that I shall not henceforth have to do a great part of the Secretaries work as well as my own: & this will make a considerable difference; the chief element of uncertainty in my present position is that I do not know how much difference there will be.

I have spun this long & rather desolate yarn about myself, because an excuse is necessary for my not saying straight out whether I intend to stand for University College or not: it is most unlikely that I shall: but I do not want to bind myself.

I should perhaps have said that every one here, Council & Staff & everyone, do all they can, to make life pleasant to me.

My wife & I hope you will come & spend a day or two with us soon. It will give us great pleasure if you will: & profit too, for we have heard nothing of Cambridge for an age.

Yours everlastingly | A Marshall

[1] Foxwell Papers.
[2] The post of Professor of Political Economy at University College, London, had been made vacant by the resignation of W. S. Jevons. Foxwell was to be eventually appointed to it.
[3] The post of Professor of Political Economy at Edinburgh University had recently been vacant. Joseph Shield Nicholson was appointed.

87. To Herbert Somerton Foxwell, 29 November 1880[1]

31, Apsley Road, | Clifton.
29 Nov 1880

My dear Foxwell,

I had no notion that names had to be sent in for University College London now. I supposed that they w^d.. be asked for about Easter. I certainly shan't sent in my name now. In fact I don't think about it, if I can help it. We had intended—if I went to London—to be very poor at all events for some years.[2] Perhaps we sh^d. both be happier so than as things are now, but until I have had time to see how the College works when the new Secretary has fairly settled down to his work, I shall not commit myself to going. So if names have to be sent in now or about now, I am out of it; & the chances are enormous that I am out of it anyhow.

Come if you can: & when you can, let us know when you can. For my wife is going to see her people at Bournemouth & wants to manage so as not to miss you.[3]

Thanks for crumbs of gossip. I hate gossip generally, but I like all you tell me: I hear very little about Cambridge.

Yours everlastingly | A. Marshall

[1] Foxwell Papers.
[2] The income of the Professorship at University College came primarily from student fees and was unlikely to exceed £150 a year. The position was in effect a part-time one. See *WSJ*, vol. 4, pp. 135, 142.
[3] Mary Marshall's parents had recently retired to Bournemouth.

88. To Herbert Somerton Foxwell, 5 December 1880[1]

31, Apsley Road, | Clifton.

My dear Foxwell,

Tell us when you know your plans: so far as we know ours we can see you with joy any time between Dec 24 & Jan 1, or between Jan 7 & Jan 14.

The more I think of the plan of taking my wife to London, the less I like it for her; though she vows she would like it for herself. She is doing a great work here: I don't see how she could be replaced: so, though I have promised her not to bind myself, I will say that I don't think it is likely I shall give another serious thought to the plan of running for London University Coll:

Yours ever | A Marshall

5 Dec 1880

[1] Foxwell Papers.

89. To Herbert Somerton Foxwell, 10 December 1880[1]

31, Apsley Road, | Clifton.
10 Dec 1880

My dear Foxwell

You must have been busy: otherwise you w^d.. not have been curious to know how I am getting on with writing. If I had been getting on at all, I should not have questioned whether to take my wife to London & poverty. In the last 12 months, I have practically done nothing in term time & next to nothing in vacation. Nearly all last vacation was taken up with College business. Henceforward it may be better: almost certainly will be.

Jowett asked us to go to stay a week with him at Xmas. We declined chiefly because I wanted to get any time I could for study: though otherwise we sh^d.. have delighted immensely in it. So you won't mind our leaving you to your books a good deal when you are with us, will you. Very glad you are coming.

Yours ever | A.M.

[1] Foxwell Papers.

90. To John Neville Keynes, 8 February 1881[1]

31, Apsley Road, | Clifton.

My dear Keynes

Will this testimonial do?[2] Speak frankly if you have any change to propose. Foxwell told me you w^d.. stand: he has not yet asked me for a testimonial.

Foxwell says that you are helping Sidgwick with his economic book.[3] Sidgwick & I differ on some questions of literary morality. For one thing we c^d.. not agree in a discussion as to the use which he (not you) w^d.. be at liberty to make of your notes of my lectures: & on hearing that he had asked you to help him with his book I asked Foxwell to give you my views on the subject. I don't know whether he has had an opportunity of doing so.[4]

Yours sincerely | A Marshall

[1] Marshall Library, J. N. Keynes Papers. Partially transcribed by Keynes, *Diaries*, entry for Wednesday February 8 where he adds. 'Marshall has sent me a wonderful testimonial.'

² See [91]. The testimonial was for the vacant Professorship of Political Economy at University College, London (see [86.2, 87.2]). Keynes dropped his plan to apply on being appointed Assistant Secretary of the Local Examinations Syndicate at Cambridge.

³ This was to appear as Henry Sidgwick, *Principles of Political Economy* (Macmillan, London, 1883). Keynes was reading the proof sheets, and his help is acknowledged in the book's preface.

⁴ After transcribing this passage in his diary, Keynes lamented 'I am immensely sorry for all that this implies. Personally, however, so far as I can remember, I have never shown Sidgwick any of what I regard as Marshall's most original work.'

91. To University College, London, 9 February 1881[1]

University College, Bristol
9 Feb 1881

Mʳ Keynes has a great natural genius for economic science, and a wide knowledge of its subject matter. He is a clear & powerful thinker, distinguished preeminently for thoroughness of intellectual character. He has a quiet but strong originality which leads him to work steadily at great issues, & which is perhaps liable to be underrated because it aims at producing that which is likely to live long rather than that which is most striking in its immediate effect. I regard him as an economist of the very highest promise.

I have heard from many quarters that he is a singularly lucid & invigorating teacher. His personal qualities are such as to make him a source of great strength to any Institution on the Staff of which he may be.

Alfred Marshall

[1] Marshall Library, J. N. Keynes Papers. See [90.2].

92. To Herbert Somerton Foxwell, 5 March 1881[1]

My dear Foxwell

Will this do? Keynes asked me for a testimonial & I determined to write to offer you one if you did not ask me for one. I don't suppose Edgeworth will ask me for one; if he did I shᵈ.. give him one, but it wᵈ.. have to be only on his power of applying the methods of exact reasoning to social questions. I have at present no means of forming an opinion as to his knowledge of the subject matter of economics.²

Thanks for your news about Sidgwick. I shall not go out of my way for him.³ And as to Edgeworth I don't much care what he does,⁴ because he does what Sidgwick does not, he enters into the spirit of the thing: & his midwifery would not be murderous.

You may be interested in the inclosed paper:[5] it will shew you how our canvass is getting on. I don't mean it as an indirect form of canvassing you.

Yours ever | A.M.

If you print your testimonials you can put any heading to mine that you like.

---

[1] Foxwell Papers. No address is given. Enclosed was the testimonial [93], dated 5 March.
[2] Edgeworth did make such a request. See [94, 95] for Marshall's response.
[3] See [90].
[4] In drawing upon Marshall's unpublished work. See [94.8].
[5] Not traced.

93. To University College, London, 5 March 1881[1]

University College, Bristol,
March 5th, 1881

Mr Foxwell is an economist of wide knowledge and of a very high order of ability, and his zeal for his subject is such that he certainly will not be content to leave it where he found it; his labours generally, but especially on the side of the history of Economic Theory, promise to have great permanent value.

He is a first-rate lecturer; his style is clear and fluent, and such as to awaken and sustain in the minds of his audience a deep interest in the subject, and a spirit of earnest inquiry. He has a very large share of that sympathy which is a chief source of the teacher's power.

He will, no doubt, provide other evidence of the eminent success which has attended the many courses of lectures he has given in different places.

He is a man of upright character, of genial disposition, and of agreeable manners; and if he should be appointed to the Chair of Political Economy at University College, London, he will, I am confident, discharge the duties of the post in such a way as to add much to the prosperity and reputation of the College.

A. Marshall

Principal of and Professor of Political Economy in University College, Bristol.

---

[1] University College, London. See [86.2]. From a printed set of Foxwell's testimonials preserved in the College archives. (Another set is in the Foxwell Papers, Kress Library, Harvard University.) The printed version differs only trivially from the manuscript original enclosed with [92] and now in the Foxwell Papers. Foxwell's other testimonials came from William Henry Bateson, Henry Sidgwick, John Venn, Thomas Edward Cliffe Leslie, James Ward, John Neville Keynes, James Stuart, and George Forrest Browne (1833–1930), archeologist and churchman, Secretary of the Cambridge Local Examinations and Lectures Syndicate.

94. To Francis Ysidro Edgeworth, 9 March 1881[1]

31 Apsley Rd., | Clifton.
9 March 1881

Dear Sir,

I have thought that I could best serve you under the circumstances by writing you a letter about your book.[2] If I had written a formal testimonial it must have been less effective than others which I have written for candidates for the same post who are known to me so intimately that I can speak of their personal qualities as well as of their knowledge of economics.[3]

If however you would prefer a testimonial, or have any other change to suggest in this letter, I will endeavour to meet your wishes.

On the question whether Walras & I discovered the theory of unstable equilibrium independently,[4] I may say that I have no doubt he did not borrow it from me; & that I could not have borrowed it from him. For I gave it in lectures even before the first edition of Prof Jevons book[5] came out; & by a lucky accident I published the central part of it in a paper of which an abstract is to be found on pp. 318–9 of Part XV [Vol. 2] of the Proceedings of the Cambridge Philosophical Society: this paper was read on Oct 20, 1873.[6] I read this 'by accident'; that is not for its own sake, but in order to explain the use of a beautiful machine for constructing a series of H^{as} with the same asymptotes that had been invented & made for me by Mr. H. H. Cunynghame.[7]

This matter is of the smallest importance, but perhaps it is as well to tell you about it. With many thanks for the great pleasure your books have given me I am yours sincerely

A Marshall

I suppose you have considered the difficulty of referring in detail to papers of mine that are not published. I fear your readers may be puzzled to know to what you refer; & so far as I have seen you have not explained. I don't think the matter is of much importance. Of course I have no objection to what you have done. I am only thinking of the possible bewilderment of your readers.[8]

---

[1] BLPES, Edgeworth Papers.

[2] F. Y. Edgeworth, *Mathematical Psychics* (Kegan Paul, London, 1881). See [95]. Edgeworth appears to have requested from Marshall a testimonial to use in applying for the vacant Professorship of Political Economy at University College, London (see [86.2]).

[3] See [91], [93].

[4] See Léon Walras, *Élemens d'Économie Politique Pure* (Corbaz, Lausanne, 1874 and 1877), leçon 7. For Marshall's earliest known treatment (*c.* 1870) of the issue see *Early Economic Writings*, vol. 1, pp. 119–59. Edgeworth, drawing on Marshall's treatment in the 'Pure Theory' chapters [59.3], tended in *Mathematical Psychics* to couple Marshall's and Walras's names coequally.

[5] W. S. Jevons, *Theory of Political Economy* [17.3].

[6] See *Early Economic Writings*, vol. 2, pp. 283–5, for the text of Marshall's abstract, 'Graphic Representation by Aid of a Series of Hyperbolas of Some Economic Problems Having Reference to Monopolies', first published in the place cited.

[7] Cunynghame's machine for drawing a family of rectangular hyperbolas (H^{as}) is not described in the *Proceedings*. It was a familiar feature of Marshall's classroom but can no longer be traced, and its principle is lost.

[8] There are several references in *Mathematical Psychics* to Marshall's privately printed 'Pure Theory' chapters [59.3]. These references are extremely cryptic and inadequate: one of many bewilderments that the baffled readers of *Mathematical Psychics* had to face.

95. To Francis Ysidro Edgeworth, 9 March 1881[1]

University College, | Bristol.
9 March 1881

Dear Sir,

I have to thank you for a copy of the proofs of your forthcoming book on 'Mathematical Psychics', from the perusal of which, as well as of your 'New & Old Methods of Ethics', I have derived the greatest pleasure. You seem to me to have gone straight to the root of the fundamental difficulties of pure economic theory; & to have dealt with them with great originality & masterly power. I trust that, as years go on, you will fully work out the important lines of thought which you have suggested; they cannot fail I think to exercise a very great influence on the growth of the science.

If you should think that this expression of my opinion can be of any service to you in connexion with your candidature for the Professorship of Political Economy at University College, London, you are at liberty to make any use of it you please.

I remain, | Dear Sir, | Yours faithfully | A. Marshall

F. Y. Edgeworth Esq.

[1] Nuffield College, Edgeworth Papers. Written to serve as a testimonial (see [94]). Edgeworth's application letter for the University College post is preserved in the College's archives.

96. To Francis Ysidro Edgeworth, (March?) 1881[1]

31, Apsley Road, | Clifton.

Dear Sir

It was on your account not on mine that I suggested that it might be worthwhile to explain what were the papers of mine to w^h.. you were referring.[2]

I have certainly no grievance: the criticism of the discussion of trades Unions in the Economics of Industry is perfectly legitimate; & though it does not convince me that I overlooked any math^l.. considerations that were material to my argument that may be my fault.[3]

I may say generally that in writing the Economics my chief difficulty was to be mathematically accurate without introducing apparently pedantic limitations

& indeed without suggesting difficulties that w^{d}.. only perplex the non-mathematical. There are many passages, particularly in the discussions on wages in Bks II & III in which a slight twist is given to the sentence in order to make it mathematically exact, or rather consistent so far as it goes with a mathematically correct statement. But in these cases I have endeavoured rather to hide than obtrude the difficulty, satisfied that harm is done by raising intricate problems in a book intended to give beginners a firm grasp of general principles. I have sometimes spent a whole day in discussing the question whether the average reader w^{d}.. be likely to see a certain difficulty: if the answer has been in the negative, I have covered the difficulty up; taking care only so to word the sentences that they shall be found on examination to be consistent with an accurate solution of the difficulty.

Yours very truly | A. Marshall

[1] BLPES, Edgeworth Papers.

[2] See [94.8].

[3] See pp. 136–7 of *Mathematical Psychics* [94.2], where the argument in book iii, ch. 6, ss. 1 and 2, of the *Economics of Industry* is criticized. Here Marshall propounds the view that 'if a rise in wages is obtained simply at the expense of profits . . . it must be self-destructive in the long run' by choking off capital accumulation (pp. 201–2). Edgeworth's criticisms defy summary, but amount to arguing that if contracts between employers as a whole and employees as a whole are viewed as the outcome of rational agreements between the two contractors then, (i) both sides must gain in terms of utility, (ii) the outcome will be indeterminate within limits.

97. To Francis Ysidro Edgeworth, 29 March 1881[1]

University College | Bristol
29 March

Dear Sir

The indeterminateness of the labour problem when there is an efficient combination on one or on both sides is a question on which I have thought a great deal. I have written a little[2] about it in the introductory chapter to those papers which Mr Sidgwick printed. If I had known that those papers would have been read by any but old pupils of mine I should have asked him to consult me as to the chapters which he selected for printing & shd have requested him not to omit the introductory chapter.[3] As it is, I prefer putting off what I have to say till the book on which I am at present engaged is ready: in fact I get so little time for work of my own that my only chance of getting on at all is to give all that little time to just those questions on which I am writing at the moment. You will however, if you read carefully between the lines, see a recognition of the difficulty in p 200 & in the first half of p 210 of the Economics of Industry.[4] I deliberated a good deal as to whether I w^{d}.. go into the matter further: but decided that as the problem was for the most part of speculative rather than practical interest, I could not give up a great space to it then: & as I have said my wife & I were very anxious not to start difficulties w^h.. we had not space to solve.

Your letter was directed right; but by a mistake of the officials it was sent to another post office & then sent back to Bristol. I found it awaiting me at College this morning; I have not your paper or book by me; but as I shall not have time to write to you this evening, I send off this letter at once.

Thanking you again for your paper & book
I am | Yours sincerely | A Marshall

I suppose you have heard that Keynes has decided not to be a candidate for the Professorship at Univ Coll Lond.[5]

---

[1] BLPES, Edgeworth Papers.
[2] 'A little' is an alteration from 'a good deal'.
[3] The surviving portions of the intended introductory chapter to Marshall's *Pure Theory* [59.3], a chapter not printed by Sidgwick, are reproduced in *Early Economic Writings*, vol. 2, pp. 117–28. There Marshall attempts to draw out 'the close analogy which the politico-commercial relations which exist between two organised industrial groups bear to those which exist between two nations' (p. 125).
[4] On p. 200 of the *Economics of Industry* it is recognized that collusion of buyers, or the particular form of an auction, might influence the price a seller receives. On p. 210 it is observed that 'the immediate issue of any trade conflict . . . [may] depend on the character and the personal relations of those who play a leading part in it, and upon a variety of other accidents, much more than upon the action of the Laws of Normal wages and profits'.
[5] See [90.2].

98. To Herbert Somerton Foxwell, 23 May 1881[1]

31, Apsley Road, | Clifton.
23 May 1881

My dear Foxwell,

I am immensely glad they have elected you.[2]

I can now speak more freely about Edgeworth. His book though it shewed great vigour, yet on the whole disappointed me. I looked at it hastily before writing him a testimonial, & lately I have read it—or at least such parts of it as I can understand—more carefully in order to review it in the Academy—I don't know whether the review has appeared yet.[3]

It is less economic, & more abstract than I had hoped & my last reading of it made me like it perhaps rather less than my first. When I saw the book, I concluded that he had no chance.[4] I thought him an infinitely young man who w^d.. be a strong competitor some day when he had studied the Real Oekonomie. But I was flabbergasted at hearing from Jowett last week that he is 40 years old.[5] Don't repeat all this even now: Ive given you scandal instead of butter: I believe I have judged your tastes rightly at all events with regard to the dislike of butter.

Yours devotedly for ever | A Marshall

My wife sends most hearty greetings.
I don't mean to hint that you like evil-speaking: I know you don't.
I am getting much stronger.

[1] Foxwell Papers.
[2] As Professor of Political Economy at University College, London. See [86, 92, 93].
[3] Marshall's review of *Mathematical Psychics* [94.2] appeared in the *Academy*, 1 April 1882. It is reproduced in *Early Economic Writings*, vol. 2, pp. 265–9. This and the 1872 review of Jevons's *Theory of Political Economy* [17.3] were the only book reviews Marshall ever wrote: but see [18.2].
[4] For Foxwell's new post?
[5] Edgeworth had read 'Greats' at Balliol under Jowett in the late 1860s.

99. To the Council, University College Bristol, 11 July 1881[1]

To the Council of
University College, Bristol.   11th. July 81.

Gentlemen,

I have long known that I am not strong enough for my present post: but I have felt bound to wait for an opportunity at which I could leave without damage to the College. That opportunity has, I think, at length arrived.

The part of my work which lies within the walls of the College presents no difficulty: but all the external work is extremely burdensome to me. I do it at a greater cost than almost anyone else would; even those social duties which would be simply an agreeable recreation to a man in good health cause me great fatigue. The result is that while on the one hand I am almost entirely neglecting studies which I am most anxious to pursue, I am on the other unable to push the interests of the College outside its walls with anything like the energy with which they could be pushed by a stronger man.

The internal organization of the College is on a basis, which, if not perfectly satisfactory, may yet serve for some years without much change. The internal work of the Principal has thus arrived at a convenient halting stage; while there is just now the most urgent need for that external work which I am not able to do properly.

I find an additional reason for thinking that this is a favourable time for retiring from my post in my belief that you have a staff of exceptional ability; and that you will have no difficulty in selecting from them, should you desire it, a Principal who will carry on the work of the College without any breach of continuity, and with much greater chance of success than I could have had.[2]

Everything that could be done by yourselves or the Staff to make my post pleasant, has been done; and I shall always feel that I owe my hearty apologies to the College for having entered upon duties which I was not strong enough to discharge. It is my one consolation with regard to the past that in all directions in which her influence could reach, my wife has more than made up for my deficiencies; and it is my chief regret with regard to the future that her work must be lost to the College.

It is with feelings of deep gratitude for the most generous and considerate treatment which I have always received at your hands, that I ask your kind permission to retire from my present position (as Principal and as Professor of Political Economy) in three months from this time.

I am, Gentlemen, your most obliged servant, | Alfred Marshall.

Copy of resolution of Council of U.C.B.[3]

'That in accepting with very great regret the resignation of Professor of Political Economy, the Council desires to record its high appreciation of the great ability, energy & devotion to the interests of the College displayed by him & M^{rs}. Marshall during the whole period of their connection with the Institution, & to express the heartiest wishes for their future welfare, & especially for the restoration of Professor Marshall's health.'

18th. July 1881

---

[1] A duplicated letter. There is a signed copy in the minute book of University College, Bristol (Bristol University Archives) and another copy (enclosed with [100]) in the Foxwell Papers.

[2] William Ramsay had joined the staff in 1880. He had seemed to Marshall an obvious successor as Principal and was to be so appointed. A detailed account from Ramsay's viewpoint is given in Morris William Travers, *A Life of Sir William Ramsay* (Arnold, London, 1956), chs. 4, 5.

[3] Added in Mary Marshall's hand to the copy sent to Foxwell.

100. To Herbert Somerton Foxwell, 24 July 1881[1]

At Mrs Stone's, Sprat Cove,
Salcombe, Kingsbridge, S Devon

My dear Foxwell,

I have resigned my post at Bristol, the letter of which I inclose a copy will tell you the chief reasons why.[2] It is the state of the finances of the College which renders the external work so imperative just now: that work I simply cannot do thoroughly well, even if I give my whole strength to it, & never open a book for study; half a days racketing about, which w^{d}.. not tire a strong man at all, makes me not only unhappy but also to a great extent useless for the rest of the day, & very often for the next day or two. I could go on with the internal work, if there were any use in that alone. But so far as organisation goes, there is nothing to be done; everything that can be done without increasing our expenditure is done; the scheme for associateships which is now ready for formal adoption completes our organisation:[3] & there is no great use in looking after the students & making them want to come to the College, while one is neglecting the external work which is necessary to enable them to have a College to come to. Also the College has just now the opportunity of putting a first rate man in my place.[4] A stranger coming from a distance c^d.. hardly do the work well: & I have not felt sure until now that if I resigned they w^d.. be able to get the right sort of man to go on. So when I was told that I sh^d.. imperil the future of the College if I resigned, I thought I ought to stay at my post at whatever cost to myself. Now it is different. It is indeed thought best that I sh^d.. abstain from indicating my successor by anything more than an unofficial expression of opinion, but I have practically no doubt as to what the Council will do. And anyhow the fact that they have at hand a man with a fair amount of local knowledge, who I think w^d.. make a better Principal for a College, in which external work is of primary importance, than any man of this age I have ever known, except Stuart[5]—this fact makes me feel that on the whole I am doing the College a service by resigning. The argument that by going I inflict an irreparable injury on the woman's side of the College, remains as strong as ever. But to repeat—what is the use of my wife's making women want to come to the College, if I can't do what is necessary to enable them to have a College to come to?

You will be curious as to our future. Of course if any post turns up that w^d.. suit us well, we shall run for it: but unless anything striking of this kind turns up, we are going to take a two years holiday. We shall let our house furnished & go to live in winter at all events about ten miles out of London in lodgings. My wife will have a season ticket to London: but I shall remain almost motionless: except perhaps occasionally when I go [to][6] the Statistical Societies Library or something of the sort. When I am in the country & can get as much fresh air as I want without going more than a few yards from the door, I can do a reasonable amount of work without pain or inconvenience of any sort: & by keeping quiet for a couple of years I no doubt shall get my wounds into a healthier state. I have not given them a fair chance yet.

I sh^d.. have liked to go on with the Economics of Trade & Government;[7] because it will be such a good opportunity for Mary & me to work together. But I suppose I must do my economic theory first: & she will help in that. We have a good many dreams of what we are going to do in these two years in the way of economic inductions: but very likely we shan't really manage much of this sort.

We are now writing under a rock, as it happens to be raining, she to Mrs Wright[8] & I to you: before us there is a thick wood of high rich trees sloping right down to the sea & almost hiding it from our sight. As soon as the shower is over we shall go to a break in the wood, & look out on what we think is the most beautiful sea coast view in England.

We are at present living in a labourers cottage our two rooms are 9 1/4 × 7 ft,

& 9 1/4 ft square respectively: but of course we are never in doors except for meals & at night; & then we have the windows wide open. We are for the first time for a very long while supremely happy, & free from anxiety. Also we are looking forward to a speedy promotion. For—though there is a little more work to be done in Bristol before we are clear of it—we expect before very long to have lodgings in a farm house: & after lodging in a labourers cottage we shall then feel that we have taken a step upwards in the world.

I ought to have told you that we are preparing a 2nd Edition of the Economics of Industry. We can't make many changes, because it is stereotyped: but we are making a few & writing a new preface: getting meanwhile much help from your corrections & notes.[9]

Yours, on behalf my Mary & myself, | eternally | A Marshall

[1] Foxwell Papers. Envelope postmarked 'JY 25 81' when forwarded from Weston-super-Mare to Foxwell who was in Switzerland.

[2] See [99].

[3] The College was not empowered to award degrees. Associateships were to recognize successful completion of a specified course of study.

[4] See [99.2].

[5] Professor James Stuart of Cambridge.

[6] Word apparently omitted.

[7] The proposed continuation of the *Economics of Industry*.

[8] Probably Mrs Richard Thomas Wright (née Mary Kennedy) who had been a fellow-student of Mary Marshall at Newnham. See [7.2]. Her husband was a Fellow of Christ's.

[9] The additional Preface to the second edition of the *Economics of Industry* is dated August 1881. The changes in the text are quite minor.

101. To Alexander Macmillan, 30 July 1881[1]

30 July 1881 | at M[rs] Stones
Sprat Cove | Salcombe, Kingsbridge | S. Devon

Dear Mr Macmillan

We have managed, we think, so as to give the printer very little trouble in altering the plates for the Economics of Industry. Our new preface will go into four pages, at all events if the type is pretty close; & we have cleared two pages by cutting out the old preface, & the note facing the beginning of the text: these two with the two blank pages there already can suffice: the only change of pagination in the book will be that the table of contents will now run from p ix to xvi instead of from p viii to xiv.[2]

There are in addition to the new preface about half a dozen considerable changes: but when there has been no blank space to afford a margin we have calculated for taking up just as many lines as we have cut out; so as not to [let][3] the disturbance run beyond the paragraphs changed.

Most of the alterations are only of one or two words; & in these cases we have taken care that those which we insert have just as many letters as those which we cut out.

I have just resigned my post at Bristol; it is what I have intended to do for a long time at the first convenient opportunity. The work of organizing the College is now done. It has a staff inferior in ability to no College of the kind, it offers a sound curriculum in the Arts & Science, & it has more than 500 students. So that there is no very pressing work to be done by a Principal sitting in his room in the College. What is wanted now is an active man who can go about the town, attend meetings, dinner parties &c; & manage, without directly canvassing for funds, to interest the rich Bristol Citizens in the College. That is what I cannot do. I am almost unconscious of my illness so long as I sit still & work moderately: but the smallest physical exertion upsets me: even going out to dinner is a great strain to me. So I have at last succeeded in convincing the best friends of the College that I am morally justified in resigning: & I am now free. Ultimately I shall probably take to some kind of teaching work again. But for the next two years or so, unless any special reason to the contrary turns up, I am going to take a holiday, & do nothing but reading & writing.

I am now sitting in an armchair looking through a wood on the wonderful coastline of Prawle point: My wife joins me in kind regards.

Yours very sincerely | A Marshall

[1] British Library, Macmillan Archive.
[2] In fact the old preface was retained.
[3] Word apparently omitted.

102. From Benjamin Jowett, 9 August 1881[1]

West Malvern
Aug 9. 1881.

Dear Professor Marshall,

I greatly lament the loss which Clifton sustains by the departure of you & Mrs Marshall.

Will you not consider the possibility of your both coming back to us as Professors of Political Economy?

I am afraid that it is impossible for us to get the 200£ which the College has hitherto given[2] continued under the embarrassed circumstance of our College funds at present. But I think it would be possible to get you elected a Fellow[3] as soon as the New Statutes come into operation. (The Fellowship is worth 200 a year.) I am not certain about this, but I should try it if I had your consent, and no doubt it would be warmly supported by H. Smith.[4]

You might receive the fees or a part of them in addition & I do not think that the residence required[5] need be more than 4 or 5 months so as to give you an almost interminable Long Vacation.

I believe that you would find Clifton or Bristol nearly as good a sphere as you could have: & I am sure that M^{rs}. Marshall would never find a better than that in which she has been already so useful & so distinguished.

Will you consider this proposal and not lightly put it aside?

It might have been better diplomacy to put off broaching the subject to you for six months—But I thought on the other hand that it might be more convenient to you to know of it beforehand, in case you should wish to make arrangements respecting your house. I have not spoken to any one but Mr Budd & our friend Wilson[6] respecting it, who warmly approve.

I hope that you are enjoying your holiday.

I should not propose that you returned to Clifton until Christmas in any case, or later if you preferred.

With kindest regards to M^{rs}. Marshall

Ever yours truly | B Jowett

---

[1] Marshall Papers.

[2] The professorial stipend, as distinct from that of the Principalship, hitherto paid to Marshall by University College, Bristol.

[3] Presumably as non-resident Fellow of an Oxford College, probably Balliol. Like Cambridge, Oxford University was drawing to the close of a period of statutory reform. See W. R. Ward, *Victorian Oxford* (Barnes and Noble, New York, 1965), ch. 13.

[4] Henry John Stephen Smith (1826–83), Professor of Geometry at Oxford, sometime Fellow and Lecturer of Balliol. Smith, like Jowett, was a prominent member of the Council of University College, Bristol, and sometimes stayed with the Marshalls.

[5] In Bristol?

[6] Francis Nonus Budd [65.4], and James Maurice Wilson (1836–1931), headmaster of Clifton College from 1879 to 1890. Wilson had been Senior Wrangler in 1859 and a Fellow of St John's College.

103. From Benjamin Jowett, 21 August 1881[1]

Dear Professor Marshall

I am glad that you have not set aside my hypothetical proposal[2] without consideration. No need to send an answer until about Oct. 12.

The point to which you refer about the payment does not seem important: Surely 200£ a year cannot be too much for the Lectures of yourself & M^{rs}. Marshall, [the][3] proportion of fees might be fixed by Council.[4]

There is another matter to which I should like to call your attention. The Professor of Political Economy at Oxford[5] is an old man, although wiry & energetic (about 76). He cannot hold out much longer. And I should think that you would have a stronger claim than any one else who is likely to be a Candidate. This may draw your thoughts towards Oxford.

The possible antagonism with M[rs]. Ramsay[6] seems to me imaginary. I do not believe that any body can quarrell with M[rs]. Marshall.

Ever yours truly | B Jowett

West Malvern until Aug. 30 | afterwards   Oxford
Aug. 21

[1] Marshall Papers.
[2] See [102.3]. Marshall's reply to Jowett's proposal has not been preserved.
[3] Word apparently omitted.
[4] That is, the Council of University College, Bristol, might fix the proportion of fees paid by students in political economy classes that was to be received by the Professor as remuneration.
[5] Bonamy Price, who was born in 1807 and had been Drummond Professor at Oxford since 1868.
[6] The wife of Marshall's successor as Principal: see [99.2].

104. From James Maurice Wilson to Mary Paley Marshall, 29 September 1881[1]

Clifton College | Clifton, Bristol.
Sep. 29/81

Dear M[rs] Marshall,

Your joint present has given me very great pleasure. We need no reminder of you; nevertheless it will often speak to us.

Edith[2] has come back full of the address:[3] it has done her good to the back bone: & will be a help to nobleness of life & true public spirit to all who read it.

I have not got ye gift of expressing myself freely either by word or letter. And so I cannot define & express ye very great gain & help your joint friendship has been to me (among hundreds more). But now yt you are going I cannot help saying something.

I preached a sermon a little while ago whereof ye burden was yt Religion was the caring much & caring always for doing one's duty, & yt all yt we commonly call religion was but accessory to this end. And no one has been of late years such a religious teacher to me as ye late Principal of Univ. Coll. Whether he finds help for his life where I do I know not, & it is a matter of secondary importance. In what is primary he has long been my master. I most earnestly hope yt he will have health & strength to continue his work. He has certainly filled his life with great interests.

You have been told often enough yt you will both leave a terrible gap. What I would rather say[4] is yt I hope both his pupils & yours (I am in both classes) will not forget what they have learnt, & yt you will be multiplied manifold in some small reflected lights: & yt others will grow up. There are many who are ye clearer & stronger in their life for having known you, & we shall not lose all this ye moment you go. Rather we shall be on our mettle.

This is poor stuff I am writing after all. But I have been occupied all ye ev[g]. & I am so tired now yt I can scarcely hold a pen.

If I can I shall come and shake hands about 11: not more.

Ever y^{rs} affec^{ntly} | J M Wilson

[1] Marshall Papers. For Wilson see [102.6].

[2] A sister of the letter writer who was a widower at this time, Edith Wilson had been a student of Mary Marshall at the College.

[3] Marshall gave a farewell address at the College in the evening of 29 September. *Memorials*, p. 16, quotes 'some notes taken at the farewell address', but their source remains a mystery. There was an extensive press report of the meeting in the *Western Daily Press*, 30 September 1881. This report included the text of an address to Marshall signed by some 80 students which reads as follows (the original is in the Marshall Papers):

> Dear Sir,—We, the Political Economy students of University College, Bristol, having heard with keen regret that you have resigned your offices of Principal of the College and Professor of Political Economy, take this means of expressing to you our deep sense of the great loss which the College generally, and its Political Economy students specially, will sustain through your resignation, and we are sure that this sense of loss will be shared by all who are interested in the progress of education in Bristol and its neighbourhood. We feel that our College has been most fortunate in having had for its first Principal one so zealous and devoted in its service as you have been, and we cannot omit to notice how admirably your work in Bristol has been supplemented by Mrs Marshall. We are certain that very much of the success which has attended the operations of the College hitherto has been due to the most valuable and indefatigable services of yourself and Mrs Marshall in promoting its interests in many ways. But it is of course in connection with your own special branch of the College studies that we feel most deeply the great loss which will be occasioned by your resignation. We wish gratefully to bear witness to the deep interest with which we have attended your lectures and classes. We have felt the great advantage of studying this most wide-reaching, important, and interesting science of Political Economy under one who is at once so completely its master and so enthusiastically devoted to it as you are. We shall never forget the very pleasant hours which we have spent with you over this most interesting study, and we are sorry indeed to think that we can no longer look forward to a renewal of these pleasant meetings with you. We shall, however, continue to be reminded of your connection with our College by your admirable work on 'The Economics of Industry'. In conclusion, we desire heartily to wish you and Mrs Marshall many years of pleasant labour in the cause of education, and especially in further prosecution of that branch of scientific research with which you and she are so specially identified, and in order that this may be so we earnestly trust that the rest which you propose now to take may restore you to complete and permanent health.   Bristol, 26th September, 1881.

[4] Followed in the original by 'yt' (i.e. 'that').

105. To Francis Ysidro Edgeworth, 1 October 1881[1]

> 31, Apsley Road, | Clifton.
> 1 Oct 1881

My dear Edgeworth,

I write from Paris. I am on my way to spend the winter in Palermo (address for some time Poste Restante Palermo).

I have long wanted to resign & have at last got leave on the ground that the internal organization of the College is practically complete & that the external work which is now the chief duty of the Principal requires great physical strength.

I am better than I was.

Wishing you well, I am, | Yours sincerely | A. Marshall

---

[1] BLPES, Edgeworth Papers. Apparently a covering letter for [106].

106. To Francis Ysidro Edgeworth, 1 October 1881[1]

1 Oct 1881

Dear Sir,

I have derived very great pleasure from reading your 'Mathematical Psychics' & your 'Old & New Methods of Ethics.'[2] You seem to me [to][3] have shewn originality & power of the highest order in handling some of the fundamental difficulties of the Pure Theories of Ethics & Economics. Should you succeed in fully working out the lines of thought which you have suggested, you will, I think, exercise a lasting influence on the growth of these sciences. You are at liberty to make any use you please of this letter.

Yours very truly | A. Marshall

Late Principal of University College, Bristol.
F. Y. Edgeworth Esq.

---

[1] Nuffield College, Edgeworth Papers. A general-purpose testimonial probably supplied for the immediate occasion of Edgeworth's unsuccessful application for the Professorship in Logic, Mental and Moral Philosophy at the newly founded University College, Liverpool. A testimonial for this post had been supplied to Edgeworth by Jevons on 21 September. See *WSJ*, vol. 5, p. 145.
[2] See [94.2], [80.4].
[3] Word apparently omitted.

107. To Herbert Somerton Foxwell, 10 October 1881[1]

Palermo
Address for the present | Poste Restante
10 Oct 1881

My dear Foxwell,

We arrived here yesterday after a roughish passage across the Mediterranean: but wonderfully well. It is a charming place: far more lovely than we had thought: though the beauty is not quite of the kind we had imagined. Until yesterday it had not rained here for 8 months—this is very unusual, they generally have some rain here in late spring. So everything is very parched up: they say the country is generally at its best about December. But even then we shan't get as much as we had hoped from the gardens & the foliage of the surrounding country. For the gardens are almost all inclosed in mud walls ten feet high; & the neighbouring country consists chiefly of rocky mountains which at present at least look as though no green thing ever lived on them, unless in a few scattered patches.

But the beauty of the mountains is almost beyond imagination by the eye that hath not seen. For their forms are most beautiful, & most various, full of the play of light & shade, of near distance, & middle distance & far distance; & rich with an endless change of full deep colours: white, red & orange are the predominant colours: but deep blues often come out in the shadows, & in spite of the drought there is even now sometimes a faint suspicion of green.

But the town is even more wonderful than the mountains: though it is true that picturesqueness of the streets is often much in debt to a peep at a mountain through the long vista of balconies on either side of the street. Of course we have not explored nearly all the town yet: but we have done a good deal by dint of taking an air cushion to the nearest tram, sitting there till it got to the end of its journey & still sitting till it got back again to some other line of trams, then getting on that & sitting that out in like manner. And I think we have already seen twenty times as many picturesque bits as I have seen in any other town. It is not only that the colour is rich: but it is generally in excellent taste. At Marseilles, there was a good deal of colour: but for the greater part it was simply loathesome. But here the Saracenic genius pervades everything; & the combinations are generally exquisite. In two or three shop windows in the chief street of the town we saw a dozen blankets for beds—something like the 'Austrian' blankets: but each of them more beautiful than any blankets we had ever seen.

We sent off our second edition of the Economics to Clay[2]—I mean the last revise of it about six weeks ago. But I suppose McMillan will not have any printed till it suits his convenience to do so. We have tried to meet as many as possible of the objections raised: & I hope you will be satisfied on the whole. It was of course impossible to alter the arrangement of Book II: so we never went thoroughly into the question whether we sh^d.. do so if we could. Perhaps we should: but it seems doubtful whether the objections that there undoubtedly are to our order w^d.. not be balanced by at least as strong objections to any other order that has been proposed. There is only one set of objections the validity of which we unhesitatingly admit but which we [have][3] not been able to pay any attention to. That is the set relating to the titles of Chaps III, IV & V of Bk II. If it w^d.. not have upset so many stereotyped plates we shd have altered the wording of these titles.[4]

We do not feel any doubt as to the exclusion of Rent from Distribution, whether the term is used as it is by Mill, or as it is in the 'Economics'. In Mill's sense, we think Land Tenure belongs to Distribution, but the Ricardian theory of rent—a mere dry algebraical formula—to the 'Mechanism of Exchange'.[5]

'Normal' is certainly not a satisfactory word: but after hundreds of hours thinking on the subject we cannot find a better. We do not think any harm is done by excluding monopoly values; Because a monopoly is itself an accident.

You propose 'competition' value, in lieu of Normal value in our sense. But surely the value of corn in Mark Lane on say Oct 10th.. 1881 is a Competition value. However our views on this point are incidentally explained a little more fully in our new preface. Again 'Market value' is a term we dislike: but we dislike a great deal more any of its rivals.

I should not have been a candidate for the Examinership at London this year even if I had been in England: because I think that it w^d.. be almost a scandal to have two Cambridge men examining together.[6] If I were an elector, I w^d.. not vote for a second Cambridge examiner, unless it happened that there were no one else in the field that w^d.. do at all. Nothing could be more pleasant to me than to examine with you: but this is a strong reason, I think, against my doing so. If all goes well, I shall strive for the high honour of succeeding you. I know that both the Math^l.. Examiners at London have been Cantabs: but that is quite a different thing. Still I am very grateful to you for thinking of me: the objection of having two Cantabs did not occur to me at first: but when it did occur it seemed insuperable.

Our plans for the future are vague. If nothing turns up to the contrary we shall stay here till March or April, then move slowly up to Germany via Florence & Venice & perhaps Naples & Rome. We propose to spend the summer in Germany; & then settle down near London. We are making no plans as to what we shall do in London. In a year something else may turn up: in fact one thing has flittered rather as though it were going to turn up.[7]

Meanwhile I am going on with 'Economic Theory'—including some curves, but making them as little prominent as possible. My wife who has never had a proper holiday since her 'degree', will have a good spell at reading. We are having about 7 cwt of books sent round by sea.

We are going to have the Times & the Economist here—I am getting to value the Times more & more every day as material for economic work—but we shall hear probably little Cambridge or Economic gossip except what we hear from him who has the most rare & valuable gift of knowing how to gossip just the right things: need I say that his initials are HSF!

Greet heartily all friends: my wife joins her greetings to mine for all Cambridge friends; & most especially for our great & good gossip.

Yours most sincerely | A. Marshall

The kindness people have shewn us as individuals & in their corporate capacities on leaving Clifton has been astonishing. My wife has realized all sorts of things including £113.18 subscribed by members of the Council: but most of this she will spend on books for the College Library.[8]

---

[1] Foxwell Papers.
[2] See [66.1].
[3] Word apparently omitted.

4 The titles are, respectively, 'Rent', 'Rent in Relation to Value', and 'Influence of Demand on Value'.

5 Distribution in both J. S. Mill's *Principles* and the Marshalls' *Economics of Industry* focuses on the question of distributing the output of marginal land between labor and capital, rent to infra-marginal land being viewed as a surplus. Mill considers distribution as dependent on whatever laws and institutions are actually present. The Marshalls consider distribution under hypothetical long-run competitive equilibrium, that is, under 'normal' conditions.

6 At this time London University was essentially nothing but an examining body. Examiners were appointed after open solicitation for applications. See *University of London: The Historical Record 1836–1912* (University of London Press, London, 1912).

7 Probably an allusion to Jowett's proposal, see [102], [103]. As the letters reproduced in Appendix III show, Foxwell was at this time unsuccessfully attempting to secure for Marshall a position at St John's College.

8 The bookcase bought to house this gift still survives, but the books are dispersed. The sum mentioned is presumably £113 18s. 0d.

108. To Charles Francis Bastable, 15 December 1881[1]

Hotel S Oliva
Palermo   15 Dec 81

Sir,

I send you a copy of my paper on 'Domestic Value'.[2] It is not an independent essay, but a fragment of an appendix of the first draft of a treatise which I began to write on Foreign Trade. It was printed with my consent, but without my supervision from the M.S.S. which ill health & other causes had made me lay on one side.

I am now taking a holiday, & am spending it in rewriting the appendix in question with some other matter, to be published as a separate book.

I have no spare copy of my paper on international trade, which is a fragment taken out of another part of the same appendix. There were not many copies printed & none of them are to be sold. In fact I am rather ashamed of their being seen at all by any but the few pupils & friends for whom they were first printed.

Yours truly | A Marshall

1 Trinity College, Dublin, Bastable Papers.
2 See [59.3].

109. To Francis Ysidro Edgeworth, 12 September 1882[1]

Ladbroke, Chine Crescent | Bournemouth
12 Sep 82

My dear Edgeworth,

Will you kindly forgive me if I do not give a proper answer to your interesting letter.[2] Life is short, & controversy is so long; that I shrink from it with dread.

I cannot see that you disprove the statement on the top of p 86 of the 'Economics'; it seems to me that you only say that it is not proved.[3] It is now more than 14 years, I think it is nearly 16 years, since I first wrote what is, I think, a rigid & complete geometrical proof of the proposition.[4] That proof has been gone over by a great number of people: & I must venture still to hold that it is valid.

I sometimes wish that I had published before Jevons' book[5] came out: as I did not, I determined to put off publishing till I could do so with satisfaction to myself; and as the cruel fates wd. have it, I did hardly any new work at economic curves between 1872 and 1881. Now I am going on again on a slow job trot: I hope to publish my justification in the course of two or three years.

I am writing as I generally do in fine weather, on the cliffs. The colour here is very good: large masses of heather both pink & red, of bright yellow gorse, with deep orange sandstone cliffs & the blue sea make a combination that w^d.. be almost too garish if it were indoors: but I think that nature out of doors can't overdo herself.

My wife sends very kind regards
Yours very sincerely | A Marshall

The next time I am making any stay in London I will let you know. But I have only spent about 5 days there in the last 5 years. I have a feeling that I ought to attend some of the Statistical Societies meetings, but I don't know if I shall manage it.[6]

[1] BLPES, Edgeworth Papers.

[2] Not preserved.

[3] The passage in question argues that an improvement in the 'arts of cultivation' may lower the total 'corn rents' received by landlords and will lower their total 'money rents', but that these rents will rise in the long run once the population response is allowed for. The nature of Edgeworth's objections can only be surmised.

[4] For Marshall's early manuscripts on the topic see *Early Economic Writings*, vol. 1, pp. 224–60.

[5] *Theory of Political Economy* [17.3].

[6] The Marshalls were to recommence teaching at Bristol in October.

110. To Herbert Somerton Foxwell, 19 January 1883[1]

31 Apsley Road | 19 Jan 83

My dear Foxwell

I hope it will be decided to complete Jevons diagrams, at all events in cases in w^h.. there is no doubt as to the figures w^h he w^d.. have used in completing them.[2] In an age in which 'quack-statistics' are frequently appearing it is I think very important to preserve & make as prominent as possible all really good work. Jevons wrote so conscientiously with so much careful preparation, & with such good judgment that I used to care for his statistical work more than for that of almost any one else

You speak of a notion of postponing his Financial to his Social essays.³ On such matters I shd say Macmillan is the best judge that can be got: & I am afraid of giving an opinion. But as you ask for one, I will say that I think it is a great advantage to bring out everything at the same time. If one half comes out first, I fancy people think they will wait till the other half comes out: & by that time the whole thing is a little stale. I think that from the point of view of both the reviewer & the private reader, there is great advantage in seeing all sides of a man at once. I think many people will be surprised at finding how important Jevons social essays are, when they come to be collected: but I don't think their full importance will be seen unless they are looked at in connection with his views on applied economics. For my part I w^d.. rather delay the more forward half than publish one part without the other.

Yours very sincerely | A Marshall

P.S. As a compromise the diagrams might be followed by a 1/2 page of statistics in a footnote bringing the figures up to date: this could be done cheaply & quickly.

I think there w^d.. be danger in continuing Jevons tables of prices in his 1865 paper⁴ unless you have much fuller information than is published of the way in w^h.. he got at them. e.g. his results differ much from those of the Economist (for a different set of commodities) for the years 60–5.

Also if the continuation of the diagrams w^d.. prima facie contradict any of the new work you are going to publish of his there ought to be something to be said against putting the figures in. If he had lived he w^d.. no doubt have continued the figures: but then he w^d.. have explained away the apparent contradiction by supplementing his theory or in some other way.

Thanks for the note about Eden.⁵ It had occurred to me that Eden may rise in price: so I am rather tempted to buy it. I will go over the copy I have here when I can get time & perhaps write to Maggs⁶ for it.

¹ Marshall Papers.

² Foxwell was editing Jevons's writings on currency, finance and commercial fluctuations at the request of Jevons's widow, Harriet Ann Jevons. These writings included many statistical diagrams. The edition eventually appeared as W. S. Jevons (ed. H. S. Foxwell), *Investigations in Currency and Finance* (Macmillan, London, 1884). For details see Rosamond Könekamp, 'The Work of Harriet Ann Jevons (1838–1910) After her Husband's Death', *Manchester School*, 50 (December 1982), pp. 379–411.

³ Jevons's 'social essays' were edited by Harriet A. Jevons and appeared as *Methods of Social Reform and Other Papers* (Macmillan, London, 1883). The expectation had been that Foxwell would complete his editing rapidly, much of the necessary work having already been performed by Jevons himself. But there ensued the first, and far from worst, of Foxwell's characteristic procrastinations.

⁴ W. S. Jevons, 'On the Variation of Prices, and the Value of the Currency Since 1782', *Journal of the [London] Statistical Society*, 28 (June 1865), pp. 294–320, reproduced in *Investigations*, pp. 119–50. Jevons's figures were not extended beyond 1865.

[5] Probably Frederick Morton Eden, *The State of the Poor* . . . (White, London, 1797) which is referred to several times in Marshall's *Principles*.

[6] Uriah Maggs, a London rare-book dealer with whom Foxwell dealt considerably. The business subsequently became the famous antiquarian firm of Maggs Brothers.

111. To Herbert Somerton Foxwell, 22 January 1883[1]

22 Jan 83

My dear Foxwell,

I had unfortunately spent a good part of Sunday afternoon in looking over Eden again & had written by Sunday nights post to Maggs asking him to let me have it.[2] I have now written to say that I w^d. prefer not being held to the purchase. If you dont hear to the contrary assume that he lets me off.

I shd like to have Malthus def^{ms}..[3] but am in no hurry for them. As to Hamilton on the National debt.[4] I am not particularly interested in the subject; & have already a huge amount of printed matter relating to it. So I think I will decline with thanks.

[1] Marshall Papers.

[2] See [110.5, 6].

[3] T. R. Malthus, *Definitions in Political Economy* (Murray, London, 1827).

[4] Presumably Alexander Hamilton, *Report on the Public Credit* (1790, 1795); *Report on a National Bank* (1790). These famous State Papers are reproduced in Alexander Hamilton, *Papers on Public Credit, Commerce and Finance*, ed. Samuel McKee Jr. (Columbia University Press, New York, 1934).

112. To Herbert Somerton Foxwell, 1 February 1883[1]

My wife is lecturing on A. Smith. She has just read Jevons on Cantillon,[2] & finds life insupportable till she has read him. I think you said you had a copy of him to dispose of. If so please let me have it; & Malthus' Definitions[3] at the same time. We forgot to give you your Sicilian plate when you were here.[4]

Yours ever | A.M.

[1] Marshall Papers. Postcard postmarked 'Clifton FE 1 83'.

[2] W. S. Jevons, 'Richard Cantillon and the Nationality of Political Economy', *Contemporary Review*, 39 (January 1881), pp. 20–7. Richard Cantillon, *Essai sur la Nature du Commerce en Général* (London, 1755).

[3] See [111.3].

[4] Presumably a gift brought from Palermo.

113. To Herbert Somerton Foxwell, 9 February 1883[1]

Don't vex yourself about Cantillon.[2] I sh^d.. not read it myself just now, if I had it. It is altogether outside my present line of work. Only Mary is going in for the history of economic theory in connection with Group D,[3] & was fascinated by what Jevons said of him. If we come to Cambridge at Easter, no doubt she will borrow the book & read some of it. On no account send it by railway. When I wrote I did not know the book was so precious; though now I think of it, I ought to have known.

I am in for 3 lectures in a workmans quarter of Bristol on Progress & Poverty.[4] I intend to avoid talking very much about George: but to discuss his subject.

Yours | A.M.

[1] Marshall Papers. Postcard, postmarked 'Clifton FE 9 83'.
[2] See [112.2].
[3] The Cambridge Higher Local Examinations were sat by some of the women taught by the Marshalls at University College, Bristol. At this time Group D covered Political Economy, Logic and Constitutional History (*Reporter*, November 2 1880, p. 97).
[4] Henry George's ideas on land nationalization, put forward in his *Progress and Poverty* (Lovell, New York, 1879) were causing quite a stir at the time. Marshall's lectures on the subject were delivered in the St Phillips Vestry Hall, Pennywell Road, Bristol, on 19 and 26 February and 3 March 1883. They were part of a largely unsuccessful attempt to interest the working classes in the new University College. Press reports of Marshall's lectures are reproduced in George J. Stigler and Ronald H. Coase, 'Alfred Marshall's Lectures on Progress and Poverty', *Journal of Law and Economics*, 12 (April 1969), pp. 118–226. Also included is the report of an unruly meeting in Oxford on 15 March 1884 where George and Marshall met face to face. For general background see Elwood P. Lawrence, *Henry George in the British Isles* (Michigan State University Press, East Lansing, 1957).

114. To Herbert Somerton Foxwell, 15 February 1883[1]

31 Apsley Road
15 Feb

My dear Foxwell,

Thanks for the Malthus:[2] It is a very nice copy.

I am sorry to hear what you say of S.J.C.: but I feel sure things will right themselves soon.[3]

Were you at Toynbee's 2nd lecture. I have heard at fourth hand that mild and gentle as he is, offence was taken at something that he said about the working classes.[4] Can you put me up to any tips as to similar rocks to be avoided.

I hear Toynbee is not well:[5] So I don't like to write to him.

Yours ever | A Marshall

Bonney wrote to me to be Secretary to Section F.[6] That filled me with confusion. I thought I had left you with the understanding that I w^d.. not like to risk taking it. As it is I fear I have given you & others useless trouble. I am so perfectly well so long as I only read & write, & so easily knocked up by knocking about, that I must stick to the resolve of living a sluggish life.

[1] Marshall Papers.

[2] See [111.3].

[3] Perhaps a reference to the financial difficulties facing the College which led to the resignation of the Senior Bursar. See E. Miller, *Portrait of a College* [11.1], pp. 96–7.

[4] Arnold Toynbee gave two lectures on 'Progress and Poverty' to a radical audience in London on 11 and 18 January 1883. The second evoked considerable hostility from much of the audience at the caution of Toynbee's suggestions for reform and his criticisms of the working classes. For a description and analysis of Toynbee's lectures see Alon Kadish, *Apostle Arnold: The Life and Death of Arnold Toynbee 1852–83* (Duke University Press, Durham, 1986), ch. 8. A written version of Toynbee's lectures, based on press reports, was published posthumously (see Kadish for details).

[5] Toynbee suffered a mental collapse after his struggles with the audience at the lecture of 18 January. He never recovered, dying—apparently of meningitis—on 9 March 1883. See ibid., ch. 9.

[6] T. G. Bonney [39.1] was Secretary of the British Association for the Advancement of Science, 1881–5. Section F was devoted to 'Economic Science and Statistics'. Its main function was the arrangement of the Section's programme at the Annual Meetings of the Association. In 1883, these were to be held (in September) at Southport with R. H. Inglis Palgrave as the President of Section F. There were four secretaries of the Section: Foxwell, W. Cunningham, J. N. Keynes, and C. Molloy (perhaps Constantine Molloy (?–1897) a Dublin lawyer). Foxwell wrote on 22 March 1883 to ask Keynes to be a Secretary, adding 'We have a first rate President in Inglis Palgrave, who is going to make a real effort to lift the Section & subject out of the disrepute into which they have fallen' (Marshall Library, J. N. Keynes Papers).

115. To Herbert Somerton Foxwell, 17 February 1883[1]

Thanks for your most interesting letter.[2] It told me exactly what I wanted to know. I am very sorry for T:, I don't admire him any the less for it. I quite agree with you that it w^d.. not be fair for any one else to bring out his papers. There is no hurry about their appearing.[3]

I am not absolutely certain that I shall not publish my lectures. I dont fancy they go over much of Ts ground.

I am very sorry indeed for the trouble I gave about the Brit. Ass^n..[4] My wife who was by at the time felt sure that you quite understood that on consideration I did not want to do it.

Yours | A M

[1] Marshall Papers. Postcard, postmarked 'Clifton FE 17 83'. 'T' refers to Arnold Toynbee.

[2] Not preserved.

[3] Toynbee's wife, Charlotte Maria, was pressing for the rapid publication of Toynbee's lectures (see [114.4]) despite his prostrated condition, and hoped that Foxwell would undertake the editorial work. The task was eventually performed by Alfred Milner (1854–1925), subsequently Lord Milner, a close friend of Toynbee. See Kadish, *Apostle Arnold* [114.4], ch. 9.

[4] See [114.6].

116. To the Editors, *The Western Daily Press*, 17 March 1883[1]

Gentlemen,—You publish to-day a letter from Mr Wallace, in which he brings
two charges against my recent public lectures.[2] The first is that I overlooked
many advantages which the agricultural labourer enjoyed a hundred years ago.
Now it happens that we have more detailed and trustworthy accounts of the
diet, dress, and mode of living of the labourer at that time than at any other,
with the exception of the last 30 years. I had re-read some of these accounts just
before my lectures, and had carefully considered all the points to which Mr
Wallace refers. A hundred years ago the labourer's common rights had already
been much curtailed; philanthropists regretted that he could not afford to rent
land on which to keep a cow; they did not propose that he should keep one on
common land. His house rent averaged 7d a week in 1770, and 1s a week a
little later on. Considering the vile accommodation that he had, this can hardly
be called a nominal rent. Mr Wallace thinks he often had milk free from the
farmers. No doubt skimmed milk was given away in some places when it was
plentiful; but so it is now. There are good reasons for thinking that the amount
of milk produced per head of the population was not much greater then than
now; while the amount per head that was consumed without passing through
the churn or the cheese vat was probably less than now. The farmer kept on an
average three pigs on the produce of every ten cows, and this fact confirms the
direct evidence of Eden and Arthur Young that the labourer did not get very
much even of skimmed milk.[3] Still, as I said in my lecture, milk was one of the
very few things with regard to which he was in some cases better off than now.
I agree with Mr Wallace that it is a pity that brown bread is not generally eaten
now. But he is, I think, mistaken in supposing that it was largely eaten a hundred
years ago. At that time only white wheaten bread was commonly eaten in the
South of England; though in the North brown bread was sometimes eaten and
porridge generally. Mr. Wallace says that the labourer got his fuel very easily.
But the fact is that wood had become so scarce that the labourer who was not
near coal mines was often terribly pinched for fuel, the cost of inland carriage
of coal being very high. The average of a vast mass of statistics collected by
Arthur Young gives £1.3s 11d as the sum expended on firing by the labourer
in 1770.[4] But the supply he got for this price was so small that in order to save
firing he went in the South of England almost entirely without warm food of
any kind, except tea.

   Mr Wallace's second attack related to the rates of interest and wages in Asia.
Mr George had said that it was a necessary and universal law that where wages
are low, interest is low. I asserted that wherever capital is scarce and population
abundant, interest will be high, though wages are low; and I said that this was
the case in Asia. Of course, bad government has been one of the causes of the
small supply of capital in Asia; and in some parts of Asia, though not in all,
want of perfect security now makes it necessary to deduct a good deal of the

insurance from the nominal rate of interest before finding the real rate. But that interest is really higher in Asia than in Europe is proved by the fact that when a railway has to build there it is cheaper to borrow the capital in Europe than on the spot. Again, when I say that wages are low in Asia, I mean, of course, not only money wages, but real wages—i.e., the food, clothing, and houseroom which the labourer obtains. Mr Wallace denies this, but I do not think your readers will expect me to prove it. Had I been wrong on all the points on which he attacks me, my main argument that the adoption of his scheme would injure the farmer and the labourer as well as the landlord would have remained practically intact.

Perhaps you will allow me to take this opportunity of explaining a quotation from Mr Gladstone's Midlothian speeches, that Mr Henry Rogers made after my last lecture.[5] It was the only objection raised in the lecture room that I did not attempt to answer at the time. According to Mr Rogers, Mr Gladstone said that French peasant proprietorship had increased the earnings 40 per cent in 14 years, while the English system has only increased it 20 per cent in 30 years. I felt sure that Mr Gladstone's meaning had been misunderstood, but could not at the time say how. I now find that he is reported to have said at West Calder that 'in 1842 the agricultural income of England was £42,000,000, and that in 1876 it was £52,000,000.'[6] But this sum includes no earnings, it is simply the rent of land. The agricultural income proper is the sum of the net incomes of all the agricultural classes, or, in other words, it is the sum of the values of all agricultural net produce. Mr Caird tells us that for the United Kingdom this amounts to about £260,000,000.[7] The complaint of the land-nationalisers is that wages are kept down by the rapid rise of rents in England. Mr Gladstone's figures have so far the opposite tendency to that which Mr Rogers ascribes to them. But Mr Gladstone further said that the agricultural income of France (by which I suppose he meant the assessed rental value) rose from £76,000,000 in 1851 to £106,000,000 in 1864. I should like to offer an explanation of this. We have Lavergne's very careful statistics as to 1847.[8] At that time rents were 25s an acre in England, and 10s an acre in France; that is, for lands of equal natural fertility they were probably in France about a third of what they were in England. The great gold discoveries were made about 1850, and from that time to 1864 there was a vast rise in prices. Meanwhile the Imperial Government had restored the security which was shaken in 1848–52; and this, of course, specially enhanced the value of land. But it was a very expensive Government, and according to general report it took every opportunity of screwing up assessments. Lastly, the free trade measures of 1860 had immensely increased the export of wine and the value of French vineyards. Under these circumstances the land system must indeed have been bad if it had prevented the assessed rental value from rising rapidly. Probably the value of the land in France will go on rising more rapidly than here; for it is still far behind and has therefore more room for improvement, and America is a market for and not a rival to

French vineyards. No one doubts that the French peasant works hard and is thrifty, but I believe that with less work the English labourer is generally better fed, clothed, and housed, and that with equal thrift he would soon become richer. I do not contend that the English system is well adapted to the French character. The fact that their wheat crops are less than half as much per acre as ours is chiefly due to the fact that wheat is a large farm crop, and that French large farms are often badly managed.

Yours, &c., | Alfred Marshall

University College, Bristol, 17th March.

---

¹ *Western Daily Press* (a Bristol newspaper), 19 March 1883. Reproduced (with some minor variations) in Stigler and Coase, 'Alfred Marshall's Lectures' [113.4].

² Alfred Russell Wallace (1823–1913), a co-promulgator with Charles Darwin of natural selection arguments, and a proponent of land reform. For the text of Wallace's letter see ibid. p. 212. The nature of Wallace's criticisms of Marshall's lectures (see [113.4]) is amply indicated by the response.

³ Sir Frederick Morton Eden, *The State of the Poor* [110.5]; Arthur Young, *A Six Months Tour through the North of England* (Strahan etc., London etc., 1770: 4 vols.); *The Farmer's Tour through the East of England* (Strahan etc., London etc., 1771: 4 vols.).

⁴ Marshall's figure is drawn from Young's *A Six Months Tour*, vol. 4, p. 438.

⁵ Henry Rogers was described in a leader in *The Western Daily Press*, 21 March 1883, as 'a veteran local politician' and a promulgator of 'the Radical view of the Land Question'. A press account of the interchange, which merely refers to 'Mr. Gladstone's speeches', is reproduced by Stigler and Coase, 'Alfred Marshall's Lectures' [113.4], p. 211.

⁶ See *The Times*, 28 November 1879, p. 10, for a full report of the speech by Gladstone at West Calder, the third of his addresses to the electors of Midlothian. The quotation occurs near the foot of the second column, as does the further statement that Marshall cites.

⁷ James Caird, *The Landed Interest and the Supply of Food* (Cassell, Petter and Galpin, London, 1880: fourth edition, a revision of the first edition of 1878), pp. 13–4. The figure refers to 1879 and represents the total value of the production of home agriculture.

⁸ Léonce de Lavergne, *Économie Rurale de la France Depuis 1789* (Guillaumin, Paris, 1860); *The Rural Economy of England, Scotland, and Ireland* (Blackwood, Edinburgh, 1855). Ch. 6 of the latter makes the kind of comparison Marshall adverts to, but the exact source of the figures he quotes is difficult to determine.

---

117. To Léon Walras, 20 March 1883¹

31 Apsley Road, | Clifton, Bristol,
20me mars, 1883

Monsieur,

J'ai beaucoup de regret à cause de ma negligence de vous bien remercier pour les brochures tres interessantes lesquelles vous m'avez envoyé.² Il y a beaucoup d'années que j'ai appliqué des logarithmes pour calculer les effets de l'achat des terres par l'État. Mais ma conclusion est opposée a la votre; ou, j'avais du dire, les votres calculations ne me semblent pas d'avoir d'application au cas d'Angleterre: parceque je crois qu'il serait impossible d'obtenir plus que 2 % et peutêtre, ne pas plus que $1\frac{3}{4}$ % *net* sur les achats. Et je crois qu'il n'y a pas de certitude que le prix de terre, *exprime en l'or*, montra sans cesse.

Le votre Serviteur oblige | A. Marshall

[1] University of Lausanne, Fonds Walras, reproduced in *LW*, letter 549. Foxwell had brought Marshall's name to the attention of Walras, who was indefatigable in promulgating his ideas (see *LW*, letter 544, 30 December 1882).

Précis: Marshall regrets his delay in thanking Walras for his interesting pamphlets. It is some time since Marshall calculated by means of logarithms the effects of land purchases by the state, but his results differed from Walras's which seem inapplicable to England where no more than a 2% return ($1\frac{3}{4}$% net) can be expected on the purchases. Nor is there any certainty that the price of land in terms of gold will continue to increase.

[2] Among the pamphlets sent by Walras must have been his 'Théorie Mathématique du Prix du Terres et de Leur Rachat par L'État, *Bulletin de la Société Vaudoise des Sciences Naturelles*, 2nd series, 17 (June 1881), pp. 189–284. Reproduced in L. Walras, *Théorie Mathématique de la Richesse Sociale* (Corbaz, Lausanne, 1883).

118. To the Editors, *The Western Daily Press*, 24 March 1883[1]

Gentlemen,—Mr Wallace does not understand my position with regard to wages a hundred years ago. In my lecture I admitted that a peck of wheat would purchase more animal food and more of a few other things a hundred years ago than now; and I admitted that he still retained some fragments of privileges which he has now lost. But I contended that a peck of wheat will now buy many things of great importance for the physical, mental and moral well-being of the labourer and his family, which it would have cost him very many pecks of wheat to purchase a hundred years ago. I concluded that his real income has risen in at least as great a ratio as his wages measured in wheat have. Mr Wallace has looked only at one side of the shield, and even in this he has pointed out nothing that I had not taken account of. The quotations he now gives do not appear to traverse my statements. It is not necessary for me to inquire in how narrow a sense the term peasantry is to be interpreted in Mr Brodrick's statement that it was once an almost universal custom among the peasantry to rent two or three acres of ground.[2] The custom had disappeared a hundred years ago as completely as it has now.

There is no reason, in our present land system, to prevent its being revived now. Mr Wallace cannot desire its revival more heartily than I do.

Again, he mistakes my point with regard to wages in Asia. It is true that while the English labourer has not enough clothes, the South Sea Islander has as many as he wants, because he wants scarcely any. No doubt those who desire a mere animal existence can have it for very little labour in a tropical climate where population is sparse. But the economists whom Mr George assails use the term real wages to mean the amount of food, clothing, houseroom, and other necessaries, comforts, and luxuries of life which the money wages will purchase.

Using it in this sense, I am not contradicted by Mr Wallace when I assert that wages in India and China are lower than in England, while interest, allowing for risk, is higher.

Yours, &c | Alfred Marshall.

---

[1] *Western Daily Press*, 24 March 1883, and reproduced with minor variations in Stigler and Coase, 'Alfred Marshall's Lectures' [113.4]. It responds to a rejoinder to [116] from Alfred Russell Wallace [116.2] published in the *Western Daily Press* on March 23. For the text of Wallace's letter see Stigler and Coase, 'Alfred Marshall's Lectures', pp. 215–6.

[2] Wallace had quoted the authority of George Charles Brodrick, *English Land and English Landlords* (Cassell, Petter and Gilpin, London and New York, 1881; for the Cobden Club), to the effect that the renting of two or three acres to farm labourers was 'but the revival of a custom once almost universal among the peasantry of England, and it is found to be fraught with manifold advantages'. See ibid. p. 429.

119. From Benjamin Jowett, 28 March 1883[1]

West Malvern
March 28/83

Dear Prof. Marshall,

The Board of Electors to the Political Economy Professorship is new, & therefore it is uncertain what line they will take. But I think it probable that they will reelect Bonamy Price who is still vigorous, (though heterodox in his political economy).[2] If I hear otherwise I will let you know.

I see that you are going to Bournemouth & think that you may like to have the opportunity of making friends with some friends of mine, Sir Henry Taylor & Lady Taylor[3] (He is the author of Philip von Artevelde). I enclose a note for them: He is a very remarkable man now in his 83rd year but vigorous & interesting.

The losses of Henry Smith[4] & Toynbee[5] are without exaggeration irreparable to Oxford, & I feel that they make the place different to me. I can no more talk over matters with them as I used to do. H. Smith was the greatest genius we have had at Oxford in my time, & A. Toynbee was one of the most promising young men in the country.

I should be glad, indeed, if anything should bring you & M^{rs}. Marshall to settle in Oxford.

With best regards to her

Ever yours truly | B Jowett

Oxford

---

[1] Marshall Papers.

[2] See [103.5]. Appointment to the Drummond Professorship was for a five-year term, renewable, and the current term expired in 1883. In the event Bonamy Price was re-elected.

[3] Sir Henry Taylor (1800–86), public servant and author of *Philip van Artevelde* (Moxon, London, 1834). Married Theodosia Alice Spring-Rice (1818?–91) in 1839 and by 1883 had retired to Bournemouth.

[4] Henry Smith [102.4] died on 9 February 1883.

[5] See [114.5].

120. To Herbert Somerton Foxwell, 30 March 1883[1]

Sunningdale | Christchurch Road, Bournemouth
30 March 83

My dear Foxwell,

M^{rs}. Toynbee, in answer to a letter of condolence,[2] says that in all the notices of Toynbee that have appeared 'his life & personality have been dwelt on mostly . . . people think of these rather than of him as an economist . . . Is not this a pity? Ought there not to be some notice printed of him as an economist'. I have answered that I have not enough knowledge either of him or of what has been said of him to enable me to do it: that economic study bears its fruit late in life, & that it may be difficult for any one to convince those who did not know him how great his promise was. But that I will pass on her suggestion to the best quarter than I can. By this I mean you: only I did not like to mention you for fear you sh^{d}. not see your way to do it.

I thought the article in the Economist was sensible, but hard.[3] That is the only notice I have seen of him except the short one in the Times.[4] The mortality among those whom the world can least afford to lose has been frightful.

We are to come up to Cambridge for a day or two on March 20th we are to stay with Taylor.[5]

I am looking forwards to nearly 6 months almost uninterrupted work at my book. I shall not spare the time that w^{d}.. be wanted for publishing my lectures on Progress & Poverty.

My wife sends her best greetings.

Yours ever | A Marshall

[1] Marshall Papers.

[2] Not traced. See [115.3].

[3] 'Death of Professor Toynbee', *The Economist*, 41 (17 March 1883), pp. 313–4: 'his spare and wasted form, hollow cheeks, and nervous clutching of the hands, while they bore ample testimony to the intense earnestness which marked every utterance, left also no doubt that he was not the man to commend orderly economic progress to an audience of which the "irreconcileable" element was certainly the most noisy, if not the most numerous . . . the cause of the poor is better aided by influence and teaching husbanded by care through a long lifetime, than by spurts of feeling, however noble, which practically end in an early grave.'

[4] *The Times*, 12 March 1883, p. 10.

[5] Charles Taylor [58.3], who in 1881 had succeeded William Bateson as Master of St John's.

121. From Charlotte Maria Toynbee, 5 April 1883[1]

Thornton Hill | Wimbledon
April 5/83

Dear Sir

I really did not mean to trouble you to take any action on my expression in my former note—please forgive me. I had not also when I wrote seen the notice in the Academy[2] which says I expect nearly all there is to say, because I am aware myself more keenly than any one perhaps how pitifully it is a fact that his work was mostly the collection of materials for future use.

Thanking you much for your kindness in sending me another note.[3]

Believe me | Yrs truly | C. M. Toynbee

[1] Marshall Papers. See [114.4, 5], [115.3], [120]. Forwarded from Bournemouth to Foxwell with the covering note 'You may be saved some trouble by seeing this. M[rs].. Toynbee's first letter certainly did ask that something sh[d]. be done.' This first letter has not been preserved.
[2] Alfred Milner, 'Obituary: Arnold Toynbee', *Academy*, 23 (24 March 1883), p. 205.
[3] Not traced.

122. To Herbert Somerton Foxwell, 10 April 1883[1]

I have made rather a fool of myself about London Univ.[2] I happened not to see any advertisement of it. But I looked in the Calendar & found that the election was at the end of April. So I have only just sent in my application; & today it is returned to me by Milman[3] with the statement that the real selection is done, though the formal election is not till April 25th.. I feel rather silly but I hope to survive.

Will the morning of Saturday April 21st suit for me to come to you to talk shop

Yours | A M.

Sunningdale, Bournemouth

[1] Marshall Papers. Postcard, postmarked '10 AP 83'.
[2] Marshall intended to apply for a vacant Examinership in Political Economy at London University.
[3] Arthur Milman (1829–?), Registrar of London University 1879–96.

123. To Herbert Somerton Foxwell, 30 April 1883[1]

31 Apsley Road

My dear Foxwell,

I am delighted to see that Keynes has got the London Examinership.[2] I hope the Moral Sciences Board will give him plenty of scope in Cambridge.[3]

You will probably have heard from Sidgwick that we are going to Oxford.[4] You were all of you so kind and good at Cambridge that we almost yielded to the temptation to go there.[5] But there is no doubt, when we come to reflect on it calmly, that we ought to go, & that in the long run we shall be glad we have gone, where there are[6] vast flocks of untended sheep without (economic) shepherds rather than where there are many able shepherds with but few sheep. I don't suppose that we will be able to get our crooks round the ankles of many of the Oxford Sheep: they are too much out of the way of treating economics as a serious study: still we can try.

Many many thanks for your kindness. The books arrived safely & wonderfully packed. I send you the electric penned statistics.[7]

Yours ever | A Marshall

[1] Marshall Papers. Envelope postmarked 'AP 30 83'.

[2] 'I have been appointed examiner in Political Economy in the University of London. I had not in the least expected it this year, as I understood that Marshall was going in. I believe that Nicholson was also a candidate' (J. N. Keynes, *Diaries*, 26 April 1883).

[3] Although Keynes did not hold a formal University appointment, he had been lecturing for some years under the auspices of the Moral Sciences Board. In December 1883 he was to be appointed University Lecturer in Moral Science at a salary of £50, a possibility broached by Sidgwick as early as July (*Diaries*, 30 July 1883).

[4] Marshall had been appointed to the Lectureship to Indian Civil Service Probationers (see [12.7]) at Balliol College, Oxford, made vacant by the death of Arnold Toynbee.

[5] It is unclear what the Cambridge prospects might have been, perhaps a University Lectureship and a College Fellowship.

[6] The word 'are' is repeated in the original.

[7] Small booklets of historical statistics prepared by means of Edison's 'Electric Pen', a stencil cutting device in use at the Bristol College. Copies survive in the Marshall Papers.

124. To John Neville Keynes, 30 April 1883[1]

31 Apsley Road | Clifton
30 April

My dear Keynes

I am delighted indeed to see that you are examiner at London.[2] If I had had to select the man out of all England whom I shd have liked best to have there, I shd.. have chosen you.

You have been a great deal in the thoughts of my wife & myself during the last few days. We shall never forget the warm feeling & the kind pleasure you took in seeing us: & you were one of the most powerful lodestones to draw us to Cambridge. But when we came to think over the matter, there was no one who acted more powerfully to send us elsewhere. We have such a perfect belief in the thoroughness & breadth & just balance of your work that you, perhaps more than any one else, seemed to make it profanity for us to push into Cambridge. The fact that you really & heartily did wish us to come back, is one of the pleasantest facts in our lives: but it is made all the pleasanter when we reflect that we shall be doing nothing still further to narrow the already far too narrow room that you have for your economic work.

I have been assuming that you have heard from Sidgwick that we are going to Oxford & that I am to give the lectures that Toynbee used to give there. But perhaps you have not heard it.[3] We had a yearning to be with our old friends at Cambridge & to try to help on the Cambridge Tripos, w^h.. we like better than any exam^n.. at Oxford. But after all Oxford is a wide & nearly empty field for economic work: & we are sure we are right in making our choice.

Yours most affectionately | Alfred Marshall

[1] Marshall Library, J. N. Keynes Papers. Keynes found the letter 'very unexpected' (*Diaries*, 1 May 1883).
[2] See [123.2].
[3] See [123.4].

125. To Herbert Somerton Foxwell, 9 May 1883[1]

I thought at first you were referring to the diagram which is the third in the list of Jevons work in Appendix II of his Th: of Pol Econ.[2] I had at the time forgotten that he had published a separate one on Banking.[3] I have never seen that & don't know what it is like: but I cant think it can be comparable in importance to the other one, that relating to the Fund, price of wheat &c. I dont see any sufficient cause for such things being charted weekly. Moreover the juice of the subject has been in a great measure brought out in Palgraves Bank rate[4] wh has an immense mass of statistics of the kind in question. The price of wheat diagram could be completed in a few hours work: & that shd I think be done. But I shd think the other is hardly worth while: The figures for the former are nearly all in ye Statistical Abstract.[5]   AM

I don't see much use in republishing the old chart without bringing it up to date.[6]

[1] Marshall Papers. Postcard, postmarked 'Bristol MY 9 83'. See [110.2] for the background.
[2] 'Diagram showing the Price of the English Funds, the Price of Wheat, the Number of Bankruptcies, and the Rate of Discount, monthly since 1731 ...' (privately published, London, 1862). See appendix II of the second edition of W. S. Jevons, *Theory of Political Economy* [59.2].
[3] 'Diagram showing all the Weekly Accounts of the Bank of England, since the passing of the Bank Act of 1844 ...' (privately published, London, 1862).
[4] Robert Harry Inglis Palgrave, *Bank Rate in England, France, and Germany 1844–78: With Remarks on the Causes Which Influence the Rate of Interest Charged: And an Analysis of the Accounts of the Bank of England* (Effingham Wilson, London, 1880).
[5] This refers to the official *Statistical Abstract for the United Kingdom*, published annually.
[6] In the upshot, the diagram on the price of English Funds etc. was brought up to date, with the exception of the bankruptcy figures where the attempt was abandoned due to the complications encountered. The diagram on the Bank of England's accounts was continued only from 1862 to 1864 as 'there were many difficulties in the way of bringing it up to date', and subsequent research had made this less vital. See *Investigations* [110.2], pp. vii, xi–xv.

126. To Herbert Somerton Foxwell, 22 May 1883[1]

My dear Foxwell,

I am rather glad of an opportunity of paying a tribute to Jevons Memory.[2] For that reason I sh^d.. prefer having my name attached to this note if it can conveniently be done.

Yours | A.M.

[Enclosure][3]

Mr. Jevons was an Economist of the highest order. In his '*Theory of Political Economy*' he explains the nature of economic quantities & their relation to one another. Work of this kind involves no startling discovery, but its effect is much greater than appears at first sight. It makes us masters of our thoughts, and founds new empires in science. A small part of his work, which was warped by his antipathy to Ricardo, will probably die away. A small part also will lose lustre when Cournot's applications of Mathematics to Economics are better known.[4] For, indeed, Jevons was, as he frankly confessed, not a skilled mathematician. Truly mathematical as was the tone of his best work, he was not at his ease when using mathematical formulae. But the great body of his work is unaffected by these blemishes; the lapse of time will but add to its lustre, and it will probably be found to have more truly constructive force than any, save that of Ricardo, that has been done during the last hundred years.

His contributions to Statistics are widely known. The pure honesty of his mind, combined with his special intellectual fitness for the work, have made them models for all time. But it is in his Essays on the applications of Economics to the theory of governmental action that his full greatness is seen. There is no other work of the kind which is to be compared to them for originality, for suggestiveness, and for wisdom. Almost every one of them contains some great new practical truth, which the world is beginning to recognise; though but few persons know their obligations to him.

---

[1] The letter is in the Marshall Papers with envelope postmarked 'Bristol MY 22 83'. The enclosure is reconstructed from a subsequent printed version, corrected for the errors noted in a postcard from Marshall to Foxwell of 6 October 1883 in the Marshall Papers.

[2] In connection with a projected appeal for a Jevons Memorial. Marshall became a member of the appeal committee which proposed to establish a studentship in memory of Jevons (*The Times*, 16 October 1883, p. 9. Also see *LW*, letters 588, 589).

[3] A printed version was circulated with the appeal under the heading 'Professor Marshall on Jevons as an Economist'. A copy is in the Jevons Papers, John Rylands University Library, Manchester. Foxwell quoted from it in his introduction to *Investigations* [110.2], p. xliii.

[4] Antoine Augustin Cournot, *Recherches sur les Principes Mathématiques de la Théorie des Richesses* (Hachette, Paris, 1838).

127. From Léon Walras, 15 July 1883[1]

Ouchy sous Lausanne,
15 juillet 1883

Monsieur et cher Collègue,

J'ai l'honneur de vous envoyer un exemplaire de mes mémoires réunis dans un volume.[2] S'il vous était possible de me faire part, en échange, de quelques-uns de vos travaux, je vous en serais particulièrement reconnaissant.

Je ne crois pas non plus que le prix des terres puisse 'monter sans cesse'[3] dans un pays quelconque, parce que je ne crois pas que la population puisse augmenter sans cesse. Mais je crois, pour l'avoir démontré mathématiquement, que le prix des terres monte dans un pays tant que la population augmente. En ce qui concerne l'Angleterre, la question est donc de savoir si le progrès économique, c'est-à-dire l'accroissement du capital et l'augmentation de la population, y est arrivé à son maximum et si la décadence est imminente. Si telle était votre opinion, je vous avoue que cela m'étonnerait.

Agréez, Monsieur et cher Collègue, l'assurance de mes sentiments dévoués.

Léon Walras

[1] Reproduced in *LW*, letter 573. Jaffé's transcription of the original draft (University of Lausanne, Fonds Walras) is adopted here.
Précis: Walras sends a volume of reprinted pieces and would be grateful to receive some of Marshall's writings in return. He doesn't believe that the price of land will always continue to rise. His proof relied on the implausible assumption that population always continues to grow. In the case of England, the question is whether economic progress, capital accumulation, and population growth, have reached their limits, with decline imminent. It would be astonishing if Marshall believed this.
[2] Presumably Walras's *Théorie Mathématique de la Richesse Sociale* [117.2], a collection of previously published pieces.
[3] See [117].

128. To Herbert Somerton Foxwell, 22 July 1883[1]

Bryn-y-mor, Parrog | Newport R.S.O *Pembrokeshire*
22 July 83

My dear Foxwell,

It is difficult to give a short answer to your flattering-coaxing letter.[2]

As general propositions I maintain that it is more important to establish truth than to confute error; & that controversy sh^d.. be left to people with sound digestions.

It seems to me infinitely more important that I should solve difficulties wh still perplex me than that I should tilt at a successful rhetorician.[3] The one thing that he says which is important, I think, is that economists are—to outward appearance at least—at loggerheads with one another. I w^d.. rather put in one brick just where it sh^d.. be in the slowly rising economic edifice than plant a hundred brickbats with the utmost dexterity exactly between the eyes of Mr George.

Still the book[4] has had so many buyers (though I doubt whether one in fifty of them has read to the end) that I almost determined to publish something about him. My weak point was that I did not know what to attack: a book as large as his own w^d.. be wanted to refute all his fallacies. But I hoped that I sh^d.. find out, in the course of my lectures at Bristol, which of his fallacies had stuck. I failed utterly.

Trying to refute George in Bristol was like throwing myself against a door that is not fastened. There was no resistance anywhere. There was plenty of enthusiasm for nationalisation of the land: if I had gone on fighting against that, I could have had opposition for ever. But there was no opposition to my attacks on George; & I practically had to leave him out of the argument.[5]

Still I was wavering: then I heard of Toynbee's death: & that disinclined me to act for the time: I did not want to say anything in any way opposed to Toynbee: & I thought I w^d.. wait. Then came the Oxford post that meant a great deal of reading about India involving a good break in my writing. Now I am writing, but in September I must begin to read India again.

When I go to Oxford I shall hold out to my pupils there the same challenge that I held out to my pupils at Bristol. I shall defy them to shew me anything in George that is new & true; also to shew me any attack of his on Mill's doctrines that is even verbally valid against that reading of Mill's doctrines that is to be found in the Economics of Industry. (It seems to me that very few even of George's false sayings are less than fifty years old.)

(As to the laws of D.R & I.R.[6] I admit that the account in the Economics of Industry is incomplete. We had intended to go into it more thoroughly in discussing American protectionist theories, in the Economics of trade & finance.[7])

Well, by this means, I shall find out which of Georges fallacies are worth attacking; & if I find that the book is not already fast loosing its hold (w^h.. I expect) I shall probably write a review article or two at Xmas or Easter.

What you say about Heitland[8] is important. I am not sure what he thinks: but if he really is taken by George, he is the only hard headed man whom I know who is. I had a talk with Beeton.[9] But I thought he was *not* hard headed. He seemed to me to swallow everything in George; & I got no nearer knowing what to attack.

Meanwhile there is an eminent economist, who believes that George is important, & on whom the eyes of the world are turned. Verily let him refute George: why not. Go in old fellow, & win.

Only do not vilify Mill. I believe that some of the modern extravagent school, by exaggerating his faults instead of bringing out his virtues, as was their duty, have done more harm to economic science than a hundred open enemies like George could do.

We have sold our house at Clifton, put our furniture in a warehouse & are spending the summer in Wales. This place suits us admirably. Good bathing, admirable sketching, river & sea boating, bracing air, perfect retirement &c. So though we had intended only to spend part of our time here, we may perhaps spend all here.

Again I say—Go in & win.

Yours very sincerely | A. Marshall

---

[1] Marshall Papers. Envelope addressed to 12 Ryder Street, London SW. Reproduced in *Early Economic Writings*, vol. 1, pp. 24–6.

[2] Not preserved.

[3] That is, Henry George.

[4] George's *Progress and Poverty* [113.4].

[5] The discussion following Marshall's Bristol Lectures on 'Progress and Poverty' is summarized in the press reports reproduced in Stigler and Coase, 'Alfred Marshall's Lectures' [113.4].

[6] That is, 'Diminishing Returns and Increasing Returns'.

[7] The proposed continuation of the *Economics of Industry:* see [34].

[8] William Emerton Heitland (1847–1935), Fellow of St John's, 1871–1935. Senior Classic in 1871: became well-known as a latinist.

[9] See [78.2].

129. To Léon Walras, 23 July 1883[1]

Newport, Pembrokeshire. 23 juillet, 1883

Monsieur et cher collègue

Je vous remercie bien de vos mémoires.[2] Je n'ai publié qu'un petit oeuvre— 'The Economics of Industry': j'aurai l'honneur de vous envoyer un exemplair quand je retourne chez moi. (Après octobre mon addresse sera 46 Woodstock Road, Oxford: je donnerai des lectures au l'Université, mais je ne m'appellerai plus Professor: je serai simplement A. Marshall)

J'ai oublié qu'est que c'est j'ai dis sur la question des rentes de terre en l'Angleterre. Je crois que sa population et son capital s'accroisseront longtemps et très rapidement. Je crois que les rentes de fermes, mesurés en blé, s'accroisseront un peu, mais je crois que c'est *possible* (je ne dis pas *probable*) que le prix de blé mesuré en *or*, diminuera plus rapidement que les rentes mesurés en blé ne s'accroisseront; et alors que les rentes mesurés en or se diminueront.[3]

Je suis été malade; et le travail d'administration à Bristol m'a empêche d'écrire. Mais j'espère d'avoir beaucoup de temps pour mes propres travaux à Oxford; et de vous envoyer après un ou deux années un traité de la théorie économique.

Agréez, Monsieur et cher collègue, l'expression de mes sentiments dévoués.

Alfred Marshall

---

[1] University of Lausanne, Fonds Walras. Reproduced in *LW*, letter 578.

Précis: Marshall thanks Walras for the volume he sent. Marshall has published only one small work, the *Economics of Industry* and will send a copy upon returning home. He explains that after

October he will teach at Oxford, no longer a professor, and gives his new address. He forgets what he had written about the income from land in England, but he certainly believes that population and capital will continue to grow rapidly there. He believes that agricultural rents in terms of wheat will rise somewhat but that the gold price of wheat could decline more rapidly, reducing rents measured in gold. Illness and administrative burdens have held back his writing but he hopes to send a treatise on economic theory in the next year or two.

[2] See [127.2].
[3] See [117, 127].

130. To Herbert Somerton Foxwell, 8 August 1883[1]

Sidgwick has written urging me to publish Prog: & Pov: lectures.[2] It is hard lines for one who hates controversy more than he does George to be forced into controversy: but I suppose I must do something at the beginning of next year. At present I am engaged in making up my own mind about difficulties. I do an average of 2 hours a day at that if I do nothing else all day: but I cant do it at all when half occupied with other things. So I cant spare time to think of George now.

As to Mill I agree that he is literary: & therefore full of error. But I think he & Ricardo contain the kernel of truth. As to definition I have written the part of the new book[3] that relates to them in a radical spirit agreeing much with Jevons. A 2/6 book[4] must be conservative in definition.

AM

You ought to answer George.

[1] Marshall Papers. Postcard postmarked 'Newport AU 8 83'.
[2] See [113.4].
[3] Marshall was now at work on his Principles.
[4] That is, the *Economics of Industry*.

131. To Léon Walras, 26 October 1883[1]

46 Woodstock Road, Oxford

Dear Sir,

At last I have returned home and send you the little book written by my wife and myself.[2]

I hope before many years are over to be able to send you a larger one.

Yours truly | Alfred Marshall

[1] University of Lausanne, Fonds Walras. Reproduced in *LW*, letter 592. Postcard postmarked 'OC 26 83'.
[2] That is, the *Economics of Industry*.

132. From Léon Walras, 28 October 1883[1]

Ouchy sous Lausanne,
28 octobre 1883

Cher Monsieur,

Je reçois avec le plus vif plaisir votre 'Economics of Industry' et je m'empresse de vous envoyer en échange mes *Éléments d'économie politique pure*[2] dans lesquels se trouve exposé le *système d'économique* qui est résumé dans mes quatre premiers mémoires.[3]

Je vois que vous avez accueilli la théorie de Jevons sur la proportionnalité des valeurs aux utilités finales dans l'échange.[4] Vous verrez dans mes ouvrages que j'ai étendu le principe de cette proportionnalité de deux marchandises à plusieurs et des produits aux services producteurs. Il en résulte que, dans un pays comme l'Angleterre où la population augmente considérablement, les utilités finales des terres augmentant considérablement, la valeur des terres augmente considérablement. Et ainsi se fait de la plus-value de la terre et de la rente se trouve à la fois constaté par l'expérience et expliqué ou démontré par le raisonnement. Excusez-moi d'insister sur ce point: il est, à mon sens, le point capital de l'économique; c'est, en tout cas, l'objet essentiel de mes travaux.

Votre respectueux et bien dévoué | Léon Walras

---

[1] Reproduced in *LW*, letter 593. Jaffé's transcription of the original draft (University of Lausanne, Fonds Walras) is followed here.

Précis: Walras thanks Marshall for the *Economics of Industry* and sends him a copy of the *Éléments*, which sets out the system summarized in the four memoirs sent previously. He sees that Marshall has endorsed Jevons's theory of the proportionality in exchange of values to final utilities. Marshall will see that Walras has extended this argument from two products to several, and also to factor services. It follows that in a country like England, with considerable population growth, the final utility of land and the value of land will rise considerably. This appreciation of land values and rents is proved by experience and demonstrated by reason. Walras apologizes for insisting on the point which he views as one of the most important in economics and central to his own work.

[2] See [94.4].

[3] The first four items in Walras's *Théorie Mathématique de la Richesse Sociale* [117.2].

[4] *Economics of Industry*, pp. 69–70: Jevons, *Theory of Political Economy* [17.3].

---

133. To Léon Walras, 1 November 1883[1]

46 Woodstock Road, Oxford.
1 November 1883.

Dear Sir

I thank you for your letter.

I cannot be said to have accepted Mr. Jevons doctrine of 'final utility'. For I had taught it publicly in lectures at Cambridge before his book appeared. I had indeed used another name viz: 'terminal value-in-use'. But following the lead of Cournot[2] I had anticipated all the central points of Jevons book, and had in many respects gone beyond him.[3] I was in no hurry to publish because

I wished to work out my doctrines on their practical side. Latterly I have been hindered by illness.

It happens however that in order to explain the use of a machine that a pupil of mine had made for me to construct a series of rectangular hyperbolas I read on October 30, 1873, before the Cambridge Philosophical Society a short paper anticipating incidentally your doctrine of unstable equilibrium.

A brief note of it is contained in Part XV of the 'Proceedings' (not the 'Transactions') of that Society.[4]

I do not wish to challenge your statement that *other things being equal* the growth of population raises rents.[5] The truth of that statement is certain; it is even indisputable. But there are many sensible Englishmen who hold that I. the best gold mines are probably already discovered II. the importation of food will continue to grow rapidly III. that 'Norman prudence' will during the next generation make its appearance among our working classes: and that therefore *gold rents* will either remain stationary or even fall. I myself think the probabilities are the other way. But it is a matter of probability and not, to my mind, of mathematical certainty.

Yours very truly, | A. Marshall

[1] University of Lausanne, Fonds Walras. Reproduced in *LW*, letter 595.
[2] See [126.4].
[3] For Marshall's earliest manuscript on value see *Early Economic Writings*, vol. 1, pp. 117–59. His claims for subjective originality seem exaggerated (see *Early Economic Writings*, vol. 1, pp. 37–52).
[4] See [94.6].
[5] See [117, 127, 132].

134. To Herbert Somerton Foxwell, 7 November 1883[1]

46, Woodstock Road, | Oxford.
7 Nov

Dear M[r] Statistical-Societies-Councillor.[2]

Would your conscience allow you to certify that Bolton King BA (of Balliol) 10 Upper Berkeley St W is a fit & proper person to become a member of the Stat[l].. Society.[3]

He was a great friend of Toynbee's, has already got a large economic library, has strong economic interests, is a man of considerable wealth & desires to become a member; but does not know any one to second his nomination.

If your conscience will let you, & you have any nomination forms, will you fill one up, & send it to me, when I will sign it, & send it on.

I am getting to care about statistics a good deal: not to work at myself: I have not the time. But I think it is just the work for rich young Oxford men who can afford to buy clerical assistance. I hope gradually to get several, & I want to make a beginning with King. I try to make my men get all the 4 statistical abstracts.[4]

I enjoyed Sunday. But it was too much for me. I mean I missed the 'let down' that I generally go in for on Sunday, & have been very washy since then. I must in future stick rigidly to the rule of not going out except on Saturday: though I forsee I shall have difficulty in doing it on the Sunday following each ad eundem dinner:[5] that is why I speak of it.

Yours ever | A. Marshall

---

[1] Marshall Papers.

[2] Foxwell had been elected to the Council of the Statistical Society on 26 June 1883. See *Journal of the [London] Statistical Society*, 46 (September 1883), p. 413.

[3] Bolton King (1860–1937) was elected a Fellow of the Statistical Society on 20 November 1883. See *Journal of the [London] Statistical Society*, 47 (September 1884), p. 398. He published articles on statistical and economic topics but is mainly remembered as a historian of Italy.

[4] This presumably refers to the annual governmental statistical compilations.

[5] Social occasions designed to promote Oxford–Cambridge ties.

135. To the Editor, *Pall Mall Gazette*, 30 November 1883[1]

Sir,—My remark that £300 a year will pay for a bachelor fellow's necessaries has, I find, reached your ears.[2] You take exception to my allowing but £60 for four months' travelling. You want to know where it can be done 'with the degree of comfort that seems to be implied in the rest of the estimate'. I have travelled for scores of months at less than £15 a month. I did not stint, but I avoided as much as possible guides, carriages, and expensive hotels. Railways did not cost me much, as I wanted to rest and to get to know land and people. Even now one can travel with abundant comfort in Western Tyrol and some other places for less than £10 a month. I think that expensive travelling cannot, as a rule, be counted among a student's necessaries. A man's 'necessaries' in the economic sense I take to be those things the want of which would be likely to diminish the efficiency of his work by a value greater than their own cost. I allowed £60 as necessary for books, leaving £180 for the rest of his necessary expenses, including illness, hospitality, and miscellaneous minor claims. I do not see that this is out of proportion to the £15 a month for travelling.

—I am, Sir, your obedient servant | Alfred Marshall.

Balliol College, Nov. 30.

---

[1] *Pall Mall Gazette*, 38 (1 December 1883), p. 2, under the heading 'The "Necessaries" of a Bachelor Fellow'. This letter is reproduced and discussed in Alon Kadish, 'Marshall on Necessaries and Travel: A Note on a Letter by Marshall in the Pall Mall Gazette', *History of Economic Thought Newsletter*, 26 (Spring 1981), pp. 15–19.

[2] The *Oxford Magazine*, 28 November 1883, had reported:

> Oxford has gained a very accomplished lecturer as well as a learned economist in Mr. Marshall. His lectures, delivered without the use of notes and with considerable impressiveness of voice and manner, have been well attended in spite of the collision of the hour with that of many Halls. Mr. Marshall enlivens the course of his lectures with little excursuses on various points. Thus, in dealing with Socialism last week he entered on the amount of income necessary for men of different rank and occupation. A careful consideration of his own circumstances had led Mr. Marshall to fix the minimum for a bachelor fellow at £300, including £60 for four months' travelling, but not horse exercise, which might in some cases be necessary.

An 'Occasional Note' in the *Pall Mall Gazette*, 38 (29 November 1883), p. 2, had drawn attention to this report adding: 'A good many people, we fancy, would be glad to know in what pleasant lands they could travel at the rate of £15 per month with the degree of comfort which seems to be implied in the rest of Mr. Marshall's estimate'.

136. To John Neville Keynes, 15 February 1884[1]

46, Woodstock Road, | Oxford
15 Feb 84

My dear Keynes,

I have just received your Formal Logic.[2] So far as I can judge, it seems to be a beautiful specimen of thorough Cambridge work, & likely to be of very great service. I think it will help to extend the scope of Formal Logic in education.

My wife joins me in kind regards to you & Mrs Keynes.[3]

Yours very sincerely | A. Marshall

[1] Marshall Library, J. N. Keynes Papers.

[2] John Neville Keynes, *Studies and Exercises in Formal Logic* (Macmillan, London, 1884).

[3] Keynes had married Florence Ada Brown, a Newnham student 1878–80, on 15 August 1882. Their famous son, John Maynard, was born on 5 June 1883.

137. To Herbert Somerton Foxwell, 10 March 1884[1]

46, Woodstock Road, | Oxford.
10 March 84

My dear Foxwell

Thankyou for your interesting letter & for your splendid lecture syllabus.[2]

Of course I sh^d.. soften down what you say as to the discontinuity between the old & the new school of economists even in the matter of laissez-faire. But bar this, I agree heartily.[3]

George disappointed me altogether.[4] He seemed to be in earnest in a way but to have absolutely no intellectual honesty—no desire for truth, but only for victory. He never attempted—so at least every one to whom I have spoken agrees—to answer a single question. He seemed to give his whole energies to rhetorical subterfuges that wd enable him to avoid answering it. Those subterfuges w^d have gone down with an uneducated audience; but not where he was. I wish I had seen him before. I sh^d.. have talked about him much less.

I think him an extremely able man: quite as much as ever: but I don't see any reason for thinking that he has that kind of ability w^h.. will make a permanent impression on opinion.

I like Oxford very much: but I have not yet got hold of many people who are willing to go through much for the sake of econ: science. I am very much hampered by not being able to go to evening meetings & talk to undergraduates & others with social freedom in other ways. This makes it very hard for me to get at the right men. I do what I can, but I *never* go out to a meal or have people in to one without suffering. Otherwise I am perfectly happy.

The next time you are coming over here whether to an ad eundem[5] or for any other purpose let us know. We want much to see you: only we shall make no stranger of you: & when a meal is over I shall leave you to talk to my wife, & go to my knitting for an hour or so.[6]

My wife sends her kind regards.

Yours ever | A Marshall

---

[1] Foxwell Papers.

[2] Probably the printed lecture syllabus for a lecture on 'Political Economy and Democracy' given by Foxwell for the Cambridge Extension Scheme at both Heckmondwike and Dewsbury, Yorkshire, on 5 and 6 March 1884. Copies of the four-page syllabus printed for each lecture are preserved in the Foxwell Papers, Baker Library, Harvard University.

[3] Foxwell had written that in the past the teachings of political economy had been characterized by 'a very dismal and ungenerous dogmatism: the once famous, now justly discredited doctrine of Laissez Faire, the Let Alone policy'. This policy 'had long been disclaimed by the leading economists of England and Germany' and 'very different views now prevail. Competition is accepted as at present the most useful economic force, but for that very reason its laws and necessary limitations are being more carefully studied, so that, like Fire, it may be the servant, not the master, of men'.

[4] Henry George had lectured at Oxford on 7 March and Marshall had been active in the discussion. For a detailed press account of the unruly proceedings see Stigler and Coase, 'Alfred Marshall's Lectures' [113.4], pp. 217–26.

[5] See [134.5].

[6] Marshall had taken up knitting as a distraction from enforced immobility, becoming an expert (see *What I Remember*, p. 24).

---

138. To Herbert Somerton Foxwell, 30 March 1884[1]

Sea View House | Niton, Isle of Wight
30 March 84

My dear Foxwell,

I think the scheme is very good—excellent in every respect save one: that is that it is not likely, without modification as to time, to catch any one who is not at a loose end; & people who are at a loose end have generally some screw loose.

I agree with you that it is very important that the first man shd be an Oxford man. But I am not a good authority to refer to: I know so very few. The only one I could recommend with any confidence is S. Ball of St Johns.[2] He is lecturing in Philosophy & professes not to be an economist. But I expect there are very few people in England who have read as much German economics as he has. His tact, & his personal influence are magnificent. Had I to act on my own limited knowledge, I shd break up the lecture into two parts one at Xmas & the other at Easter, & put on pressure to overcome Ball's shyness & make him lecture. If he absolutely refused, but not till then I shd ask him if he knew anyone else that w^d.. do. He w^d.. be very likely to.

If Ashley[3] *is the man I am thinking of,* he w^d.. not do at all: he w^d.. have his heart in the work, but not much else. Bolton King[4] of course you know of: he is able, but already has his hands full: & I dont know whether he wd lecture well. (There may be good men who went down before last October. Of them of course I know nothing.)

The Land Reform Union has just asked me to 'hold a public debate with H. George in some London Hall next week'. It w^d.. have upset me & prevented my doing any writing during the vacation so I refused. Otherwise I think I shd have accepted. We flourish here. I hope you are giving yourself some rest.

Yours very sincerely | A Marshall

---

[1] Foxwell Papers. This letter was enclosed by Foxwell in a letter to Alfred Milner [115.3] which was returned to Foxwell after it failed to reach Milner. It is concerned with the organization by the recently established Toynbee Trust of an inaugural set of lectures. See Kadish, *Apostle Arnold* [114.4], pp. 230–1. Foxwell was a member of the Trust's committee and Marshall took Sidgwick's place on it in 1888.

[2] Sidney Ball (1857–1918), lecturer in philosophy and Fellow of St John's College, Oxford, since 1882. Foxwell, in his covering note to Milner, observed that 'Marshall would not speak as strongly as he does if Ball were not perfectly safe on the Economical side.'

[3] Presumably William James Ashley. Foxwell reported to Milner that 'Sidgwick has come to the conclusion that Ashley's impediment in his speech makes it unsafe for us to try him as a first experiment.'

[4] See [134.3].

---

139. To Herbert Somerton Foxwell, 29 April 1884[1]

46, Woodstock Road, | Oxford.
29 April

My dear Foxwell,

I have but just got your letter: it almost always saves time to address as above.

Many thanks for your very kind congratulations: also for those of Ward & MacAlister.[2]

I feel no sort of grievance against S.J.C. I don't know what the College could have done for me. I have a grave grievance against the old statutes that made me resign my fellowship on marrying: but the College could not help that.[3]

Balliol has raised my salary as lecturer to £200: on the ground that my teaching is not confined to Indian Students.[4] The Fellowship has no salary attached to it. But it gives all the other rights of a full Fellowship: e.g. a seat among the governing body: & thus it differs from an 'honorary fellowship'. We do very well: & are absolutely happy.

My wife is just now more than happy: almost mad with joy.[5] I too am very glad. I think Cambridge must follow.

It is insane—in my view—for the two great Universities to be able to find time to examine unkempt urchins of 12 all over the country, & not to be able to supply a decent exam[n] for the higher work of our local colleges. I feel sure that these have a vast future before them. Why should Oxford & Cambridge abnegate the post of leadership & leave London & Manchester to direct all the higher work except that small amount that is done by residents at Oxford & Cambridge. Probably this will shock you. But think over it, as a favour to me. When are you coming to Oxford?

Yours ever | A Marshall

Since I wrote this Mary has come in from Somerville Hall.[6] She says the Students are going to have a torch light procession of triumph. She is going to it.

[1] Foxwell Papers.

[2] Marshall had just been elected to a three-year non-stipendiary Fellowship at Balliol. (Kadish, *Apostle Arnold* [114.4], p. 18 n.) Ward is probably James Ward. Donald MacAlister (1854–1934), Senior Wrangler 1877, was a Fellow of St John's from 1877 to 1934. He became a leader of the medical profession and was knighted in 1924.

[3] These Statutes had been revised since Marshall's departure in 1877. However Foxwell's Fellowship was under the old statutes and had to be resigned on his eventual marriage in 1898. SJC is St John's College.

[4] For the details of Marshall's compensation at Balliol see Kadish 'Marshall on Necessaries and Travel' [135.1].

[5] Oxford had just voted to admit women students, whether resident in Oxford or not, to sit for certain of the Honours examinations. Arrangements were to be undertaken by the Oxford Delegacy for Local Examinations. See Vera Brittain, *The Women at Oxford* (Macmillan, New York, 1960), pp. 66–70.

[6] An Oxford college for women.

140. To Harriet Ann Jevons, 1 June 1884[1]

46, Woodstock Road, | Oxford.
1 June, 84

Dear M[rs] Jevons,

I have to thank you for the most valuable book w[h] you have sent me.[2] It was delivered in the first instance to an 'Alfred Marshall' at Keble College,[3] & I have only just received it.

I already know a good deal of it almost by heart; & as time goes on I shall get to know the rest of it in the same way.

I think the manner in w^h it is brought out reflects great credit on its editors;[4] it is a splendid tribute to the memory of the great man who has passed away.

Well as I know his writings I am always coming across some new side remark w^h seems to me full of suggestion, & in advance of the time. I am ever more & more convinced that since Ricardo there has been no one to rival him either in England or any other country as an original economist.

Yours very sincerely | A. Marshall

---

[1] Original in the Jevons Family Papers. Substantially reproduced in Könekamp, 'The Work of Harriet Ann Jevons' [110.2].

[2] W. S. Jevons, *Investigations in Currency and Finance* [110.2] which had just been published.

[3] *Oxford University Calendar* for 1884 records an Alfred Marshall as a commoner at Keble College.

[4] Although Foxwell was technically the editor, he credited Mrs Jevons with a significant part of the work and she supplied a preface. See *Investigations*, pp. xliv, xvii–xviii.

---

141. To Herbert Somerton Foxwell, 15 November 1884[1]

46 Woodstock Road
Oxford   15 Nov

My dear Foxwell,

It has just occurred to me that the V.C. cannot be expected to acquaint the other electors for the P. E. Professorship that I am a candidate.[2] So I am writing to them. Will you kindly address & post this letter to Inglis Palgrave.[3]

I do not know whether you are an elector: but I presume not any more than I am.[4] But McLeod does not know that I am not an elector & has sent me his testimonials again. I think I must have had nearly half a dozen copies of the first volume of them. But they are strong.[5]

I shall hear of you from Mary.

Yours ever | A. Marshall

The Master[6] writes to say that if Professor then I may be Fellow of St. Johns. Should I wish it? he asks. Of course I have written to say yes most muchly. I shd feel like a swallow getting back to its old eaves.

---

[1] Foxwell Papers. The envelope is postmarked 'Oxford No 17 84'.

[2] The sudden death of Henry Fawcett on 6 November had left the Professorship of Political Economy at Cambridge vacant. The 'V.C.' (Vice Chancellor), an *ex officio* member of the Board of Electors to the Chair, was Norman McLeod Ferrers (1829–1903) Master of Caius College.

[3] Not traced.

[4] Marshall, Foxwell, and Inglis Palgrave had in 1883 been members of the standing Board of Electors to the Chair (*Reporter*, 29 October 1883). But Marshall was no longer listed on the Board when the formal announcement of the vacancy appeared (*Reporter*, 18 November 1884). As it transpired, Inglis Palgrave was also a candidate and did not act as an elector.

[5] Henry Dunning Macleod was a perennial candidate (he had stood for the chair when Henry Fawcett was elected in 1863). His printed application and testimonials were impressive, at least in scale, being virtually of book length.

[6] Charles Taylor [58.3], Master of St John's.

142. To Herbert Somerton Foxwell, 20 November 1884[1]

46 Woodstock Road
20 Nov

My dear Foxwell,

You really ought to be a candidate. I have told Cunningham, who wrote to ask if I was a candidate ten days ago, & Nicholson who has just written, that I think they ought to stand, that each of them has a chance. I say the same emphatically to you. However much to my advantage it might be for you not to stand I cannot bear the thought of your standing out on my account.

I wish I had thought of the difficulty about letting the electors know before writing to the V.C.[2] I should then have sent round a collographed circular letter w^h.. w^d. obviously require no answer. I am sorry that I implied that I wanted you to tell me whether you were a candidate. I had intended to avoid doing so.

I have a good deal of gossip to tell you at some time.

Yours ever | A Marshall

[1] Foxwell Papers.
[2] See [141.2].

143. To Léon Walras, 1 December 1884[1]

46 Woodstock Road Oxford
1 Dec 84

Dear Sir,

I thank you for your paper on 'Monnaie d'Or &c'[2] wh. I shall read with pleasure when I get time.

Yours truly | A Marshall

[1] University of Lausanne, Fonds Walras. Reproduced in *LW*, letter 618.

[2] Léon Walras, 'Monnaie d'or avec billon d'argent régulateur. Principes proposés à la conférence monétaire pour la prorogation de l'Union Latine' (1884). A pamphlet subsequently published in the *Revue de Droit International et de Legislation Comparée*, 16 (December 1884), pp. 575–88. (See *LW*, letter 606 n. 2.)

144. To Herbert Somerton Foxwell, 1 December 1884[1]

46, Woodstock Road, | Oxford.

My dear Foxwell,

I quite sympathize with the tone of your letter.[2] If a candidate has any thoughts of withdrawing he ought at once to inform all other possible candidates that he knows of. It is true that on the 17th. & 18th I opened the question whether I ought to try for the post I so much coveted. I spent a sleepless night on the 17th & decided on the 18th.. that it was clear I should stand. In the night of the 18th.. I felt I had not thrashed out the question, I discussed it confidentially with two people on the 19th.. & by the 20th came to the conclusion that there is a very wide margin of reasons in favour of standing. From the 20th.. to today I have never had an instants doubt. And it is absolutely certain that if alive on the 13th I shall stand. When in doubt I consulted a few people in the strictest confidence. I can't imagine how the rumour got about. When in doubt I gave up all preparation for lectures & thought of the pros & cons nearly all day & nearly all night; because I felt that if the question was an open one I must publish the fact. If I had thought that I shd take long to make up my mind I shd certainly have written to you & others to say so. If I had decided not to stand I shd have instantly sent a 'multiple' telegram to the V.C. Sidgwick you, Cunningham & Keynes; & another to Nicholson.[3] And I shd have tried to get a note about it in the next days Times.

But to you I repeat: be a candidate I must take my chance.

I wish Palgrave were not standing. I thought he could not free himself from his business sufficiently. He is a tremendously strong candidate particularly on one side of the subject.[4]

Please tell any one whom you may see that it is, so far as human things can be certain, absolutely certain I shall be a candidate.

All the arguments for withdrawing turned out to be weaker & the arguments against it stronger than I expected. I can now hardly imagine how I came to have a doubt.

I am writing against time. I don't see any way to say anything about Japan[5] just now.

Yours ever | A. Marshall

---

[1] Foxwell Papers. Envelope postmarked 'DE 1 84'.

[2] Foxwell's letter has not survived, but it appears to have chided Marshall's failure to communicate (rumoured) doubts about his standing for the chair, doubts which could have led to Foxwell's own candidacy. The election was to take place on 13 December.

[3] That is, Norman Ferrers [141.2], Henry Sidgwick, William Cunningham, John Neville Keynes, and Joseph Shield Nicholson, all the last three being possible applicants for the chair.

[4] Inglis Palgrave was a banker and a specialist in monetary economics.

[5] This word is unclear and could conceivably be 'Johns' (St John's College).

145. To Herbert Somerton Foxwell, 13 December 1884[1]

46, Woodstock Road, | Oxford.

13 Dec

My dear Foxwell,

I thank you very much for telegraphing.[2] I don't want to know details. I think it is always best not even to be able to guess who have voted against one.[3]

Shall you be at the Statistical Society on Tuesday?[4] I shall be there. If I don't see you there I shall try to look in on you for a very few minutes on Wednesday at St Johns—ie if you are up. We are to lunch with Miss Clough[5] & shd come to you, I think, just after.

We are going to take advantage of the mild weather & try to find a house, or if not that then Lodgings for next Term. We propose to come home on Wednesday.

I have thought of not lecturing till the May Term: except of course giving my inaugural lecture. I sh^d.. advertise myself as prepared to give informal instruction on (say) Saturday morning & Monday afternoon. For the May Term lectures I have thought of 'Rent profits & wages'.[6]

I shd like to talk with you about this: also if I have an opportunity with Keynes.

Yours in haste | A. Marshall

---

[1] Foxwell Papers.

[2] Marshall had just been elected Professor of Political Economy at Cambridge, Foxwell having been one of the electors. See [141, 142, 144].

[3] Keynes recorded (*Diaries*, 13 December 1884):

> Election to the Political Economy Professorship. Yesterday a p.c. [postcard] from Foxwell 'It is by no means certain. Will let you know as soon as possible'. This afternoon I got rather fidgetty about the result; but in the evening another p.c. came from Foxwell, 'Marshall is elected'. The other candidates were Inglis Palgrave, Macleod, Cunningham, Levin [12.4] and Hooppell.

> (Robert Eli Hooppell (1833–95), then Rector of Byers Green, County Durham, had taken a first in the Moral Sciences Tripos of 1856, but was hardly a serious candidate.)

[4] The Statistical Society met on 16 December 1884 to hear a paper by J. Stephen Jeans entitled 'On the Comparative Efficiency and Earnings of Labour at Home and Abroad'. Neither Marshall nor Foxwell is recorded as participating in the discussion. See *Journal of the* [*London*] *Statistical Society*, 47 (December 1884), pp. 614–65, for a full report.

[5] Probably the Principal of Newnham, Anne Jemima Clough [78.2]. Mary Marshall was to return to Newnham as a lecturer in 1885, serving in this capacity until 1908.

[6] Marshall gave two lecture courses in the May Term: an elementary one on 'The Distribution of Wealth' and an advanced one on 'Some Difficult Points in the Theory of the Distribution of Wealth' (*Reporter*, 21 April 1885, p. 601).

146. From Benjamin Jowett to Mary Paley Marshall, 14 December 1884[1]

address Oxford
Dec 14, 1884

Dear M^{rs}. Marshall

I am like you pleased but sorry at your leaving Oxford:

There can be no question that you were right in standing: I wish we could have had you at Oxford but time & seasons would not agree.

Thank you for all your affection & kindness towards me, which has been a great pleasure to me during the last few years of life.

I think that you & he have taken for your own one of the most interesting subjects of human knowledge and of the greatest practical importance, & that you will have the best opportunity of teaching it. I should like to give him one piece of advice (though I have no business to give it, nor do I expect him to take it) which is not to overlay his 'Opus Magnum'with Mathematical forms or symbols: or to imagine that in such subjects these can be real instruments of discovery, however natural they may be to his own mind as a mathematician. I was very glad to hear that they were to be relegated to the appendix.

With best regards to him | Believe me | Yours truly & affectionately | B Jowett

[1] Marshall Papers. Separate portions are reproduced in Evelyn Abbott and Lewis Campbell, *The Life and Letters of Benjamin Jowett, M.A. Master of Balliol College* (Murray, London, second edition, 1897), vol. 2, p. 246, and their *The Letters of Benjamin Jowett* . . . (Murray, London, 1899), p. 215. The printed address 'Mentmore, Leighton Buzzard' is struck out.

147. To Herbert Somerton Foxwell, 23 December 1884[1]

My dear Foxwell,

The 2nd Resolution turns out to be harmless, for it does not mention the M Sc Tripos: and as to the rule about setting papers—that will not hurt me personally though I am convinced that it is ultra vires, & founded on no authority of Statutes, & will probably be resisted by other Professors.[2] If so I shall follow suit, not because I think the Professors ought not to set papers, but because I think they ought not to be 'regulated' into setting them. But I shall not stir in this matter, unless it is to follow the lead of others.

So Sidgwick & I are at peace again. He is very good, in spite of his 'regulating'.[3] I think either Cunningham or Keynes will come here. I dont know w^h..: I think Cunningham wd get the larger class at all events at first & Keynes wd do most good to those he did get. So I am not taking a side on the matter, further than I can help.[4]

Yours ever | A.M.

[1] Foxwell Papers. Envelope postmarked 'Oxford DE 23 84'.

² The General Board of Studies at Cambridge was attempting to revise and systematize the rules governing the rights and responsibilities of University Professors and Lecturers. The precise resolution is not readily identifiable in the formal record (*Reporter*, 18 March 1884, 9 June 1885). Henry Sidgwick represented the Moral Science Board on the General Board of Studies which had considerable powers of purse.

³ There had recently been a stormy meeting of Marshall and Sidgwick, now the Knightsbridge Professor of Philosophy. Sidgwick recorded:

> He came here on December 17, called on us, heard my view of the lectures required, then suddenly broke out. I had produced on him the impression of a petty tyrant 'dressed in a little brief authority' (Chairman of the Board of Moral Science) who wished to regulate, trammel, hamper a man who knew more about the subject than I did. I tried to explain, and we parted friends; but the explanation was imperfect, correspondence ensued and on Tuesday (23) I received from him a long and very impressive letter, analysing my academic career, and pointing out that the one source of failure in it was my mania for over-regulation. (Arthur Sidgwick and Eleanor Mildred Sidgwick, *Henry Sidgwick: A Memoir* (Macmillan, London, 1906), p. 394.)

Unfortunately this correspondence with Sidgwick has not been traced. Marshall's suspicions were doubtless inflamed by Sidgwick's considerable dabblings in political economy since about 1878.

Marshall must have discussed matters with Foxwell when visiting Cambridge, for writing on 19 December from Oxford (Foxwell Papers) he requested 'Be sure you do not tell anyone what I said about Sidgwick's monomania. It is enough for me to have to fight his wish to regulate my lectures on his model; it w^d.. be a great pity to have any personal element introduced into the official controversy.'

⁴ Marshall's neutrality as to the choice between John Neville Keynes and William Cunningham as his successor at Balliol seems feigned. He was soon actively promoting Keynes. See [149.2].

148. From Benjamin Jowett, 25 December 1884¹

West Malvern
Dec. 25. 1884

My dear Marshall,

I write to thank you for your kind letter:² It has been a great pleasure & happiness to me to have known you & M^rs. Marshall: Thank you again & again for your never-failing affection to me & for your attachment to the College.³

We shall greatly miss you at Oxford: the Undergraduates say to me 'Who will teach Political Economy to us now?' I have no doubt that there is an excellent field for teaching it, both at Oxford & Cambridge, partly because it is 'in the air' now, & also because it enters so largely into various University examinations: I think you are to be congratulated on the subject of your Professorship both on this account, & also because I believe that an immense deal may really be effected by it for the good of all classes. We shall be able by the help of Political Economy to look Commercial movements in the face, to predict them a few days or weeks beforehand & to make the best use of the interval.

Which is the most sensible man & which is the best teacher?—Keynes or Cunningham? We cannot offer much salary not more than 150–200£ a year: But the lecturer, if he succeeds, would have a good chance of obtaining Price's chair which must be vacant in 2 or 3 years time, as Price is not likely to be reelected.[4]

Will you be surprized at my attacking you about Symbols? (rather unfair, just when you are leaving us and in a letter to your wife).[5] I seem to see that various persons such as De Morgan & Boole[6] have tried to apply mathematics to subjects which did not admit of their use & have rather deluded themselves & others: (Henry Smith[7] had this feeling about such attempts). Now I do not object to their application to Political Economy, provided they are not regarded as a new method of discovery, but only as a mode of expressing a few truths or facts which is convenient or natural to the few whose minds easily adopt such symbols. Political Economy is human & concrete & should always be set forth in the best literary form: the language of symbols may be relegated to notes & appendices.

I have worried you enough about this matter, in which I have always fancied, perhaps erroneously there might be a danger to your 'opus magnum'. Wishing you success in the best sense for your work & your life.

Believe me My dear Marshall | Every yours most truly | B Jowett

---

[1] Marshall Papers. Reproduced in *Early Economic Writings*, vol. 1, pp. 27–8. Partly reproduced (with 'commercial' misread as 'communist') in Abbott and Campbell, *The Letters of Benjamin Jowett* [146.1], pp. 215–6.

[2] Not preserved.

[3] Balliol.

[4] See [103.5], [119.2].

[5] See [146].

[6] Augustus de Morgan (1806–71) and George Boole (1815–64), mathematicians and logicians.

[7] See [102.4].

149. To John Neville Keynes, 28 December 1884[1]

For the next few days → 1 Beacon Terrace | Sidmouth.
28 Dec

My dear Keynes,

There will be certainly plenty for you to do at Cambridge. Should you go to Oxford, I shall not be able to pick my work with quite the same freedom that I shall if you stay: & on personal grounds I shd be deeply grieved at your going.[2]

But during the last week I have [been][3] drifting to the conclusion i that if you stand you will be elected ii that if you are elected you will be glad of it.

Unfortunately I had not thought enough, as I ought to have done, of the difficulty you might find yourself in if you tried Oxford, did not like it, & yet had your retreat cut off. I ought to have written suggesting that you might take the work on trial for six months. Markby told me that he thought of proposing that to whoever was appointed. I know he w^d.. assent to it. You might keep your Cambridge house, & perhaps some of your Cambridge work.

Unfortunately the telegraph office is closed or I w^d.. have telegraphed both to you & Markby. But from a letter I have had today from the Master of Balliol,[4] I *think* that there will be no precipitate action.

I do want you to consider this: you have, what I have not, the strength to carry through the work single handed at Oxford. You w^d.. be alone there. There is no one else who has given the best part of his life to mastering economic theory. On the other hand teachers of history abound there; there is a plethora of them. Putting aside all personal considerations, that seems to me (& I think it will to others) to be a sufficient ground for believing that you are the man wanted. And if others think you are the man wanted, then surely you may be bold enough to think it probable you will succeed. If you do succeed you will probably[5] be Professor in three years time. I say 'probably' only; because so many are the chances of life, that I don't think it right to speak strongly in such a matter.

I fear I may have expressed myself badly in talking to Mrs Keynes as to the need of facility for 'public speaking.'[6] Most lecturers at Oxford read their lectures, those who do not, make large use of notes. There is such a demand for trustworthy teaching of economics in Oxford; so strong a feeling among the undergraduates that there is not much good in hearing those who have taken it up so to speak as a plaything, that with your singular power of lucid exposition, you w^d.. be certain to get hold of the best of them. If you have any want of oratorical power—& on this point I have no information beyond what Mrs Keynes said—it w^d.. only influence the numbers at the fag end of your class. And they do not matter.

I pray you then to consider whether you could not give Oxford a six months trial.

I am writing to Markby a short note telling him of what I am writing to you: & I am saying the same thing to the Master of Balliol, whose letter asking for further information about you has arrived by this mornings post.[7]

If you do go to Oxford you will have the formation of a very considerable part of the thought & feeling of the English people in your own hands

Yours—more unselfishly than | you know | Alfred Marshall

We could not have lived in the centre of the town with any comfort, at least I could not. I take every day two or three walks of 1/4 or 1/2 mile: I cannot get much further. And it makes all the difference to me whether this walk is amid houses or in the fields

---

[1] Marshall Library, J. N. Keynes Papers.

[2] Marshall had called on Keynes on 16 or 17 December. Finding Neville away, he had urged on Mrs Keynes [136.3] the desirability of Neville applying for the Balliol post that Marshall was vacating. As Mrs Keynes explained in a letter to her husband,

He feels that in persuading you in any way to consider it he is acting most unselfishly because there is no one he is more anxious to keep here—but at the same time he is not altogether satisfied with your position here (he does not at all like you to be spending your energies on the Local Exam. work [90.2])—while there is such a fine career for the right man.

That Cunningham had already decided to apply may have heightened Marshall's interest in 'running' Keynes, though Marshall did not 'wish it to be known that the first suggestion came from him'. Marshall's campaign was followed up by a telegram to Keynes on 20 December suggesting that he enquire for the details of the post, and by a letter (not preserved) received by Keynes on 22 December in which Keynes records Marshall as writing 'I have described you very minutely to Dr Markby . . . I think there is little doubt that either you or Cunningham will be asked to come here. Each has his own claims. I know, & perhaps Dr Markby guesses wh I think the stronger'. Keynes wrote to Marshall on 26 December saying that he did not wish to be a candidate. On the 29th: 'In the morning a telegram came from Marshall again urging me to offer myself for Oxford. I telegraphed back that I could not see my way to doing so, and in reply to a second telegram I wrote.' (See [150].) On 30 December Keynes received the present letter from Marshall. (See *Diaries*, entries for 18, 20, 22, 23, 26, 29, 30 December.) William Markby (1829–1914), Reader in Indian Law at Oxford, 1878–1900, and Fellow of Balliol was in general charge of the Indian Civil Service probationers at Balliol. He had served as Judge of the High Court of Calcutta, 1866–78, and was to be knighted in 1889.

[3] Word apparently omitted.

[4] See [148].

[5] Altered from 'almost certainly'.

[6] Presumably this took place in the interview of 16 or 17 December.

[7] Marshall's note to Markby and response to Jowett have not been traced.

150. From John Neville Keynes, 29 December 1884 (incomplete)[1]

My dear Prof. M.

Since receiving your second telegram, I have again been in a state of great uncertainty as to what I ought to do, but on the whole I have decided not to write further to D^r.. Markby.[2] If it were a question of lecturing for the May term only I think I might undertake—as you suggest—to lecture at Oxford temporarily without committing myself to any permanent change in my Cambridge work.[3] I have so much on my hands that this arrangement does not seem to me to be possible unless I had practically made up my mind that it was a first step towards giving up Cambridge altogether. To do this would mean so much in every way that I seem to want weeks to think it over in all its aspects before being prepared to make such an important change, & at present as I said in my letter of Friday last I cannot persuade myself that the chances of my succeeding in doing good work at Oxford are sufficient to warrant me in giving up the work I have at Cambridge. This being the case I cannot of course do anything to lead D^r. M. to offer me the appointment. I wish now I had talked the whole matter over with D^r. S.[4] I did not do so because I was afraid I shd find myself hinting at the part you had taken in suggesting it to me.

The work in connection with the Local Examinations[5] is particularly heavy—

& I have arranged to give a course of lectures on Pol. Econ. to the Civil Service students[6] & another at Newnham besides the continuation of a course on Logic in connection with my University lectureship.[7]

[1] Marshall Papers. From a copy or draft kept by Keynes.

[2] See [149.2].

[3] This possibility must have been broached by Marshall before he wrote [149] which Keynes received only on 30 December. See [149.2].

[4] Drs M. and S. are Markby and Sidgwick.

[5] Keynes was Assistant Secretary of the Local Examinations Syndicate in Cambridge. See [90.2].

[6] That is, the probationers for the Indian Civil Service resident in Cambridge, for whom special courses were provided. For information on the scheme see Stefan Collini, Donald Winch, and John Burrow, *That Noble Science of Politics* (Cambridge University Press, Cambridge, 1983), pp. 354–7.

[7] See [123.3]. Keynes's transcription ends at this point.

151. To William Graham Sumner, (1884?)[1]

I have to thank you for your excellent little book of suggestive questions on economics.[2] I have been using and have been getting a good many of my pupils to get your 'Social Classes'.[3] I found it a most fascinating book, though I am not quite so thorough an advocate of *Laisser faire* as you are.

[1] Reproduced from Starr, *William Graham Sumner* [26.8], p. 502, where the letter is said to have been written 'from Oxford'.

[2] W. G. Sumner, *Problems in Political Economy* (Holt, New York, 1884).

[3] W. G. Sumner, *What Social Classes Owe to Each Other* (Harper, New York, 1883).

152. To Robert Forsyth Scott, 2 February 1885[1]

17 Chesterton Road, | Cambridge
2 Feb 1885

Dear M[r] Bursar,

You are aware that I should be very glad to obtain the lease of, say, 1/3rd acre on Grange Road, adjoining on the north the site let to M[r] Ball,[2] in order to build on it a small house. It would be of red brick, covered with red tiles. It would be designed by M[r] J. J. Stevenson;[3] & I should not propose to spare any expense necessary for making its architectural effect pleasant. But my requirements as to space are small, & M[r] Stevenson tells me that they can be well met by spending £1000 that sum to include all extras.

You have told me that the College Surveyor[4] recommends that no house of less value than £2000 should be built on that part of the College property: but at the same time, you kindly offered to bring my application before the Council. At first I was unwilling to avail myself of your offer: for the fact that I am a member of the College makes me wish not to ask the Council to make any exception in my favour.

But since seeing you, I have gone with Mr Stevenson to look at all the available sites in the neighbourhood of the Grange Road & the Madingley Road. And it seems possible that for reasons, not perhaps strictly within the province of the College Surveyor, the Council may think it best not to sanction the rule proposed by him. For (with the doubtful exception of a small piece belonging to Gonville & Caius College) the land in question is, I think, the only available building ground with a gravel soil near St John's & Trinity Colleges & the Literary Schools. There will I think always be many engaged in College or University work, & who wish to be near it, but who are unwilling to live on a clay soil. The proposed rule would prevent such men from getting what they want, unless they should be prepared to live in very expensive houses; & on the plan of allowing an acre for each large house, there would not be room for very many even of those.

The special advantages which a gravel soil near the Colleges has, do not increase proportionately with the size of the plot on which the house is built. I for one should be very willing to pay for 1/3 acre at a considerably higher rate than the £30, which the Surveyor has recommended[5] when a whole acre is let for one large house.

Possibly the Council may think that the College would not lose by having on an acre three houses of £1000 value instead of one of £2000; provided *firstly* that the smaller houses were built in architectural harmony with the larger, & secondly that they paid ground rent at a higher rate.

While then I would on no account ask the Council to make any concession to me on personal grounds; I should be much obliged if you w^d.. ask them to consider on general grounds whether it is advisable to exclude houses, such as that which I wish to build, from the site in question.

If they do not, perhaps you will allow me hereby to apply through you to them for a lease of the plot referred to at the beginning of this letter.[6]

I am Dear Mr Bursar | Yours truly | A. Marshall

The Senior Bursar | St John's College.

---

[1] St John's College Archives. Robert Forsyth Scott (1849–1933) served as Senior Bursar of St John's College from 1883 to 1908, when he became Master. Peter D. Groenewegen drew my attention to this letter and the consequent correspondence, not reproduced here.

[2] Walter William Rouse Ball (1850–1925), mathematician and Fellow of Trinity.

[3] John James Stevenson (1831–1908), student of Sir Gilbert Scott, a well-known architect who did much work for the Oxford and Cambridge Colleges.

[4] John Carter Jonas, land agent of Cambridge and London.

[5] This figure represents the annual ground rent associated with the leasehold.

[6] The College Council declined to deviate from its surveyor's recommendation with regard to any site in the desired Grange Road area. After prolonged negotiation a College-owned site located on the north side of the Madingley Road was leased to Marshall as the site for his proposed house. Balliol Croft was built there and occupied in the autumn of 1886: see [183.2]. Meanwhile, the Marshalls rented 'Firenze', 17 Chesterton Road.

153. To the Society for Promoting Industrial Villages, 2 February 1885 (incomplete)[1]

I trust that the Society for Promoting Industrial Villages may prosper in the very arduous task it has undertaken.[2] I think the most effective and just remedies for the overcrowding of London, and, in a smaller degree, of some other large towns, are gradually to increase the security with which sanitary regulations are enforced; and at the same time to help those who cannot earn high wages in the town to move with their work into the country, where house and garden rent are cheap.—Professor Marshall (Cambridge) 2nd February 1885.

[1] Printed in an 1885 brochure of the Society preserved in the BLPES, Solly Papers. The Society was formed in 1884, and apparently wound up in 1889, and had offices at 12 Southampton Street, Strand, London WC. Its aim, as set out in the same brochure, was

> to draw together for counsel and common action all those who deploring the condition of vast numbers of the population of London and other large towns, are of the opinion that the evils complained of are greatly aggravated by the constant influx of the unemployed from country districts. It is believed that this depletion of the country and congestion in the towns might be prevented, to the great benefit of both urban and rural England, if more employment were found for the country people in and around their homes, by market gardens, cottage or cooperative farms, home industries, and local manufactures.

The moving spirit was the Reverend Henry Solly (1813–1903) who was active in the labour movement and in social reform. Founder of the Working Men's Club and Institute Union 1862 and editor of *The Beehive* 1869–70. Author of *Rehousing of the Industrial Classes; or Village Communities v. Town Rookeries* (Swan Sonnenschein, London, 1884). See Henry Solly, *These Eighty Years* (Simkin and Marshall, London, 1893: 2 vols.). The aims of the Society were similar to ideas Marshall had expressed in 'Where to House Them', *Contemporary Review*, 45 (February 1884), pp. 224–31, part of a Symposium on 'The Housing of the London Poor': reprinted *Memorials*, pp. 142–51, under the title 'Where to House the London Poor'—see especially pp. 149–50.

[2] Marshall made a £5 donation to the Society, according to a list of subscribers in the brochure, and made further smaller subscriptions until the Society's demise.

154. To Herbert Somerton Foxwell, 13 February 1885[1]

Firenze,
Chesterton Road, Cambridge 13 Feb

My dear Foxwell

Cunynghame is a mystery. I did not enjoy the joke, because I was anxious to hear the men talk sensibly; & I knew I shd have to sacrifice the whole of today as a penalty for going to an evening meeting : but otherwise I daresay I might have liked it.[2]

I too knew something of the Guernsey meat market. I had been puzzled to know how a sensible people could have allowed so odious a monopoly to come into existence. On similar terms one might be willing to build the Cambridge people a market at a cost of £100,000. It wd cost them £1,000,000 before many years were over.[3]

Cooper[4] sends his 'very kind regards'.

Yours ever | A. Marshall

[1] Foxwell Papers. Envelope postmarked 'FE 13 85'.

[2] Cunynghame appears to have visited Cambridge to address the economic students.

[3] The reference is to the covered meat and fish market built in St. Peter Port, the principal town of Guernsey. The details involved have not been discovered.

[4] Probably Charles James Cooper, admitted to St John's in 1870, but eventually migrating to Trinity. He obtained a Whewell Scholarship in International Law in 1874, two years after Foxwell had done so.

155. To John Neville Keynes, 16 February 1885[1]

Firenze, | Chesterton Road, | Cambridge
16 Feb

My dear Keynes,

I have found the abstract of my lectures on 'Economic Theory' for last Term. I give the heads of it on the adjoining paper. You will be able to steer your course pretty well now without the memorandum I made for the 'Advanced Course.'[2]

You will recollect that

i   some of the best students B.As chiefly have come to no lectures save the 'Economic Theory'
ii that of those who proposed to come to the 'General Course' & the 'Economic Theory', many attended irregularly
iii that scarcely any of them read systematically
iv that Pennell,[3] who I still think is the ablest of the Indians there, & perhaps some others whom you may have, did not come to the economic theory.

Please not to call me Prof Marshall: Marshall is enough in all conscience.

Yours ever | A. M.

P.S. I am getting to recollect what I had intended to lay chief stress on in the advanced course

i   difficulties in the Theory of value, & of wages & rent with special reference to Mill Bk IV[4]
ii further working out of the theory of crises & overproduction
iii the difficult parts of the theory of taxation, with special reference to the problems started by Adam Smith in Book V.[5] (But not with minute reference to his opinions about them: these I proposed to leave chiefly for 'informal instruction.')

I had proposed to give quite half the time to this because questions of taxation open up all the earlier difficulties & are therefore specially well suited for a revision course: also as it happened I had said next to nothing about them in the 'Economic Theory' course.

---

[1] Marshall Library, J. N. Keynes Papers. Keynes was to take over in the Easter Term some of the Oxford teaching which Marshall's resignation left unprovided for. See [162.3] for the details of this arrangement.

[2] The items referred to cannot be identified, but a printed brochure for Marshall's Oxford Lectures in 1884–5, preserved in a scrapbook in the Marshall Papers, indicates that Marshall planned to teach a General Course (2 hours per week) in all three terms, a course on Economic Theory (2 hours per week) in the Michaelmas term, and an Advanced Course (one hour per week) in the Lent term. It appears that Keynes took over the Advanced Course, which was postponed until the Easter term. See [162.3].

[3] Aubrey Percival Pennell of Christ Church, B.A. 1886, had entered Oxford in 1883 as a candidate for the Indian Civil Service. He was to become deputy commissioner for Burma.

[4] Of J. S. Mill's *Principles*.

[5] Of the *Wealth of Nations*.

156. From Benjamin Jowett to Mary Paley Marshall, 22 February 1885[1]

Ball. Coll.

Feb 22/1885

Dear Mrs Marshall,

I have delayed longer than I intended answering your very kind letter[2] as I am afraid that busy people sometimes do with friends, because they know that they will not be offended. Will you forgive me & let me thank you most heartily for your present of a charming reading table & some knitted work.

I am glad to hear that you are happily settled in Cambridge & am not sorry to hear that you have left a part of your heart behind you at Oxford. The friendship of you & your husband has been a great blessing & good to me—And not to me only: for your departure is considered a general loss both to the political economy & the Society of the place.

(It occurs to me to mention a propos of nothing that I have some books of Mr Marshall's on Political Economy (Socialism &c) which I will keep for a few weeks longer, if you do not want them.)

You & Mr Marshall must come & see me next term: There is nothing that I like better than introducing my friends to one another, and I sometimes feel that nobody has better friends than I have: That is my experience of life: Excuse this piece of Egotism.

Oxford is going to admit ladies to the Musical Degree: & we are fighting over the Examinations which it is desired to specialize by all the faculties, whether with due regard to the interests of general education I am doubtful—We are also about to have a Medical School, which Dr Acland who has hitherto prevented it, is obliged to swallow, not without many wry faces.[3] I must likewise tell you, what may, perhaps, have a faint interest for your husband, that the College having the 'Singular privilege of electing its own Visitor' yesterday elected the Lord Justice Bowen[4] to that office (an old fellow of the College).

Thank you for the papers containing the account of the Conference.[5] I have always thought that the Economists[6] carried Laissez faire to an extreme & that the Government ought to do for us what it can do & we cannot. But now the pendulum is swinging too far in the opposite direction & hopes are being roused which after causing a[7] great deal of disturbance must end in disappointment. We want to have the question of laissez faire versus government interference more illustrated by facts—Of course the question is very different in different countries.

I have been reading 3 biographies—all of them well done & very interesting. George Elliot—R. W. Emerson & the Count Pasolini[8]—the latter I had not heard of before. He seems to have been one of the best sort of Italians.

Will you give my kindest regards to your husband & Believe me
Yours most truly | B Jowett

If you are disposed to run over to Oxford for a day or two at any time it would give me great pleasure to see you.

---

[1] Marshall Papers. Substantially reproduced in Abbott and Campbell, *Letters of Benjamin Jowett* [146.1], pp. 216–8.

[2] Not preserved.

[3] Jowett served as the Vice Chancellor of Oxford University, 1882–6. The creation of a medical school was on his personal agenda (Abbott and Campbell, *Life and Letters* [146.1], vol. 2, p. 214). On the formal establishment of a new Faculty of Medicine (Medicine had previously in the Faculty of Natural Science) see *Oxford University Gazette*, 26 May, 9 June 1885. Henry Wentworth Acland MD (1815–1900) was Regius Professor of Medicine. The proposal to allow the Delegacy of Local Examinations to use the First Examination for the Bachelor of Music for the Oxford University Examination for Women had recently been approved: see *Oxford University Gazette*, 3, 10, 17 and 24 February 1885.

[4] Charles Synge Christopher Bowen (1835–94). Baron Bowen, who had been a Fellow of Balliol from 1858 to 1862, was at this time Lord Justice of the High Court of Appeal.

[5] Probably the celebrated Industrial Remuneration Conference which had met in London 28–30 January 1885. Marshall had been a participant and had delivered a conference paper on 'How far do Remediable Causes Influence Prejudicially (a) the Continuity of Employment, (b) the Rates of Wages'. This is not one of his more penetrating essays, and was rather ill-judged for the somewhat radical mood of the occasion, but among the four appendices accompanying it—'Overcrowding in Towns, the Interdependence of Industries, A Standard of Purchasing Power, Theories and Facts about Wages'—is an important restatement of his views on distribution theory (reproduced in *Guillebaud*, pp. 598–614). Marshall's entire contribution is reproduced in Sir Charles W. Dilke (ed.), *Industrial Remuneration Conference: The Report of the Proceedings and Papers* (Cassell, London, 1885; reprinted Kelley, New York, 1967, with a useful introduction by John Saville). See also summaries of Marshall's participation in discussion, ibid., pp. 76–9, 213–4.

[6] Possibly 'the Economist', the magazine of that name, but most probably an allusion to the British Classical School of Economics.

[7] The word 'a' is repeated in the original.

[8] That is, George *Eliot*, Ralph Waldo Emerson [25.17], and Count Guiseppe Pasolini (1815–76), President of the Senate of Italy. Most probably the books were: John Walker Cross, *George Eliot's Life Related in her Letters and Journals, Arranged and Edited by her Husband J. W. Cross* (Blackwood, Edinburgh, 1881); Daniel Moncure Conway, *Emerson at Home and Abroad* (Trübner, London, 1883); Count Pietro Desiderio Pasolini, *Memoir of Count Pasolini—Compiled by his Son* (Longmans Green, London, 1885).

157. To the Society for Promoting Industrial Villages, 19 March (1885?)[1]

Memorandum

I agree generally with the pencil marks by Mr Hole.[2] Sanitary inspection must I think be in the main *official*.

I am afraid of too highly differentiating the Committees at first. A complex organisation of committees each doing one part of the whole may be effective hereafter: but I shd not like to begin with it. I w^d.. rather that at first each little colony sh^d.. be started guided & helped by one committee: the Society being a common meeting ground for all Committees (or private individuals) that might take part in the movement; but not attempting to work them into an organized whole at present.

I think it is doubtful whether we are quite ready for the joint stock company part of the programme. Anyhow I w^d.. keep that distinct from the rest.

I w^d.. begin by not climbing too high: so as not to fear a fall.[3]

19 March   Alfred Marshall

[1] BLPES, Solly Papers. A handwritten memorandum. For background see [153.1].
[2] James Hole (1820–95), social reformer, was on the Society's Council. See the article on him in Joyce M. Bellamy and John Saville (ed.), *Dictionary of Labour Biography*, vol. 2 (Macmillan, London, 1974), pp. 183–5.
[3] The Society's schemes were to prove less than successful. On 25 May 1887, Foxwell—a Vice President and Council member of the Society—wrote to Henry Solly [153.1]: 'I have reluctantly come to the conclusion that the Society will never have any practical influence. We have failed to get hold of the British public: & having failed, the best thing we can do as I think, is to stand aside, in the hope that others may be more fortunate'. He added that Marshall was also of the view that it was 'hopeless to struggle on' (BLPES, Solly Papers).

158. From Léon Walras, 2 April 1885[1]

Ouchy sous Lausanne,
2 avril 1885

Tous mes remerciements, Monsieur, pour l'amical envoi de votre intéressant discours inaugural[2] et tous mes compliments aussi au sujet de la haute situation scientifique qui vous a été faite et par suite de laquelle vous avez été amené à le prononcer. Je m'en réjouis d'autant plus que cela me permet d'espérer pour un avenir prochain le trâité complet d'économique dont vous m'avez parlé. A cet égard, permettez-moi de vous signaler un ouvrage de grande valeur qui paraît en ce moment en Allemagne: *Mathematische Begründung der Volkswirts-chaftslehre* (Leipzig, Engelmann) par M. W. Launhardt, Directeur de l'École Polytechnique à Hanovre.[3]

Votre respectueux bien dévoué | Léon Walras

[1] Reproduced as *LW*, letter 644. Jaffé's transcription of the original draft (University of Lausanne, Fonds Walras) is followed here.

Précis: Walras thanks Marshall for his interesting Inaugural Lecture and compliments him on its scientific stance. He looks forward to receiving soon the economic treatise previously mentioned by Marshall,and draws his attention to Launhardt's valuable work recently published in Germany.

[2] Marshall's Inaugural Lecture had been delivered at the Senate House on 24 February 1885. It was published in May: *The Present Position of Economics: An Inaugural Lecture* (Macmillan, London, 1885). The text is reproduced in *Memorials*, pp. 152–74. Walras must have received a preliminary version. Keynes thought the lecture 'a decided success' but heard that it 'caused (for different reasons) displeasure to Cunningham, Sidgwick and Ward' (*Diaries*, entry for 24 February 1885).

[3] Carl Friedrich Wilhelm Launhardt had published the cited book earlier in 1885.

159. To Herbert Somerton Foxwell, 20 April 1885[1]

17 Chesterton Road, Cambridge
20 April

My dear Foxwell

If the Statistical Society really is in straits, I will be prepared to speak for 20 minutes 'on the use of the graphic method'.[2] I might not have time to write a paper but I should have time between the end of my lectures here & the Jubilee to arrange my thoughts & draw a picture or two. And at the worst I would write the paper—perhaps from shorthand notes—afterwards.

I don't want to: but I am ready to do it if there is need & even distress.
Yours | A.M.

[1] Foxwell Papers. Postmarked 'AP 22 85'.

[2] The Statistical Society was planning a meeting in London in June to mark its 50th anniversary. Marshall's paper 'On the Graphic Method of Statistics' was published in the *Jubilee Volume of the [London] Statistical Society* (Stanford, London, 1885), pp. 251–60, and is reprinted in *Memorials*, pp. 175–87. He was somewhat chagrined to discover that the paper had to be in print before the meeting (undated letter, Foxwell Papers), observing

when you asked me to read the paper, I said I w^d.. not undertake to 'read' it, but I w^d.. undertake to be ready to 'speak' something. I did not know that it was necessary to have what I said written & never dreamed of having it printed before hand. Why did you not then tell me that it was the custom to do so.

160. To the Editor, *The Times*, 30 May 1885[1]

The Present Position of Political Economy

Sir,—I fancy I recognize the hand of one of our ablest economists in the article in *The Times* of to-day with the above title,[2] and it is therefore with all deference that I would venture to defend one position assailed in it. Referring to my belief that the older economists had underrated the chances of rapid improvement through overlooking the fact that 'poverty is a chief cause of the weakness which is the cause of poverty,'[3] he says that, if so, 'we seem confronted by an endless chain of misery, the seeing of which, and not the omission of seeing it, may have been the reason why the older economists did not look for a large upheaval of the working classes.'

The substance of their argument was, I think, this:—A rise in the wages of the working classes will lower the interest on capital and the earnings of the higher ranks of industry. This will diminish the rate of growth of capital and of the higher ranks of industry; therefore the demand for the labour of the working classes will diminish, and their wages will fall back to the old level. The great change made by the present generation of economists lies, as I hold, in refusing to accept unconditionally the first step of this argument.

If it be true that poverty is the chief cause of weakness, and that a rise of wages is likely to increase strength, there is room for hope that the higher-waged labour will not be dear labour. If so, there will be no check to the growth of capital and of the higher grades of industry, and therefore the rise in wages may be maintained till the time is ripe for making a new step forwards. Thus where your reviewer sees an endless chain of misery, I think I see the hope of escape from it.

I quite agree with him that it was never more important than now to insist on the futility of philanthropy which cares only for increasing happiness and diminishing misery, and pays little regard to the effect of its action on character. The present unpopularity of the older economists is, as he rightly says, partly due to the courage with which they proclaimed this. But while reckless philanthropy is as rampant as ever, there is a great modern growth of wise and far-seeing effort to help people to strengthen themselves and thus permanently to raise themselves.

And there is a constant improvement in the way in which wages are spent. As a cup of salt water increases thirst, so an ill-spent rise in wages deepens misery. But in the main increased wages are used to improve the physical, mental, and moral strength of the present and the rising generation. In so far as they are so used, high wages are a cause of that efficiency and 'social morality' which enable wages to be permanently high.

Your reviewer complains that while I value highly the organon of discovery of the older economists, I seem to speak slightingly of their results. I did not intend to do so, for I hold that most of their results were, so far as they went, true when they were written, and that many of them are true now. It is the universality and not the truth of their results that I rank so far below that of their organon. I wanted to argue that, whether their doctrines are true or not, no good work can be done without the aid of the analysis and methods of reasoning which have been slowly wrought out by their great genius.

Alfred Marshall.

Cambridge, May 30.

---

[1] Printed in *The Times*, 2 June 1885.

[2] The long and thoughtful review of Marshall's now-published Inaugural Lecture [158.2] in *The Times*, 30 May, was unsigned. Marshall probably suspected Leonard Courtney, known to be a leader writer for *The Times*, as the author, as in fact he was: G. P. Booth, *Life of Leonard Courtney* (Macmillan, London, 1920), pp. 229–30.

[3] 'The poverty of the poor is the chief cause of that weakness and inefficiency which are the cause of their poverty', *Memorials*, p. 155. Marshall is in turn quoting the paraphrase of this sentence in *The Times* article.

161. To Herbert Somerton Foxwell, 8 June 1885[1]

Firenze, | 17 Chesterton Road, Cambridge.
8 June 85

My dear Foxwell

I believe Turnbull will take the Secretaryship of the Industrial Village Society[2] if it is offered to him. If so, he is heaven-sent. He has large private means, the desire to devote his life to a great public cause, & a thorough knowledge of farming theoretical & practical. He has gone through the Cirencester College to improve his power of managing his friend Sir George Sitwell's estate—of which he remains the agent, though he has given up all other agencies. He is young—say 35—full of energy & of great practical power.[3]

He hesitates for two reasons: first he does not know enough about the Society to be sure that it is a thing he can take as his purpose in life : secondly he does not know whether he w^d.. not have to be in London more than he wishes to be. I think if he took it he w^d.. put in an assistant secretary to be in the office all day & every day but I believe he w^d.., under the Council, be the real working force.

He will call on you later on in the week. Perhaps you will let Mr Morley[4] know about him, if you have an opportunity. He has written to the Society for papers: if when he gets them he is still inclined to go further, I shd like him to call with a letter of introduction from you or me on Mr Morley.[5]

Yours ever | A.M.

---

[1] Foxwell Papers.

[2] See [153.1].

[3] Peveril Turnbull was the friend and agent of Sir George Reresby Sitwell (1860–1943), father of Osbert, Sacheverell, and Edith Sitwell. The family seat was Renishaw Hall, Derbyshire. Osbert recalled Turnbull and his wife as 'cultivated and intelligent': *Left Hand Right Hand* (Little Brown, Boston, 1944), p. 251.

[4] Samuel Morley (1809–86), businessman and philanthropist. A Member of Parliament for Bristol 1868–85, and a prominent supporter of the Society.

[5] Nothing seems to have come of the proposal. Indeed, the incompetence and dishonesty of its successive secretaries was to be one cause of the Society's demise. See Solly, *These Eighty Years* [153.1], vol. 2, pp. 558–9.

162. To John Neville Keynes, 18 June 1885 (incomplete)[1]

I have been staying at Balliol with the Master.[2] He & everyone spoke very warmly of you: said you had been a great success; & that they were very anxious you shd go on for the next three terms on the same plan as in the last term.[3] Markby[4] who is very eager about it, said that when he last saw you, he feared it wd not be possible to get the money for a second teacher: and of course as your time is so limited Phelps[5] or some one like him is indispensable. Markby was full of apologies as to the small pay offered. But I told him that you wd understand the situation; and that if you declined, it wd not be on account of the smallness of the pay; but I very much hoped you would not. Popular gossip says that there is pretty sure to be a vacancy in the chair of P.E. at Oxford in less than three years:[6] and that if you go on as you have begun your chance will be a very good one. Of course gossip must be taken only for what it is worth: but it is worth something. You know I never pay compliments when I can help it; & I dont want to make invidious comparisons between you & others who might be asked to do the work if you declined. But considering the particular lacuna there is in Oxford teaching & Oxford thought on Economics, I feel strongly that you are the right man to fill it; & on public grounds I am very very anxious you shd fill it. Phelps was among those who spoke warmly of you & hoped that you wd go on.[7]

[1] From a copy transcribed by Keynes (*Diaries*, entry for 18 June 1885). The original seems not to have survived. Keynes adds the postscript 'This letter has encouraged me altho' my answer must still be in the negative'.

[2] Benjamin Jowett.

[3] The account of Marshall's campaign to persuade Keynes to move to Oxford can be continued here beyond the date, 28 December 1884, to which it was previously taken (see [149.2]). On 31 December Keynes received a further letter (not preserved) from Marshall urging that he take the Oxford post temporarily. Keynes records Marshall as writing 'Consider whether anyhow you wd not be wise in giving up the Local Exam[n] work. But if you find any difficulty in answering this, don't worry yourself over it. Too much worry of that kind wd upset you. Then try if you can't make temporary arrangements.' On 5 January 1885 Keynes received a definite offer of 'the Oxford work for two terms'. He wrote to decline on 8 January. On the 11th: 'In the afternoon M[rs] Marshall called. She & her husband had evidently set their hearts on my going to Oxford'. Four days later a postcard arrived from Marshall,

On public ⎤ grounds I am awfully sorry ⎤
   private ⎦   glad ⎦

followed by a telegram 'if still least doubt, telegraph & I return to-morrow—quite convenient every way—Please speak frankly'. But Keynes's mind was made up. However, on 31 January Marshall called to propose that Keynes go to Oxford one day a week, and by 10 February it was 'practically settled that I am to go to Oxford once a week next term. They will give me £40.' On 17 March Keynes dined at the Marshalls', meeting Dr and Mrs Markby, and on 28 March he was 'beginning to write my Oxford Lectures—wh I hope subsequently to expend [sic] into a book on "The Method of Political Economy"'—the germ of Keynes's eventual *Scope and Method*. On 19 April he called on Marshall, staying for three hours. 'He told me something about resident Balliol fellows; & gave me advice for reading about India'. Keynes's first lecture at Oxford was given on Saturday 25 April and his last on Saturday 6 June, when Keynes concluded that 'on the whole my lectures at Oxford have been successful, altho' I have not appreciated the Balliol society, who might I think have paid me rather more attention'. (*Diaries*, entries for the indicated dates. See also letters of 2 January and 15 February to Keynes from W. Markby, Marshall Library, J. N. Keynes Papers.) For a general account of the whole episode see Robert Skidelsky, *John Maynard Keynes, 1, Hopes Betrayed 1883–1920* (Macmillan, London, 1983), pp. 59–61.
[4] See [149.2].
[5] Lancelot Ridley Phelps of Oriel College, Oxford, had also been involved in the teaching of political economy to the Oxford probationers for the Indian Civil Service. He was to assume full responsibility for this after Keynes withdrew.
[6] Bonamy Price had been re-elected in 1883 to a further five-year term as Drummond Professor. Further re-election must have seemed improbable given his age. (See [103.5, 119.2, 148].)
[7] Keynes's transcription ends at this point. Although invited by Markby to continue the arrangement for the next academic year, Keynes declined. Marshall wrote, in a letter (not preserved) that was received by Keynes on 23 June, 'I am very sorry. However I expect they will now ask Foxwell. If he consents, well. If not, I shall puff and blow at you again on public grounds' (Diaries, entries for 17 and 23 June 1885). It is not clear whether Foxwell was asked, but he certainly did not teach at Oxford.

163. From Francis Amasa Walker to Mary Paley Marshall, 3 October 1885[1]

Since I wrote you last, I have crossed the Atlantic Ocean once and the American Continent twice.

We had a pleasant, and, for the Red Star Line, a rapid, passage, on the Westernland, leaving Antwerp on the 1st of August, and 'tying up to the wharf' in New York on the evening of the 11th, too late, however, to enable us to get away to Boston that night.

The prodigals were welcomed home. The Fairchilds consented to take Miss Sally back, and Mrs. Walker, after looking Lucy over, decided to receive her, just the same as if she hadn't been careering around over the face of Europe.[2] The girls, on their part, were heartily glad to get home, while remaining glad that they went abroad.

As for me, there was no rest for my weary feet. An old engagement carried me off, on the 20th of Augt. to California. Fortunately, Mrs. Walker's curiosity about the other side of the country was sufficient to overcome her reluctance to travel in my company; and, fortunately, also, a maiden sister voluntarily undertook the martyrdom of managing our household in my wife's absence. So, we started for the Pacific, stopping a half day, only, at Denver, and a day at Salt Lake City. In California we were the guests of Governor Stanford, who has it in view to found a new university, on that coast, and wished to confer with me about it.[3]

The Stanfords are immensely wealthy, and having lost their only child, have turned their thoughts to applying what would have been *his* fortune to educational uses.

We stayed in California three weeks, going around somewhat, to see the unique agriculture and industry of that country, which is so unlike our own, or your own. When I left California two weeks ago, there had not been a drop of rain over the whole extent of the State for four or five months, and none was expected for weeks to come. Think of that, ye Britishers, who carry an umbrella if you are going around the corner, for half an hour.

We came directly 'through' on our return trip, our longest stay being an hour and a half at Chicago. All our children were well and glad to see us; and after five or six days of paper hanging and painting, we are now happily settled in our places for the winter.

I do wish you and Prof. Marshall could come over the water this winter, and visit us and look over our big country. But if it is *the book* which stands in the way, I will not complain, for the book has rights superior even to those of the United States of America. I wish I could lend your husband a little of my superabundant vitality to enable him to do his work more at leisure and with more pleasure than his delicate health allows.

We look back—Sally and Lucy and I, to our visit in Cambridge, with the deepest pleasure. You were ever so kind to my girls, and I shall never fail to cherish a most grateful sense of it.

---

[1] Reproduced without salutation and closing in James Phinney Munroe, *A Life of Francis Amasa Walker* (Holt, New York, 1923), pp. 307–8. Neither the original nor the preceding correspondence have been traced. The date is provided by Munroe. Mrs Marshall much later recorded

> I have a very vivid recollection of the visit which Professor Walker paid us in the summer of 1885, when he brought with him his daughter Lucy and her friend Miss Fairchild. He was the life of every party and he seemed to have a great power of enjoyment which infected those he was with and made him a most delightful guest.

(Presumably taken from a postscript to a letter of reminiscence written by Marshall at Munroe's request: see ibid., p. 309. The surviving portion of Marshall's (1922?) letter is reproduced in Vol. 3.) In a letter to Walker of 25 September 1885 Marshall had congratulated him on the volumes of the 1880 Census, supervised by Walker: 'They are indeed a wonderful work; and must fill all European statisticians with envy' (quoted ibid., p. 198, original not traced).

[2] In recognition of his laborious services since 1881 as President of the Massachusetts Institute of Technology, Walker had been given leave and $1,000, with the suggestion that he inspect the technical schools of Europe. He left for Europe in May and at some point must have called on

the Marshalls in Cambridge. He and Marshall had met previously in New Haven (see [26]). Walker married Exene Stoughton in 1865 and had seven children, Lucy being his elder daughter. Sally Fairchild is not further identified.

³ Leland Stanford (1824–93), railroad magnate and founder of Leland Stanford Junior University, subsequently Stanford University, in Palo Alto. See Orrin Leslie Elliott, *Stanford University: The First Twenty-Five Years* (Stanford University Press, Stanford, 1937), especially pp. 21–2.

164. From Edward Carter Kersey Gonner, 6 November 1885¹

57 Finchley New Road. | N.W.
6. xi. 85.

My dear Professor Marshall,

Do you not think that it would be possible to get some publisher to start a monthly economic journal?² As far as I can see the great difficulty with regard to economics arises from the fact that there is no common recognition of any *scientific* truth. There is still less knowledge of the history of political economy and of the various teachers under whose influence it has attained its present position. Now a monthly magazine would aid in remedying these defects. It could treat of Economic theory and also point out the historical side of the question. At present political economy rarely finds utterance in a magazine except to enforce some proposition which has been made the subject of political battle. Consequently very little progress is made.

If it is true that pol Econ. is a so generally interesting [subject]³ as is often said there should be no difficulty in finding a public to support such a magazine. It would not really be in rivalry with any other magazine or journal as the Economist treats of other tho' equally valuable matter. My idea is that its work might lie in three directions—

(1) Development of economic theory
(2) The historical developmt of pol. econ.
(3) Reviews

Believe me,
Very faithfully yours, | E. C. Gonner.

¹ Foxwell Papers. Sent to Foxwell by Marshall under cover of [165]. Gonner had come under Marshall's influence as a student at Oxford.
² Foxwell's interest in starting a new journal had already been communicated to Keynes: 'Foxwell has been in to talk to me about a Journal of Economics that he has an idea of starting or getting started' (*Diaries*, entry for 13 March 1885).
³ Word apparently omitted, or 'a' left in inadvertently.

165. To Herbert Somerton Foxwell, 8 November 1885[1]

17 Chesterton Road, Cambridge.
8 Nov 85

My dear Foxwell

The writer of this[2] is an Oxford man 1st.. class Hist: Schools, with a great interest in economics.

He is not quite first rate: but if the economics magazine is halting for want of an editor, he might perhaps do.

I have told him that I am sending you this letter.

Yours | A.M.

[1] Foxwell Papers.
[2] Gonner's letter [164] was enclosed.

166. To Léon Walras, 8 December 1885[1]

On the last page of my paper on The Graphic Method of Statistics[2] for

OT read PT
Ot   ”   Pt.

A. Marshall

[1] University of Lausanne, Fonds Walras. Reproduced in *LW*, letter 689. Postcard postmarked 'DE 8 85'.
[2] See [159.2]. The correction is rather crucial, for it was in this paper that Marshall introduced— quite unobtrusively—his concept of demand elasticity, and the mistake made the graphic measure of elasticity incorrect. Walras must have received a preliminary copy since the error is corrected in the published version.

167. From Benjamin Jowett, 5 January 1886[1]

Oxford Jan 5

My dear Marshall

Will you & M[rs]. Marshall give me the great pleasure of a visit at Oxford on Sat Jan 23 when I hope to have Welldon,[2] the new Master of Harrow and M[r]. & M[rs]. Humphrey Ward[3] staying with me?

At Oxford, as you know, we follow the Cambridge lead sometimes with uncertain steps. At Cambridge I see that you have made a very important change lately by admitting affiliated students to a degree after two years residence.[4] I have always been in favour of this change myself, but the University is against it, having almost a Superstition in favour of residence. But I do not quite see how to stop at the limit which Cambridge has chosen. Must not every body (say over 19 or 20 to keep out schoolboys) be allowed to start from the commencement of his second year if he offers a higher standard of attainment?

Will you tell me what is thought at Cambridge about this question and what is the exact change made? Also will you kindly send me any papers which bear upon it? Such a change as I spoke of above to which the Cambridge move seems to lead may have a very great effect on the future of both Universities.

With kindest regards to M^rs. Marshall

Believe me | Ever yours | B. Jowett.

---

[1] Marshall Papers. Partly reproduced in Abbott and Campbell, *Letters of Benjamin Jowett* [146.1], pp. 218–9. The fact that 23 January was a Saturday, together with other details, establish the year as 1886.

[2] James Edward Cowell Welldon (1854–1937), Senior Classic 1877 and a Fellow of King's since 1878, was headmaster of Harrow School from 1885 to 1898. Jowett was celebrated for his house parties, which strove to introduce the promising to the famous. See Abbott and Campbell, *Life and Letters* [146.1], vol. 2, pp. 48–51.

[3] Thomas Humphrey Ward (1845–1926) and Mary Augusta (Arnold) Ward (1851–1920). 'Mrs Humphrey Ward' is celebrated as a novelist.

[4] The provision permitting prior extension study sufficient for an Affiliation Certificate to count in lieu of a year's residence at Cambridge had passed the University Senate on 10 December 1885. See *Reporter*, 9 June, 22 and 27 October, and 15 December 1885. Also see Harrison, *Learning and Living* [13.2], pp. 243–4.

---

168. To the Editor, *The Times*, 11 February 1886[1]

Political Economy and Outdoor Relief

Sir,—It is often said that political economy has proved that outdoor relief must do more harm than good; I venture to question this. When outdoor relief was given simply to avoid the expense of indoor relief, it no doubt did great harm. For it was managed carelessly—so as to foster improvidence and make life too pleasant for those who wanted to get through it without doing any hard work. This was in the long run expensive to those who paid the Poor rates and injurious to those on whom they were spent. Economists protested against this short-sighted policy, and welcomed Mr. Goschen's Act of 1870,[2] which, while distributing the burden of indoor relief over the whole of London, kept each union responsible for its own outdoor relief. Some economists are on the whole glad that it has resulted almost in the entire abolition of outdoor relief in many unions. But there are others who regard this result with misgivings.

In administering the criminal law it is considered better to let a thousand guilty escape than to punish one who is innocent. Perhaps we go too far in this; but I think that we go too far in the opposite direction in administering the Poor Law. For we are not yet ready with an organized system of private charity to prevent the homes of honest workers from being broken up by a season of misfortune, and to save from the workhouse those to whom its stagnation and ribaldry are most repulsive. I know that some people deny this and maintain that even in East London kindly provision is made for all truly deserving cases; but their test of merit seems to me to be unreasonably severe. I should not lay much stress on my own opinion on this subject if it did not seem to be that of all working men without exception, the best of them as well as the worst. At Socialist lectures I have been struck by the amused smile with which the *bonâ fide* working men generally receive the extravagances of the orator; but when he talks of the cruelty of cutting off outdoor relief indiscriminately in order to save the rates, every face flushes and every eye gleams. The question whether we are to have order or tumult will be decided not by the well-to-do and not by the residuum, but by the honest working man. A policy which tends to enlist his sympathy with those who are no friends of order is either a great duty or a great blunder.

The economic arguments against the old outdoor abuse do not seem to me to justify us in saying that discrimination must be left to private charity, and that the Poor Law officers may use none but must treat those that have done all that can be fairly expected of them on the same plan as the lazy, the improvident, and the vicious; and that where out relief is still allowed the law should require, as it at present does, the whole income that is derived from any little savings, or from club money or good-conduct pensions, to be deducted from it.

On the other hand, political economy does, I think, prove that if relief works at full wages are started to employ ten thousand men, and kept going for a few years, the result will be that ten thousand extra families will drift into London. This will mean further overcrowding, more children brought up without healthy play, more race deterioration, and in the long run larger crowds of people out of work. We may take warning from the results of Baron Haussmann's public works in Paris.[3] Works that are not in themselves necessary, but are undertaken in order to give employment, should be such as can be suspended at any time. The pay should be enough to afford the necessaries of life, but so far below the ordinary wages of unskilled labour in ordinary trades that people will not be contented to take it for long, but will always be on the look-out for work elsewhere. I for one can see no economic objection to letting public money flow freely for relief works on this plan.

Cambridge, Feb. 11.   Alfred Marshall.

---

[1] Published in *The Times*, 15 February 1886.

[2] George Joachim Goschen as President of the Poor Law Board had introduced the 'Poor Law-Equalization of Rate Bill' into Parliament in 1870.

[3] George Eugene Baron Haussman (1809–91), builder of modern Paris. The grandiose schemes set in train by Louis Napoleon proved financially draining, leading to Haussman's resignation as prefect in 1870.

169. To John Llewelyn Davies, February 1886 (incomplete)[1]

... I have gradually become convinced that the main evil of our present system of aid of the poor is its failure to enlist the co-operation of the working classes themselves. It is because I believe that the working classes alone can rightly guide and discipline the weak and erring of their own number that I have broken silence now. . . .[2]

But the feeling that the Residuum ought not to exist and that they will exist till the working classes themselves have cleared them away . . . has coloured my whole life and thought for the last ten years. I care about it more than about all other political questions put together. . . .

The peril is really very great. Soon the control of the working classes over Imperial and Local Government will cease to be nominal and become real.[3] If they had learnt to look for guidance to the C.O.S.[4] people, they could have been shown how to use out-relief rightly, and not to abuse it. As it is, I believe they *will* abuse it.

I remain,

Yours most respectfully and sincerely, | Alfred Marshall.

I do not think undeserving people often get out-relief: but I think that the House is in many ways less disagreeable to them than to those of clean minds.

[1] Reproduced in *Memorials*, p. 373. The original has not been traced. The *Memorials* version heads the letter 'Balliol Croft, Cambridge, Feb. 1886'. But either the address or the date must be incorrect as the move to Balliol Croft did not take place until August (see [183.2]). It seems probable that Davies wrote to Marshall concerning [168], so that a February date would be plausible. A letter from Davies on outdoor relief appeared in *The Times*, of 19 February 1886. Davies (1843–1916), classicist, theologian, clergyman, and alpinist, was the brother of Sarah Emily Davies [85.1] and a former Fellow of Trinity College, Cambridge. He was at this time vicar of Christ Church, Marylebone.

[2] Probably an allusion to [168].

[3] The franchise reform of 1884 had increased the electorate from 3 to 5 million and introduced for the first time the principle of 'one man one vote'. See, for example, R. C. K. Ensor, *England 1870–1914* (Clarendon, Oxford, 1936), pp. 87–8.

[4] The Charity Organization Society, which aimed to coordinate private attempts to relieve the poor. Florence Ada Keynes and Mary Paley Marshall were both active in the Cambridge branch, and Marshall was a warm supporter.

170. To Arthur Herbert Dyke Acland, 26 February 1886[1]

17 Chesterton Road, Cambridge
26 Feb. 1886

My dear Acland,

I don't think my views on Labour Statistics are worth much: but as you ask for them, here they are.

American experience shows, I think, that a Labour Statistics Bureau may be of great service provided it does not attempt too much.[2] I would have it aim at collecting only a few results at first, but subjecting those to a severe ordeal. It would be slow work at first: but nothing trustworthy can be got till certain disputed points of principle have been settled. When this has been done for a few representative trades, the work can easily be extended to others.

My own plan would be to issue to employers and employed at the chief centres of, say, the machine making trades, forms to be filled up, shewing not only the rates of wages in each branch, but the proportion of workers who get each rate, with separate columns for additions through overtime and piece work, and for deductions through short time. On this basis a draft Report for each such centre should be issued; local papers would no doubt gladly print it. Then notice should be given that a representative of the Bureau would hold a court at a certain time, say in the town hall; and hear arguments to shew that the figures in the draft Report were too high or too low: reporters being present. Then the Bureau should sum up and deliver judgment in its final report.

The process would at first be tedious; but I have so many hundred square yards of wage statistics which I don't much believe, that I would gladly exchange some of them for as many square inches of figures that had been tried in open court in this way.

I agree with you that lists of blue books[3] ought to be more accessible.

Yours very truly, | A. Marshall

---

[1] Printed in *Memorials*, p. 372. The original has not been traced. Acland (1847–1926) had been Senior Bursar of Balliol during Marshall's time there and had recently been elected Member of Parliament for the Rotherham constituency, serving from 1885 to 1899. He was an energetic proponent of educational reform and a supporter of the cooperative movement.

[2] The US Bureau of Labor, established in the Department of the Interior in 1884, became the present Bureau of Labor Statistics in 1913.

[3] British government reports and publications.

171. To the Vice Chancellor, Cambridge University, 15 March 1886[1]

17, Chesterton Road,
15th March, 1886.

Dear Mr Vice-Chancellor,

I desire to offer through you to the University a 'Political Economy Prize' of £15 in each of the next five years to be spent in economic books; and to be awarded by an examination in Political Economy open to all members of the University under the standing of M.A. I should wish that the Examiners be directed to publish the names of those who acquit themselves in a manner deserving honourable mention; and that the first award be in June, 1887.

I hope that a prize may be offered under these or similar arrangements during the whole of my tenure of my chair: but, as the scheme is in some respects a new experiment, I think it best to ask the Senate to sanction it for five years only in the first instance.

I propose to put the sum of £10 each year in the hands of the Vice-Chancellor for the expenses of the examination. I should be glad that this money should be placed at the disposal of the Moral Sciences Board; who have consented, should the scheme be approved by the Senate, to conduct the proposed examination; which in their view should consist of the papers on 'Political Economy' in Part I., and on 'Advanced Political Economy' in Part II. of the Moral Sciences Tripos.[2]

My reason for making this proposal is that our present examinations do not allow scope for all the interests that are connected with economic studies. Provision has indeed been made for the most important of them by the Moral Sciences and Historical Triposes; and to their broadening and stimulating influence much of the recent progress of English Political Economy is due. But the Science has many sides. On some sides the best preparation is to be found in Natural Sciences studies, on others in Mathematical and on others in Legal; while the speculations of Aristotle and Plato often direct the attention of Classical students to the subject. The events of our own age are leading all thoughtful men constantly to read and talk on economic problems, especially if they intend to become ministers of religion or are looking forward to a political career. Thus Economics holds a singular position. It is, I think, the only subject of which the unsystematic study in the University exceeds the systematic: the only one which finds a great portion of its ablest and most diligent students among those who are preparing for, or have graduated in, Triposes in which it is not represented. I want to supply an Examination which, by offering public recognition of thorough work, will help to steady and systematise this unsystematic study. To do this effectively its standard must be high: but it must be confined to the Science itself, so that it may not repel men who can spare but a limited time from their own pursuits. Those who enter for it will, I trust, often be led on to the philosophical and historical studies which are intimately connected with Economic Science.[3]

I am, | Dear Mr Vice-Chancellor, | Yours faithfully, | Alfred Marshall.

The Rev. | The Vice-Chancellor,
Christ's College Lodge, | Cambridge.

---

[1] Printed in the *Reporter*, 4 May 1886. The original does not appear to have been preserved. The Vice Chancellor at this date was Charles Anthony Swainson (1820–87), Master of Christ's College and Lady Margaret Professor of Divinity.

[2] The prize was accepted on the stated terms, except that the recipient was allowed to spend it on books of any description. See *Reporter*, 25 May and 8 June 1886. It was known as the Marshall Prize and was to be replaced by the triennial Adam Smith Prize in 1891. The Marshall Prize was awarded to S. M. Leathes of Trinity in 1887, J. M. E. McTaggart of Trinity in 1888, A. W. Flux of St John's in 1889 and James Welton of Caius in 1891. No award was made in 1890. None of

these recipients was at the time a candidate for the Moral Sciences Tripos. Welton subsequently became Professor of Education at Leeds University. Stanley Mordaunt Leathes (1861–1938), a Fellow of Trinity from 1886, stayed on to become a lecturer in history at Cambridge, leaving in 1903 for the Civil Service Commission. He was knighted in 1919.

[3] Marshall's ambitions to enlarge the basis for teaching his subject had already been announced in his Inaugural Lecture [158.2]: see *Memorials*, pp. 171–4.

172. To Herbert Somerton Foxwell, 24 March 1886[1]

My position is that a Colonial Customs League[2] is impracticable, & w^d.. probably cost us more than w^d.. pay for the child of every poor man a start in life: that the economic arguments to prove that it wd give employment to the unemployed seem to me bad in every way.

But I have always said I sh^d.. be glad if the English people were willing to pay £10,000,000 a year for anything that wd retain the friendship of our colonies. (India I do not regard as a colony.)

I was afraid from what you said at the Guildhall that I advocated buying cheap & selling dear.[3] I do what I can to buy dear & sell cheap in many cases. My contention is that any law made to prevent people from dealing with one another, who want to—they not being helpless women, children, &c—will be evaded & ∴ do more harm than good   A.M.

[1] Foxwell Papers. Postcard, postmarked 'Cambridge MR 24 86'.

[2] The specific proposal or discussion alluded to here remains unclear. Imperial preference had not yet become a prominent issue in public debate. For the pertinent background see Benjamin H. Brown, *The Tariff Reform Movement in Great Britain, 1881–95* (Columbia University Press, New York, 1943), ch. 4.

[3] This probably refers to a meeting held at the Guildhall, Cambridge, on 5 March 1886. This was intended 'to discuss the question—"Do any economic or moral forces keep the wage-earning class in a permanently depressed cond^n., &, if so, by what means can these forces be most efficaciously counteracted?" Sedley Taylor who had called the meeting opened with a paper & then there were speeches. Marshall spoke with some effect, but had by no means got to the heart of the question when his time was up. Foxwell spoke sensibly. Cunningham not so.' (J. N. Keynes, *Diaries*, see entries for 5 and 9 March 1886.) Keynes found the topic 'far too big' and judged the affair 'almost a fiasco'. Sedley Taylor (1834–1920), a sometime Fellow of the College who lived in Trinity for most of his life, was at this time an enthusiast for profit sharing. See his *Profit Sharing Between Capital and Labour: Six Essays* (Kegan Paul, Trench, London, 1884). His main interests lay in music, however.

173. To Herbert Somerton Foxwell, 27 April 1886[1]

Dear Foxwell,

I think the history of the Pol Econ Club is most interesting: far more so even than I had supposed from what little I had heard of it: I shd be very much obliged if you w^d.. put me in the way of becoming a member, either by proposing me yourself or by telling me how to proceed.[2] I suppose that other things being equal it wd be well that one at least of the proposers sh^d.. be a member of old standing. I shd like Courtney[3] as well as any body. I think he w^d.. be willing.

I will bring Nicholson's papers[4] the next time I am passing. His position seems to me very similar to Jevons': I agree with almost all he says: but I don't get much further.

Yours ever | A Marshall

27 April

[1] Foxwell Papers. Envelope postmarked 'Cambridge AP 27 86'.

[2] The Political Economy Club, founded in 1821, had periodic dinner meetings in London at which a designated member introduced discussion on an announced topic. As Professor of Political Economy at Cambridge, Marshall was entitled to be an honorary member, as were various other Professors of the subject elsewhere—Foxwell had become an honorary member in 1882 upon obtaining the Professorship at University College, London. Marshall became a member of the Club in 1886, but it is surprising that he had not been elected earlier. The Club published occasional volumes recording its activities. 1 (1860), 2 (1872), 3 (1881), and 4 (1882) were available at this time. For a comprehensive treatment see Political Economy Club, *Minutes of Proceedings 1899–1920, Roll of Members and Questions Discussed 1821–1920, with Documents Bearing on the History of the Club: Centenary Volume* (vol. 6 of the Club's Publications: Macmillan, London, 1921).

[3] Marshall had hoped to be Foxwell's guest at a meeting of the Club on 8 May 1885 when Courtney was to introduce the question, but a sore throat kept him at home. (Marshall to Foxwell, 6 May 1885, Foxwell Papers.)

[4] Probably a reference to J. S. Nicholson's answers to the questions on the subject of currency and prices circulated by the Royal Commission on the Depression of Trade and Industry of 1886. See the Commission's Third Report, Appendix C (0.22035, App. 2). Marshall's replies are reproduced as pp. 3–16 of his *Official Papers*.

174. To the Editor, *The Statist*, 24 May 1886[1]

Bi-metallism

Sir: I think you have somewhat misapprehended my remarks at the meeting of the Bankers' Institute to discuss Mr. Giffen's paper on 'Bi-metallism.'[2] I did not make it sufficiently clear that my scheme for an authoritative index number had no connection with what I call true bi-metallism.

I said that I regarded what is ordinarily called bi-metallism as very likely to be unstable; for, if the cost of producing gold were to exceed the cost of producing that amount of silver which the currency laws made its equal in value, gold mining would cease, though of course some gold would still be found with the silver. What gold there was would then be absorbed almost entirely by war chests and for the purposes of art and ornament. Nothing would induce English and other civilised people to carry about much more silver than they do now. Not being able to get gold they would insist on having (convertible) notes, and there being very little gold in store these would be chiefly on a silver basis. Thus so-called bi-metallism would in my opinion be very likely to degenerate into silver monometallism, silver coins being used for small change and silver paper for the chief work of business.

I argue that if we are to have a great disturbance of the currency for the sake of bi-metallism we ought, I think, at least to secure that we get it. And for that purpose I suggested a modification of Ricardo's 'Proposals for an economical and secure currency' (pp. 397–454 of McCulloch's edition).[3] He proposes that, except for small change, we should use paper money on a solid gold basis; but that, as the gold basis is wanted only for foreign trade, it should be in the form, not of coins, but of stamped bars of considerable weight. I proposed to wed a silver bar of, say, 2,000 grammes to each gold bar of, say, 100 grammes; the Government being ready to buy or sell a wedded pair of bars in return for a fixed sum of its currency. (It would be somewhere about £29 for England.) This would be true bi-metallism. It would require no international contract; but if adopted by several nations would constitute by itself a working international currency for large transactions. It would soon lead to the adoption of a currency of uniform denomination in all these countries, by which business would be further transacted. It would not attempt to exercise any influence on the relative values of the metals. This was my first plan.[4]

My second plan had no connection with my first. It involved no change of any kind in the currency. In fact it was very similar to that which I understood you, sir, to propose in your last week's number.[5] It was that the Government should publish an authoritative 'Index Number,' and, based on it, an (approximately) uniform standard of purchasing power. It would then empower (but not compel) A, when lending £100 to B say in 1886, to contract for the return at some future time, say in 1896, not of £100, but of money which had in 1896 the same purchasing power which £100 had to 1886. The standard could be used also for rents, wages, interest, &c. I wished to keep these, the main outlines of the plan, as free as possible from complications; but my view is that after a time we might take some further steps in the direction of giving greater stability to trade and industry. Modifications of the standard might be made for special purposes; agricultural contracts, for instance, being arranged in terms of a unit of general purchasing power with specially heavy weights attached to the prices of agricultural produce. So again for contracts in mining industries, &c. And this would lead to more scientific sliding scales for wages than those now in use.

Whether these latter complications are introduced or not, this scheme seems to me to be of far more practical importance to the industry of the country than bi-metallism of any kind. It does not require Government to interfere with contracts, but only to give facilities for forming them on a reasonable basis. I may add that I alluded to it some time ago at the Industrial Remuneration

Conference (*See* Report, pp. 78–9 and 185–6).[6]
I am, Sir, &c., Alfred Marshall

Cambridge, 24th May.

[1] Printed in *The Statist*, 17/431, 29 May 1886, p. 592.
[2] The text of the paper by R. Giffen, 'On Some Bi-Metallic Fallacies', *Journal of the Institute of Bankers*, 7 (June 1886), pp. 397–429, is followed by a detailed report of the discussion (pp. 430–59), which is in turn followed by 'Additional Notes by Mr Giffen' (pp. 460–6). Marshall's comments (pp. 447–51) make the proposals outlined in the letter. These proposals were alluded to in an anonymous article, 'A Practical Conclusion from the Appreciation of Gold', *The Statist*, 17/430 (22 May 1886), pp. 556–7. An opponent of bimetallism, *The Statist*, raised the 'practical objection' to Marshall's first proposal (symmetalism) that 'it involves, according to his own admission, an extensive reconstruction of our whole monetary system' (p. 556).
[3] David Ricardo, *Proposals for an Economical and Secure Currency* . . . (Murray, London, 1816): James Ramsey McCulloch, *The Works of David Ricardo* (Murray, London, 1846; new edition 1871).
[4] Marshall's two proposals were to be described at greater length in his 'Remedies for Fluctuations of General Prices', *Contemporary Review*, 51 (March 1887), pp. 355–75, reprinted in *Memorials*, pp. 188–211. See also *Official Papers*, pp. 9–15, 28–31.
[5] See the 22 May article referred to in n. 2 above.
[6] See Dilke, *Industrial Remuneration Conference* [156.5]. The first of the page references should be 178–9.

175. To Herbert Somerton Foxwell, 29 May 1886[1]

29 May
My dear Foxwell
    Sidgwick came to me after last Board meeting & spoke thusly:—
    'If you & Foxwell think that the Advanced P.E. papers w^d.. be improved

by having the history of early economic theory
    &   the   "   "   "   "   facts

taken out of it & put into Pol: Phil: I will consent: though I am not anxious for the change. If the change is made I shd wish it to be as much as possible on your (F & Ms) responsibility not on mine; I shd like you to agree on suggestions for the necessary alteration of the schedule, & also on books to be recommended. One reason why I am not ready to take the responsibility for the change is that I do not see my way to naming books w^h.. I myself like.'
    I have been very busy, or I shd have come to you before. Having missed you this morning, I write.
    If early history be defined as that before 1770, & a good roomy berth can be found for it under the head of Pol: Philos I sh^d.. be mildly in favour of the change. But I am not rampant about it.
    What say you?[2]
    The Statist & I are rubbing our jowls together over the notion that so called Bimetallism w^d.. be likely to degenerate into Silver Monometallism.[3]

I saw Walford's Catalogue[4] in your rooms. It made my mouth water.
Yours quite ever | A Marshall

---

[1] Foxwell Papers. Envelope postmarked 'Cambridge MY 29 86'.
[2] It does not appear that any formal change was made by the Moral Sciences Board. Foxwell would hardly have been prone to support the proposal.
[3] See [174].
[4] A bookseller's catalogue?

176. To Francis Ysidro Edgeworth, 17 June 1886[1]

West Cliff, Lower Sheringham, | N^r Cromer
17 June 1886

My dear Edgeworth,

Just the same question has been asked me by Ashley,[2] whom perhaps you know. My answer can be but a slight one. My information has been got gradually, a great deal of it from conversation; I have crossexamined people (normally conversant with India) who have started by saying that prices & wages in India were ruled by custom & have got them to admit that the custom always changed in substance, if not in outward form, whenever there was any considerable Ricardo-economic reason why it sh^d.. And I have picked up hints here & there in my reading, some of wh I have noted down: but most of them have simply gone to form my general impressions.

The only books that I think I recommended to Ashley were W Hunters.[3] But it now occurs to me that there are a good many more in Phears Aryan Village (Macmillan).[4]

Of course there are price lists for wholesale purchases in India as in England: but I don't want to lay too much stress on this.

I have just seen your post card.[5] I expect you know the books I shd be most inclined to recommend viz in English Cossa's *very* brief account (MacMillan), Ingrams article on Pol Econ in the Encyclopaedia (his literary but unscientific mind seems to me to have absorbed useful results out of the German historians with regard to Pre-Adam-(Smith)ite times, though most of what he says as to the last hundred years seems to me to be nonsense).

In German I strongly recommend Kautz Geschichtliche Entwickelung der Nat. Oekon: of course there is Roschers vast Geschichte der Pol Oekon in Deutschland.

Yours sincerely | A Marshall

Glad to see you are to be a Statistical Councillor.[6]

---

[1] BLPES, Edgeworth Papers.
[2] There is no record of William James Ashley's request. The mutability of custom and the applicability of Ricardian theory to non-commercial societies were to be prominent issues in Marshall's disagreements with Ashley, and especially with William Cunningham.

[3] Sir William Wilson Hunter (1840–1900) was a prolific writer on Indian topics. His most general work is *The Indian Empire: Its People, History and Products* (Trübner, London, 1882).

[4] Sir John Budd Phear [51.8], *The Aryan Village in India and Ceylon* (Macmillan, London, 1880).

[5] Not preserved. Apparently a request for advice on treatments of the history of economics. The works referred to are: Luigi Cossa, *Guide to the Study of Political Economy* (Macmillan, London 1880: translated from the second Italian edition); John Kells Ingram, 'Political Economy', *Encyclopaedia Britannica, Ninth Edition*, vol. 19 (Scribners, New York, 1885), pp. 346–401; Gyula Kautz, *Die Geschichtliche Entwicklung der National-oekonomik und ihrer Literatur* (Gerold, Vienna, 1860); Wilhelm Georg Friedrich Roscher, *Geschichte der Nationalökonomik in Deutschland* (Oldenburg, Munich, 1874).

[6] See *Journal of the [London] Statistical Society*, 49 (September 1886), p. 523, for Edgeworth's election to the Council of the Society.

177. To Robert Giffen, 25 June 1886[1]

Firenze, | Chesterton Road, | Cambridge.
25 June 1886

Dear Mr Giffen,

I have not yet made clear, I fear, my proposal about linked bars of gold & silver.[2] For in the notes you have added to the report of the discussion at the Bankers Institute,[3] you speak of my proposing the use of certificates.

But what I meant to propose was a paper currency—the only legal tender —based on linked bars of gold & silver. No doubt there w^d.. be great opposition to the adoption of so strange a scheme: & I do not myself advocate it *positively* but only *relatively* to the so called Bimetallic scheme. If however it were once introduced, there would be no difficulty about floating the paper: as it w^d.. be the only money (except of course copper & silver token coins). The essence of the plan is that it w^d.. not try to fix the value of gold relatively to silver; & therefore not relatively to the currency which w^d.. be fixed at a mean between the values of gold & silver.

I quite admit the validity of your objections to the second scheme[4] as it stands. I did not want to overweight my proposal by going into details; but my complete scheme includes provision for recasting the basis of the index number at fixed intervals. I am a little shy of talking about this, because I find myself changing my mind as to the best way of carrying out this part of the plan.

Yours very truly | Alfred Marshall

[1] Marshall Papers.

[2] See [174].

[3] See [174.2]. Giffen (p. 466) was 'not very much taken' with the proposal which he understood Marshall to make for 'a combination of gold and silver in bars against which Governments should issue certificates', fearing that such certificates could not be floated.

[4] Giffen (p. 466) very much liked the index number proposal but observed that the behaviour of the price index over long periods might be very dependent upon unpredictable changes in the technology of producing the various goods it covered.

178. From Robert Giffen, 28 June 1886[1]

June 28th 1886

Dear Mr Marshall

I am much obliged to you for your note of the 25^{th 2} but I fear I have no time to answer it. I am more interested perhaps than you imagine about both your suggestions. About the first, namely, the linked bars of gold & silver, I may say that I was speaking not perhaps with strict accuracy of your issuing 'certificates' against the linked bars; still I should regard the issue of what you describe as paper money against them practically as the same thing. Paper money as far as I know is only in three forms:—first, a certificate, like the gold and silver certificates of the United States' Government; second, a promise to pay a distinct sum of money on demand or a distinct thing; & third, a promise to pay a distinct sum of money or a distinct thing but not on demand. The equivalent of the latter is expressed by some foreign issues of paper, not in the form of a distinct promise but by the use of an expression as 'worth so much' or some phrase of that sort. For the strict purposes of the discussion, however, any of these forms which are admissible come to much the same thing & I should [equally]³ object to them on the grounds I have stated in my notes. I do not think they could be floated. You say that they would be the only legal tender & again that they would be the only money, except of course copper & silver token coins. Nevertheless I doubt if, in some communities, they could be floated even on these terms, or at any rate whether they could be floated so as to exclude the use of either gold or silver separately & the issue of paper money by individuals & corporations against deposits of gold or silver. My belief is that gold & silver, especially gold, are in demand for certain definite & separate purposes & that whatever legal enactments may be, this natural demand can never be entirely got rid of. Any attempt to create money or currency without regard to this natural demand breaks down at a point: the demand remains & the metal is continued to be used for the purposes of money in spite of the enactment of any other kind of money.

A very long time ago I entertained some such idea as you have, in fact I believe it was suggested at one time by one of the Herschells, but I am unable to give the reference;⁴ on considering it however I was unable to see my way & from what I have seen of business since & the feelings of business men on such subjects, I [become]⁵ more & more convinced that they will not look at any thing except a particular metal as standard money & certificates or promises to pay on demand based on that metal; anything else will be considered by the better class of business people as unsound money & I say this in spite of the vogue which bi-metallism has at present achieved.

As to your second suggestion I should like very much indeed that you would develop it more fully. I believe that in consequence of the great increase of population & great development of industry during the last century & which is still going on, a new condition as regards money is coming into existence. The tendency I believe will be for prices to fall more quickly from period to period & from generation to generation than they have ever done in the history of mankind & that these changes of prices are more material than they ever were to commercial men just because business itself is so enormously extended. Some of the difficulties of this fall may be met by the use of index numbers in the way you suggest & it is therefore expedient that schemes of this kind should be discussed & developed.

   Yours very truly | [Robert Giffen]

[1] Marshall Papers. An unsigned copy discovered with [177] at the Board of Trade, where Giffen headed the Statistical Department from 1876–97.
[2] See [177].
[3] Illegible word.
[4] The reference Giffen had in mind has not been identified. Possibly he was alluding to Farrer Herschell (1837–99), Solicitor General 1880–5 and Lord High Chancellor 1885 and 1892–5, who as Lord Herschell chaired the Gold and Silver Commission of 1887–8 [214.5]. But the Herschel family seems much more likely. Sir William Herschel (1738–1822), the famous astronomer, had considered in 1801 the relationship between sun spot activity and the price of wheat. His son, Sir John Herschel (1792–1871), astronomer and scientist, who served as Master of the Mint, 1850–5, seems the most likely candidate. But Sir John's sons, William James (1833–1917), Alexander Stuart (1836–1907), and John (1837–1921), all of whom displayed a strong scientific bent— William pioneered the use of fingerprints for identification—are also possibilities.
[5] Word apparently omitted.

179. To Herbert Somerton Foxwell, 17 July 1886[1]

                    Villa Rosa | Lower Sheringham | N^r Cromer
                                                            17 July
My dear Foxwell,

   You have inclosed nothing in your letter. But I had a long talk with Miller's young man[2] in Cambridge last winter; & have nothing to add to what I said then. I think lectures are good: an economic journal on scientific lines good: but I am against spending money on a new journal on popular economics.

   I am glad your lectures went off well.

   An idea came into my head to take the opportunity of the British Ass^n.. to say something, I rather want to say, about 'General Overproduction.' But Martin[3] has sent me the list of papers already arranged for. It is so vast, that I am not inclined to add another. I have not quite decided: but nearly: It w^d.. keep my book back by a chapter.[4]

   Yours quite ever | A Marshall

[1] Foxwell Papers.
[2] Probably Robert Miller (?–1898) an engineer who had made a fortune in Australia and returned to settle in Edinburgh. He financed anonymously the Industrial Remuneration Conference of 1885 [156.5] and was anxious to further social enquiry and discussion. He was apparently prepared

to provide £150 a year for the promulgation of economic thinking. Miller's 'young man' remains unidentified. See Frederic Harrison, *Autobiographic Memoirs* (Macmillan, London, 1911: 2 vols.), vol. 2, pp. 296–8. Miller's money also helped finance a series of lectures, given at various venues in Scotland in the summer of 1886, in which Foxwell was a participant, lecturing on 'Irregularity of Employment and Fluctuation of Prices'. The lectures were published as John Burnett and others, *The Claims of Labour* (Cooperative Printing, Edinburgh, 1886). See J. M. Bellamy and J. Savage, *Dictionary of Labour Biography*, vol. 2 [157.2], pp. 73–4.

[3] John Biddulph Martin, a London banker who wrote on monetary topics. The British Association for the Advancement of Science was to meet at Birmingham in September with Martin serving as President of Section F.

[4] Marshall did not read a paper. See [180].

180. To Herbert Somerton Foxwell, 26 July 1886[1]

Sheringham
26 July 1886

My dear Foxwell,

I have been thinking a good deal about your suggestion that I shd. urge Keynes to edit an economic journal supported by Miller's money.[2] I shd. be very glad if he wd.. But Miller's letter[3] & what his young man told me in Cambridge lead me to fear that he might want more room for people like Wallace[4]—to say nothing of Hyndman[5]—than either Keynes or I shd think right. What I hoped might happen was

i You & others to start an association for bringing out a Journal: with an editorial committee of wh. (say) Keynes wd.. be secretary & paid editor (say £50) a year.

ii People in general invited to subscribe. I think a good many people wd.. guarantee £10 to £20 a year. Miller might then be asked to contribute some or all of his £150 to this: but the tone of the association wd.. be settled independently of him. Cannot something of this kind be done?

I don't think £150 a year is enough to start it. I think there ought to be *at least* £300 for the first year, perhaps £150 for the second & after a few years it ought to pay its way. My one conviction is that it is better to do nothing than to do it on the cheap.

I have determined to go on with my book for the present at least. You know my views will appear on some points about money in the next volume of the Depression of Trade Com^n.. Reports.[6] So I am writing to Martin to say I won't read a paper at Birmingham.[7]

We get into our new house early in August. General Walker is coming to us on Aug 10th..[8]

Yours ever | A Marshall

[1] Foxwell Papers.
[2] See [179.2].

[3] Not traced.

[4] Probably Alfred Russell Wallace [116.2].

[5] Henry Mayers Hyndman (1842–1921), socialist leader and follower of Marx.

[6] See [173.4].

[7] See [179.3].

[8] Francis Amasa Walker had held the rank of Brigadier General in the American Civil War. On 13 August Keynes 'lunched with the Marshalls meeting General Walker. He is a great talker but very interesting; and thoroughly genial' (*Diaries*).

181. From Charles Booth, 18 October 1886[1]

2 Talbot Court | London E.C
18 October 1886

Dear Sir,

I have received your very kind note[2] of the 15th. & am encouraged by it to venture on asking a favour from you.

I am now engaged (with some others) on an attempt to describe analytically the industrial & social status of the population of London: that is, to state the proportions in which different classes exist, with the actual present condition of each.

It is a very difficult undertaking & any results obtained will be much open to criticism of all kinds.

What I wish to ask for from you is criticism, *in advance*, on the method adopted.

It is proposed to piece together information from as many different sources as possible, so as to make the evidence check & complete itself so far as possible. The framework of the enquiry will be found in the facts obtainable from the School board visitors, who, among them, provide something very like a house to house visitation in the poorer districts, & who usually know the occupation & something of the condition of life of every family, where there are school children, in the lower middle class & all below it.

As a trial I have completed a preliminary analysis, from school board information, of a sub-registration district in the East End of London with 20,000 inhab & it is this analysis which I desire to submit to you before going further with the work as much depends on the soundness of the system adopted.

I hope you will excuse the liberty I am taking in asking this favour from you. I had intended to make the request through my friend M[r] Arthur D Acland[3] with whom I believe you are acquainted, & who is associated in the present attempt; but M[r] Acland is out of town & on receiving your note I decided to write direct.

I am | Yours very truly | Charles Booth

[1] University of London Library, Booth Papers. Substantially reproduced in Thomas Spensley Simey and Margaret B. Simey, *Charles Booth: Social Scientist* (Oxford University Press, Oxford, 1960), p. 86, which provides further background. Booth was at this time just embarking on the extensive enquiries leading to his monumental nine-volume study *Life and Labour of the People in London* (London, 1891–1903).
[2] Not traced.
[3] See [170.1].

182. From Charles Booth, 20 October 1886[1]

2 Talbot Court EC | London
20 October 1886

Dear Sir

I am much obliged for your kind consent, & now enclose by book post:

(1) Notes on the method adopted
(2) Schedules for S[t] Pauls sub. reg. dist.
(3) Summary
(4) Classified list of occupations.

The first three explain themselves; the fourth contains all the occupations we have yet come across.[2] The list under each heading will become much longer as we proceed but enough is done to indicate how all sorts of occupations will be dealt with.

I feel I am pressing too much on your good nature in sending you such a mass of materials, but I do not see how to make it any less if our plan is to be fairly laid before you. Pray take your own time & do not hesitate to send the most unfavourable criticisms that occur to you.

The clergy of the neighborhood[3] so far as I have yet obtained their views, consider the picture given far too favourable & I think myself that class 3 in labour is exaggerated at the expense of class 2.[4]

I obtained yesterday the scheduled results of the Mansion House relief[5] given in this neighborhood & it would seem from a hasty comparison that, if my figures are correct, not less than half of classes 1, 2 & 3 were relieved. The comparison can be made more exactly when our figures are extended to cover the same area as that dealt with by the Mansion House Committee for S[t] Georges in the East, & may also be made elsewhere in London.

Yours very truly | Charles Booth

Alfred Marshall Esq

[1] University of London Library, Booth Papers.
[2] 'accross' in the original.
[3] Original spelling.

[4] Booth divided the working classes into six classes (subsequently labelled A–F), the three lowest being those without regular earnings. See his 'The Inhabitants of Tower Hamlets (School Board Division) Their Condition and Occupations', *Journal of the Royal Statistical Society*, 50 (June 1887), pp. 326–91, especially pp. 329–33. The reported discussion of this paper (pp. 392–401) includes interesting remarks by Marshall (pp. 392–6).

[5] The Lord Mayor's relief fund had organized a preliminary inquiry into poverty. See Belinda Norman-Butler, *Victorian Aspirations: The Life and Labour of Charles and Mary Booth* (George Allen and Unwin, London, 1972), p. 71.

183. To Oscar Browning, 27 October 1886[1]

Balliol Croft, | Madingley Road, Cambridge.[2]
27 Oct 86

My dear Browning,

With the concurrence of the Moral Sciences Board, I write to say that I should be very glad to act on the suggestion made to me by you that the 'Pryme' collection of books shd be deposited with the Historical books in the Gallery of the Philosophical Societies Library. Will you kindly lay before the Committee which manages the Historical collection this my request that they will kindly receive them on deposit.[3]

I calculate that the books will fill about 100 feet of wall space: say, the space between two windows of the gallery, & possibly the space under a window in addition. Many of the books are paper pamphlets, & the lower shelves had therefore, I think, best be inclosed with doors.

Had they gone into the Moral Sciences Lecture room I proposed to spend £25 on providing bookshelves &c. I shall be glad to hand over that sum to your Committee for the purpose of firstly providing a bookplate with Professor Pryme's name on it, secondly providing bookshelves & cupboards; & thirdly in case there should be any surplus, binding some of the books.

I have a good slip catalogue made by Mr Rogers[4] of the University Library. But of course there are as yet no labels on the backs of the books.

Yours sincerely | Alfred Marshall

Oscar Browning Esq.

[1] King's College, Cambridge, Browning Papers.

[2] This is the first letter addressed from the house which was to be home to the Marshalls for the remainder of their lives. The full address was 'Balliol Croft, 6 Madingley Road, Cambridge'.

[3] On 11 May 1886 the Special Board for Moral Science had reported to the Vice-Chancellor that:

The late Professor Pryme having left a collection of books the catalogue of which he describes as 'one of the catalogues made by George Pryme first Professor of Political Economy in the University of Cambridge of a portion of his Library, bequeathed by him for the use of all future Professors of that Science'; the Board recommend that Professor Marshall be authorised to put up in Room No. 5 of the Literary Schools lock-up cases to contain the above collection; that he be at liberty to grant the use of a key of the cases to any student at his discretion; and that this be deemed due custody of the books (*Reporter*, 25 May 1886).

This report was discussed by Senate on 14 October, when Marshall further explained that the deeming of 'due custody' was 'the vital point of the Report, and if it were not conceded he did not see what could be done'. He explained that 'the books had long lain in boxes in the room next the Vice-Chancellor's room' and that the passage quoted in the Report was the only known instruction relating to them. The University Librarian was unwilling to accession them temporarily, while the Moral Sciences Board wished to retain the option of adding them to a Moral Sciences Library, should one be formed. Hence the current proposal. (*Reporter*, 19 October 1886).

The alternative proposal to house the Pryme Library with the History books was probably made by Browning after the 14 October discussion and was the one adopted. The Library of the Cambridge Philosophical Society had been taken over by the University in 1881 and was housed in the New Museums near the Cavendish Laboratory. The Literary Lecture Rooms and Selwyn Divinity School, where lecture room 5 came to be Marshall's peculiar territory, were on Trinity Street, directly across from the gateway of St John's. The building is now known as the Selwyn Divinity School.

[4] Not further identified.

184. To John Bates Clark, 29 October 1886[1]

Many thanks for your interesting 'Philosophy of Wealth'[2] I have found out Miss Rand and Miss Johnson:[3] & my wife & I have had great pleasure in welcoming them.

Yours very truly | Alfred Marshall

[1] Columbia University Library, J. B. Clark Papers. Postcard postmarked 'Cambridge OC 29 86'.
[2] J. B. Clark, *The Philosophy of Wealth: Economic Principles Newly Formulated* (Ginn, Boston, 1886).
[3] Helen Chadwick Rand and Mary Augusta Johnson were Americans studying at Newnham College during 1886–7.

185. To Macmillan and Company, 13 November 1886[1]

Mess[rs] MacMillan & Co   13 Nov 1886

Dear Sirs

We will at some time talk out the question of the copyright of the Economics of Industry in other than English speaking countries.[2] I think the author ought always to retain in his own hands the power of authorising translations.

It is not a matter of £.s.d: but of something much more important & the principle seems to me to be one of the highest importance.

I notice that our Agreement makes no mention of translations: though it does of copies sold in America.

Meanwhile I sh[d].. like to write to the gentleman who is going to translate the Economics of Industry into Marathi: suggesting that he shd introduce some paragraphs about India: will you therefore kindly return me his letter, as I have forgotten his name.[3]

Yours truly | Alfred Marshall

[1] British Library, Macmillan Archive. From Balliol Croft.

[2] Further correspondence (not reproduced here) in the Marshall Papers indicates:

    (i)   The issue was precipitated by a request of 16 October to Marshall from one Ramon R. Plastounoff for permission to make a Russian translation.

    (ii) 'Macmillan & Co.' responded on November 15 'We think there is not the slightest difference of opinion between us as to the power of the author to authorise translations'.

[3] Not identified. The names 'Nasik' and 'Mr Vinayakappji Gupte' are mentioned in Macmillans' 15 November letter.

186. To Herbert Somerton Foxwell, 17 November 1886[1]

17 Nov

Dear Foxwell

Prymes Pamphlets turn out to be far more numerous than I had thought. I fear that it will be necessary to follow the plan adopted in the University Library & Trinity Library of binding often 15 or 20 together, in more cases than you w^d.. like. I hope this won't make you throw up the job in disgust. You may even yet alter my views: but at present I feel that when I have spent £30 all told on the collection, the final utility of any further binding will have (to me) a lower economic measure than its expenses of production. Meanwhile we want a Pryme book plate badly. I want to consult you about that. I don't want to have the Historical Library book plate put in them.

I reckon thus,

catalogue rather over	£5
bookplate, moving & perhaps labelling	£5
binding	£20
	£30

Be gentle & don't storm at me too much.

Yours | A. M.

[1] Foxwell Papers. From Balliol Croft. See [183]. Writing on the same day to Oscar Browning, Marshall stated that 'Pryme's pamphlets are more numerous than I had thought. I am going to get Foxwell to help me with them'. He opposed Browning's suggestion that there be two bookplates: 'it w^d.. injure the books, drive Foxwell wild, & really be unnecessary'. An earlier note of 28 October to Browning had intimated amendment of the budget proposed in [183]: 'I am glad that shelves will probably be provided gratis for the Pryme Collection. There is room for spending any amount of money on binding the books.' (King's College, Cambridge, Browning Papers.)

187. From Léon Walras, 25 November 1886[1]

Lausanne, 3 Square de Georgette,
25 novembre 1886

Monsieur et très honoré collègue,

Je fais imprimer en ce moment une théorie de la Monnaie[2] qui sera précedée d'une petite préface dans laquelle j'ai saisi une occasion qui s'offrait à moi de citer les économistes qui font entrer la considération de la *Final Utility* dans la théorie de la valeur d'échange. Je vous ai rangé parmi ces économistes; et j'ai indiqué d'après les explications que vous m'avez fournies il y a 3 ans, comment vous aviez précédé Jevons sur ce point.[3] J'y ai fait figurer aussi M. Edgeworth en raison de son *Mathematical Psychics*.[4]

Il me semble d'après ce que m'a dit Edgeworth que je pourrais citer également M. le Prof. Henry Sidgwick en raison de ses *Methods of Ethics* et de ses *Principles of Political Economy;*[5] mais je n'ai point ces ouvrages entre les mains et je crains de commettre peut-être une erreur. J'ai écrit, il y a huit jours à M. Foxwell pour le prier de me renseigner; [mais je ne reçois pas de réponse] de lui; pouvez-vous le faire à [sa] place?[6] Dans le cas où M. Sidgwick [nous] appartiendrait effectivement, je vous prierais de me fournir le titre exact ainsi que le lieu et la date de publication des ouvrages de lui que je puis mentionner. J'aimerais également connaître le titre exact de M. Sidgewick comme professeur à Cambridge.

Excusez-moi, Monsieur et cher collègue, du dérangement que je vous cause. Dès que je le pourrai, je vous enverrai ma préface. Elle vous prouvera, je crois, que l'économie dont j'ai parlé valait la peine d'être saisie et que la doctrine de la '*Terminal Value in Use*' (puisque c'est ainsi que vous l'appeliez) est en train de faire très bien son chemin dans le monde.

Croyez-moi je vous prie votre respectueux et bien dévoué | Léon Walras

---

[1] Reproduced in *LW*, letter 749. Jaffé's transcription of the original draft (University of Lausanne, Fonds Walras) is followed here. The square brackets enclose words supplied by Jaffé in lieu of illegible or omitted words.

Précis: Walras announces that he will shortly publish a work on the theory of money, in the preface of which he will take the opportunity to list those economists introducing the final-utility theory of exchange value. Marshall will be included, his anticipation of Jevons being indicated in accordance with his earlier letter [133]. Walras will also include Edgeworth and wonders if he should include Sidgwick, but is unfamiliar with his works. He wrote to Foxwell eight days ago for advice on this, but has had no reply and asks whether Marshall would be willing to help instead. The exact title and publication date of pertinent works of Sidgwick would be needed: also Sidgwick's precise title in Cambridge. Walras apologizes for the trouble he is causing and will send a copy of his preface. Marshall will see that the theory is well worth mastering and that the doctrine of 'terminal value in use', to use Marshall's term, promises to make its way in the world.

[2] L. Walras, *Théorie de la Monnaie* (Corbaz, Lausanne, etc., 1886).

[3] See [133].

[4] See [94.2].

[5] See [14.2], [90.3]. The misspelling of Sidgwick is presumably Walras's.
[6] The letter to Foxwell and Foxwell's eventual reply are reproduced in *LW*, letters 744, 750.

188. To Léon Walras, 28 November 1886[1]

28 November 1886

Dear Prof Walras,

Foxwell's father died recently. But Sidgwick tells me he has sent a message to you through him.[2]

I am glad you are going to collect and complete your economic writings.

As to Jevons and myself I do not claim to have anticipated him as to the doctrine of final utility, but to have learnt what I learnt from anybody, from Cournot, not from him.[3] I gave the doctrine in lectures before Jevons published it. But it is quite likely that he gave it in lectures as early as I did, or earlier.

Wishing your new book all success,

I am | Yours sincerely, | Alfred Marshall

[1] University of Lausanne, Fonds Walras. Published as *LW*, letter 751. From Balliol Croft.
[2] See *LW*, letter 750.
[3] See [133], [126.4].

189. From Francis Amasa Walker, 29 November 1886[1]

In the course of another week my publishers, the Messrs. Scribner, will send you a copy of my work on the History of the Second Army Corps,[2] which has given me indescribable pains and suffering during the past three or four years, in the collection of materials amid vast heaps of rubbish, or in determining with approximate accuracy the course of a thunderbolt on some summer's evening of 1862 or 3 or 4.

It is all done now, for weal or woe, the book has been ordered to press. Please let a copy stand on your shelves, if not out of interest in the fortunes of the body of troops whose history I have sought to narrate, then, in remembrance of me.

I sent you a week or two ago, or more, a copy of the 1st n°. of the Harvard Quarterly Journal of Economics.[3] The publisher will hereafter send the nos. to you, on issue, as I am desirous you should get the magazine, for our sake, not yours. I shall, also, send you, about Decr. 15, a copy of the new Scribner's Magazine, in which I have an article on Socialism.[4] As I wrote Foxwell, it is not deep, but only seeks to draw certain lines on the surface which may help the 'popular reader' of economic literature, to place himself, at any time, with reference to this make of government initiative and enterprise—'orient himself' would be the fashionable word.

I have been monstrously busy ever since my return from England, first, with my trip to California, and then, in finishing my book, but I have found time to think very often of my visit to Cambridge, and of your and Mrs. Marshall's great kindness to me.[5]

My school year has opened, in every way, fortunately. Our annual Catalogue will be sent you next week, so that you may see how unlike an English University is a Yankee School of Technology.[6]

---

[1] Printed, ostensibly in full but without salutation or closing, in Munroe, *A Life* [163.1], pp. 263–4. The date is provided by Munroe.

[2] Francis A. Walker, *History of the Second Army Corps in the Army of the Potomac* (Scribner, New York, 1886).

[3] The first issue of the *Quarterly Journal of Economics*, 1, is dated October 1886.

[4] Francis A. Walker, 'Socialism', *Scribner's Magazine*, 1 (January 1887), pp. 107–19. Reprinted in Walker's *Discussions in Economics and Statistics*, ed. Davis R. Dewey (Holt, New York, 1899).

[5] See [180.8]. Walker had made a second visit to California to advise Leland Stanford in August–September 1886. See Elliott, *Stanford University* [163.3], p. 26.

[6] Walker was at this time President of the Massachusetts Institute of Technology. Two further letters to Marshall from Walker of 1887 (no date as the first page was lost) and 20 January 1888 are substantially reproduced by Munroe, *A Life* [163.1], pp. 305–6 and 320–1. The originals have not been traced. These letters are not reproduced below since they throw little light on the relationship of the correspondents, being essentially expositions of Walker's views on, respectively, the Interstate Commerce Bill and the American political scene. The next letter of Walker's reproduced below is [323].

---

190. To Karl Pearson, 13 December 1886[1]

13 Dec 86

Dear Sir,

I have long wished to make your acquaintance & have hoped that some accident might bring us together. At last I venture to ask you if you would come to see me some time when you are in Cambridge. Perhaps it might be convenient for you to dine with me in Hall at St John's on some day during our Christmas 'Festivities', w^h.. last from Decr 27 to Dec 31 inclusive. If you think you could come on the 27th—'St John's Day'—I shd be glad to know early: but for the other days of the 'Festivities' no notice is required.

I have just this moment been looking at Bax's paper on you in his 'Religion of Socialism':[2] & that suggested to me that I shd wait no longer for an introduction from accident.

Yours truly | Alfred Marshall

---

[1] University College, London, Pearson Papers. From Balliol Croft. Pearson, 3rd Wrangler in 1879, had established a reputation for brilliance in his time at King's.

[2] Ernest Belfort Bax, 'The Two Enthusiasms: An Answer to Mr. Karl Pearson', in his *The Religion of Socialism; being Essays in Modern Socialist Criticism* (Sonnenschein Lowery, London, 1886). Bax comments on Pearson's lecture, *The Enthusiasm of the Market Place and of the Study* (South Place Ethical Society Publications, 5, London, 1885).

191. From Benjamin Jowett to Mary Paley Marshall, 30 December 1886[1]

Balliol College:
Dec 30. 1886

Dear Mrs Marshall

I was very much pleased to hear from you & to find that you had not forgotten me or the episode of your life at Oxford.

I think that your husband is one of the happiest of men in having a subject of study which deeply interests him & which deeply interests the world at the present day and besides being speculative may be the source of untold benefits to the multitude of men. And you share his happiness & interests in a manner that hardly falls to the lot of any other woman and I hope that you will not allow him to write anything that is not perfectly intelligible and which cannot be expressed in words without symbols: You remember that I was always an enemy to the Mathematical formulae—He will reply that I do not understand them which is very true. But I remember that H Smith[2] was equally opposed to them & I think that all attempts of any kind to express ideas by numbers & figures have failed & will always fail because they are not in pari materia—things indefinite cannot be measured by things definite though they may be sometimes illustrated by them. Therefore I was very glad to hear that the doctrine of numbers was to be relegated to the Appendix.

I do not think that I have seen or written to you since General Walker came to see me.[3] I was very much pleased & interested in him. He seems to deserve all you said in praise of him.

I hope that you like the new Master of Trinity:[4] He is a very good man & quite devoted to his work, religious, but not at all illiberal; & therefore I should expect him to do a great deal for the Undergraduates: His wife was a charming person & would have been a great help to him in his new position. Though not very learned or able he has a touch of genius & is very accessible to new ideas.

The Ladies Colleges & their education seem to flourish at Oxford in a quiet way. I always hope that they will not desert accomplishments, for what they consider solid attainments. It seems to me that they should be united & that there ought to be no opposition between. We all of us need solid knowledge, & a solid method of working, but we don't require much of this solid food: I am afraid of overworking & of destroying elasticity. I should like the Ladies' Colleges to be distinguished as places of Society & good manners, and also to be schools of music, which seems to me to have great power in forming the character—But I suspect that you would not agree in this view of ladies' education, or rather of a part of it. For I do not deny that the other side of regular attainments must be included.

I shall look forward to a visit from you & Alfred in the Spring or at any time when you are able to offer.

Will you give my kindest regards to your husband & best wishes for the new year

I have told a Bookseller to send you some of Count Tolstoi's[5] novels as a very small new years gift. I hope that you will like them.

Believe me | Ever yours truly | B Jowett

I should like very much to hear what your husband thinks about bimetallism— I am afraid that his plan[6] would be too agreeable to the American Silvermongers & very disagreeable to the Indian Cultivators of the Soil.

[1] Marshall Papers. Partially reproduced in Abbott and Campbell, *Life and Letters* [146.1], vol. 2, pp. 315–6, where it is dated 20 December.

[2] See [102.4].

[3] See [180.8].

[4] Henry Montagu Butler (1833–1918), Master 1886–1918, had previously been headmaster of Harrow School.

[5] Count Lev Nikolayevich Tolstoy (1828–1910).

[6] See [174].

192. To Francis Ysidro Edgeworth, 11 January 1887[1]

11 Jan 87

My dear Edgeworth,

I found I could not put 'purchasing power' before my currency theories. I tried writing on that plan: but it failed & I had to put $1\frac{1}{2}$ days work into the fire.

So I have stuck to my old original plan, & have written an article on my currency theories winding up with a couple of pages on purchasing power. That will I hope appear on the first of March & then I shall be at your service, if you care to have me.[2] The Pol: Econ: Club discussion on the matter is in about 3 weeks time.[3]

I found the subject grow: I don't know what the Editor will say to the length of my article. I did all I could to keep it down. And had to squeeze especially at the end.

The article is not long: but I think Editors don't like technical articles unless they are very short. Yrs ever | A Marshall

[1] BLPES, Edgeworth Papers. From Balliol Croft. The letter deals with the writing of Marshall's paper on 'Remedies for Fluctuations of General Prices' [174.4].

[2] Perhaps an allusion to the Section F Committee of which Edgeworth was secretary. See [202.1].

[3] On 4 February, Marshall was to lead a Political Economy Club discussion on his question 'What monetary System is best calculated to avoid the evils which are now caused by changes in the value of Gold and Silver?' (Political Economy Club, *Centenary Volume* [173.2], p. 112.)

193. To the Editor, *The Times*, 17 January 1887[1]

The Royal Commission on Trade Depression

Sir.—I have been struck, as you have been, by the way in which the chief report of the Royal Commission on the Depression of Trade reflects the broad wisdom, the clear judgement, and the genial temper of Lord Iddesleigh.[2] While professing myself almost completely in agreement with it (except, perhaps, on the railway rates question),[3] I should like to add my tribute of gratitude for the instruction to be got from the minor reports and observations. But among these there are one or two remarks which are for various reasons likely to influence public opinion, and on which I ask leave to say a few words.

The most important, perhaps, is Professor Price's objection to Clause 82, which says, 'It must be for the country and the workman himself to decide whether the advantages of the shorter hours (as compared with those worked in foreign countries) compensate for the increased cost of production and diminished output. We believe that they do'. On this he argues that 'shorter hours of labour do not, and cannot, compensate to a nation for increased cost of production or diminished output. They tax the community with dearer goods in order to confer special advantages on the working men. They protect him, and that is a direct repudiation of free trade. The country is sentenced to dearer and fewer goods.'[4] No doubt it is right to protest against the common doctrine that shortening the hours of labour is a remedy for low wages and irregularity of employment. But since, after all, production is for men, and not men for production, it may be better to have shorter hours even if this should entail some loss of wealth to the whole community and some loss of wages also. And in many trades even shorter hours would increase efficiency in several ways, among others by enabling the worker to hold himself better in hand, and therefore to manage more delicate and complex machinery. As the report itself proves, the suffering has been generally the least among those workers whose hours are the shortest, and greatest among those who, having had a less fortunate start in life, are fit only for work of such low quality that it can be done almost equally well whether they are tired or not, and who consequently are compelled to work long hours. It is perhaps not true that men are the servants of machinery; but we shall not have made machinery completely the servant of men till we have arranged that machinery should work long hours, and that men in alternate shifts should work short hours. In this movement I see a great hope for the improvement of the human race, and still I call myself a free trader.

Secondly, in a quotation made by Mr. Jamieson, and apparently approved by some others,[5] from the brilliant paper which Mr. Sauerbeck recently read before the Statistical Society,[6] it is argued that the income-tax returns show a falling off in national prosperity. The income assessed per head of the total population was, it states, £9 5s. in 1845, £11 1s. in 1855, £13 2s. in 1865, £17

5s. in 1875, and £17 9s in 1885, the increase being only 2.3 per cent. in the last decade. But taking Mr. Sauerbeck's own figures, we find that the purchasing power of money had risen in the ratio of 96 to 72 in the ten years 1875 to 1885, so that £17 9s. in 1885 was equivalent to £23 9s. at the prices of 1875. That is, the income of the well-to-do rose in the last decade, not 2.3 per cent., but 33.5 per cent. No doubt the returns in 1875 were deficient in some respects; but, on the other hand, there were then many bubble incomes, which existed only in the fond hopes of those who did not know that they were beaten.

Thirdly, the main report implies that, provided the total wealth of the country be increasing, a fall of profits is not an unmixed evil, since it indicates a tendency to a more equal distribution of wealth. To this an objection is made (p. xxvi) that 'profitable industry is the source of wealth', and that 'the stimulus of profit being removed production must ultimately diminish.'[7] The second statement is no doubt true when duly conditioned. But the first is so worded as to suggest the notion that the profits on capital are the only important source of accumulation. The exceptionally high authority of the names that are appended to it may make this statement help to keep alive what I had thought was a rapidly decaying economic error. German writers take to themselves credit for showing that much of Ricardo's reasoning was vitiated by his neglecting all sources of accumulation other than profits. But in fact Richard Jones had anticipated them by showing—greatly to Dr. Whewell's delight—that taking the history of the world as a whole, rent and the earnings of labour have been a much more important source of accumulation than profits.[8] No doubt Ricardo's assumption was, in this as in so many other cases, suggested by the particular circumstances of England in his time—for then the landowners were not a saving class, and the earnings of labour even among the middle classes afforded little margin for saving. But the landowning classes drink much less and save more than they used to do, considerable savings are made from wages, while the professional classes now, perhaps, save more in proportion to their incomes than the trading classes.

All the reports are full of suggestions, but I must not take up more of your space. I will only add my regrets that, being bound up with other matters, they are not to be had for a less price than 2s. 4d. Could they not be published separately in octavo form for a few pence?

Cambridge, Jan. 17.   Alfred Marshall.

---

[1] Printed in *The Times*, 18 January 1887.

[2] Lord Iddesleigh (1818–87), better known as Sir Stafford Northcote, had served as Chairman of the Royal Commission on the Depression of Trade and Industry whose *Final Report* (C.4893), dated 21 December 1886, had recently been published. Bonamy Price and George Jamieson (1843–1920), an authority on China, were among the members of the Commission.

[3] See pp. xxii, xxv of the *Report*. The Commission took the view that British railways rates were neither excessive nor unduly discriminatory.

⁴ This is the entire extent of Price's dissent (*Report*, p. xliii). The parenthesized remark in the quotation from Clause 82 (*Report*, p. xxi) is Marshall's. Also the original reads 'or diminished output'.

⁵ See p. xxxii of the *Report*. Jamieson's dissent, pp. xxviii–xxxvi, deals mainly with the interpretation of the statistical record.

⁶ Augustus Sauerbeck, 'Prices of Commodities and the Precious Metals', *Journal of the* [*London*] *Statistical Society*, 49 (September 1886), pp. 581–648, see p. 624.

⁷ See *Report* clauses 34–42 and 54–5 (pp. xi–xiii, xv–xvi). The objection is raised in a minority dissent (pp. xxvi–xxvii) signed by Jamieson, Inglis Palgrave and three other members of the Commission.

⁸ Richard Jones, *Literary Remains* [51.4] especially pp. 34–47 and 363–73. Whewell's 'delight' is hardly displayed in his prefatory memoir to this work and Marshall's allusion remains obscure.

194. To the Editors, *The Western Daily Press*, 21 January 1887¹

Shall University College be Starved to Death?

Sirs,—I have heard with consternation that the council of University College, Bristol, have been compelled by want of funds to give notice of dismissal to their Professors of English and Classical Languages, Literature, and History. May I, as one who owes much to the kindness of Bristol citizens, venture to entreat them, for their own sakes, and for the good fame of their great and glorious city, to rouse themselves to avert this disaster. I believe that there are no institutions in the world in which such high and thorough adult education is given, at so small a total cost to the community, as our local colleges; and foremost among them for efficiency combined with economy has been University College, Bristol. It has helped the rising generation of Bristolians to get that scientific knowledge, the want of which is constantly causing Englishmen to be beaten by foreigners, who, though often inferior in energy and power of origination, have learnt in local universities and technical institutes how to make the most of their resources, and how to enter into and to anticipate the wants of consumers in other lands. It has helped to raise the standard of culture, to give to young men interests and amusements that raise them instead of lowering them. And to the daughters of Bristol it has opened opportunities for education, which, taken altogether, are unsurpassed. It has always seemed to me that those women who are able to get all the highest education they want without leaving their homes, and breaking themselves away from the associations of domestic life, are singularly fortunate. And I have often pointed with a happy pride to the splendid classes of women at Bristol.

But now I am told that this is to be stopped; that the salary of the literary instructors, already low, is to be as far reduced that the College cannot expect, except by an accident, to attract men of sufficient ability to do properly the extremely difficult task of imparting higher instruction to adults. Surely this is a mistake even from the purely business point of view of keeping up the value of Bristol and Clifton property. There is no town in England which seems to me to offer as great advantages to those who are not tied down to live in any particular place, as Bristol and Clifton. The life, the energy, the variety, the pleasant intercourse of a town are combined with a pleasant climate and most beautiful scenery. It has excellent schools; let it only have a first-rate college for adults, and its prosperity as a residential town seems to be ensured. Will not those who own the land, and those whose trade depends on the prosperity of the town and its suburbs, contribute to the very small sum that is wanted to prevent so deep an injury as that now threatened? But I cannot believe that it is possible. The generous inhabitants of Bristol, remembering the noble traditions of their city, will not for so small a sum part hastily with men who have given the prime of their lives to faithful services under great difficulties; they will not consent to have it said that Bristol thinks that a second-rate college is good enough for her needs. A few years more of courage, and then endowments will grow up from legacies and in other ways; and one more truly great and noble deed will have been added to the records of Bristol history.

Cambridge, Jan. 21st.   Alfred Marshall.

---

[1] Printed in *The Western Daily Press*, 25 January 1887. On the College's financial difficulties see Cottle and Sherborne, *The Life of a University* [42.2], pp. 17–24.

195. From Thomas Burt to Mary Paley Marshall, 16 February 1887[1]

Feb 16th 1887

Dear Mrs Marshall,

Accept my hearty thanks for your very kind letter. I will gladly fall in with any arrangements you & Professor Marshall make.

I am in a great fix. When I accepted the invitation to visit Cambridge I said I foresaw only one thing that might prevent me from fulfilling my promise. A dispute was pending in the coal trade of North'd[2] & if it resulted in a strike I thought it would be difficult for me to leave the north. Unfortunately a strike has taken place.[3] This is regretted on every ground. Nowhere has so much been done as in Northumberland to adopt more rational methods of adjusting differences.

My time & strength are absorbed in this wretched struggle & I do not quite see how I can get away. I am now leaving for Newcastle, and I shall see how the land lies. I have not yet written to Mr Shepherd[4] to explain my position.

I am glad Mr Burnett can attend.

With thanks & kind regards I am very truly yours | Thos Burt

P.S I have been in London only a few days on special business.

[1] Marshall Papers. No address given. Burt had promised to address a meeting of the Society for the Study of Social Questions on 'Trades Unions' in Cambridge on 26 February, presumably being invited to stay at Balliol Croft. He did not attend the meeting, the Chairman reading a letter from Burt 'regretting that owing to great pressure of work he was unable to fulfil his promise to be present'. The principal speakers in the event were John Burnett (1842–1924) 'Late Secretary of the Amalgamated Society of Engineers', and W. H. Hey (1839–1907), the'Secretary of the Society of Iron Founders'. See *Cambridge Review*, 9 March 1887, pp. 259–60.

[2] Northumberland.

[3] The strike commenced on 27 January and agreement was reached on 24 May. See *The Times*, 26 January (6d), 4 April (7f), 13 April (5e), 25 May (10d).

[4] William Fleetwood Sheppard (1863–1936) of Trinity was one of the Society's committee members.

196. To John Neville Keynes, (February?) 1887[1]

My dear Keynes

My wife & I find it very hard to see Laughlin's points,[2] & perhaps we underrate the strength of his attack. W^d.. you kindly read the enclosed letter, & see if you think it does really answer him.[3]

Do you think it is worthwhile to keep in that long paragraph about Cairnes, grades &c?[4] After writing it I feel much inclined to cut it out bodily, partly for the sake [of][5] brevity & partly to avoid being drawn into a controversy.

Excuse my bothering one who is so busy as you are; but our conversation the other day made me wish to get your views.

Yours ever | Alfred Marshall

[1] Marshall Library, J. N. Keynes Papers. From Balliol Croft.

[2] See J. Laurence Laughlin, 'Marshall's Theory of Value and Distribution,' *Quarterly Journal of Economics*, 1 (January 1887), pp. 227–32, a criticism of the *Economics of Industry*.

[3] See [197].

[4] Only a brief mention of the issues raised in Cairnes's *Leading Principles* [17.4], is retained in [197].

[5] Written '&' in the original.

197. To the Editor, *Quarterly Journal of Economics*, 25 February 1887[1]

Sir,—In spite of my rule not to engage in controversy, I must ask your leave to state briefly that the courteous attack made by Professor Laughlin in your last number,[2] on the Theory of Value and Distribution contained in the *Economics of Industry*, is founded on a misapprehension.

He supposes that the aim of that theory is to substitute expenses of production for cost of production as a regulator of value. But that is not the case. Mill used the phrase, 'cost of production,' in two senses, to represent sometimes the efforts and sacrifices required for producing a commodity, sometimes the money measures of these sacrifices. In the former use, he showed how cost of production tends, under certain circumstances, to regulate value. But, when he says that cost of production tends to equal value, he must use the phrase in the latter sense; for an exchange value or a price cannot equal an effort, though it can equal the money measure of that effort. Finding that the double use of the phrase led to confusion, I proposed to use 'expenses of production,' in lieu of 'cost of production,' in the latter sense. (My reasons are given at some length in the *Fortnightly Review* for April, 1876,[3] where I originally suggested the phrase.) In doing this, I did not think I was saying anything that was substantially new, but simply writing out more clearly what Mill had meant. Assuming competition to be free, I regard cost of production, in the first use of the term, as determining the (normal) expenses of production, and these as determining (normal) value absolutely in those cases in which the cost, and therefore the expenses, of production are independent of the amount produced. In those cases in which the cost, and therefore the expenses, of production are liable to vary with the amount produced, and therefore to depend, in some measure, indirectly on demand, I regard cost of production, through its influence on (normal) expenses of production, as acting, in conjunction with Demand, to determine the amount it is worth while to produce, and at the same time (normal) price.

Mr. Laughlin says that, in the *Economics of Industry*, 'the subject of value is treated before that of distribution.' If he will look again, he will find it is not so. The object with which the book was written was, as stated in the preface to the second edition, 'to show that there is a unity underlying all the different parts of the theory of prices, wages, and profits. . . . This law of normal value has many varieties of detail, and takes many different forms. But, in every form, it exhibits value as determined by certain relations of demand and supply, and cost of production as taking the chief place among the causes that determine supply.' (See, also, Book II., Chaps. VI. and XIII.)[4] It was essential to this purpose to put the general theory of normal supply and demand before that of distribution, but both are included under the one head of value. The discussion of value is opened before that of distribution, but finished after it. The argument, therefore, does not, as Mr. Laughlin thinks, imply the circular reasoning of determining wages by expenses of production and expenses of production by wages.

I cannot enter here into the discussion of the relation between different grades. I can only remark that I consider Cairnes's treatment of them to be neither as original nor as completely thought out as it appears to Mr. Laughlin. The question of compact industrial groups, of which the question of grades is a part, is itself but one side of a very large problem on which I have much to say, but for which there was no room in the *Economics of Industry*. (See, however, pp. 107, 108, 131, 132, and 206–13.)

No doubt there is much that is faulty in exposition in the *Economics of Industry*. I am at present engaged on a larger book, in which I am allowing myself more room, and hope I may make my meaning clearer. In conclusion, I will ask Mr.

Laughlin to remember that the use of the phrase 'expenses of production,' in lieu of 'cost of production,' is to be regarded as offering, not a new theory, but merely a verbal amendment. The main object which my wife and I had in writing the *Economics of Industry* was, I repeat, to show that there is a unity underlying all the different parts of the theory of prices, wages, and profits. I am, sir,

Yours truly, | Alfred Marshall.

Cambridge, England, Feb. 25, 1887.

[1] Printed in the *Quarterly Journal of Economics*, 1 (March 1887), pp. 359–61. Laughlin's brief rejoinder follows (pp. 361–2).
[2] See [196.2].
[3] 'Mr Mill's Theory of Value' [18.3].
[4] These chapters are entitled 'Distribution' and 'Relation of Normal to Market Value' respectively.

198. To John Neville Keynes, (5?) March 1887[1]

My dear Keynes,

Croom Robertsons letter[2] does not convince me. I think his three or four readings are unnecessary. I don't believe other editors do it. What does it matter whether there is absolute uniformity throughout? Why not let each writer spell &c as he likes?

I shd in any case suggest that the journal shd appear as the Harvard journal[3] does on 1st Feb, May (August?), November. That wd.. put the work almost entirely into the vacation.

As to the small print,[4] that is of course a very heavy item, if compiled by the editor or even under his superintendence. But the notion was that if we had small print, it wd.. be looked after in departments by the associated editors.

So I say dont decide straight off.

Yours | A.M.

The Economist will be a little late this week. It attacks me for proposing that Government shd.. publish an ideally perfect unit. I want to write to say that while discussing the conditions of a perfect unit, I proposed that Government shd start with a rough & simple method.[5]

On second thoughts I wd suggest *15th* Jan, April July, Oct.

[1] Marshall Library, J. N. Keynes Papers. From Balliol Croft.
[2] George Croom Robertson (1842–92), Professor of Mental Philosophy and Logic at University College, London, since 1866 and first editor of *Mind*. The letter concerns the proposal (see [180]) that Keynes should edit a projected economics journal. Foxwell had raised the matter with Keynes on 22 January and though he 'declined definitely' Marshall had pressed him strongly on 15 February to reconsider. Keynes had reluctantly promised to go so far as to ask Croom Robertson to tell him something of his experience as an editor of *Mind*. Robertson's reply reinforced Keynes's resistance when Marshall and Giffen pressed him further on 13 March. (*Diaries*, entries for the dates indicated.)

[3] *Quarterly Journal of Economics.*
[4] The notes and information section of the proposed journal.
[5] Marshall subscribed to the *Economist*, Keynes to the *Statist*, which they then exchanged. The issue in question is that of 5 March: see [199.2].

199. To the Editor, *The Economist*, 8 March 1887[1]

A Tabular Standard of Value.

Sir,—You attribute to me the proposal that a Government Department should set to work to construct a scientifically accurate unit of purchasing power: and you have an easy task in proving that such a scheme is impracticable.[2] So fully conscious of this was I, that I deferred till all my main argument was over any inquiry as to the conditions of a scientifically exact unit. I introduced that inquiry by saying that 'for the present we must be content with very rough methods, and improve them gradually as our statistical departments got their work into shape. It is enough that even in its simplest and most easily workable form the unit gives a tenfold better standard of value than that afforded by the precious metals.'[3] And, at the end of the inquiry, I conclude that 'we cannot hope to get a standard of purchasing power that is free from great imperfections.'[4] You are thus mistaken in supposing that I propose to substitute for Jevons' simple kind of unit a very complicated one.[5] I propose to take the simplest kind of unit, with only such improvements as we can see our way to introducing safely at once, and to let it gradually develop itself with the progress of statistical science and practice. Again, you prove that a man buying tea or drawing a cheque on his bankers would have to deal in terms of the currency, and not in terms of the unit. No one, so far as I know, has ever proposed that the unit should be used except for deferred payment: current business would be left to the currency.

But while you have thus combated proposals which I have not put forward, you have said nothing to invalidate my main argument. That argument is (1) That evils of a fluctuating standard for deferred payments are chiefly of modern origin; but that now they are of overwhelming importance; (2) That these evils would be but very slightly diminished by the adoption of gold and silver instead of gold alone as the basis of our currency; (3) That even so rough-and-ready a tabular standard as that published by yourself from year to year would give a far better standard for deferred payments than even a stable bi-metallic currency; (4) That fixed-ratio mintage is not what it claims to be, a stable bi-metallism. I propose an alternative scheme for basing our currency on gold and silver, which, though more uncouth at first, would, I believe, be stable, and have many other advantages. Whether this be so or not, I contend that we ought not to alter our currency in a hurry, but take a little more time to look round us. An authoritative tabular unit might be introduced at once for use by those who liked it in arranging for deferred payments. It would at first be on a simple basis;

the Department would take care not to reach out beyond its strength, but, as all other statistical departments do, would gradually improve its methods as its strength increased and its experience accumulated. This is my proposal. I submit that you have not shown reason for believing that its advantages would not exceed its disadvantages. It is no new proposal, but the benefits to be gained by it are far greater now than when it was first made, and the difficulties in the way of its optional use are less.—I am, Sir, yours truly, | Alfred Marshall.

Cambridge, 8th March.

¹ Printed in *The Economist*, 12 March 1887, p. 339.
² See 'A Tabular Standard of Value', *The Economist*, 5 March 1887, pp. 303–4, commenting on Marshall's 'Remedies for Fluctuations in General Prices' [174.4]. *The Economist* argued that Marshall's proposed Tabular Standard was 'impossible and impracticable' and 'as unreliable a thing as it is possible to imagine'.
³ *Memorials*, p. 207, where 'got' is 'get'.
⁴ *Memorials*, p. 211, where 'that' is 'which'.
⁵ W. S. Jevons, 'A Tabular Standard of Value', ch. 25 of his *Money and the Mechanism of Exchange* (King, London, 1875).

200. To Herbert Somerton Foxwell, 10 March 1887¹

No I am not candidate for the examinership² & I do not suppose I ever shall be. Nicholson has asked me for a testimonial for it: & I have given him one.³

Thanks for your kindly sayings. Our difference is very slight. I think it is premature to push for fixed-ratio-mintage regarded even as a half way house.

But I quite think a time *may* come after we have tried quarter way houses such as £1 notes, & have got to know the lie of the country better, when it may be well to advocate fixed-ratio-mintage as a half way house. So regarded its stability becomes of secondary importance.

I hope however that we may discover a better half way house, if the question is properly discussed.

Yours | A.M.

¹ Foxwell Papers. From Balliol Croft. Foxwell wrote on the envelope (which was not mailed) 'Marshall on Bimetallism Mar. 10 1887'.
² Of London University.
³ Not traced.

201. To the Editor, *The Economist*, 16 March 1887¹

A Tabular Standard of Value

Sir,—You seem to be surprised at my saying that while I wish current business to be left to the currency, I should like salaries and wages to be fixed in units in many cases.[2] The explanation is, that, to quote again from my original account of my plan, 'Salaries and wages, unless when governed by a sliding scale, generally retain their nominal value more or less fixed, in spite of trade fluctuations; they can seldom be changed without much friction, and worry, and loss of time.'[3] That is to say, salaries and wages are in many cases not current business properly speaking, but are more or less ruled by implicit contracts, understandings, and trade customs, which range over a long period. Under the present system, their real value 'falls when prices are rising and the purchasing power of money is falling, so that the employer pays smaller salaries and wages at the very time when his profits are largest in other ways';[4] and *vice versâ*, when trade is bad and prices low, wages and salaries of the old nominal value rise in real value above their normal level. This causes extra pressure on the employer just when he has the least power of bearing it, and thus increases the number of the unemployed in times of depression. I do not, therefore, plead guilty to your charge of inconsistency.

The rest of your criticisms[5] deal with difficulties which have not been overlooked, but which cannot be adequately discussed in a letter.—I am, Sir, yours truly, | Alfred Marshall.

Cambridge, March 16.

[1] Printed in *The Economist*, 19 March 1887, p. 368.
[2] *The Economist*, 12 March 1887, had commented (p. 335) on the letter from Marshall [199] published in the same issue, expressing puzzlement as to how wages, taxes, etc. could be fixed in terms of 'the unit' (as Marshall had implied in his article: see *Memorials*, pp. 198–9) while at the same time all current transactions used currency. That is, *The Economist* entirely failed to grasp the concept now known as 'indexation'.
[3] *Memorials*, p. 191.
[4] *Memorials*, p. 191, where 'pays smaller salaries and wages' appears as 'pays smaller real salaries and wages than usual'.
[5] *The Economist's* other complaints were that a general price index might not measure accurately the purchasing power of money wages, and that 'the very feature of his plan which he regards [as] its special merit is in fact, a fatal defect'. That is, evolutionary improvement in the construction of the unit would undermine its authority and credibility.

202. To Francis Ysidro Edgeworth, 16 March 1887 (incomplete)[1]

16 March

My dear Edgeworth

As is my wont I shall write to you with perfect frankness & without reserve.

Foxwell did not take away your paper. So I have read over carefully your introductory Memorandum & have dipped into the body of the paper in a few places. I am now going to take the paper to him, as I shd not be able to do anything more at it during the next few days. I will ask to be allowed to see it again after he & Sidgwick have seen it.

My first sight conclusion is then that the whole inquiry (including even those *few* points on w^h I do not think I shall ever entirely agree with you) is most valuable & important; & is well worthy of all pains that can be spent on it: but that insofar as it is new & original it is better suited for a paper by you than for a Report.

The Report shd I think be terse, judgematic, & err if at all on the side of being common place. The new work in this paper is very important: but it shd appear as yours, & not as that of the Committee for two reasons. (i) you ought to have the credit of it (ii) if it has to be discussed in Committee you will lose your freedom, will not be able to present it as you think best; while the Committee w^d.. have to sit twice a week for three months in order to discuss it properly, & w^d.. not discuss it properly even then.[2]

In my view the report shd deal almost exclusively with the first of your[3] . . .

I regard the question of the relation between the bullion basis & the credit superstructure of money as incapable of being treated with numerical exactness for practical purposes because

i the forms of credit change much faster than we can get statistics for them in England.

ii no solution is of practical use which does not include the whole civilised & *uncivilised* world.

Also I think the question is not *set*. I think it is even more unsuited for discussion by a Committee than that w^h.. is before us, & that we have already three times as much to do as we can manage without straying further afield.

I regard the problem as of fascinating interest but don't want to discuss it now.

Yours straightly | Alfred Marshall

[1] BLPES, Edgeworth Papers. From Balliol Croft. The letter is concerned with the preparation of a report by the 'Committee for Ascertaining and Measuring Variations in the Value of the Monetary Standard', established in 1886 by Section F of the British Association for the Advancement of Science. Edgeworth was Secretary of the Committee, while Marshall was a member, as were Foxwell, Nicholson, Palgrave, Sidgwick, J. B. Martin, and Stephen Bourne, statistician and author of *Trade, Population and Food: A Series of Papers on Economic Statistics* (Bell, London, 1880).

[2] In the event the Committee decided to present a preliminary report, drawn up by Edgeworth, to which was appended a long 'Memorandum by the Secretary'. See *Annual Report of the British Association, 1887*, pp. 247–301. The Committee also recommended that it should be reappointed and that Giffen should be made a member.

In 1888 a second report drawn up by Giffen was submitted, with another very extensive memorandum by Edgeworth adjoined (*Annual Report . . . 1888*, pp. 181–232). In 1889 there was a brief third report and another lengthy memorandum from Edgeworth (*Annual Report . . . 1889*, pp. 133–64) after which the Committee did little, although it reported briefly in 1890 (*Annual Report . . . 1890*, pp. 485–8). Edgeworth's extremely interesting contributions are substantially reproduced in F. Y. Edgeworth, *Papers Relating to Political Economy* (Macmillan, London, 1925), vol. 1, pp. 195–343.

[3] One or more folded sheets appears to be missing, only two such sheets having survived.

203. To Francis Ysidro Edgeworth, (18?) March 1887 (incomplete)[1]

Giffen was here from Saturday to Monday. I think his insight is marvellous. He says that the tabular unit is admirably discussed in a paper on 'Weights & Measures' by Sir George Shuckburgh Evelyn in the Proceedings of the Royal Society for 1798!![2] You shd certainly look that up.

Yours very sincerely | Alfred Marshall

I want you clearly to understand that I think your paper is even in its present form *splendid* as a paper, though not as a report; & that when the commonplace part is taken out & worked up into a report, there will remain the materials for a first rate paper. You might perhaps call it a Memorandum as Palgrave did in a somewhat similar case.

I had a hard weeks work last week. Then Giffen stayed with me then the Master of Balliol.[3] Then I had a number of things to do under high pressure, & now I am unfit for work for a few days. So please dont write to me till next week. I am going to read novels & drink hot water till Monday & then I hope to set to at my book.

To my mind the last 20 or 30 pages of your paper are of exceptional value. I am much excited to know how your . . .

[1] BLPES, Edgeworth Papers. Only one folded sheet survives. Keynes met Giffen at the Marshalls' on Sunday the 13th so that a dating of about 18 March seems the most plausible (*Diaries*, entry for 13 March).

[2] Sir George Shuckburgh Evelyn, 'An Account of Some Endeavours to Ascertain a Standard of Weight and Measure', *Proceedings of the Royal Society of London* (1798), pp. 133–82, especially pp. 175–6. This paper was noted in one of the Committee's reports (see *Annual Report of the British Association, 1888*, p. 184. Also see W. S. Jevons, *Investigations* [110.2], p. 122 (a passage originally published in 1865)).

[3] Jowett.

204. From Benjamin Jowett to Mary Paley Marshall, 11 April 1887[1]

Address Oxford
April 11. 1887

Dear M[rs]. Marshall,

It was very good of you to write to me; & I am very glad to hear that you are beginning to improve. Anything is interesting to me which relates to you or Alfred who show so much regard & affection for me.

I should have been at Bournemouth too, as I have been for the last twenty years at this time of the year, if Sir H. Taylor[2] had been alive. To me & to many he is a great loss—so good & kindly & free from jealousy and also though half forgotten in this generation, one of the first literary men of our time.

I am staying with Tennyson[3] who is full of vigour & energy—writing & hoping to write as long as he lives. In mind I do not see the slightest decline—memory good as ever & conversation as lively & charming. He only wants what we are all of us rather in search of—repose & freedom from visitors—He is much gentler & kinder than formerly. I fear that he sometimes feels very sadly the death of Lionel.[4]

It gave me great pleasure to see you at Cambridge. I think that you have built yourselves a model house & have found a model way of life—I very much admire your plan of living upon nothing—The only claim that interferes with it is the claim of Society which in certain positions you cannot get rid of. But I think that you & Alfred make as near an approach to the Early Christians as is possible in the 19th Century.

Ever yours sincerely | B Jowett

[1] Marshall Papers. Reproduced in Abbott and Campbell, *Life and Letters* [146.1], vol. 2, p. 322.
[2] See [119.3].
[3] Alfred Lord Tennyson (1809–92), the Poet Laureate, who at this time lived at Farringford, Freshwater, Isle of Wight.
[4] Lionel Tennyson, youngest son of the poet and a rising star in the India Office, had died in April 1886 from illness contracted on a visit to India.

205. To Macmillan and Company, 12 April 1887[1]

12th April 1887

Messrs. MacMillan & Co.,

Gentlemen,

I am writing a book on 'Economics', which will cover about the same ground as Mill's Political Economy,[2] and will probably be of about the same length, or a little shorter. I propose to publish it in two volumes octavo; of which the first will, I hope, appear this autumn and the second about two years later.

This book will be the central work of my life; & I shall regard it differently from anything I have written or may write. Partly for this reason, & partly because I think I may want to publish a very cheap popular edition of it, or of some part of it, at no very distant date, I should like to retain control over the copyright.

May I ask you whether you can accept it on the 'half-profits,' or 'royalty' system, with the condition that the copyright lapses to me after four (or five) years from the publication of the *second* volume?

I shd like the price of the octavo edition to be not very high: partly because books on economics are read by many students whose means are small, & who are not taking the subject up for examination, so that they avoid high priced books on it.

I should also wish to be free to use it in writing a new edition of the 'Economics of Industry' and in writing the long promised 'Economics of Trade and Finance'.[3]

Mathematics cannot now be avoided in some branches of economics; but I have stowed them away in an appendix at the end of either volume: some diagrams w^h.. do not require a knowledge of mathematics have been inserted in the footnotes.

I enclose a table of contents: & am sending separately a draft more or less rough of a little more than half the first volume.[4]

Yours very faithfully, | Alfred Marshall.

[1] British Library, Macmillan Archive. From Balliol Croft. Printed in C. W. Guillebaud, 'The Marshall–Macmillan Correspondence over the Net Book System', *Economic Journal*, 75 (September 1965), pp. 518–38, at p. 519, and in *Early Economic Writings*, vol. 1, pp. 88–9. A more prolix draft preserved in the Marshall Library reads (with paragraph breaks omitted):

I am writing a book on 'Economics' which will be of about the same size as Mill's Political Economy & will cover nearly the same ground. The main purpose of my life has been for the last 15 years & will be for the future to write this book and gradually to improve it that it may do for this generation something like what Mill's book did for its [this sentence struck out]. I propose that the first edition should be in two volumes octavo, but I may want to pubish a popular edition of it at no very distant period. I should like therefore the copyright to revert to me after four or five years from the publication of the second volume. (I propose to bring out the first volume this autumn, & the second about two years later.) I wish also to be free from the first to make any use of it that may seem advisable in preparing a new edition of the 'Economics of Industry' & in writing the long promised 'Economics of Trade & Finance.' Will you kindly tell whether you w^d.. be willing to publish the book subject to these conditions on the half profits or the royalty plan. I shd be willing to agree to any reasonable arrangement for my bearing the greater part of the expense of advertising the book during (say) the two years preceding the lapse of the copyright to me. The price of the octavo edition shd I think be fixed as low as possible. Many of its readers w^d.. probably be people of the student class whose means are limited; but who yet were not taking up economics for examination. It therefore shd not follow the rule of scientific books that appeal to a small class of specialised readers who must have them at any price. [The last three sentences replaced the previous: 'I should be glad to have the price of the library edition fixed as low as possible. Considering the class of readers who w^d.. be likely to buy it, a rather low price wd be I think advisable in the pecuniary interests of the book.'] The modern age requires some use of mathematics in the higher branches of economics: but lest they shd deter the general reader I propose to put them into a small Math Appendix [this word replaces the previous 'Note'] at the end of either volume. I propose also to illustrate some of the reasonings in the text by the use in the footnotes of the graphic method so far as it can be easily followed by those who have no knowledge of mathematics. I inclose a table of contents, & am sending a draft more or less rough of about two thirds of the first volume. Yours very truly.   A.M.

[2] J. S. Mill's *Principles*.
[3] See [34, 50].
[4] Neither item seems to have been preserved. However a note of 1 October 1887, preserved in the Marshall Papers, gives the intended contents of volume 2 and of the final book of volume 1,

Volume 2 will probably contain: Book VII Foreign Trade; Book VIII Money and Banking; Book IX Trade Fluctuations; Book X Taxation; Book XI Collectivism; Book XII Aims for the Future. Mathematical Appendix.

Book VI Value Distribution and Exchange: Ch. I Introduction; Ch. II Central Problem; Ch. III Central Problem continued; Ch. IV Field of Employment for Capital and Labour; Ch. V Rent in relation to value; Ch. VI Rent continued, Agricultural Rent, Land Tenure;

Ch. VII Rent continued, Influence of Progress on Rent; Ch. VIII Earnings; Ch. IX Earnings continued; Ch. X Interest; Ch. XI Earnings of Management, including Cooperation; Ch. XII Wholesale & Retail Prices; Ch. XIII Secular Changes, Pressure of Population; Ch. XIV Conclusion, containing summary reference to influence of Trade Unions and notice of Trade Combinations etc.

206. From Macmillan and Company, 14 April 1887[1]

Macmillan & Co.
Bedford Street. Covent Garden.
London April 14, 1887.

Dear Sir,

We write to say that we shall be very glad to publish your book on 'Economics' on the terms you propose and we enclose a draft of an agreement containing a clause which we think will meet your views as to possible termination of the arrangement after a certain period. You will observe that the last clause is so worded that the arrangement may be continued without a fresh agreement in case notice is not given five years from the date of the publication of the second volume, but the agreement is terminable by notice at the expiration of certain periods which we leave it to you to fix: we should be glad however if you would agree to make the periods not less than three years.

If you will kindly read through the draft and let us have it back again either approved or with any modifications you think fit to suggest we will have it copied & sent to you in duplicate for signature.

Shall we send you back the Ms.? We gather from what you say that it is not yet ready for the printer. We think that when you saw M[r]. Alexander Macmillan you said that you wished to have your book printed at the Pitt Press.[2] Is that so?

We are, dear Sir, | Yours truly, | Macmillan & Co.

Prof. Marshall,
Balliol Croft,
Madingley Road,
Cambridge.

---

[1] Marshall Papers. Printed in Guillebaud, 'Marshall–Macmillan Correspondence' [205.1], pp. 519–20.

[2] The University Press in Cambridge. For details of the unusual partnership arrangement between the Press Syndicate and the Clay printing firm, with C. J. Clay [66.1] holding the appointment of University Printer, see Sydney Castle Roberts, *A History of the Cambridge University Press, 1521–1921* (Cambridge University Press, Cambridge, 1921); Michael H. Black, *Cambridge University Press, 1584–1984* (Cambridge University Press, Cambridge, 1984).

207. To Herbert Somerton Foxwell, (April?) 1887[1]

I shd have said last night that I based my request to MacMillan for a return of the copyright to me after 5 years on the ground that this book was the central work of my life, that I expected to spend a great deal of the rest of my life in gradually improving it &c. Thus he treated the book as an exceptional case: & I don't know whether he w^d.. consider it fair to have what he consented to in this case quoted against him in another.

I think on the whole it w^d.. be best to let any application made him come as an independent suggestion.

Let me know as soon as it is settled whether you read a paper at the P.E. Club on May 6th.[2]

Yours | A.M.

[1] Foxwell Papers. From Balliol Croft. The letter apparently relates to the arrangements for publication of the inaugural monograph for the Toynbee Trust [138.1]. This study of industrial arbitration was to appear as L. L. F. R. Price, *Industrial Peace: Its Advantages, Methods, and Difficulties. A Report of an Inquiry made for the Toynbee Trustees* (Macmillan, London, 1887). The present letter was filed by Foxwell with other letters on this matter. Marshall had written to Foxwell on 31 January 1887: 'I shall be very glad to write a short preface, as you request on behalf of the Toynbee Trustees, to Price's essay'. But on 26 June, having received proofs, he lamented to Foxwell 'I had no notion till I tried how difficult it is to write a Preface to another man's essay: I spent a long time over it: & about half like the result' (Foxwell Papers).

[2] In fact, Giffen introduced the question at the meeting of the Political Economy Club on 6 May 1887. (The only other 6 May meetings prior to 1900 were in 1892 and 1898.)

208. To Charlotte Maria Toynbee, 7 May 1887[1]

7 May

Dear Mrs Toynbee

M^r. Foxwell wrote last night just before starting to London asking me to write to you about the photograph.[2] My doing so is not strictly in order: but it will save time.

Before I left Oxford I tried to get a duplicate of the photo in the Balliol Common Room. I was shown a small one w^h. I understood was reduced from it ; though from your letter to M^r. Milner[3] it appears that the small one was the original. I thought it inferior to the large one & did not buy it. Since then I have always intended to get one of the larger size to go into a panel in my study: but have put it off. I thought it w^d. save time if I could get one here to compare with the small one, & telegraphed to Hills & Saunders Oxford for one: they telegraphed back that I must apply to their Eton house. I telegraphed there & was told they had no photograph of M^r. Toynbee. On this I wrote to M^r. Foxwell, suggesting three courses.

i   To send the small photo to MacMillan

ii to ask you whether you thought the large photo had been taken from an improved copy of the small one, & was better; if so whether you could get the loan of the Balliol copy or in any other way supply one to MacMillan: also whether you thought there was anything to be said for substituting the photo that you yourself prefer. (I may remark here that I think a personal friend of Toynbee's w^d. care more for the portraits being like him than for anything else: his own memory & imagination w^d. enable him to fill in what was wanting. But for the general public I think one sh^d. select that portrait w^h. as it stands, gives the most pleasant impression & suggests the most attractive character.)

iii In case he sh^d. find after consulting with you & others that no available photo was thought satisfactory, to drop the proposal altogether.

I mean that so far as I am concerned I sh^d. be unwilling to press the proposal unless it met with the cordial approval of others, especially of yourself. But I myself think that the small photo you sent, though not so good as my memory of that in the Balliol Common room, is one that it w^d. do people good to have seen.[4]

As to the preface, I propose

i to give some account of the Toynbee trust (M^r. Milner & M^r. Acland[5] have promised to supply me with materials)

ii to say something about my own impression of Toynbee & of his influence on Oxford (this w^d. not be very long, but rather emphatic)

iii to quote a passage from P. 149 of 'The Industrial Revolution' & thus to pass to the subject of the Essay.[6]

Yours sincerely | [Alfred Marshall]

[1] Foxwell Papers. From Balliol Croft. From an unsigned transcript in Mrs Marshall's hand, presumably sent for Foxwell's information.

[2] It was hoped to include a portrait of Arnold Toynbee in the inaugural monograph for the Toynbee Trust—Price's *Industrial Peace* [207.1].

[3] Not traced. For Milner see [115.3].

[4] This appears to have been the photograph, ostensibly signed by Toynbee, eventually used as the book's frontispiece. Marshall remarked of it in his preface that it is 'reproduced from the best likeness of him that there is; but it is not quite satisfactory, it does not adequately represent the beauty and strength of his character. It will however help those who knew him to freshen their own memories of him, and will enable others to form some imperfect notion of what he was' (p. viii).

[5] See [170.1].

[6] Marshall's preface (pp. v–xxvi) is reproduced only partially, and with significant alterations, in *Memorials*, pp. 212–26, under the title 'A Fair Rate of Wages'. The original version quotes extensively a letter from Milner describing the establishment and goals of the Trust (pp. v–vi) and follows (pp. vii–ix) with Marshall's assessment of Toynbee's work and character. It did not include the proposed quotation from Toynbee's posthumous *Lectures on the Industrial Revolution in England: Popular Addresses, Notes, and Other Fragments by the Late Arnold Toynbee—with a Short Memoir by B. Jowett* (Rivington, London, 1884: second edition 1887).

209. To Members of the Cambridge University Senate, 12 May 1887[1]

To the Members of the Senate

I venture respectfully to protest against the publication with the authority of the University of the last sentence on p. 93 of the recent Report of a Conference on Local Lectures. It refers to a proposed three years' course of local lectures on Economics in which the first year is devoted to English economic history down to the repeal of the Corn Laws; the second to the main body of economic science and the third to its literary history; and then says:—'There would be no serious objection to reversing the order of the first and second year where it was *necessary*, though to proceed from a knowledge of the facts to the theories that explain them is the natural order and far the best where it can be managed.'[2]

I object to this statement firstly, because it implies that the study of facts can be entirely separated from scientific reasoning; and this is, I consider, impossible. For instance, an account of the economic changes in the first twenty years of this century must be bald and meaningless, unless some explanation is given of the mutual bearing of the different events; and that involves a constant use of analysis and reasoning.

I object to it secondly because it implies that 'the facts' with which economics are concerned are those of English history before 1848. I hold that these are only some of the facts with which the economist has to deal, and that for many purposes they are not so important as those connected with the condition of England and other countries in our own age.

Recent developments of the telegraph and the cheap press, of steam communication and steam manufacture, of science and of popular education, have led economic causes to group themselves in new ways and to bring about results which our fathers could not foresee. Those whose time for economic studies is short are, I think, not fairly treated if they are taught only how to deal with problems that have now but little direct practical interest, and to work out theories which were suggested by conditions of life that have passed away. All this is thoroughly well worth doing, but not at the expense of the vital task of analysing and explaining the economic phenomena on which the weal or woe of our own generation depends. Having followed the extension lectures on economics from the beginning,[3] and having myself lectured for five years at Bristol, I make bold to express the opinion that the twenty-four lectures which are assigned to this task are wholly insufficient for it: and that if there is a three years' course, two out of the three years should be given to it where there is no special reason to the contrary.

If any plan is to be officially advocated by the University, I would suggest that it should be that of devoting the first year to setting forth so much of general economic science as is required for the analysis and explanation of the simpler phenomena of modern times. The class would have some knowledge of them before-hand, but it would be ill-organised. The lecturer should help them to arrange their knowledge and to trace the relations of cause and effect among familiar facts. The task would involve the constant use of the historical and comparative method. He would always be adding to their knowledge new facts drawn from various countries and various stages of civilisation: he would use some of them to explain how the conditions under which we live have grown up; he would use all of them to illustrate and shew the application of general principles of economic reasoning. The more difficult parts of the subject should be postponed to another course on general economics, but even this should avoid abstract theories as far as possible. For indeed a second course of twenty-four lectures will barely suffice to finish the explanation of the most important economic facts of our own time. This course might come either before or after a third years' course on economic history.

I do not urge that the University should impose this arrangement on the country. For I doubt the advantage of adopting an official programme of general application. I incline to think that advice is better given unofficially and with reference to the special circumstances of each case. One of the chief of these is the supply of lecturers available at the time. I admit that an untried lecturer can be more safely trusted to deal with the outlines of past history than with the facts of his own time, and that in discussing modern economic problems much mischief may be done by an injudicious lecturer who has not yet learnt the limits of his own knowledge. If this has once happened at any lecture centre, it will be a long time before another course on general economics is wanted there. Should there ever be a scarcity of tried lecturers it might therefore be well to fall back on some such plan as that proposed in the Report; but I believe there are very few economists in England, Germany or any other country who would subscribe to the statement that it is 'the natural order and far the best when it can be managed.'[4]

Alfred Marshall

May 12, 1887.

---

[1] A printed flysheet. From a copy in the Cambridge University Archives, Guard Book on Local Examinations and Local Lectures, where copies of the items mentioned in nn. 2 and 4 are also to be found.

[2] Cambridge University Local Lectures, *Report of a Conference in the Senate House Cambridge on the Affiliation of Local Centres to the University and Other Matters, March 9 1887* (Syndics of the University Press, London, 1887). The appendix (pp. 89–94) includes suggested 'Sketches of Courses to Cover Periods of Three Years'. The suggested course for Political Economy (p. 93) reads

FIRST YEAR

Michaelmas Term. English Economic History, from the making of Domesday Survey to the Suppression of the Monasteries, including both events.

Lent Term. English Economic History, continued to the repeal of the Corn Laws.

The purpose of this course would be to shew clearly how our existing industrial society, and existing industrial relations came into being.

SECOND YEAR,

Michaelmas Term. The Modern Theory of Political Economy: Value, Prices, Credit, &c., Foreign Exchanges.

Lent Term. Applied Political Economy, Rents Profits, Wages, Taxation, &c. with special reference to Trade Statistics in the Town where the Lectures are held.

THIRD YEAR.

Michaelmas Term. The History of the Doctrines of Political Economy. The Mercantile Theory. The Physiocrats, Adam Smith, Ricardo.

Lent Term. The History of the Doctrines of Political Economy. The Early French Socialists. Robert Owen. Lassalle. Karl Marx and the International. Katheder Socialisten.

Laveleye, or Ely, or Rae. *Socialism.*

There would be no serious objection to reversing the order of the first and second year where it was *necessary*, though to proceed from a knowledge of the facts to the theories that explain them is the natural order and far the best where it can be arranged.

³ See [13.3].

⁴ A printed flysheet to Senate Members from the Secretary of the Local Examinations and Lectures Syndicate, George Forrest Browne [93.1], dated 13 May 1887, was issued in reply to Marshall's. Browne emphasized that the suggested sketch was far from a definite proposal and that it dated from before Marshall's return to Cambridge. He promised that Marshall would be consulted before 'anything so ambitious as a three years' course on Economics is proposed to a Lecture Centre'. This storm in a teacup blew over, but Cunningham, although not mentioned, must have seen it as just one more move by Marshall against the historical approach to economics. See Audrey Cunningham, *William Cunningham, Teacher and Priest* (SPCK, London, 1950), pp. 64–5.

210. From Charles Booth, 22 May 1887¹

Gracedieu Manor, | Leicester.
22 May 1887

Dear Professor Marshall

I am very much obliged to you for sending me Mr Herbert Mill's letter & the report of his Liverpool address.² May I keep the former? The latter I return herewith.

I have not reached the constructive stage myself, & would rather keep out of it except so far as is needed to forecast the information which is required. I should suppose that suitable members for a self supporting Agricultural Community would not be very easily found & that only under the influence of an enthusiasm or religious fervour of some kind could such a community be worked successfully. Its success would be a tour de force—the same capital with the same energy & capacity of management (without the enthusiasm) would in any other field of industry provide a good living for 100 families, if the capital & management were given gratis. And at best, with capital & management given & religious enthusiasm to boot, I doubt if more than a bare subsistence would be got out of an agricultural community growing their own food & spinning & weaving their own clothes.

Your analysis of London industry (in 'The housing of the London Poor')[3] seems to me admirable & the constructive portion of your paper is of very great interest to me. I trust we[4] may meet again sometime, as there are many points which I should like further developed, & I should be glad to learn in what ways I could work for you while continuing my East End Enquiry.[5]

My plan is to let my secretaries go on with the Hackney Division, which contains another 400,000 people & completes the East End, doing it on much the same plan as I have used for Tower Hamlets, but with some improvements & to apply to the whole East End an investigation into the leading industries & into the habits of life as well as industry of the different classes.

I shall not open up any new problem but simply enlarge the total field to which the special work will apply.

Yours sincerely | Charles Booth

[1] University of London Library, Booth Papers.
[2] No clue as to these has been discovered. The individual referred to is presumably Herbert V. Mills (not Mill), a Congregational minister, author of *Poverty and the State, or Work for the Unemployed. An Enquiry into the Causes and Extent of Enforced Idleness, together with the Statements of a Practicable Remedy Here and Now* (Kegan Paul, Trench, London, 1886). An advocate of self-contained communities, he founded in 1892 the Starthwaite Home Colony in Westmorland. See Dennis Hardy, *Alternative Communities in Nineteenth Century England* (Longman, London, 1979), pp. 111–14.
[3] Marshall's 1884 paper, 'Where to House Them' [153.1], had been reprinted recently as a pamphlet (Metcalfe, Cambridge, 1887) under the title 'Where to House the London Poor': see *Memorials*, pp. 142–51.
[4] Apparently written as 'me'.
[5] See [181, 182].

211. To Henry Sidgwick, 7 June 1887[1]

7 June 87

My dear Sidgwick,

My wife & I think it w[d].. be a mistake to ask the Senate to admit women to degrees until the great changes of recent years have had more time to establish themselves & to work out their full effects. And we think that no more stringent conditions should be required of women when they are candidates for degrees than when they are candidates for degree examinations.[2]

Speaking for myself only, I will add that I do not wish this to become a mixed University. I think that the genius of women is different from that of men, & that this difference is a great benefit to the human race, & the foundation stone of existing institutions. I fear that if women took part in the government of Cambridge, it would cease to be fully adapted to the wants of men, & would degenerate; while yet it never can become thoroughly suitable to the wants of women. I think it is our duty to welcome women heartily as guests with full access to the educational advantages of the place, at least so long as they have no University of their own. When here they should have the best help in the highest work they can do. But they should be encouraged to choose their studies with reference to their own wants, & not to go out of their way to imitate men.

As at present advised I should vote for the proposal to grant degrees if it were found possible so to frame it that it could not be used as a step towards obtaining for them a share in the government of the University, & if it did not tend to assimilate their studies to those of men, as regards preparing for pass examinations.[3] Otherwise I should vote against it.

Yours very truly | Alfred Marshall

[1] Newnham College, Cambridge. From Balliol Croft. For the circumstances giving rise to this letter see Rita McWilliams–Tullberg, *Women at Cambridge* [7.2], pp. 85–91. For different reasons, Marshall and Sidgwick were allied at this time in opposing a campaign to admit women to Cambridge degrees. Sidgwick made use of Marshall's letter after deleting the two sentences after 'mixed University', whose sentiments would hardly be to his taste.
[2] Women had been formally admitted since 1881 to the Tripos examinations for honours without having to take the Previous examination.
[3] Women had not at this time been admitted to the examinations for the Ordinary (or Pass) Degree.

212. To Richard Theodore Ely, 16 June 1887[1]

16 June 87

Dear Sir,

I have to thank your Association very much for electing me one of its first honorary members.[2] I esteem the honour highly: & I shall value much the publications w^h.. I am privileged to receive.

It will give my wife & me great pleasure if you, or any other of the leading members of your Association should be able to spend a day or two with us & see 'old' Cambridge.

Yours very truly | Alfred Marshall

Prof Ely
Sec: American Economic Ass^n..

[1] State Historical Society of Wisconsin, Ely Papers. From Balliol Croft.
[2] Marshall was listed as an honorary member of the American Economic Association, of which Ely was Secretary, in the latter's report to the Association's Second Annual Meeting, held 21–5 May 1887. See *Publications of the American Economic Association*, 3/3 (July 1888), p. 72 (p. 222 of the full vol. 3).

213. From Benjamin Jowett to Mary Paley Marshall, 3 July 1887[1]

W. Malvern | Address Oxford
July 3/87

Dear M^{rs}. Marshall,

If you have not yet fled away to the Continent will you & the Professor come and pay me a tête à tête visit on Thursday for a few days.[2] It would give me great pleasure to see you & to hear how the Professor gets on with his 'opus magnum'.

I am getting better of my illness but am still much weaker than I used to be, which provokes me for I have numberless things to do. I have adopted your husband's old practice of working for ten or fifteen minutes at a time which I think answers.[3] With best regards to both

Ever yours | B Jowett

[1] Marshall Papers.

[2] A postcard to Foxwell of 7 July informed him that the Marshalls were 'starting in a few minutes for Guernsey where we expect to arrive next Saturday week—Thence probably straight to Manchester'. The route to Guernsey was indicated as London, Dieppe, Rouen (3 days), Le Havre, Caen, Granville, Guernsey. (Foxwell Papers.)

[3] See *Memorials*, pp. 4–5.

214. To Herbert Somerton Foxwell, 21 July 1887[1]

Le Condré | St Peters in the Wood, Guernsey.

21 July 87

My dear Foxwell

The weather here is very pleasant: my wife is happy painting: I am happy writing: I don't want to go to dusty Manchester on Aug 27:[2] I w^d.. rather stay here till Sep 15 or 25.

But I want to meet Menger & Boehm Bawerk;[3] & to see the Manchester Factories: so I am irresolute.

I don't want you to write me a long letter about the B. Ass: but if you have any printed agenda paper you could send me either to keep or on loan, I w^d.. be thankful. Also if you can tell me of any one besides those two whom I shd want to meet, & who will be there.

One plan occurred to me to stay here, & ask them to[4] look me up at Cambridge before they left England in case they stay a good time here.

I have got about 40 pages in type, & shall go on printing till I get 100 or so. Then I shall pause a little. I have still nearly 100 pages of Vol I which are not yet even in first draft: & though I know pretty well what I am to say in them, I dont want to run the risk of having to contradict on p 500 what is said on p 50 more flatly than is absolutely necessary.

I wonder what you are doing.

I am so sorry we shan't get Courtney's exam^n of McLeod in Vol I of ye Gold & Silver Report.[5] It must have been worth hearing if Courtney was in form.

Yours quite ever | Alfred Marshall

[1] Foxwell Papers.

[2] The annual meetings of the British Association for the Advancement of Science were to commence in Manchester on this date.

[3] Neither Carl Menger nor Eugen von Böhm Bawerk appears to have actually presented a paper to Section F, although Walras did (*in absentia*). See *LW*, letter 802.

[4] Followed in the original by a further 'to'.

[5] Henry Dunning Macleod had appeared as a witness before the 'Royal Commission Appointed to Inquire into the Recent Changes in the Relative Values of the Precious Metals', known colloquially as the Gold and Silver Commission. He had been examined by the Commission, of which Leonard Courtney was a member, on Monday 18 July 1887. See Questions 7174–7398 of the *Second Report* (C. 5248, 1888). The *First Report* (C. 5099) was published in 1887. Marshall was subsequently to appear as a witness, giving his famous three days' evidence on 19 December 1887 and 16 and 23 January 1888. This was printed, with supporting memoranda, in the Appendix (C. 5212–I, 1888) to the *Final Report* (C. 5212, 1888) and is reproduced in *Official Papers*, pp. 17–196.

215. To Herbert Somerton Foxwell, 9 August 1887[1]

Dear Foxwell

Your letter just arrived. By sending specially to catch this evenings post I shall get my answer to Cambridge by Wednesday second post.

As to general adviser & counsellor:[2] I w^d.. put

i   Goschen
ii Giffen
iii Foxwell, Nicholson & Palgrave.

The first two are absurd. I guess Nicholson wd not go. There might be some chance of Foxwell or Palgrave. Foxwell is unmarried & Palgrave might like a change.[3]

Of course there are also City men with some knowledge of economics: but I speak only of those whom I know.

As to Professor: a young man wont know banking: a middle aged man might: but if he is willing to go he wd be self-proved a muff & not fit: I think among young men ready made the best I know so far as knowledge goes is Soyeda:[4] but of course they know all about him.

I think they must either take a German who knows a great deal & wont come to much; or if they are to do what is best for them as well as for us a young able English man with pluck & intellectual enterprise, & good judgement & lastly an agreeable temper. I feel I don't know exactly the right man. The three that occur to me are[5]

Sorley
Price LLFR
Leathes

Sorleys weak points are I shd say his promiscuousness, his readiness to get up anything & perhaps a little awkwardness of manner that may—I don't know that it does—indicate a little cantankerousness.

Leathes' weak point is I think his want of dash & outward show of energy.
Price has not much studied finance.

There I have written out my ignorance. The fact is you know every one I know
& many whom I don't know: & I answer more because as you say the question
is of vital importance than because I can add anything worth having to what
you know.

But before you tell anyone the salary is £1000 a year make sure that this is
not Stuarts innocent translation of 5000 yen, which is, or was, a very different
thing. I know of a man who thought he had a grievance because in a case like
this he did not find out the difference till too late.

Thanks for what you say about Manchester.[6] It is attractive. I think I shall go.
So glad you have got to know Birch:[7] I wish [I][8] had: I took a fancy to him.
Yours in almighty haste | Alfred Marshall

As to counsellor how about some retired official e.g. Sir T.H.F.[9]

---

[1] Foxwell Papers. Envelope postmarked 'Guernsey AU 9 87'. The postscript was written on the envelope.
[2] James Stuart had been approached by the Japanese government, which was seeking an economic adviser and/or university teacher of economics for a three-year contract at a salary of £1,000 per year. Stuart had approached Foxwell on the matter and Foxwell had in turn sought Marshall's advice. Foxwell himself was tempted by the possibility (see for example Keynes's *Diaries*, entry for 28 August 1887).
[3] Is Marshall being arch?
[4] Juichi Soyeda (1864–1929), Japanese banker and statesman, who, as a non-collegiate student in Cambridge from 1885–7 and a member of the Cambridge Economic Club, had come under Marshall's influence.
[5] All three had come under Marshall's influence, L. L. F. R. Price at Oxford and W. R. Sorley and S. M. Leathes [171.2] at Cambridge. Both Price and Sorley were at this time lecturers under the Toynbee Trust [138.1].
[6] See [214.2].
[7] Probably John W. Birch (1825–97), Governor of the Bank of England 1879–81, who was a member of the Gold and Silver Commission [214.5].
[8] Word apparently omitted.
[9] Sir Thomas Henry Farrer.

---

216. To Herbert Somerton Foxwell, 22 August 1887[1]

Le Condré, St Peters in the Wood
Guernsey 22 Aug 87

My dear Foxwell,

You will laugh at my fickleness: I do myself rather: but circumstances chuck
me about. After writing to Manchester to engage rooms,[2] I began to wind up
my M.S.S. preparatory to taking a long haul at ye Bluebook on Gold & Silver.[3]
Then I made a calculation of what I have to do to get my Vol I out before ye

Easter Term, & found that I should be hard pressed for time even if I had no interruptions.

So I am writing to Manchester offering to pay whatever profit is necessary on my lodgings.

I am sorry: because I expect this meeting will be the best Section F has ever had: & perhaps better than any it ever will have for the next ten years.

But going there w^d.. lose me much time. It w^d.. make me fill my head with currency problems & break off the continuity of my work at my book. I am always wasting time by partly discussing in one chapter questions that I afterwards find shd go into another, perhaps a couple of hundred pages away. Now I know what there is in every chapter yet first-drafted (about 4/5 of whole). But if I go to Manchester, I shall have forgotten by the time I return to my book. I feel I am boring a good deal: to say nothing of making myself a trifle ridiculous. But that won't hurt much.

I have for the same reason abandoned my notion of asking any foreigners to stay with me in September: unless you want to get up a party then, & then I will go shares. As at present advised I stay here till middle of September—lovely climate never too hot, never too cold, charming sketching: my wife getting to know ye rocks by heart & painting them twice as easily as when she came here—But if you want to get up a party & [it]^4 w^d.. make any difference to you, we will come back earlier, say by the 10th.. I shall take no steps unless I hear from you. I have 3 spare beds you know: one of them very small.

Edgeworths draft report^5 is able & entertaining. But I don't suppose you will adopt it. I think the original proposal of merely asking to be reappointed & calling attention to F.Y.E's excellent Memorandum is the best.

As to banks. Have you gone in for their Statistics. I make out that in England (other than large towns) there is about a bank to every 1000 families: surely that w^d.. be enough if they were properly distributed. I wonder whether there are a million people who are more than five miles from a bank. I shall look in the Times to see about 'Prof Foxwell's striking paper on £1 notes'.^{6}

Yours foolishly | Alfred Marshall

^{1} Foxwell Papers.
^{2} For the meetings of the British Association. See [214.2].
^{3} The First Report of the Gold and Silver Commission. See [214.5].
^{4} Word apparently omitted.
^{5} For the British Association Committee on which all three were serving. See [202.1, 2].
^{6} Foxwell did not present such a paper.

217. To Francis Ysidro Edgeworth, (August?) 1887^1

My dear Edgeworth,

I ought to have calculated my resources before. I find I shant get my Vol I out next Spring if I don't stick to it like a leach. So I have sorrowfully given up hopes of going to Manchester.

I can hardly say what I think of your draft report by letter. Indeed I have not been able to give my mind to the questions raised in it properly.

I think it is very able & interesting: though I shd prefer the omission of all about metaphysics.

But as at present advised I am in favour of a mere formal Report.

I shd like it to refer to you in appreciative terms, & as you may not like to give this message yourself I will write to Giffen about it.[2]

But I will wait a day or two to see if I hear anything from you or Foxwell.

Yours ever | Alfred Marshall

---

[1] BLPES, Edgeworth Papers, no address. The letter relates to the report of the British Association Committee. See [202.1, 2].

[2] This letter has not been traced. In a further letter to Edgeworth of 6 September, written en route from Guernsey to Cambridge, Marshall indicated 'I cordially concur in what has been done' by the Committee. (BLPES, Edgeworth Papers.)

218. To Herbert Somerton Foxwell, 23 September 1887[1]

23 Sep 87

My dear Foxwell,

You said yesterday, if I understood you rightly, that Sidgwick was thinking of resigning his post as a Toynbee Trustee that I might find room there.[2] I don't like to broach the subject to him until he broaches it to me. But I do not like to let the remark pass without saying that

i   I think Sidgwick is eminently the right man in the right place in the Trust.

ii The reasons w^h.. caused me originally to refuse to go on it are still in existence, though weaker. Committee meetings still knock me up, though I can stand more of such work than I could.

iii In some respects my not being on the Trust enables me to give advice more freely to employés of the Trust. &

iv I w^d.. not go on in Sidgwicks place. If he proposed it, I shd thank him heartily but decline.

Yours ever | A.M.

---

[1] Foxwell Papers. From Balliol Croft.

[2] See [138.1]. Marshall did in fact become a Trustee in 1888 (Papers of the Toynbee Memorial Fund, Greater London Record Office).

219. To Macmillan and Company, 28 September 1887[1]

28 Sep 87

Gentlemen

I write to report progress as to my book

100 pp are in type.[2] I expect to have 150 more at the press before long. Then I must turn my attention to other things for a couple of months. In the succeeding four months I hope, if not unexpectedly interrupted to give my whole time to the book & get it out. If I do not finish it (Vol. I) by Easter, it will have to stand over till the summer, or wh is the same thing, the Autumn.

Mr Clay[3] suggested that I shd write to you my views as to paper, in order that he may be able to take down some of the type.

I like for a book of this kind, wh will probably consist of about two volumes of 600 pp. each, a strong but close lying paper. Green's larger history (1878)[4] has the sort of paper I like: but I should not object to its lying a little closer, if it could do that without losing strength & opacity.

I leave the number of copies to be decided by you. I take it for granted that in the case of a book like this, of wh the second edition is sure to differ materially from the first, it is best not to stereotype.

Yours very truly | Alfred Marshall

Mess[rs]. MacMillan & Co.

I do not like a very white paper: but I do not like any touch of pink. I prefer an almost imperceptible grey or buff.

---

[1] British Library, Macmillan Archive. From Balliol Croft.

[2] From this time on in his association with Macmillan's, Marshall seems to have dealt directly with the University Printer in Cambridge [206.2] without passing material through Macmillan's for editorial scrutiny and advice. Decisions as to what to set up in type and when to do so seem to have been left entirely to him.

[3] Probably C. J. Clay [66.1], University Printer.

[4] John Richard Green, *History of the English People* (Macmillan, London, 1878–80; 4 vols.).

220. To John Neville Keynes, (12?) October 1887 (incomplete)[1]

Many thanks for your notes on sheet 4. Some of them are extremely important: particularly that about Bastiat's date.[2] I thought he wrote about 1835: but was wrong. As to your constructive suggestions: I regret only the time they may cost you: to me they are great & unmixed kindnesses & benefits.

---

[1] From a partial transcript in Keynes's diary (entry for 13 October 1887). Keynes had recorded on 8 October that Marshall was giving him proof sheets to read, the beginning of a long bombardment with them. Keynes's initial reaction to the book on 13 October was that 'I think it will come up to the high expectations that have been raised with regard to it. It is evidently

the work of a man whose knowledge of his subject is profound.' None of Keynes's comments on Marshall's proofs have survived, but many of Marshall's letters to Keynes up to June 1890 involve reactions to them.

[2] The 100 or so pages in type at this time comprised little beyond book i of *Principles* (*1*), which then included the historical chapters eventually relegated to appendices A and B in the fifth edition of 1907. The reference to Bastiat is probably that on p. 63n. of *Principles* (*1*) (see *Guillebaud*, p. 759) which was modified to read 'Half a century later Bastiat published, in opposition to the socialists, an extravagant doctrine to the effect that the natural organisation of society under the influence of competition is the best . . . that can be theoretically conceived.' Claude-Frédéric Bastiat (1801–50) published his *Sophismes Économiques* in 1845 and 1848 and his *Harmonies Économiques* partly in 1848 and 1849. They were published fully only posthumously. (See [15.4, 72.8].)

221. To John Neville Keynes, (October?) 1887[1]

My dear Keynes

The slips you now have are intended to go to the printers; & unfortunately I have told him that everything in red ink is a correction of the side notes. Columns 38–41 were waste. Columns 42–4 I did over again: it only took me a few minutes: still perhaps it wd be best for you in future to write with a soft pencil, as my wife does; then it can be rubbed out in an instant.

I had doubted whether to include Scheel with Ingram. But after what you say, I have looked at the 2nd Ed^{n}.. of Schönberg. I find Scheel has written a new introduction of a much less carping character than what he had said before. So I have left him out.[2]

Do you mind looking at the illustrations I have added to ye note on column 44[3] & criticising them freely.

Yours thankfully | A.M.

[1] Marshall Library, J. N. Keynes Papers. From Balliol Croft. The letter concerns the proofs of book i, ch. 5 of *Principles* (*1*).

[2] This almost certainly relates to the footnote on pp. 73–4 of *Principles* (*1*) dealing with J. S. Mill's controversy with Auguste Comte (see *Guillebaud*, pp. 764–5). Here mention of J. K. Ingram's restatement of Comte, the 'methodenstreit', and Schönberg's *Handbuch* are all retained: Gustav Schönberg, *Handbuch der Politschen Ökonomie* (second edition, Laupp'sche, Tübingen, 1885–6, 3 vols.; first edition 1882, 2 vols.). See Keynes's *Scope and Method*, p. 133n. for a discussion of similar matters, including reference to the views of Hans von Scheel.

[3] Most probably the footnote on p. 77 of *Principles* (*1*). See *Guillebaud*, p. 147.

222. To John Neville Keynes, (October?) 1887[1]

My dear Keynes

Many thanks: the more directly & 'dogmatically'[2] you speak the greater your kindness.

I must however bother you: for what you say about measurability requires careful consideration & I do not understand it.

Marriage & suicide are crucial instances. I say, in so far as they are measurable they are fit for the economic calculus. e.g. they are so fit (i) in countries in which a bride is generally bought, having a 'normal' price for any given rank of life, with bargainings in w^h.. the seller tries to get a little more than the average price (because her teeth are very white) or the buyer tries to pay a little less because she has a slight cast in the eyes. (ii) in countries in which a rich man condemned to death is allowed to produce a substitute & buys at ye normal price, more or less, some poor affectionate wretch who wd rather have his family happy & die himself than live with them in misery.

As to the conservative–liberal difficulty.[3] Political convictions cannot be bought, or measured, I hold. But take the case of voting by shareholders in a Joint Stock Company, where the motives[4] of voting have in them no element of duty:—I think they could be measured (if it were worthwhile). E.G. it is said if you keep the minimum share at £500, the chances are that a majority of the shareholders will find it pays to come to the meetings, & the company is likely to be better managed than if £10 shares are distributed over a large body of holders.

Tell me frankly if you consider this defence valid.

I think Nathan seems very able: I also have (or had last Thursday when I took the names) Napier, Gillend, Moreland, Wilkinson.[5]

My class is not very large, but of higher average quality than usual.

Yours ever | AM

I send you back these pp, together with column 38 in which I had already referred to Mill on motives.[6]

I have made no changes on 'measurability' yet. I am waiting to hear from you again. In any case, I shall explain more carefully.

Ten minutes sufficed to undo all the harm you did by writing in red ink. Please write in pencil freely whenever that plan works: e.g. when the change is the omission or change of a word or a stop.

In references it is good to use a scale, I think, like that wh I inclose. e.g., 'P 39 L 47' is found at once with a scale.

I may be going to London Tomorrow afternoon, returning on Wed evening.

---

[1] Marshall Library, J. N. Keynes Papers. From Balliol Croft. The letter concerns the proofs of book i, ch. 6 of *Principles* (*1*).

[2] Closing quotation mark omitted in the original.

[3] See the footnote on pp. 83–4 of *Principles* (*1*) (*Guillebaud*, p. 144).

[4] Altered from 'objects'.

[5] Probably Arthur Edward Nathan BA 1889, Alan Bertram Napier BA 1889, Robert Woodburn Gillan (not Gillend) BA and LLB 1889, William Harrison Moreland (Indian Civil Service 1889, Law Part I 1889), and Richard James Wilkinson (Historical Tripos 1889). None of these students took the Moral Sciences Tripos.

[6] See *Principles* (*1*), p. 65: *Guillebaud*, pp. 764–5.

223. To the Editors, *Cambridge Review*, December 1887[1]

Sirs,—Mr. Sedley Taylor's quotation from Mansel's Phrontisterion[2] has reminded me of some extracts I read in a commonplace book many years ago,
from an apparently forgotten paper of Mansel's on *The Dynamics of a Parti-cle*.[3]
He begins by parodying Euclid's Definitions and Postulates. Here are a few
Definitions:—

Plain superficiality is the character of a speech in which, any two points being
taken, the speaker is found to lie wholly with regard to those points.

Plain Anger is the inclination of two voters to one another who meet together,
but whose views are not in the same direction.

When a Proctor meets another Proctor, making the votes on one side equal
to those on the other, the feeling entertained by each side is called *Right Anger*.

Obtuse Anger is that which is greater than *Right Anger*.

His Postulates are:

Let it be granted;

That a speaker may digress from any one point to any other point.

That a finite argument (i.e. one finished and disposed of) may be produced
to any extent in subsequent debates.

That a controversy may be raised about any question and at any distance
from that question.

I am, Sirs, yours truly, | Alfred Marshall.

[1] Printed in the *Cambridge Review*, 9/215 (7 December 1887), p. 134.

[2] Sedley Taylor, 'Mansel's "Phrontisterion"', *Cambridge Review*, 9/213 (23 November 1887), pp.
99–101, with a letter of correction 30 November, p. 117. Henry Longueville Mansel, 'Scenes from
an unfinished drama, entitled Phrontisterion, or Oxford in the 19th Century', published
anonymously in 1852 and republished in H. L. Mansel, *Letters, Lectures and Reviews, including the
Phrontisterion* (Murray, London, 1873). Mansel's piece is a spoof on University reform. Mansel
(1820–71), theologian and metaphysician, was Professor of Ecclesiastical History at Oxford 1866–8
and Dean of St Paul's, 1868–71. On Sedley Taylor see [172.3]. Taylor, 'Believing that many of
your readers would gladly make acquaintance with Mansel's incisive humour', disclaimed any
desire to lampoon recent Cambridge developments, wishing only to provide 'easier access to
materials for hearty laughter'. Nevertheless, Alon Kadish has chosen to interpret Marshall's letter
as a riposte to an implicit attack by Taylor (Kadish, *Historians, Economists and Economic History*
(Routledge, London, 1989), pp. 155–6).

[3] This piece has not been traced. It is not included in Mansel's *Letters, Lectures, etc.*

224. To Herbert Somerton Foxwell, 12 December 1887[1]

                                                                    12 Dec 87

My dear Foxwell

Wicksteed is one of the very few men whom I w^d.. rather see than
not even when I am busy.[2] But I cannot stand even him just now. I seem to be
perpetually climbing sand-hills. As soon as I get interested in one subject & am

making progress in it, somebody orders me off to some other branch of inquiry.

I have now got a week before the 19th..³ to put my thoughts on currency into order, & I cannot go into Jevons' supply curves—wh I have forgotten all about, only I know I thought he was rather clumsy—just for the present.⁴

Here is a proposal. Ask Wicksteed to stay with you for the 27th.. Let him be *my* guest in Hall for that night: you ask some-one else. You chaperone him to breakfast &c next day.

The only hitch is this. If after the 19th.. I feel washed out, & the weather is attractive, I shall go from London to Torquay for a short stay. My wife has just started to go there to be with her mother. But at the worst you could then take Wicksteed into Hall on the 27th.. with my invitation.

Why did not you turn up on Friday at Giffens?

Yours muchly | A.M.

You may write in pencil any rude remarks you like on the inclosed copy of the answers I sent to ye Commission.⁵

Thank Beeton⁶ for me for his kind invitation.

---

¹ Foxwell Papers. From Balliol Croft.
² Keynes recorded. 'Wicksteed to spend the night with us. Foxwell, Beeton & Ward joined us at dinner. Wicksteed is extremely clear headed & knows what he is about in Political Economy. I am interested in his curves' (*Diaries*, entry for 20 December). P. H. Wicksteed, *Alphabet of Economic Science, Part I Elements of the Theory of Value or Worth* (Macmillan, London, 1888) was to appear shortly. For Beeton see [78.2].
³ Marshall was due to give evidence to the Gold and Silver Commission. See [214.5].
⁴ Perhaps Wicksteed wished to discuss this topic.
⁵ For Marshall's Preliminary Memorandum to the Gold and Silver Commission see *Official Papers*, pp. 19–31. The formal transmittal letter (p. 19) was dated 9 November 1887. It is not reproduced here.
⁶ Wicksteed's 'Economic Circle' had been meeting fortnightly at Beeton's Hampstead home since October 1884. The regular participants included the writer and dramatist George Bernard Shaw (1856–1950), Foxwell, Cunynghame, Edgeworth, and Sidney Webb, while Marshall seems to have shown up on occasion. See R. S. Howey, *The Rise of the Marginal Utility School 1870–1889* (University of Kansas Press, Lawrence, 1960), pp. 118–30 (where Cunynghame is confused with Cunningham). It is a pity that records were not kept of this remarkable seminar.

---

225. To John Neville Keynes, 13 January 1888¹

13 Jan 88

My dear Keynes

I was very glad for ye sake of $\tau\sigma\ \pi\hat{\alpha}\gamma$² to hear that you intend to be a candidate for the Oxford Prof^P..; though sorry on patriotic & personal grounds.³

I send you proofs of my Book III.⁴ The Press were clamouring for copy; so I sent them some; though I am too full of 'gold & silver' to prepare it properly.⁵

Take your time about correcting ye proofs.[6]
Yours affectionately | Alfred Marshall

[1] Marshall Library, J. N. Keynes Papers. From Balliol Croft.

[2] 'The whole'.

[3] The Drummond Professorship of Political Economy at Oxford had been rendered vacant by the death of Bonamy Price on 8 January. On receiving Marshall's letter, Keynes observed 'This is the first I had heard of my having made up my mind on the matter' (*Diaries*, entry for 13 January 1888).

[4] Keynes had been reading the proofs of book ii in November, observing that 'I can't say that I think this book on Definitions particularly good; and his style is often atrocious' (*Diaries*, entries for 16, 24 November 1887).

[5] See [214.5].

[6] Later the same day or on the following morning Marshall wrote again, saying 'You certainly should stand for Oxford, if you would take the post shd you be elected. I think Rogers is first favourite. But it must do you good, & can't do you harm to stand' (*Diaries*, transcribed in the entry for 14 January 1888, original letter not traced). J. E. Thorold Rogers, who had held the chair from 1864–8 was to be elected as Price's successor.

226. To John Neville Keynes, (26?) January 1888[1]

My dear Keynes

I happen to have to write to Markby,[2] on Junior Bursar (Balliol) business: so I will tell him about you. That will be on the whole better than writing to Jowett. I will wait about writing to him till I can send him some proofs of your book.[3]

I forgot to say *confidentially* that Creighton,[4] talking to my wife, spoke of your chance at Oxford as good. He too said Rogers was out of it.

On second thoughts you may let me have my Bk III proofs again at your leisure, it will be best to get it into rough polish before you go over it.

Yours ever | A.M.

Another thing I forgot. Some people at Oxford are said to be trying to get Laveleye[5] to stand. I am very much against that. My line in writing to Markby is—*if you go out of Oxford*   i don't take Laveleye   ii do take Keynes.

[1] Marshall Library, J. N. Keynes Papers. Partly transcribed *Diaries*, entry for 27 January 1888. From Balliol Croft.

[2] See [149.2].

[3] This refers to the proofs of an early draft for Keynes's *Scope and Method*, an outgrowth of the lectures he had given in Oxford in 1885: see [162.3]. The book was not to appear until 1891.

[4] Mandell Creighton (1843–1903), historian and bishop, then Dixie Professor of Ecclesistical History at Cambridge, presumably retailing Oxford gossip.

[5] Emile de Laveleye the Belgian economist.

227. To John Neville Keynes, 7 February 1888[1]

7 Feb 88

My dear Keynes,

I have glanced rapidly through your proofs.[2] I think them excellent. The only general suggestion wh occurs to me is that I shd prefer references of a controversial nature to the opinions of individuals being relegated to footnotes. But I am aware that my opinions on this class of subjects are somewhat extreme. I go to Oxford on Saturday to stay with the Master of Balliol.[3] I should like to take these proofs with me, & any others that may be ready, & to be authorized to show them, if occasion offers, & even to lend them if they should be asked for.

You will I suppose send copies of the proofs to the electors. Of course they will be inundated with printed matter & wont read many pages of any one. The only object therefore of hurrying on with the proofs is to make it clear that you did not set to work to write your book on hearing of poor Price's death.[4] Subject to this not very important condition, I think quality is more important than quantity.

I am behind hand with my Memorandum for the Commission.[5] I had promised it by todays post: but it is not half finished yet; as I have had to expand its scope. So I cant do anything else till I have sent that off. When I have, I will read through your proofs carefully.

I have heard certain miscellaneous gossip about Oxford since I last wrote—none of it very important.

I think Cunningham is in the main right. I think the feeling in Oxford is against Rogers: but outside is in his favour; & a small responsible body of electors may pay more attention to outside opinion than to local opinion. Nevertheless outsiders who favour Rogers, do not, so far as I have observed, understand the real nature of the objections felt to him. They think it is political bigotry: w^h.. it is not.

I don't think McLeod has a fraction of a chance. Palgrave is very strong on one side, but only on one side.

My own order of probability—not my order of merit, I mean not the order in wh I shd myself vote, by a long way—is[6]

Phelps
Rogers
Keynes
Foxwell (if he stands) } oeq:
Cunningham
Price
Palgrave } oeq:

This is confidential of course.

Keep up your strength. In particular if asked to meet any Oxford men who come to Cambridge on Sunday next for the *ad eundem*[7] don't work at proofs & fag yourself out before hand. Keep yourself bright. Read this to Mrs Keynes. Tell her to do her duty & then obey her dutifully.

Yours ever | A.M.

My only reason for thinking that Foxwell may possibly stand is that he speaks as if he wd not dream of doing so: & he generally abandons rather quickly any very strongly held opinion.

[1] Marshall Library, J. N. Keynes Papers. From Balliol Croft.

[2] See [226.3]. Keynes observed on 24 January 1888, 'I am thinking of taking the two first chapters [sic] of my book to press even though they will not have received my final revision. I shall then have something in print to send the electors.' Two of the slips had come back by 28 January. (*Diaries*, entries for the dates indicated.)

[3] Jowett.

[4] See [225.3].

[5] Marshall was preparing for the Gold and Silver Commission [214.5] a lengthy 'Memorandum as to the Effects which Differences Between the Currencies of Different Nations have on International Trade'. He had already prepared on 13 January a shorter 'Memorandum on the Relation Between a Fall of the Exchange and Trade with Countries which have not a Gold Currency'. See *Official Papers*, pp. 170–95.

[6] Among these possible candidates, only Phelps, Rogers, and Langford L. F. R. Price (not to be confused with Bonamy Price whose death had led to the election) would count as 'Oxford men'. However Palgrave, who had escaped a university education, had family connections with Oxford.

[7] See [134.5].

228. To John Neville Keynes, (14?) February 1888[1]

Tuesday morning

My dear Keynes

I am sending a message to the Historical Board instead of going.[2] I expect we had better put off our interview about the Mo Sc Tripos[3] till the weather is more suitable.

I was not very fortunate at Oxford. I missed Bryce[4] who was here; & I did not see Markby.[5] I still think Phelps is the most likely of the Oxford men—bar Rogers. But I think his chance is less & Rogers' much greater than I did before going. I am rather reverting to my original opinion that the odds are slightly in favour of him as against the field. I spoke always in his favour. But I managed to get out a good strong sentence or two about you to anyone to whom I spoke on the subject. The Master[6] seemed pleased to have a copy of your proofs: & I have sent the second copy to Giffen.

Yours ever | A.M.

[1] Marshall Library, J. N. Keynes papers. No address given. The letter is partly transcribed by Keynes, *Diaries*, entry for Saturday 18 February, apparently shortly after receipt.

[2] Marshall was an *ex officio* member of the Historical Board.

[3] Proposals for reform of the Tripos were afoot. See [229], [231].

[4] James Bryce (1838–1922), scholar and statesman, who was at the time both an MP and Regius Professor of Civil Law at Oxford.

[5] See [149.2].

[6] Jowett.

229. To John Neville Keynes, (15?) February 1888[1]

My dear Keynes

Tell me frankly if there is anything in this Testimonial w[h] you wd like amended. I will rewrite it with great pleasure. My chief difficulty was to account for the fact that you had not yet written more. I don't know whether you think I have said the right thing about that.

If not, say so at once.

There are four chapters in type w[h] you have not had. But they have not yet had even a rough polish put on them, & I fear they wont till about the end of the Term. I don't know whether to send them to you now or not.

I am writing a line to Sidgwick to tell him my chief objection to his scheme[2] & to say that I wd gladly revert to ye Tripos of 1873, or something of the sort.[3]

I am not a good judge as to whether people are more likely to read things in pages than in slips. Perhaps they are. Anyhow I would try to get the proofs sent off[4] before long. I have no copy to read: but I shall get back Giffens tomorrow.[5]

You will of course now write to him.

Yours ever | A.M.

[1] Marshall Library, J. N. Keynes Papers. Referred to by Keynes, *Diaries*, entry for 18 February 1888, where he observes 'Marshall's testimonial is far too flattering'. The testimonial has not been traced.

[2] Sidgwick's scheme involved separating the Moral Science Tripos into two parts which could be taken in separate years. (Keynes, *Diaries*, entry for 29 February 1888.) Marshall's letter to Sidgwick has not been traced. See also [235.5].

[3] The Moral Sciences Tripos had been divided in 1883 into Part I and Part II, both taken together. Candidates took five of the six subjects in Part I, but chose only two of the six subjects in Part II: see [231.5] for further details. It was thus easy for candidates to evade serious work in political economy. Before this, the Tripos had simply covered the four subjects Moral and Political Philosophy, Mental Philosophy, Logic, and Political Economy, all carrying the same weight. See *Reporter* 9 June 1874, 11 May 1880, 8 June 1880, 15 February 1881.

[4] Presumably to the Oxford electors: see [227].

[5] See [228].

230. From Robert Giffen, (15?) February 1888 (incomplete)[1]

I have been asked by two friends already to give testimonials for the Oxford Professorship & have thought it prudent to decline. I should be testimonialising too much. I have however given permission to both gentlemen to give a reference to me & I shall gladly do the same for Mr Keynes if he thinks it would be useful to him, & I shall be happy, if I am asked by the electors, to say what I know of him. I need not tell you that I have the highest opinion of Mr Keynes formed on what I saw of him at Cambridge[2] & on what you & others have told me; but hardly in any case enough materials for a testimonial. What I could say if I am referred to would be much better. I have not quite read through the proofs you have sent me, but I shall do so & return them to you probably to-morrow. I am glad for my own sake I have seen them, & I shall look out for Mr Keynes in future more than I should otherwise have done. I must not express good wishes for the success of any particular candidate, but I am quite sure if Mr Keynes is elected he will be a most creditable appointment.[3]

---

[1] From a transcript by Keynes to whom Marshall passed the letter (*Diaries*, entry for 18 February 1888). The original has not been traced.

[2] See [203.1].

[3] Keynes submitted testimonials only from his superior at the Local Examinations and Lectures Syndicate (G. F. Browne [93.1]), Marshall, J. S. Nicholson, and an old one from H. Fawcett. In addition, H. S. Foxwell, Giffen, W. Markby [149.2], and James Bonar were probably listed as referees. Henry Sidgwick preferred not to be named as his brother William was a candidate. (*Diaries*, entry for 18 February 1888.)

231. To John Neville Keynes, 18 February 1888[1]

18 Feb.

My dear Keynes,

I remain of the opinion I expressed to you yesterday that I shd cordially concur in any slowly matured scheme for reorganizing the Moral Sciences Tripos, which was approved by teachers of the other Moral Sciences, provided it made no great change in the position which Political Economy holds: but that I should oppose uncompromisingly any proposal for diminishing its weight in the second half of the examination.[2] I am increasingly of opinion that a short study of Political Economy seldom does much good, & not infrequently does much harm. It is not till a man is about to take his degree that his work at economics generally becomes of any substantial value.

I understand that it is wished that Part I shd be taken in a different year from Part II, & that the importance of Metaphysics shd be diminished in the first half & increased in the second.[3] Without having any strong views on the matter, I am inclined to think that both these changes may be wise.

But on further consideration I have abandoned the notion I hastily adopted yesterday that (as I think you first suggested) the arrangement [be that] of the Natural Sciences Tripos.[4]

I certainly am not inclined to suggest any new plan without longer consideration, & probably not at all. But I have sketched a plan which represents my present opinions so far as I have any.

If you like you may show this to Sidgwick or any other member of the Board.

Yours ever | Alfred Marshall

[Enclosure]

Part I

Psychology and elements of Metaphysics
Logic
Ethics
Pol Econ
Two papers in each: either every candidate to select three subjects, or as I am inclined to prefer every candidate to do all.

Lastly a paper of Essays.

Part II

Metaphysics
Psychology
Logic
Ethics & Politics, or 'Sociology'
Political Economy & Statistics.

Each candidate to select two subjects.
Each subject to be treated historically as well as constructively: The historical element in Psychology might be much less than in Metaphysics, & so on. But that might be left to take care of itself.[5]

If the Theory of Political Economy before the time of Adam Smith is to be treated at all, it should I think go into the fourth group. Modern Political Economy will have quite enough of an historical element if modern changes & modern statistics are treated carefully. I incline to think that one of the chief subjects for the study of advanced economists shd be Statistics & that these shd be treated not as a separate department of knowledge, but as a language in which certain classes of problems can best be expressed.

If *a* Foxwell pushes for the early history of P.E. *b* Sidgwick does not wish to take it with Politics, might it be represented in the Mixed Essays papers only??

---

[1] Marshall Library, J.N. Keynes Papers. No address given.
[2] See [229.2, 3].

³ This presumably describes Sidgwick's proposal. See [229.2].

⁴ Words apparently omitted in haste. The Natural Sciences Tripos served as an umbrella for different paths of specialization.

⁵ At the time, Part I covered (i) Moral and Political Philosophy, (ii) Psychology, (iii) Metaphysics, (iv) Logic, (v) Political Economy (vi) General Philosophical Essays. Candidates took five of these. Part II covered (i) History of Ancient Philosophy, (ii) History of Modern Metaphysical Philosophy, (iii) History of Modern Ethical Philosophy (iv)Advanced Psychology and Psychophysics, (v) Advanced Logic, (vi) Advanced Political Economy. Candidates took two of these. (*Reporter*, 11 May 1880, 15 February 1881.)

232. To John Neville Keynes, 24 February 1888¹

24 Feb 88

My dear Keynes,

I think your testimonials though few are vigorous.²

I only wish you had either omitted 'Fellow of St John's Cambridge', or recollected to insert 'sometime Fellow of Balliol',³ in my designation.

It was my fault: I ought to have reminded you.

I am now at last making some progress with my book. I will send you Book III in a few days unless I hear to the contrary.

I have read some of your proof more carefully. I think it is extremely good: but I shall venture to make one or two suggestions of a general character about it: especially as to your references to the Germans.

Yours ever | AM

¹ Marshall Library, J.N. Keynes Papers. From Balliol Croft.

² See [230.3].

³ See [139.2]. Marshall had been elected a Professorial Fellow of St John's on his return to Cambridge. See [141].

233. To John Neville Keynes, 1 March 1888¹

March 1 88

My dear Keynes,

I suppose the 28ᵗʰ.. was only the day for sending in names. I thought it was the day of election.² I now expect they wont meet till Saturday.³

I am ashamed to trouble you with my proofs. But I⁴ take you at your word. I send you two chapters on agriculture wh I had put in type last October in order to get Mʳ Bullock Hall's⁵ criticism on the purely technical parts.

Book IV Ch I, a short introductory chapter on Supply in general will be in type soon. At present I have been at work on the Chap on 'Capital.' I have completely rewritten it for about the eighth time, reintroducing a great part of what I had in it some time ago. It has a historical Note, the only one wʰ.. I am at present inclined to introduce.⁶ I will send you a proof of it when I get it. It will contain implicitly suggestions as to the way of handling German definitions w^{h}.. it may be interesting to you to consider with reference to your own book: though very likely you may not think I have chosen the right plan.

Please write your notes on the proofs themselves.

Yours ever | A M.

---

[1] Marshall Library, J. N. Keynes Papers. From Balliol Croft.

[2] 28 February was the deadline for applications for the Oxford chair.

[3] Since 1 March was a Thursday, this would appear to refer to 10 March. The election took place on 16 March (see *The Times*, 17 March 1888 (13d)).

[4] Followed with a further 'I' in the original at a turn of page.

[5] In *Principles* (*1*), book iv, chs. 2 and 3 were entitled 'The Fertility of Land' and 'The Fertility of Land, continued. The Law of Diminishing Return'. William Henry Bullock-Hall (1837–1904) had been a student at Balliol 1856–60 and was a local agriculturalist, residing at Six Mile Bottom near Newmarket.

[6] The 'Historical Note on Definitions of the Term Capital' was attached in *Principles* (*1*) to book ii, ch. 5, on 'Capital'.

234. To John Neville Keynes, (March?) 1888[1]

My dear Keynes

I think you may like to see these testimonials of Palgraves wh I have just got. I think the delay is against Phelps & in favour of Rogers & the non-Oxford men.[2]

I have got entangled in my Book IV; & cannot, as I had intended, send over Book three this week. So I send you back an unaltered copy. Please write on it either in ink, or wh is perhaps better in pencil: but don't bother about misprints & small points: as Price[3] & my wife have looked out for them. I could lend you a copy of my three days evidence[4] if you like. I have two copies: & they wont be published for a long while.

Yours ever | A.M.

---

[1] Marshall Library, J.N. Keynes Papers. No address given.

[2] See [227].

[3] Langford L. F. R. Price is acknowledged co-equally with Keynes as assisting with the proofs of the *Principles*. See the Preface to *Principles* (*1*) (*Guillebaud*, p. 37).

[4] See [214.5].

235. To John Neville Keynes, (March?) 1888[1]

My dear Keynes,

Dont spoil your trip[2] by bothering yourself about my Proofs, when not inclined for them. I send you my reformed Ch on Capital.[3] It is a spare copy: & if you don't return it, I shan't mind. I shall work on at Book IV for the next two or three weeks & try to get that ready for the press: then I shall return to Books II & III.

I am getting very excited about Oxford.[4]

Yours ever | A.M.

I don't at all like Sidgwicks new M. Sc Tripos Scheme.[5] In particular I dislike the change which he has silently made of allowing a man to take Part II on Moral & Metaphysical Philosophy alone, without extending a similar grace to other subjects. But I think the scheme is every way bad.

[1] Marshall Library, J. N. Keynes Papers. No address given.

[2] Keynes was visiting Germany, Austria, Italy, and Switzerland between 15 March and 11 April.

[3] Book ii, ch. 5 in *Principles (1)*: see [233].

[4] See [233.3].

[5] This was probably a modification of Sidgwick's earlier scheme [229.2] but the details are not clear. The Minutes of the Moral Science Board indicate that the proposal by Sidgwick to separate the two parts of the Tripos and make certain other changes was discussed on 29 February 1888. There was further discussion in the meeting of 28 April, but it was not until the meeting of 15 May that new proposals arose. Then Sidgwick moved and Cunningham seconded a motion to make 'the study of philosophy including metaphysics' compulsory in Part II. The motion tied 3–3. For the final stages of the reform of the Tripos see *Reporter*, 2 February 1889, pp. 481–3; 5 March 1889, pp. 505–7; 19 March 1889, pp. 571–3, 593–6. Also see Appendix IV below.

236. To John Neville Keynes, 17 March 1888[1]

17 March 88

My dear Keynes

You will have heard that Rogers is elected.[2] He had great claims on Oxford, independent of the value of his work.[3] Markby[4] is here, in lodgings. He was sorry to miss you, & will I think write to you; he w[d].. have liked you to be elected, I think.

The next point to be considered is that of editing the proposed economic quarterly.[5] The salary is to be £100. It may not last for ever: but very likely it will: & anyhow it will get you into the way of writing on economic subjects in journals, w[h].. will always enable you to earn a good sum, if you want to, by work that is worth doing for its own sake. So I intend to bully you into giving the matter serious consideration. You are the right man for the work, & it is very important work.

Yours most sincerely | Alfred Marshall

I had addressed your envelope to *A.M.* JNK. But that good Italomaniac my wife compelled me by the terror of her wrath to use Italian words.[6]

[1] Marshall Library, J.N. Keynes Papers. From Balliol Croft.

[2] See [225.3], [233.3].

[3] J. E. Thorold Rogers had held the Drummond chair from 1863 to 1868 but then had failed to be re-elected, Bonamy Price having been run successfully against him, partly on political grounds. This was widely felt to have been an injustice. For details see Neil B. de Marchi, 'On the Early Dangers of Being Too Political an Economist: Thorold Rogers and the 1868 Election to the Drummond Professorship', *Oxford Economic Papers*, 28 (November 1976), pp. 364–80.

[4] See [149.2].

[5] See [180, 198.2]. Keynes observed 'Marshall is on at me again about editing the economic journal, but I have told him that it would worry me beyond measure' (*Diaries*, entry for 10 April 1888).

[6] Keynes was in Italy from 26 March to 6 April but the point remains obscure. Possibly 'à Monsieur' had been used when 'a Signor' would have been appropriate? (Suggested by Peter Groenewegen.)

237. From James Edwin Thorold Rogers, 19 March 1888[1]

Oxford Mar 19

My dear Mr Marshall,

I believe that my reelection to my ancient office is acceptable to all parties. It has extinguished in me at last, all remembrance of a wrong done twenty years ago, which many who took part in the injury, have regretted to me.[2]

I am glad that you find my facts useful. It is very possible that I may err in my inferences. But I take my stand on my facts. The mischief which has been done to a true Pol. Econ. by autobiography & Metaphysics is incredible. I hope in the volume of lectures I gave here in the past year[3] to point some of this out, and I think one ought to do so, to the best of ones powers, without fear or favour.

I hope in the course of the summer to begin compiling for my last two vols.[4] in those precious archives of Kings & S. Johns. These archives relieve the former corporation from the charge of contributing four centuries of unproductive consumption.

Yours faithfully | James E. Thorold Rogers

[1] Marshall Papers. Presumably in response to a letter of congratulation, not traced.

[2] See [236.3].

[3] J. E. Thorold Rogers, *The Economic Interpretation of History: Lectures Delivered in Worcester College Hall, Oxford, 1887–8* (Unwin, London, 1888).

[4] At this time six volumes of Rogers's monumental *A History of Agriculture and Prices in England* had been published. A final volume was to be published posthumously (Clarendon, Oxford, 1866–1902).

238. To John Neville Keynes, (April?) 1888[1]

My dear Keynes

My wife is reading your chapters[2] this afternoon. I will read them tomorrow.

You returned my papers on India. I had a vague impression that you asked to be allowed to keep the notes on Ricardo longer.[3] But I am probably mistaken.

I must have lent them to some one else. But I cannot conceive who it was. Don't trouble any more about it.

I am writing to Caldecot[4] to say that I wish he w^d.. work out his original plan for putting the four subjects i Psychology ii Logic iii Philosophy (Mental & Moral) & iv P. E on an equal footing; & that I w^d.. rather see P.E. turned out of the M Sc Tripos altogether, than have the Tripos so manipulated as to cause the greater part of the students for it to give their third year—the only time when they are at all fit to see the bearing of economic questions—exclusively to Philosophy. In my opinion there w^d.. be less harm in putting Philosophy exclusively into the first & second years than in giving it the monopoly of the third: But of course I don't advocate that.

Yours ever | A.M.

[1] Marshall Library, J.N. Keynes Papers. From Balliol Croft.

[2] See [226.3, 227.2, 232].

[3] Neither the papers on India nor the notes on Ricardo have been identified.

[4] Alfred Caldecott (1850–1936), first class in the Moral Sciences Tripos 1879 and Fellow of St John's. He became Professor of Logic and Mental Philosophy at King's College, London, in 1891. The Minutes of the Board of Moral Science do not record any motion by Caldecott. The misspelling of the name is Marshall's.

239. To John Neville Keynes, (25?) April 1888[1]

My dear Keynes

My wife will look over the letter I have written to you,[2] & send it on with her own comments tomorrow or Saturday. The more I look at your proofs[3] the more do I think that they are excellent, but that they can be made better.

Yours ever | A M

[1] Marshall Library, J. N. Keynes Papers. From Balliol Croft. Partly transcribed by Keynes, *Diaries*, entry for Saturday 28 April 1888.

[2] See [240].

[3] See [226.3, 227.2].

240. To John Neville Keynes, 26 April 1888[1]

26 April

My dear Keynes

I think there is most excellent material in these two chapters. But I don't think you have made the most of them. They are a sort of introduction; & introductions always have to be re-written many times. I don't know enough of the other chapters to give more than a very rough shot at a plan for rearranging the material in it. But I will pluck up my courage & here goes :—

Ch I Introductory

A survey of the past (not a formal history) enough to show how economic science has got into a tangle, & requires to [be]² saved from the follies of its friends & attacks of its enemies (See my wife's note A):³ Showing how Cairnes set himself to this task,⁴ but how the position having developed the work has to be done anew, saying simply how you propose to do it, & what good you expect people to get from what you have to say.

Ch II your present Ch IV. & so on to the end of your present Ch X.

Then your present Ch II & lastly the constructive part of your present Ch I.

In short have you not put the cart before the horse, in putting your account of the resources of economics after your account of the method in wh it uses those resources.

Surely you have to speak dogmatically on controversial questions in Ch I, while the defence of your positions will come, according to your present arrangement in later chapters.

Our minds are a little different. Yours is more orderly than mine: & when we differ on a point of this kind, it is more likely that you are right than I. But perhaps what is most likely is that the right solution lies somewhere between us, but much nearer to you than to me.

I wᵈ.. suggest that after taking a little time to turn over the utterances of Balliol Croft, you shd come & have a talk.

Yours very sincerely | Alfred Marshall.

I have no doubt that the book will be the best on the subject, & will have a large circulation even if you bring it out as it is.

['Enclosure']⁵

General remarks

A new book on the subject ought to be very German & based more on 'new School' difficulties as felt in Germany & in America & England. Too much prominence is given to the doctrines of writers who [are]⁶ sinking out of memory; too little in comparison is said in anticipation of the difficulties of the coming generation.

On the German side too little is said of the historical origin of a great part of the science, e.g. cameral wissenschaft.

As regards general pitch of the book :—I shd be inclined to try to separate α the didactic from the controversial, & β that part wh is designed to help the beginner & clear away the prejudices of the vulgar (including the working man), from that wh is designed to remove the subtler mystifications from the minds of those who have already considered for themselves the philosophic problems of 'the many in the one & the one in the many' as applied to Social Science.

ex requires to be expanded or explained[7]
f   more suitable for footnote
o   perhaps omit
s   simplify the diction.

[Enclosure by Mary Paley Marshall]

P. 3 | I s^{hd}. have thought something might be said as to *why* there is so much more dispute as to the method of studying P.E. than there is about studying anything else. It always seems to me that some apology is needed for talking about Economic method, when we never bother ourselves about method in other sciences

P. 10. I think this is a little hard on 'common-sense' for it supplies many important inductions. Also P 11.

P. 12 I dont like this § on the definition of P.E w^h goes into so much detail & criticism, coming in the middle of this introductory Ch; w^h otherwise is so general. Might it not be better to give a short preliminary definition here enough for the present purpose & then put off its definition § 7–10 till you come to Ch. on definition? It seems to me to make a great break with the continuity of the chapter as it stands.

I s^{hd}. myself make a separate Ch of *the definition of P.E.* & treat it more thoroughly showing how it had gradually grown & changed, & make the German school more important—In a book on method, I think the definition of the subject s^{hd} be made a conspicuous part.

P. 36–7. I think one or two illustrations w^d. lighten it up here.

Since writing this I have read my husbands letter & agree with what he says as to general arrangement & to his new pencil notes.[8]   MPM

[1] Marshall Library, J. N. Keynes Papers. From Balliol Croft. Quoted in *Diaries*, entry for Saturday 28 April 1888. Keynes and Marshall had a discussion about Keynes's book on Saturday 21 April which left Keynes depressed:

> He practically wants me to give a year to studying the Germans and then to rewrite entirely. On one or two points I think he is right that if I say anything at all I ought to be more thorough. He also thinks that some of the points I raise for discussion are obsolete. Here I cannot agree with him. I think I can effect some improvement by eliminating as far as possible the *personal* controversial elements, making use of controversy mainly as a means for bringing out my own views.

By the next day Keynes was consoling himself with the thoughts that 'I think he [Marshall] has hardly done justice to the good points of my book. I think I can claim for it clearness & definiteness. Another thing is that I never can rely much on Marshall's judgement. His views are nearly always exaggerated on one side or the other.' By Saturday 28 April he concluded 'I was unduly depressed after my conversation with Marshall'. (*Diaries*, entries for 21, 22, 28 April 1888.)

[2] Word apparently omitted.

[3] The note concerning p. 3 in the enclosure from Mary Paley Marshall has against it an 'A' in the margin.

[4] John Elliott Cairnes, *The Character and Logical Method of Political Economy* (Macmillan, London, 1857).

[5] This was possibly given to Keynes during the discussion on Saturday 21 April as it is partly transcribed in *Diaries*, entry for that date. Marshall's note was written in pencil on a page proof for Keynes's title page. Keynes eventually abandoned these proofs and rewrote completely so that it is impossible to relate the detailed points to the final text of *Scope and Method*.

[6] Word apparently omitted.

[7] Presumably a key to notations written on the returned proof.

[8] Possibly Marshall's 'enclosure', which was in pencil, but more probably additional notes, perhaps written on the proofs, that were not preserved.

241. To John Neville Keynes, (7?) May 1888[1]

Dear Keynes

I send you these papers.[2] I shd like to add to what I said yesterday, that I have no intention of making an attack on Sidgwick's method of conducting Mo Sc Board business unless I can not help it.

Also all my indignation against him is confined to a rather narrow area. It is Sidgwick as a university politician & to some extent as a writer on economics that I quarrel with. All the rest of Sidgwick, I expect I think as highly of as you do.

Yours ever | A.M.

[1] Marshall Library, J. N. Keynes Papers. From Balliol Croft. Quoted by Keynes in *Diaries*, entry for 8 May 1888.

[2] Probably relating to Moral-Science Board business, but not identified. The proposed reform of the Moral Sciences Tripos was causing considerable friction between Marshall and Sidgwick, who was chairman of the Moral Sciences Board.

242. To the Council, King's College, London, 21 May 1888[1]

From Alfred Marshall
Professor of Political Economy at the University of Cambridge.

May 21, 1888

Hearing that my friend, Mr. Edgeworth, proposes to be a candidate for the vacant Professorship of the Principles and Practice of Commerce in Kings College, London, I have pleasure in expressing my opinion that he is extremely well qualified for the post. He has a thorough knowledge of economic science; he is a very able man with accurate habits of thought, and would discharge the duties of the Chair with great care and conscientiousness.

(signed Alfred Marshall)

[1] From a printed set of testimonials provided by Edgeworth, King's College Archives. A further set is in Nuffield College, Oxford, Edgeworth Papers. Edgeworth, who was already Lecturer in Logic at the College, was promoted. Marshall had written a substantively identical testimonial for Edgeworth on 24 March 1888 for an Examinership in Political Economy of the University of London (BLPES, Edgeworth Papers).

243. To John Neville Keynes, 23 June 1888[1]

23 June

My dear Keynes,

I am an awful nuisance & if you strike, I shall have no ground for complaint. But I shd be much obliged if you w^d.. look through this paper of Nicholson's[2] & the rough draft of my answer. Nicholson's Note seems to be of old date. But he did not send me a copy : & I have only just got one. Murray[3] wants a short answer from me to be printed for private circulation among the Commission. Neither Nicholson's Note nor my reply are to be published.[4]

This interruption to my book is awfully disgusting, & I make my answer as short as possible. Will you kindly consider i whether I am bound to go any further than I have gone ii whether anything I have said will irritate Nicholson & can be omitted iii anything else that occurs to you.

I have been bothered by visitors: & tomorrow I shall be more or less engaged till about five o'clock. But I w^d.. like to talk out this point, if you will kindly let me, & also some other papers that Murray has sent me confidentially. So I propose to bring those papers along on Monday morning, arriving at your house about 10.30, & asking you to give me an hour or so.[5] You will be interested in the other papers.

Make pencil notes freely on my MS.S.

Yours bothersomely | A. M.

[1] Marshall Library, J. N. Keynes Papers. From Balliol Croft.

[2] Nicholson had written for the Gold and Silver Commission [214.5] a 'Note on the Effect of a Fall in the Gold Price of Silver on General Gold Prices'. The Note was not reproduced in the Commission's Report.

[3] George Herbert Murray (1849–1936), civil servant, who was Secretary of the Commission; knighted in 1899.

[4] A four-page 'Note by Professor Marshall on Professor Nicholson's Paper' dated 30 June 1888 was in fact included among the supplementary materials published with the Commission's *Final Report* (C.5212, 1888). It is not reproduced in *Official Papers*. It restates the general views Marshall had already presented to the Commission.

[5] 'Marshall was with me nearly the whole of the morning talking over another paper he has written for the currency commission. He has got into controversy with Nicholson' (*Diaries*, entry for Monday 25 June 1888). The 'other papers' Marshall sought to discuss cannot be identified.

244. To Robert Harry Inglis Palgrave, 27 June 1888[1]

27 June 1888

My dear Palgrave

I am very glad McMillan have undertaken the Dictionary.[2]

I hope all will go well. I don't expect to be able to do anything to speak of for it myself. But I will retain as benevolent an attitude as a neutral can, who is so engaged on domestic politics (his own books) that he can't go in for an active policy in foreign affairs.

Yours very sincerely | Alfred Marshall

---

[1] Palgrave Family Papers. From Balliol Croft.

[2] The *Dictionary of Political Economy*, edited by Palgrave, was to be published by Macmillan (London) in three volumes between 1894 and 1899.

245. To John Neville Keynes, 20 August 1888[1]

Fylingdales
20 Aug

My dear Keynes,

After long delays wh are partly due to my fault, partly that of the Press, I send you the first four of a batch of chapters on 'Industrial Organization': the fifth relating to 'Business Management' is at the Press & I will ask them to send you a proof direct.[2]

Please to write your comments on them in pencil as far as may be convenient to yourself.

There remains in Book IV a final chapter summing up the conditions of Supply.[3] Then comes Book V short & nasty; on the 'General Theory of the Equilibrium of Demand & Supply': & then Book VI wh is to be very much like Book II of the Economics of Industry.[4]

Up to the beginning of 'Organization of Industry' is 300 pages, from there to the end of the Volume I think 300 more.[5] It's a long job.

I wonder whether my wife or I can be of any service to you.

After Tuesday the 28th our address for two or three weeks will be

Cliffgrove | Staithes | Yorkshire.

I suppose you will be taking another trip soon.

I wonder what you think of Booths & my Census Memorandum.[6]

There is no truth in the report in the Times[7] that [I][8] intend, or ever did intend, to read a paper on the Census at the British Assn.

Yours very sincerely | Alfred Marshall

---

[1] Marshall Library, J. N. Keynes Papers.

[2] In *Principles (1)*, book iv, chs. 8, 9, 10, 11 were entitled 'Industrial Organization', 'Industrial Organization, continued. Division of Labour. The Influence of Machinery', 'Industrial Organization, continued. The Concentration of Specialized Industries in Particular Localities', 'Industrial

Organization, continued. Production on a Large Scale'. Ch. 12 was entitled 'Industrial Organization, continued. Business Management'.

[3] Book iv, ch. 13 of *Principles (1)*, entitled 'Conclusion. The Law of Increasing in Relation to that of Diminishing Return'.

[4] Book ii of the *Economics of Industry*, entitled 'Normal Value', was mainly devoted to the long-run theory of distribution.

[5] It turned out to be 450 pages more.

[6] Marshall and Charles Booth, concerned that the 1891 population census should use an improved occupational classification and better methods, had apparently sent 'letters of enquiry' to various individuals and organizations. The matter was eventually taken up by the various statistical societies, leading to a deputation to the Chancellor of the Exchequer: see [255.6]. For pertinent information see Marshall's comments (pp. 461–3) on G. B. Longstaff, 'Suggestions for the Census of 1891', *Journal of the Royal Statistical Society*, 52 (September 1889), pp. 436–58, followed by 'Discussion', pp. 459–67. Also see ibid., pp. 384–8 for a report on the Society's own initiative.

[7] See the article 'The British Association', *The Times*, 15 August 1888 (4a): 'Professor Marshall will invite the attention of the section [Section F] to the necessity of amending the occupation returns of the census'.

[8] Word apparently omitted.

246. To John Neville Keynes, 27 August 1888[1]

Address for ⎫	Cliffgrove
next two or ⎬ →	Staithes R.S.O.
three weeks ⎭	Yorkshire

27 Aug 88

My dear Keynes

Thankyou very much for looking over my proofs.

I have given up the hope of bringing out my vol I in January but I still hope to get it out in March.

All but 200 pages are now with the printer, or next door to being so. There remains 200, of which about half are I think in good condition, but the other 100 have some of them to be written & the rest to be rewritten.

I am now busy with diagrams which swarm in the latter half of Book V.

I had said to Booth that I thought it w^d.. be good to have a discussion of the Census at Bath.[2] He told Elliott,[3] who consented cordially: & Booth said he, Elliott, wanted me to read it; though I guess he was sharp enough to know that Booth was the right person really. But Booth did not send on that part of the message. I told Booth I could not: & he told Elliott so.

I know that: but nothing more.

Yours ever | A.M.

[1] Marshall Library, J. N. Keynes Papers.

[2] See [245.6].

[3] Thomas Henry Elliott, a member of the organizing committee.

247. To the Editor, *Quarterly Journal of Economics*, (August?) 1888[1]

Business Profits and Wages

Mr. Macvane prefaces his note on the above subject in the last number of this *Journal*[2] by the statement that his aims in writing are to make his own position clear and to abstain from controversy. I do not think he attains the former of these two aims. He certainly does not attain the latter; for he proceeds to give a paraphrase of my views on this subject, and to find fault with them.[3] I do not wish to trespass on the patience of the readers of this *Journal* further than to say that I abide by my doctrines as expounded by myself, but that I do not accept the paraphrase of them given by Mr. Macvane.

Alfred Marshall.

[1] Published under the indicated heading in the correspondence section of the *Quarterly Journal of Economics*, 3 (October 1888), p. 109.

[2] Silas M. Macvane, 'Business Profits and Wages: A Rejoinder', *Quarterly Journal of Economics*, 2 (July 1888), pp. 453–68. Macvane's criticisms of the views of Marshall and Walker had been launched in his 'The Theory of Business Profits', ibid., 2 (October 1887), pp. 1–36, and were initially addressed by Marshall in his 'Wages and Profits', ibid., 2 (January 1888), pp. 218–23 (reproduced in *Guillebaud*, pp. 822–7).

[3] Macvane had criticized from a wages-fund perspective the views on distribution set out in the *Economics of Industry*.

248. To John Neville Keynes, 29 September 1888[1]

29 Sep 88

My dear Keynes

In order to get more time free for my book in the Lent Term I want to change the arrangements of my lectures. Will you therefore kindly make the following alterations when revising the Mo: Sc: list for publication in this Terms Reporter.[2]

(i) Transfer 'Competition Combination & State Interference' from Lent to Easter Term

(ii) Insert for Lent Term 'Advanced Economic Theory (Continued)'.

The change will not affect the number of lectures I give, but only their arrangement.

I have been going slowly lately. I daresay I shall look you up at the Syndicate Building[3] before long & try to get a chat.*

Yours ever | A. Marshall

* I must go to the Press on Tuesday or Wednesday morning.

[1] Marshall Library, J. N. Keynes Papers. From Balliol Croft.

[2] See *Reporter*, 8 Oct 1888. Lists of lectures offered by the Board for Moral Science were published in the *Reporter* each term, covering the remaining portion of the academic year.

[3] Keynes had an office there in connection with his work for the Local Examinations and Lectures Syndicate. See [90.2].

249. From Henry Hardinge Cunynghame, 4 October 1888[1]

Special Commission, 1888
Royal Courts of Justice
Oct 4 . 1888

My dear Marshall.

I finished the hyperbolagraph[2] last night and am happy to say that it works exceedingly well. I send you one of its performances in copying ink & about 40 or 50 reproductions which will probably last you two or three days?

The accuracy may be seen by inspection, for instance, observe the curve whose area is 16 square inches, & where it cuts the 6 and 4 ordinates. Again take the curve whose area is 4 squ inches, & observe where it cuts the 4 & 8 ordinates. Test the diagram how you will & I believe you will no where find it a line breadth out.

If you wish to turn them into diagrams for a book, then it may conveniently be done by drawing the diagram out either on one of the collographs or else on a piece of tracing cloth placed over one of them. This should then be sent me, & with the machine I will draw out what hyperbolas are so indicated, on the big scale. They will then be reduced by means of photography to the requisite size & done into blocks by one of the well known photo-zinc-cut processes. If they were reduced by 1/2 this wd. make the lines 1/10th of an inch apart. If this is too fine, they cd be made coarser.

Y^s. affec. | H. Cunynghame.

---

[1] Marshall Papers.

[2] A device for drawing a grid of rectangular hyperbolae—presumably an adaptation of the machine shown to the Cambridge Philosophical Society in 1873: see [94]. Marshall must at this time have been preparing the monopoly diagrams for book v, ch. 13, of *Principles (1)* which utilised such grids.

250. To John Neville Keynes, (24?) October 1888[1]

Private

A–D have come. I don't much like them. The sample article on Value is, I think very unsatisfactory.[2] I am inclined to hold as much aloof as possible. I now understand what you said about it. We must have a talk before *R.H.I.P* appears on the scene. If there is not some change I fear *R.I.P* may be the end of all.

Yours A.M.

Low Barometer & Mo Sc Board[3] together have done me up.

---

[1] Marshall Library, J. N. Keynes Papers. From Balliol Croft.

[2] RHIP (i.e. Palgrave) had constructed a list of entries for the letters A–D in the proposed *Dictionary of Political Economy* [244.2]. Keynes had observed, 'Palgrave has sent me his list of proposed terms for his dictionary with the approximate space assigned to each. He asks for criticisms. On the

whole the list seems to me badly drawn up. I think Palgrave is hardly the man for the work. He has not a sufficiently all round knowledge of political economy' (*Diaries*, entry for 28 September 1888). On 12 October Keynes found Palgrave's specimen entry on value 'poor'.

[3] The first meeting of the academic year was on 24 October 1888, when reform of the Tripos was still under inconclusive consideration.

251. To John Neville Keynes, 26 October 1888[1]

26 Oct 88

My dear Keynes

I intended to tell you that I acted deliberately in applying the curves only to problems of Normal Values & not to Market values.[2] Market curves can be drawn: but [I][3] shd agree with Wicksteed that they could never have a shape that w^d.. correspond to the Law of Increasing return.[4] And I don't think they w^d.. be of much practical use. I considered whether I w^d.. introduce 'market' curves, & explain the differences between them & Normal curves: but thought I shd only bother the reader.

And now I want to ask your kind advice on a difficult point.

What I say about *Derived* Demand & Supply Book V Ch V §§1, 2 & 4[5] is, in my own conceited opinion, new & important: but the exposition gave me a great deal of trouble & is I fear unsatisfactory yet. In particular I have taken an illustration in the text (not in the footnote) about plasterers which I knew at the time was not in perfect logical harmony with the assumption that the curves apply only to periods sufficiently long to allow free action to the normal forces of supply (in this case the growth of plasterers). I took that particular illustration partly because it is a striking one, partly because I shall want it a good deal in Book VI: and I thought that if I apologized for & explained away this logical change of point of view, I s^{hd}.. bother the readers: & that if I said nothing about it probably no one w^d.. find it out. Also I took care to say nothing of the possibility of the supply curves sloping downwards towards the right. (I have suppressed hundreds of possible queer cases of that sort for fear of overburdening the book by statements of the conditions by w^h.. they had to be safeguarded.)

Now the question I want to ask is:—wd it be best

    a to explain the change of venue involved by the plasterers' illustration
or *b* to destroy it ruthlessly
or *c* run the risk of detection by lynx eyed (or minded) readers.[6]

I send papers on Monopolies.[7] There is something wrong with the supply curve in Fig 37 (as also in Figs 20 & 29): & they must be redrawn. But the curves don't affect the argument.[8]

Yours ever | A.M.

P.S. I find that a line RT wh I had intended to have in the two figs 34, has dropped out. But references to it remain in the argument. I can do without it. Please substitute the slips 72–7 wh I now inclose for those w^h.. you have.^{9}

For greater clearness I propose to put the first two paragraphs of §3 on slip 60, before the last paragraph of the preceding section. (Verbal changes will be necessary.) My object is to emphasize the fact that the marginal note at the bottom of slip 60 applies with greater or less force to all supply schedules.^{10}

I am making hardly any progress with my work just now. So you won't get Bk VI Ch 1 as soon as I hoped.

I have not read the slips for the last half of Book V. There may be bad flaws in them.

^{1} Marshall Library, J. N. Keynes Papers. From Balliol Croft. Partly reproduced, *Guillebaud*, p. 400.

^{2} This seems to refer to the proofs of book v, ch. 2, of *Principles (1)*, entitled 'Temporary Equilibrium of Demand and Supply'.

^{3} Word apparently omitted.

^{4} Wicksteed had attacked Marshall's supply curves in a paper presented to the 'Economic Circle' [224.6] on 16 October. Keynes recorded 'Florence and I went to London, staying the night with Beeton at Hampstead. Afterwards a meeting of Wicksteed's Economic Club. Wicksteed read a paper criticising Marshall's supply curves. Foxwell, Henry Cunynghame & Edgeworth were present. I was much interested at meeting the two latter'. (*Diaries*, entry for 16 October 1888.) Two weeks later Cunynghame rose to Marshall's defense with a paper 'Some Remarks upon Demand and Supply Curves and Their Interpretation, Read at Mr. Beeton's House, 9 Maresfield Gardens, Hampstead, October 30th 1888' (privately printed). From this, Wicksteed's objections seem to have taken a rather jejune form: the supply curve 'must always rise. For in any state of things the manufacturer will always make the easiest first'. Cunynghame's own solution, which he developed into H.H. Cunynghame, 'Some Improvements in Simple Geometrical Methods of Treating Exchange Value, Monopoly, and Rent', *Economic Journal*, 2 (March 1892), pp. 35–52, did not entirely satisfy Marshall.

It should be noted that Wicksteed's *Alphabet* [224.2] dealt only tangentially (pp. 108–24) with supply, which fell into 'the "theory of production" or "making" rather than into that of the "theory of value" or "worth"' to which the book was devoted (p. 109).

^{5} When *Principles (1)* appeared, this material was in book v, ch. 6, 'Joint and Composite Demand: Joint and Composite Supply'. Guillebaud's version of the letter makes the alteration silently.

^{6} In the event, Marshall inserted the following qualification 'This case has important practical bearings, which give it a special claim on our attention; but we should notice that, referring as it does to short periods, it is an exception to our general rule of selecting illustrations in this and the neighbouring chapters from cases in which there is time enough for the full long-period action of the forces of supply to be developed.' *Principles (1)*, p. 431; *Principles (8)*, p. 382.

^{7} This probably refers to the proofs of book v, ch. 8, of *Principles (1)*, entitled 'The Theory of Monopolies'.

^{8} Figure 37, *Principles (1)*, p. 463, appears as Figure 35 in *Principles (8)*, p. 483. Figures 20 and 29, *Principles (1)*, pp. 424, 444, appear as Figure 38, *Principles (8)*, p. 806, and Figure 29, *Guillebaud*, p. 532.

^{9} Figures 34 and 35 of *Principles (1)*, pp. 448, 449, are identical to Figures 33 and 32 of *Principles (8)*, pp. 473, 469.

^{10} This probably refers to pp. 445–6 of *Principles (1)*, reproduced on *Principles (8)*, pp. 465–7, with the two original paragraphs of section 3 being amalgamated into one.

252. To John Neville Keynes, 16 November 1888[1]

16 Nov 88

Dear Keynes

I have calculated pages & find I cant bring out Vol I before Easter. So now I shall want, with a shamed face, to change back & lecture in the Lent Term.[2] And while about it I can somewhat alter the subject of the lectures so as to make them suit the historical men,[3] if you are in any doubt as to whether you w^d.. like to give a special set of lectures for them.[4]

In any case I s^{hd}.. change the title somewhat; because I have about a foot thickness of Blue books that I want to read before lecturing *in extenso* on Government Interference. And though I don't suppose I shall do much at my book in the Lent Term, I could not read the Blues then with any satisfaction.[5]

On this plan I shall get the Easter Term free for my Book VI & my address on Cooperation,[6] w^h.. will be very much on the subject of Book VI, will almost write itself.

If you don't lecture to the Historical men, I shall just go on with my Monday & Fridays course taking the second half of Mill as my text book, & putting difficulties on to the Wednesdays.[7] If you do lecture to them, I shall probably go over somewhat the same ground; but pitch my key note a little higher so as to get nearer to the wants of those BA's &c who are now attending my elementary as well as my advanced class.

Will you dine in Hall[8] with me on the 27th before Leslie Stephen's address.[9] Answer please when we meet.

Yours ever | A. Marshall

I have been looking up my old notes on Cournot[10] & find I have gone at some length into the question whether the marginal expense of production is to be regarded as $\phi(x)\Delta x$ or as $\Delta\{x\phi(x)\}$ where $y = \phi(x)$ is $=^n$ to supply curve, y, being price & x amount of commodity. I will let you see the notes some time.

---

[1] Marshall Library, J. N. Keynes Papers. From Balliol Croft.

[2] See [248].

[3] Candidates for the Historical Tripos.

[4] No lectures by Keynes were listed by the Historical Board. He lectured on logic for the Moral Science Board and also regularly taught a separate political economy course for Indian Civil Service candidates.

[5] Marshall's lectures were listed identically by both Moral Science and History Boards. The lecture lists in the *Reporter*, 14 January 1889, show Marshall as lecturing in the Lent Term on 'Trade and Finance' (the continuation of his general course) on Mondays and Fridays at 12.00, and on 'Advanced Economic Theory (continued)' on Saturdays at 12.00. He was shown as not lecturing in the Easter Term. Previously (see [248]) he had been listed as teaching the general course in the Easter rather than the Lent Term, and covering in it 'Competition, Combination and State Interference'.

[6] Marshall was due to give the Presidential Address to the Cooperative Congress at Ipswich on 10 June 1889. For the text of his address see his 'Cooperation', *Memorials*, pp. 227–55.

[7] Marshall usually taught 'Advanced Economic Theory' on Wednesdays at 12 and presumably still planned at this point to do so in the Lent term.

[8] That is at St. John's College.

[9] Leslie Stephen gave an address on behalf of the Universities Settlement Association and Toynbee Hall in St John's College Hall on 27 November 1888. Philip Lyttleton Gell (1852–1926) of Balliol, Chairman of the Universities Settlement Association, also spoke and Marshall moved the vote of thanks. See *Cambridge Review*, 22 and 29 November 1888. Keynes did dine at St John's and judged Marshall's performance 'excellent' (*Diaries*, entry for 27 November 1888).

[10] These notes are reproduced in *Early Economic Writings*, vol. 2, pp. 302–5. $=^n$ stands for 'equation'.

253. To John Neville Keynes, 8 December 1888[1]

8 Dec 88

My dear Keynes,

I am quite ashamed to ask you to look at M.S.S. of mine when you ought to be doing your own book. But the case is one in w^h.. I do very much want advice:—

The inclosed[2] was part of the first systematic account of my views on value (I can't fix the date but I believe it was 1870. I know for certain it was before 1874). In them I have divided markets according to lengths of periods A, B, C, D (for short statement see p 24,1) and make the supply curve a horizontal straight line for A, necessarily inclined positively for B & C, & of all sorts of shapes for D. (There is some exaggeration in the D figures as I drew them.)[3]

Substantially I believe the account given in these papers to be right & that given by Wicksteed[4] (as I understand it) to be wrong. I have however a great deal more to say about the D curves some of which is already in slip; & some of w^h.. was to have come later, but will now go anyhow into Books IV & V.

In writing the chapters on 'Domestic Values' in the Appendix to my Treatise on Foreign Trade,[5] I left out about A: B: C: D; partly because they do not bear directly on foreign trade problems. And when writing my present Book V, I decided after some doubt to do the same.

But now I am inclined to think that my fear of over-complexity has led me to adopt a course wh is likely to be misunderstood; & I am doubtful whether I ought not to bring back again the substance of A: B: C: D.

Ought I?

I dont want you to write an answer if it w^d.. take you long.

At all events if you are likely to be in Cambridge about the 19th, I will come to Harvey Road[6] on the day after I return & ask for a verbal answer.

Your apologetic & grateful Bore | Alfred Marshall

[1] Marshall Library, J. N. Keynes Papers. From Balliol Croft. Reproduced in *Early Economic Writings*, vol. 1, pp. 119–20, and substantially in *Guillebaud*, p 365.

[2] Reproduced with an editorial introduction as 'Essay on Value' in *Early Economic Writings*, vol. 1, pp. 119–59.

[3] The C and D curves are closely related to the short- and long-period normal supply curves introduced in *Principles* (*1*).

[4] See [251.4].

[5] 'The Pure Theory of Domestic Values'. See [59.3].

[6] Keynes resided at 6 Harvey Road, some one and a half miles from Balliol Croft.

254. From Benjamin Jowett to Mary Paley Marshall, 19 December 1888[1]

Longleat, Warminster
Dec 19. 1888

Dear Mrs Marshall,

I feel as if I were guilty of an offense in not answering your kind letter. I have thought of you & Alfred many times during the last month, but being lazy, & rather tired, I had not the energy to write. If the same thing ever happens to you, I hope you will forgive me: and will understand that little neglects of this sort, though ungracious do not imply any dimunition of regard or affection:

I am sorry to hear that your long vacation was not a perfect success. I remember going to the region in which you were settled[2] about 30 years ago with Mr Lyulph Stanley[3] then a youth. I did not much care about the places. With the exception of Whitby Abbey everything was modern & not interesting. I look upon you as going to the Sea for the benefit of the book, as some people go for the sake of their children, and it is of great importance to choose the right air for the book. And you are probably already thinking of where you will go next year. The long vacation is a joy for ever, at least it is always coming back.

I sometimes think that you are two of the happiest people I have ever known: In the first place you have in common a most delightful pursuit: 2 a charming society: 3 you have made for yourselves (for which I especially commend & envy you) a perfectly simple way of life, without trouble & without expense, 4) you may look forward to doing a great deal of the kind of good which is most needed in this miserable world, good for the poor: good for the many, 5) and lastly you are beginning both of you to have good health of which no one knows the blessing who has not felt the want of it.

How is the Book? that like the child is the darling of the house—and a much less troublesome creature than most children. I hope to see it launched in the world in the course of the coming year.

I hope you received the Evidence.[4] I used to talk about it to Lord Lansdowne[5]—who has, I think settled down pretty much upon the line which Alfred indicates—viz to let the Indian currency alone, unless there are any visible signs of the further depression of silver? He is clear headed about this & about other things & will I think do well.

With best regards to Alfred | Ever yrs affectionately | B Jowett

[1] Marshall Papers. Reproduced in Abbott and Campbell, *Life and Letters* [146.1], vol. 2, pp. 341–2.

[2] The North Yorkshire coast.

[3] Edward Lyulph Stanley (1839–1925) sometime student and Fellow of Balliol. He later became Baron Stanley and Baron Sheffield. See Abbott and Campbell, *Life and Letters*, vol. 1, pp. 333, 352.

[4] The evidence before the Gold and Silver Commission [214.5]?

[5] The Fifth Marquess of Lansdowne (1845–1927), educated at Balliol, Governor-General of Canada 1883–8, Viceroy of India 1888–93.

255. To John Neville Keynes, 20 December 1888[1]

20 Dec 88

My dear Keynes

I have to thank you very much for your letter.[2] I had no intention of denying any of the propositions in it: but the fact that it seemed necessary to you to state them, proves that if I go into a formal classification at all, I must be as you say much more explicit. So far as I recollect I had intended to treat the case of a book or newspaper on the plan of charging to each copy after the first only the direct outlay on it. In this particular I have changed my views as to what is most convenient, & propose to go on difft lines.[3]

I think now I shall probably leave Bk V almost exactly as it is, but bring together immediately after it the analysis of the difficulties of Cost of Production into a separate short Book before the long Book on 'Distribution & Exchange' instead of scattering them over that Book.[4] I began to write a Book with that title in the middle of last Term: but found difficulties in arrangement & gave it up. But though awkward, it will enable me to be explicit; & on the whole I have decided to try to get on with that plan. The chief change I shall make in Bk V is to say that the conditions under wh the supply curve can be inclined negatively will be discussed finally in the new Bk VI.

Your kindly letter is as usual immensely useful: those parts of it w^h.. criticize opinions I had not intended to express are as useful as any.

I dont think however we entirely agree. Because I do not accept Cunynghames position at all. He seems to me to try to cut the Gordian knot, & to fail. This applies to his first Part as well as his second.[5] You will understand what I mean when you see my (new) Bk VI.

The deputation[6] went off well.

I am getting an increased conviction of the importance of giving a larger place in Logical papers to those difficulties of investigation w^h.. actually occur in real life, & a smaller place to semi-scholastic questions however good they may be as a mere gymnastic.

Perhaps we shan't agree on this.

Yours most ever | A.M.

[1] Marshall Library, J. N. Keynes Papers. From Balliol Croft.

[2] Not preserved. Keynes's private reactions to reading Marshall's proofs during the autumn of 1888 might be noted here (*Diaries*, entries for the dates indicated).

Some more proof sheets from Marshall. I think that some parts of his book will be very good indeed, but that other parts will be poor. (15 September 1888.)

A long call from Mrs Marshall. She says that Marshall values extremely my criticisms on his book, & that he always looks forward to them with the greatest interest. (8 October 1888.)

I am now working at rather a heavy installment of Marshall's proof sheets (with the curves in the notes). The arrangement seems to me bad, & I am not altogether well satisfied with this part of the book, though portions of it are very good indeed. The form of the argument & the composition want Sidgwick's finish. (3 November 1888.)

Called on Marshall & had a talk with him for an hour or so on various topics. I always find a talk with him rather wearing. I think it is partly because he is so faddy, and because he attaches such importance to trifles. (11 November 1888.)

[3] This appears to relate to the classification of cost which is dealt with mainly in book vi, ch. 6, of *Principles (1)*.

[4] This solution was adopted in *Principles (1)* where the new book vi was headed 'Cost of Production Further Considered'. In the second edition of 1891 and thereafter this material was integrated with book v rather than with the final book (now again book vi) as Marshall had originally planned.

[5] See [251.4]. Cunynghame dealt with supply first, then symmetrically with demand. For supply, he distinguished a family of 'quantity-intensity curves' each arraying in increasing order the production cost of the successive units produced, given a specified total production. The supply curve or 'curve of final cost' was interpreted as the locus of all those points, one to each intensity curve, at which total quantity produced equals the total quantity for which the intensity curve is defined. No adequate explanation of why intensity curves differ was offered, the most obvious possible justification being external economies or diseconomies.

[6] On 11 December a deputation of teachers of political economy and representatives of statistical societies had waited on the Chancellor of the Exchequer (Goschen) to urge 'the desirability of obtaining at the next census more accurate statistics, particularly in relation to the industrial pursuits of the community; also to urge that in future the census should be taken quinquennially'. Marshall is reported as urging 'the importance of having an occupational census of a continuous character . . . They wanted to be better able to distinguish the skilled from the unskilled workers, and to know what trades were in existence.' (*Morning Post*, 12 December 1888.) See also *The Times* (same date; 10a) and [245.6].

256. To the Editor, *The Times*, 26 December 1888[1]

The Manchester Chamber of Commerce and Protection

Sir,—It seems that at least one-twentieth of the Manchester Chamber of Commerce are agreed that imported goods 'of a nature and kind which we ourselves produce' should 'pay the legal proportional share of the burden of Imperial and local taxation which they would have paid if produced or manufactured in the United Kingdom'.[2] Surely they cannot think that a person who buys a Swiss watch escapes paying on it the Imperial and local taxes which he would have paid if he had bought an English watch? The Swiss watch had to be bought with the products of English labour in some form or other. Let us suppose that a parcel of cutlery was sent abroad in exchange for it. Then, since the English cutlery manufacturer must have paid his share of English rates and taxes just as fully as the English watch manufacturers do, the imported watch has paid its share of English national burdens just as much as the English watch would have done. If special taxes were levied on it, it would be taxed twice. That would not, *prima facie*, be fair trade.

If we gave a drawback on our exports equal to the rates and taxes which they have paid in the process of production, then it would be true that imported goods would have an unfair advantage in competing with those produced at home. But as it is they all pay their share, whether or not they are 'of a nature and kind which we ourselves produce'.

By the way, it would be interesting to know in what language the resolution was first drafted, and who is responsible for the attempt to translate it into the Queen's English.[3]

Cambridge, Dec. 26,   Alfred Marshall.

[1] Printed in *The Times*, 28 December 1888.

[2] See *The Times*, 20 December 1888 (12c) for an account of the Chamber's resolution, proposed by H. F. Hibbert. A letter from William Fogg in *The Times*, 26 December 1888 (5b), explained that the resolution had been engineered by some 50 or 60 'fair traders', mostly new members, and did not represent the dominant opinion of the Chamber's 1,030 members: 'Manchester the birth-place and home of free trade, cannot allow this stigma to lie'.

[3] An allusion to the resolution's less than elegant wording or a hint of foreign influence?

257. To John Neville Keynes, 15 January, 1889[1]

                                                      15 Jan
My dear Keynes

I return your exam[n] papers with thanks. I have ticked those questions w[h].. seem to me to come within the scope of the proposed paper on 'Inductive Logic, Th: of Probabilities; Th: of Statistics'.[2]

I can see no real difficulty in the matter.

I shd wish all papers in Part II (not in Part I) to be long enough to allow for slight differences between the casts of mind of individual students.

Yours A.M.

I have quite decided to bring that part of the old Book VI (on 'Distribution & Exchange') wh relates to difficulties as to Cost of Production into a place by itself as a new Book VI putting off Distribution & Exchange to be Book VII. I shan't send anything more to the press till I have got Book VI nearly written. I have quite decided that I can see no reason for modifying the substance of anything I have said about unstable equilibria. But I shall make my explanations fuller.

By the way you may like to see the inclosed,[3] & return it at your leisure.

I think I spoke to you some time ago of Pantaleoni[4] as seeming to me to have much truer mathematical instincts than Jevons, Walras Launhardt & Co, & I may now add Wicksteed.[5] But I have not told him that.

[1] Marshall Library, J. N. Keynes Papers. From Balliol Croft.

[2] Marshall was at this time pushing a proposal to permit political economy students to substitute the study of logic and methodology for that of metaphysics in Part II of the Moral Sciences Tripos (see [235.5]). Apparently he had been looking over old examination papers with a view to drawing up a specimen paper. Keynes was not entirely enthusiastic: 'Marshall wants one of the Advanced Logic papers to be taken in lieu of Metaphysics by P.E. specialists. I rather hesitate to agree as it may mean that logic examiners will have less freedom in setting their questions.' (*Diaries*, entry for 1 December 1888.) In a further note of 17 January (also in the J. N. Keynes Papers) Marshall observed.

> I think (i) those questions w^h.. profess to be on inductive logic in the papers you sent me are fairly well suited for those students of economics who may come in from the Math: or Nat: Sc: Tripos, & (ii) in the interests of the main body of Mo Sc men it w^d.. be well to increase the importance in Part II of Inductive Logic (+ Probabilities + Statistics) relatively to formal &c Logic.

[3] Not identified.

[4] Maffeo Pantaleoni's *Manuele di Economia Pura* (Barbèra, Florence, 1889; translated as *Pure Economics*: Macmillan, London, 1898) reproduced with Marshall's consent some of the diagrams from the privately printed 'Pure Theory' chapters [59.3]. No correspondence has survived.

[5] P. H. Wicksteed's *Alphabet* [224.2] had appeared recently. Keynes's reaction had been more favourable: 'I am reading Wicksteed's *Alphabet of Economic Science*. There is perhaps over much mathematics & some points may be worked out in needless detail—but he has a wonderful power of clear exposition, & many of his illustrations—homely as they are—are excellent' (*Diaries*, entry for 16 December 1888).

258. To the Editor, *The Times*, 23 January 1889[1]

Bimetallism

Sir,—My opinions on the subject of bimetallism are already published at great length, in the appendix to the final report of the Commission on Gold and Silver;[2] and I had no desire to enter into the battle that is now being waged in your columns. But Sir Louis Mallet, in the letter published by you to-day, mentions me as one of those who have 'substantially approved the bimetallic theory,'[3] and I fear this may lead to some misapprehension. I am often asked whether I hold the quantity theory of money, or the cost of production theory. I agree with Mill in accepting both;[4] I think that either of them, when properly explained, includes the other; they are but two sides of one great truth. I think that an international agreement to coin gold and silver freely at a fixed ratio would exercise a strong force tending to equalize the market values of the metals; and so far I go with 'the bimetallic theory'; but I do not go with it so far as to think that the force would be practically irresistible. It probably would be strong enough to maintain itself for a long time, if the ratio adopted were 20 or 22 to one; but not if it were $15\frac{1}{2}$ to one.

No one denies that the last ratio differs widely from the cost of production ratio, by which I mean the ratio which is required to keep the annual production of the precious metals at about the same relative proportion as the existing stocks of them. But the extreme advocates of bimetallism, looking only at the direct effects of this divergence, argue that the existing stock of gold would suffice to sustain fixed ratio mintage at $15\frac{1}{2}$ for many years, even though the annual supply of fresh gold should diminish fast. That is where I separate myself from them; for, though the direct effects which this divergence exerts on the production of gold might, perhaps, do no very great harm for some years, the indirect effects which it exerts on the scramble for gold would, I think, be likely to destroy the scheme almost as soon as it was adopted. A few bimetallists might think that gold was not over-rated; but the majority of the world would think it was. Civilized peoples, as well as semi-civilized, would regard the hoarding of gold as a good investment. Governments would join, as they do now, in the scramble, army chests and bank cellars, private hoards and goldsmiths' safes would, I fear, take so much as to render the sovereign very shortly as obsolete as the dodo. All this supposes the 'bimetallic' law actually to come into effect; but, of course, it might be made inoperative from the very first by the refusal of bankers, which, I think, would be justifiable under the circumstances, to make contracts except in gold.

If, however, the international agreement were based on a ratio of 20 to one, or, still better, of 22 to one, its strength would, I think, be obviously greater than that of the forces opposed to it. There would be no general opinion that gold was over-rated: few enthusiasts would hoard gold, the majority of people would go on very much as they do now. The existing scramble for gold would, perhaps, not be stopped, but it would not be violently increased, as it would be under the $15\frac{1}{2}$ ratio. There would, of course, be minute fluctuations of the gold price of silver in the market about its central value; but they would do no harm, and bankers, when they came to look at the matter calmly, would see that it was not worth their while to refuse to make bargains in currency. The very fact that the agreement was known to be strong would take away their strength from the forces opposed to it. It would be almost sure to last long, and might last very long. When it fell through, public opinion might be ready for some more truly scientific scheme. And, though I myself have a hankering for true bimetallism, instead of that 'final-ratio-mintage',[5] or 'alternate metallism', which has usurped the name, I have no objection to the experiment being tried of fixed-ratio-mintage at 20 or 22 to one.

Some, however, regard the 'theory of bimetallism' as including the doctrine that the fall in the gold price of silver gives a proportionate bounty to the Indian cultivator of wheat. That is not part of the bimetallic theory, but a morbid excrescence from it. 'N.' cannot denounce too emphatically that doctrine as 'utter nonsense'.[6]

Cambridge, Jan. 23.   Alfred Marshall.

[1] Printed in *The Times*, 25 January 1889.
[2] See [214.5].
[3] Sir Louis Mallet (1823–90), civil servant and economist, was a member of the Gold and Silver Commission. See his letter 'Is Bimetallism Nonsense', *The Times*, 23 January 1889, where he cites Sidgwick, Marshall, Foxwell, and Nicholson as having 'substantially approved the [bimetallic] theory'. Mallet was responding to anonymous letters in *The Times* signed 'N' and 'X' (21 January 1888 (12a, b)) critical of the bimetallist position adopted by the Commission. There was extensive correspondence, reportage, and editorializing on bimetallism and the experience of English versus Indian agriculture in *The Times* during the second half of January and early February.
[4] See J. S. Mill's *Principles*, book iii, chs. 7–9.
[5] 'Final' is probably a misprint for 'fixed'.
[6] This alludes to an earlier letter from 'N': *The Times*, 15 January 1889 (10d).

259. To the Editor, *The Times*, 31 January 1889[1]

Sir,—Mr. Chaplin[2] complains that I deny his conclusions, but do not grapple with his arguments as to the 25 per cent. bounty on Indian wheat. He forgets that he and I argued the matter out at a sitting of the Royal Commission on Gold and Silver, and with your permission I will quote the end of the discussion.[3] The questions are, of course, his, and the answers mine:—

'Question 9,801.—You have submitted, then, that the position of the English grower is worse by 10s. a quarter than it was when his wheat was £2 a quarter ?—No; I have not admitted that.

'Question 9,802.—But is that capable of dispute?—Yes; because that assumes that the prices of other things are the same. Supposing that the wages and rents had fallen in proportion to the fall of other commodities, he would not be affected at all, he would simply use fewer counters, and he would pay away proportionately fewer counters.

'9,803.—But I gathered from you that the position of the Indian grower at all events was this, that the rupees that he got were as valuable to him as ever they were, inasmuch as they would buy as much as they did at any other period?—Certainly.

'9,804.—Very well, to that extent he must be a gainer, must he not, as compared with the English producer, in so far as he is receiving the same price for his wheat as compared with the English grower, who is losing 10s. a quarter?—I deny that the English grower is losing 10s. a quarter.

'9,805.—But in price, I mean?—But price does not matter. Supposing the price of everything were doubled, nobody would be any richer; it is simply a question of using more counters. Of course, in so far as the English farmer is not able to reduce his fixed charges, in so far he is suffering. He has to go without income which, by a better distribution of wealth, tends more and more in the favour of the working classes; for this fall of prices causes the wealth of the country, in my opinion, to be more equally distributed than it would be if the high prices of 1873 had been maintained.'

That, then, is my answer. I admit that a bill for 1,000 rupees is worth just as much to the Indian ryot as it was in 1873: but I contend also that the statistics of prices show it also to be worth just as much to the English farmer as it was then. Taking Mr. Chaplin's figure, I will suppose that the ryot and the farmer received 20 rupees and £2 respectively in 1873; and that in 1888 the ryot still got 20 rupees, the farmer only £1 10s. If so, each of them now gets 25 per cent. less gold than before, each of them gets about as much silver as before, and each of them gets about the same power of purchasing commodities in general as before.

Statistics prove that this is so. Ricardo proves that it must be so.[4] For if a fall of 25 per cent. in silver gave a bounty of 25 per cent. to Indian producers of wheat, and, of course, therefore, to Indian producers of other commodities, Indian goods underselling all others would give rise to such a preponderance of bills drawn in favour of India as could only be met by a flow of scores of millions of pounds' worth of the precious metals annually to India. There has been no such flow; therefore there has been no such bounty. It is true that some time ago there was a slight excess in the purchasing power of the precious metals in India as compared with England, and therefore there was a slight bounty on sending Indian goods to England in exchange for them, and a perceptible increase in the flow of them to the East; but that was practically over long ago.

No one denies that since in England we use about 25 per cent. less yellow counters for any transaction than we used to do, those who have to pay fixed charges of any number of counters suffer; borrowers lose, creditors and fixed-wage receivers gain. If there were any branch of production in which the *entrepreneur* was hit exceptionally hard, that particular branch might for a while be undersold; but as a fact farmers are not in this exceptional case. We now give Indian wheat the precedence over most other Indian goods, the producers of which have equally whatever bounty arises out of the fall of silver, for two reasons. The chief is that the cost of carrying Indian wheat to England has fallen more than the cost of bringing here any other important Indian product. Wheat is the only bulky export of India which is generally grown in places that have no water carriage; and therefore it had to wait for the making of the railways. The other cause is that the methods of preparing Indian wheat for the English market have very much improved in recent years. These causes happen to have coincided generally with the fall in the value of silver, but statistics prove that there is no sort of agreement between the changes in the prices of wheat and of silver in the London market, whether we take the figures from year to year, from month to month, or from week to week. If I wanted facts I should rely on these; but Ricardo's reasoning is enough for me.

Alfred Marshall.

[1] Printed in *The Times*, 31 January 1889.

[2] Henry Chaplin (1840–1923), politician and sportsman, had been a member of the Gold and Silver Commission [214.5]. He was a vehement supporter of bimetallism and a vigorous proponent of the view that gold monometallism and the consequent fall in the gold price of silver had seriously hurt British agriculture since 1873. He featured prominently in the copious discussions of these matters in the columns of *The Times*, January–February 1889. Marshall is responding to a letter from Chaplin appearing in *The Times*, 28 January 1889, chiding the editors, unnamed 'correspondents', and 'an authority so eminent as that of a Professor' in the way Marshall indicates. Chaplin's argument ran as follows.

The price of wheat, which formerly was £2 a quarter, has dropped to £1.10s., and the rupee which was, roughly speaking, worth 2s., has fallen now, for the sake of argument, let us say to 1s. 6d. . . . £1 10s., in gold, with the rupee at 1s. 6d., will exchange for as many rupees as £2 with the rupee at 2s. Consequently the Indian grower is getting now precisely the same number of rupees as when wheat was making £2 instead of £1.10s. a quarter, which is the price to-day. Those rupees will purchase for the Indian grower as much as they ever did before. . . . The Indian producer realizes at the present moment just the same amount that he realized before, while the English grower is receiving £1 10s., instead of £2 for every quarter that he sells. The question is reduced, then, to this very narrow issue—Will £1 10s. to-day go as far, in all respects [in England], as £2 did before?

Indisputably not, Chaplin asserts.

[3] See *Official Papers*, pp. 84–5.

[4] Ricardo's *Principles*, ch. 7.

260. To John Neville Keynes, 7 February 1889[1]

7 Feb 89

Dear Keynes

I promised not to worry you any more about the Editorship of the Economic Journal.[2] But I just tell you that either Edgeworth or Price[3] will probably be asked very shortly to undertake it at a salary of £100. Either will probably accept. Foxwell told me this, & asked whether there was any use in putting pressure on you for the last time. *Every* one would *very much* prefer you.[4]

So now | Yours | A.M.

[1] Marshall Library, J. N. Keynes Papers. From Balliol Croft.

[2] See [180, 198.2, 236].

[3] L. L. F. R. Price, that is.

[4] Keynes commented: 'It is very good of Marshall to give me a final chance of reconsidering the question—but I cannot see my way of accepting the offer' (*Diaries*, entry for 11 February 1889). F. Y. Edgeworth was appointed.

261. From Sidney James Webb, 28 February 1889[1]

27 Keppel St. | Bedford Square
28 Feby/89

Dear Mr Marshall

I had not forgotten my promise to send you the papers of the Fabian Society. I enclose its present prospectus, which includes a careful definition of Socialism, in its completely realised form. I will send you copies of its two recent pamphlets in a day or so.[2]

I do not quite understand your remarks as to Co-operation, (but I do not, of course, expect further elucidation by letter). My paper on Co-operation[3] was intended as an excursus in economic science. I do not gather that you dispute my assertion that modern economists are compelled to withhold their assent from the Co-operators' delusion, that an indefinite extension of voluntary co-operation would result in the elimination of the power of the owners of the means of production to levy a tribute on the workers. If I am wrong in my economics I shall be glad to be corrected.

My 'attitude' to Co-operation (which is not at all hostile) has nothing to do with this scientific point. I think the Co-operators have some grounds of complaint against the Economists for not making this point clear to them.

As to your doubt whether 'the path indicated by modern Socialists is a *practicable* one'—the answer is *solvitur ambulando.*[4] The history of the past generation supplies the proof. I did not know that your 'Experience was to the opposite': I think the great majority of economists are with us on this point, as well as all statesmen.

Your difficulty appears to be in realising adequately that the course of social evolution is making us all Socialists against our will. You cannot doubt that it is 'practicable' for a municipality to own gasworks or tramways, and so on. You cannot doubt the practicability of a Factory Act, or an Income Tax levied practically on Rent, Interest and Salaries only. Yet extend these, and you have an enormous stride towards Collectivism. We may differ as to time (and this is unimportant, for time itself will settle that), but I believe we agree absolutely in Economics, and practically in politics. And I am accepted by the Socialists as one of them.

Yours very truly | Sidney Webb

[1] BLPES, Passfield Papers. Reproduced in Norman Mackenzie (ed.), *The Letters of Sidney and Beatrice Webb* (Cambridge University Press, Cambridge, 1978), vol. 1, p. 124. Marshall's letter, to which this responds has not been traced. The two were probably brought into contact by the 'Economic Circle' [224.6].

[2] Not precisely identified: *Fabian Essays on Socialism*, ed. George Bernard Shaw (Scott, London, 1889), was in preparation at this time. It included Webb's essay 'The Historical Basis of Socialism'.

3 Probably Webb's 'Economic Limitations of Cooperation', *Cooperative News*, 12 January 1889. See also pp. 49–54 of Webb's 'Socialism in England', *Publications of the American Economic Association*, 4/2 (April 1889).
4 Let experience decide.

262. To John Neville Keynes, 3 April 1889[1]

Read Postcript first

3 April

My dear Keynes

I have hunted high & low for my copy of the Leipzig Jahrbuch 1883 containing Schmollers Methodologie:[2] but I cant find it. However you can get it out of the University Library. The reference to it is given on page 1 of the third pamphlet of the Carl Menger Volume.[3]

I find also that I cant lend you Sax's Wesen und Aufgaben der Nat: Oekon:[4] because it is bound up with some other things that I must take with me. I think it is in the University Library. If not I will lend it to you later.

Happy thought. Postcript

Instead of sending this with the books I shall send it to London to say:— Will you stay over Friday in London & dine with me at 6.55 at the Pol Econ Club at Lincolns Inn fields entrance to Inns of Court Hotel on Friday.[5] I leave here on Friday morning, stop in London & on Saturday go to Dorsetshire.

Yours | A.M.

1 Marshall Library, J. N. Keynes Papers. From Balliol Croft. Keynes, taking to heart Marshall's advice [240] about the importance of German methodological views, was attempting to master them with Mrs. Keynes's aid. 'Every evening Florence reads me some pages from Menger on the Method of Political Economy' (8 September 1888). 'Florence & I are irritated but amused by Menger's repetitions. He is very dogmatic, & he gives very few illustrations, but he keeps on saying the same thing over and over again in almost the same words' (17 September 1888). 'Florence is beginning to translate Cohn to me. It is difficult German' (28 September 1888). Subsequently, 'Florence has been reading to me Schmoller on Menger, & is now reading Menger on Schmoller. He is most abusive, & makes us roar with laughter' (17 July 1889). Later, they were 'doing some more German (Lexis and Sax) on a new plan—not reading anything to me, but writing marginal notes in the books' (10 August 1889). (*Diaries*, entries for the dates indicated.)
2 Gustav von Schmoller, 'Zur Methodologie der Staats und Sozialwissenschaften', *Jahrbuch für Gesetzgebung, Verwaltung und Volkswirtschaft im Deutschen Reich* (1883), pp. 974–94.
3 Marshall's practice was to have pamphlet collections bound. Presumably he had already loaned Keynes this volume containing Carl Menger's pamphlets.
4 Emil Sax, *Das Wesen und die Aufgaben der Nationalökonomie* (Holder, Vienna, 1884).
5 On Friday 5 April the Political Economy Club held a discussion on wages, led by J. E. C. Munro. See Political Economy Club, *Centenary Volume* [173.2], p. 115.

263. To John Neville Keynes, 27 May 1889[1]

27 May 89

My dear Keynes

Strangely enough I had decided last night to write to you this morning about my lectures.

My book goes slowly; & just now indeed I am not working at it at all. Cooperation has filled my mind for some time, & will do so till Term is over.[2] (Book VI 'Cost of Production' is partly printed but there is not much use in your seeing it till there is some near prospect of your being able to have the latter half.) I expect to get my Vol I out before Xmas or anyhow immediately after. But I dont want to lecture very hard in the October Term.

I want however to keep my hold on the Historical men: they are Kittle–Kattle; & yet important.

So I propose to adapt my general course in October & Lent terms to their needs: wh by the bye coincide with part of the needs of the BA's.[3]

I don't know what Foxwell is going to do: but you will know soon. I think it w^{d}.. be a good plan for you to talk with him, if you feel inclined; but I have not myself found him receptive of suggestions: I presume however that he may be left to cover, either in this or the coming year, the History of Economic Theory: & perhaps the History of Economic Institutions.

There remain to be given Lectures to Poll Men;[4] (I hope to take a turn at these some time myself, but I don't want to do it this year) & lectures on Advanced Economic Theory, including the higher part of Statistics—I mean all that is not suitable [for][5] men of the Historical type,—intelligent, more or less earnest, but not very profound.

Now if you[6] like to put yourself down for any part of Advanced Economic Theory for the Michaelmas Term, I will undertake to leave that part out of my lectures on Advanced Theory in the remaining two Terms; &, if you like, I will make the title of these courses more specific, so as to make it clear that I shall not go over the ground you have chosen.

I know you dont want to lecture in the Lent Term: & with this abominable arrangement of having the Triposes in the middle of the Easter Term that Term is not well suited for beginning a course of advanced lectures: though a course already begun can be wound up in that Term. Still if you sh^{d}.. for any reason strongly prefer to lecture in the Easter Term, I w^{d}.. put four lectures a week into the Lent Term & leave the Easter Term free.

The objections to that from the point of view of the men are

i   there w^{d}.. be no Advanced Theory in the Michaelmas Term &
ii some men might want to come to both of my courses in the Lent Term & find it too much.

Or is there anything else that you can suggest, consistent with my keeping my course for the Historical men undisturbed: I think I had better do that.[7]

Yours very much | Alfred Marshall

[1] Marshall Library, J. N. Keynes Papers. From Balliol Croft.
[2] See [252.6].
[3] See [252].
[4] These were usually taught by Foxwell.
[5] Word apparently omitted.
[6] Followed by a further 'if you' in the original.
[7] In the lecture list published in the *Reporter*, 7 October 1889, Marshall is shown as teaching 'Advanced Economic Theory' in the Lent Term (W at 12) and 'Advanced Economic Theory (continued)' in the Easter Term (M, F at 12). He was due to teach his general course in the Michaelmas and Lent Terms (M, F at 12), covering 'Value, Money, Foreign Trade' in the Michaelmas Term and 'Commercial Fluctuations, Taxation, Economic Functions of Government' in the Lent. This course was taken by candidates for both the Historical and Moral Sciences Triposes. Keynes was not listed as teaching Advanced Political Economy.

264. From Edward Carter Kersey Gonner, 5 June 1889[1]

Victoria University | University College, Liverpool
5. VI. 89

Dear Professor Marshall,

I cannot but think that it is the very greatest of pities that all English Economic students are still left dependent on foreign Reviews & Magazines for the development of their Economic theories & for the registry of Economic fact. It seems to me that the lack of such a review is of the greatest disadvantage to the cause of English Economic Science. We are cut off from one another in a way which is unknown to the students in any other study whether scientific or historical. This is not the case in foreign countries where reviews & journals exist. Personally I don't believe that the work being done for Palgrave's Dictionary[2] would interfere one whit with the work which would have to be done for such a review. The sphere of each work seems to me quite separate.

In such a review there would I imagine be some four original articles of length. These I am sure would come in sufficient number. Then there would be notes & short comments on theories etc or points of research not worked out thoroughly & lastly of course reviews etc. So far as I can see there would be no difficulty in any of these quarters & any difficulty that might present itself would only be such as to require a little patience & a little energy to overcome. I really do think the matter one of importance as while we are all working in isolation we can achieve but little of that which it might be our lot to achieve. For my part I am willing and anxious to do all that I can to assist in making such an under-taking successful—but I do not think it ought to be delayed. What do you think?

Very truly yours | ECK Gonner.

I am *getting on slowly* with my edition of Ricardo.[3]

[1] Foxwell Papers.

[2] See [244.2].

[3] This appeared as David Ricardo, *Principles of Political Economy and Taxation*, ed. by E. C. K. Gonner (Bell, London, 1891).

265. To Beatrice Potter, 2 July 1889[1]

2 July 89

Dear Miss Potter,

I send you my gossiping address[2] on the great subject wh you are setting yourself to get to the bottom of. I have not ceased to regret that you have not chosen a path in wh the broad heavy masculine foot cannot tread; & in wh therefore your energetic & thorough methods of work w^d have a scarcity value. But as that is not to be, I look forward with joyful expectation to your study of the Cooperative Movement: I am sure that it will have a permanent & a cosmopolitan interest.

Yours very truly | Alfred Marshall

[1] BLPES, Passfield Papers. From Balliol Croft. Beatrice Potter, later Webb, who had been assisting Charles Booth in his study of London Poverty [181.1], proposed to write a book on cooperation. On a visit to the Cambridge home of Mandell Creighton [226.4], she conversed with Marshall who urged her to work on some problem connected with female labour. For her amusing record of this conversation, and for her portrait of the ill-at-ease Marshall presiding over the Cooperative Congress in Ipswich see Beatrice Webb, *My Apprenticeship* (Longmans Green, London, 1926), pp. 338–41, 354–61.

[2] See [252.6].

266. To John Neville Keynes, 23 July 1889[1]

St Magloire
23 July

Dear Keynes

I send you the remainder of BK VI on Cost of Prod^n.. BK VII is on the way: but it[2] limps shockingly.

You will see that the first of these Chapters has[3] already had some suggestions made on them: but you can write freely on all. I shall send another copy to the Press. Prices pencil notes I have not looked at.[4] Some of his verbal amendments seem to me generally scarcely required: but he has sharp eyes; & often finds errors such as 'its' instead of 'theirs' when all we three[5] have failed to note them.

I sent a copy of my Coop^n.. address[6] to Auspitz.[7] It has just come back marked 'Gestorben'. Poor fellow!.

We like this place: especially does my wife. Hope you prosper.

I will send you soon Brentano's latest attack on the 'orthodox school'.[8] He has you know great vogue: so his illogicalisms are noteworthy. I presume you have the English Translation (Universal Review) of his last years attack.[9] If not I will send that too.

Yours ever | AM

[1] Marshall Library, J. N. Keynes Papers. From Bordeaux Harbour, Guernsey.
[2] Followed by a further 'it' in the original.
[3] Originally this had been written 'the first two of these three Chapters have'.
[4] See [234.3].
[5] Keynes and the two Marshalls.
[6] See [252.6].
[7] Rudolf Auspitz lived until 1906, so the news of his demise was premature.
[8] Probably Lujo Brentano, 'Une Leçon sur L'Économie Politique Classique', *Revue d'Économie Politique*, 3 (1889), pp. 1–22.
[9] Lujo Brentano, *Die Klassische Nationalökonomie* (Duncker and Humblot, Leipzig, 1888). This lecture was translated as 'The "Last Word" on Political Economy', *Universal Review*, 2 (September–December, 1888), pp. 340–56. The author's name is rendered Eujen Brintano!

267. To John Neville Keynes from Mary Paley Marshall, 10 August 1889[1]

St Magloire | Bordeaux Harbour | Guernsey
10 Aug 89

Dear Mr Keynes

Thankyou very much for your suggestions. They will be most helpful & I think we agree with nearly all of them. I think we have practically decided not to make any fundamental changes at present. This could not be done without retarding the Big Book[2] w^h. would be a great evil.

With kindest remembrances to M^{rs}. Keynes

Yours very sincerely & gratefully | M P Marshall

[1] Marshall Library, J. N. Keynes Papers. Keynes had recorded 'I am looking through the *Economics of Industry* with a view to sending suggestions to Mrs Marshall for the new edition of the book' (*Diaries*, entry for 3 August 1889).
[2] The Marshalls' familiar name for the *Principles*, sometimes abbreviated to B.B. (not to be taken as an abbreviation for Böhm Bawerk).

268. To John Neville Keynes, August 1889[1]

My dear Keynes

I dont think we disagree about *method*. I dont think you say anything about it in your proofs with wh I dont agree. But we differ about *people*. I hold that the 'classical' economists knew their facts: but only put an abstract of them in their shop front. Also I dont think they were nearly as abstract as you do. Even since I wrote my own earlier chapters[2] I have altered a little in this direction in consequence of a more careful study of what they say about wages.

And I have gradually become convinced that whenever the Irish man Cliffe Leslie undertook to set right the English economists about the facts of English life, he was wrong in consequence of the paucity of the facts at his disposal: though he made a show of knowledge by putting all he knew in the shop window.

I wish I had a spare copy of my earlier chapters at hand. But they are very much on the same lines as *The Present Position of Economics*[3] so far as this point goes :—a little kinder to Ricardo & Co, though as I have said not quite so kind as I am inclined to now.

Yours ever | AM

Slip 2   New sentence at top | 'particular scope' Qe[4] omit particular.[5]

Addition A.[6]   I like the substance of this very much but fancy the form might be with advantage altered *somewhat* in this direction after 'either school'—'The sharp contrast wh is found in their formal statements of method seems to have been partly due in some cases to the spirit of controversy, & in nearly all cases to a desire to insure that that side wh they thought specially important, shd be brought prominently before the attention of the reader. And that they did thus exaggerate their differences is proved by the fact that when they come to close quarters with the same particular problems they nearly always treat them very much in the same fashion. They all make a careful study of the facts of the case, & they all break up the problem if it is a difficult one into its component parts, & break the difficulty of one part after another before they come to a general conclusion as to the whole'—I have not tried to express myself well but only to indicate my general notion.

Slip 8 Note.   I wonder whether the similarity of intellectual character between Senior & Bagehot strikes you as strongly as it does me.[7] Both had a singularly wide knowledge of the world: both were sketchy writers; both had brilliant aperçus & both were generally holding on by the tails of two aperçus that were struggling in opposite directions at the same time. So it seems to me.

Slip 9   'hypothetical'.[8] You know I contend that all sciences except pure mathematics are hypothetical in the sense in wh economics is.

Slip 9   Question at end of 3ʳᵈ ¶. I am not sure whether induction is a 'method' or 'a means'. Also the wording hardly makes it clear enough that the sentence is governed by the 'is regarded' of a few lines higher up.

Slip 9 at bottom.   I think it is a great pity to call Sidgwick *Dr.*[9] In Germany the term Dʳ. conveys no honour: & I think it will be so here. But I only say this as an empty protest. I dont expect you to pay heed. Every German Profʳ is a Dʳ.. but never calls himself so.

Slip 10 line 4 'essentially' Qe 'thoroughly' or 'entirely'.

Slip 10 end of last ¶. Qe 'Again Cairnes himself. . . . slave labour' & continue establishes some important doctrines by a careful inductive study of facts in wh he makes very little use of deductive reasoning.[10]

Slip 10 Top of Second ¶ Distribution is so technical & non-natural a word that I always give it a D.

Going back to Note B.[11] I shd be inclined to add something to the effect that discussions as to cause & effect are less liable to engender partisan heat than discussions as to moral duty: & it is a good plan for people to agree as long as they can, & fight only when they must.

Addition C. Stopping rather obscures the fact that in the 'T.O' you [are] referring to the Principles.

Addition D is I think excellent though I shd myself elaborate the influence of Ricardo's followers on the excellent Blue books &c of wh the German hist school have made such good use.

Addition E. You know von Thünen's[12] *metier* was that of an agricultural reformer. His abstract economics came in by the way. He was up to his eyes in facts about rye & manure & so on.

Slip 11 footnote 'Schönberg's article on *die Volk^t*—is in his Handbuch.[13]

---

[1] Marshall Library, J. N. Keynes Papers. From Guernsey. Keynes had abandoned the earlier proofs [227.2] for the first two chapters of his *Scope and Method*. Macmillan and Co. having by now agreed to pubish the book, he initiated the setting up of new proofs on 1 August 1888. By 17 August five chapters had gone to the Press and by 27 August criticisms from Marshall and Nicholson were being received. Keynes went in for extensive revision, regardless of cost, and worked sporadically at the unfinished chapters (the book eventually had ten chapters) until the end of 1890. The book finally appeared early in 1891, the preface being dated 12 December 1890. Marshall appears to have read and commented on Keynes's proofs right through this period, but since Marshall's letters are not all dated, and since the proofs were often revised substantially after he saw them, there are some difficulties in ordering his comments and relating them to the final text. (See *Diaries*, entries for 1, 8, 10, 17, 22, 23, 27, 28 August, 2, 5, 11, 23, 28, 30 September, 5 October, 4 November 1888; 1 April, 8, 24 July, 5, 24 September, 6, 9 October, 5 November, 19 December 1890.) The present letter and the next one most probably comment on the new proofs of ch. 1, 'Introductory'. Keynes recorded 'Criticisms from Marshall & Nicholson on Chapter 1. Marshall thinks I have been unfair to the English school (in my manner of comparing it with the German), & to Mill in particular' (*Diaries*, entry for 27 August 1888).

[2] Book i, chs. 4–7 of *Principles (1)*.

[3] See [158.2].

[4] Marshall apparently uses 'Qe' as an abbreviation for 'Quaere' or 'I question whether'.

[5] See *Scope and Method*, p. 4.

[6] See ibid., pp. 8–10. In the finished work, ch. 2 had notes A, B and ch. 4 had notes A, B, C. But the 'additions' referred to here seem to have been eliminated or embodied in the text.

[7] See ibid., pp. 12, 16 n.

[8] See ibid., p. 16.

[9] In ibid., Sidgwick is referred to sometimes as Professor and sometimes as Dr.

[10] See ibid., pp. 18–19.

[11] Marshall probably meant to amend 'Note B' to 'Addition B', as he did in the cases of 'Additions C, D, E' which he had originally written as 'Notes C, D, E'.

[12] See ibid., p. 21.

[13] See ibid., p. 22 n. (Schönberg, 'Die Volkswirthschaft', in his *Handbuch* [121.2].)

269. To John Neville Keynes, August 1889[1]

My dear Keynes

I have had to rewrite what had been intended to be the first chapters of Book VII. This is partly due to rearrangement wh has caused delay; but now I am going on.

I find we differ more than I thought & have expressed my views freely: you will I fear not be convinced.

I object in toto to the distinction between German & English. I think the distinction, started by Walker[2] who is without any special knowledge, & cant read German, is utterly inappropriate.

Suppose you were[3] to compare the English chemists of 1800–40 with the German chemists of 1840–90 & call the methods of the former English & the latter German, you w^d.. I think change what is fundamentally a difference of time into one of geography. Every one of your contrasts & oppositions is too sharp for me. Your quotation from Dunbar on slip 14[4] expresses my view. I wish you had put it first, & made it your text; & then explained the minor differences which have grown up around substantial agreement; but which have been exaggerated by the heat of controversy

Then again I think you are most harsh & unfair to your own countrymen. What German has ever had one half of the knowledge of the facts of life possessed by McCulloch the bête-noire of those who call the 'English' school abstract

What country has a mass of economic statistics to be compared to ours. Those very Germans who abuse us, go for their facts to those very men whom they revile.

I think the picture you give is in general effect a libel on England. What country produced Arthur Young & Eden, Anderson, Porter, Tooke, McCulloch & McPherson?[5] What country can show a series of statistical volumes to be compared to our Journal:[6] What German investigations are nearly as realistic, statistical & ethical, as our Blue books especially our recent ones. What private German has done work as good as Booth's Life & Labour?[7]

Eh??

Yours most frankly. But with great admiration on all points bar this | A.M.

I don't deny that the aggregate economic activity in Germany at present is three times that in England, & the trained economic ability even greater in proportion.

I inclose a paper of notes by my wife. We agree on almost every point.

I have sent the first two Chapters of Book VII to the press some time ago. The Note on Ricardo had been arranged to go at end of BK VII.

I have just decided to put it at end of BK VI.[8]

[Enclosure by Mary Paley Marshall]

S^{p}. 7 & 8[9]

I think the account given of the English exposition of method is rather extreme. I think Mill w^{d} only have subscribed to it in his earlier days, & I fancy Bagehot w^{d} take some exception to 'the economic man'. Mills longer title to his Principles[10] shows that he considered P.E. as having an applied side.

I think that it should be brought out that the German school have devoted a much greater part of their energy to talking about method than the English; & that the trifling amount that has been said by the English doesnt i represent the view of English Economists as a whole on the subject of method & ii doesnt at all represent the methods w^{h} have been adopted by English economists; the best work in England has been done by the best available methods without troubling to say what the method is.[11]

Out of the 4 you mention Cairnes is the only one who set himself to write on method.[12]

The greater part of what has been *written* on method in England has been done by the anti-Mill Ricardo side. e.g. Cliffe Leslie etc.

The method pursued by the English School of P.E is not at all represented by what has been written on method.

---

[1] Marshall Library, J. N. Keynes Papers. Probably sent from Guernsey. See [268.1] for the background.

[2] F. A. Walker, *Political Economy* (Holt, New York, 1883), part i.

[3] Written 'where' in the original.

[4] In *Scope and Method* Dunbar is only cited (p. 29 n.) and paraphrased (pp. 216–7 n.) in the following words: 'the method to be employed in carrying economic science into regions never penetrated by Ricardo is simple; it is only necessary to draw from the actual observation of affairs fresh premisses relating to forces of the secondary order'. See C. F. Dunbar, 'The Reaction in Political Economy', *Quarterly Journal of Economics*, 1 (October 1886), pp. 113–33.

[5] That is, Frederick Morton Eden, James Anderson, George Richardson Porter, Thomas Tooke, John Ramsay McCulloch, and David McPherson.

[6] The *Journal of the* [*London*] *Statistical Society* (since 1887 the Royal Statistical Society).

[7] See [181.1].

[8] The 'Note on Ricardo's Theory of Cost of Production in relation to value' is appended to book vi, ch. 6 (pp. 529–36) in *Principles (1)*.

[9] Slips 7 and 8?

[10] The full title of J. S. Mill's *Principles* is 'The Principles of Political Economy with some of their Applications to Social Philosophy'.

[11] The remaining comments are struck through.

[12] See [240.4].

270. To John Neville Keynes, 27 August 1889[1]

St Magloire
27 Aug

My dear Keynes,

I expect your plan is the best:—a short note on Consumers Rent & then anything you like to say later on about Rent-Consumers. Thanks.[2]

I knew 'Shew' was the older spelling: e.g. in the bible. But I stick to my guns, & maintain I was right not only in defending Show, but in holding that no modern authority wd say that Shew is preferable—or even strictly speaking defensible.

It was Todhunter[3] who first called my attention to the matter. I had been taught Shew in my youth: but he wd not allow it.

I am troubled a little about your reference to Bagehots 'Postulates'.[4] The fact is I have always been rather ashamed of the part I played as to that. I met Mrs Bagehot at dinner, & more with a view to being polite, than of set purpose, asked her whether she had thought of publishing the two chief essays separately at a low price. She shortly afterwards wrote that she was going to do so; & asked me to write a preface implying that she relied on me to do it, in consequence of what I had said to her. So I wrote very unwillingly. But really I am not in sympathy (intellectually) with Bagehot. He is most brilliant; but very hasty & in reading him I alternately agree & admire much, & differ & admire a little. I could not go into that, partly because Mrs Bagehot w^{d} not have liked it, partly because I had not time. The result was a short & utterly empty preface; & to speak quite frankly I am a little ashamed of having special attention called to it by your kindness.

Yours ever | AM.

The Press have been longer than I have known them about setting up my Bk VII ch I. It has not come from them yet.

---

[1] Marshall Library, J. N. Keynes Papers. From Guernsey.

[2] Inglis Palgrave had requested Keynes to write an entry on Consumer Rent for the A–D Section of the *Dictionary* [244.2], suggesting the possibility of the two-part treatment indicated by Marshall. The A–D entry, due by December 1889, proved to be the only one on Consumer Rent.

[3] The mathematician Isaac Todhunter (1820–84) had been a teacher and colleague at St John's. See Appendix II.

[4] Marshall had written a short preface (pp. v–viii) to Walter Bagehot, The *Postulates of English Political Economy* (Longmans, London, 1885). The nature of Keynes's allusion to it remains unclear. Mrs Elizabeth Bagehot was the eldest daughter of James Wilson (1805–60), first editor of *The Economist*. Her husband had died in 1877. Keynes refers to Bagehot frequently in *Scope and Method* but there is no mention of Marshall's preface.

271. To John Neville Keynes, September 1889[1]

My dear Keynes

I think your Chap I is excellent now. I do not mean that on any point I sh^d.. say exactly what you have. But I think it represents excellently your point of view; & my own differences from it are never more than half the breadth of a hair. And it is not useful to hair-split. There is however one point on wh I think you might be a little clearer:—the sentence on slip 12 'It will be observed &c'[2] shd I think come in some form or other at an earlier stage. In fact you have tacitly implied that these characteristics are all entirely dependent, are in fact different sides of the same thing. Now it is true that if you are ethical you must be realistic. But if you were to strike out about a dozen pages from Booth's *Life & Labour*[3] (as some people—not I—think he wd have been well advised to do) you w^d.. have a very realistic piece of economic work, but not at all an ethical one.

I am not sure that I shd not strike out 'ethical' from the heading of §3[4] & introduce the connection between ethics & realism later on.

I don't think Böhm Bawerk has written anything on method: but I regard him as more important than Sax, though less original & (but don't repeat this) less genuine than Menger.

As at present arranged we leave here on Tuesday 10th.. & expect to get home *about* the 18th.. having no letters forwarded meanwhile. I think you had better not send me anything later than by the *three* oclock post on Friday.

I will send you some more slips of my own before I go.

The last time my wife read your proofs first; this time, I have read them first.[5]

Yours ever | A.M.

The discussion is about *method*. Now is there an *ethical* method? There is an ethical tone & an ethical *scope*. Do you not rather run method & scope together in what you say about 'ethical'?

---

[1] Marshall Library, J. N. Keynes Papers. From Guernsey. Quoted by Keynes (*Diaries*, entry for 4–5 September 1889).

[2] See *Scope and Method*, pp. 22–3, especially p. 22 n.

[3] See [181.1].

[4] In *Scope and Method* this is 'The conception of political economy as an ethical, realistic, and inductive science'.

[5] Mrs Marshall added the note 'I have now read them & cannot find any fault. MPM'.

272. To John Neville Keynes, (September?) 1889[1]

My dear Keynes,

I take an extreme position as to the *methods* & *scope* of economics. In my new book I say of *methods* simply that economics has to use every method known to science. And as to scope, I say 'Economics is a study of mans actions in the ordinary business of life it inquires how he gets his income & how he uses it.'[2]

I extend 'income' so as to include non-exchangable 'goods';[3] & generally I never discuss any line of division or demarcation except to say that nature has shown no hard & fast lines, & that any lines man draws are merely for the convenience of the occasion: & shd never be treated as though they were rigid.

So I am not a good judge of the views expressed by your more orderly nature. I have simply indicated where we differ. But I don't think it will do for you to pay much attention to what I say. What Nicholson says is likely to be far more helpful to you.

If I had to write on this subject I shd keep the Chapter & notes of about the same length as you have. But I shd ignore almost all opinions wh seemed to me clearly wrong, & I shd spend the space saved on a history of the broader movements & changes in attitude of the science with regard to the topics under discussion, trying to bring out the correlation between the history of economic science & of economic conditions.

Yours ever | A.M.

The chapter seems to me good. But the point of view is too different from mine to enable me to say quite confidently how good.

I doubt whether you had better bother yourself more about my views on these subjects. But if you want to know them more in detail the best way perhaps wd be for me to lend you my Book I over again

---

[1] Marshall Library, J. N. Keynes Papers. From Balliol Croft. Marshall had been reading chs. 2 and 3 of *Scope and Method* during September. Both he and Nicholson found ch. 2 'longwinded'. A short undated note from Marshall in the Keynes papers reads 'Dear Keynes. Perhaps you may as well look at our notes before we talk. You will then be able to extract our meaning more fully. We both [i.e. Alfred and Mary] think the Chapter very good, but dragging, rather in §§4, 5. Yours ever A.M.' This probably relates to ch. 2, 'On the Relation of Political Economy to Morality and Practice'. About ch. 3, 'On the Character and Definition of Political Economy Regarded as a Positive Science', Keynes observed 'Marshall thinks that in chapter 3 I attempt to draw too hard & fast lines.' The present letter appears to relate to that chapter. (See *Diaries*, entries for 23, 28 September 1889.)

[2] A paraphrase rather than a direct quotation of the opening statement (p. 1) of *Principles (1)*.

[3] See book ii of *Principles (1)*.

---

273. To Léon Walras, 19 September 1889[1]

19 September 1889

Dear Sir,

I have to thank you very heartily for your new edition of Elements d'Econ. Pol.[2] I have not myself retired from the conclusion that I think I communicated to you some time ago, viz that the right place for mathematics in a treatise on Economics is the back-ground. But I think it is most desirable that different seekers after truth should take different routes; & I rejoice much that the pure mathematical route is being developed by your great ability & energy.

Yours very truly | Alfred Marshall

---

[1] University of Lausanne, Fonds Walras. Printed as *LW*, letter 922. From Balliol Croft.

[2] L. Walras, *Éléments d'Économie Politique Pure* (second edition: Guillamin, Paris, etc., 1889).

274. To Ludwig Joseph Brentano, 1 October 1889[1]

1 Oct. 89

Dear Sir,

I have to acknowledge the receipt of your courteous letter.

The remark in my recent letter to Dr. Schwiedland[2] was not public & was not volunteered. It was elicited by a sentence in his previous letter to me in wh he quoted you as an authority on recent English history to which Englishmen must bow.

Under these circumstances I trust I may be excused for not endeavouring to substantiate the remarks wh I made to D[r]. Schwiedland. I could not do so without writing a long & rather controversial letter. And in addition to my habitual dislike to controversy, the pressure of a book wh I am writing, & wh in spite of all my efforts, makes slow progress has forced me to make a rigid rule against controversy of all kind.

I will not close this letter without taking the opportunity of saying that widely as we differ about the history of economic theory & economic phenomena in England during the present century, I have the greatest respect for your character & for the influence wh you have[3] exerted over the sentiments of the rising generation of economists; & that I find myself in cordial agreement with much that you have written.

Yours very truly | Alfred Marshall

I hope to have the pleasure of sending you at the beginning of the next year Vol I of the book I am writing, nearly six hundred pages of wh are in type already. It is not controversial, but it contains an expression of my views on several of the points to wh your recent Addresses[4] refer.

It is possible that, feeling a little irritated I used rather strong expressions about my disagreement with you. I have no recollection of the words I used in writing to D[r] Schwiedland.

---

[1] Bundesarchiv, Koblenz, Brentano Papers. From Balliol Croft. Printed substantially in H. W. McCready, 'Alfred Marshall: Some Unpublished Letters', *Culture*, 15 (September 1954), pp. 300–8, at p. 303.

[2] 'Eugen Peter Schweidland (1863–1940?) was a minor Austrian economist, professor at the Technical University in Vienna and author of books on social insurance' (McCready, ibid. p. 303 n.). Marshall's correspondence with him has not been traced. See also *Economic Journal*, 13 (March 1903), pp. 154–5.

³ Followed by another 'have' in the original (at a turn of page).

⁴ McCready (p. 303 n.) cites L. J. Brentano, *Über die Ursachen der Heutigen Socialen Not: Ein Betrag zur Morphologie der Volkwirtschaft* (Liepzig, 1889). But see also [266.8, 9].

275. To John Neville Keynes, 11 October 1889[1]

11 Oct 89

My dear Keynes,

As you were kind enough to call my attention to Cunningham's paper, I send you the inclosed correspondence.[2] I maintain that in the passage about Indian rents he represents himself as quoting the substance of something said by me; & that he is not justified in persisting in publishing a statement that I hold an opinion w^h I tell him I do not hold.

Still the matter is rather small: & as at present advised I propose to do nothing further.

This is not private.

Yours very sincerely | A.M.

¹ Marshall Library, J. N. Keynes Papers. From Balliol Croft.

² The correspondence is not preserved but is presumably that alluded to in William Cunningham, 'The Comteist Criticism of Economic Science', *Report of the British Association for the Advancement of Science, 1889*, pp. 462–71, especially 462 n., 470 n. In this paper, delivered to Section F of the British Association at Newcastle upon Tyne in September, Cunningham had quoted critically the views expressed in Marshall's Inaugural Lecture [158.2] and had charged (pp. 469–70) that 'Professor Marshall, instead of accepting the description of mediaeval or Indian economic forms as they actually occur, sets himself to show that the accounts of them can be so arranged and stated as to afford illustrations of Ricardo's law of rent'. The printed version added to this statement the footnote: 'As I was sorry to learn that Professor Marshall considered himself aggrieved by the criticism contained in this sentence, I offered to introduce any disclaimer he might send.' He reported that Marshall had asked him to say that 'the references which I have made to him imply that he takes a position with regard to the historical school different from that which he does take'. At Marshall's request he included fuller quotations from Marshall's Inaugural Lecture. Marshall also wished to add the statement that 'Mediaeval and Indian land tenure systems are of great interest from many points of view, and that the study of the relations in which they stand to the Ricardian theory is an essential part, but only a small part of the duty of the economist in regard to them.'. Cunningham, while trusting that 'the explanation now given may correct any misapprehension which has gone abroad' interpreted Marshall's objections as largely vindicating his, Cunningham's, original position. The net effect was hardly mollifying.

276. To an unknown correspondent, 20 October 1889[1]

20 Oct 89

Dear Sir

Speaking generally I agree with your criticism of Marx.[2] His theory of value is in my opinion a series of *petitiones principii*.

But I owe much to him. I read his book in 1870, & his extracts from English blue-books—garbled though many of them are—were of great service to me. Now everyone knows about the state of factory labour early in the century; in 1870 very few people had given their attention to it.

M Laveleye[3] is a man of warm & generous instincts, & has great knowledge of international public affairs. But I do not regard him as an authority on the strictly scientific side of economics. Please however not to repeat this.

As to Ricardos theory of Cost of production, the Note[4] on the sheet I inclose will show you my position. The sheet is part of a volume wh is passing through the press. Perhaps I may ask you kindly to return it not later than a week hence.

Yours very truly | Alfred Marshall

[1] Marshall Papers. From Balliol Croft.
[2] Karl Marx, author of *Das Kapital*.
[3] Emile de Laveleye.
[4] See [269.8].

277. From the Editors, *Cambridge Review*, 24 October 1889[1]

Dear Professor Marshall,

I trust that the impatience with which so distinguished an economist as you must naturally have expected the appearance of a letter has not caused you serious inconvenience. But in our society where so many are so great the business of selection is indeed hard, and you will I am sure be ready to pardon. In writing to you, I need scarcely begin by reminding you of the satisfaction which Cambridge felt when it was known that Mr. Alfred Marshall had been persuaded to take possession of the chair of Political Economy, vacated by the death of Professor Fawcett. A heavy task indeed to wear the armour of the mighty dead, for armour cannot, like clothes, be taken in to suit the new lodger, but in this heavy task who shall say that you have not triumphed? True that the Moral Sciences Tripos has dwindled by the growth of its more attractive younger brethren,[2] and now pale Death seems to mark it for its own. And indeed to be numbered among the departed were better than to live in a state of intermittency, or sustained solely by some slight competition from Girton or Newnham, and thus to become a very scorn of men. But it is not for me to discuss the Moral Sciences Tripos. The fading away of it is surely to be laid at the doors of those who will neither make merry or mourn therein to the piping and wailing of yourself and the Professor of Moral Philosophy.[3] For indeed your lecture room is itself a proof, be the Moral Sciences Tripos what it may, that Economics have a hold indeed on the Cambridge mind. So well can I picture you to myself as you lay bare the intricacies of Normal Value to beginners, or speak to the more advanced of Banking and Money and the Economic Functions of Government. Each difficulty modestly cleared away in words that come now fast now slow, gaining emphasis by the increased quietness with which they are delivered. Nor are you without a sense of humour and the power of leavening a dull lump or so with it. When at times you stray from the narrow paths of the Science of Economics and tell us of the Stock Exchange, of 'Brums' and 'Berthas,' of the peddlings of Jew and Greek, of Wall Street and American operators, you shew a touch and more of the driest wit. With eyes directed abstractedly towards the ceiling (some say you are often among the clouds), and a voice so tiny and quiet that all ears are kept astretch, is the story told. And when the eyes descend again upon the class we see by the twinkle there, that we and you are laughing together. Permit me to recall to you an occasion on which you gave notice that at the next lecture you would treat on the curves of demand mathematically for those who would please to attend, 'only an elementary knowledge of mathematics will be required,' and then you gave time to those who had recently floored the additionals to preen themselves and think they would certainly come, before you observed with the upward gaze and sly air 'I don't think it will be much use for anyone to come who has not a fairly complete knowledge of differential and integral calculus.' A sadder and a wiser class, among whom was I, went from that room thinking perchance that after all, elementary was a relative word. I wonder now do you have that little joke with each succeeding generation, or was it only played once?

But in general we, I speak as a beginner, leave your room, and, at your recommendation, go hot foot and buy your book;[4] and what a charmingly innocent little book it seems, in its modest sage-green cover, price 2/6. One imagines as one reads in the preface that it was a work designed for use in extension lectures, and carelessly glances at the end to see its number of pages, that it will fall an easy victim to a day or two of moderate reading. Was ever so complete a take in? Oh, wretched little book! You who contain matter so closely packed, and, on first acquaintance, so confusing; abounding with definitions so long, and travelling to all appearances in circles as complete as ever circles were. Humiliation is good, and thou dost bring it with thee. Truly I loved thee not, nor even now have I o'ercome my first prejudice, though I have long looked upon thy bygone terrors with a fairly even mind.

And having spoken of the Professor in the lecture room and of the Professor's book, may I go further and speak of the Professor at home?[5] We thank you for your kindness and readiness in solving our difficulties, if we bring them to you as you sit in your study at Balliol Croft, a study all books, with scarce room for Professor and student. You meet us at the door as we are shewn in, do not know our names, never seem to recognise that we have been before, shake hands hesitatingly, and are with some difficulty started to talk: we learn much from your talk. Or else, plunging into statistics and dragging out that great MS. volume[6] wherein are preserved figures upon figures, you will shew us curves, curves telling us of cotton and iron and rupees and measles, and to all seeming yet stranger mixtures than these. What does not that book contain: can it tell us of variations of the weather and of the boat race, whereon you are basing a theory that we win the boat race whenever a wet Lent term provides enough water in the Cam for us to row upon; or of the relative merits of Professors and undergraduates? I daresay it can. If you told me it was all there I should feel no surprise. A wonderful volume.

I fear I have spoken but inadequately to you. If so, remember the task was difficult, and look on my letter with kindly eyes. You are prone, as you showed us but lately, to accuse a brother economist of misrepresenting you in connection with the British Ass., and art seemingly sore on the matter.[7] If I too have misrepresented you, I pray you have me excused.

---

[1] Printed in the *Cambridge Review*, 24 October 1889. Unsigned. Number 9 in a series of 'Letters to Lecturers'. It might be questioned whether such an open letter can reasonably be construed as 'correspondence', but its intrinsic interest may excuse its inclusion.

[2] The Tripos was sat successfully by 7 men and 4 women in 1886, 5 men and 5 women in 1887, 3 men and 2 women in 1888, and 2 men and 5 women in 1889.

[3] Henry Sidgwick was then the Knightsbridge Professor.

[4] The *Economics of Industry*.

[5] Marshall's practice, frequently announced in the *Reporter*, was to be 'at home' to all interested students from 4–7 p.m. Mondays and Thursdays during Term.

[6] Marshall's 'Red Book' of statistical charts and chronologies 'was arranged so that if a pin were run through its many pages at any given year the pin-hole would show what was happening that year in Philosophy, Art, Science, Industry, Trade, etc.' (*What I Remember*, p. 20). It is preserved in the Marshall Library.

[7] See [275.2].

---

278. To John Neville Keynes, 17 November 1889[1]

17 Nov 89

My dear Keynes

At last we return your proofs.[2]

You will see that I agree generally with the latter half,[3] but that so far as the former half[4] is concerned I differ a little on two grounds.

i I think Mill[5] really held the position wh you hold, & not the position that the study of economic affairs can be isolated

ii I now differ from you both in holding (what I did not always hold) that the economic man does so little good service & causes so much trouble that on practical & tactical (not theoretical) grounds, it is best to do without him.

And even in the latter part you seem to me to concede too much to the popular opponents of economics. I think it most important to make clear that the narrowness charged against economists is to be found almost exclusively in the writings of people who were not economists, but who had dabbled in economic literature enough to be able to quote without their context passages that wd serve them a good turn [towards][6] their own dirty ends by their own mean & cruel manouvres.

The first part is I think perhaps too long & too prominent. I am not sure the general effect wd not be improved by putting the second part first. I like the second part very much, the first part only moderately.

Yours ever | A.M.

[1] Marshall Library, J. N. Keynes Papers. From Balliol Croft.
[2] Apparently the proofs of ch. 4 of *Scope and Method*, 'On the Relation of Political Economy to General Sociology'.
[3] Probably ss 3 and 4 which deal with 'Examples of economic problems requiring for their complete solution a realistic treatment' and 'Distinction between political economy and other social enquiries'.
[4] Probably ss 1 and 2 which deal with 'Conflicting views of the relation between economic science and the general science of society' and 'The place of abstraction in economic reasoning'.
[5] See John Stuart Mill, 'On the Definition of Political Economy and on the Method of Investigation Proper to it', Essay V in his *Essays on Some Unsettled Questions of Political Economy* (Longmans, London, 1844); also his *System of Logic* [74.3], book vi. For Keynes's discussion of Mill's views see *Scope and Method*, pp. 112–14.
[6] Word apparently omitted.

279. To John Neville Keynes, 26 November 1889[1]

26 Nov

My dear Keynes,

As you will see from this inclosed sheet[2] I regard Consumer's Rent as a sum of money not as an amount of utility.

I hold that Jevons' great error[3] was that of applying to utility propositions that are only true of price. It was here that he thought himself most profound: & it is because I think he was wrong in this one point in wh he differed from his predecessors Von Thünen & Cournot, that I consider his claims to greatness do not to any considerable extent rest on his Theory of Pol Econ

I can see no connection between the loss of Consumers Rent & the loss of Total Utility resulting from a tax, unless it is known whether the commodity taxed is one consumed by the rich by the poor or by all classes alike.

If you think it best to put in a full account of Consumers Rent at once, I shd be very glad that you shd make any use you like by quotation or otherwise of the inclosed sheet.

If you make any references at all it shd be to the privately printed papers issued in 1879[4] & to (Book III ch IV & Book V ch VII & VIII (Qe)[5] of *Principles of Economics*. But in all matters follow your own judgment; that is sure to be best.

I write hastily; but with many thanks for the kind trouble you are taking

Yours very sincerely | Alfred Marshall

Perhaps you might introduce something about the matters discussed in my Book III Ch IV §2[6] on your page 5.

[1] Marshall Library, J. N. Keynes Papers. From Balliol Croft. Partly reproduced by *Guillebaud*, p. 260. See [270.2] for the background.

[2] Probably proofs for *Principles (1)*, book iii, ch. 4, 'The Measurement of the Utility of Wealth'.

[3] See Jevons, *Theory of Political Economy* [17.3].

[4] *The Pure Theory of Domestic Values* [59.3].

[5] Chs. 7 and 8 of book v in *Principles (1)* were entitled 'Theory of Changes in Normal Demand and Supply, with some of its Bearings on the Doctrine of Maximum Satisfaction' and 'The Theory of Monopolies'. For 'Qc' see [268.4].

[6] This deals with 'Corrections to be made: firstly on account of differences in the wealth of different purchasers. Secondly on account of elements of collective wealth which are apt to be overlooked'.

280. From John Neville Keynes, 2 December 1889 (incomplete)[1]

I have never overlooked the difficulties involved in comparing the satisfaction yielded by a given expenditure to different purchasers. But I had not realized that you attach so fundamental an importance to defining C.R.[2] as a sum of money & not an amount of utility. It seems to me to be only a question at what point the above difficulties shd be introduced.[3]

My view was that just because the money does not accurately measure the utility, where different persons are concerned, it was better not to introduce the idea of measurement at the outset by taking it into the definition & that for different individuals the money measure is imperfect although under certain conditions it may afford a rough practical approximation towards the truth.[4]

There was another difficulty that I felt & that caused me to word the definition as I did—you say (on p. 176. The few lines preceding the bracket—& the bracket)[5]—

But if he buys instead of coal some substitute—say wood—that substitute will yield a consumers' rent after the same manner—though probably to a different amount—as the coal.

If, however, we suppose him not to buy coal because he neither needs it nor any substitute (or because neither it nor any substitute can be got)—so that he has £7 more to spend on the same commodities as those upon wh he has previously spent the remainder of his income, his demand for these commodities will be affected & therefore the consumers rent afforded by them. We shall have a change from AC to A'C' [see Fig.]

However I will rewrite the article & if I am not boring you too much send it to you again. It is your views[6] I want to expound & of course wd not consent to send anything to Palgrave which you did not regard as rightly representing you.

I am not here charging you with any confusion, but expressing my view that the other order of procedure is equally free from confusion. It seems to me very clearly put in Wicksteed's exposition of Jevons pp.[7]

I may add that the phrase 'total burden of a tax' was taken from the heading

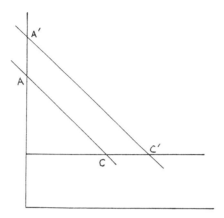

of Ch. 2 of the Pure Theory of (Domestic) Values.[8] I have felt I must write the above as some justification for what must have seemed to you simply an error—But burn when read & don't trouble.

[1] Marshall Library, J. N. Keynes Papers. From a draft retained by Keynes. Headed 'Letter to Marshall 2 Dec/89'.
[2] That is, Consumer Rent.
[3] This sentence was inserted then struck through.
[4] An earlier variant had read: '. . . better not to introduce the idea of measurement into the definition at all. But to indicate subsequently—as you go on to do—that after all the money measure is the best we can have & that under certain cond^{ns} it affords a rough practical approximation towards the truth'. Another deleted variant opened the paragraph with 'You define consumers rent as the economic measure of surplus pleasure. This is accurate so far as the individual is concerned—but it seems equally accurate if we define C.R. as an amount of utility. In any case we have to point out subsequently . . .' (continuing as in the other variant).
[5] What follows is a paraphrase rather than a quotation from *Principles* (*1*), p. 176. See *Guillebaud*, pp. 258–9, for the text of this page. In Marshall's example the consumer buys 7 tons of coal when the price is £1 per ton, receiving a total utility of £10 + 7 + 5 + 3 + 2 + $1\frac{1}{2}$ + 1 = £$29\frac{1}{2}$ and a consumer rent of £$29\frac{1}{2}$ − 7 = £$22\frac{1}{2}$.
[6] Altered from 'doctrine'.
[7] See Wicksteed's *Alphabet* [224.2], especially pp. 68–77.
[8] See [59.3] where the heading is 'The Total Burden of a Tax. Consumers' Rent'.

281. To John Neville Keynes, 2 December 1889[1]

2 Dec 89

My dear Keynes

I hope I did not imply that you confused hedonics & economics. I did not at all mean to. What I meant was that the very fact that my protest against Jevons' systematic confusion between the two has been (deliberately) a silent one, makes me very anxious that my Consumers Rent shd not be run up into his Total Utility. I had that prominently in view when writing on the Burden of a Tax in my old Treatise on Foreign Trade.[2] I wanted to make clear that economic statistics have nothing to do with Utility, but only with its rough money measure.

I considered for a long time whether I wd discuss the difficulty you raise about the change of consumers rent derived from other things consequent on a diminished purchase of coals. Perhaps I shall in consequence of the difficulties having struck you insert a line or two in the Mathematical Appendix to say: If he spends less on coals, the marginal utility of money for other purchases will be affected to an infinitesimal degree:—infinitesimal because, as stated in the text (p   ),[3] the whole of this class of reasonings is strictly valid only on the assumption that the purchases under discussion are small relatively to the purchasers whole wealth.

My solution of the difficulty then seem to be different from yours: not opposed to it. For I prefer to work on a different hypothesis from yours. I think however that if you pursued the matter far, you might be compelled to adopt my hypothesis.

Yours very sincerely | A.M.

My book do grow: Oh! it do grow! B.B.Bother it!!!

P.S. My wife can't find the passage in the text quoted above. I feel sure I wrote it: but I may have intended to transfer it to some other place & then forgotten it.[4] So I have just written an addition to Note VI of the Appendix[5] wh I inclose for your v kind criticism. Don't hurry to return this. I have to preach at the Pol Econ Club in London on Trades Unions next Friday & shant be back till following Thursday.[6]

---

[1] Marshall Library, J. N. Keynes Papers. From Balliol Croft. Partly reproduced in *Guillebaud*, pp. 260–1.

[2] See *The Pure Theory of Domestic Values* [59.3].

[3] The citation was left blank for reasons indicated later. But at some point there was a revision in blue pencil to read 'as stated (Q Sec P5)'—presumably a reference to proof sheets.

[4] The passage in question appears to be book v, ch. 2, s. 3, of *Principles* (1).

[5] The following sentences appear to have been added to Note VI of the mathematical appendix to *Principles* (1).

> It should be noted that, in the discussion of Consumers' Rent, we assume that the marginal utility of money to the individual purchaser is the same throughout. Strictly speaking we ought to take account of the fact that if he spent less on coals, the marginal utility of money to him would be less than it is, and he would get an element of Consumers' Rent from buying other things at prices which now yield him no such Rent. But these changes of Consumers' Rent (being of the second order of smallness) may be neglected, on the assumption, which underlies our whole reasoning, that his expenditure on any one thing, as, for instance, coals, is only a small part of his whole expenditure.

[6] Marshall led a discussion at the Political Economy Club on 6 December 1889. His question was 'How has the power of Trade Unions to influence rates of wages and hours of labour been affected by the Social and Economic changes of recent years?' (*Centenary Volume* [173.2], p. 116).

282. To John Neville Keynes, (December?) 1889[1]

My dear Keynes,

I think your paper[2] is excellent & much better than I could have written myself.

I have only one suggestion to make. You say, as I shd, 'agricultural rent is the excess of the *value* &c': therefore analogy as well as my own preference wd surely lead you to express consumer's rent not 'in kind' but in value or money.[3]

If any apologies are due they are from me to you.

Yours ever | A.M.

[1] Marshall Library, J. N. Keynes Papers. From Balliol Croft.
[2] Keynes's entry on Consumers' Rent for Palgrave's *Dictionary*. See [270.2].
[3] The final version of Keynes's entry, which is nothing but a simplified restatement of Marshall's views, reads 'The term *Consumers' Rent* is seen to be employed analogically: agricultural rent is the excess of the value of the total produce obtained . . . over what is required to remunerate the farmer . . . consumers' rent is the excess of the money equivalent of the satisfaction derived . . .'. Difficulties associated with non-constancy of the marginal utility of money go unmentioned, but there is a caution about making interpersonal comparisons.

283. To John Neville Keynes, 20 December 1889[1]

Very many thanks for your careful criticisms. They will be of great use. They will make me round off the edges of what I say about Mill &c: though I still think his Book IV[2] is the best thing for its size there is on the subject.

Yours ever | AM

You notice that in BK IV he speaks of wages as depending on produce, not on capital directly.[3]

[1] Marshall Library, J. N. Keynes Papers. From Balliol Croft. Postcard, postmarked 'DE 20 89'. An undated letter of this period in the Marshall Library, J. N. Keynes Papers, not reproduced here, as it is mainly concerned with minor business, contains the sentences: 'I had forgotten the passage in Ricardo p 97 to w[h].. your pencil note refers; though I find that I had put a ? against it. It w[d].. be out of place, I think, for me to go into detail about Ricardo Ch IX, so I have cut out the reference to it altogether. Many thanks for that, & other suggestions.'
[2] Book iv of Mill's *Principles* is on the 'Influence of the Progress of Society on Production and Distribution'.
[3] Thus, Mill's book iv was broadly consistent with later marginal-productivity approaches to distribution and largely free of wages-fund taint.

284. To John Neville Keynes, January 1890[1]

My dear Keynes

I have nothing to send you alas! My next chapter is just going to the Press. But my vacation has not been very satisfactory. I have just had a sore throat myself on a small scale. That keeps me away from Foxwell: I don't feel I have much power of resistance to infection.

I agree generally about the correspondence in the Times.[2] But I admire & respect Giffen in spite of his conspicuous faults. And the only part of H.S.F's letter w^h I did not like was that in wh he imputed to Giffen a half-dishonest desire to stifle discussion.[3] I regard that suggestion as absurd as well as unkind. I don't respect Scrutator.[4]

It was not very long ago that I told Foxwell I wished his party wd drop the $15\frac{1}{2}$ ratio: it was that, I said, wh kept me away from them. To wh he announced that he had never heard any serious person propose bimetallism at any other ratio. But he has changed his ground completely now.[5]

When Giffen's letter in the Times appeared I wrote to say that I wished he wd draw a distinction between '$15\frac{1}{2}$' & '22' bimetallism.[6] I thought he had proved e.g. that the former w^d create a panic in the city; but not the latter.

I will try to call on Whitting.[7] I have no official *locus standi* in the matter of the £10 after it has once passed from my hands; & therefore I am a little afraid of writing to him.

Yours ever | A.M.

Of course I paid Whitting each year a single cheque for £25.

[1] Marshall Library, J. N. Keynes Papers. From Balliol Croft. Quoted by Keynes (*Diaries*, entry for 28–9 January 1890).

[2] There had been an extensive and heated correspondence on bimetallism in *The Times* December 1889–January 1890.

[3] Keynes observed. 'There has been lately in The Times a vigorous controversy on Bimetallism, initiated by Giffen, to whom Foxwell wrote what was in my opinion a very able & crushing reply' (*Diaries*, entry for 28–9 January 1890). Giffen had followed up his article, 'A Problem in Money', *Nineteenth Century*, 26 (November 1889), pp. 863–81, with a long letter to *The Times*, published 26 December 1888, vigorously attacking the bimetallic tendencies of the report of the Gold and Silver Commission [214.5] and arguing that bimetallism could not work. Foxwell's 'crushing' rejoinder appeared on 7 January 1889. There were further letters from Giffen, dealing with various aspects of the controversy, on 6, 31 January and 1 February. Foxwell had written: 'it is very much to be regretted that Mr Giffen did not submit his views to the [Royal] Commissioners, by whom they would certainly have been received with due attention and, what is more important, subjected to a searching and careful examination. Mr Giffen, however, has preferred to appeal to the public'.

[4] Anonymous letters of 17, 20, and 24 January, signed 'Scrutator' reflected no great credit on their author, who patronizingly took for granted a lack of connection between money and prices and between metallic money and 'bankers' money', the latter taken as entirely determined by the desired value of transactions.

[5] Foxwell's letter had taken the position that the bimetallists aimed only for a sustainable gold price of silver, whatever it might be, and that their goal was not to raise this price. For Marshall's views see [258].

[6] Marshall's letter to Giffen has not been traced.

[7] Frederick Whitting (1854–1911) was the Secretary of the Financial Board of the University. Keynes had been examining for the annual Marshall Prize [171]. Marshall's yearly payment of £25 included £10 for the costs of examining.

285. To Herbert Somerton Foxwell, 17 February 1890[1]

17 Feb 90

My dear Foxwell

I had a great hunt for a consecutive gold-price history of silver when I was preparing the picture wh I ultimately put into my article in the Contemporary for March 1887.[2] I mention there the very unsatisfactory makeshift to wh I was reduced. In my search I came across a good many isolated facts. Perhaps I ought to have kept note of them but I didn't.

French literature is no doubt the right place to hunt in: but I know very little of it.

The only things I can put my hand on now that it may interest you to look at are

   i   Tooke's *High & Low Prices* Appendix IV pp 7–10
   ii Tooke's *History of Prices* Vol II pp 387–8
   iii a number of isolated notices in this book of Helferichs, wh I send because perhaps you have not got it. (See e.g. pp 243–4.)[3]

Giffen & I had a talk on this subject two or three years ago. We joined in lamenting a lack of proper data. But of course I do not take such things much to heart.

Yours ever | A.M.

[1] Foxwell Papers. From Balliol Croft.
[2] 'Remedies for Fluctuations in General Prices' [174.4]. See *Memorials*, p. 195.
[3] Thomas Tooke, *Thoughts and Details on the High and Low Prices of the Last Thirty Years* (Murray, London, 1823), and *A History of Prices and of the State of Circulation from 1793–1837* (Longman, Orme, Green and Longmans, London, 1838), vol. 2: more appropriately, pp. 384–5. Johann Alfons Renatus von Helferich, *Von den Periodischen Schwankungen im Werth der Edeln Metalle von der Entdeckung Amerikas Bis zum Jahr 1830* (Schrag, Nuremberg, 1843).

286. To Herbert Somerton Foxwell, 19 March 1890[1]

Wed morning

My dear Foxwell,

Palgrave writes very urgently that a day's discussion at the British Ass[n] shd be given to

'the establishment of
   a an economic society
   b an economic Journal—as an organ for discussion of economic subjects'.

I shd be inclined in favour of the proposal if it had the support of all those interested, but not otherwise.

What say you? | A.M.

¹ Foxwell Papers. From Balliol Croft. Envelope postmarked 'MR 19 90'. Marshall was serving as President of Section F of the British Association for the Advancement of Science. The 1890 Annual Meeting was to be held in Leeds, 3–10 September. Palgrave's letter has not been preserved.

287. To Herbert Somerton Foxwell, 22 March 1890[1]

22 March 90

My dear Foxwell,

I am writing to you
&
Palgrave
$\left.\begin{array}{c} \\ \\ \end{array}\right\}$

to suggest that, if you approve, it wd be a good plan for me to send round a collograph circular (as soon as I know how stand the matters I was asked to inquire about); & at the end to say   It is proposed that after the formal business is over, the meeting shd resolve itself into a committee for discussing the questions whether the time is ripe for the formation of an econ^c ass^n $\left\{\begin{array}{c} \& \\ or \end{array}\right\}$ the foundation of an economic journal; & if so, on what lines they shd be organized.

I am writing to Palgrave on my own responsibility to say that I, as an individual, much hope that he won't send out his circular[2] till some attempt of this kind has been made to secure united action.

Yours ever | A.M.

Next meeting fixed 4 p.m. on Tuesday April 15: day chosen specially to suit you.

¹ Foxwell Papers. From Balliol Croft. Foxwell, Inglis Palgrave, and E. C. K. Gonner were urging Marshall to use the Section F Committee of the British Association as an *ad hoc* committee on the founding of an economic association and journal. The others involved would have been H. Sidgwick, J. Bonar, R. Giffen, J. S. Nicholson, J. E. C. Munro, T. H. Elliott and J. B. Martin. Meanwhile, an Oxford group, supported by W. Cunningham, was independently moving ahead with plans for a new journal, the *Economic Review*, intended to have an ethical slant and Christian tone. See A. W. Coats, 'The Origins and Early Development of the Royal Economic Society', *Economic Journal*, 78 (June 1968), pp. 349–71; Alon Kadish, *The Oxford Economists in the Late Nineteenth Century* (Clarendon, Oxford, 1982), pp. 185–92; Alon Kadish and Richard D. Freeman, 'Foundation and Early Years', in John D. Hey and Donald Winch (eds.), *A Century of Economics: 100 Years of the Royal Economic Society and the Economic Journal* (Blackwell, Oxford, 1990).
² Not traced.

288. To Herbert Somerton Foxwell, (March?) 1890[1]

St John's College | Cambridge

Dear F.

You ought to see Gonners document[2]—I made sure you had done so. It is first page that I don't like. No harder task can well be conceived than that of drawing up an epoch-making circular of this kind. It is not unkind to say that his shoulders are not broad enough for the task. Mine certainly are not.

I don't want to include 'mere' business men. But I dont want to exclude Bank Directors & others of the class who are for me at least the most interesting members of the Pol Econ Club. I have always heard before what the academic economists say. It is the men of affairs from whom I learn. Poor Edgeworth w^d.. not waste his *great* strength as much as he does if he w^d.. study the minds of men of affairs & learn from them to get a sense of proportion. However I only ask that the matter shd be decided by the meeting & not by a fiat issuing from you & Gonner. I dont feel strongly about it.

Yours ever | A.M.

[1] Foxwell Papers.

[2] Gonner had apparently drafted a circular on the proposed economic association. See [287.1].

289. From Macmillan and Company, 27 March 1890[1]

Macmillan & Co.
Bedford Street, Covent Garden.
London Mch 27 1890

Dear Sir,

We are sending today specimens of binding for your 'Principles of Economics' in the colours either of which we shall be happy to adopt.

As regards the price of the book if it is fixed in accordance with what we take to be sound commercial principles, i.e. if we put the highest price on the volume that could be asked without injury to the sale we should suggest 18/-. But we are anxious to meet the views you expressed when you last called here and we propose therefore that the retail price should be fixed at 16/-. We shall also be happy to contribute towards the present you think of making to the principal Public Libraries by charging you 8/- a copy for any that you buy for that purpose.

We are,

Prof A Marshall,   Yours truly,
Cambridge   Macmillan & Co.

[1] Marshall Papers. Reproduced in Guillebaud, 'The Marshall-Macmillan Correspondence' [205.1], p. 520.

290. To Macmillan and Company, 1 April 1890[1]

1 April, 1890.

Gentlemen,

I like very much the bindings you have kindly sent me. I w^{d}.. however suggest one or two slight alterations, if you see no objection to them.

(i)   'Principles' should I think be subordinated to 'Economics' a little more than it is. Perhaps it might be in a type scarcely larger than 'Marshall'.

(ii) I should like about 1/2 inch more space between the lines at the top & 'Principles'.

(iii) I am one of those who hold that the true 'architectural' principle of book binding is that the cover is one whole & not two panels fastened together by a back. And therefore I do not like to see the lines on the two boards going right round them. I prefer the plan you have adopted in Bryce's *Commonwealth*,[2] in wh the only lines on the boards are continuations of those on the back.

I like the colours, as well as the letterings, very much. But I prefer the one I return (I assume that the made-up copy is useless to you: if not, I will return it at once).

Thank you much for fixing 16s instead of 18s as the price. I should have preferred 14s; but I know you have gone as far as I can reasonably expect in my direction.

Messrs. MacMillan & Co   Yours very truly | Alfred Marshall

[1] British Library, Macmillan Archive. From Balliol Croft. Reproduced in Guillebaud, 'The Marshall–Macmillan Correspondence' [205.1], pp. 520–1.
[2] James Bryce, *The American Commonwealth* (Macmillan, London, 1888).

291. To John Neville Keynes, 2 April 1890[1]

2 April 90

My dear Keynes,

I have at last completed my discussion of Demand & Supply in relation to Capital [and][2] Business Power. It has spread over three long Chapters;[3] the remainder of wh I hope to send you in a couple of days. Please don't return any till you get all. During the months November–January when I am sure I had (Influenza)$^{1/n}$ where n is perhaps *3* or *4*, my work was so flabby that I destroyed most of it, & am ashamed of what is left; & at the end though I was a little brighter I wrote so fast that I dont like those Chapters. They seem to me too long winded: & as space is becoming very valuable I shd be glad of suggestions as to parts that you think shd be cut out or curtailed. I have already cut out one or two things.

I send the table of contents as far as printed, not for you to correct, but to show you the geography. You may like to know that there remain one Chapter on Demand & Supply in relation to Land;[4] & one or two winding up chapters.[5] I shall have to leave out much that I had wanted to get in.

I wonder how your book gets on; & whether, if it is not out before September, you could not read part of it—say on Economics in relation to Statistics, at the British Asso^n..[6] Do!.

I have some more books on Statistics that I think it possible you might come to look at if you are passing this way. But it is hardly worth while to send them on spec.

Yours very sincerely | Alfred Marshall

---

[1] Marshall Library, J. N. Keynes Papers. From Balliol Croft.

[2] Word apparently omitted.

[3] Book vii, chs. 7–9, of *Principles (1)*.

[4] This had become two chapters, book vii, chs. 10, 11, when *Principles (1)* appeared.

[5] There were eventually two when *Principles (1)* appeared: book vii, ch. 12 'General View of the Theory of Value', and book vii, ch. 13, 'The Influence of Progress on Value'.

[6] See [286.2].

292. To John Kells Ingram, 2 April 1890[1]

2 April 1890

Dear Prof Ingram,

I have to preside over the British Association at Leeds next September, & am making out a draft list of the leading papers that will be read there. May I venture to ask you to read one. It would afford very great gratification to myself & others if you would do so.[2]

Yours very truly | Alfred Marshall

---

[1] Public Record Office, Northern Ireland, Ingram Papers. From Balliol Croft.

[2] It appears, according to a further letter of 21 June from Marshall, that Ingram had envisaged a paper on women's wages. In the event he appears not to have attended. See [312.2].

293. To Herbert Somerton Foxwell, 10 April 1890[1]

10 April 90

My dear Foxwell,

Strangely enough Ingram[2] wrote last Tuesday urging me to start an association to publish translations of foreign books. He was most urgent.

I hope you will approve of what I have done.[3]

W^d.. not your copy of the later issue of Gossen be of use to you.[4] Its binding is too grand for me. I hardly realised how grand it was, and I wd be *quite glad* to give it back in exchange for a plainly bound, or an unbound copy.

I hope you are receiving 'betterments' from your 'Environment'.[5]
Yours quite ever | Alfred Marshall

[1] Foxwell Papers. From Balliol Croft.
[2] Translations and reprints were among the activities a new economic association might undertake, and both Foxwell and Inglis Palgrave had urged them at various points. See Coats, 'Origins and Early Development' [287.1]. Ingram's letter has not been traced.
[3] See [287].
[4] A second but unchanged edition of Gossen's forgotten 1854 classic had appeared following its rediscovery and popularization by Jevons and Walras: H. H. Gossen, *Entwickelung der Gesetze des Menschlichen Verkehrs* . . . (Prager, Berlin, 1889).
[5] The letter was addressed to St John's College 'to be forwarded', but it appears not to have been.

294. To Members of the Committee of Section F, 10 April 1890[1]

After considering the tenour of the conversation on this subject at our last meeting, and after some consultation with Prof. Foxwell and Mr Palgrave I propose to move that on Tuesday next, as soon as the necessary business has been disposed of, we resolve ourselves into a special meeting for the discussion of the following questions:—

(i)   Has the time come for founding an English Economic Journal somewhat similar in character to the American Quarterly?[2]

(ii) Has the time come for founding an English Economic Society, or Association; which shall have as its main objects the encouragement of research and discussion, the publication of monographs, the translation of foreign works and the republication of English works that are out of print?

(iii) If so should its general lines be those of an English 'learned' society; or of the American Economic Association, which holds meetings only at rare intervals, and the membership of which does not profess to confer any sort of diploma?

(iv) Should the Journal be published by such Society or Association (if formed), and edited under the direction of a committee appointed for that purpose by this Council?

(v)   Shall we appoint a small subcommittee to convene a meeting to discuss, and take action on these questions, and to invite to it (1) all members of the Council of the Royal Statistical Society; (2) all members of the Political Economy Club; (3) all who have been, or are, lecturers on economics in any university or public college in the United Kingdom together with ourselves and any other persons whose presence may seem to the Subcommittee specially desirable?

Balliol Croft, Cambridge: Alfred Marshall
10 April 1890

[1] Reproduced in the note [by John Maynard Keynes], 'The Society's Jubilee 1890–1940', *Economic Journal*, 50 (December 1940), pp. 401–9 at pp. 401–2. The original, which was presumably duplicated for circulation to the committee members [287.1], is untraced.

[2] The *Quarterly Journal of Economics*.

295. From Macmillan and Company, 15 April 1890[1]

Macmillan & Co.
29 & 30 Bedford Street, Strand
London, W.C., April 15th, 1890.

Dear Sir,

You may possibly have seen some suggestions we made towards a plan for reducing the retail prices of books and also the discounts allowed to the trade, in order that books might be sold for the prices at which they are advertised. At present as you are aware it is usual for booksellers to allow their customers a discount of 2^d. and sometimes 3^d. in the [shilling][2] from advertised prices. This system is the cause of two evils: in the first place books have to be made (nominally) ridiculously expensive in order that there may be plenty of margin for taking off discounts, & in the second place the system of allowing discounts to retail purchasers has fostered a spirit of competition among booksellers so keen that there is not enough profit in the business to enable booksellers to carry good stocks or to give their attention to bookselling proper. They have to supplement their profits by selling 'fancy goods' Berlin wool etc., & are in many cases, in the country especially, driven out of business altogether.

Our theory is that the proper thing to do is only to allow the retail bookseller such a discount from the published price as will give him a fair profit if he gets full price for a book. This, of course, would enable publishers to make books, nominally, cheaper. We have adopted the plan in isolated cases but always with large books selling for several guineas—& it has met with the approval of the better class of booksellers. We should like to try the same plan with a book of general interest intended for wide sale & it has occurred to us that your *Principles of Economics* is well suited for the purpose. It is not a book that would in any case come in the way of the 'cheap-Jack' booksellers who are the only opponents of our scheme & we think, therefore, that there is no fear that the experiment would have any ill effect on the sale of the book itself. It would however be an experiment & we should not like to make it without your full approval. Our idea would be to make the price 12s. 6d. *net* instead of 16s.[3] and the trade price would be 10s 5d. with a further discount at settlement averaging 5 per cent. We shall also abolish the 'odd copy'—i.e. 25 books will not be charged as 24 or 13 as 12 1/2.

Perhaps you will kindly let us know your views.
We are yours | very truly, | Macmillan & Co.

Professor Marshall | Cambridge

[1] British Library, Macmillan Archive: from Macmillan's copy. Reproduced in Guillebaud 'The Marshall–Macmillan Correspondence' [205.1], pp. 521–2, and in Sir Frederick Macmillan, *The Net Book Agreement 1899 and the Book War 1906–1908* (Macmillan, London, 1924) where Sir Frederick claims to have been the letter's author. Marshall's acceptance of the proposal made in this letter was to give the *Principles* a minor place in publishing history.
[2] Written $1/- in the original.
[3] See [289].

296. To John Bates Clark, 7 May 1890[1]

7 May 90

Dear Sir

As President for this year of the Section of Economics & Statistics in the British Association, I venture to endorse the inclosed invitation of the Leeds Committee.

I fear I shall be unable to see much of the foreign guests at Leeds; & in August I shall not be at Cambridge. But I shall be here from Sep 15 to Sep 25; & if you shd care to pay a short visit to this town, it wd. give my wife & me great pleasure to see you. Our own house, wh is not large, may be full; but in any case we shd be glad to provide lodgings of some sort in the neighbourhood.

Yours very truly | Alfred Marshall

Prof J B Clark

[1] Columbia University Library, J. B. Clark Papers. From Balliol Croft.

297. To Herbert Somerton Foxwell, 2 June 1890[1]

2 June 90

My dear Foxwell,

You must have been in a hurry when you read my draft letter:[2] otherwise you could not have supposed that I compared the 'popular' magazines, with the publications of the 'Organization'. Later on I say that a main source of Englands economic troubles is the absence of opportunity for 'Englishmen who have something to say that is too technical for the ordinary magazines & too short for a book'.[3]

Nor can I understand how you can deny that English magazines are the best 'popular' magazines that treat of economics. That they are so is I believe the universal opinion of Germans & Americans as well as of Englishmen, or rather those few Englishmen who read foreign magazines much. Cohn[4] for instance, the best judge of 'popular' economic writing perhaps in Germany spoke enthusiastically about them.

However I have always disliked the 'self-conscious' comparison in detail of our own merits & demerits with those of other countries with wh Gonner began.[5] (This particular passage has passed your criticism unchallenged several times.) And so I have cut out all the details bodily.

Next the plan of putting Council of Stat S^y.. before lecturers was I think your own proposal. And I think it a reasonable course; because the order of precedence in these matters is generally that of age & dignity: ie the inverse of that of activity & practical influence. However, to please you, I have inverted the order.[6]

The old men are rapidly dying off & losing their energy: we want to start so as to include them: in a very few years those who are now the younger men of the movement will be its old fogies.

The 17th.. will enable Munro to come & suits Elliott best. So I am deciding on that day, though Palgrave wont be able to be present then.[7]

Yours vermicularly | trodden but turning | Alfred Marshall

Bohm Bawerk   Schmoller & Hadley are coming to British Ass^n. Some answers not yet received. Oh! also probably Pantaleoni.[8]

[1] Foxwell Papers. From Balliol Croft.

[2] This refers to the first draft of Marshall's open letter concerning the proposal to form an economic association. This draft has not been traced, but copies of the second, third and fourth drafts and the final version are preserved in the Royal Economic Society Archives. The final version is reproduced as [326] to which variorum notes on the earlier versions are attached.

[3] This phrase was retained through all versions including the final one.

[4] Gustav Cohn the German economist, an expert on railways and public finance, who had spent some years in England, mainly studying railways.

[5] Marshall's draft appears to have drawn on an initial one written by E. C. K. Gonner. See [288.2].

[6] See [294]. This inversion is in effect in all subsequent versions.

[7] See [287.1].

[8] Only Arthur Twining Hadley is recorded as communicating a paper to Section F in Leeds. (*Report of the British Association for the Advancement of Science, 1890*, pp. 898–929.) However, Keynes did subsequently dine at the Marshalls with Maffeo Pantaleoni and Hadley (*Diaries*, entry for 15 September 1890).

298. From Carl Menger, 8 June 1890[1]

Wien

8 Juni 1890

Hochgeehrter und lieber Herr College

Ich danke Ihnen vorallem für die freundliche und mich hoch ehrende Einladung zur Theilnahme an der diesjährigen Jahresversamlung der British Association, insbesondere aber für Ihre gütige Einladung, Sie in Cambridge zu besuchen. Leider bin ich nicht sicher, ob es mir heuer möglich sein wird, nach England zu kommen. Ich bin ein viel geplagter und viel beschäftigter Mann.

Gewinne ich heuer die Zeit, ein englisches Seebad zu besuchen, so käme ich sicher nach Leeds und würde mich herzlich freuen, den Kreis von ausgezeichneten Gelehrten persönlich kennen zu lernen, deren Bestrebungen den meinen so verwandt sind und deren Schriften ich mit so grossem Interesse verfolge. Ist es mir, wie ich besarge, heuer nicht möglich, diesen Plan auszuführen, so komme ich nächstes Jahr nach England, dass ich seit 12 Jahrennicht mehr besucht habe, und nichts würde mich mehr freuen, als Sie bei dieser Gelegenheit persönlich kennen zu lernen.

Mit herzlichen Grüssen | Ihr ergebener College | Prof. Carl Menger

[1] Marshall Papers.

Précis: Menger thanks Marshall for an invitation to the meeting of Section F in Leeds, but being busy and harassed doubts whether he will be able to attend unless in conjunction with a holiday at the English seaside. He will visit England next year if not this, 12 years having elapsed since his last visit. He would like to meet English economists, whose work he follows, and particularly to make Marshall's acquaintance.

He appears not to have attended the Leeds meeting.

299. To John Neville Keynes, (June?) 1890[1]

Dear Keynes

I send first half of my last chapter. Have you a copy of my table of contents. I fancy I sent you one & said you might keep it.[2] But I have spoilt the only copy I can find of my own; & so shd be rather glad to steal yours if you have one.

Yours | A.M.

Wd you let me know what you think on the following Questions—it being taken for granted that an economic journal is desired by *all* parties:—

  i Shd an economic organization if started undertake at starting anything beyond the Journal; or shd it begin with that & gradually go on to other things
 ii If it shd do nothing else at first, shd the organization in the first instance be a private assemblage of persons who know one another; & afterwards gradually expand into an organization

This last plan was my own original hobby. I dropped it in deference chiefly to Foxwell & Gonner & as I thought Nicholson.[3] But I find now I had mistaken Nicholsons views; & am inclining to revert to my old hobby.

Since I wrote this letter Foxwell has returned Ashley's and Nicholsons: wh I send.[4] Please let me have them back by Monday.

[1] Marshall Library, J. N. Keynes Papers. From Balliol Croft.
[2] See [291].

³ See [287.1, 294].

⁴ Letters not traced. Marshall had forwarded W. J. Ashley's letter to Foxwell as 'full of the most valuable suggestions' (letter of 11 June, Foxwell Papers).

300. To John Neville Keynes, (June?) 1890[1]

My dear Keynes,

I am very glad of all your news.

I shall probably set few papers or none during the October Term, a good many during the Lent Term & perhaps a few—of a kind not to poach on Berry's ground[2]—in the May Term.

But these are only first thoughts; & I may change my plans before the next edition of the Lecture list comes out.[3]

I don't in the least know when I shall get away from Cambridge.

The Economic Assⁿ plans[4] are 'unanimous' pretty well: but I fear muddled through haste. A new proposal to get to work at once was carried in spite of my protests that feared we shd get into a mess: & now I come to take a general view of my instructions I find them not a well organized whole—to put it mildly!

Its a long story. If you are staying in Cambridge I will come & fetch your proofs & tell you Association gossip. Its a long story. Send me a line if you are going to leave Cambridge soon.

Yours gladly | A.M.

I am going to write to Browne[5] to ask to be let off taking in the Lecture Extension Visitors. This Economic Assⁿ.. business in July[6] is the last straw that breaks the camel's back!

¹ Marshall Library, J. N. Keynes Papers. From Balliol Croft.

² Arthur Berry was due to teach for the first time a course on 'Diagrammatic and Mathematical Treatment of Economic Theory' in Easter Term 1891. He continued to teach it until 1900, after which W. E. Johnson took it over. (The title became 'Diagrammatic Treatment of Pure Economic Theory' in 1896. The 'Pure' was inserted in 1892.)

³ See *Reporter*, 6 October 1890. Marshall was down to teach his General and Advanced courses in the Michaelmas and Lent Terms only.

⁴ See [287.1, 294].

⁵ G. F. Browne [93.2] was Secretary of the Local Examinations and Lectures Syndicate. Presumably the Marshalls had offered visitor accommodation at Balliol Croft.

⁶ At this time it was planned to have the inaugural public meeting to found the new economic association on 23 July. See [326.2].

301. To the Editor, The Economist, 28 June 1890[1]

The Stock of Gold in the United States.

Sir,—You say in your note on this point,[2] that as the visible supply of gold in the States is only £84,000,000; the total stock cannot be, as has been estimated, £138,000,000; since 'there can be nothing like £54,000,000 in actual circulation.' I presume that the amount in actual circulation is very small, but is it certain that the amount hoarded or half-hoarded is *une quantité négligéable?* I was told some time ago that there was a good deal of hoarding of gold among the illiterates in the States, and especially the negroes who had got a little new wealth in the Western States. I cannot say whether my informant was right, but it seems to me a matter worth inquiring into.

Alfred Marshall.

[1] Printed in *The Economist*, 28 June 1890, p. 830.
[2] See *The Economist*, 21 June 1890, pp. 788–9.

302. To Herbert Somerton Foxwell, 28 June 1890[1]

28 June

My dear Foxwell,

Keynes is coming to dinner on the 5th.. & I think we shall ask Sidgwick & Cunningham, & perhaps the wives.[2] I much wish you wd come & talk out the Ass^n..: but I don't want you to do what you don't like. If you really think it would be disagreeable to you to see Giffen just now, you might return to Cambridge on Monday the 7th.. & ask Dunbar to spend Monday night with you. (We have asked him only for the Saturday to Monday, & propose to leave Cambridge ourselves by the 5.50 train on the Monday at the latest.)

I scarcely know of any one who is certain to be at the meeting in July:[3] & I know of three very important persons who will probably or certainly not be able to come viz Sidgwick Bonar & Palgrave.[4]

The more I think about the editorship the more I think that if we 'marry in haste, we may repent at leisure', & I dont believe that even if we have our meeting in July we shall be able to get the Editor to work till October: unless indeed you wd like the one man power & appoint Giffen as Dictator to arrange every thing!!![5]

I don't want to argue about Giffen: but it is easier to believe that the Marquis of Granby misunderstood him than that he contradicted himself.[6] For instance Giffen may have been talking to him on the supposition that the U.S. w^d.. sell their gold: a contingency wh he excludes when he says free coinage of silver *by itself* w^d.. have very little effect on prices.

I could say more: but don't want to Kontrovert.

So write to me at Toynbee Hall[7] to say whether you will dine with us on Saturday the 5th.. I hope you will: but w[d].. rather you didn't come against your will.

Yours ever | A. Marshall

Goschen's Secretary answers that G: has 'Sympathy' with the movement: but I fancy he thinks it is rather cheeky to ask him when Parliament is sitting—and fussing.[8]

Remember me kindly to Hoare.[9]

[1] Foxwell Papers. From Balliol Croft.

[2] Keynes recorded that 'Florence & I dined with the Marshall's, meeting Professor [C. F.] Dunbar of Harvard—a very quiet man, one who evidently weighs his words before speaking, but very likeable. Sidgwick & the Cunninghams completed the party' (*Diaries*, entry for 5 July 1890).

[3] See [300.6].

[4] See [287.1].

[5] See [284.3] on a possible source of ill feeling.

[6] This probably relates to a private discussion reported by Foxwell. The Marquis of Granby, Henry John Brinsley (1868–1925), was a Member of Parliament from 1885 to 1895, when he entered the Lords as Lord Manners. In 1906 he succeeded his father as eighth Duke of Rutland. From 1885 to 1888 he had served as Private Secretary to the Prime Minister, Lord Salisbury.

[7] The occasion of Marshall's visit to Toynbee Hall in London's East End is unknown. He was a familiar face there.

[8] George Joachim Goschen was at this time Chancellor of the Exchequer.

[9] Alfred Hoare (1850–1938), banker, educated at St John's (14th Wrangler, 1873), who lived at Charlwood Farm, Sharpthorne, East Grinstead. Marshall's letter was addressed to Foxwell at 'Charlewood Farm, Forest Row, Sussex'.

303. To Herbert Somerton Foxwell, 5 July 1890[1]

5 July 1890

Dear Foxwell

M[r] Goschen, while expressing much sympathy with our movement, would be unable to take the Chair at our meeting if it is held in July.[2] M[r]. Courtney, while quite willing to come if at the time he should find himself disengaged, has 'no reasonable expectation of being free any afternoon in the week except Saturday.'[3] Nearly half of those specially interested in the movement, with whose plans I am acquainted, do not expect to be able to attend a meeting in July. And lastly, further discussion has given cause for thinking that several Committee meetings must be held after the semi-public meeting before the Editor can be elected & fairly settled to his work; that these meetings could not be held in August, & that the interests of the Journal w[d]. be prejudiced by a long interval of inaction following our semi-public meeting. On this grounds I suggest that we should revert to the decision, carried almost unanimously at our April meeting, that the semi-public meeting sh[d]. be postponed to the autumn. Of those whom I have consulted, two acquiesce in the change & the rest are decidedly of opinion that it should be made. M^r. Elliott in particular, who moved the resolution to hold the meeting in July, authorises me to say that he is in favour of the change, & that resolution, it will be remembered, was carried by a majority of one. Unless I hear from you shortly to the contrary, I shall assume that you acquiesce in the change, & unless you hear from me to the contrary within a week you may conclude that no further action will be taken in the matter till we meet again at Leeds.[4]

Yours very truly | Alfred Marshall

[1] Foxwell Papers. No address. A collograph circular with the recipient's name inserted in ink. Presumably the same letter was sent to all members of the organizing committee [287.1]. An identical letter to Bonar is in the Royal Economic Society Archives.
[2] See [300.6].
[3] Letter not traced. As a public figure, Leonard Courtney's involvement, like Goschen's, was desired to give weight to the enterprise.
[4] See [286.2].

304. From Macmillan and Company, 7 July 1890[1]

Macmillan & Co.
Bedford Street, Covent Garden,
London July 7 1890.

Dear Sir,

We have received the thickness copy of your book from the University Press and also an approximate estimate of the cost of printing. The book is now so much larger than it was when we wrote to you about the price some two months since,[2] that it seems to us it would be reasonable to increase the price from 12/6 net: which was then decided upon, to 14/-. A closely printed volume of 800 pages like yours would ordinarily be priced at 18/- or 21/-.

We enclose for your approval, a draft of a paragraph for this week's 'Athenaeum'.[3]

We are yours truly, | Macmillan & Co.

Prof: Marshall | Balliol Croft | Cambridge.

[1] Marshall Papers.
[2] See [295].
[3] See [305.2].

305. To Macmillan and Company, 8 July 1890[1]

8 July 90

Gentlemen,

I have to thank you for the care & skill you have shown in preparing a notice of my book. You have done it much better than I could have. But the latter part seems to me not perfectly accurate; & yet I don't see how to improve it without being prolix. I like the first half, & I think it is sufficient. A short notice is always more likely to be read than a long one; and I shall be quite contented with the first half only, down to 'of the age.' I think that is very good, & shd myself stop there. But if you think it advisable to add the third sentence, I shd accept your judgment: only I shd wish 'In accordance with English tradition' to be omitted, as it is likely to raise a controversy when prefixed to the compressed sentence which follows. In that case, you would run on from 'of the age' to 'The author regards—guide in life': & stop there.[2]

As to the price of the book, I told you when I saw you in London recently that it wd contain 49 sheets.[3] (I had told you at first it wd. be 46 or 47 sheets; & afterwards had written[4] to say it would be $47\frac{1}{2}$; if I recollect right.) I had wanted to talk out a proposal for keeping the price at its old level, in case you shd think the book was now too big to be retained there under ordinary arrangements. But I understood you to say it would not be necessary to enter on the question.

A net price of 14s corresponds, for the large town buyer, to a full price of 18s: and therefore if published at 14s it will be rather above than below the customary price. It is true that when we met you had not before you an estimate of the cost of printing; & my corrections of the press have certainly been heavy. I should have preferred to talk the matter out. But time presses, & you will be wanting to advertise a price at once. And therefore I make the definite proposal that I should pay £20 as a special contribution to the extra expenses of printing, and that the net price should be 12/6. I should prefer this course to raising the Net price to 14s. But while saying this, I think it only right to add that if you entertain a *strong* objection to so large a book appearing at that price, I shall feel bound, though unwillingly to yield to your decision, & accept a net price of 14s.

I do not think it will be necessary for you to communicate with me again before advertising the price of the book: but I may as well add that I expect to sleep tonight at the Great Northern Hotel, Leeds, & tomorrow at St. Enoch's Hotel, Glasgow.[5]

I will write shortly about presentation copies.

Yours very truly | Alfred Marshall

---

[1] British Library, Macmillan Archive. From Balliol Croft. Reproduced in Guillebaud, 'The Marshall–Macmillan Correspondence' [205.1], pp. 523–4.

[2] The final version of the notice, published in the *Athenaeum*, 12 July 1890, p. 64, reads:

> Messrs. Macmillan & Co. will publish immediately the first volume of Prof. Alfred Marshall's long-expected treatise on the 'Principles of Economics'. It is an attempt to present a modern version of old doctrines with the aid of the new work, and with reference to the new problems of the age.

A similar statement appeared in *The Times* of the same date (p. 6). The original version has not been traced.

[3] A sheet comprised 8 pages or 16 sides: 49 × 16 = 784 pages. *Principles* (*1*) had 754 pages plus preliminaries of 28 pages and two pages of advertisements, 784 in all.

[4] Letter not traced.

[5] The Marshalls were embarking on a Scottish vacation.

306. From Macmillan and Company, 9 July 1890[1]

July 9, 1890.

Dear Sir,

We will send the paragraph about your book to the literary papers abbreviated in accordance with your suggestion.

As to the price we are willing that it should stand at 12/6 *net* and we will accept a payment of £20 from you towards the cost of corrections which as you know have been very large.

We shall be glad to have your list for presentation copies at your convenience.

We are

Professor Marshall,   Yours very truly,

Cambridge.   Macmillan & Co.

[1] British Library, Macmillan Archive. From a copy retained by Macmillans. Reproduced in Guillebaud, 'The Marshall–Macmillan Correspondence' [205.1], p. 524.

307. To Francis Ysidro Edgeworth, 10 July 1890[1]

Glasgow

Thursday evening

My dear Edgeworth,

I got your letter in time but only just in time to write a letter of wh I inclose a copy.[2]

We are wandering at our own sweet will & sending telegrams once in twenty four hours to our servant to say where we shall be 36 hours later. Thus we know that in about 36 hours hence we shall probably be leaving Loch Awe Hotel. But where we shall go then we have not a ghost of a notion. We are on a search not much more easy than that of the Holy Grail: ie. lodgings sweet & simple in a very beautiful place which others have not yet found out. Please calculate the chance of our finding them in six shots ie in investigations conducted from six centres; of wh Loch Awe Hotel is to be the first.

You will now be able to become a Honorary member of the Pol Econ Club.[3] We don't meet again till December. I think Courtney will propose you

Yours ever | AM.

[1] BLPES, Edgeworth Papers.

[2] See [308].

[3] Marshall seems to be taking Edgeworth's election to the Tooke Professorship for granted. It was one of the professorships carrying with it honorary membership of the Political Economy Club.

308. To the Principal, King's College, London, 10 July 1890[1]

10 July 1890

Dear Sir

Having just heard that my friend Prof Edgeworth is a candidate for the Tooke Chair of Economics & Statistics, I venture to write to you to say that in my opinion he has shown himself to be an economist of great ability & originality; while his contributions to the theory of Statistics have already given him a European reputation, & are likely to leave a permanent record in the history of the science. I think therefore that he is specially well fitted to fill this double chair w^h.. has been established so aptly to commemorate the memory of Tooke: & it will be a source of great gratification on public as well as on private grounds, if I sh^d.. hear that the choice of the electors has fallen on him.

I have the honour to remain | Dear Sir | Yours very faithfully | Alfred Marshall

The Rev | The Principal
Kings College

---

[1] BLPES, Edgeworth Papers. From a copy in Mrs. Marshall's hand. Addressed from Balliol Croft, but probably posted elsewhere. The Tooke Professorship had been held since 1859 by J. E. Thorold Rogers who had recently resigned it. Edgeworth had been Professor of Political Economy at King's College since 1888: see [242].

309. To John Neville Keynes, (14?) July 1890[1]

Blair | Dalmally, NB
Tuesday

Dear Keynes

This is a farm on the moors, near Loch Awe with only one house within two miles of it. Scenery consists of big mountains, bigger moors, & biggest clouds. We got here yesterday. I read your proofs today. Tomorrow I am going to address myself gravely & seriously to the question:—What the dickens am I to talk about on Sep 4?[2]

I have done as I w^d.. be done by: sought for passages in wh I could find something I did not completely agree with: & expressed my disagreement in the short bark of an expostulating fox terrier.[3]

But I think it is very good as a whole. The first four slips are perhaps a trifle heavy: the rest seem to read much more easily. My wife is finishing her share at them: if it rains she will finish quickly: if by any odd chance it shd be fine, she will let them wait till it rains again.

W^d.. you mind noting the day at wh my book comes to you. I want to utilize you as a Macmillan-velocity-meter.[4]

Yours ever | AM.

[Postscript by Mary Paley Marshall]

P.S. Wednesday. I have just been through the proofs, & have put my initials to the few remarks, other than purely verbal ones, w^h. I have been able to make. I think the two first sections of each chapter are rather heavy, but that all the rest is very interesting, & I like the note at the end greatly. If possible I think it w^d be better to have more sections; they are at present very long, considering the difficulty of the subject. I agree with all my husbands remarks.

The Economist shall leave here tomorrow.[5]

[1] Marshall Library, J. N. Keynes Papers. NB (North Britain) is a synonym for Scotland. Almost certainly written on Tuesday 14 July, but the following Tuesday is conceivable.

[2] Marshall was then due to give in Leeds his Presidential Address to Section F of the British Association for the Advancement of Science: see [286.2]. He finally elected to speak on 'Some Aspects of Competition'. For the text see *Memorials*, pp. 256–91.

[3] These comments, which were probably written on the proofs, appear not to have been preserved. The proofs are likely to have been those of chs. 6, 7, and 8 of *Scope and Method*, entitled 'On the Method of Specific Experience in Political Economy', 'On the Deductive Method in Political Economy', and 'On Symbolic and Diagrammatic Methods in Political Economy'. At this stage, ch. 8 was only a note to ch. 7 on mathematical methods. Keynes observed 'Nicholson writes—"... . The note on mathematical methods is very good, but I think it should be lengthened & made into an independent chapter with some examples ...".". Marshall & Mrs Marshall also pronounce the mathematical note very good, & so I think I shall give it more prominence by making it into a chapter in accordance with Nicholson's advice. But I do not think I shall add examples ...' (*Diaries*, entry for 21–4 July 1890).

[4] Keynes received his presentation copy of *Principles* (*1*) between 21 and 24 July, judging it 'a very handsome volume' (*Diaries*, entry for 21–24 July 1890).

[5] See [198.4].

310. To Ludwig Joseph Brentano, (July?) 1890[1]

Dear Prof. Brentano,

I am in Scotland, whither I have retreated to hide myself from all men, to rest, & to write my address as President of Section F (Economics & Statistics) of the British Association.[2] That Address, alas!, I have not yet begun. So I shall not be visible till I go to Leeds on Sep 3rd for the meeting of the Association. Even when there I shall be so busy that—not being very strong—I have told the few foreign economists who will be there that I do not expect to be able to see much of them at Leeds; but that if they will come to see me at Cambridge for a few days beginning Sep 15th.. I shall be glad; & one or two are coming.[3] My house is small: but I can get extra sleeping accommodation in the neighbourhood.

I am authorized to ask you to be present at the meeting at Leeds, if you shd care to do so; and I shall be very glad if you will join our small party on the 15th Sep at Cambridge.

Yours very truly, | Alfred Marshall

[1] Bundesarchiv, Koblenz, Brentano Papers. No address. Reproduced in McCready, 'Marshall: Letters' [274.1], p. 304.
[2] See [309.2].
[3] See [297.8].

311. To Macmillan and Company, 22 July 1890[1]

22 July 90

Gentlemen,

I have to thank you for a copy of my book.[2] I think the wrapper is an excellent finishing touch to your part of the work which has all been admirably done, & for wh I am under very great obligations to you. I suppose it was the doubt about the price which has prevented you from advertising it as shortly to appear; but I am sure that in this matter also you will proceed with your usual vigour & judgement. I must thank you also for the notices of the *Economics of Industry* at the end of the new volume.[3] I have put on a separate slip of paper[4] suggestions for a modification of them whenever you may again be issuing them in any form. Fawcett's book is extremely attractive & easy reading: but I doubt whether it is really 'more detailed' than the closely packed—perhaps too closely packed— *Economics of Industry*.

As regards the presentation copies of the new book,[5] you have acted with great generosity for which again I tender you my hearty thanks. Every now & then new names are likely to occur to me of people to whom for one reason or another I shd like to give the book. And I shall therefore be much obliged if you will kindly send to Balliol Croft at your convenience a dozen copies of the book for my private use, on the understanding that you charge my separate account with them: I must, please, insist on this condition.

There are however two new foreign reviews to wh perhaps the book shd be sent by you. They are *L'Économie Sociale*, & the more important *Annals of the American Academy of Political & Social Science*. Prof Dunbar tells me that this last is meant as a kind of 'Western' counterblast to the two already existing 'Eastern' Quarterlies.[6] As you are acting for his Journal, you may be interested to look at the notice of them on pp. 434–5 of its July number.[7]

I remain | Yours very faithfully | Alfred Marshall

Mess[rs] MacMillan & Co.

[1] British Library, Macmillan Archive. Addressed from Balliol Croft, but presumably sent from Scotland.
[2] The exact publication date of *Principles (1)* remains uncertain, and perhaps the very idea of a precise date is dubious. Publication had been announced as immediate on 12 July [305.2], while on Thursday 24 July *The Times*, in 'Books of the Week', included an extensive discussion, tantamount to a review, of Marshall's book described as having been published 'this week' (i.e. between Monday 21 July and Wednesday 23 July). The date 18 July is given in a letter of 25 August 1924 from Daniel Macmillan to John Maynard Keynes (King's College, Cambridge,

J. M. Keynes Papers) where the initial printing is given as 2,000: the source of this information is unclear. See also *Memorials*, pp. 503–4.

[3] The first of the two pages of advertisements concluding *Principles* (*1*) was largely devoted to extracts from reviews of the *Economics of Industry*. The quotation from the *Westminster Review* (January 1880), ran 'The book, we venture to predict, will prove useful both to those who have no leisure to study the larger text-books, and also as an introduction to the subjects in the case of students who hope to proceed to the more detailed works of Mill or Fawcett'. Other reviewers quoted (from *The Times, Athenaeum, Spectator, Academy, Cambridge Review, Liverpool Daily Post*) displayed a more just appreciation of the book's qualities.

[4] Not traced.

[5] A rough draft for the list of individuals to be sent copies (Marshall Papers) involves some 75 names including family members, leading economists at home and abroad, Cambridge colleagues, and acquaintances in public life.

[6] C. F. Dunbar edited Harvard's *Quarterly Journal of Economics*. The other 'Eastern' Quarterly must be the *Political Science Quarterly*, edited at Columbia.

[7] *Quarterly Journal of Economics*, 4. The cited pages include brief descriptions of both new journals.

312. To John Kells Ingram, 22 July 1890[1]

Scotland: address uncertain
22 July 90

Dear Professor Ingram,

I deeply regret the news contained in your letter.[2]

Our proposed meeting is postponed till the Autumn.[3] I have been much pressed for time; & in my hurry I forgot to write to tell you of the change. I am very sorry for having done so.

It is very difficult to know what to do about meetings. If they are frequent, the society will practically become a London Society; & may fall chiefly into the hands of people whose time is not very important. Just those people, whether academic students of economics or men of affairs who wd be likely to speak with knowledge & a high sense of responsibility w^d.. be those least likely to find time to attend frequent meetings: at least so some of us think.

I don't feel at all sure wh will prove the best in the long run. But as it is easier to change from annual to monthly meetings than *vice versa*, I am inclined to vote for beginning with the former—if indeed we are to have any meetings other than business meetings.

Yours very truly | Alfred Marshall.

[1] Public Record Office, Northern Ireland, Ingram Papers.

[2] Probably his withdrawal from the meetings of the British Association and the proposed Economic Association as a result of his wife's death.

[3] See [303].

313. From Benjamin Jowett, 24 July 1890[1]

Ball Coll
July 24. 1890

My dear Marshall

I was delighted to get your book[2] this morning & to find it so full of interest. I congratulate you on having written such a book. It will be of great value both to capitalists & to the working classes. It seems to me to be just what was wanted to mediate between the old political economy & the new, or rather between the old state of industrial Society & the new. Neither employers nor employed have any reason to regard you as otherwise than a friend. Ricardo himself would not have objected to have his a priori reasonings supplemented & modified by your facts.

Also I think the book excellent in an Educational point of view: It is very clear & interesting & goes back to great principles. It answers implicitly the question so often asked: 'What is the relation of Political Economy to Ethics'? I think the style admirable—I am also pleased to see that you have not over-loaded the subject with Mathematics, and have rather diminished than increased its technicality.

Every page, I open, seems to me to contain something good—e g 369–371[3]—I often think of the difficulty of rising in life & how to lessen it—The Universities & education do something to diminish it but business much more, especially if some noble sense of philanthropy could be introduced into it.

I hope that having the Book out you will have a well-earned holiday: a landing place before you go up the next flight of stairs—But I know by experience that no one ever takes advice about health. I suppose we are all so conceited that we imagine the world cannot go on without us at least in our own spheres.

Have you gone to Robin Hood's Bay?[4] or whither?

The two days which I spent at Cambridge leave a charming recollection in my mind.

Will you give my kindest regards to M^rs. Marshall? I cannot sufficiently thank you both for your goodness & affection to me. I shall hope to write to her when I have read more of the Book.

I remain   My dear Marshall
Ever yours | B Jowett

---

[1] Marshall Papers. Reproduced in Abbott and Campbell, *Life and Letters* [146.1], vol. 2, pp. 378–9.

[2] *Principles* (*1*).

[3] Pages 369–71 of *Principles* (*1*) covers most of book iv, Ch. 12, s. 11, summarized in the analytical table of contents as 'The working man's opportunities of rising. He is hindered less than at first sight appears, by his want of capital; for the Loan-Fund is increasing rapidly. But the growing complexity of business is against him' (p. xx).

[4] The small resort on the North Yorkshire coast.

314. To James Bonar, 25 July 1890[1]

My dear Bonar,

I am sorry you won't be present at the meeting; firstly because I think you might be converted to an open Society. No one, to whom I have spoken, except Foxwell, Edgeworth and yourself thinks a close society would be safe and the general opinion of those with whom I have conferred is that a close society would be inundated by Quacks, who could not be kept out, unless the society was so small as to be little more than a private club: but that Quacks would not care to come into a society which was open to all: and would not do much harm there, if they did come in.

Yours very truly | Alfred Marshall

25 July

[1] Written from Scotland. Reproduced in the note 'The Society's Jubilee' [294.1] at p. 404. Original not traced. Concerning the proposed economic association, etc. See [287.1].

315. From Macmillan and Company, 25 July 1890[1]

July 25, 1890.

Dear Sir,

In case the review of your book in yesterday's *Times* happens to have met your eye we write to explain that the copy which was sent to that paper appears through an unfortunate accident to have had the sheet containing the analytical contents omitted in the binding.[2] We at once wrote to the Editor who has inserted a note on the subject in today's paper (page 10, column 6).

We are,
Yours very truly,
Macmillan & Co.

Professor Marshall.

[1] British Library, Macmillan Archive. From a copy retained by Macmillans. Reproduced in Guillebaud 'The Marshall–Macmillan Correspondence' [205.1], p. 525.
[2] *The Times* 'review' [311.2] had complained of the lack of a detailed table of contents.

316. To Macmillan and Company, 28 July 1890[1]

Willowbank, Taynuilt | N.B.
28 July 90

Gentlemen,

The net result of the binder's mistake as to the Times' copy of my book is, I think, rather good than bad. Thank you for acting so promptly about it.

I enclose this letter from Mr Chamberlain, wh seems to me rather strange: but I suppose his request shd be granted, as the London Edition of the New York Herald is substantially an independent paper.[2] I leave the matter however for you to decide.

I enclose also a cutting from the Western Morning News.[3] The statement that the advertised price is the wholesale price seems to me a gratuitous folly. But perhaps you may think that if so important a newspaper can make such a mistake, it may be well to repeat some explanation of what is meant. I leave the matter entirely in your hands.

There is however one point on wh I am myself not quite clear, though perhaps I ought to be. It is whether retailers of books published net will be able to charge different prices to those who pay cash, & to those who have the prices entered in the Day Book & Ledger & ultimately in a bill. On general principles I am a strong advocate of inducements being given by the retailer to the customer to pay cash; though I myself never do pay cash for books, partly because the books that I order are out of the way books, in many instances, of wh neither I nor the bookseller know the price before-hand. But I think that your task of accustoming the public to net prices has been made more difficult by Ruskin's action.[4] For instance I bought the other day of Messrs. MacMillan & Bowes a 7/6 book of Ruskin. Inside the cover was marked '7/6 cash, 8/6 credit.' I pay quarterly, & so I suppose I shall ultimately pay 9/10 × 8/6 for it.[5] That seems to me an awkward arrangement. And if, as I suppose, it will not be necessary on the new *net* system, I think it will be worth while to explain that to the public.

It is quite beyond my range to make any definite suggestion on this subject: for I really do not understand the trade. But I think you may perhaps be interested in knowing what, speaking in ignorance as I do, I shd be inclined to advocate. It is that (i) the published price shd be that at w^h the retailer can afford to sell the book on *short* credit: i.e when he has all the expense of entering it in his books, but has not his capital locked up for any considerable time. (ii) The purchaser who pays instant cash shd get 1d in the shilling discount. (iii) The purchaser who demands a long credit shd pay an addition of 5% per *half*-year: the common charge of 5% a year is, I think, altogether insufficient; but I don't think it w^d.. be very easy to get people to adopt this last suggestion.

Another point that may ultimately require explanation is the relation of the new net system to that of the monthlies. They are sold at 25% discount in London, but at full price even for cash over the counter, I believe, in Cambridge & elsewhere. This has always puzzled me.

Yours very truly | Alfred Marshall

[1] British Library, Macmillan Archive. Reproduced in Guillebaud, 'The Marshall–Macmillan Correspondence' [205.1], pp. 525–6. Guillebaud addresses it from Balliol Croft, but the printed heading is struck through. Taynuilt, North Britain (i.e. Scotland), is on Loch Etive.

[2] Mr Chamberlain, not otherwise identified, appears to have been on the London editorial staff of the New York Herald and to have requested a review copy of *Principles* (*1*). See [317].

3 A Plymouth newspaper.

4 John Ruskin [25.21] had arranged for his books to be supplied to the public by mail at the same price as to the trade. Booksellers were expected to add some 10% to this price to compensate their services.

5 The calculation implies that a 10% discount is received for paying quarterly.

317. From Macmillan and Company, 30 July 1890[1]

July 30, 1890.

Dear Sir,

We do not know Mr. Chamberlain and as a rule we think it undesirable to send presentation copies of books to individuals connected with newspapers. We are however sending a copy addressed to 'The Editor of the N.Y. Herald (London Edition)' and if Mr. Chamberlain is the person to whom such books are sent for review it will no doubt reach him.

We do not think that it is worth while to take any notice of the muddle-headed paragraph from 'The Western Morning News.' We hear on all sides that the booksellers are delighted at the terms on which your book has been published and that is the important thing. Neither do we think it wise to lay down regulations as to discount for cash etc. It would be impossible to enforce them and we think such things had better be left for settlement between the booksellers and their customers.

We are, dear Sir,
Yours very truly,
Macmillan & Co.

Professor Marshall.

1 British Library, Macmillan Archive. From a copy retained by Macmillans. Reproduced in Guillebaud, 'The Marshall–Macmillan Correspondence' [205.1], p. 526.

318. From Gustav Schmoller, 6 August 1890[1]

Professor Dr. Gustav Schmoller
Berlin W.

Postamt 62. Wormserstrasse 13.
Den 6ten August 1890

Geehrtester Herr Kollege!

Zu meinem grossen Bedauern muss ich Ihnen anzeigen, dass ich im September nicht nach England kommen, also Ihr Meeting in Leeds nicht besuchen,und Ihr Gast in Cambridge, wie ich so sehr gewünscht hatte, nicht sein kann.

Meine Gesundheit war in den beiden letzten Monaten so schlecht, dass mein Arzt vollständige Schonung und Ruhe verlangt, ich soll nach Tyrol gehen und dort in den Bergen mich ausruhen und erholen. Ich kann Sie versichern, dass es mir sehr schmerzlich ist, so nicht das Vergnügen Ihrer persönlichen Bekanntschaft zu haben. Ich würde mich um so mehr gefreut haben, Sie zu sprechen, als ich aus Ihrem eben erhaltenen 'principles of economics' ersehe, wie gut Sie auch in der deutschen Litteratur Bescheid wissen. Ich danke Ihnen bestens für die gütige Zusendung Ihres Werkes von dessen Lektüre ich mir viel Freude und Belehrung verspreche. Da ich heute abreise und es heute früh erst erhielt, konnte ich nur flüchtig bis jetzt darin blättern. Mein Buch 'zur Gewerbe- und Socialpolitik der Gegenwart' werden Sie wohl erhalten haben.

In der Hoffnung Sie später einmal persönlich kennen zu lernen, und mit nochmaligem Danke für Ihre Güte bin ich

in ausgezeichneter Hochachtung | Ihr | ergebenster | Gust. Schmoller

[1] Marshall Papers.

Précis: Schmoller regrets that he cannot attend the Section F meeting in Leeds, or visit Marshall in Cambridge, but his doctor has enjoined a period of rest in the Tyrol. He has just received a copy of the *Principles* and is impressed by Marshall's knowledge of the German literature and would like to make his acquaintance. He trusts that his recent book (Duncker and Humblot, Leipzig, 1890) has reached Marshall.

319. From Edwin Robert Anderson Seligman, 22 August 1890[1]

Columbia College | New York
Aug 22 1890

Professor Alfred Marshall,

Dear Sir,

Permit me to thank you for the 'Principles' which you were kind enough to send me and the perusal of which I have just completed. It is a remarkable work—remarkable for the knowledge displayed as to the latest advances in continental researches as well as for the holding fast to what is best in the old classical doctrines. It will be an excellent antidote to those extreme votaries of the historical school who see no good but in details—but it will at the same time open the eyes of the uncompromising adherents to the undiluted doctrines of the classicists. So much of what has been written of late in Germany—as e.g. Cohn's recent volumes[2]—while stimulating are yet so undecided and imprecise in their conclusions that it is refreshing to read the logical clear cut chapters in your work. I had already for some time set my students to work especially on Mangoldt[3] & Thünen,[4] & I now feel doubly sure that in many respects they hit the right path.

I am looking forward with interest to your next volume in the hope that it will contain a discussion of the principles of finance. I myself am at work at a comprehensive study on finance in 2 or 3 volumes,[5] but want to avail myself of your work. Do you expect to get it out within a few years?

I shall see that your book gets the review that it deserves. As I consider J. B. Clark as in some respects the ablest economist we have on this side, I shall get him to undertake the review for the Political Science Quarterly.[6]

Yours very truly | Edwin R A Seligman

¹ Columbia University, Seligman Papers.

² Gustav Cohn, *System der Nationalökonomie* (Enke, Stuttgart: vol. 1. *Grundlegung*, 1885, vol. 2. *Finanzwissenschaft*, 1888); *Nationalökonomische Studien* (Enke, Stuttgart, 1886).

³ Hans Karl Emil von Mangoldt, *Grundriss der Volkswirtschaftslehre* (Maier, Stuttgart, 1863).

⁴ Johann Heinrich von Thünen, *Der Isolierte Staat . . .* (Leopold, Rostock, 1826–63; 3 vols.).

⁵ This project was never brought to publication.

⁶ Clark's review of *Principles* (*1*) appeared in vol. 6 (March 1891). See also his review of *Principles* (*2*) in the same volume (December 1891), p. 740, and pertinent correspondence between Clark and Seligman in Joseph Dorfman, 'The Seligman Correspondence', *Political Science Quarterly*, 56 (1941), pp. 107–240, 270–86, 392–419, 573–99, at pp. 111–13.

320. From Benjamin Jowett to Mary Paley Marshall, 18 September 1890[1]

Address | Ball. Coll.
St Andrews
Sep 18. 1890

Dear M^{rs}. Marshall

I think that you and your husband have a right to be very happy this vacation. I perceive that the Book[2] has been very much appreciated, and that the Presidency of the Economic Section has gone off extremely [well].[3] Does not Mr Percival[4] call you the great economists (I always speak of you in the Dual or Plural number) and distinguishes the Socialism of which he approves from that which he disapproves, the former being that of 'our great Economist Marshall': In which I agree, but I do not like the name because it is misleading.

And now could you not under the pretence of studying the Metayer System or something of the sort, or Egyptian or Indian Agriculture take a six month's holiday? It would be very wise and you would come back with renewed strength & full of new ideas?

I read a day or two ago a very remarkable account of the life of Arthur Young prefixed to the reprint of his travels in France:[5] I was delighted with it. I dare say that you know it: I shall enroll him among heroes & great men. Is there any body like him living now.

I think that you & Alfred are very fortunate in having for the pursuit of your lives a great living science which is also growing & contains many obscure points, & which has, perhaps, a nearer bearing on the welfare of mankind than any other. Do we really know the laws of Currency or even of supply & demand? And is there or not still a great deal to be cast out like the distinction of Home & Foreign Trade & endless attempts to make differences of degree into differences of kind & useless & pedantic efforts to use words always in the same sense: I am glad to see that there is a considerable element of Hegelianism in the book which I am sure helps to emancipate us from many verbal arguments & distinctions.

I hope that you & Alfred will run over & see me sometime during the Term.

I have had a very uneventful vacation having staid at Oxford until about 3 weeks, and having drudged away long enough at Plato[6] have been[7] paying visits at Scotch friends houses among others at Lord Rosebery's.[8] I like him & have a very high opinion of him: He told me that there was nothing he liked so well as studying hard, & he has certainly a great deal both of knowledge & reflection. He is not at all unmanageable in the direction of property. Some day I shall hope to have the opportunity of making him acquainted with you.

With most kind regards to your husband.

Believe me | Ever yours | B Jowett

---

[1] Marshall Papers. Reproduced in Abbott and Campbell, *Life and Letters* [146.1], vol. 2, pp. 380–1.

[2] *Principles* (*1*).

[3] Word apparently omitted.

[4] Abbott and Campbell render Percival as 'Punch', but there seems little doubt that 'Percival' is correct. John Percival (1834–1918), first headmaster of Clifton College from 1862 to 1879, and at this time headmaster of Rugby School. In 1895 he became Bishop of Hereford. Marshall had first been brought into contact with Percival by teaching mathematics briefly at Clifton College in 1865 and contact was renewed when Marshall became Principal of University College, Bristol, in 1877. See *Memorials*, p. 5.

[5] M. Betham-Edwards (ed.), *Travels in France by Arthur Young During the Years 1787, 1788, 1789*, with an introduction, biographical sketch and notes by the editor (Bell, London; second edition 1889). See especially pp. xxix–li.

[6] Jowett was at this time revising his translation of Plato's *Dialogues* for a third edition. See Abbott and Campbell, *Life and Letters*, vol. 2, chs. 11, 12.

[7] 'Be' in the original.

[8] The fifth Earl of Rosebery (1847–1929), at this time Chairman of the London County Council, was Foreign Secretary briefly in 1886 and again in 1892, becoming Prime Minister in 1894 and serving for just over a year. His principal seat was at Mentmore near Leighton Buzzard but he had Scottish properties. He was a scholar and author by avocation. The reading of the name as 'Rosebery' seems correct, and is adopted by Abbott and Campbell, but is subject to some doubt.

321. To John Neville Keynes, 20 September 1890[1]

20 Sep 90

My dear Keynes,

I think this Chapter[2] is excellent. Its illustrations are numerous & suggestive; & its whole style is forcible, clear & effective.

My criticisms do not come to much. I have only two points of any importance to urge.

One is an old point. You make all your contrasts rather too sharply for me. You talk of the inductive & the deductive methods:[3] whereas I contend that each involves the other, & that historians are always deducing, & that even the most deductive writers are always implicitly at least basing themselves on observed facts. And in consequence you *first* allow to the inductive method pure & simple more by far than I shd allow to it, & similarly for the deductive method: and *afterwards* take back a great deal of what you have allowed by saying that after all deduction involves induction & *vice versa*. Thus in the end you come to pretty nearly the same result as I sh^d..: but you start by saying things that seem to me not true. It is a mere question of arrangement: but I think it is a very important one practically. I think the right order is *first* to emphasize the mutual dependence of induction & deduction, & *afterwards* to show in what kinds of inquiry the economist has to spend the greater part of his time in collecting arranging & narrating facts, & in what kinds he is chiefly occupied in reasoning about them & trying to evolve general processes of analysis & general theories which shall show the Many in the One & the One in the Many.

My second point is that you continually use the word *theory* where I shd use *analysis*. This seems to me in itself to cause confusion wh is increased by the fact that later on you exclude modern facts from history;[4] & yet you do not boldly say that they are part of theory. If they are then I agree with you that a study of theory shd come before a study of history.[5] But I do not myself like to put the case in this way. My own notion is

i   Begin with Analysis, which is an essential introduction to all study of facts whether of past or present time; with perhaps a very short historical introduction.

ii   Go on to call to mind the students knowledge of the economic conditions in wh he lives. Show the relations in wh they severally stand to one another & carry analysis further, making it more real & concrete.

iii   Build up a general theory or process of reasoning applicable to Value Money Foreign trade &c, with special reference to the conditions in wh the student lives, & pointing out how far & in what ways, it can be made to bear on other conditions.

iv   Give a general course of economic history.

(v   Qe.[6] Return to economic theory & carry it further.)

vi   Consider economical conditions in relation to other aspects of social life.

vii   Treat of the economic aspects of practical questions in general & social reform in particular.

§v. may come almost any where; or, for some classes of students, may be omitted altogether.[7]

Such are the hobbies of | Yours very sincerely | Alfred Marshall

Yes! I think it is a bad plan for students to have two consecutive hours teaching on the same subject. They get weary. So it w^d. I think be a good plan for you to change your hours if you can easily do so.[8]

[1] Marshall Library, J. N. Keynes Papers. From Balliol Croft. Largely reproduced in Ronald H. Coase, 'Marshall on Method', *Journal of Law and Economics*, 18 (April 1975), pp. 25–31 at pp. 26–7.

[2] Ch. 9 of *Scope and Method*, entitled 'On Political Economy and Economic History', which has two substantial notes attached. Keynes quotes this letter as relating to his 'history chapter' (*Diaries*,

entry for 22–4 September 1890). He adds that Marshall 'makes some criticisms, but as regards the most important of them, he seems to me only to say in a different way very much what I have tried to say myself'.

[3] These terms are used by Keynes throughout *Scope and Method*.

[4] Keynes does not go quite so far in *Scope and Method*, but see pp. 273, 307–9.

[5] See *Scope and Method*, pp. 269–73.

[6] Qe stands for Quaere (or question).

[7] Marshall's comments seem to have led Keynes to insert the following statement.

> There has been some dispute as to whether the study of economic history should precede that of economic theory or *vice versa*; it may also be argued, as a third alternative, that since their dependence upon one another is mutual, the study of the one and the other should be carried on more or less *pari passu* . . . so far as elementary study is concerned, it seems best that some treatment of general economic science in its simplest and broadest outlines should come first. (*Scope and Method*, pp. 272–3).

[8] The lecture list eventually published for the Michaelmas Term 1890 (*Reporter*, 6 October 1890) shows Marshall teaching the Advanced course on Saturdays at 12 and Keynes teaching Political Economy (Papers) Saturdays at 10.

322. To John Neville Keynes, 2 October, 1890[1]

2 Oct 90

My dear Keynes.

I think the Chapter[2] is *very* interesting to advanced students: but it is more critical than constructive & is perhaps not so well suited to beginners as the Notes.[3] They are extremely interesting. But perhaps a few of them might be developed a little more. When method has to be inculcated by specimens (as is I think right with Statistical method), a few specimens set forth with great fullness of detail seem to me more instructive than a larger number more hastily treated.

I shd myself say that Statistics was the science of the method of reasoning from quantitative data to conclusions. Eg Keppler's laws[4] are typical illustrations of the method. And I shd say it potentially an abstract or universal science; but in so far as it is this it is really a branch of Mathematics and practically the kinds & the groupings of the difficulties met with in reasoning from quantitative data vary so much with the subject matter of those data, that only a very small part of the complete science of Statistics w^d consist of its general or introductory chapter. The greater part w^d.. consist of chapters in w^h.. the concrete peculiarities of such data in different subject matters were made prominent.

I.e. there w^d.. be chapters on Sanitary statistics, on Statistics in their application to Biology (heredity, race characteristics &c), on Economic Statistics & so on.

And I shd hold that any one of these chapters together with the general or introductory chapter, may conveniently be regarded as a separate science, in the same way as we regard *Human* Anatomy, or *Hydro*-Mechanics as a separate science.

Ought not you to say something as to the great use of Statistics in connection with Concomitant Variations, pointing out how *one* table of Statistics will seldom go beyond supporting 'post hoc ergo propter hoc': while a sufficient number of them afford the known guarantee against the improper use of this formula. I don't go into detail, (though it is a point on wh I am inclined to be rather urgent), because I have given my views on it in the Jubilee Stat[1].. Number to wh you have already referred.[5] I argue that the graphic method has special advantages for this use of Statistics: but that is not my main point.

In conclusion let me congratulate you heartily. I am sure the book will be very widely read, & of great service. I hope & think it will probably be translated: & every way redound to your fame & honour.[6]

Yours congratulatorily | Alfred Marshall

---

[1] Marshall Library, J. N. Keynes Papers. From Balliol Croft.

[2] Ch. 10 of *Scope and Method*, which is entitled 'On Political Economy and Statistics'. This, with its appended note, completed the book.

[3] Ch. 10 of *Scope and Method* has only a single note: 'On Some of the Precautions Requisite in the Use of Statistics in Economic Reasonings'. But this effectively comprises four separate notes: (i) Conditions of the reliability of statistical data, (ii) The interpretation of simple statistics, (iii) The range of statistics, (iv) The grouping of statistics.

[4] The celebrated laws of planetary motion propounded by Johannes Kepler or Keppler (1571–1630).

[5] [159.2], reproduced in *Memorials*, pp. 175–87. See *Scope and Method*, p. 322 n.

[6] After transcribing these last two sentences in his diary, Keynes observed 'I know there is great exaggeration here, & that out of kindness & friendliness Marshall writes in a style of exaggeration in order to encourage me. Still on the whole he cannot think the book contemptible, or as bad as I am myself sometimes inclined to think it' (*Diaries*, entry for 2 October 1890). *Scope and Method* appeared early in 1891, its preface being dated 12 December 1890.

323. From Francis Amasa Walker, 16 October 1890[1]

More and more I enjoy, more and more I admire your work.[2] The spirit and tone of it are admirable. The elevation and dignity of sentiment are quite as impressive as the strength and severity of the thinking.

You have made a great, a very great, book, which will, I am confident, exhibit the characteristic of a few books, namely, the capability of growing more and more upon the mind of the public.

I am much impressed by the enormous advantage you have over a man like myself, for example, in being a mathematician and a physicist. I shall have to qualify that remark. The advantage I have in mind comes chiefly from your being a physicist. I don't so much envy the mathematician, tho' I can readily see that he has a great power of illustrating economic truths, and of expressing them in terms at once compact in themselves and familiar and welcome to many minds.

But the physicist (who might, I suppose, conceivably be not even a good mathematician) has a truly enormous advantage in studying the phenomena of industrial society, in watching the propagation of economic shocks, in tracing the lines of fracture from commercial or financial disasters, in appreciating and estimating the degree and the direction of industrial forces making for good and of industrial disturbances making for harm.

I have been much impressed by this thought as I read your work. It seemed to me that only a man who had profoundly studied the mechanics of heat, light, and sound could exhibit so much insight into the nature of economic forces and so much at once of capacity and of restraint in judging and even estimating their effects upon human society.

---

[1] Printed, possibly incompletely, and without salutation or closing, in Munroe, *A Life* [163.1], pp. 342–3. The original has not been traced. The date is provided by Munroe.

[2] *Principles* (*1*).

324. From Benjamin Jowett, 20 October 1890[1]

Ball. Coll.
Oct. 20—1890

My dear Marshall,

Will you & M^{rs}. Marshall give me the pleasure of a visit on Sat Nov 29 when I hope to have Mr Balfour staying with me?

Whom do you think the best candidate for our Professorship of Political Economy?[2] Is any one superior to Edgeworth? He has written to ask me to support him so far as I have any influence.

I hope that you & Mrs Marshall are well & are enjoying the success of your book. I gave it to Lord Rosebery:[3]

Ever yours | B Jowett

---

[1] Marshall Papers.

[2] The death of J. E. Thorold Rogers on 12 October had made vacant the Drummond Professorship at Oxford.

[3] See [320.8].

325. From Thomas Burt, 24 October 1890[1]

35 Lucerne Crescent
Oct 24th 1890

Dear Professor Marshall,

I thank you for your very kind letter. What a pleasure it would be to visit Cambridge again and to spend a few hours once more with you and M^{rs}. Marshall. Circumstances, however, 'that unspiritual god' will not allow me to accept your friendly invitation. As you know our recess is very short, and all my available time will be occupied. On Nov 12.th 13.th 14th I have to be in Edinburgh to attend meetings of the Royal Commission on Mining Royalties.[2]

I am reading your book with the deepest interest. 'Some books are to be tasted' &c says Bacon. Yours requires and deserves time, and that is rather a scarce commodity with me just now. But I shall manage. The other day I breakfasted with Rev Moore Ede who had the Bishop of Durham[3] as his guest. What charming men they are! I do not see why we should apply that epithet exclusively to women! Both of them spoke very enthusiastically of your book.

I trust M^{rs}. Marshall and you are well.

With kind regards to both. | I am every truly yours | Thos Burt

[1] Marshall Papers. On printed stationery of the Northumberland Miners' Mutual Confident Association, Newcastle upon Tyne. Burt was at this time a Member of Parliament.
[2] Burt was a member of the Commission.
[3] Brooke Foss Westcott (1825–1901), sometime Fellow of Trinity College, Cambridge, and Regius Professor of Divinity at Cambridge, 1870–90.

326. To potential members of a proposed economic association, 24 October 1890[1]

Proposal to Form an English Economic Association

Dear Sir,

I have been requested to invite you to attend a private meeting at University College, London, on Thursday November the twentieth to discuss proposals for the foundation of an Economic Society or Association, and, in conjunction therewith, of an Economic journal, and to take action thereon. The chair will be taken by the Right Hon. the Chancellor of the Exchequer[2] at 5 o'clock.

The need of an economic journal has long been felt in England. Every other country in which economic studies are pursued with great activity, offers facilities for the publication of thorough scientific work by persons who have not the time, or are unwilling, to write a formal treatise. Since isolated pamphlets, however able, seldom obtain any considerable circulation, Englishmen who have something to say that is too technical for the ordinary magazines, and too short for a book, are sometimes compelled to give their views to the world in the columns of a foreign periodical, or as a publication of the American Economic Association; but more frequently they put it aside till an opportunity should offer for working it out more fully and publishing it as a book; and that opportunity too often does not come.[3] A strong and widespread feeling[4] that English economists, and especially the younger men among them, are thus[5] placed at a great disadvantage through the want of any easy means of communication with one another, has led to the holding of many private meetings and discussions on the subject in Oxford, Cambridge, London, and possibly elsewhere;[6] and lately the matter has come under consideration of the Committee of Section F (Economics and Statistics) of the British Association.[7] It is as the result of these discussions that I have been requested to issue the present invitation to you.

It was at first proposed to collect a guarantee fund, and to issue the journal as a private concern. But latterly the feeling has been growing that some security should be afforded that the journal should always represent all shades of economic opinion, and be the organ not of one school of English economists, but of all schools; and it is thought that this end will be best attained by the publication of the journal under the authority of an Economic Association. It is suggested that it should be conducted by a salaried Editor, who should have full power as to matters of detail,[8] but should from time to time confer on matters of general principle with a Committee of the Association, appointed for that purpose.

It has been suggested that as a rule each number of the Journal might contain one long article, or monograph, and two or three shorter articles, together with reports from foreign correspondents, and a detailed bibliography of current economic literature, besides some miscellaneous matter. It is proposed also that extra numbers should occasionally be issued containing reprints of rare works that have historical interest, or translations of foreign pamphlets.

The Association might gradually enlarge the scope of its action. It might supply a common meeting place for English economists, and bring them together from time to time. It might increase its issues of economic publications.[9] And lastly, if its funds sufficed for the purpose, it might do good service by promoting economic investigations, especially such as cannot well be undertaken by Government departments, and yet involve considerable expense; for the ability, the inclination and the means to carry on investigations, such as that which is now being made on 'The Labour and Life of the People in London',[10] are seldom united in one person.

Almost the only question on which a difference of opinion has so far shown itself is whether or not the Association should be open to all those who are sufficiently interested in Economics to be willing to subscribe to its funds. If the Association should hold[11] meetings for discussion, the further question would arise whether they should be at frequent intervals, say once a month, or more rarely, say once a year. There are some who think that the general lines to be followed should be those of an English 'learned' Society, while others would prefer those of the American Economic Association, which holds meetings only at rare intervals, and the membership of which does not profess to confer any sort of diploma.

The meeting on November the 20th[12] will be asked to decide Firstly, whether it is desirable to found an Economic Society or Association which shall undertake at once the issue of a journal; and (supposing this question to be answered in the affirmative) Secondly, whether, for the present, it shall hold any meetings other than business meetings; and if any, then at what intervals: Thirdly, what shall be the conditions of membership; and any other questions that may arise.

The meeting will further be asked to appoint a committee to give effect to its decisions.[13]

It is proposed to invite to that meeting (1) all lecturers on Economics in any University or public College in the United Kingdom; (2) the members of the Councils of the London, Dublin and Manchester Statistical Societies; (3) the members of the London Political Economy Club, together with a few other persons, besides members of the Committee of Section F of the British Association.[14]

I have the honour to remain, | Dear Sir, | Yours faithfully, | Alfred Marshall.

Cambridge, 24 Oct. 1890.

[1] A printed circular, reproduced in 'The Society's Jubilee' [294.1], pp. 402–4. Copies of the original are in the Marshall Papers and the Royal Economic Society Archive. The latter also has printed copies of the second, third and fourth drafts circulated to the organizing committee [287.1]. The first two were dated June while the last is undated. The intended circulation is indicated in the last paragraph of the circular.

[2] G. J. Goschen. In previous drafts the name was left blank. The date was set as Wednesday July 23 in the second and third drafts but left blank in the fourth. None of the drafts gives a time. Reference to an economic journal was inserted in the third draft.

[3] 'ever come' in the second and third drafts.

[4] 'And so strong has been the feeling' in the second draft.

[5] 'thus' omitted in the second draft.

[6] The second draft reads 'one another, that a number of private meetings and discussions on the subject have been held in Oxford, Cambridge . . .'.

[7] 'consideration of the members of the Organizing Committee' (third draft; also fourth draft with the omission of 'Organizing'). The second draft reads 'at last the matter came under consideration at an informal gathering of the Organizing Committee.'

[8] 'as to detail' in the second and third drafts.

[9] The second draft had read 'This is all that it is proposed that the Association should undertake at first; but it might gradually enlarge the scope of its action. Besides increasing its issues of economic publications, it might ultimately supply a common meeting place for English economists and bring them together from time to time.'

[10] See [181.1].

[11] 'ultimately hold' in the second draft.

[12] The date was left blank in the fourth draft and given as July 23rd in the previous ones.

[13] In the second draft this paragraph reads: 'The meeting on July 23 will be asked to decide (among other things) the condition of membership of the Society or Association.' The words in parentheses were inserted by hand.

[14] In the second draft the last phrase is placed immediately after the word 'meeting'.

327. To Lancelot Ridley Phelps, 31 October 1890[1]

31 Oct 90

My dear Phelps,

I am sure you have done what you thought was the best for all. But I had thought that by the rather strong expression of opinion on wh I had ventured (that I thought it was important both for your & for us that the difference between our aims shd be emphasized),[2] I had indicated a hope that you wd take some such title as 'The Journal of Social Reform'. I really believe you wd have succeeded better if you had. But if you think your title is best for your purposes, we ought not to ask you to change it.

I do not know what we shall adopt. But I am myself thinking of proposing

The British Journal
of
ECONOMICS[3]

Yours very sincerely | Alfred Marshall

---

[1] Oriel College, Phelps Papers. From Balliol Croft. Phelps was an organizer of the forthcoming Oxford-based *Economic Review* [287.1].

[2] Parentheses not in the original.

[3] The title finally adopted was the *Economic Journal*.

328. To Lancelot Ridley Phelps, 5 November 1890[1]

5 Nov 90

My dear Phelps,

I cannot recollect what I wrote.[2] But I know I was feeling very stupid & unwell. Scotland did not agree with me, & my British Ass[n]. Address sat on me like a nightmare. So I am quite sure that if you did not gather my meaning clearly, the fault was mine & not yours. I desire the success of your journal, as you originally described its aims to me, almost as much as I do that with wh I am more directly connected. But undoubtedly the way wd have been easier for us if you had been able to adopt a title which itself suggested that the two journals are designed to meet different wants, to supplement one another & not to compete with one another.

Yours very sincerely | Alfred Marshall

---

[1] Oriel College, Phelps Papers. From Balliol Croft.

[2] Marshall must have written to Phelps in July or August, but his letter has not been traced.

329. To John Biddulph Martin, 7 November 1890[1]

Dear Martin

I write to invite you to a meeting to make arrangements for the 20th.. It will be held by permission in the Statistical Society's offices at 4 p.m. on Wednesday next Nov. 12th.. The following questions will be raised

i   Are the inclosed Resolutions satisfactory?

ii Should they be circulated in the body of the Hall or only on the platform?
(The majority of the answers to my last circular were in favour of
circulating them in the body of the hall. But two members of the Committee
think it w^d.. be a mistake to do so: so the question had better be discussed
orally.)

iii Are the suggested movers & supporters approved. (Of course I have not
as yet invited any one & the inclosed paper is *strictly confidential*).

iv What names shall be suggested for the Council under Resolution IV.
(Informal discussions have seemed to show that it w^d.. be best to make
the list a rather large one of say 15 or 20 members to start with, & to leave
to the Council itself the question of appointing an executive Committee).

The appointment of a Secretary, & several minor details will also be discussed.
Yours very truly | Alfred Marshall

7 Nov 1890

Many thanks for your telegram. I have twice tried to catch Foxwell in vain. I
have left the figures about books[2] with him, & asked him to return them when
he has read them.

[Enclosure][3]

Resolutions

The following Resolutions will be submitted as a basis of discussion:

I. That it is expedient to form an Association for the advancement of
economic knowledge by the issue of a Journal (of which at least four numbers
shall appear annually), and other printed publications; and by such other means
as the Association may from time to time agree to adopt.[4]

Proposed by the Right Hon. G. J. Goschen, M.P.

Supported by Professor Sidgwick and Mr Palgrave.[5]

II. That any person who desires to further the aims of the Association,
consents to obey its rules,[6] and is approved by the Council, be admitted to
membership; and that the annual subscription be fixed for the present at one
guinea.

Proposed by the Right Hon. L. H. Courtney, M.P.

Supported by Mr Giffen[7] and Prof. Edgeworth.

III. That those present constitute themselves members of the Association;
and that a Committee be now appointed to draft Rules and to submit them to a
Meeting of the members to be called as soon as may be practicable: members
of this Committee to be members of the first Council of the Association, and to
have power to add to their number. Future appointments to the Council to be
made by the Society[8] in General Meeting.

Proposed by the Right Hon. Sir John Lubbock, Bart., M.P.[9]
Supported by Professor Foxwell and Mr Martin.
   IV. That the following be members of the Committee:—[10]

[1] Royal Economic Society Archive. A collographed letter with the recipient's name and the postscript added by hand. Presumably similar letters were sent to other members of the organizing committee [287.1].

[2] The nature of this information is unclear.

[3] A printed sheet marked 'Proof. Private and Confidential'. A revised proof and an identical final version are also in the archives. Alterations are noted below.

[4] The final version dropped the parenthesized phrase.

[5] The final version read 'Supported by Professor Marshall, Mr Giffen and Dr Cunningham'.

[6] The final version dropped this phrase.

[7] 'Professor Sidgwick' replaced 'Mr Giffen' in the final version.

[8] 'Association' replaced 'Society' in the final version.

[9] Sir John Lubbock (1843–1913), fourth Baronet and first Baron Avebury. Fellow of the Royal Society (for work in biology) and Member of Parliament for London University 1880–1900.

[10] In the final version, IV read 'A Resolution nominating members of the Committee will be | Proposed by Mr Palgrave | Supported by Professor Munro'.

330. To Herbert Somerton Foxwell, 10 November 1890[1]

                                                   Monday

My dear Foxwell,

   Nicholson won't be there.[2] Before you wrote I had come to the conclusion that room must be made for Cunningham somehow.

   I am opposed to Graham whom I regard as a *very* weak man. We shall say that Ingram & Bastable support the scheme heartily.[3] But I think we ought to have a resident Oxford man—either Phelps or Price.[4]

   I incline to propose that Cunningham be put in for an early resolution; & that we print Resolution V vote of thanks to Chairman & to the Council of Univ Coll, & get Martin to propose that.[5]

   In my opinion the three most important names on the paper are Goschen's, yours & Giffens, & after them Sidgwicks.

   We may not be able to chat tomorrow.

   So I scrawl this | Yours A.M.

[1] Foxwell Papers. Envelope postmarked 'NO 10 90'. From Balliol Croft. See [326] and the enclosure to [329].

[2] At the 20 November meeting.

[3] William Graham (1839–1911), Professor of Philosophy and Political Economy at Queen's College, Belfast, 1882–1909. Primarily a philosopher. J. K. Ingram and C. F. Bastable might also be viewed as representing Irish concerns.

[4] L. L. F. R. Price.

[5] For a full account of the 20 November meeting, including Marshall's remarks, see *Economic Journal*, 1 (March 1891), pp. 1–14.

331. To John Kells Ingram, 15 November 1890[1]

15 Nov 90

Dear D[r] Ingram

Will you be able to take part in our meeting to found an Econ[c].. Association on the 20th..? I much hope you will. But if not will you kindly write a short note w[h] can be read, if the Chairman thinks fit. I ask only for a short one, for our work will be long & our time brief.

Yours very sincerely | Alfred Marshall

---

[1] Public Record Office, Northern Ireland, Ingram Papers. From Balliol Croft.

332. From Benjamin Jowett to Mary Paley Marshall, 30 December 1890[1]

address | Balliol College
Dec 30, 1890

Dear M[rs] Marshall,

Accept my best thanks for the pretty little pocket book which you & Alfred have sent me. I shall not forget you when I use it: You & a few other persons always remind me how little I do for my friends & how much they deserve at my hands.

I am delighted to hear that the treatise on Political Economy, the child of so many hopes and anxieties, has made such a prosperous start in the world. And don't fear the work of revision. It is not really laborious: the labour was in the original concoction, and great improvement is possible because the author has more command of his subject and can see his own defects when he comes fresh to them after an interval. I should like to have new editions of books greatly altered every five years. Only one wishes that no one would read the first edition after the second has appeared; but I have a little expedient to meet this difficulty also (I cannot say that it has been very successful hitherto, but I believe it will be)—I allow every one who delivers up a copy of the first edition to buy the second at half price.[2]

May not 'we authors maam'[3] agree together about American Copyright? But it seems too good to be true.

I am glad that you were pleased with M[r] Balfour.[4] I am sure that he & Alfred have a great deal more in common than either of them have with M[r] Labouchere[5] or even with Sir William Harcourt.[6]

It seems to me that the College is getting on as well as its friends could wish & better than its enemies who seem to be rather numerous & malevolent [would desire].[7] I tell you this because you live at Balliol Croft & may find some little interest in it.

When I come next to Cambridge I have set my heart on making an excursion to Ely with you which I have not seen for a long time.

'The Evil One', that is the Post[8] has come to fetch me away. With love to Alfred I remain Dear Mrs Marshall

Yours truly & affectionately | B Jowett

[1] Marshall Papers. Substantially reproduced in Abbott and Campbell, *Life and Letters* [146.1], vol. 2, pp. 389–90.

[2] In 1892 Jowett followed this practice for the third edition of his translation of Plato's *Dialogues*. See *Life and Letters*, vol. 2, p. 405.

[3] Disraeli's quip to Queen Victoria.

[4] See [324].

[5] Henry Dupré Labouchère (1831–1912), journalist and politician.

[6] Sir William Harcourt (1827–1904), who had served under Gladstone as Solicitor General, Home Secretary, and Chancellor of the Exchequer. Whewell Professor of International Law in the University of Cambridge from 1869 to 1887.

[7] Words apparently omitted.

[8] Perhaps 'Pest'.

APPENDIX I
Alfred Marshall's Family

Family matters enter only tangentially into Marshall's surviving correspondence, so that an abbreviated description of the pertinent individuals and their relationship to him is all that seems needful here.[1]

Marshall's parents, William Marshall (1812–1901) and Rebecca Marshall née Oliver (1817–78) were married in 1840 and had five children. Alfred, who was born on 26 July 1842, was the second. The oldest son, Charles William born in 1841, left for India at age 17, returning later in life to settle in England at Bathford. Agnes, born 1845, went out to India sometime after 1875 to assist her brother Charles. She died there relatively young, perhaps in 1884. Alfred's younger sister, Mabel Louise, born in 1850, lived until 1912, while the fifth sibling, Walter, born in 1853 died of tuberculosis in South Africa in 1874 before completing his studies at Cambridge, where he had been a member of Peterhouse.

Charles Marshall married Lucy Guillebaud and had two sons, William who became a doctor and Arthur who died of wounds received in the First World War. Mabel Louise married Erneste Guillebaud (1856–1907), brother of Lucy. A student at Cambridge, where he had been a member of Trinity (BA 1881), he served as Rector of Yatesbury, Wiltshire, from 1889 until his unexpected death in 1907. William Marshall lived with them there in his latter years as a widower.

The Guillebauds had four sons. The oldest, Harold (1888–1941), read classics at Cambridge 1907–10 (Pembroke) and was then dragooned by his uncle into a further year studying economics. He became a churchman and missionary, serving for some years in Rwanda. Next came twins, Walter Henry (1890–1973) and Claude William (1890–1971). Each became a member of St John's, their uncle's college, after initial study in Manchester. Walter took the Natural Sciences Tripos and Diplomas in Agriculture and Forestry, becoming an expert with the Forestry Commission. Claude took the Economics Tripos and won the Adam Smith Prize of 1914. He became a well-known Cambridge economist, Fellow of St John's, and editor of his uncle's *magnum opus*. The youngest son Cyril (1893–1915) suffered ill health and died as a youth.

Alfred's father William Marshall was the eldest of the six surviving children born to William Marshall (1780–1828) and his wife Louisa, née Bentall, who died in 1825. Alfred's paternal grandfather had a chequered career, and upon his early death in reduced circumstances his young family came under the care of their mother's brothers, John Bentall of London and Thornton Bentall of

Totnes. Of the five siblings of Alfred's father, four were boys. Two of these, Edward (1817–62) and Thornton (1822–61), died relatively young, Edward after a promising career in the Royal Navy and Thornton in the antipodes after service as an army surgeon. The other two of Alfred's paternal uncles must have been better known to him. Henry (1821–80) was in business, first in India and after about 1860 in England. Charles Henry (1820–74) prospered as a pastoralist and businessman in Australia, revisiting his native country on occasion. He it was who enabled Marshall by a loan to enter Cambridge University as an undergraduate in 1862, and whose legacy of £250 made possible the four-month-long tour of North America that Alfred undertook in 1875. But among his father's siblings it was Alfred's Aunt Louisa Maria (1818–1907) who played the largest role in his life. Mary Paley Marshall reports:

> A was devotedly fond of his Aunt Louisa. She made the care of her brothers & their families her first duty in life. She refused several offers of marriage because she wished to remain a center of the large family & to keep them all together. She did this to the end of a long life. . . . [Alfred] was so overworked at school & by his father that his life was saved by his Aunt Louisa with whom he spent his long summer holidays at Kenton Cottage, near Dawlish. She gave him a boat & a gun & a pony, & by the end of the summer he returned home brown & well.[2]

Alfred's father, something of a domestic tyrant, had an unremarkable career as clerk, and eventually cashier, at the Bank of England. A man of intelligence and ability, but little common sense, he rode strange hobby horses and his literary pretensions manifested themselves in odd and idiosyncratic publications. Alfred was much closer to his mother who provided the warmth his father lacked. She came from a humble family—her father being a butcher—with which little contact seems to have been maintained. The Marshall family, clinging somewhat precariously to its middle-class status—Alfred's father had described himself on marriage as 'gentleman'—must have frowned on the imprudence of such a match.

Alfred married Mary Paley (1850–1944) in July 1877, the marriage being without issue. The daughter of the Reverend Thomas Paley (1810–99), sometime Fellow of St John's and Rector of Ufford 1847–81, and of his wife Ann Judith née Wormald, Mary Paley was among the first group of women students at what was to become Newnham College in Cambridge. She was the second-born of four siblings, with an older sister and two younger brothers, one of whom—George Knowles Paley (1860–1938)—became a barrister on the North East Circuit. There is no indication that Mary maintained close ties with her siblings after marriage, although she did periodically visit her parents in Bournemouth to where they moved after her father retired.

Family concerns do not seem to have loomed large in Marshall's life. As Mary Marshall recorded, 'He loved his mother, his sister Mabel and his Aunt Louisa.

I don't think that as time went on, he really cared very much for anyone else, except some of his former pupils'—and, it should be added, Mary herself.[3] But he took an avuncular interest in the youthful Guillebauds, especially after their father's death in 1907, treating them as 'honorary pupils', and advising and guiding them in a somewhat Polonian manner.[4]

Mary taught economics at Newnham for many years, and also at Bristol, and was active in Cambridge social life. But—aided by the redoubtable servant Sarah Payne, first acquired in Bristol—she devoted herself above all to smoothing Alfred's way and sheltering him from the petty vexations of life.[5] Whatever regrets she may have had about the sacrifice of her own interests and ambitions, the marriage seems to have been one of true devotion.[6]

---

[1] For further details see J. M. Keynes, 'Alfred Marshall 1842–1924' *Memorials*, pp. 1–65 (also in the *Economic Journal*, 34 (September 1924), pp. 311–72, and in J. M. Keynes, *Essays in Biography: Collected Works*, vol. 10 (Macmillan, London, 1972)); W. R. Scott, 'Alfred Marshall 1842–1924', *Proceedings of the British Academy*, 11 (1924–5), pp. 446–57; C. W. Guillebaud, 'Some Personal Reminiscences of Alfred Marshall', *History of Political Economy*, 3 (Spring 1971), pp. 1–8; R. H. Coase, 'Alfred Marshall's Mother and Father', *History of Political Economy*, 16 (Winter 1984), pp. 519–27; R. H. Coase, 'Did Marshall Know Where He Was Born?' *History of Economics Bulletin*, 7 (Summer 1986), p. 34; R. H. Coase, 'Alfred Marshall's Family and Ancestry', in R. McWilliams Tullberg (ed.), *Alfred Marshall in Retrospect* (Elgar, Aldershot, 1990). As Coase's discoveries make clear, there are minor inaccuracies and misrepresentations in the accounts set out by Keynes and Scott which relied heavily on notes provided by Mary Paley Marshall. The entire body of evidence on family background is reviewed at considerable length in P. D. Groenewegen's important recent biographical study of Marshall, *A Soaring Eagle: Alfred Marshall 1842–1924* (Elgar, Aldershot, 1995).

[2] Notes for J. M. Keynes, King's College, Cambridge, J. M. Keynes Papers.

[3] Notes for W. R. Scott, Marshall Papers.

[4] See the letters to Arthur Marshall and Harold and Claude Guillebaud reproduced in Vol. 3.

[5] See J. M. Keynes, 'Mary Paley Marshall, 1850–1944', *Economic Journal*, 54 (June–September 1944), pp. 268–84; reprinted in J. M. Keynes, *Essays in Biography: Collected Works*, vol. 10; Mary P. Marshall, *What I Remember* (Cambridge University Press, London, 1947).

[6] Additional biographical studies pertaining to Marshall which might be mentioned here for completeness are John K. Whitaker, 'Alfred Marshall: The Years 1877–1885', *History of Political Economy*, 4 (Spring 1972), pp. 1–61, and 'What Happened to the Second Volume of Marshall's *Principles*? The Thorny Path to Marshall's Last Books', in John K. Whitaker (ed.), *Centenary Essays on Alfred Marshall* (Cambridge University Press, London, 1990); Peter D. Groenewegen, 'Alfred Marshall and the Establishment of the Cambridge Economic Tripos', *History of Political Economy*, 20 (Winter 1988), pp. 627–67, and 'Teaching Economics at Cambridge at the Turn of the Century: Alfred Marshall as Lecturer in Political Economy', *Scottish Journal of Political Economy*, 37 (January 1990), pp. 40–60. Mention should also be made of the reminiscences by F. Y. Edgeworth, C. R. Fay, E. A. Benians, and A. C. Pigou, that were included in *Memorials*, pp. 66–90. Two monographs in which Marshall's activities feature prominently are: John Maloney, *Marshall, Orthodoxy and the Professionalisation of Economics* (Cambridge University Press, Cambridge, 1985); Alon Kadish, *Historians, Economists and Economic History* (Routledge, London, 1989).

APPENDIX II
Marshall's Testimonials for the Principalship of University College Bristol, June 1877

As was the custom of the time, Marshall submitted a printed set of testimonials as part of his application for the Principalship of University College Bristol. Three of these testimonials which took the form of letters addressed to Marshall were reproduced as letters [37–9] above. The remaining testimonials, which are of considerable interest for the light they throw on Marshall at this early stage in his career, are reproduced below.[1]

1. From the Rev. Dr. Bateson, Master of St. John's College, Cambridge.

I have much pleasure in recommending to the most favourable consideration of the Council of University College, Bristol, the qualifications of Mr. Alfred Marshall, M.A., Fellow and Lecturer of St. John's College, who informs me that he is a Candidate for the office of Principal of the College.

I have long known Mr. Marshall and I have a great admiration for his character, which is remarkable for its great simplicity, earnestness, and self-sacrificing conscientiousness.

Having distinguished himself in the Mathematical Tripos of 1865 by obtaining the place of second Wrangler, he soon devoted himself to the study of Moral Science, more especially Political Economy. To this subject he has applied himself with indefatigable labour both by study and inquiry at home and abroad and by journey on the Continent of Europe and in the States of America.

In his office of College Lecturer he has rendered valuable and important service, always exercising a refining influence and making his subject and his class-room attractive and popular.

I may add that he is one who would on no account accept service where he could not work heartily and effectively, and I cannot picture to myself a field of work which would not benefit largely by his superintendence and co-operation.

W. H. BATESON,

Cambridge, 20th June, 1877.   Master of St. John's College.

2. From Anne J. Clough, Principal of Newnham Hall, Cambridge

June, 21, 1877.

I have much pleasure in saying what I know of Mr. Alfred Marshall of St. John's College, Cambridge.

Mr. Marshall was one of our first Lecturers when I came to Cambridge in October, 1871. He had a very remarkable influence on his class. He induced them to work steadily and seriously, and they were all much interested in the subject.

I feel sure that he would throw himself into any work he undertook with great energy, and that he would be very likely to make it a success.

ANNE J. CLOUGH,
Principal of Newnham Hall, Cambridge.

3. From Henry Fawcett, MA, MP, Professor of Political Economy in the University of Cambridge   51, The Lawn, South Lambeth Road.

TO THE COUNCIL OF UNIVERSITY COLLEGE, BRISTOL

Gentlemen,

As I have known Mr. A. Marshall of St. John's College Cambridge very intimately for many years, I am enabled to state with great confidence that few people have devoted themselves with greater assiduity to the study of economic science. The amount of knowledge which he has accumulated on the subject is most varied and extensive.

His high Mathematical attainments which were proved by the fact that he was second Wrangler in 1865, have no doubt greatly contributed to the success with which he has studied political economy.

Mr. Marshall has not only a thorough knowledge of the theory of the subject, but he is a most patient accumulator of facts bearing on economic principles. Many of these principles he has elucidated by most elaborate and exhaustive statistical investigations.

HENRY FAWCETT,
June 23, 1877.   Professor of Political Economy, Cambridge.

4. From H.S. Foxwell, M.A., Fellow and Lecturer of St. John's College, Cambridge

St. John's College, Cambridge, June 25th, 1877.

I have great pleasure in expressing, however inadequately, the very high opinion I have of Mr. Marshall's qualifications as an Economist.

For the last six years he has delivered courses of lectures upon every branch of the science, which have long been conspicuous among the very best lectures delivered in the University, and have been attended by all the most advanced and many of the other students of political economy for both the Historical and Moral Sciences Triposes.

I had the privilege of attending some of those courses, and have since then been constantly in the habit of resorting to Mr. Marshall for advice and direction; and I find it difficult to convey my sense of his ability, or of the obligations under which he has laid me and my fellow pupils. For years we have looked up to him as our leader and adviser in all matters connected with Economic Science; and those of us whose duty it has been to lecture for the University in the large towns on this subject owe what success we have had to his careful training and constant assistance.

Mr. Marshall has an unusually wide knowledge of the literature of the subject, English and Foreign, scientific and statistical: he has taken great pains to obtain a practical and first-hand knowledge of the conditions of various industries in England and the United States; and he has brought the mathematical power of a second Wrangler to bear on the elaboration of the abstract theory of the science. It is in this last respect perhaps that his originality is most unmistakeable and therefore best known; but I venture to think that his more laborious investigations into the practical applications of economic doctrine and into the historical connection of economic ideas and social conditions will prove to be equally original, and of still greater value.

At a critical period in the history of economics Mr. Marshall seems to me to be one of the very few (still fewer since the unfortunate death of Mr. Bagehot), who have grasped the true notion of the limits and function of the science; and I do not hesitate to express my conviction that there is no one living better qualified or more likely to advance it.

H. S. FOXWELL, M.A.

Fellow and Lecturer in Moral Science of St. John's College, Cambridge; late Lecturer on Political Economy at University College, London; late Examiner of the Moral Sciences Tripos; late University Lecturer on Political Economy under the Extension Scheme.

5. From the Ven. Dr Hessey, Archdeacon of Middlesex, &c., late headmaster of Merchant Taylor's School

41, Leinster Gardens, Hyde Park, W., June 23, 1877.

I have much pleasure in bearing my testimony to the ability, vigour, and general merits of Mr. Alfred Marshall, M.A., one of my former pupils.

Mr. Marshall received his education from me at Merchant Taylor's School, and at his leaving in June, 1861, after a very distinguished career, and obtaining our chief Mathematical Prize, and the position of Third Monitor, was offered a scholarship at St. John's College, Oxford, which, under the then existing system, would have led in three years to a Fellowship. With characteristic independence and consciousness of mental power, he declined this opening, and accepting a Parkin's Exhibition of smaller value, which is given annually to the best Mathematician leaving for Cambridge, he determined to trust his fortunes in that University. He was not mistaken. He gained a Scholarship in St. John's, Cambridge, in that same year, and a Foundation Scholarship in 1862.

At his degree in 1865, he came out Second Wrangler, and was immediately elected a Fellow of his College. Since 1869 he has held the office of Lecturer in the Moral Sciences in that Society. You will hear from other sources of the manner in which he has discharged his duties, both in this position and in the other functions incumbent upon him, how varied are his accomplishments and range of reading, and what an influence he exercises for good in the University; but I cannot help observing that the man who has wrought thus, and succeeded thus, appears to be singularly fitted by his energy and special attainments for the post of Principal and Professor of Political Economy in a new College, such as that of University College, Bristol. The courage and judgment which have marked his own course would be invaluable when applied to the guidance of a rising institution. I may add that I have a high opinion of Mr. Marshall's integrity and sense of duty, and that I am persuaded that he would more than justify the greatest expectations that could be formed of him.

J. A. HESSEY, D.C.L.,

Archdeacon of Middlesex, late Boyle Lecturer in H. M. Chapel at Whitehall, and Bampton Lecturer in the University of Oxford, sometime Head Master of Merchant Taylor's School.

6. From Henry Sidgwick, MA, Prelector of Moral and Political Philosophy in Trinity College, Cambridge

Hill Side, Chesterton Road, Cambridge, June 20th.

I have known Mr. Alfred Marshall intimately for several years, and I believe that he possesses, in rare combination, the qualities that are likely to be most valuable in such a post as the Principalship of University College, Bristol. On the one hand he is a man of originality and genuine scientific interests, eminently qualified to advance the boundaries of knowledge in any department to which he applies himself. Although he has as yet published little, the importance of his economic studies is already recognised by competent judges; and I doubt not that his forthcoming work, of which the greater part is already completed, will give him at once a high position among living English economists.

At the same time his zeal for social improvement, especially in the direction of education, is at least as strong as his zeal for the advancement of science.

For the last seven years I have been associated with him both in the teaching of Moral Sciences to the members of this University, and also, through his voluntary assistance, in the scheme for extending academic instruction to women which has gradually developed itself here during that period. In both departments I have found him a most effective and valuable colleague, unsparing of his time and trouble, a very interesting and stimulating teacher, with a natural gift for contriving and adapting schemes of organization, thoughtful in collecting the different elements needing consideration in any practical question, quick in seizing those of chief importance, and inventive in meeting difficulties.

For more than seven years all the students who have taken high honours in moral sciences have obtained their instruction in political economy almost entirely from him.

If he is elected, the loss to his subject here will be great; I trust, however, that the gain to Bristol will more than compensate for it. I know no man who sympathises more thoroughly with the aims and hopes of the founders of this new College: or is likely to devote himself more conscientiously to ensure, so far as in him lies, their successful realization.

HENRY SIDGWICK,

Prelector of Moral and Political Philosophy in Trinity College, Cambridge.

7. From the Rev. V. H. Stanton, MA, Fellow of Trinity College, &c.

June 25th, 1877.

TO THE COUNCIL OF BRISTOL UNIVERSITY COLLEGE.

Gentlemen,

Hearing that my friend Mr. A. Marshall, Fellow and Lecturer in Political Economy of St. John's College, Cambridge, proposes to offer himself as a candidate for the Principalship of Political Economy, I have much pleasure in bearing testimony to those of his qualifications which are well known to me.

I myself attended two courses of his lectures on Political Economy after I had taken my B.A. degree, and I have repeatedly gone to him for advice since. I believe him to be even already very likely unsurpassed among English Political Economists in learning; he has also a very clear perception of the true method and scope of the science and of the requirements of its actual condition; and he is most completely devoted to his work as a student and professor of it. He has not yet had time to publish, but I feel sure that if he is appointed to the Professorship of Political Economy in Bristol College, he will do honour to the College. As a teacher I found him very suggestive.

As for Mr. Marshall's fitness for the more general work of Principal, I know that he is earnest for all educational progress, and would work heartily for it. Especially I know that he has followed with warm interest, and thoroughly understands the working of, 'Cambridge Local Lectures,' for I have myself been closely connected with that scheme.

I am, Gentlemen, yours faithfully, | V. H. STANTON, M.A.

Fellow of Trinity College, Cambridge, formerly Lecturer in Political Economy appointed by the 'Cambridge Local Lectures' Syndicate, and late Hon. Sec. to that Syndicate.

8. From I. Todhunter, MA, FRS, Lecturer and Late Fellow of St John's College, Cambridge

St. John's College, Cambridge.

I have known Mr. Marshall during the whole of his residence in St. John's College. His eminent mathematical ability is attested by his position as second Wrangler in the Mathematical Tripos for 1865. As I was one of the Moderators for that year, I had the best opportunity for judging of his powers and attainments, and I formed a very high opinion of them.

Since taking his degree in 1865, Mr. Marshall has devoted much time to the subject of Political Economy and kindred studies. I have been sometimes associated with Mr. Marshall as a College Examiner in the subjects which are grouped here under the name of Moral Sciences; and it was obvious that he had cultivated them with the resources of an acute and vigorous mind.

On account of his conspicuous ability, his wide and varied knowledge, and his zeal as a teacher I consider Mr. Marshall to be eminently qualified for the post he desires to obtain.

I. TODHUNTER,

June 21, 1877. St. John's College, Cambridge.

---

[1] Professor R. D. Collison Black kindly provided a transcript. The original printed set from which this transcript was made appears to have been in the Marshall Library but its present whereabouts are unknown. The original letters do not seem to have been preserved, and no copy of the testimonials is to be found in the scant archives of University College, Bristol. J. M. Keynes quoted from the testimonials in his memoir on Marshall (*Memorials*, p. 27). On Anne J. Clough see [78.2]. James Augustus Hessey (1814–92), classical scholar and divine, was headmaster of Merchant Taylors' School from 1845 to 1870. The other letter writers are identified in the Biographical Register above.

APPENDIX III
Foxwell's Initiative

As the Marshalls left Bristol in October 1881, Herbert Somerton Foxwell approached Charles Taylor [58.3], the new Master of St John's College, about the possibility of a lecturing appointment for Marshall. The initiative seems to have come to nothing, but Foxwell's two letters, reproduced below, are very illuminating.[1]

St. John's College, | Cambridge.
Oct. 6. 1881.

My dear Master

I believe you know that M^r. Marshall has been obliged to resign the Principalship of University College Bristol, because the state of his health makes it impossible for him adequately to discharge those more external & active duties which are just now the most important ones attaching to the office.[2]

The consequence is that he finds himself obliged to depend entirely for support upon his private means. Speaking without exact information, I believe these means to be small, & certainly not such as it is seemly that so able & deserving a member of our body should be compelled to exist upon, if it is reasonably possible for us to enlarge them.

I am well aware that this is in many respects, to which I need not further allude, a very unfortunate time to make any proposal implying a new charge on the College income. But I think this is a case in which, if the money can possibly be spared, the College may by a small expenditure not only sensibly improve the position of one of its late fellows engaged in research of first rate importance, but also do a great service, indirectly perhaps even more than directly, to economic & historical teaching in the University.

What I would venture to suggest to the Master & Seniors is briefly this:— There is at present a subject prescribed for study under the schedule of the Moral Sciences Tripos, on which there is no resident competent to lecture. The subject is described as 'the diagrammatic expression of [economic] problems in pure theory, together with the general principles of the mathematical treatment applicable to such problems.' Let M^r. Marshall be invited to give (at least) one course of twenty lectures a year upon this subject. In return for this work, which is of exceptional interest & difficulty, he might perhaps be offered £100 a year; £50 of which might fall as a new charge on the College income, while the remaining £50 would be provided from the addition which the College was kind enough to make to my stipend, when M^r. Marshall's departure left me in sole charge of the Moral Science teaching in the College; & which naturally reverts to him when by his return he again shares the responsibility with me.

I have the best reason to know that if the Master & Seniors found themselves able to adopt this proposal, their action would be most heartily welcomed by those engaged in the teaching or study of the Moral Sciences here: & not by them only, but also by many distinguished economists outside the University, to whom M^r. Marshall's present position is a cause of very real & often expressed regret.

It is only right to add that in making this suggestion, I am acting entirely on my own responsibility, & cannot say how the offer if made might be received by M^r. Marshall to whom the matter has never even been so much as hinted at.

It is not necessary for me to remind those who know M^r. Marshall that the value of his presence here is not to be estimated by the duties he has stipulated to perform, but perhaps I ought to mention, what may not be so generally known, that he is now recognized in Cambridge & elsewhere as the founder of a distinct economic school, & that a large proportion of his pupils are now holding important educational posts, or have in other ways become men of mark.

It appears to me that the University is precisely the place for men of this quality: & that educational endowments cannot be better applied than to their support.

I would therefore beg that this proposal may be laid before the Master & Seniors: hoping that they will regard it merely as a general suggestion, possibly faulty in detail, or even impossible of immediate execution, but at least deserving their favourable consideration.

I remain, my dear Master, | Yours very truly | H. S. Foxwell.

St. John's College, | Cambridge.
Oct. 15. 1881

My dear Master

I have just heard from Marshall who is at Palermo in Sicily, where he proposes to winter, & then return to live near London: but he describes himself as unsettled.[3]

I thought it was important to mention in regard to the matter that will be discussed on Monday, that his health is considerably improved. He says so in his letter and also in a speech made on occasion of a presentation.

I have enclosed the account of the proceedings,[4] because it explains thoroughly the reasons which led him to leave Bristol, & also shows the high opinion people had of him there. Please let me have it again at your convenience.

From what I know of Marshall I feel sure that mental worry, partly connected with the finance, & partly with the disagreeable personalities of one or two non-university men on the staff, at Bristol, was a principal cause of his illness. A student's work & a student's pay is all he wants to bring him round, at least sufficiently to do work of first rate quality & importance.

£113.18.0 was collected & presented to Mrs. Marshall before they left Bristol. Yours very truly | H. S. Foxwell.

[1] The originals are in the Archives of St John's College (D104:109–10). Peter Groenewegen drew my attention to them.

[2] See [99].

[3] See [107].

[4] The press report of the farewell meeting [104.3]. The press cutting was apparently never returned to Foxwell.

APPENDIX IV
The 1889 Debate on Reform of the Moral Sciences Tripos

The Senate debate of 7 March 1889 on the Report of the Special Board for Moral Sciences led to the following remarkable interchange between Cunningham, Marshall and Sidgwick (*Reporter*, 19 March 1889, pp. 593–6). This interchange is interesting not only for the substantive differences revealed, but also because it highlights issues that were to dog the continuing debate on curricular reform until the position of economics was finally settled by the establishment in 1903 of a new Tripos in Economics and Politics. The Report being discussed recommended that the two Parts of the Moral Sciences Tripos be made independent, and that those specializing in economics for Part II be permitted to substitute Political Philosophy for the otherwise-required subject of Metaphysics (see [229.3, 231, 235.5]).

Dr. Cunningham . . . objected to the regulation which allowed the substitution of Political Philosophy for Metaphysics in the case of Economic students who took up the second part of the Tripos. The reason alleged for this special arrangement was that Political Economy was independent of Metaphysics and that those who engaged in the study of Political Economy need not necessarily make any great advance or take any great interest in Metaphysics. It seemed to him that in the interests of Political Economy as a study, it was unfortunate so to accentuate a severance of this kind: so far as he could judge of Political Economy in the present day, there were a great many Metaphysical questions underlying it, and those who went out to the world as specialists in it should have some insight into the treatment of these Metaphysical questions. There was a large part of Political Economy which must deal with socialistic difficulties, and behind all these lay the question, What is meant by an individual? How far an individual was to be considered as a sort of monad, or as itself formed by social surroundings, were most important problems in relation to the whole controversy of socialism. Thus in order to take a sound view with regard to socialism, there ought to be preparation in the study of Metaphysics. Similarly a great many of the burning questions in modern Economics related to the appropriate method of study, and they could not be thoroughly treated without trenching on metaphysical problems as to the nature of knowledge. The same was true with regard to the attack which was commonly made on Political Economy as not forming an independent science. English Political Economy had been very much tinged with Metaphysical notions which Comte, who was its most effective critic, regarded as out of date. The only answer to his criticism was to shew that Metaphysics were not out of date but had a real value still, and Political Economy would very much gain in strength if this line could be taken. He deprecated very strongly any attempt at severance between Economic and Metaphysical study, as it was important in the interest of Political Economy to accentuate the connection with Metaphysics.

He did not say that everybody interested in Political Economy should necessarily approach it through Metaphysics; there were a large number of Economic questions which might be treated without Metaphysics. At the same time the University already provided for such students, and he thought it unfortunate to provide twice in a similar fashion. A student with interest in Political Philosophy but not in Metaphysics was already encouraged to study Political Economy in conjunction with Jurisprudence and History for the Historical Tripos. Since that scheme had been so recently framed, it required very strong justification to start another examination with a similar arrangement. . . . He had had a good deal to do with teaching Political Philosophy. . . . and it did not seem to be a satisfactory subject in itself. When a similar course to that now proposed was tried in the Moral Sciences Tripos, it was thought to be so very unsatisfactory that it was discarded. . . .

Professor Marshall agreed with a great deal of what Dr Cunningham had said, but he took a different position with regard to Metaphysics. He thought that if a student who was making Political Economy his main subject, chose to read Metaphysics, he would be the better for it, but Metaphysics was not adapted for compulsory study. Looking at the history of Economics, one did not find that those who had approached it from a metaphysical standpoint had contributed very much to its progress; almost all economists had worked on lines separate from Metaphysics, and many had even indicated a certain distinct severance of their minds from metaphysical questions. It was true that the Scotch school of economists had a good deal of interest in Philosophy; but Philosophy was a broad term, and it must be borne in mind that under the proposed regulations students would study some branches of Philosophy, though not Metaphysical Philosophy. They would study Ethics and Logic. He did not himself see that Metaphysics did throw a very important light upon questions of scientific method. And as to the question whether a man was to be regarded as a monad, that must indeed come before all students of Ethics and Economics in some way or other; he did not object to anybody treating it as a metaphysical question, but he should prefer not to treat it so; and he objected to making its metaphysical treatment compulsory. It seemed to him therefore, on the whole, that if they retained the Moral Science Examination as the chief examination in Economics they should not make Metaphysics compulsory. There was a great deal to be said for separating to some extent these two branches of moral science, the mental and metaphysical side, and the social side; though they had long been united in the Moral Sciences Tripos. Ere long a time might come when they would be ready to have a political sciences school. Schools of this kind were already thriving in America. America had two economic journals, and the recent intellectual activity in America in Economics had been very wonderful; he thought the growth of political sciences schools was partly the cause and partly the result of this movement. They might soon have such a school here, and it would very likely be connected with, but not identical with, the Historical Tripos. He thought it would be a pity even in this case to exclude Economics altogether from the Moral Sciences Tripos, because he thought everybody should look on social questions more or less from the ethical side; and some persons might prefer to give their chief attention to the philosophical aspects of the study. It was important that those who had such a preference should be allowed to follow it. But in addition they should have a Political Science Tripos, in which there would be an element of History, but not so much History as was wanted for those students who were going to carry on historical research in after life. He had heard many able historians talk with contempt of those who called themselves historical students, and who did not know how to read ancient MS.; and this seemed to him a reasonable position to take. But an historical student so defined was not a typical or representative student of Economics. Economic conditions were changing so fast, and the rate of change was increasing so fast, that the Economic student was more and more taken up with recent and contemporary history, and had every year less time to spare for Mediaeval History. Therefore he could not admit that the wants of the ordinary Economic student could be met by an examination in which Mediaeval History was as prominent as in the present Historical Tripos, admirable as this was for its own purpose. He thought that the scheme now proposed for the Moral Sciences Tripos, though not altogether satisfactory, and though in many respects to be regarded as a transitional stage, was yet the best step on the whole they could take. The plan was not exactly what he himself wanted. He wanted to give much more freedom of choice, but opinions on the Board differed and the plan now adopted seemed to be an excellent compromise. With regard to the particular paper that would be allowed as a substitute for Metaphysics, three proposals were brought before the Board; one that it should be a paper on Economic History, another that it should be a paper on Advanced Scientific Method with special regard to statistics, in order that they might be worked at by mathematicians who take up the study of Economics after their degrees; and a third that it should be a paper on Political Philosophy. He himself voted for the papers in the order in which he had mentioned them; but he cordially accepted the decision of the Board.

Dr. Sidgwick . . . had a strong sympathy with what had fallen from Dr Cunningham with regard to the desirability of students of Political Economy also studying the theory of the nature and conditions of knowledge and of the relation of the individual to the universe, included in the term Metaphysics. At the same time he was compelled to say that after an experience of 20 years he agreed with the conclusion stated by Professor Marshall, that Metaphysics was a subject exceedingly well suited to men whose minds were adapted to it, but exceedingly bad when forced upon minds not so adapted; and he thought the rest of the Board were unable to resist the evidence brought forward by Professor Marshall, partly from his own experience, to shew there were students anxious to devote themselves to a full and complete study of Political Economy, and who might with advantage be encouraged to take up that subject, who still had very clearly an unmetaphysical turn of mind. Therefore, after much deliberation and thought, he had come to the conclusion that the exact regulation here made was on the whole the best. It was to be observed that it did not indicate that a student of Political Economy ought not to study Metaphysics, for it was left completely open for him to do that. . . . He need not enter fully into the various arguments that led them to choose Political Philosophy as an alternative. He thought it would be generally felt by anyone who approached the subject from the outside, that if a student took up Ethical Philosophy and Political Economy, the study of Political Philosophy, connected as it was on the one side with Ethics and on the other side with Political Economy, was one that was naturally and properly combined with the two. He felt, with Dr Cunningham, the difficulty in teaching it, though he thought the experience to which Dr Cunningham referred related rather to a different form of study, the history of Political Theories, which used to stand as an advanced branch, and which they had not proposed to include in Political Philosophy as here defined. He agreed however with Professor Marshall in thinking it probable that in the course of a few years they would feel a desire to construct a Political Sciences Tripos: and if they were moving in that direction, it seemed clearly advantageous that the subject of Political Philosophy should be maintained in the Moral Sciences Tripos.

APPENDIX V
Is London Healthy?

The following short note published under Marshall's name in the *Pall Mall Gazette*, 13 April 1887, has the air of a letter to the editor and seems worth reproducing given its general inaccessibility.

Is London Healthy?
By Professor Alfred Marshall.

It is true that the death rate of London is only a little above the average. But people die of consumption in Torquay and Mentone, not because those places are specially unhealthy, but because those who have weak lungs go to them. In like manner many people live long in London, not because London is healthy, but because their exceptional health and strength induced them to come to London. There are more than a million people living in London who were born elsewhere. Most of them when they came were picked lives, the strongest member of their several parishes; those who, having the best income-earning power, and being the least liable to illness, had most to hope and least to fear from playing for the high stakes of London life. More than half a million London-born people are living elsewhere, and of these a great part went away because they felt themselves unequal to the strain of London life. The death rate of women in London between the ages of fifteen and twenty-five is remarkably low, and this seems to be due to the two facts that the conditions of life of domestic servants are favourable, and that young people who come to London to earn their living are likely to go home as soon as they get ill; they thus swell the death rates of healthy country parishes. But next, when we say that London is unhealthy, we mean not so much that Londoners die prematurely, as that they live enfeebled lives. Want of fresh air, of light, and of healthy play does not kill directly, but it lowers vitality. Of course mortality is higher in those urban districts which have no proper drainage system than it is in London. But I contend that, so far as the statistics of mortality throw light on the question at all, they tend to show that London is very unhealthy; because, though the Londoners are for the greater part picked lives, and though they have all the resources of wealth to help them, yet their expectation of life is below the average. If those who migrate into London could take their health and their strength and their good incomes to some other part of England, they would, I contend, be far more likely to have a vigorous progeny in the next generation. The complaint against London is similar to that against India. It attracts many of the best lives in the Empire:

it uses up their strength, and returns them and their children comparatively feeble. This evil will be increased if the prison spaces are used to add to the density of the population of London: it will be diminished if they are used for healthy recreation; and this fact makes the right interpretation of the London death rate important just now.